Loosening the Grip

A HANDBOOK OF ALCOHOL INFORMATION

Eighth Edition

JEAN KINNEY, M.S.W.
www.projectcork.org
Lecturer, Community and Family Medicine
Dartmouth Medical School

Illustrations by
Stuart A. Copans, M.D.

McGraw Hill

Boston Burr Ridge, IL Dubuque, IA Madison, WI New York San Francisco St. Louis
Bangkok Bogotá Caracas Kuala Lumpur Lisbon London Madrid Mexico City
Milan Montreal New Delhi Santiago Seoul Singapore Sydney Taipei Toronto

The McGraw·Hill Companies

Higher Education

LOOSENING THE GRIP: A HANDBOOK OF ALCOHOL INFORMATION, EIGHTH EDITION
Published by McGraw-Hill, a business unit of The McGraw-Hill Companies, Inc., 1221 Avenue of the Americas, New York, NY 10020.

This book is printed on acid-free paper.

3 4 5 6 7 8 9 0 FGR/FGR 0 9 8 7

ISBN-13: 978-0-07-297275-7
ISBN-10: 0-07-297275-0

Editor in Chief: *Emily Barrosse*
Publisher: *William Glass*
Executive Editor: *Nicolas R. Barrett*
Director of Development: *Kathleen Englberg*
Developmental Editor: *Carlotta Seely*
Executive Marketing Manager: *Pamela S. Cooper*
Managing Editor: *Jean Dal Porto*
Project Manager: *Catherine R. Iammartino*
Art Director: *Jean Schreiber*
Senior Designer: *Kim Menning*
Text Designer: *Caroline McGowan*
Cover Designer: *Yvo Riezebos*
Cover Credit: *Cover art and text cartoon art copyright © Stuart A. Copans, M.D.*
Media Project Manager: *Ron Nelms*
Associate Production Supervisor: *Jason I. Huls*
Composition: *10/12 Times Roman, by Cenveo*
Printing: *45# New Era Matte, Quebecor World Fairfield, Inc.*

Library of Congress Cataloging-in-Publication Data

Kinney, Jean, 1943–
Loosening the grip : a handbook of alcohol information / Jean Kinney ; illustrations by Stuart A. Copans.— 8th ed.
p. cm.
Includes bibliographical references and index.
ISBN 0-07-297275-0 (softcover : alk. paper)
1. Alcoholism—United States—Handbooks, manuals, etc. 2. Alcoholism—Treatment—United States—Handbooks, manuals, etc. I. Title.
HV5292.K53 2006
362.292—dc22 2005050496

www.mhhe.com

Contributors

Stuart A. Copans, M.D.

Illustrator

Dr. Copans, a child psychiatrist, was a lecturer in an alcohol counselor training program, discussing the effects of alcohol abuse on the family—the early sign of what has since become a major professional interest. He has directed a residential adolescent substance abuse program, in a Dartmouth-affiliated teaching hospital, and is currently in private practice and a consultant to schools on issues of adolescents.

Jean Kinney, M.S.W.

Jean Kinney, lecturer in Community and Family Medicine at Dartmouth Medical School, was the Associate Director of the Alcohol Counselor Training Program at Dartmouth conducted between 1972 and 1978, the program that was the impetus for this text. Upon the completion of the training program, she joined Project Cork, a program established to develop and implement a model curriculum for medical student education. In 1999, Jean Kinney was the first recipient of the NIAAA's Senator Harold Hughes Award, in recognition of these educational efforts in translating scientific work into clinical practice. She publishes a substance abuse website for health-care professionals.

Fred C. Osher, M.D.

Chapter 12, Other Psychiatric Considerations: Suicide, Co-occurring Psychiatric Illness

Dr. Osher entered the field of psychiatry after serving as the medical director of a detoxification center in Detroit, a setting that sparked his continuing interest in substance abuse issues. He was an early member of the New Hampshire Psychiatric Research Center, which has been a leader in the area of the care of those with psychiatric illness and substance abuse problems. From there he moved to the Substance Abuse and Mental Health Services Administration (SAMHSA), and has since joined the

University of Maryland in Baltimore, where he is an Associate Professor and Director for the Center for Behavioral Health, Justice,and Public Policy. He is also affiliated with the Department of Psychiatry of the Johns Hopkins Medical School.

Trevor R.P. Price, M.D.

Chapter 3, Alcohol and the Body
Chapter 6, Medical Complications

Dr. Price entered psychiatry after training in internal medicine. His interest in alcohol was sparked during his tenure at Dartmouth Medical School, when he was a member of the faculty for the Alcohol Counselor Training Program. Dr. Price has been on the faculty of Dartmouth Medical School, the University of Pennsylvania School of Medicine, and the Medical College of Pennsylvania and Hahnemann Medical School. He has recently traded being a department chair for private practice, and to again have the opportunity to provide patient care.

Donald A. West, M.D.

Chapter 12, Other Psychiatric Considerations: Section on Psychotropic Medications
Chapter 13, Other Drugs of Abuse

Dr. West, Associate Professor of Pychiatry at Dartmouth Medical School, is actively involved in coordinating substance abuse services at the Dartmouth Hitchcock Medical Center and is medical director of the short-term psychiatric unit at the Medical Center. He originally came to Dartmouth on a half-year sabbatical from the University of New Mexico, which he spent with the substance abuse treatment team, and the area apparently began to look like home.

By the time a text has reached its Eighth Edition, it becomes difficult to sort out and separate the particular contributions of individual people. Those listed above assumed responsibility for revising and updating material for this edition. Much of what remains incorporated here is, however, the product of others who contributed to earlier editions, and whose work remains.

Gwen Leaton

Co-editor, previous editions

Gwen Leaton was involved in the Alcohol Counselor Training Program as a research assistant. Following the completion of the Counselor Training Program, she held positions in several other education and training programs. Gwen was intimately involved in the development of the initial text as well as subsequent revisions. Gwen died in early 1999.

Frederick Burkle, Jr., M.D., M.P.H., FAAP, FACEP

Chapter 11, Adolescents, previous editions

Dr. Burkle, a lecturer to the counselor trainees at Dartmouth Medical School, came to a psychiatry residency program at Dartmouth Medical School after a practice in pediatrics. He has long since left chilly New England and is a Professor of Pediatrics and Surgery at the University of Hawaii John A. Burns School of Medicine and Professor of Public Health at the University of Hawaii School of Public Health.

Richard Goodstein, M.D.

Chapter 11, The Elderly
Chapter 12, Suicide Evaluation and Prevention

Dr. Goodstein, another member of the training program faculty at Dartmouth, after establishing and directing a Psychiatric Services Crisis Clinic within the Dartmouth Hitchcock Medical Center, moved south. He joined the Carrier Foundation as Vice President of Medical Education, has been on the faculty at the Rutgers Medical School, and is currently senior director of medical partnerships at Merck & Co. in Pennsylvania.

Hugh MacNamee, M.D.

Chapter 11, Adolescents, previous edition

Dr. MacNamee was an associate professor of clinical psychiatry in the Division of Child Psychiatry at Dartmouth until his death in 1984. Material on adolescents incorporated here reflects lectures he gave to the alcohol counselor trainees. His eminently practical stance and uncommon common sense were always much in evidence. Some things really cannot be improved on. His influence continues too through other contributors who trained under him.

For Sarah Horton, with love

God of Compassion, if anyone has come to Thine altar troubled in spirit, depressed and apprehensive, expecting to go away as she came, with the same haunting heaviness of heart; if anyone is deeply wounded of soul, hardly daring to hope that anything can afford her the relief he seeks, so surprised by the ill that life can do that she is half afraid to pray; O God, surprise her, we beseech Thee, by the graciousness of Thy help; and enable her to take from thy bounty as ungrudgingly as Thou givest, that she may leave her sorrow and take a song away.

Author Unknown

Brief Contents

Contents

Preface

> Material on alcohol and alcoholism is mushrooming. There are books, articles, scientific reports, pamphlets. On present use, past use, abuse. Around prevention, efforts at early detection, effects on the family, effects on the body. When, where, why . . .
>
> And yet, if you are in the helping business and reasonably bright and conscientious and can find an occasional half hour to read but don't have all day to search library stacks, then it's probably hard for you to lay your hands on the information you need when it would be most helpful.
>
> This handbook is an attempt to partially remedy the situation. It contains what we believe is the basic information an alcohol counselor or other professional confronted with alcohol problems needs to know and would like to have handy. The work here isn't original. It is an effort to synthesize, organize, and sometimes "translate" the information from medicine, psychology, psychiatry, anthropology, sociology, and counseling that applies to alcohol use and alcoholism treatment. This handbook isn't the last word. But we hope it is a starting point.
>
> Preface, *Loosening the Grip,* First Edition, 1978

In the period since the publication of the first edition of this handbook, what was then described as rapid growth in the literature has become a veritable deluge. Consequently, the demands upon those in the helping professions are even greater. To be current would entail not only scanning the literature from the disciplines mentioned, but also looking at the many new journals of the alcohol and substance abuse fields.

Since the first edition of *Loosening the Grip,* there have been many changes in the alcohol field. Possibly the most notable one is that there is no longer a distinct alcohol field in the way that was true in the 1970s. There is now a field of substance abuse, which represents a merging of the previously separate worlds of alcohol treatment and drug treatment.

Beginning with the first edition of this book, there have continued to be queries on the title. Yes, there is a story behind it. When Gwen Leaton, my coauthor for the first six editions, and I were preparing the original text, an apt title did not leap forth. Somewhere along the line, in casual conversation someone recounted the comment of an alcoholic struggling to get sober. This alcoholic, discussing her drinking in a rather defiant and belligerent fashion, said, "If God didn't want me to drink, He'd knock the glass out of my hand!" One of us jokingly commented that we hoped whoever was present had supplied the obviously perfect retort, "He will; all you have to do is loosen your grip." Somehow that metaphor caught the simplicity and the complexity, the ease and the difficulty, the "holding on" and "being held" that are a part of alcohol problems.

An almost mandatory conclusion for book prefaces is an exhaustive listing of "all the persons whose support and assistance. . . ." Trusting that families, friends, and professional colleagues know who they are, here there is a slight departure from that tradition. In fact, many of the most significant contributions to this work have been made by individuals whose names and identities, such as the woman in the example just given, are in many instances unknown—substance abuse clinicians, those in the 12-step groups, members of the clergy, school counselors, the medical profession—all those who have been responsible for the strides in our collective understanding and clinical practice, all those whose efforts in their professional and private lives make loosening the grip possible. There is the continuing presence of Gwen Leaton in this work. Having been a two-decades-long collaborative effort, revising the text to eliminate the "we's" was difficult; those that remain continue to be appropriate.

Jean Kinney

HIGHLIGHTS OF THIS EDITION

Story of Alcohol Presented in New Way

The introduction to the topic of alcohol is now divided into two separate chapters. Chapter 1, Alcohol, focuses on the historical background and describes the changing views of alcohol throughout the years. It also includes historical background on other drugs, such as tobacco and marijuana. Chapter 2, Alcohol and Its Costs, current drinking patterns, problems associated with use, and provides international comparisons. As two separate chapters, the many-faceted topic of alcohol becomes more manageable and focused.

Focus on Drugs Boxes

Most chapters include Focus on Drugs boxes, which highlight a drug other than alcohol and compare or contrast that drug with alcohol. This addition broadens the text's coverage of other drugs of abuse and offers additional topics for discussion.

Demographic Changes in Alcohol Use

As society changes, so does the use of alcohol and other drugs. This edition discusses, the drug-free workplace, club drugs, binge drinking, and the genetic basis for alcoholism. This approach offers valuable information an insight for new counselors.

Alcohol Use in Context

By highlighting environmental and cultural influences, gender differences, and sexual orientation, this edition presents a real-life view of alcohol and shows all the factors that need to be taken into consideration in treatment use disorders.

New or Expanded Topics

Chapter 1: Alcohol

1. Separate discussion of historical background of alcohol
2. Addition of historical material on other drugs
3. History of tobacco use in the United States
4. History of marijuana use
5. Changing views of alcohol over time

Chapter 2: Alcohol and Its Costs

1. Current information on patterns of alcohol and other drug use
2. International comparisons of alcohol use and effects

Chapter 3: Alcohol and the Body

1. Ingestion and Metabolism
2. Highlighting of alcohol's action on the body

Chapter 4: Alcohol Dependence

1. Examination of implications of disease concept
2. Current research of different "types" of alcohol dependence
3. Diagnostic criteria for other drug use disorders

Chapter 5: Etiology of Alcohol Dependence

1. Cross-cultural comparisons of drinking patterns
2. International comparisons of impact of alcohol policy changes

Chapter 6: Medical Complications

1. Alcohol-cocaine interactions
2. Latest research on many medical complications associated with alcohol use

Chapter 7: The Behavior of Dependence

1. Comparison/contrast of emergence of alcohol problems to other drugs

Chapter 8: Effects of Alcohol Problems on the Family

1. Expanded consideration of impact on family
2. Impact of other drug use on family
3. Effects of child's alcohol/drug use problem on parents and family unit
4. Impact of smoking on other family members

Chapter 9: Evaluation and Treatment Overview

1. Manual-guided treatment
2. Screening instruments for drug problems

Chapter 10: Treatment Techniques and Approaches

1. Newest treatment approaches and drug therapies
2. Impact of marijuana on driving

Chapter 11: Special Populations

1. Update on patterns of use and nature of problems in various population segments

2. Adolescents: problems with diagnostic criteria; smoking cessation issues
3. College students: binge-drinking facts and myths; performance-enhancing drugs among college athletes; possibilities and limitations of common college approaches; nicotine use
4. Women: effects of other drug use during pregnancy; women-only treatment approaches; women and children in treatment
5. Workplace: comparison of alcohol and drug problems; drug testing in the workplace setting

Chapter 12: Other Psychiatric Considerations

1. Current information on comorbidity of substance use and other psychiatric problems
2. Update on psychotropic medications used in treatment of mental health problems

Chapter 13: Drug of Abuse Other Than Alcohol

1. Most recent data on drugs of abuse, epidemiology and associated problems, and treatment approaches
2. History of drug control policies
3. Frameworks for underpinning classification of drugs
4. Drugs associated with "raves"
5. Table comparing toxicity/lethality of different drugs of abuse
6. Factors that underlie drug classification schema
7. Performance-enhancing drugs used by athletes
8. Expanded discussion of legal drugs such as nicotine and caffeine

Chapter 14: Odds 'n' Ends

1. Professional role
2. Role of computer in workplace: ethical issues and guidelines for e-mail with clients and other electronic communications

SUCCESSFUL FEATURES

Alcohol and College Life

This edition continues its in-depth coverage of alcohol use in colleges and universities. It presents the natural history of alcohol problems among college students, discusses issues related to college athletes, and addresses the protective factors built into the college environment.

Drugs Other Than Alcohol

The chapter dedicated to drugs other than alcohol surveys the major drug classes, discussing their acute and chronic effects. It also examines the patterns and social costs of drug use and offers an overview of treatment and screening for drug use.

Various Treatment Approaches

This new edition continues to present the different treatment approaches available today, including treatment via the Internet, treatment matching, screening tests for adolescents, Alcoholics Anonymous, self-help, group therapy, and other non-12-step treatment programs.

Readable Style

With a writing style that is conversational and easy to follow, this text draws readers in and leads them through its broad coverage of the topic in terms of age groups, social institutions, and counseling options.

Integrated Approach

By synthesizing information from medicine, psychology, psychiatry, anthropology, sociology, and counseling, this text presents a broad view of alcohol use and treatment of alcoholism.

SUPPLEMENTS

Instructor's Resource CD-ROM

This CD includes the Instructor's Manual, Computerized Test Bank, and PowerPoint presentation designed to accompany *Loosening the Grip: A Handbook of Alcohol Information.*

Instructor's Manual

With chapter outlines and Internet resources for each chapter, this manual offers information for use in the classroom and for further exploration by students. It also provides related links in the following areas: medicine, alcohol, other drugs of abuse, patters of substance abuse, clinical guides, curricula, policy and white papers, and international data.

Computerized Test Bank

The test bank is available on the Instructor's Resource CD-ROM as Word files and with EZ Test **computerized testing software.** EZ Test provides a powerful, easy-to-use test maker to create printed quizzes and exams. EZ Test runs on both Windows and Macintosh systems. For secure online testing, exams created in EZ Test can be exported to WebCT, Blackboard, PageOut, and (beginning fall 2005) EZ Test Online. The EZ Test CD is packaged with a Quick Start Guide; once the program is installed, users have access to the complete User's Manual, including multiple Flash tutorials. Aditional help is available at www.mhh.com/eztest.

PowerPoint Presentation

The chapter-by-chapter PowerPoint presentation is a helpful teaching aid that can be modified to meet the needs of individual instructors and their courses.

Internet Resources

Online Learning Center
www.mhhe.com/kinney8e

This website offers resources to students and instructors. It includes downloadable ancillaries, web links, student quizzes, additional information on topics of interest, and more. Resources include:

For the instructor

1. Downloadable PowerPoint presentation
2. Instructor's Manual
3. PageOut

For the student

1. Interactive quizzes
2. Chapter-related readings
3. Chapter outlines
4. PowerWeb

Course Management Systems

www.mhhe.com/solutlons

Now instructors can combine their McGraw-Hill Online Learning Center with today's most popular course-management systems and McGraw-Hill's PageOut. The McGraw-Hill Online Learning Center has also been converted into a cartridge that can be used in most course management systems. Our Instructor Advantage program offers customers toll-free telephone support and unlimited e-mail support. Instructors who use 500 or more copies of a McGraw-Hill textbook can enroll in our Instructor Advantage Plus program, which provides on-campus, hands-on training from a platform specialist. Consult your McGraw-Hill sales representative to find out what other course management systems are easily used with McGraw-Hill online materials.

PowerWeb

www.dushkin.com/online

The PowerWeb website is a reservoir of course-specific articles and current events. Students can visit PowerWeb to take a self-scoring quiz, complete an interactive exercise, click through an interactive glossary, or check the daily news.

PowerWeb is packaged with many McGraw-Hill textbooks. Students are also granted full access to McGraw-Hill's Student Site.

Primis Online

www.mhhe.com/primis/online

Primis Online is a database-driven publishing system that allows instructors to create content-rich textbooks, lab manuals, or readers for their courses directly from the Primis website. The customized text can be delivered in print or electronic (eBook) form. A Primis eBook is a digital version of the customized text (sold directly to students as a file downloadable to their computer or accessed online by a password).

PageOut: The Course Website Development Center

www.pageout.net

PageOut, free to instructors who use a McGraw-Hill textbook, is an online program you can use to create your own course website. PageOut offers the following features:

- A course home page
- An instructor home page
- A syllabus (interactive and customizable, including quizzing, instructor notes, and links to the text's Online Learning Center)
- Web links
- Discussions (multiple discussion areas per class)
- An online gradebook
- Links to student web pages

Contact your McGraw-Hill sales representative to obtain a password.

Taking Sides: Drugs and Society, Sixth Edition

www.dushkin.com/takingsides

McGraw-Hill/Dushkin's *Taking Sides* series currently comprises 22 volumes with an instructor's guide with testing material available for each volume. The *Taking Sides* approach brings together the arguments of leading social and behavioral scientists, educators, and contemporary commentators, forming 18 to 20 debates, or issues, that present the pros and cons of current controversies in an area of study. An Issue Introduction that precedes the two opposing viewpoints gives students the proper context and historical background for each debate. After reading the debate, students are given other viewpoints to consider in the Issue Postscript, which also offers recommendations for further reading. *Taking*

Sides fosters critical thinking in students and encourages them to develop a concern for serious social dialogue.

ACKNOWLEDGMENTS

The editor and the publisher would like to thank the following instructors for reviewing *Loosening the Grip.* Their comments and suggestions have been very helpful.

For the Eighth Edition

Warren P. Allen
Western Oregon University

Cliff Garoupa
Fresno City College

Bruce Hayden
Florida International University

Bob Hayes
Lewis-Clark State College

Donald Krzyzak
Jane Addams College of Social Work

Alfred Lyons
St. Petersburg College

Candy S. McCorkle
Spring Arbor University

For the Seventh Edition

Jerome L. Short
George Mason University

Janette Simon
Upper Iowa University

Merry J. Sleigh
George Mason University

Joseph Stano
Springfield College

CHAPTER 1

Alcohol

ONCE UPON A TIME . . .

Imagine yourself in what is now Clairvoux, high in the Swiss hills. Stone pots dating from the Old Stone Age have been found that once contained a mild beer or wine. The beverage probably was discovered very much as fire was—by a combination of nature plus curiosity. If any watery mixture of vegetable sugars or starches, such as berries or barley, is allowed to stand long enough in a warm place, alcohol will make itself.

No one knows what kind of liquor came first—wine, beer, or mead—but by the Neolithic Age it was everywhere. Tales of liquor abound in folklore. One story relates that at the beginning of time the forces of good and evil contested with each other for domination of the earth. Eventually the forces for good won out. But a great many of them were killed in the process, and wherever they fell, a vine sprouted from the ground, so it seems some felt wine to be a good force. Other myths depict the powers of alcohol as gifts from the gods. Some civilizations worshiped specific gods of wine. The Egyptians' god was Osiris; the Greeks', Dionysius; and the Romans', Bacchus. Wine was used in early rituals as libations (poured out on the ground, altar, and so on). Priests often drank it as part of the rituals. The Bible, too, is full of references to sacrifices, including wine.

Ramses III distributed beer to his subjects and then told them the tingling they felt radiated from him.

From ritual uses the drinking of wine spread to convivial uses, and customs developed. Alcohol was a regular part of meals, viewed as a staple in the diet, even before ovens were invented for baking bread. The Assyrians received a daily portion from their masters of a "gallon" of bread and a gallon of fermented brew (probably a barley beer). Bread and wine were offered by the Hebrews on their successful return from battle. In Greece and Rome, wine was essential at every kind of gathering. Alcohol was found to contribute to fun and games at a party—for example, the Roman orgies. Certainly its safety over water was a factor, but its effects also had something to do with it. It is hard to imagine an orgy where

Persia. Malcolm, in his "History of Persia," relates that wine was discovered in that kingdom in the reign of Janisheed, who attempted to preserve grapes in a large vessel. Fermentation occurred, and the king believed that the juice was poison and labeled it as such. A lady of the palace, wishing to commit suicide, drank from it. She was pleased with the stupor that followed and repeated the experiment until the supply was exhausted. She imparted the secret to the king and a new quantity was made. Hence, wine in Persia is called "delightful poison."

William W. Spooner

The Cyclopaedia of Temperance and Prohibition. New York: Funk & Wagnells, 1891.

everyone drank water or welcoming a victorious army with lemonade. By the Middle Ages, alcohol permeated everything, accompanying birth, marriage, death, the crowning of kings, diplomatic exchanges, treaty signings, and councils. The monasteries became the taverns and inns of the times, and travelers received the benefit of the grape.

The ancients figured that what was good in these instances might be good in others, and alcohol came into use as a medicine. It was an antiseptic and an anesthetic and was used in combinations to form salves and tonics. As a cure it ran the gamut from black jaundice to knee pain and even hiccups. St. Paul advised Timothy, "No longer drink only water, but use a little wine for the sake of your stomach and your frequent ailments." Liquor was a recognized mood changer, nature's tranquilizer. Biblical King Lemuel's mother advised, "Give wine to them that be of heavy hearts." The Bible also refers to wine as stimulating and cheering: "praise to God, that He hath brought forth fruit out of the earth, and wine that maketh glad the heart of man."

FERMENTATION AND DISCOVERY OF DISTILLATION

Nature alone cannot produce stronger stuff than 14% alcohol. Fermentation is a natural process which occurs when yeasts combine with plants, be it potatoes, fruit, or grains. The sugar in the plants, exposed either to wild yeasts from the air or to commercial yeasts, produces an enzyme, which in turn converts sugar into alcohol. Fermentive yeast cannot survive in solutions stronger than 14% alcohol. When that level is reached, the yeast, which is a living thing, ceases to produce and dies.

It may not cure you, but it will make you feel better
Rhazes discovers distilling

In the tenth century, an Arabian physician, Rhazes, discovered distilled spirits. Actually, he was looking for a way to release "the spirit of the wine," which was welcomed at the time as the "true water of life." European scientists rejoiced in their long-sought "philosopher's stone," or perfect element. A mystique developed, and alcohol was called the fountain of youth, eau-de-vie, aqua vitae. Usequebaugh, from the Gaelic *usige beath,* meaning breath of life, is the source of the word "whiskey." The word "alcohol" itself is derived from the Arabic *al kohl.* It originally referred to a fine powder of antimony used for staining the eyelids and gives rise to speculation on the expression "Here's mud in your eye." The word evolved to describe any finely ground substance, then the essence of a thing, and eventually it came to mean "finely divided spirit," or the essential spirit of the wine. Nineteenth-century temperance advocates tried to prove that the word "alcohol" is derived from the Arabic *al-ghul,* meaning ghost or evil spirit.

Distilled liquor wasn't a popular drink until about the sixteenth century. Before that, it was used as the basic medicine and cure for all human ailments. Distillation is a simple process that can produce an alcohol content of almost 93% if it is refined enough times. Remember, nature stops at 14%. Start with a fermented brew. When it is boiled, the alcohol separates from the juice or whatever as steam. Alcohol boils at a lower temperature than the other liquid. The escaping steam is caught in a cooling tube and turns into a liquid again, leaving the juice, water, and so on behind. Voila—stronger stuff—about 50% alcohol.

Proof as a way of measuring the strength of a given liquor came from a practice used by the early American settlers to test their brews. They saturated gunpowder with alcohol and ignited it: too strong, it flared up; too weak, it sputtered. A strong blue flame was considered the sign of proper strength. Almost straight alcohol was diluted with water to gain the desired flame. Half and half was considered 100 proof. Thus, 86-proof bourbon is 43% alcohol. Because alcohol dilutes itself with water from the air, 200-proof, or 100%, alcohol is not possible. The U.S. standards for spirits are between 195 and 198 proof.

ALCOHOL USE IN AMERICA

Alcohol came to America with the explorers and colonists. In 1620, the *Mayflower* landed at Plymouth because, as it says in the ship's log, "We could not now take time for further search or consideration, our victuals having been much spent, especially our bere." The Spanish missionaries brought grapevines, and before the United States was yet a nation, there was wine making in California. The Dutch opened the first distillery on Staten Island in 1640. In the Massachusetts Bay Colony, brewing ranked next in importance after milling and baking. The Puritans did not disdain the use of alcohol, as is sometimes supposed. A federal law passed in 1790 gave provisions for each soldier to receive a ration of one-fourth pint of brandy, rum, or whiskey. The colonists imported wine and malt beverages and planted vineyards, but it was Jamaican rum that became the answer to the thirst of the new nation. For its sake, New Englanders became the bankers of the slave trade that supplied the molasses needed to produce rum. Eventually whiskey, the backwoods substitute for rum, superseded rum in popularity. Sour-mash bourbon became the great American drink.

This is a very brief view of alcohol's history. The extent of its uses, the ways in which it has been viewed, and even the amount of writing about it that survives give witness to the value placed on this strange substance. Alcohol has been everywhere, connected to everything that is a part of everyday life. Growing the grapes or grains to produce it is even suspected as the reason for the development of agriculture. Whether making it, using it as a medicine, drinking it, or writing about it, people from early times have devoted much time and energy to alcohol.

WHY BOTHER?

So alcohol happened. Why didn't it go the way of the dinosaurs? Think about the first time you ever tasted alcohol. Some people were exposed early. Some may have been allowed a taste of Dad's beer, along with sharing his pretzels when he watched Monday night football. Some sneaked sips at the first big wedding or a party they attended. For some, alcohol was served at home as part of special meals, with kids getting a small glass of wine. For others, alcohol was seen very infrequently at home, if at all. They may not have tried alcohol until middle school or high school, whether at a friend's house or a party.

A significant part of our introduction to alcohol occurs through movies, as well as ads on television or in magazines. In addition to any firsthand early experience, these sources also mold our understanding of what alcohol is and how it is a part of adult life.

When you tried that first sip of Dad's beer, you didn't like the taste. But you took a sip every time it was offered. As the ads tell you—*as you're fighting your way to the top, it helps to have a taste of what's up there.*

In middle school, too often you found that parties were as much torture as fun. You felt awkward; conversation didn't come easily; you never felt comfortable. Then one time, someone brought some orange juice spiked with vodka. That went down easily; the effects were nice. *To keep the party going, keep the best on hand.*

By the time you got your driver's license, your folks had had more discussions than you could begin to count about drinking. They were particularly concerned about the dangers of drinking and driving. Your friends, too, had all heard the same spiel. You knew your parents were concerned and what they said made sense. But still, it seemed that there must be *some* reasonable exceptions. After all, you were all together at Zarah's house; no one was going to be driving. There might have been a brief flash of guilt, but "really," nothing was going to happen. *On your night of nights, add that sophisticated touch.*

Or perhaps your family didn't drink. Maybe they *just* didn't, and it really wasn't that much a part of the community you lived in. Or rather than neutral or disinterested, they may have been opposed to alcohol. They gave you lots of reasons: "people who drink get into trouble" or even "God's against it." You looked up to your folks, or were scared of them, or you really believed that part about God's stand. Among your friends, as odd as it may sound, the issue never really came up. Then came college, the army, or a job and your own apartment. Suddenly it seemed as if everyone drank something, sometime, somewhere. They weren't dropping dead at the first sip or getting into too much trouble that you could see. There may have been a few "incidents," but people mostly laughed and brushed it off with "Aaah, he was plastered." Lightning didn't strike. You didn't see the devil popping out of the bottle. Just the opposite—everyone seemed to be having a lot of fun. *When the gang gets together . . . bowling, fishing, sailing, hiking, swimming, everywhere.*

It could be that you grew up with wine being served at meals. At some time you were initiated into the process as a matter of course. You never gave it a second thought. You might have had a religious background that introduced you to wine as a part of your ritual acceptance into adulthood or as a part of your particular church's worship.

With time, age, and social mobility, the reasons for continuing to drink become more complex. It is not unusual to drink a bit more than one can handle at some point. After one experience of being drunk, sick, or hung over, some people decide never to touch the stuff again. For most, however, something they are getting or think they are getting out of alcohol makes them try it again. Despite liquor's effects on us, most of us search for an experience we have had with it, want to have with it, or have been led to believe that we can have with its use. *As an essential part of the Good Life, __________ cannot be excelled.*

Theories of Alcohol Use
It's an attempt to recapture the security of feeding at the breast.
It is an attempt to deal with the anxiety of an unstable environment.
It is an attempt to gain more power
It's an attempt to reach an altered state of consciousness

Theories to Explain Alcohol Use

Those trying to explain drinking behavior have always been more interested in alcoholism (alcohol dependence) than in explaining alcohol use per se. Nonetheless, various theories were advanced in the past to explain the basic why behind alcohol use. Probably all contain some truth. They are included here to provide a historical perspective. They resurface from time to time as "new" ideas and may be assumed by the uninformed to explain alcoholism.

"It calms me down, helps my nerves. It helps me unwind after a hard day." This explanation can be thought of as the anxiety thesis. In part it is derived from Freud's work. Freud concluded that, in times of anxiety and stress, people fall back on things that have worked for them in the past. In theory, the things you will choose to relieve anxiety are those you did when you last felt most secure. That lovely, secure time might last have been at Mom's breast. It has been downhill ever since. In this case, use of the mouth (eating, smoking, drinking) is chosen to ease stressful situations.

Another version of the anxiety thesis came from Donald Horton's anthropological studies. He observed that alcohol was used by primitive societies either ritually or socially to relieve the anxiety caused by an unstable environment. Drunken acts are acceptable and not punished. The greater the environmental stress, the heavier the drinking. Accordingly, in this view, alcohol's anxiety-reducing property is the one universal key to why people drink alcohol. This theory has by and large been rejected as the sole reason for drinking. Indeed, with the advances in biological research on alcohol's effects, it is now realized that alcohol doesn't, in fact, actually reduce anxiety. At best it partially masks it.

Another theory that surfaced was based on the need for a feeling of power over oneself or one's environment. Most people don't talk about this, but take a look at the heavy reliance of the liquor industry on macho models, executive types, and beautiful women surrounded by adoring males. People in ads celebrate winning anything with a drink of some sort.

The power theory was explored by researchers in the early 1970s, under the direction of David McClelland. They examined folktales from both heavy- and light-drinking societies. Their research indicated that there was no greater concern with relief from tension or anxiety in heavy-drinking societies than in those that consumed less. To look at this further they conducted a study with college men over a period of 10 years. Without revealing the reasons for the study, they asked the students to write down their fantasies before, during, and after the consumption of liquor. The stories revealed that the students felt bigger, stronger, more influential, more aggressive, and more capable of great sexual conquest the more they drank. The conclusion was that people drink to experience a feeling of power. This power feeling was seen as having two different patterns, depending on the personality of the drinker. What was called *p-power* is a personal powerfulness, uninhibited and carried out at the expense of others. Social power, or *s-power,* is a more altruistic powerfulness, power to help others. This s-power was found to predominate after two or three drinks; heavier drinking produced a predominance of p-power.

Another theory arose during the late 1960s at the height of the counterculture, with its wave of drug use, particularly psychedelic drugs. This approach, as discussed by Andrew Weil, claimed that every human being has a need to reach out toward a larger experience. People will try anything that suggests itself as a way to do that—for instance, alcohol, drugs, yoga, or meditation. Some drugs were then commonly said to "blow your mind" or were designated as "mind-expanding drugs." Evidence cited for seeking altered states of consciousness begins with very young children, who whirl, hyperventilate, or attempt in other ways to produce a change in their experience. When they are older, people learn that chemicals can produce different states. In pursuit of these states, alcohol is often used because it is the one intoxicant we make legally available. The "drug scene" was viewed as another answer to the same search. Weil suggested that this search arises from the "innate psychological drive arising out of the neurological structure of the human brain." His conclusion was that we have put the cart before the horse in focusing attention on drugs rather than on the states people seek from them. Thus, he suggested that society acknowledge the need itself for an altered state of consciousness and cope with it in a positive rather than a negative way.

If all be true that I do think,
There are five reasons we should drink;
Good wine—a friend—or being dry—
Or lest we should be by and by—
Or any other reason why.
DEAN OF CHRIST CHURCH, OXFORD
Reasons for Drinking, 1689

Another perspective on factors that may contribute to alcohol use focuses on stresses associated with modern, everyday life—be it in the pressures of making it in the corporate world, corporate downsizing, or the changes in family structure. Use of alcohol is seen as one response to stress. Other responses to stress include hypertension, ulcer disease, and migraine headaches. Accordingly, stress management has become popular as a technique to help people develop alternative, less destructive means of coping with stress.

More recently a factor that has been considered to shed light on reasons for drinking is the role of *expectations*—that is, what individuals believe that alcohol will do to or for them. For the most part, researchers now are less interested in identifying factors within the individual that motivate alcohol use. More attention is being directed toward the social setting in which people find themselves, to identify factors associated with patterns of use. For example, attention is turning to the roles of peers in determining adolescents' decisions to use alcohol, the influence of parental standards in setting norms for their teenagers' drinking, and the impact of legislative approaches.

In vino veritas.
PLINY

In general, the accepted stance now seems to be a "combination of factors" approach. One inescapable fact is that, from the very earliest recorded times, alcohol has been important to people. Seldon Bacon, former head of the Rutgers School of Alcohol Studies, made a point worth keeping in mind. He called attention to the original needs that alcohol might have served: satisfaction of hunger and thirst, medication or anesthetic, or fostering religious ecstasy. Our modern, complex society has virtually eliminated all these earlier functions. Now all that is left is alcohol the depressant, the mood-altering drug, the possible, or believed, reliever of tension, inhibition, and guilt. Contemporary society has had to create new needs for alcohol to meet.

We take a drink only for the sake of the benediction.
PERETZ

Myths

In thinking about alcohol use, remember that myths, a variant of expectancies, are equally important to people. Many think that alcohol makes them warm when they are cold (not so), sexier (in the courting, maybe; in the execution, not so), manlier, womanlier, cured of their ills (not usually), less scared of people (possibly), and better able to function (only if very little is taken). An exercise in asking people what a drink does for them will expose a heavy reliance on myths for their reasons. Whether factually based or not, myths often influence people's experience of alcohol use. Whatever the truth in the mixture of theory and myth, enough people in the United States rely on the use of alcohol to accomplish something for them to support a virtual $100 billion industry.

ALCOHOL PROBLEMS: THE FLY IN THE OINTMENT

Alcohol is many-faceted. With its ritual, medicinal, dietary, and pleasurable uses, alcohol can leave in its wake confusion, pain, disorder, and

HE'S ALWAYS GOT AN EXCUSE. TODAY HE'S AFRAID THE ANTEATERS WILL EAT THE ANTS.

tragedy. The use and abuse of alcohol have gone hand in hand in all cultures. With the notable exceptions of the Muslims and Buddhists, whose religions forbid drinking, temperance and abstinence have been the exception rather than the rule in most of the world.

As Sin or Moral Failing

Societies have come to grips with alcohol problems in a variety of ways. One of these regards drunkenness as a sin or a moral failing and the drunk as a moral weakling. The Greek word for drunk, for example, means literally to "misbehave at the wine." An Egyptian writer admonished his drunken friend with the slightly contemptuous "Thou art like a little child." Noah, who undoubtedly had reason to seek relief in drunkenness after getting all those creatures safely through the flood, was not looked on kindly by his children as he lay in his drunken stupor. The complaints have continued through time. A Dutch physician of the sixteenth century criticized the heavy use of alcohol in Germany and Flanders by saying, "That freelier than is profitable to health, they take it and drink it." Some of the most forceful sanctions have come from the temperance movements. An early U.S. temperance leader wrote that "alcohol is preeminently a destroyer in every department of life." As late as 1974, the New Hampshire Christian Civic League devoted an entire issue of its monthly newspaper to a polemic against the idea that alcoholism is a disease. In its view, the disease concept gives reprieve to the "odious alcohol sinner."

As a Legal Issue

Many see the use of liquor as a legislative issue and believe misuse can be solved by laws. Total prohibition is one of the methods used by those who believe that legislation can sober people up. Most legal approaches through history have been piecemeal affairs invoked to deal with specific situations. Excessive drinking was so bad in ancient Greece that "drinking captains" were appointed to supervise drinking. Elaborate rules were devised for drinking at parties. Another perennial favorite has been control of supply. In 81 C.E., a Roman emperor ordered the destruction of half the British vineyards.

The sin and legal views of drunkenness often go hand in hand. They have as a common denominator the idea that the drunk chooses to be drunk and is therefore either a sinner or a ne'er-do-well, who can be handled by making it illegal to drink. In 1606, intoxication was made a statutory offense in England by an "Act for Repressing the Odious and Loathsome Sin of Drunkenness." In the reign of Charles I, laws were passed to suppress liquor altogether. Settling a new world did not dispense with the problems resulting from alcohol use. The traditional methods of dealing with these problems continued. From the 1600s to the 1800s, attitudes toward alcohol were low-key. Laws were passed in various colonies and states to deal with liquor use, such as an early Connecticut law forbidding drinking for more than half an hour at a time. Another law in Virginia in 1760 prohibited ministers from "drinking to excess and inciting riot." But there were no temperance societies, no large-scale prohibitions, and no religious bodies fighting.

America's Response to Alcohol Problems

Drinking in the colonies was largely a family affair and remained so until the beginning of the nineteenth century. With increasing immigration, industrialization, and greater social freedoms, drinking became less a family affair. Alcohol abuse became more open and more destructive. The opening of the West brought the saloon into prominence. The old, stable social and family patterns began to change. The frontier hero took to gulping his drinks with his foot on a bar rail. Attitudes began to intensify regarding the use of alcohol. These developments hold the key to many modern attitudes toward alcohol, the stigma of alcoholism, and the wet-dry controversy. Differing views of alcohol began to polarize America. The legal and moral approaches reached their apex in the United States with the growth of the temperance movement and the Prohibition amendment in 1919.

Temperance and Prohibition

The traditional American temperance movement did not begin as a prohibition movement. The temperance movement coincided with the rise of social consciousness, a belief in the efficacy of law to resolve human problems. It was part and parcel of the humanitarian movement, which included child labor and prison reform, women's rights, abolition, and social welfare and poverty legislation. Originally it condemned only excessive drinking and the drinking of distilled liquor, not all alcoholic beverages nor all drinking. It was believed that the evils connected with the abuse of alcohol could be remedied through proper legislation. The aims of the original temperance movement were largely moral, uplifting, and rehabilitative. Passions grow, however, and before long those who had condemned only the excessive use of distilled liquor were condemning all alcohol. Those genial, well-meaning physicians, business owners, and farmers began to organize their social lives around their crusade. Fraternal orders, such as the Independent Order of Good Templars of 1850, grew and proliferated. In a short span of time it had branches all over the United States, with churches, missions, and hospitals—all dedicated to the idea that society's evils were caused by liquor. This particular group influenced the growth of the Women's Christian Temperance Union (WCTU) and the Anti-Saloon League. By 1869, it had become the

Equal suffrage. The probable influence of women's suffrage on the temperance reform can be no better indicated than by the following words of the Brewer's Congress held in Chicago in 1881: Resolved, That we oppose always and everywhere the ballot in the hands of woman, for woman's vote is the last hope of the prohibitionists.

WILLIAM W. SPOONER

The Cyclopaedia of Temperance and Prohibition. New York: Funk & Wagnalls, 1891.

National Prohibition Party, the spearhead of political action, which advocated the complete suppression of liquor by law.

People who had no experience at all with drinking got involved in the crusade. In 1874, Frances Willard founded the WCTU in Cleveland. Women became interested in the movement, which simultaneously advocated social reform, prayer, prevention, education, and legislation in the field of alcohol. Mass meetings were organized, to which thousands went. Journals were published; children's programs taught fear and hatred of alcohol; libraries were established. The WCTU was responsible for the first laws requiring alcohol education in the schools, some of which remain on the books. All alcohol use—moderate, light, heavy, and excessive—was condemned. All users were one and the same. Bacon, in describing the classic temperance movement, says there was "one word for the action—DRINK. One word for the category of people—DRINKER."

By 1895, many smaller local groups had joined the Anti-Saloon League, which had become the most influential of the temperance groups. It was nonpartisan politically and supported any prohibitionist candidate. It pressured Congress and state legislatures and was backed by church groups in "action against the saloon." Political pressure mounted. The major thrust of all these activities was that the only real problem was alcohol and the only real solution was prohibition.

In 1919, Congress passed the Volstead Act, the Eighteenth Amendment, ushering in Prohibition. What exactly did Prohibition prohibit? This act made the commercial manufacture, sale, and transportation of alcoholic beverages illegal. It did not ban the possession of alcoholic beverages nor make it illegal to produce either beer or wine for personal consumption. The act had 60 provisions, was messy and complicated, and no precedent had been set to force the public cooperation required to make it work. Prohibition remained in effect from 1920 to 1933.

Prohibition shaped much of the country's economic, social, and underground life. Its repeal under the Twenty-First Amendment in 1933 did not remedy the situation. While there was a decline in alcoholism under Prohibition, as indicated by a decline in deaths from cirrhosis, it had failed nonetheless. The real problems created by alcohol were obscured or ignored by the false wet-dry controversy. The quarrel raged between the manufacturers, retailers, and consumers on one side and the temperance people, many churches, and women on the other. Those with alcohol problems or dependent on alcohol were ignored in the furor. When Prohibition was repealed, the problem of abuse was still there, and those dependent on alcohol were still there, along with the stigma of alcoholism. The other legacy of Prohibition was the development of underground crime syndicates. When no longer needed to provide alcohol, they took on other illicit activities, and later came to play a major role in drug trafficking.

The front door of the Boston Licensing Board was ripped down by the rush to get beer licenses the day Prohibition ended.

Another approach to alcohol problems is that of denial. This stance arose after the failure of Prohibition and is still not totally out of fashion. Problems arising from conflicting values and beliefs are often handled with euphemisms, humor, ridicule, and the delegating of responsibility to others.

Our inconsistent attitudes toward alcohol are reinforced in subtle ways. For example, consider the hard-drinking movie heroes. There's the guy who drinks and drinks and then calls for more, never gets drunk, out-drinks the bad guys before he offs them, and gets the girl in the end. Then there's Humphrey Bogart, who is a drunken mess, wallowing in the suffering of humanity until the pure and beautiful heroine appears, at which point he washes, shaves, gets a new suit, and they live happily ever after.

Drunkenness Versus Alcoholism

It is important to see that alcohol dependence is not separate from alcohol. Dependence does not spring full-blown from somewhere. It is generally a condition that develops over time. Alcohol is available everywhere. A person really has to make a choice *not* to drink in our society. In some sets of circumstances one could drink for the better part of a day and never seem out of place. Some brunches have wine punch, Bloody Marys, or café brulée as their accompaniment. Wine, beer, or a mixed drink is quite appropriate at lunchtime. Helping a friend with an afternoon painting project or even raking your own lawn is a reasonable time to have a beer. Then, after a long day comes the predinner cocktail, maybe some wine with the meal. Later, watching a tape with friends, drinks are offered. And surely, some romantic candlelight and a nightcap go hand in hand. For most people this would not be their daily or even weekend fare, but the point is that none of these scenarios would cause most people to raise an eyebrow. The accepted times for drinking can be all the time, anywhere. Given enough of the kind of days described, the person who chooses to drink may develop problems, because alcohol is a drug and does have effects on the body.

Food without drink is like a wound without a plaster.
BRULL

Is alcoholism, which in medicine and counseling is now termed "alcohol dependence," a purely modern phenomenon, a product of our times? There are no references to alcoholics as such in historical writing. The word "alcoholism" was first introduced in 1849. Magnus Huss, a prominent Swedish physician, wrote a book on the physical problems associated with drinking distilled spirits, titled *Chronic Alcoholic Illness: A Contribution to the Study of Dyscasias Based on My Personal Experience and the Experience of Others.* (The term "dyscasias" is no longer used. Even when this work was published, the meaning of the term was a bit vague, covering a combination of maladies and generally used to describe those thought to have a "poor constitution.") In using the term "alcoholism," Huss was following the common scientific practice of using "ism" as a description of a disease, especially those associated with poisonings. While recognizing the host of medical complications, he thought that the culprit was distilled spirits and not associated with fermented beverages.

Temperate temperance is best. Intemperate temperance injures the cause of temperance.
MARK TWAIN

PORTRAIT OF A MAN WHO
SWears He will Never
HAVe another drink

Wine is a bad thing,
It makes you quarrel with your neighbor.
It makes you shoot at your landlord,
It makes you—miss him.

While the word "alcoholism" is a relatively modern one, there are vague references as far back in time as the third century that distinguish between being merely intoxicated and being a drunkard. In a commentary on imperial law, a Roman jurist of that era suggested that inveterate drunkenness be considered a medical matter rather than a legal one. In the thirteenth century, James I of Aragon issued an edict providing for hospitalization of conspicuously active drunks. In 1655, Younge, an English journalist, wrote a pamphlet in which he seemed to discern the difference between one who drinks and one who has a chronic condition related to alcohol. He says, "He that will be drawn to drink when he hath neither need of it nor mind to it is a drunkard."

History of Alcohol Treatment Efforts

The first serious considerations of the problem of inebriety, as it was called, came in the eighteenth and nineteenth centuries. Two famous writings addressed the problem in what seemed to be a new light. Although their work on the physical aspects of alcohol became fodder for the temperance zealots, both Dr. Benjamin Rush and Dr. Thomas Trotter seriously considered the effects of alcohol in a scientific way. Rush, a signer of the Declaration of Independence and the first surgeon general, wrote a lengthy treatise with a nearly equally lengthy title, *An Inquiry into the Effects of Ardent Spirits on the Human Body and Mind, with an Account of the Means of Preventing and the Remedies of Curing Them.* Rush's book is a compendium of the attitudes of the time, given weight by scholarly treatment. The more important of the two, and the first scientific formulation of drunkenness on record, is the classic work of Trotter, an Edinburgh physician. In 1804, he wrote *An Essay, Medical, Philosophical, and Chemical, on Drunkenness and Its Effects on the Human Body.* He states: "In the writings of medicine, we find drunkenness only cursorily mentioned among the powers that injure health. The priesthood hath poured forth its anathemas from the pulpit; and the moralist, no less severe, hath declaimed against it as a vice degrading to our nature." He then gets down to the heart of the matter: "In medical language, I consider drunkenness, strictly speaking, to be a disease, produced by a remote cause, and giving birth to actions and movements in the living body that disorder the functions of health." Trotter did not gain many adherents to his position, but small efforts were also being made at that time in the United States and elsewhere.

Around the 1830s, in Massachusetts, Connecticut, and New York, small groups were forming to reform "intemperate persons" by hospitalizing them, instead of sending them to jail or the workhouse. The new groups, started by the medical superintendent of Worcester, Massachusetts, Dr. Samuel Woodward, and Dr. Eli Todd, did not see inebriates in the same class with criminals, the indigent, or the insane. Between 1841 and 1874, 11 nonprofit hospitals and houses were set up. In 1876, *The*

Journal of Inebriety started publication to advance these reformers' views and findings. These efforts were taking place against the background of the temperance movement. Consequently, there was tremendous popular opposition from both the church and the legislative chambers. The journal was not prestigious by the standards of the medical journals of that time, and before Prohibition the hospitals were closed and the journal folded.

Another group also briefly flourished. The Washington Temperance Society began in Chase's Tavern in Baltimore in 1840. Six drinking buddies were the founders, and they each agreed to take a friend to the next meeting. Within a few months, parades and public meetings were being held to spread the message: "Drunkard! Come up here! You can reform. We don't slight the drunkard. We love him!" At the peak of its success in 1844, the membership consisted of 100,000 "reformed common drunkards" and 300,000 "common tipplers." A women's auxiliary group, the Martha Washington Society, was dedicated to feeding and clothing the poor. Based on the promise of religious salvation, the Washington Temperance Society was organized in much the same way as the ordinary temperance groups, but with a difference. It was founded on the basis of one drunkard's helping another, of drunks telling their story in public. The society prospered all over the East Coast as far north as New Hampshire. A hospital, the Home for the Fallen, was established in Boston and still exists under a different name. There are many similarities between the Washington Society and Alcoholics Anonymous (AA): alcoholics helping each other, regular meetings, sharing experiences, fellowship, reliance on a Higher Power, and total abstention from alcohol. The society was, however, caught up in the frenzies of the total temperance movement, including the controversies, power struggles, religious fights, and competition among the leaders. By 1848, just 8 short years after being founded, it was absorbed into the total prohibition movement. The treatment of the alcoholic became unimportant in the heat of the argument.

Recognition of the alcoholic as a sick person did not reemerge until comparatively recently. The gathering of a group of scientists at Yale University's Laboratory of Applied Psychology and the Fellowship of Alcoholics Anonymous, both begun in the 1930s, were instrumental in bringing this about. Also in the 1930s, a recovering Bostonian, Richard Peabody, first began to apply psychological methods to the treatment of those with alcoholism. He replaced the terms "drunk" and "drunkenness" with the more scientific and less judgmental "alcoholic" and "alcoholism." At Yale, Yandell Henderson, Howard Haggard, Leon Greenberg, and later E. M. Jellinek founded the *Quarterly Journal of Studies on Alcohol (QJSA)*—since 1975 known as the *Journal of Studies on Alcohol.* Unlike the earlier *Journal of Inebriety,* the *QJSA* had a sound scientific footing and became the mouthpiece for alcohol information. Starting with Haggard's work on alcohol metabolism, these efforts marked the first attempt to put the study of alcohol and alcohol problems

Alcohol is a very necessary article. . . . It makes life bearable to millions of people who could not endure their existence if they were quite sober. It enables Parliament to do things at eleven at night that no sane person would do at eleven in the morning.
GEORGE BERNARD SHAW, 1907

in a respectable, up-to-date framework. Jellinek's masterwork, *The Disease Concept of Alcoholism*, was a product of the Yale experience. The Yale Center of Alcohol Studies and the Classified Abstract Archive of Alcohol Literature were established. The Yale Plan Clinic was also set up to diagnose and treat alcoholism. The Yale Summer School of Alcohol Studies, now the Rutgers School, educated professionals and laypeople from all walks of life. Yale's prestigious influence had far-reaching effects. A volunteer organization, the National Council on Alcoholism (NCA)—now renamed the National Council on Alcohol and Other Drug Dependence (NCADD)—also grew out of the Yale School. It was founded in 1944 to provide public information and education about alcohol, through the joint efforts of Jellinek and Marty Mann, a recovering individual who became the NCA's first president.

On the other side of the coin, Alcoholics Anonymous was having more success in treating alcoholics than was any other group. AA grew, with a current estimated membership of over 2 million in both America and abroad. Its members became influential in removing the stigma that had so long been an accompaniment of alcoholism. Lawyers, businesspeople, teachers—people from every sector of society—began to recover. They could be seen leading useful, normal lives without alcohol. (More will be said in Chapter 9 on the origins and program of AA.) The successful recoveries of its members unquestionably influenced the course of later developments.

Public Policy and Alcohol

An alcoholic is someone you don't like who drinks as much as you do.
DYLAN THOMAS

Changing perceptions of the alcohol problem have become the foundation for public policy. Alcoholism is now recognized as a major public health problem. At the center of the federal efforts has been the National Institute of Alcohol Abuse and Alcoholism (NIAAA), established in 1971. The NIAAA at its founding became a major sponsor of research, training, public education, and treatment programs. The legislation creating the NIAAA was a landmark in our societal response to alcoholism. This bill, the Comprehensive Alcohol Abuse and Alcoholism Prevention, Treatment, and Rehabilitation Act of 1970, was sponsored by the late Senator Harold Hughes, himself a recovering person. Beyond establishing the NIAAA, the legislation created what might be called a bill of rights for those with alcoholism. It recognized that they suffer from a "disease that requires treatment"; it provided some protections against discrimination in the hiring of recovering alcoholics. That protection was further extended through passage of the Americans with Disabilities Act of 1990, designed to protect those with disabilities from discrimination.

In a similar vein, the Uniform Alcoholism and Intoxication Treatment Act, passed by Congress in 1971 and dealing with the issue of public intoxication, was recommended for enactment by the states. This act mandated treatment rather than punishment. With it, public inebriation was no longer a crime. These legislative acts incorporated the emerging new views of alcoholism and alcohol abuse: it is a problem; it is treatable.

On the heels of this legislation, there was a rapid increase during the 1970s in alcoholism treatment services, public and private, both residential and outpatient. In addition, each state mandated alcohol and other drug abuse services that focused on public information and education as well as treatment. Similarly, community mental health centers that received federal support were required to provide alcohol services. Also, health insurance coverage began to include rather than exclude alcoholism treatment services for its subscribers.

In the 1990s, concern about rising health-care costs, increases that consistently exceeded the rate of inflation, brought about efforts to limit coverage for many medical services. Alcohol and other drug abuse services that were covered disproportionately felt the ax. Insurance providers were increasingly reluctant to cover residential care. Thus, the earlier, most common form of treatment, the 28-day residential program, ceased to be the dominant treatment model. The result has been more outpatient treatment and the closing of many inpatient treatment programs because of empty beds. Many professionals recognize that inpatient care need not be the universal standard. However, it is critical for some patients.

Alcohol Treatment Professionals

With the increase in alcohol services, a new professional emerged, the alcohol counselor. These professionals formed the backbone of treatment efforts. With the increasing professionalism, the term "counselor" is more commonly being replaced by the term "therapist" or "clinician." Alcohol counselors' associations were formed in many states. The early distinction of separating alcohol and drug counselors has gone by the boards. In some instances alcohol-drug counselor associations certify alcohol counselors; in others, state licensing boards have been established. To promote uniformity of standards as well as facilitate recognition of credentials between states and across different certification groups, a voluntary organization—the National Certification Reciprocity Consortium—was established in the 1980s by various certification groups.

Interest in counselor credentialing began in the mid-1970s. A decade later, physicians in the substance abuse field began to examine the same questions. What qualifications should a physician have to work in the field? Is personal experience, the primary route by which many physicians initially entered, sufficient? The question was answered, just as it had been with alcohol counselors, with a clear no. Thus, the first steps were taken among physicians to establish a physicians' credentialing process. At this time there are several physician groups for those professionally involved in the alcohol and drug fields. The largest of these organizations, the American Society on Addiction Medicine (ASAM) began to offer a certification examination for members in the treatment of substance abuse. Other efforts have been launched to create a medical

Work is the curse of the drinking classes.
OSCAR WILDE

specialty in "addiction medicine," which would be analogous to other medical specialties, such as orthopedics, pediatrics, or family practice, and which would by definition entail a standardized training sequence and a process to award certification. ASAM has been in the forefront of this effort. The creation of a new medical specialty is a long process. It requires the approval and sanction of the Board of Medical Specialties, the national group that oversees the component member boards. Similarly there are credentials for nurses in the substance abuse field. In combination, these efforts testify to the concern for creating standards and the recognition of a core knowledge base and associated clinical skills. They represent an effort to bring those medical personnel engaged in the care of alcohol and other drug abuse patients fully into the medical mainstream.

All excess is ill, but drunkenness is the worst sort.
WILLIAM PENN

Education for all helping professionals on substance abuse has become more common, with a proliferation of workshops, special conferences, courses, and degree programs. Concern about professional education and standards has not been restricted to those whose primary professional involvement is in substance abuse. It has been increasingly recognized that a core knowledge base and associated clinical skills need to be part of any helping professional's training. Thus, the federal Alcohol and Drug Institutes and the Center for Substance Abuse Treatment (CSAT) have initiated programs to improve professional education among physicians, nurses, and social workers. These efforts have included designing model curricula, preparing curriculum materials, and working with the associated professional societies to promote the inclusion of education on alcohol and other drugs by these professions.

With the emergence of alcohol-drug treatment as a new health-care service, efforts were initiated to develop standards, not only for treatment personnel but also for treatment agencies. In 1984, the Joint Committee on the Accreditation of Health Care Organizations first established minimal standards for alcohol rehabilitation programs. Other groups, such as the Commission for Accreditation of Rehabilitation Facilities (CARF), also began to accredit substance abuse services. These efforts have resulted from, and at the same time have contributed to, our society's response to alcohol and other drug use as a major public health problem.

Bacchus has drowned more men than Neptune.
THOMAS FULLER

Problems of Alcohol Use and Public Policy

The focus on alcohol dependence during the 1980s broadened to include the larger issues of alcohol problems and alcohol use. Previously, the public's attitude could have been summarized as "The only real alcohol problem is alcoholism and that wouldn't happen to me." Now alcohol problems are not seen as so far removed from the average person. Driving while intoxicated has captured public attention. This alcohol-related problem can touch anyone. The concern about driving while intoxicated seems to have spilled over to intoxication in general. Intoxication has become less acceptable and is as likely to elicit disgust as to be considered funny or amusing. Other alcohol-related issues also have hit the public policy agenda.

The lobby for warning labels on alcoholic beverages saw its efforts succeed in 1989. The extent to which these labels have actually had an impact on drinking patterns is unclear, but it seems to have been modest. In 1999, the system of warning labels almost took a hit. The Wine Institute, a trade association of California vintners, convinced the Treasury Department's Bureau of Alcohol, Tobacco and Firearms, whose mission is to regulate the marketplace and collect taxes, to allow an "educational label," a "nonwarning label," for wine. The language proposed was as follows: "The proud people who made this wine encourage you to consult your family doctor about the health effects of wine." (The word "effects" had to be substituted for the Wine Institute's originally proposed "benefits.") This initiative was mounted purportedly in response to some research suggesting that consumption of wine in moderate amounts may have protective health benefits, including a reduced risk of heart disease. To take the wine manufacturers at their word, it seemed only "fair" that this information should be publicly available.

Periodically the Departments of Agriculture and Health and Human Services issues *Dietary Guidelines for Americans*. At the point of the most recent updating, the wine industry made recommendations similar to those outlined in the previous paragraph. Alcohol was first mentioned in the *Guidelines* issued in 1980, when moderate use was urged. The third version, in 1990, added another caveat: that the use of alcohol is not recommended. However in 1996, in light of evidence on potential benefits of moderate use, it was proposed that mention be made of "a lower risk of heart disease associated with moderate drinking for some individuals." To further expand on this, it was proposed that they also note that "alcoholic beverages have been used to enhance the enjoyment of meals by many societies throughout history." This move by the wine industry did not escape the notice of Congress and public health officials. Thus, they succeeded in blocking the introduction of "educational labels."

Advertising

Questions are increasingly being raised about the advertising of alcohol. The industry's advertising budget for 1998 was $1.1 billion. However, what one thinks of as advertising is literally only the half of it. In reporting advertising costs, typically such costs refer to what the Federal Trade Commission (FTC) terms "measured" media—TV, magazines, and newspapers. Other forms of advertising are termed "promotional expenses." For "well-promoted brands," traditional advertising represents only one-third of the total advertising/promotion budget, so the total promotional *and* advertising budget for alcohol in reality is closer to $3.3 billion. Promotional efforts include:

- Sponsorship of cultural, musical, and sporting events.
- Internet advertising.

- Displays for retail outlets. Window and interior displays for stores, bars, and restaurants are a significant expense. These costs are not restricted to printing costs. The retailers and bar owners are also paid to display these materials.
- Distribution of items with brand logos. One of the lesser known jobs available to a college student is as a beer company's representative. The job includes passing out all manner of things with the beer company's logo—from posters to beer mugs, back-packs, T-shirts, hats, and Frisbees. The list goes on and on. One study on tobacco is instructive. It involved a survey of middle and high school students in rural New England. One-third reported owning a cigarette promotional item. While only 4.5% reported taking such an item to school that day, 45% reported seeing such an item on the day of the survey. Students don't have to read a magazine or watch TV to be exposed to advertisements; they only have to walk down the hallways of their schools.
- Product placements in movies and TV shows. That beer in a movie doesn't have a made-up generic logo, the Bud Lite, Corona, or Sam Adams doesn't get there because the prop department selected it at random. Special companies exist to promote the use of products in entertainment productions, be they cell phones, cars, or alcoholic beverages. This is no small issue; after all, 93% of the 200 most popular movie rentals for 1997 and 1998 depicted alcohol use. Interestingly, in the same movies only 12 showed any long-term consequences of alcohol use, and less than half (49%) depicted any short-term negative outcomes.
- Catalogs and other direct mail communications.
- Price promotions, such as sales, coupons, and rebates.
- Trade promotions directed at wholesalers and retailers. More than one small convenience store owner has paid for a child's college education from the special payments that come from placing advertising materials prominently.

The United States is the leading beer-producing country in the world. Production in 1996 equaled 23,700,000 metric tons.

World Health Organization. *Global Status Report on Alcohol.* Geneva, Switzerland: 1999.

The money spent for just the advertising component is virtually equivalent to that spent on advertising for all other beverages combined—from milk to fruit drinks. The suspicion is that, contrary to the industry's claims, advertising does not simply represent companies' efforts to capture a larger share of the existing market by encouraging drinkers to switch brands. Rather, advertising is also directed at increasing the market size. That means promoting use among those who are nondrinkers or very light drinkers.

Targeting Underage Drinking

Of special concern is the targeting of young people. The use of animated characters is just one case in point. Might the Budweiser frogs be considered an effort to prime the pump for future consumers? Then there is the placement of advertising. Decisions about where to place advertisements are carefully considered by manufacturers or businesses.

Magazines and television shows can provide very detailed information about their readers or viewers, with a breakdown by age, income, education, geographic region, and ethnicity. This allows advertisers to target very specific populations. It happens that many of the publications selected for alcohol advertising are placed to hit the youth market, including those under 21 years of age. A substantial proportion of these ads are for liquor. There is concern that the television advertising is growing dramatically. In just 2 years, the number of liquor ads on cable TV grew 630%, from 513 to more than 33,000.[1] The proportion of ads placed on programs viewed by a significant proportion of underage youth is growing. In 2003, each of the 15 shows most popular with teens had had alcohol ads, at a cost estimated at $30 billion. Beyond having these young readers envisioning alcoholic beverages in their futures, one can't imagine that the size of the underage market has totally escaped the beverage industry. A report issued in 2003 points out that underage drinking represents 19.2% of all alcohol consumption. Of the estimated total of 50.52 billion drinks consumed annually in the United States, that means 9.7 billion drinks for those under age 21. That translates into 26.6 million drinks *daily* by those not legally old enough to consume alcohol. The annual bar tab for underage drinking? $22.5 billion.

A related issue is the creation of new beverages that are seen as appealing to younger people. One such example is the wine coolers introduced in the 1980s. More recent arrivals are drinks designed to mimic some old-fashioned nonalcoholic beverages. First introduced in England, they have since crossed the Atlantic. There are Two Dogs Alcoholic Lemonade; Mrs. Pucker's Citrus Brew; Hucker's Alcoholic Cola (with a 15% to 20% alcohol content); and TGI Friday's Lemon Drop Drink, with its 40% alcohol content. The newest arrival is "alcopops." These are neon-colored single servings, packaged in test-tube-style plastic vials. Or how about six-packs of "Jello-shots"—plastic tumblers of gelatin, fruit-flavored and laced with vodka? These have hit the U.S. market and are being stocked on grocery shelves amid their look-alike traditional nonalcoholic counterparts. Labels typically include cartoon characters or closely resemble the design of many of the old favorites, such as Kool-Aid.

One of the more outrageous efforts to introduce nontraditional beverages occurred in Australia. The new offering was Moo Joose—alcoholic milk. The manufacturer, Wicked Holdings Pty Ltd, envisioned a beverage containing more than 5% alcohol by volume, to be available in flavors of chocolate, banana, strawberry, and coffee and mimic flavored milk. The following were set forth as positive features: (a) "Milk with its component proteins is likely to produce feelings of satiation that may limit the amount consumed"; (b) "It is possible that the milk content

[1]In September of 2003, the beverage industries announced a reform of their advertising codes, restricting TV ads to those shows with fewer than 30% of underage viewers. However, it is doubtful that this goal will be met without major changes. The distillers have a voluntarily imposed ban on advertising liquor on the major broadcasting networks, but the cable networks are fair game.

may reduce the rate of absorption of alcohol into the walls of the stomach and small intestine and act like food in delaying the rate of absorption"; (c) "The fact that the fat content is low is likely to make more attractive [*sic*] to young women . . . Low sugar levels are also an attraction to young women in the 18+ age group." Also mentioned as positive features of Moo Joose were its proposed four-pack packaging, which would supposedly foster moderation, as well as narrow-necked bottles with screw tops that would minimize the chances of other persons spiking the drink.

Among those speaking on Moo Joose's behalf was a major Australian substance abuse group. The Alcohol & Drug Foundation explained its support for Moo Joose by noting that any incidental alcohol problems would be more than offset by declines in drinking resulting from its anticipated prevention campaign conducted jointly with the beverage industry. The licensing group was unconvinced by these arguments and Wicked Holding's application was denied, on the basis that it represented an unacceptable risk to the health and well-being of young people. This particular case is an instance of concerns that have been expressed about the potential for problems in *any* beverage industry and substance abuse field collaboration. (See Chapter 14 for further discussion.)

Beyond targeting the youth market, some companies have developed advertising campaigns directed toward women and minority groups. The content of the ads is another source of concern. Even by advertising standards, many are blatantly sexist, depicting women in a demeaning manner and promoting the stereotypes of male behavior that contribute to sexual harassment.

Targeting Developing Countries

Another concern is the alcohol beverage industry's (especially the distillers') sales promotion in developing countries. With a declining domestic market, one way to maintain profits is to increase foreign sales. Along with economic development, many countries have begun to experience a significant increase in alcohol-related problems. Western patterns of alcohol use, now being introduced, are often very different from traditional practices. (See Chapter 5.) One question raised by efforts to increase sales in developing countries is an ethical one. Is there any justification for introducing alcohol problems into countries already struggling with the problems of poverty, malnutrition, inadequate health care, high rates of maternal and infant mortality, and illiteracy? There is another, even more basic question. This arises in response to breweries now being built in developing countries, usually financed by international groups. Here the concern is not a future rise in alcohol problems. The brewing process itself requires significant amounts of scarce resources—water and grain. Any diversion of water from agricultural use or town/village water supplies or activities that reduce the amount of grain for food can have a devastating immediate impact on people's health and well-being.

Changing Norms

There is a counterbalance, sort of, for the alcohol industry's effort to have its product appear in the hand of Johnny Depp or Renée Zellweger. These are the public service announcements to promote responsible use. In addition are efforts to alter the manner in which alcohol use is portrayed in the media, especially television programming. Network film features aired in prime time with alcoholics as major characters are no longer news. Even on the soap operas, in addition to several of the major characters who are active alcoholics, now there are also characters in recovery. Overall, from soaps to cop shows, drinking behavior is portrayed with a bit less glamour and more realism than in the past. These changes were sparked in part by a major public educational campaign conducted out of the Harvard School of Public Health. This campaign is geared toward working with movie and television writers, directors, and producers to incorporate alcohol-related themes. For example, the project promoted incorporating the designated driver into prime-time television shows.

Presumably the people of North America and Hawaii stumbled upon alcohol produced through the natural process of fermentation, as did people elsewhere. However, it never became a part of these native cultures. What factors may have fostered this societal rejection of alcohol?

Health and fitness has become a major national interest. Witness the rise in exercise classes, the emergence of personal trainers, gym and health center memberships, nutritional supplements, alternative medicine, aromatherapy, and the latest low-carb diets. The alcohol beverage industry has responded to these fitness concerns. It is ironic that the industry is spending an undisclosed portion of its $1 billion advertising budget to promote lower-alcohol-content beverages! Along with the lite beers, near beers, and wine coolers, there has been a marked growth in the sales of bottled water, sparkling water, and nonalcoholic beers and wines.

In sum, significant changes are taking place in how the majority view alcohol problems and what constitutes appropriate alcohol use. A book published in the mid-1980s, *How to Control Your Social Drinking* was probably a first. The introduction noted it was not intended for alcoholics, for whom controlled drinking is not recommended, but for a social drinker who may find it is easy to overindulge in a drinking society. Basically, it offered hosts, partygoers, and top-level business executives a compilation of tips and techniques to keep consumption down, while discussing the benefits of moderation. The book's significance is not that it contained any startling or new information, but simply that it was published and seen as a topic of sufficient general interest to generate book sales.

OTHER DRUG USE

Alcohol is the psychoactive substance most widely used in the United States.[2] Even though alcohol arrived along with the first European colonists, it is not the oldest psychoactive drug used in North America.

[2]The patterns of alcohol and other drug use are described in the next chapter.

That honor goes to tobacco, a plant native to North America, and only introduced to the rest of the world through trade between the Virginia colony and England.

Tobacco

Among Europeans, the earliest use of tobacco was as snuff—powdered tobacco that was sniffed—the preferred form of the tobacco among the upper classes. Though not as fashionable, tobacco was also smoked, by breaking the leaves and stuffing them into a pipe. From Europe these forms of tobacco use were transported to the American colonists. By the early 1800s, other forms of tobacco were becoming more popular; for example, chewing tobacco gradually began to replace snuff. By the end of the century, the annual per capita consumption of chewing tobacco was 2.8 pounds. In terms of tobacco smoking, cigars came to replace pipes. Imported from Europe, cigars were rather expensive and were a status symbol, a hallmark of the upper class. A cigar is still the mark of a tycoon. Consider the cartoons depicting the well-to-do, portly, bushy-mustached, white-haired businessman wearing a suit, complete with vest and pocket watch, and smoking a large cigar. Or consider the characters long associated with the Monopoly game.

There are a vast number of things and customs . . . which do not contribute . . . the slightest to mental, moral, or physical advancement, and which serve only as a diversion, a relaxation, an amusement, or a consolation. Why destroy them?

A tobacco lobbyist, 1919

When they first appeared in the 1850s, cigarettes were viewed with disdain, and considered "the smoke" of the lower classes. Cigarettes were first adopted by urban immigrants and particularly adolescent boys. Initially sold individually not in packs, cigarettes were far less expensive. That the cigarette wasn't the choice of any "real" man was made clear by its name, formed by adding the feminine suffix "ette" to "cigar." Despite the stigma, circumstances made cigarette use more common. The Civil War battlefields were not well-suited to leisurely smoking a cigar; a quick smoke was the safer option. In the latter part of the 1800s periods of economic depression placed cigars out of reach of many who switched to cigarettes. The invention of the Bonsack cigarette manufacturing machine and a new style of marketing really promoted the adoption of cigarettes.

During the Depression, the average family spent as much as 6.9% of its income on tobacco.

With the possible exception of Super Bowl hoopla, it is almost impossible for those living in the 21st century to appreciate the impact of the earliest cigarette marketing. Surely a first-rate textbook on marketing could be written drawing on nothing other than the efforts of the tobacco industry over the years. Much of what we now think of as advertising was introduced by the tobacco companies. They were the first to place full-page spreads in magazines that reached virtually every household in the way that TV does now. Of course, tobacco companies had the example of the patent medicine manufacturers to build upon. The potential for mass production, coupled with aggressive marketing to create demand, very rapidly catapulted cigarettes into becoming the primary route for nicotine administration. How successful? Over a 50-year period, production didn't just double or triple. Between 1889 and 1949, it grew by an astronomical 2,000%.

During World War II tobacco farmers were exempt from military service because they were considered essential workers.

Beyond advertising, the tobacco companies used other promotional techniques successfully. They were the among the first to give away cards of entertainment figures, the predecessor of the next century's baseball cards. In a stroke of genius, in both WWI and WWII, cigarettes were provided free to soldiers as part of their basic rations. This promotion to young men, clearly succeeded; in the 1950s, 80% of all men were smokers. Marketing to women began in the 1920s and '30s. The number of women who smoked doubled in a decade.

Isn't it rather too bad that an organization [the WCTU] which undoubtedly did so much good in the fight against the saloon should . . . fly off on such a tangent? The liquor and tobacco problems are as different as the sun and the moon.

Tobacco industry editorial, 1921

Undoubtedly a self-reinforcing cycle was set in motion. Cigarettes were on a roll. The more people who smoke, the more acceptable the behavior, and, in turn, the more smoking is interwoven into public life in ways large and small. In the public's mind smoking was defined as a behavior which denotes a host of desirable traits—whether its being "with it," macho, liberated, sexy, athletic, or any of the other attributes depicted in cigarette ads.

As there were anti-alcohol voices, so too there were some opposed to tobacco. In comparison to alcohol, there were some significant differences. For one, tobacco products were sold in a wide variety of places—from general stores, to candy stores, to cigar stores—most of these settings were well integrated into community life. So there wasn't the equivalent of the bar or saloon as a target for attack. In fact, many at the time considered cigar stores as wholesome alternatives to saloons. Interestingly too, distinctions were made between different tobacco products. The tobacco prohibition movement typically focused exclusively on cigarettes. In the 1890s, several states banned cigarette sales, but these first laws did not apply to cigars or chewing tobacco. Whether these bans could have been maintained in light of the subsequent heavy advertising campaigns is doubtful. But the return of a generation of WWI veterans who had become addicted to their daily ration of nicotine significantly redefined the image of the smoker.

Although some of the opposition to smoking was based on health concerns, until the mid-20th century, these were generally dismissed as without any foundation. Then the solid scientific basis for these health concerns was evident. In 1964, the landmark Surgeon General's *Report on Smoking and Health* painstakingly laid out the health problems associated with smoking. Along with public health efforts, such as education and promotion of smoking cessation, governmental efforts were made to restrict the tobacco industry's promotional activities. For example, in 1963, with the Surgeon General's report clearly on the horizon, the tobacco industry had to curtail advertising to the youth market, and in the following year agreed to cease other media advertising. In some instances these limitations were ignored; in other instances, alternative marketing methods were adopted. In addition, the tobacco companies followed a duplicitous course. In public they challenged the scientific evidence for health problems and the addictive nature of nicotine, while at the same time withholding information from their own studies of health effects. Companies also went through the motions of creating "safer" cigarettes,

while simultaneously manipulating nicotine content, which was the ingredient that hooked smokers and kept them coming back for more.

In 1994, the state of Minnesota filed the first in what became a set of complicated lawsuits against the major tobacco manufacturers, involving both the federal and state governments. These cases raised a host of questions pertaining to product safety, the role of government in regulation, and manufacturers' responsibility for liabilities. The goal of the states was to recover costs for their health-care expenditures for smoking-related illnesses. The 1998 Master Settlement Agreement (MSA) between states and the tobacco industry involved billions of dollars which helped fund prevention and smoking cessation efforts. The publicity these cases received also was a source of public education, further diminishing public acceptance of smoking and promoting acceptance of further regulation.

In later chapters the acute and chronic effects of drinking and other drug use are discussed. However, differences between alcohol and nicotine—the addictive ingredient of tobacco—warrant mention here. Differences in the public perceptions of alcohol and nicotine are, in part, explained by the differences in their pharmacological effects. Nicotine has a much greater risk of addiction than alcohol. Although most people who use alcohol can properly be described as social drinkers, a "social smoker" is quite rare. On the other hand, nicotine does not have an intoxicating effect similar to that of alcohol. An evening of heavy smoking may make someone reek, but that isn't comparable to drunkenness. Cognitive function isn't impaired by smoking: for years smoking in the workplace was common. If as many people had been drinking at their desks as were then smoking there, the business community would have screeched to a halt! Probably the single behavioral change associated with smoking is the edginess and tension of short-term abstinence that is a sign of physical dependence. It is what prompts the smoker to announce, "I'm going out for a cigarette." The significant problems associated with smoking develop over the long haul. Of course, the hook with tobacco is that the highly addictive nature of nicotine assures the smoking continues long enough to develop health problems.

Marijuana

Marijuana is American hasheesh. . . . You can grow enough marijuana in a window box to drive the whole population of the United States stark, staring, raving mad.
WILFRED BLACK

Dope: the Story of the Living Dead. New York: Star & Co., 1928

Unlike nicotine and alcohol, which have been part of the American landscape since colonial times, marijuana is a far more recent arrival. Derived from the plant *cannabis sativa,* marijuana is native to central Asia. Anthropologists and historians have traced its spread throughout the world. As early as 3000 B.C.E., it was known in China. Seemingly it was never widely used for its psychoactive effects, and it was considered an inferior medicine. The response in India, a millennium later, was more enthusiastic. Cannabis was adopted both as a sacred plant and as a medicine capable of curing all major ills while also promoting vital energy.

From India, cannabis spread to Persia in the eighth century B.C.E. While known in both ancient Greece and Rome, records suggest that the major interest was for its fiber to manufacture rope. Apparently, its use for pleasure was dismissed as a poor substitute for wine or beer.

The reception of cannabis in the Middle East was more positive, especially as the rise of Islam had led to the ban of alcohol. The term "cannabis" comes from the Persian *kanabas*. The extract from the plant was called hashish, which is Arabic for "grass." After the fall of Rome, Persia represented the center of learning and the sciences. During this period, a number of writings speak of its therapeutic uses. It was recommended for diverse problems, ranging from curing earaches, to easing epilepsy and dissolving flatulence. Also, it was recommended for stimulating appetite and producing a craving for sweets. For literally centuries, Islamic scholars and clerics debated whether it was appropriate to use hashish for pleasure. Finally the answer came in the seventeenth century: No. The thinking was that its psychoactive properties were similar to those of wine, thus it too clouds the mind and interferes with prayer. This resulting prohibition continues—except for medical uses—and in most Islamic countries is incorporated into law.

Over a several-century period, Arab incursions introduced cannabis into North Africa and Europe. In Europe cannabis was never particularly popular for its psychoactive properties. Interest was largely restricted to its use as a medicine. But as a medicine, it was deemed lacking. In England, physicians found the compounds imported from India had widely varying strengths, and thus were unreliable. Overall they were considered less effective than other available medications, such as opium and its derivatives. American physicians, following the example of British colleagues, imported cannabis extracts from India, and were a bit more inclined to use them for an array of conditions. Cannabis was incorporated into the many available patent medicines whether sold in an array of stores, by traveling salesmen, or by mail order. Compared to other ingredients—coca, alcohol, opium, morphine, and later heroin—in these various tonics, pills, balms, powders, elixirs, and extracts, cannabis was virtually an inert ingredient! In the later efforts to ban patent medicines and control drug use, cannabis was not one of the ingredients being primarily targeted. While prescribed with declining frequency, it was only in 1942 that cannabis was removed from the list of drugs approved for medical purposes.

Despite hemp being grown from colonial times, recreational or nonmedical cannabis use was largely unknown in the United States until the last century. Cannabis as a psychoactive substance was introduced to the American continent in the 1600s, by slaves from West Africa brought to Brazil. However, it was never adopted by either the Portuguese colonialists or native peoples of Brazil. Nonetheless, use continued and, over time, gradually spread along the coasts. In the early 1900s, cannabis, under the name marijuana, indicating its Latin American roots, was

Mexican Family Goes Insane

A widow and her four children have been driven insane by eating the marijuana plant, according to doctors, who say there is no hope of saving the children's lives and that the mother will be insane for the rest of her life.

The mother was without money to buy other food for the children, whose ages range from 3 to 15, so they gathered some herbs and vegetables growing in the yard for their dinner. Two hours after mother and children had eaten the plants, they were stricken. Neighbors, hearing outbursts of crazed laughter rushed to the house to find the entire family insane. Examination revealed that the narcotic marijuana was growing among the garden vegetables.

New York Times, July 6, 1927

FOCUS ON DRUGS

Drugs Other Than Alcohol

In thinking about drugs other than alcohol, several phenomena are worth considering:

- **The role of processing.**
  It has been observed that substances used in the form in which they are naturally produced tend to be less problematic than any processed derivatives. For example, nature produces alcohol at a maximum concentration of 14%; distillation is needed to achieve alcohol contents that can approach 100%. Chewing coca leaves, common for centuries in the Andes mountains, doesn't produce the same effects as cocaine. And, heroin is more than a different form of opium.

  Related to this is the emergence of pharmaceutical formulations, some of which are based on naturally occurring substances and others of which are wholly synthesized. A number of the most problematic substances in the twenty-first century were products touted in the nineteenth century as miracle, wonder drugs. Early on cocaine was declared to be a safe, nonhabituating product, well suited to treating opiate withdrawal. Yessssss. Heroin was marketed as a vast improvement for treating coughs, especially those associated with tuberculosis, epidemic at the time. Other drugs of abuse that have been created in the laboratory as pharmaceuticals include the barbiturates, amphetamines, the benzodiazepines. These were always controlled substances, legally available only by prescription. For many years these drugs were manufactured at levels far exceeding the number of legitimate prescriptions that could be written, making it apparent that they also were manufactured for the illicit drug trade.

- **The role of technology.**
  Just as the greater potency that accompanies processing increases risk, so too does the technology used in drug administration. The prime example is the syringe. In case you think that everything that could be invented has been, how about a machine that allows you to inhale alcohol? Just imagine the possible advertising slogans: "Tired of old-fashioned sipping or even gulping? Why use such a long route to get the alcohol into the bloodstream?" A machine called AWOL, short for Alcohol Without Liquid, was introduced at a trendy New York bar in the summer of 2004. The contraption resembles an oversized asthma inhaler attached to an oxygen tank. It disperses liquor as a vapor in an oxygen mist. Don't worry that you may inhale too rapidly—a dial can be set to regulate the rate of alcohol vapor dispensed. It's difficult to imagine this becoming popular. Remember that earlier some asked, "Who would ever stick themselves with a needle?" For the moment, the use of AWOL is stymied by fine print in the liquor licensing regulations, such as alcohol having to be dispensed from its original containers. However, as one alcohol researcher wryly commented, "The group we should worry about most is the one that isn't legally allowed to drink alcohol in the first place."

- **Legal status.**
  Classification of psychoactive substances either as licit or illicit is not based exclusively or even primarily on their pharmacological properties. During the course of your readings here, consider several questions. If it were possible to erase all previous history and attitudes and start afresh, if you were asked to designate classes of drugs to be licit, which would you choose? What factors would you consider to be important in making these assignments? Which things would you see as important in defining harm? And harm to whom? Are there harms that are introduced or avoided by the legal or illicit status of a substance? To what extent can these be diminished? In which column would alcohol, tobacco, and caffeine be found, your licit or illicit list?

Everything that can be invented has been invented.
COMMISSIONER, U.S. OFFICE OF PATENTS, 1899

introduced into the American southwest by Mexican settlers and into New Orleans by sailors from Mexican and Caribbean ports. From the first, marijuana was very suspect and aroused concerns. In part this was consistent with the efforts to control patent medicines, restrict the use of opiates and cocaine, and ban alcohol. It was consistent too with international conferences and treaties in the early 1900s directed to curtailing international trade in opiates. However, the major factor at work was racism. As portrayed by the press, law enforcement, and other public officials, marijuana was exceedingly dangerous and highly addictive, prompting uncontrolled violence and causing insanity, along with virtually every social ill one could imagine. This was the era that introduced phrases such as "drug fiend" into our vocabulary.

In light of this clear marijuana "threat," by 1932 more than 10 states had enacted laws to ban its use. Despite the fact that marijuana was used primarily by the marginalized, and racial and ethnic groups, there was a sense of urgency to protect the broader society. Beyond the perceived dangers associated with its use, another factor was at work. There was the fear that marijuana, if it remained legal, might fill the niche left by the prohibition of alcohol and banning of narcotics. With the passage of the Harrison Act in 1914, narcotics and cocaine had been classified as controlled substances available only for medical purposes and by prescription. (See Chapter 13 for further discussion of drug control.)

The subsequent movement of marijuana into the mainstream of American culture might be seen as having occurred in two stages. The first was its association with the blues and jazz, and the bohemian scene. The second was its adoption by the sixties counterculture. Ironically, the earlier success in defining marijuana as deviant and unacceptable, along with the exaggerations about its effects, probably helped make it the psychoactive substance of choice for a movement with the mantra "Don't trust anyone over 30."

RESOURCES AND FURTHER READING

Abel EL. The Gin Epidemic: Much ado about what? *Alcohol and Alcoholism* 36(5):401–495, 2001.

Alcohol History Database <http://www.scc.rutgers.edu/alcohol_history>
Note: Contains bibliographic records for over 600 monographs, pamphlets, and journals from the 19th and early 20th centuries dealing primarily with the American Temperance and Prohibition movements.

Alcoholics Anonymous. *Alcoholics Anonymous Comes of Age.* New York: AA World Service, 1957.

Austin G. *Alcohol in Western Society from Antiquity to 1800.* Oxford UK: Santa ABC-Clio Information Services, 1985.

Bacon S. The classical temperance movement in the U.S.A. *British Journal of Addiction* 62:5–18, 1967.

Burnham JC. *Bad Habits. Drinking, Smoking, Taking Drugs, Gambling, Sexual Misbehavior, and Swearing in American History.* New York: New York University Press, 1993.

Center on Alcohol Marketing and Youth. *Youth Exposure to Alcohol Ads on Television, 2003.* Washington DC:

Georgetown University, Center on Alcohol Marketing and Youth, 2004.

Chafetz M. *Liquor, The Servant of Man.* Boston: Little, Brown & Co, 1965.

DP: The Washingtonians. *AA Grapevine* 27(9):16–22, 1971.

Foster SE, Vaughan RD, Foster WH, Califano JA. Alcohol consumption and expenditures for underage drinking and adult excessive drinking. *Journal of the American Medical Association* 289(8):989–995, 2003. (46 refs.)

Gahlinger P. *Illegal Drugs: A Complete Guide to Their History, Chemistry, Use, and Abuse.* New York: Plume/Penguin, 2004.

Horton D. Alcohol use in primitive societies. In Pittman DJ, White HR, eds: *Society, Culture, and Drinking Patterns Reexamined.* New Brunswick NJ: Rutgers Center of Alcohol Studies, 1991.

Inciardi J. *The War on Drugs II.* New York: Mayfield Publishing Company, 1992.

Lender ME, Kamchanappe KR. Temperance tales, antiliquor fiction and American attitudes toward alcoholics in the late 19th and early 20th centuries. *Journal of Studies on Alcohol* 38(7):1347–1370, 1979.

MacAndrew C., Edgerton R. *Drunken Comportment.* Chicago: Aldine, 1969.

McClelland D, et al. *The Drinking Man.* New York: The Free Press, 1972.

Munro G. An addiction agency's collaboration with the drinks industry: Moo Joose as a case study. *Addiction.* 99(11):1370–1374, (31 refs.)

Munro G., Learmonth A. 'An unacceptable risk': the problem of alcoholic milk. *Drug & Alcohol Review,* 23(3):345–349, 2004. (26 refs.)

National Institute on Alcohol Abuse and Alcoholism. *Tenth Special Report to U.S. Congress on Alcohol and Health.* Washington DC: U.S. Government Printing Office, 2000.

Rorabaugh W. *The Alcohol Republic: An American Tradition.* New York: Oxford University Press, 1979.

Schaffer A. Vaporize me. Is inhalable alcohol a good idea? *Slate.* September 2004. <slate.msn.com>

Sournia JC. *A History of Alcoholism.* Cambridge MA: Basil Blackwell, 1990.

Weil A. Man's innate need: Getting high. In: *Dealing with Drug Abuse.* Ford Foundation: New York, 1972.

CHAPTER 2

Alcohol and Its Costs

I have very poor and unhappy brains for drinking. I could well wish courtesy would invent some other custom of entertainment.
WILLIAM SHAKESPEARE
Othello

In the United States, statistics on who drinks—what, where, and when—have been kept since 1850. However, comparisons between different historical periods are difficult. One reason is that only since 1950 have statistics been gathered methodically and impartially. Another reason is that there have been changes in the way the basic information is organized and reported. A century ago, reports included numbers of "inebriates" or "drunkards." In the 1940s through the 1960s, "alcoholics" were often a designated subgroup. Then came the 1970s and another change. "Heavy drinkers" or "heavy drinkers with a high problem index" began to replace "alcoholics" as a category in reporting statistical information. In the 1980s, "dependence" replaced "alcoholism." Currently the *National Survey on Drug Use and Health*, a national survey conducted by the federal government that assesses alcohol and other drug use patterns, gathers data on whether people use alcohol and other drugs, and how frequently—in their lifetimes, in the past year, and in the past month. If someone has used alcohol in the past month, he or she is considered a *current drinker.* For current drinkers there are also questions about the amount people drink. Those who report having had five or more drinks on one occasion during the past month are termed *binge drinkers.* If someone has had five or more drinks on at least five occasions the past month, he or she is categorized as a *heavy drinker.* With the changes in ways of describing drinking patterns, the tasks of identifying changes in drinking practices and comparing different periods are not easy ones.

WHO DRINKS WHAT, WHEN, AND WHERE

Out of the maze of statistics available on how much Americans drink, where they drink, and with what consequences, some are important to note. It is now estimated that 70% of men and 60% of women are drinkers, having had a drink at some point in the past year. They constitute about 65% of the adult population. The proportion of current drinkers, those who have had a drink in the past month, is smaller, about half of the population. Historically, per capita consumption rose dramatically in the decade following Prohibition, increasing by over 50%. While less dramatic and despite some modest ups and downs, overall consumption continued to rise through the 1970s, peaking in the early 1980s. Since then, alcohol consumption has declined. Consumption in 1998 was the lowest since 1962. Despite very slight increases, consumption through 2002 remained at a record low. The decline in total alcohol consumption is due almost entirely to liquor's having become less popular. Since 1977, liquor consumption has dropped by 39%. Notably, the decline in liquor sales has not been counterbalanced by a corresponding increase in either wine or beer consumption. The per capita sales of wine and beer have remained fairly steady. Part of the overall decline in per capita consumption is due to changes in the age distribution. As a country, we are growing older, and older people drink less. Canada estimates that as much as 7% to 17% of its drop in per capita consumption is due to changes in the age distribution.

In 2000, the statistically average American consumed the equivalent of 2.18 gallons of pure ethanol. The alcohol content varies by type of beverage. Accordingly, of the total alcohol consumed, 30% of the ethanol consumed came from liquor, 14% from wine, and the remaining 56% from beer.

A word of caution: All of these figures describe the statistically average American. However, it is important to realize that the average American is a statistical myth. It isn't as if we all awake each New Year's Day to find our annual allotment for alcohol sitting on the doorstep. The typical American does not, in fact, drink his or her statistical quota. First of all, recall that approximately one-third of Americans do not use alcohol at all. The remaining two-thirds show a wide variation in alcohol use. Thus, 70% of the drinking population consumes only 20% of all the alcohol. The remaining 30% of the drinkers consume 80% of the alcohol. Most significantly, one-third of that heavy-drinking 30%, or less than 7% of the total population, consumes 50% of all alcohol. Picture what that means. Imagine having 10 beers to serve to a group of 10 people. If you served these to represent the actual consumption pattern described, you'd have the following: 3 people would sit empty-handed; 5 people would share 2 beers. That leaves 2 people to divide up 8 beers. Of those 2 people, 1 person would take 2 and the other person would get a whole six-pack.

The same pattern holds for underage drinkers. As someone who examined the data on adolescent drinking noted, there is "the myth that 'all' youth drink" and the impression that "many are binge drinkers." In fact, adolescents who have five or more drinks per occasion represent a small minority of all adolescents—in 2002 that was approximately 3.5% of those 12–14 years old and about 18% of those 15–17. Equally important, this

amounts to 81.5% and 88.5%, respectively, of all alcohol consumed by people in those age groups.

Drinking Patterns

Patterns of alcohol consumption vary according to a number of demographic factors. Based on information for 2003, among the key factors are the following.

Gender

Women are more likely to be nondrinkers than are men. Furthermore, they drink less frequently than men; when they do drink, they typically consume less. Twenty percent of women, versus 14% of men, are lifelong abstainers. In terms of drinking frequency, in the past year, 71% of the men report having had a drink, versus 62% of women. In the last month, 57% men have had a drink, but only 45% of women. Men are twice as likely to be heavy drinkers than are women, with 31% of men compared to 15% of women having had five or more drinks per occasion at least once in the past month, the definition of binge drinking.

Age

Levels of alcohol consumption vary with age. In 2003, the highest level of alcohol use in the preceding month was found among 21-year-olds, at 71%. The proportion of current drinkers declines with age. Among those 55 years and older, less than half have had a drink in the past month, and the percentage for those 65 and older drops below 40%. The oldest age group, those over age 65, has the largest percentage of lifetime abstainers, approximately 22%. This is twice the proportion of lifelong abstainers for those ages 21–55.

For both men and women the proportion of heavier drinkers is highest in the 18–25 age group. While age 21 represents the legal drinking age, current drinking begins far sooner. Current drinking is reported by 20% of those age 15, and 56% of those 20 years old. The age group with the highest portion of heavy drinkers is 21 years old, with one out of every five having had more than five drinks on five occasions in the past month. By way of comparison, the rate of heavy drinking among 30-year-olds is 10%; among 50 years old, 6%; and among those 65 and older, 1.5%.

Race

Among racial and ethnic groups, whites have the highest proportion of drinkers. This is true for both men and women. In 2003, among whites 70% report drinking in the past year, as compared to 61% of Native Americans, 60% of Hispanics, 55% of Blacks, and 54% of Asian-Americans. For current drinking, whites have the highest percentages (55%) and

The description of drinking patterns in this section represent a snapshot of drinking in the year 2002. This kind of data is cross sectional. It compares individuals with different characteristics whether by age, or gender, or residence, at the same moment in time. A caution: A common error is using this type of data to think about differences over time. However, as makes sense if you think about it, it is an error to presume that the drinking of this year's 20-year-olds can predict the drinking of future 20-year-olds. Nor is today's 40-year-old a good predictor of how our 20-year-old will drink two decades from now. Any group's alcohol or drug use is influenced by the particular era in which they grew up as well as the situation at the time. For example, the elderly of a generation ago had a higher rate of lifetime abstinence than today's elderly. This is commonly attributed to the fact that the previous generation grew up in the era of Prohibition.

Asian-Americans the lowest rate (37%). While there are differences in the proportion of drinkers between racial and ethnic groups, the larger differences are in the frequency of drinking and frequency of heavy drinking. Native Americans are the racial/ethnic group with the highest rate for both binge (28%) and heavy drinking (9%). The Native American rate for heavy drinking is 15% higher than that for whites, 47% greater than that reported by Hispanics, virtually double the rate for Blacks, and is about 2 and a quarter times higher than that for Asian-Americans.

Education

Alcohol use increases for both men and women with higher levels of education. In 2003, among those age 26 or older, approximately two-thirds of college graduates are current drinkers, as opposed to only one-third of those without a high school education. On the other hand, the reverse is true for the proportions involved in heavy drinking. About 7% of those with less than a high school education report heavy drinking, compared to roughly 4% of college graduates. That is almost a 60% difference.

Family Income

The proportion of drinkers rises with family income. However, the proportion of heavy drinking episodes is twice as high among those whose household income is below the national median income than among those above this level.

Geographic Region

In the South, 39% are abstainers, not having had a drink during the past year. This is about 15% more abstainers than in other regions. The Northeast has the greatest number of lifetime drinkers, 88%, and the greatest percentage of current drinkers, 57%. The part of the country with the lowest rate of monthly drinkers is the South, with 46%. In terms of heavy drinkers, five or more drinks per occasion on five or more occasions in the past month, the highest rate is in the Midwest, with 8%, with the South having the lowest rate, 6%.

If the numbers who abstain are not included in calculating consumption, the South has the highest level of consumption, and the lowest rate is in the Northeast. Beyond absolute differences, regions differ by whether their levels of consumption are dropping, rising, or remaining unchanged. From year to year these changes are relatively minor. They are seen as related to patterns of people's moving. With more younger people, who tend to drink more than older persons, now moving south, the average age of the population declines, and the level of alcohol consumption rises accordingly.

Type of Community

Additional differences in drinking patterns are seen in relation to the type of community in which people live—whether suburban, rural, or metropolitan. Current (past month) use is higher in metropolitan areas (54%) and lowest in rural areas (41%). However, the highest rate of binge drinking occurs in the smaller metropolitan areas, those with fewer than 250,000 residents (27%.) These smaller metropolitan communities also have the highest rate of heavy alcohol use (9%), a rate 40% higher than that in the largest metropolitan areas, and 72% higher than rural areas.

However, the picture is a bit different for adolescents and young adults. Rural areas have the highest rate of both current drinking and binge drinking within the 12-to-17-year-old group. This is a rate approximately 25% higher than that found in metropolitan areas. However, in the next age group, those 18–25, the highest level of current drinking moves from the rural areas to the smaller metropolitan areas. When it comes to binge drinking, the highest rate is found in the smaller metropolitan areas.

Marital Status

The lowest proportion of drinkers is found among those who are widowed. This is probably related to age, with the widowed being more likely to be older and, thus, in the age group with the lowest proportion of drinkers. The proportion of drinkers is essentially the same among those who are married, separated or divorced, or never married. However, the picture is different when one looks at heavy drinkers. The highest rate of heavy drinking episodes is found among those never married, 8.7%, closely followed by those who are divorced, 7.9%. This is close to four times the rate of heavy drinking found among those who are married or widowed.

Religion

Protestant conservative religious denominations have the lowest percentage of members who drink, 53.6%. The religious groups with the highest proportion of members who use alcohol are Jews, 92%; followed by Catholics, 79%; and liberal Protestant groups, 73%. On the other hand, although Jews have the biggest proportion of drinkers, less than 0.1% are heavy drinkers. The highest levels of heavy drinking are reported by Catholics and those whose religious affiliation is noted as "other." Both drinking and rates of heavy drinking vary according to the importance placed upon religion. Only half of those who consider religion very important drink, only a third are weekly drinkers, and only 1.5% report occasions of heavy drinking. On the other hand, among those for whom religion is "not at all" or "not really" important, about 53% are weekly drinkers and 9% are heavy drinkers.

We take a drink only for the sake of the benediction.
PERETZ

International Comparisons

How do drinking patterns in the United States compare with those of other countries? Comparisons of drinking patterns between countries are difficult. For example, a quarter of men and over a third of women in

FIGURE 2.1 Recorded adult (15+) per capita consumption 1970–1996 by economic region (in liters of pure alcohol). World Health Organization, Substance Abuse Department. *Global Status Report on Alcohol.* Geneva: World Health Organization, 1999, p. 19.

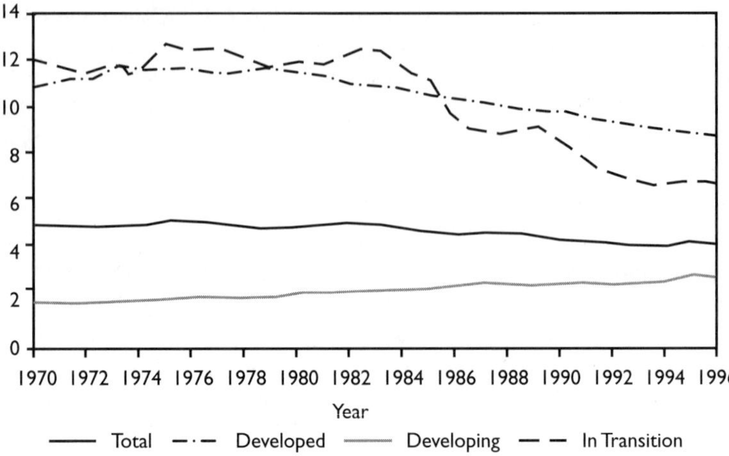

Ireland are nondrinkers. On the other hand, in Denmark 98% of men and 94% of women drink, so the alcohol consumed within a country is spread over very different portions of the population. A far more useful form for reporting such information would be the per capita consumption among the drinking population; however, no one uses that format.

Internationally, alcohol consumption in industrialized countries has generally declined. A decade ago, per capita consumption, for example, had virtually halved in Italy, going from 13.7 liters of absolute alcohol in 1970 to 8.7 liters in 1990. At the same time, consumption in economically underdeveloped countries is rising. Thus, there is a convergence of drinking patterns around the globe. This is shown in figure 2.1.

ALCOHOL PROBLEMS

Abuse and Dependence

The most recent federal estimate is that 7.7% of all those age 12 or older have a serious alcohol problem, consistent with a diagnosis of alcohol dependence or abuse. Within this group, about 17% have an additional drug problem. (The rate of problems among adolescents ages 12 to 17 is essentially the same, 7.8%, which represents more than 3 million teenagers.) Thus, in the United States an estimated 18.1 million people have a significant problem with alcohol.

For every person with an alcohol problem, it is estimated that four family members are directly affected, which means that approximately 73.6 million family members are touched by alcohol. Serious alcohol problems are significantly more common than illicit drug problems. For each person with an illicit drug problem, there are five persons with a serious alcohol use.

During the 1970s and 1980s, a number of national polls included questions about alcohol problems. During that period an ever increasing number of those interviewed indicated an alcohol problem in the immediate family. In 1972, about 1 out of every 10 people (12%) said that a member of the immediate family had a problem with alcohol. Six years later, about 1 person in 4 (24%) said that an alcohol problem had adversely affected his or her family life. In 1983, that figure rose to 1 out of every 3. Only 1 year later, the figure reported by a Harris poll was that 38% of all households reported being beset by alcohol problems. In 1988, a survey conducted for the NIAAA found that 43% of the population reported having a family member with alcoholism. These changes in large part probably reflect the increased recognition by families of alcohol problems in their midst, rather than representing a dramatic rise in the occurrence of these problems.

Beer ranks fourth, behind soft drinks, coffee, and milk, in total beverage consumption in the United States.

In terms of which families are affected, those who are separated or divorced are more likely to report a family member with an alcohol problem. Those separated or divorced are three times more likely to report having had an alcoholic spouse. Younger adults are also more likely to report having an alcoholic family member than are older adults. The proportions are 42% for those under age 45 versus 26% of those over age 65. In any of these figures, there is not much precision in distinguishing between alcoholics and those who are nonalcoholic but have had alcohol-related problems. These nonalcoholic problem drinkers might include the one-time drunken traffic offender who appears in court or the person who, when drunk for the one and only time in his or her life, puts a foot through a window and ends up in a hospital emergency room. But the suspicion is that, when reporting "troubles," people are not referring to those who miss work after a particularly festive New Year's Eve.

Among those who are alcohol dependent, under 5% are among the homeless, the modern counterpart of what was at one time termed "skid row." At least 95% of problem drinkers are employed or employable; they are estimated to constitute 10% of the nation's workforce. Most of them are living with their families. The vast majority live in respectable neighborhoods and are homemakers, bankers, physicians, salespeople, farmers, teachers, computer programmers, and clergy. They try to raise decent children, go to football games, shop for their groceries, go to work, and rake the leaves.

Economic Costs Versus Economic Benefits

Although they constitute only a small portion of the drinking population, alcohol abusers and alcoholics combined cost the United States a huge amount of time and money each year. In assessing these costs, government statistics rely heavily on data gathered during the census, conducted every 10 years. The quantity of information generated may take several years to analyze. When dealing with national counts of anything, from population figures to the numbers of licensed drivers to the quantity of alcohol sold, the data are almost always an estimate. The figures are derived from the most recent data available or are inferred from other

Applying Cost-Benefit Analysis to Cannabis

Cost-benefit analysis has led some in Australia to openly muse about the impact of regulating and taxing cannabis. The cannabis industry in Australia is the same financial size as its gold industry, twice the size of its wine industry, and three-quarters the size of the nation's beer industry. An obvious question is: Why leave a $5 billion industry off the books and in the hands of criminal elements? Beyond the loss of revenue, there is another issue. Despite all the drug control efforts, most Australians say marijuana is easy to get. Furthermore, of the 50,000 cannabis arrests in 2001–2002, approximately three-quarters were for simple possession. So scarce law enforcement resources are diverted from violent and other serious crimes; and the fines generated do not cover law enforcement costs. Furthermore, the current one-stop-shopping system, meaning a single illicit drug market, combines marijuana with more serious drugs such as heroin, amphetamines, and cocaine, raising the question of whether this has the effect of making these other drugs more accessible.

Editorial. *Drug and Alcohol Review* 23: 139–141, 2004

Table 2.1 Social Costs of Alcohol Use, 1998*

	$ (in Billions)	% of Costs
Reduced productivity in the workplace	87.7	47.8
Reduced productivity in the home	15.0	8.2
Motor vehicle crashes	20.9	11.3
Comorbidities (related illnesses)	15.9	8.6
Unintentional injuries (excluding auto)	17.6	9.6
Crime	7.2	3.9
Fetal alcohol syndrome	11.2	6.0
Treatment for alcoholism	8.5	4.6

From: NIAAA. *Seventh and Tenth Special Reports to Congress on Alcohol and Health,** Rockville MD, 1994 and 2001.
*This chart is organized by categories that made sense to laypeople. But the figures are updated with information from the tenth report.

numbers. From time to time, the federal government revises the manner in which it calculates particular figures. Thus, changes do not necessarily reflect a decline in alcohol problems and their costs but may instead reflect a different way of gathering the data. The most recent estimates of the economic costs of alcohol problems are presented in Table 2.1.

The other side of the cost coin is economic revenues. The total alcohol tax revenues raised by federal and state authorities in 1998 was $18.2 billion. It should be noted that in 1987, federal tax rates on distilled spirits were raised for the first time in 34 years. The tax on liquor was then raised 20%. Nonetheless, alcohol, especially distilled spirits, continues to be a true bargain. Because inflation has outstripped any federal and state tax increases, the real price of distilled spirits has been cut by nearly half. The real cost of beer has dropped 20%, and the cost of wine has dropped almost 25%. Alcoholic beverages have become so inexpensive that their prices are essentially the same as those of nonalcoholic drinks. Correspondingly, while the costs of soda tripled the costs of alcoholic beverages have not quite doubled, putting them in the same price range. The net effect of all this is that the typical American can drink more but can spend less of the total family income to do it.[1]

How do the social benefits of alcohol use compare with its social costs? Social benefits include tax revenues, wages, salaries, and income generated directly by the manufacture and sales of alcohol or indirectly

[1]This is based on a population in 1998 of 272.4 million, age 15 and above, the age used by the federal government in calculating per capita consumption rates.

via the hospitality industry plus philanthropic contributions by the alcohol beverage industry. These social benefits have not been systematically calculated, as are the social costs associated with drinking. Nor have there been efforts to calculate alcohol's benefits to individuals.

A rough calculation of the cost-benefits of alcohol can be made by comparing the figures for social costs, \$184.6 billion, and for social benefits—that is, the alcohol-generated tax revenues, \$18.2 billion. Thus, for every dollar of taxes generated, there is a corresponding cost to society of \$10.14. In other words, if all the alcohol sold in the United States in 1999—which was 605.9 million gallons of ethanol—were treated as if it had all been marketed as gallons of pure alcohol, the social cost would be \$310.80 per gallon. The social benefit per gallon under the same reckoning would be \$30.64. Translate those gallons of pure alcohol into fifths of 80-proof liquor. That would represent 1,512,969,421 fifths. The bill to society per fifth would be \$125.00; the benefits in the form of taxes, \$12.30 per fifth.

Other attempts have been made to consider the social costs of alcohol use, especially with respect to health-care costs. One study with the provocative title "The Taxes of Sin: Do Smokers and Drinkers Pay Their Way?" was concerned with just that question. A variety of costs related to drinking and smoking were examined—for example, the monetary impact of early death due to smoking and heavy drinking. The study found that, if smokers and drinkers die early, the amount of money they have paid into retirement plans and social security in part becomes available to subsidize the benefits of others. The conclusion was that smokers do pay their way, but those with alcoholism do not. At best, taxes on alcohol were found to cover about half of the expenses generated by those who drink heavily.

Personal Costs

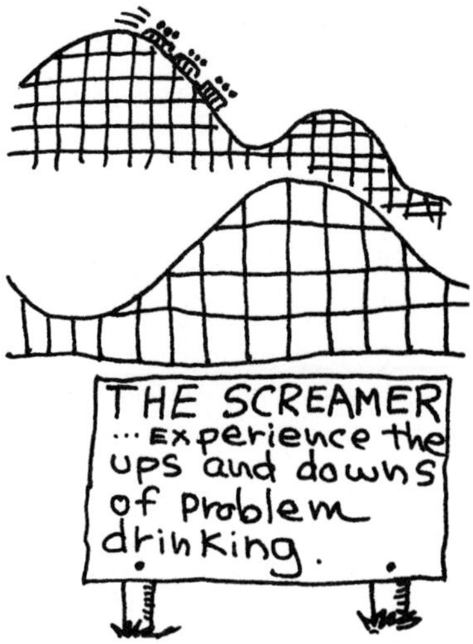

The personal cost of alcohol problems is tremendous. It is estimated that alcohol-related deaths may run as high as 10% of all deaths annually. Heavy drinking reduces life expectancy. The mortality rate of those with alcoholism is 2½ times greater than that of nonalcoholics. Those with alcoholism also have a higher rate of violent deaths. Drinking figures prominently in both accidental and violent death, for alcoholics and nonalcoholics alike. As many as 75% of all unintentional injuries are alcohol-related, including motor fatalities, falls, drownings, fires, and burns.

Injuries

Alcohol use is implicated in injuries. Studies have repeatedly shown that those who have been drinking have a greater likelihood of landing in an emergency room. This is true of all age groups. One statewide study of trauma center patients found that, of those 12–17 years old, 12.8% were alcohol positive; of those 18–20 years old, 47.0% were alcohol positive;

and the proportion of those 21–25 years old reached 64%. Another large study drew on the insurance records of more than 1.5 million people covered by the health insurance plans of 70 large corporations. For those with a history of an alcohol problem, 46% had been hospitalized as the result of injury in the prior 3 years. When a history of other drug use was added to the alcohol use, the risk for injury rose to 58%.

It is the upheaval of prior norms by a society that has finally recognized that it must change its habits and do whatever is required, whether it means a small change or a significant one, in order to stop the senseless loss inflicted by drunken drivers.
ROBERT N. WILENTZ, CHIEF JUSTICE, NEW JERSEY SUPREME COURT
Majority opinion in a 6 to 1 ruling that a host may be held liable for serving alcohol to persons later involved drunk-driving incidents, June 27, 1984.

The risk of injury increases with rising blood alcohol levels, indicated as BAC (blood alcohol concentrations). Thus, for bicyclists, the risk of injury is 5 times greater for those with a BAC higher than 0.02. At a BAC of 0.08 or higher—the level set by law for driving while intoxicated—the chances of injury are 20 times higher.

Another factor related to the risk of injury is the age at which people start drinking. For those who started drinking before age 14, as opposed to those who delay drinking until age 21, there is a five times greater risk of having an alcohol-related injury, and an over three times greater likelihood of an alcohol injury in the past year.

Motor Vehicle Fatalities

The number of fatalities involving alcohol has been steadily declining. Of the 42,116 traffic fatalities in 2001, 30.5% were alcohol-related. The figure for alcohol-related traffic fatalities includes deaths of not only drivers but also passengers and pedestrians. The figure also includes accidents involving bicycles and motorcycles as well as cars and trucks. This 2001 figure represents a 24-year low. The rate of decline has been highest among younger drivers, among whom the level of alcohol fatalities has essentially been cut in half. Nonetheless, alcohol-related fatalities are not evenly spread across all drivers. Approximately 75% of alcohol-related fatalities occur among those between the ages of 16 and 44.

Women have always had far fewer alcohol-related fatalities than men, but differences by gender have been narrowing. In fatal motor vehicle accidents involving a pedestrian or bicyclist, the odds are greater that it will be the bicyclist or pedestrian, not the motorist, who has been drinking. The rates of alcohol-related pedestrian deaths are higher in rural areas than in urban and suburban locales. The severity of injuries and the associated length of a hospital stay too are related to alcohol consumption at levels of 0.10 or above.

Annually in the United States there are more than 82 million drinking-driving trips, at blood alcohol concentrations of 0.08 percent and higher, the legal level for intoxication. There are only 1.5 million arrests for drinking and driving each year.

Alcohol and the outcome of an accident are related in several other ways. Drinking is likely to decrease the use of protective devices, such as seat belts and motorcycle safety helmets. With intoxicating levels of alcohol, the use of helmets declines by one-third. In a major urban area, in which bicycle use is rising, fully 70% of riders who had been drinking prior to an accident were not wearing helmets. Also, medical care for those who have been drinking and sustain injuries is likely to be more complicated. For accident victims with a similar severity of injuries, those who had been drinking had lower blood pressure and lower PCO_2 (the latter is a measure of blood gases and both are indexes for shock).

Thus, their medical condition was more fragile and likely to lead to problems if resuscitation and/or emergency care were delayed.

Falls

Drinking increases the risk of both death and injury from falls. A review of all studies of deaths from falls showed alcohol involved in 15% to 63% of the groups studied. As blood alcohol rises, the risk of falls increases. Compared with those who have not been drinking, those with a 0.10 blood alcohol content (BAC) have a 3 times greater risk of a fall; with a BAC of 0.16 or above, the risk is 60 times higher. Of the injuries commonly associated with falls, fractures of the ribs and vertebrae are 16 times higher for people who are heavy chronic drinkers than for nonproblematic or "social" drinkers. One study following people over a decade found that the likelihood of a fatal fall increased in proportion to the number of drinks an individual had reportedly consumed on a "typical" drinking occasion. Among the elderly, already vulnerable to falls, having two or more drinks per day further increases the risk of falls by 25%.

Burns and Fires

Drinking increases the risk of injury and death by burns and fires. Burns and fires cause about 5,000 deaths annually. Half of the people who die in house fires have high BACs. A review of recent studies shows that between 33% and 61% of people who died as a result of burns had been drinking. Approximately one-quarter of burn injuries involved people who were drinking. Alcohol use also appears to have an impact on the outcome of burn injuries. Among burn victims, those with a positive BAC had virtually twice the proportion of fatalities. The likelihood of death increases with higher BACs. In addition, it has been found that those diagnosed as alcoholic had a 3 times higher rate of mortality and died with smaller burns. So both alcohol consumption at the time of the fire and alcoholism influence survival rates. For home fires involving cigarette smoking, alcohol, too, is likely to be a factor.

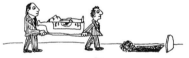

Water Mishaps

Bacchus has drowned more men than Neptune.
THOMAS FULLER

Drinking is involved in a significant percentage of deaths from drowning. Among young males, alcohol is a significant contributing factor in 50% of all drownings. In boating-related drownings, one study found 45% of the victims had a positive BAC, and 22% were legally intoxicated. Studies have shown that boat operators who are suffering from fatigue due to sun, wind, glare, and wave motion are 10 times as likely to miss course correction signals if they are also legally intoxicated. Furthermore, those legally intoxicated (with a 0.01 BAC) are at a 10 times greater risk of death in boating accidents. Boat passengers who have been drinking are at increased risk also. Alcohol similarly plays a role in diving accidents, many of which result in spinal cord injury and paralysis. Diving injuries that result in spinal cord injury are four times as likely to involve intoxicated divers. Not surprisingly, blood alcohol levels as low as 0.12 impair divers' judgment and, at levels of 0.4, impair the ability to perform dives.

Air Traffic Safety

The impact of alcohol has also been considered with respect to air traffic safety. No alcohol-related accidents have occurred among the major commercial airlines, but alcohol use has been a factor in a small percentage of other aviation accidents. Experimental studies show that alcohol levels as low as 0.025 reduce a pilot's ability to perform essential tasks.

The Workplace

Alcohol has been implicated in injuries in the workplace in a variety of work settings. An Australian study found that, among fatal workplace injuries, 65% of those injured had a BAC of 0.05 or higher, and another 16% had measurable blood alcohol levels. In addition, drinking outside work also has an impact on the workplace. Higher overall levels of drinking are associated with higher numbers of workmen's compensation claims. The increase is seen at 14 or more drinks per week.

Suicide

Alcohol plays a significant role in suicide. Studies indicate that, in one-third of suicide attempts, the individual had been drinking. In slightly over one-third of successful suicides, the individual had a positive BAC. Drinking is also associated with more lethal means of suicide—particularly, the use of firearms. Alcohol is associated more often with impulsive suicides than it is with premeditated suicides. Among adolescents a pattern of binge drinking is associated with suicide. Finally, there is a clear association between alcohol abuse and alcohol dependence and rates of suicide. The risk increases with other drug use and the presence of psychiatric disorders.

Violence

There is a clear link between alcohol and violence. Of the estimated 11.1 million victims of crime each year, in 1 out of 4 the perpetrator was reported to have been drinking. By comparison, despite the popular myths to the contrary, in only 1 out of 20 cases were other drugs involved. Drinking also increases the likelihood of being the victim of violence. In as many as 67% of all homicides, the victim, the assailant, or both have been drinking. The more serious the crime and the more serious the injuries, the more likely that alcohol is involved.

If once a man indulges himself in murder, very soon he comes to think little of robbing; and from robbing he comes next to drinking and sabbath breaking, and from that to incivility and procrastination.
THOMAS DE QUINCEY, 1839

Drinking is a major factor in family violence. Violence against partners is twice as likely to involve alcohol than are incidents of violence committed against strangers. In couples whose relationships have included aggressive episodes, physical aggression is four times more likely to involve alcohol than is verbal aggression. Alcohol is also a precipitating factor in child abuse, beatings, and other family violence. It is estimated that alcohol is implicated in two-thirds of all cases of family violence. In cases of domestic violence, the likelihood of severe physical aggression is more than 11 times higher on days of men's drinking than on days where there is no drinking. Fifty percent of patients treated in emergency rooms as a result of violence-related injuries had been drinking within the 6 hours before the incident.

As discussed in the most recent *Special Report to the U.S. Congress on Alcohol and Health,* there are a variety of patterns of violence. The occurrence of violence differs with drinking patterns—for example, with binge drinkers versus steady heavy drinkers—and with the acceptance or nonacceptance of violence in families. Similarly in work on violence and children, what is being discussed as violence can encompass or refer to only some of the following: physical abuse, sexual abuse, psychological abuse, neglect, maltreatment, and abandonment.

Crime

Alcohol use is reflected in national crime statistics. Its role in homicide and family violence has been noted, and it is a significant factor in assaults in general. Alcohol is involved in both attempted and completed rapes. For 50% of the rapists and for 30% of the victims, alcohol is a prominent feature. In cases of robbery, up to 22% of the offenders have been drinking. The current estimate of the total national bill for alcohol-related crimes and misdemeanors is over $10 billion. The relationship between alcohol and crime is evident, too, in where crimes occur. City blocks with bars have been found to have higher rates of assaults, robberies, and rapes than city blocks without bars. The relationship between crime and alcohol use is not wholly clear. For example, one question raised is whether those who have been drinking are simply more likely to be apprehended. Or does the alcohol-crime relationship possibly reflect patterns of law enforcement? The current thinking is that a variety of interacting factors play a role, such as expectancies, personality factors, the social context, and the pharmacological properties of alcohol.

Best while you have it use your breath,
There is no drinking after death.
JOHN FLETCHER, C1616
ENGLISH PLAYWRIGHT

Health Care and Alcohol

Alcohol has a significant impact on both health-care delivery and health-care costs. The following list summarizes some significant points:

- Studies have consistently shown that a minimum of 20% of all hospitalized persons have a significant alcohol problem, whatever the presenting problem or admitting diagnosis. That is an absolute minimum. In some institutions, the proportion is apt to be higher.

The Veterans Administration (VA) estimates that 50% of all VA hospital beds are filled by veterans with alcohol problems.

- In terms of health-care costs, the American Medical Association in 1993 issued a report stating that, of the annual $666 billion that Americans spend on health care annually, $1 out of every $4 is related to caring for those who are victims of alcohol and other drug problems.
- Some people incur a disproportionate share of health-care costs. One large-scale study of hospital costs found that a small proportion of patients, only 13%, had hospital bills equal to the remaining 87%. The distinguishing characteristic of the high-cost group was not age, gender, economic status, or ethnicity. The distinguishing characteristic of high-cost users was that they were heavy drinkers and/or heavy smokers. A follow-up study found that high-cost users also had multiple hospitalizations. In general, patients with a history of alcoholism have significantly more repeated hospitalizations than do those without such a history.
- When health-care costs for untreated alcoholics and their families are compared with those of families without alcohol dependence, the difference is striking. The families with alcohol dependence have 100% greater medical costs. In the 1-year period prior to treatment for alcoholism, the health-care costs for untreated alcoholism are over 300% of those of the general public. Such a pattern of increasing medical care immediately prior to diagnosis is true for many chronic diseases, including diabetes, hypertension, heart disease, and respiratory illnesses.
- The children of those with alcoholism too have higher than anticipated health-care costs. A study conducted by the Children of Alcoholics Foundation found that children of alcoholics had a 25% greater rate of health-care utilization than their peers. Furthermore, if hospitalized, their stay in a hospital was 29% longer; the hospital bills for their care were 36% greater.
- Following alcohol treatment, there is a rapid decline in the total family's health-care costs.
- As alcohol problems contribute to health care costs, so too does the failure to diagnose alcohol problems. For example, interventions among hospitalized patients reduces readmissions. Every dollar spent on brief interventions leads to a savings of $19 in future costs for rehospitalization. In a single military hospital it was estimated 1 year's missed diagnoses generated an additional $10 million in hospital expenditures.

It is unfortunate and ironic that, of all these health-care costs, only a small proportion—approximately 13%—represents expenditures for rehabilitation or treatment of the primary alcohol problem. The bulk of the costs is for treatments of alcohol-induced illness and trauma. Equally

FOCUS ON DRUGS

Heroin: It's a Small World . . .

It might come as a surprise that subsistence farmers living half a world away, each cultivating less than 100 acres that yield an annual total income of $2,520, who live in a country with few miles of paved highways, with only one commercial airport, and essentially no commercial transportation system, are the source of over 75% of the world's heroin.[1] These approximately 264,000 farmers produce a crop with an estimated street value of $30 billion.

During the second half of the 1990s, Afghanistan became the world's largest source of illicit opium poppy cultivation and its derivative, heroin. In recent years it has produced more than 3,000 metric tons annually. And production is increasing. In 2003, about 80,000 hectares—each of which is equivalent to 100 acres—was devoted to poppy cultivation, an increase of 8% over the previous year. A United Nations survey conducted in 2003 found that 43% of the non-poppy-growing farmers indicated they planned to do so the following year. If in fact they did, the portion of farmers' land devoted to poppy cultivation would rise from 27% in 2003 to more than 40% in 2004. Poppy cultivation has spread throughout the country, with poppy now grown in 28 of the country's 32 provinces.

Farmers' income from poppy cultivation, at $1.02 billion, is the equivalent of 20% of Afghanistan's total legitimate gross national product. Tack onto that figure the profits from processing the opium into heroin and transporting it to the borders, and the value rises to $2.3 billion. The total income from heroin—from the point of planting seeds to the processed heroin reaching the country's borders and entering the international drug trade—is equivalent to half of Afghanistan's total legitimate economy. Since the typical rural family consists of 6 or 7 people, opium cultivation plays a direct role in the livelihood of an estimated 1.7 million rural people, about 7% of the total population. This doesn't include those engaged in trading opium at bazaars, refining it into heroin, or trafficking it to the country's borders.

For individual farmers, there are a number of reasons to plant poppy:

- Land that is poorly suited for virtually any other crop is perfect for poppy. Poppy thrives in sandy soil and on steep hillsides that assure good drainage. Cultivation requires little if any fertilization or irrigation.
- Poppy cultivation is well suited to small plots.
- Growing wheat, the major alternative cash crop, at best can generate only 2% of the income that comes from poppy cultivation.
- The net income of poppy farmers is estimated to be about three and a half times greater than that of non-poppy farmers.
- Poppy farmers have access to credit that isn't otherwise available. The majority of this credit is *not* provided by opium traders; indeed only 30% is. Most credit is extended by traders and shopkeepers.
- Strict adherence to Islamic law prohibits charging interest. Thus the credit arrangements generally involve advance sale of the next year's crop at an agreed upon price known as the "salaam price." About half of poppy growers reported having obtained credit. One of the results is that to repay a loan, the farmer is obligated to cultivate poppy the following year.
- Opium production benefits laborers, too. The average daily wage for opium harvesting is $6.80, more than twice that paid for wheat harvesting.

Contrary to what might be expected, families who grow poppy have smaller landholdings than non-poppy-growing farmers. The average family plot available for all its cultivation is about 2 hectares. Less than 30% of this is used for poppy. The rest is used to raise livestock, or planted in other crops, either for the family's own use or to provide a cash crop for sale at the local bazaar.

The majority of the farmers (80%) report that they decide what to plant on the land they own, rent, or work as sharecroppers. There is not now—or is the proper word "yet"?—an organized drug cartel that controls the areas. "Taxes" are, however, levied by regional officials, payable in cash or in kind, commonly equivalent to 1/10 of the opium harvest. But the amounts are variable, depending upon the particular region, and such things as ethnic group membership, kinship relationships, and friendships.

[1] As this book was in press, the figure was raised to 90% based on 2004 data.

(Continued)

FOCUS ON DRUGS

Continued

Afghan farmers are well aware that poppy cultivation is illegal. That they can be responsive to bans is quite clear. Production dropped dramatically, by 90%, in a single year (2001) in response to a ban instituted by the Taliban regime. With the overthrow of the Taliban, production immediately bounced right back, essentially to the pre-ban level. At the same time, cultivation also spread to new areas of the country. A new ban issued in 2002 was essentially ignored. Farmers readily acknowledge their cultivation of poppy is motivated by financial incentives. There is no other crop that can provide comparable income. Also, they point out that the UN-sponsored food programs conducted in their country have distributed bread made with foreign wheat, wheat imported by the UN! In addition, promises of external aid if they refrain from poppy production have yet to be honored.

The questions this raises for defining what represents enlightened drug control policy are seemingly limitless. What? How? If?

What would be the cost for buying off the Afghan farmers? How would the monies required to reimburse farmers compare to the current military expenditures in the war on terror? If poppy production were reduced in Afghanistan where might cultivation be transferred? Does poppy cultivation translate into a problem of drug use within Afghanistan?

United Nations Office on Drugs and Crime; Government of Afghanistan's Counter Narcotics Directorate. *Afghanistan: Farmers' Intentions Survey 2003/2004.* Vienna, Austria: United National Office on Drugs and Crime. February 2004. <www.unodc.org/unodc/en/crop_monitoring.html>

United Nations Office on Drugs and Crime; Government of Afghanistan's Counter Narcotics Directorate. *Afghanistan Opium Survey 2003.* Vienna, Austria: United National Office on Drugs and Crime, 2003. <www.unodc.org/unodc/en/crop_monitoring.html>

disturbing is the NIAAA's estimate that 85% of the nation's alcoholics and problem drinkers are not receiving any formal treatment. Even if one were to factor in those who enter AA and who have had no involvement in formal treatment (approximately 60% of the 2 million members of AA), that only reduces the untreated portion by another 5%.

A more recently recognized health-care cost is the expenditures that result from fetal alcohol syndrome (FAS) and fetal alcohol effects (FAE). It has been estimated that the costs for treatment and the special education, training, and required support services adds over $10 billion to the nation's health-care costs. These infants grow to become children and eventually adults who continue to require care.

If one considers the federal dollars spent on health research, alcohol abuse is a health concern that has historically gotten short shrift. When alcohol abuse is compared with other diseases, such as heart disease and cancer, the amount of federal research dollars spent on alcohol research is not proportional to the economic costs or to the numbers of those affected. In the early 1990s, 15 times more money was spent on heart disease research than on alcoholism and alcohol abuse research. And the amount spent on cancer research was 35 times greater, although the associated costs are only three-quarters as great as those associated with alcohol abuse and alcoholism.

One of the big questions is how alcohol and other drug use problems will fare in the rapidly changing U.S. health-care system. Despite numerous studies that demonstrate that treating alcoholism is cost-effective and that any treatment is better than no treatment, alcohol problems along with other drug use often constitute the only major diseases not routinely covered by health insurance. There is more awareness of the toll that alcohol dependence and alcohol abuse can take in our public and private lives, yet there remains a bias that such problems are "different" from other medical illnesses. When health-care reform emerged on the national agenda during the first Clinton administration, many national groups submitted position papers to influence how alcohol and other drug problems would be addressed within health-care reform. These statements tried to convey two messages. One was the importance of not having a dual standard of care, one for traditional medical problems and a different one for substance abuse, as if the latter were not a real or legitimate medical condition. The other message emphasized the potential savings that can result if substance abuse is treated, rather than waiting for the emergence of its medical complications. While an overarching national plan was not effected, forces for change were set in motion. Unfortunately, the dual standard of care that was feared has become the norm, as managed care has come to dominate the landscape. The degree to which this view goes unchallenged will testify to the extent to which we have come to recognize alcohol abuse and other drug problems as health concerns rather than moral issues.

RESOURCES AND FURTHER READING

Social Costs and Social Policy

Addictive Behaviors 28(9): entire issue, 2003. Note: Thematic issue on interpersonal violence and substance use.

Alcohol Epidemiologic Data System, Nephew TM, Yi H-y, Hoy AK, Stinson FS, Dufour MC. *Apparent per Capita Consumption: National, State, and Regional Trends, 1977–2000.* Surveillance Report No. 62. Bethesda, MD: National Institute on Alcohol Abuse and Alcoholism, 2003. (37 refs.)

Alcohol Epidemiologic Data System, Yi H-y, Williams GD, Dufour MC. *Trends in Alcohol-Related Fatal Traffic Crashes, United States, 1977–2001.* Surveillance Report No. 65. Bethesda, MD: National Institute on Alcohol Abuse and Alcoholism, 2003. (52 refs.)

American Medical Association. *Factors Contributing to the Health Care Cost Problem.* Chicago: American Medical Association, 1993.

Canfield DV, Hordinsky J, Millett DP, Endecott B, Smith D. Aviation—Prevalence of drugs and alcohol in fatal civil aviation accidents between 1994 and 1998. *Aviation, Space, and Environmental Medicine* 72(2): 120–124, 2001. (8 refs.)

Cherpitel C, Borges GLG, Wilcox HC. Acute alcohol use and suicidal behavior: A review of the literature. *Alcoholism: Clinical and Experimental Research* 28(5 Supplement 1): 18S–28S, 2004. (87 refs.)

Children of Alcoholics Foundation. *Children of Alcoholics in the Medical System: Hidden Problems, Hidden Costs.* New York: Children of Alcoholics Foundation, 1990.

Cook PJ, Moore MJ: Violence reduction through restrictions on alcohol availability. *Alcohol Health and Research World* 17(2):151–156, 1993.

Driscoll TR, Harrison JA, Steenkamp M. Review of the role of alcohol in drowning associated with recreational aquatic activity (review). *Injury Prevention* 10(2):107–113, 2004. (66 refs.)

Greenfield TK, Graves KL, Kaskutas LA. Alcohol warning labels for prevention: National survey findings. *Alcohol Health and Research World* 17(1):67–75, 1993.

Gruenewald PJ: Alcohol problems and the control of availability: Theoretical and empirical issues. In: Hilton ME, Bloss G, eds.: *Economics and the prevention of alcohol-related problems, NIAAA Research Monograph 25,* Rockville, MD: National Institute on Alcohol Abuse and Alcoholism, 1993.

Hingson R, Heeren T, Jamanka T, Howland J. *Age of drinking onset and unintentional injury involvement after drinking.* Washington DC: National Highway Traffic Safety Administration, 2001. (25 refs.)

Hingson R, Winter M. Epidemiology and consequences of drinking and driving. *Alcohol Research & Health* 27(1): 63–78, 2003. (30 refs.)

Hoffmann NG, DeHart SS, Fulkerson JA. Medical care utilization as a function of recovery status. *Journal of Addictive Diseases* 12(1):97–108, 1993.

Holder HD. Changes in access to and availability of alcohol in the United States: Research and policy implications. Addiction 88(Supplement): 67S–74S, 1993.

Johnston LD, O'Malley PM, Bachman JG. *Monitoring the Future Study, National Survey Results on Adolescent Drug Use. Overview of Key Findings, 2003.* Rockville MD: National Institute on Drug Abuse, 2004.

Jones NE, Pieper CF, Robertson LS. The effect of legal drinking age on fatal injuries of adolescents and young adults. *American Journal of Public Health* 82(1):112–115, 1992.

Kerr, WC, Greenfield TK, Bond J, Ye Y, Rehm J. Age, period, and cohort influences on beer, wine, and spirits consumption trends in the U.S. National Alcohol Survey. *Addiction* 99(9):1111–1120, 2004. (32 refs.)

Kung HC, Pearson JL, Liu XH. Risk factors for male and female suicide decedents ages 15–64 in the United States—Results from the 1993 National Mortality Followback Survey. *Social Psychiatry and Psychiatric Epidemiology* 38(8):419–426, 2003. (50 refs.)

Manning WG, Keeler EB, Newhouse JP, Sloss EM, Wasserman J. The taxes of sin: Do smokers and drinkers pay their way? *Journal of the American Medical Association* 261(11):1604–1609, 1989.

Miller TR, Lestina DC, Smith GS. Injury risk among medically identified alcohol and drug abusers. *Alcoholism: Clinical and Experimental Research* 25(1):54–59, 2001. (23 refs.)

Mukamal KJ, Mittleman MA, Longstreth WT, Newman AB, Fried LP, Siscovick DS. Self-reported alcohol consumption and falls in older adults: Cross-sectional and longitudinal analyses of the cardiovascular health study. *Journal of the American Geriatrics Society* 52(7):1174–1179, 2004. (27 refs.)

National Center for Injury Prevention and Control. *Injury Fact Book 2001–2002.* Atlanta: National Center for Injury Prevention and Control, 2002. [Note: This is the most recent edition, available as of 2004.]

National Institute on Alcohol Abuse and Alcoholism. *Tenth Special Report to U.S. Congress on Alcohol and Health.* Washington, DC: U.S. Government Printing Office, 2000.

National Institute on Drug Abuse, Office of Applied Studies. Results from the 2003 *National Survey on Drug Use and Health: National Findings.* Rockville MD: Substance Abuse and Mental Health Service Administration, 2004.

Neumark YD, Van Etten ML, Anthony JC. "Alcohol dependence" and death: Survival analysis of the Baltimore ECA sample from 1981 to 1995. *Substance Use & Misuse* 35(4):533–549, 2000. (26 refs.)

Pirkola SP, Suominen K, Isometsa ET. Suicide in alcohol-dependent individuals: Epidemiology and management (review). *CNS Drugs* 18(7):423–436, 2004. (138 refs.)

Porter RS. Alcohol and injury in adolescents. *Pediatric Emergency Care* 16(5):316–320, 2000. (15 refs.)

Rehm, J, Gmel G, Sempos CT, Trevisian M. Alcohol related morbidity and mortality (review). *Alcohol Research and Health* 27(1):39–51, 2003. (125 refs.)

Sinclair JD, Sillanaukee P. The preventive paradox: A critical examination (commentary). *Addiction* 88(5):591–595, 1993.

Storer RM. A simple cost-benefit analysis of brief interventions on substance abuse at Naval Medical Center Portsmouth. *Military Medicine* 168(9):765–768, 2003. (9 refs.)

CHAPTER 3

Alcohol and the Body

	Calories
Beer, 12 oz	*173*
Martini, 3 oz, 3:1	*145*
Olive, 1 large	*20*
Rum, 1 oz	*73*
Sherry, sweet, 3 oz	*150*
Fortified wines	*120–160*
Scotch, 1 oz	*73*
Cola, 8 oz	*105*
Pretzels, 5 small sticks	*20*
Lemon, slice	*3*

The Joy of Cooking

It is widely recognized that alcohol is more than a beverage. Alcohol is a drug. When ingested, it has specific and predictable physiological effects on the body—any body, every body. Usually attention is paid to the physical impact of chronic use or what happens with excessive use. Often overlooked are the normal, routine effects on anyone who uses alcohol. Let us examine what happens to alcohol in the body—how it is taken in, how it is broken down, and how it thereby alters body functioning.

INGESTION AND ABSORPTION

The human body is well engineered to change the foods ingested into substances needed to maintain life and provide energy. Despite occasional upsets from too much spice or too much food, in general, this process goes on without a hitch. The first part of this transformation is called digestion. Digestion is like a carpenter who dismantles an old building, salvages the materials, and uses them in new construction. Digestion is the body's way of dismantling food to get raw materials required by the body. Whether alcohol can be called a food was at one time a big point of controversy. Alcohol does have calories. One ounce of pure alcohol contains 210 calories. To translate that into drinks, an ounce of whiskey contains 75 calories, and a 12-ounce can of beer contains 150 calories. Alcohol's usefulness as a food is limited, however. Sometimes alcohol is described as providing empty calories. It does not contain vitamins, minerals, or other essential nutrients. Also, alcohol can interfere with the body's ability to use other sources of energy. As a food, alcohol is unique in that it requires no digestion. Since alcohol is a liquid, no mechanical action by the teeth is required to break it down. No digestive juices need be added to transform it into a form that can be absorbed by the bloodstream and transported to all parts of the body.

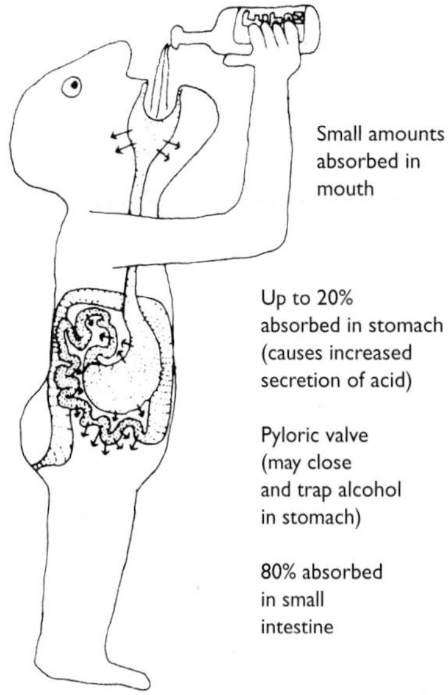

ABSORPTION OF ALCOHOL

What happens to alcohol in the body? Surprisingly, absorption of alcohol begins almost immediately with a very small amount taken up into the bloodstream through the tiny blood vessels in the mouth. But the majority goes the route of all food when swallowed—into the stomach. If other food is present in the stomach, the alcohol mixes with it. Here, too, some alcohol seeps into the bloodstream. Up to 20% can be absorbed directly from the stomach, and another small portion is metabolized in the stomach. The remainder passes into the small intestine to be absorbed. The amount of food in the stomach when drinking takes place has important ramifications. Alcohol is an irritant. It increases the flow of hydrochloric acid, a digestive juice secreted by cells of the stomach lining. Anyone who has an ulcer and takes a drink can readily confirm this. This phenomenon explains the feeling of warmth as the drink goes down. The presence of food dilutes the alcohol and tends to diminish its irritant properties.

The amount of food in the stomach is an important factor in determining the speed with which the alcohol is absorbed by the bloodstream. A rapid rate of absorption is largely responsible for the subjective feeling of being intoxicated—thus, the basis for the advice, "Don't drink on an empty stomach." How much and how quickly alcohol is absorbed depends both on the total amount of alcohol in the stomach's contents and on the relative proportion of alcohol to food. The greater the amount of alcohol and the smaller the amount of food in the stomach, the more rapidly the alcohol is absorbed into the bloodstream and the higher the resulting blood alcohol level. A sex-based difference also seems to influence blood alcohol levels. This is related to differing amounts of an enzyme, gastric *a*lcohol *deh*ydrogenase (ADH), produced by the stomach lining that promotes the breakdown of alcohol. Because women have significantly lower levels of this enzyme, more of the alcohol they drink remains available to enter the small intestine and be taken up by the blood. Therefore, when women and men consume equivalent amounts of alcohol, women have a higher blood alcohol concentration.

See. I don't drink on an empty stomach. I alway have a couple of beers to line it before I really start to drink.

In addition to the impact of food in the stomach, the rate of absorption varies with the type of beverage. The higher the concentration of alcohol in a beverage (up to 50%, or 100 proof), the more quickly the alcohol is absorbed. This partially explains why distilled spirits, with their higher alcohol content, have more apparent "kick" than wine or beer. In addition, wine and beer contain some food substances that slow absorption. On the other hand, carbon dioxide, which hastens the passage of alcohol from the stomach, may increase the speed of absorption. As a result, champagne, sparkling wines, and drinks mixed with carbonated soda may give a sense of "bubbles in the head."

Now, on from the stomach to the pyloric valve. This valve controls the passage of the stomach's contents into the small intestine. It is sensitive to the presence of alcohol. With high concentrations of alcohol, it tends to get "stuck" in the closed position—a condition called *pylorospasm.* When pylorospasm occurs, the alcohol trapped in the stomach may cause sufficient irritation and distress to induce vomiting. This is what accounts for much of the nausea and vomiting that may accompany too much drinking. A stuck pylorus valve also may serve as a self-protective mechanism. It may prevent the passage into the small intestine of what might otherwise be life-threatening doses of alcohol.

BLOOD ALCOHOL CONCENTRATION

In considering the effects of alcohol, several questions come to mind. How much alcohol and in how large a person? How fast did the alcohol get there? Is the blood alcohol level rising or declining? Let us consider each of these in turn.

First, let's consider the concentration of alcohol in the blood. One tablespoon of sugar mixed in a cup of water yields a much sweeter solution than a tablespoon of sugar diluted in a gallon of water. Similarly, consuming a drink with 1 ounce of alcohol results in a higher blood alcohol level in a 100-pound woman than in a 200-pound man. In fact, it is virtually twice as high. Her body contains less water than his. Even if they are of the same weight, the amount of water in the woman's body is less than in the man's. For that reason, when they consume the same amount of alcohol, her blood alcohol level will be higher than his. The second factor is rate of absorption, which depends both on the amount and concentration of alcohol in the stomach and on how rapidly it is ingested. So if you quickly drink a scotch on the rocks on an empty stomach, you will probably be more giddy than if you drink more alcohol more slowly—say, in the form of beer after a meal. Even with a given blood alcohol level, there is greater impairment the faster the level has been achieved. Impairment is based on both the amount absorbed and the rate of absorption. The rate of absorption determines how fast the alcohol reaches the brain. Finally, on any drinking occasion, there are different effects for a particular blood alcohol level, depending on whether the blood alcohol level is going up or coming down.

Once in the small intestine, the remainder of the alcohol (at least 80% of that ingested) is very rapidly absorbed into the bloodstream. The bloodstream is the body's transportation system. It delivers the oxygen and nutrients that the cells require for energy and picks up wastes produced by cell metabolism. By this route, too, alcohol is carried to all parts of the body.

Although blood alcohol levels are almost universally used as the measure of alcohol in the body, this does not mean that alcohol merely rides around in the bloodstream until the liver is able to break it down. Alcohol is both highly soluble in water and able to pass rapidly through cell walls. Therefore, it is distributed uniformly throughout the water content of all body tissues and cells. For a given blood alcohol level, the alcohol content of the tissues and cells varies in proportion to the amount of water they contain. The alcohol content of liver tissue is 64% of that in the blood; of muscle tissue, 84%; of brain tissue, 75%. It takes very little time for the tissues to absorb the alcohol circulating in the blood. Within 2 minutes, brain tissues will accurately reflect the blood alcohol level.

BREAKDOWN AND REMOVAL

The removal of alcohol from the body begins as soon as the alcohol is absorbed by the bloodstream. Small amounts leave unmetabolized through sweat, urine, and breath. The proportion of alcohol in exhaled air has a constant and predictable relationship to the blood alcohol concentration—which is the basis for the use of breathalyzers. These routes, at most, account for the elimination of only 5% of the alcohol consumed. The rest has to be changed chemically and metabolized to be removed from the body.

In 1990, a joint Italian-U.S. research group, headed by Mario Frezza and Charles Lieber, published new findings on metabolism. This was front page news, particularly because they identified differences between men and women. The breakdown, or metabolism, of alcohol occurs in a multistep process. The first step is its biochemical conversion to acetaldehyde. The enzyme that accomplishes this is called alcohol dehydrogenase, referred to as ADH. Before Frezza and Lieber's work, this enzyme was thought to be present and active only in the liver. They, however, identified a gastric form of ADH, referred to above. The breakdown of alcohol that occurs in the stomach is termed "first-pass metabolism." For nonalcoholic men, the amount of alcohol that can be metabolized by the stomach may be as great as 30% of the alcohol consumed. Nonalcoholic women metabolize only half that amount in the stomach. Therefore, greater proportions of alcohol enter the bloodstream of women.[1] For both sexes at all ages, a history of chronic heavy alcohol use leads to a significant decrease in first-pass metabolism.

The acetaldehyde that is formed is itself acted on in the second step of metabolism, by still another enzyme called aldehyde dehydrogenase. Aldehyde dehydrogenase, too, is present in both the stomach and the liver. Then, very rapidly the acetaldehyde produced is further metabolized into acetic acid. This is dispersed throughout the body, where it is broken down in cells and tissues to become carbon dioxide and water. The following diagram illustrates the chain of events:

---

[1]Some preliminary research suggests possibly this sex-based difference may be apparent only among young adults, and then reverse in later life.

FOCUS ON DRUGS

Route of Administration—So What?

"Route of administration" is the term for how a drug is taken into the body. There are a number of ways that apply to all drugs, not just drugs of abuse. For example, prescribed medications may be taken *orally*. Often there are further instructions, such as "Take with eight ounces of water" or "Take on an empty stomach," or "Take with meals." Some pills have coatings and others are gel capsules because the medication has to navigate the digestive system. Some medications may be administered via *inhalers,* for example with asthma or allergy medications. Also drugs may be *injected.* Here too there are variations—just under the skin, or into a large muscle (usually the arm or the buttock), or intravenously. Or drugs can be *absorbed through the skin,* via patches, as in some pain medications or the nicotine patch. For all medications, the particular route of administration is selected to assure that drugs are delivered efficiently and effectively, that a drug is not removed from the body before it can do its job, and that a drug is delivered at the proper rate.

To apply this efficiency and effectiveness principle to drugs of abuse, consider, marijuana. When marijuana is smoked in a joint, approximately 30% of the active ingredient that provides the desired effect, THC,[*] is destroyed by the heat involved with smoking. Another 20% to 40% is lost in sidestream smoke, the amount released in the smoke between puffs. So this route of administration might be considered very inefficient. Between 50% and 70% of the active ingredient never reaches the user. When smoking marijuana, people typically hold their breath. By holding their breath users maximize the amount that enters the bloodstream from the lungs. While a lot of the THC may have been lost, what does reach the lungs very rapidly passes into the bloodstream. Despite the loss of at least half of the psychoactive ingredients, smoking is an effective route to deliver the marijuana to the brain. With smoking the effects of the drug are felt more immediately than if the marijuana were ingested orally, as happens when it is added to brownies or some other food and has to traverse the digestive system.

With drugs of abuse, the target organ from the user's perspective is the brain. The bloodstream is the body's mechanism for delivering the drug's active ingredients to the brain. On entering the bloodstream the drug is very quickly delivered to the brain. Therefore, the most efficient delivery system is the one that gets the drug into the bloodstream the most rapidly. When drugs such as cocaine are snorted, they are absorbed into the bloodstream from the mucous membranes of the nose. Drugs that are inhaled or smoked enter the bloodstream through the lungs. Intravenous administration places the drug directly into the bloodstream.

The route of administration also has significance in terms of the kinds of problems that can result from use. For some substances, the dangers that come from the route of administration are greater than the effects of the drug itself. Nicotine is a prime example. Many long-term health problems are tied to *smoking,* not to nicotine. The addictive properties of the nicotine prompt the continuation of the dangerous practice of smoking. Injection as a route of administration is very efficient. Intravenous administration places the drug directly into the bloodstream. Injection, while very efficient, presents significant problems such as the risks of infection which accompany nonsterile techniques. The common practice of sharing needles too is very dangerous as it is a very efficient way of transferring bloodborne viruses, such as HIV/AIDS and hepatitis B and C.

When prescription drugs are drugs of abuse, the route of administration is likely to differ from what the manufacturer intended when formulating the drug for medical use. This introduces an additional twist. OxyContin®, a pain medication is a case in point. OxyContin is a semisynthetic opioid prescribed for chronic, severe pain. The medication's active ingredient is oxycodone, which is the basis of other pain medications, such as Percodan®. However, unlike the other pain preparations, OxyContin is formulated in a time-release form. The benefit for patients is that the medication needs to be taken only twice a day instead of possibly as many as six times per day. As it is equivalent to several doses of these other drugs, OxyContin contains between 10 and 160 mg of oxycodone, compared with the 5 mg of oxycodone contained in Percocet. OxyContin is manufactured as a tablet. When used as a drug of abuse, it is crushed and then ingested, snorted, or diluted in water and injected. In the process of crushing the time-release action is disarmed, so the full amount of the opioid is available immediately. Used in this fashion, OxyContin provides a rush similar to that associated with heroin.

---

[*]Sixty-one substances found only in marijuana are called cannabinoids. One of these cannabinoids accounts for virtually all of marijuana's effects; it is delta-9-tetrahydrocannabinol. The abbreviation is THC.

Alcohol → acetaldehyde[2] → acetic acid → carbon dioxide and water

Almost any cell or organ can break down the acetic acid that is formed. But only the liver or the stomach can handle the first two steps. These first steps depend upon the availability of a substance known as NAD^+, which must be present for the enzyme ADH to do its job. This essential substance, or cofactor, is present only in the liver and stomach. The rate of metabolism—that is, how quickly metabolism takes place—is determined by the availability of this cofactor. It is not in infinite supply or immediately present in sufficient quantities to accomplish the metabolism of alcohol in one fell swoop.

As alcohol is oxidized to acetaldehyde, the cofactor NAD^+ is changed; it is converted to NADH. As this occurs, the proportion of NADH to NAD^+ increases. The change in the relative amounts of these two substances has a number of important biochemical ramifications, which are discussed in Chapter 6.

The best thing about losing 45 lbs. is that how it only takes two beers to get drunk.

Generally the rate at which food is metabolized depends on the energy requirements of the body. Experience will confirm this, especially for anyone who has taken a stab at dieting. Chopping wood burns up more calories than watching videos. Eat too much food and a storehouse of fat begins to accumulate around the middle. By balancing our caloric intake with exercise, we can avoid accumulating a fat roll. Again, as a food, alcohol is unique. It is metabolized at a constant rate irrespective of the amount present or the body's metabolic needs. The presence of large amounts of alcohol at a particular moment does not prompt the liver to work faster. Despite alcohol's potential as a fine source of calories, increased exercise (and hence raising the body's need for calories) does not increase the speed of metabolism. This is probably not news to anyone who has tried to sober up someone who's drunk. It is simply a matter of time. Exercise may mean only that you have to contend with a wide-awake drunk rather than a sleeping one. He or she is still intoxicated. The rate at which alcohol is metabolized may vary a little between people. It will also increase somewhat after an extended drinking career. Yet the average rate is around 0.5 ounce of pure alcohol per hour—roughly equivalent to one mixed drink of 86-proof whiskey, or a 4-ounce glass of wine, or one 12-ounce can of beer. The unmetabolized alcohol remains circulating in the bloodstream, "waiting in line." The presence of not yet

[2]It is at this point that disulfiram (Antabuse®), a drug used in alcoholism treatment, acts. Disulfiram stops the breakdown of acetaldehyde by blocking acetaldehyde dehydrogenase. Thus, acetaldehyde starts to accumulate in the system. It is very toxic, and its effects are those associated with an Antabuse reaction. A better term would be "acetaldehyde reaction." The toxicity of acetaldehyde usually isn't a problem, since it breaks down faster than it is formed. But disulfiram does not allow this to take place so rapidly—thus the nausea, flushing, and heart palpitations. It has been observed that Asians often have such symptoms when drinking. These are seemingly based on genetically determined metabolic differences. In effect, some Asians may have a genetically determined built-in Antabuse-like response.

metabolized alcohol in the blood, and hence the brain, is responsible for its intoxicating effects.

ALCOHOL'S ACUTE EFFECTS ON THE BODY

What is the immediate effect of alcohol on the various body organs and functions?

Digestive System

Alcohol is an irritant. This explains the burning sensation as it goes down. Alcohol in the stomach promotes the flow of gastric juices. A glass of wine before dinner may thereby promote digestion by priming the stomach for food. But with intoxicating amounts, alcohol impedes or stops digestion. It can be irritating to the lining of the stomach and small intestine.

Circulatory System

In general, acute use of alcohol has relatively minor effects on the circulatory system in healthy individuals. In moderate amounts, alcohol is a vasodilator of the surface blood vessels. The vessels near the skin surface expand, which accounts for the sensation of warmth and flush to the skin that accompany drinking. Despite the subjective feeling of warmth, body heat is lost. Thus, whoever sends out the St. Bernard with a brandy cask to aid the cold, snow-stranded traveler is misguided. Despite the illusion of warmth, a good belt of alcohol will likely further cool off the body.

Kidneys

Anyone who has had a couple of drinks may well spend some time traipsing back and forth to the bathroom. The increased urine output is not caused by alcohol's direct action on the kidneys, nor is it due simply to the amount of liquid consumed. This phenomenon is related to the effect of alcohol on the posterior portion of the pituitary gland, located at the base of the brain. The pituitary secretes a hormone, called ADH, *an*tidiuretic *h*ormone that regulates the amount of water the kidneys excrete. When the pituitary is affected by alcohol, its functioning is depressed. Therefore, too little of the hormone is released, and the kidneys produce a larger than normal amount of dilute urine. This effect is most pronounced when alcohol is being absorbed and the blood alcohol level is rising.

Liver

The liver is very sensitive to the acute effects of alcohol. (See Chapter 6 for more information about the long-term effects of alcohol on the liver.) It has been demonstrated that for any drinker, not just heavy drinkers, even relatively small amounts of alcohol (1 to 2 ounces) can lead to rapid accumulation of fat in liver cells.

The liver performs an incredible number of metabolic functions—a very important one is its role in maintaining a proper blood sugar level. Sugar (the body's variety, called glucose) is the only source of energy that brain cells can use. Because the brain is the master control center of the body, an inadequate supply of glucose in the brain can have far-reaching consequences.

When alcohol is present in the body, the liver preferentially devotes its "attention," so to speak, to metabolizing it. This may interfere with the normal liver function of maintaining a steady, adequate supply of blood sugar. In the liver there is a stored form of glucose (glycogen) that usually is readily available to be converted to glucose. However, if one has had an inadequate diet, or has not eaten much for a day or two, glycogen may not be adequate. At such times the liver normally would employ a more complicated biochemical process to transform other nutrients, such as protein, into glucose. This process is called gluconeogenesis. However, in the presence of alcohol this complicated maneuver is blocked. In such cases hypoglycemia can result. In a hypoglycemic state the concentration of sugar in the blood is abnormally low. As a result, the brain is deprived of its proper nourishment. Symptoms include hunger, weakness, nervousness, sweating, headache, and tremor. If the blood sugar level is sufficiently depressed, coma can occur. Hypoglycemia may be more likely to occur and may be more severe in individuals who already have liver damage from chronic alcohol use. But it can occur in otherwise normal people with healthy livers who have been drinking heavily and have not been eating properly for as little as 48 to 72 hours.

In individuals with adequate diets, other metabolic effects of alcohol may cause abnormally high levels of blood glucose. This is called hyperglycemia, which is a state similar to that occurring in diabetics. In view of its potentially significant effect on blood sugar levels, the possible dangers posed by alcohol for the diabetic are obvious.

The liver also plays an important role in the metabolism of other drugs. The presence of alcohol can interfere with this role and be responsible for some alcohol-drug interactions. The liver enzyme ADH is essential to the metabolism of alcohol. Quantitatively, it is the liver's major means of metabolizing alcohol. The liver does have a "backup" system, however. This secondary system is called the cytochrome P450, or MEOS (microsomal ethanol oxidization system). It is located in intracellular structures called microsomes. While termed a backup system for metabolizing alcohol, it is believed that this secondary system begins to help out significantly in removing alcohol only after long-term heavy drinking. It is mentioned here because it is a major system in metabolizing other drugs, including many prescription drugs. Thus alcohol's effects on this system may affect the ways in which many drugs are metabolized by the liver, which can have clinical importance.

Acutely, the MEOS activity is inhibited dramatically by the presence of alcohol. Therefore, other drugs may not be broken down at their usual rates. If other drugs in the system have depressant effects similar to that of alcohol, the central nervous system will be subjected to both simultaneously. However, with some drugs there are additional potential problems. Suppose someone is taking a prescription drug, such as phenytoin (Dilantin) or warfarin sodium (Coumadin), at set intervals. The presence of alcohol may acutely interfere with the metabolism of such medications; thus, when the next scheduled dose is taken, substantial amounts of the earlier dose may remain and cumulative toxic effects may occur.[3]

Central Nervous System

The major acute effect of alcohol on the central nervous system (CNS) is that of a depressant. The common misconception that alcohol is a stimulant comes from the fact that its depressant action disinhibits many higher cortical functions which are what place a brake on various actions. It does this in a somewhat paradoxical fashion. Through the depressant effects of alcohol, parts of the brain are released from their normal inhibitory restraints. Thus, behavior that would ordinarily be censured and inhibited can occur. Acute alcohol intoxication, in fact, induces a mild delirium which is a fully reversible acute brain dysfuntion. Thinking becomes fuzzy; orientation, recent memory, and other higher mental functions, notably impulse control, are altered. An electroencephalogram (EEG) taken when someone is high typically shows a diffuse slowing of normal brain waves associated with this mild state of delirium. For the light and even relatively heavy occasional drinker these acute effects are, of course, completely reversible. Regular heavy use over time presents a substantially different story.

Precisely how alcohol affects the brain and thereby influences behavior is not fully understood. Research indicates that alcohol exerts a major effect on the physical structure of nerve cell membranes, an effect that alters their functioning. These changes may be transient with acute alcohol intake, may persist with chronic use, or may lead to other changes in the structure and function of nerve cells as they compensate and adapt to the continued presence of high levels of alcohol. These effects on nerve cells, directly caused by the presence of alcohol, are

[3]With chronic alcohol use, the activity of the MEOS is speeded up. In this instance various drugs are broken down faster, so higher doses must be administered to achieve a given therapeutic effect. (See Chapter 6 for more about alcohol-drug interactions.)

presumed to play a major role in causing the behaviors seen with acute intoxication. They are also believed to be the basis for the phenomena of craving, tolerance, withdrawal, and loss of control that are the key features defining alcohol dependence.

Alcohol significantly affects the production and activity of many different neurotransmitters, which act as chemical messengers in the brain. Neurotransmitters allow the cells in the brain to send messages from one cell to another. Thus they are the basis of the brain's communication system. Each cell has a "message sending" end and also a "message receiving" end. Neurotransmitters are what allow messages to cross the spaces between cells, called synapses, and activate the receptors on the "receiving" nerve cells.

Several neurotransmitter systems are believed to be particularly important in mediating the effects of alcohol. Alcohol decreases the levels of one of the brain's major inhibitory transmitters, *GABA*. This causes a slowing of the communication across the synapse. The effects of alcohol on GABA may contribute to the disinhibition of behavior. Alcohol also hastens the breakdown and removal of the noradrenergic neurotransmitter, *norepinephrine*. This chemical is known to be involved with activation and stimulation of the nervous system, and the fight-or-flight response to threats. The removal of this stimulating neurotransmitter may help explain the calming or relaxing effects of alcohol.

In addition, alcohol depresses the activity of *serotonin* in some regions of the brain. Decreased levels of serotonin have been linked to behaviors associated with intoxicated states, depression, anxiety, poor impulse control, aggressiveness, and occasionally suicidal behavior. Finally, the presence of alcohol increases the level of endogenous (meaning naturally and normally occurring) opiate-like substances, known as endorphins. This in turn may lead to increased dopamine activity, especially in the parts of the brain known to be involved in generating feelings of pleasure and well-being. Recent research indicates that other brain receptors—particularly the nicotinic and cholinergic receptors—may contribute to alcohol's reinforcing properties. To further complicate this, alcohol appears to affect neurotransmitters in some sections of the brain more than those in other sections.

Without question, the brain is the organ that is most sensitive to the acute effects of alcohol. This sensitivity is what being "high," drunk, intoxicated, or impaired is all about. The neurophysiological basis of intoxication is not yet fully understood. Without a doubt the intensity of the effect is directly related to the concentration of alcohol in the blood and hence the brain, but even here there are several other factors to be considered.

The degree of intoxication is dependent on whether the blood alcohol level is rising, falling, or constant. It is known that the CNS and behavioral effects of a given blood alcohol concentration (BAC) are greater when the blood alcohol level is rising. This is called the Mellanby effect. It is almost as if there were a small "practice effect," the development of a short-term adaptation or tolerance, by the nervous system to alcohol's presence acutely. Thus, for a given BAC, there is more impairment if the blood level is rising than with the same BAC if the level of alcohol in the blood is falling. Another possible effect of ingesting a large amount of alcohol is disturbances in memory. With BACS in the range of 0.20 or above, the ability to form memories of events is impaired. The person may have absolutely no memory of events, or memories may be partial and spotty. Although commonly referred to as alcohol blackouts, the medical term is anterograde amnesia involving short-term memory. Women are more likely than men to experience these disturbances in memory. (See Chapter 6 for further discussion of blackouts.)

The drug alcohol is a CNS depressant. It interferes with the activity of various brain centers and neurochemical systems—sometimes with seemingly paradoxical results. A high BAC can suppress CNS function across the board, even to the point of causing respiratory arrest and death. At lower doses it may lead to the activated, giddy, poorly controlled, and disinhibited behaviors that are typical of intoxication. This is not due to stimulation of CNS centers that mediate such behavior. Rather, it is attributable to the indirect effect of the selective suppression of inhibitory systems that normally keep such impulsive behaviors in check.

Watch or recall someone becoming intoxicated and see the progression of effects. The following examples refer to the CNS effects in a hypothetical "average" male. Of course, the observed effects of differing numbers of drinks over an hour in any given person may vary considerably. However, the type and severity of behavioral effects that do occur are a direct function of the amount of alcohol consumed; they progress in a fairly predictable fashion.

The drinks used in the following examples are a little under one-half ounce of pure alcohol, the equivalent of a 12-ounce beer, a 4-ounce glass of wine, or an ounce of 86-proof whiskey. Many generous hosts and hostesses mix drinks with more than 1 ounce of alcohol, even in the context of a quite proper cocktail party. Then there are college fraternity parties. They often ladle out large quantities of spiked punch of unknown—but usually high—alcohol content. Or there are the adolescents living in rural New England who, at an impromptu party out in the woods, simply pass the bottle around. So, as you read on, don't shrug off the "10-drink" section as an impossibility.

One Drink

With 1 drink, the drinker will be a bit more relaxed, possibly loosened up a little. Unless he chugged it rapidly, thus getting a rapid rise in blood alcohol, his behavior will be little changed. If he is of average height and weighs 160 pounds, by the end of an hour his blood alcohol level will be 0.02. (The actual measurement is grams %, or grams/100 milliliters. For example, 0.02 g% = 200 mg%.) An hour later all traces of alcohol will be gone.

Two and One-Half Drinks

With 2½ drinks in an hour's time, the party-goer will have a 0.05 blood alcohol level. He's high. The "newer" parts of the brain, those controlling judgment, will have been affected. That our friend has been drinking is apparent. He may be loud, boisterous, and making passes. Disinhibited, he is saying and doing things he might usually censor. These are the effects that mistakenly cause people to think of alcohol as a stimulant. The system isn't really hyped up. Rather, the inhibitions have been suspended, due to the alcohol's depression of the parts of the brain that normally put the brakes on. At this time our friend is entering the danger zone for driving. With 2½ drinks in an hour, 2.5 hours will be required to completely metabolize the alcohol.

Five Drinks

With 5 drinks in an hour, there is no question you have a drunk on your hands, and the law would agree. A blood alcohol level of 0.10 is now more than sufficient to issue a DWI in any state. By this time the drinker's judgment is nil ("Off coursh I can drive!"). In addition to the frontal regions of the brain controlling judgment, the cerebellar centers controlling muscle coordination are also impaired. There's a stagger to the walk and a slur to the speech. Even though the loss of dexterity and reaction time can be measured, the drinker, now with altered perception and judgment, may claim he has never functioned better. For all traces of alcohol to disappear from the system, 5 hours will be required.

Ten Drinks

A drunken night makes a cloudy morning.
SIR WILLIAM CORNWALLIS

This quantity of alcohol in the system yields a blood alcohol content of 0.20. More areas of the brain than just the judgment, perceptual, and motor centers are affected. Emotions are probably very erratic—rapidly ranging from laughter to tears to rage. Even if your guest could remember he had a coat—which he may not because of memory impairment—he'd never be able to put it on. For all the alcohol to be metabolized, 10 hours will be required. He'll still be legally drunk after 6 hours.

Sixteen Drinks—2 Six-Packs and 4 Beers

With this amount of alcohol the drinker is stuporous. Though not passed out, nothing the senses take in actually registers. Judgment is gone, coordination wiped out, and sensory perception almost nil. With the liver handling roughly 1 ounce of alcohol per hour, it will be 16 hours, well into tomorrow, before all the alcohol is gone.

Twenty Drinks—Not Quite a Fifth of Whiskey

At this point the person is in a coma and dangerously close to death. The vital brain centers that send out instructions to the heart and breathing apparatus are partially anesthetized. At a blood alcohol level of 0.40 to

0.50, a person is in a deep coma and entirely unresponsive. At a BAC of 0.60 to 0.70, breathing ceases and death occurs.

ACUTE OVERDOSE AND TOXICITY

With alcohol, as with many other drugs, an acute overdose may be fatal. Usually this occurs when very large doses of alcohol are consumed within a very short period of time. Rapid absorption of the ingested alcohol leads to a rapid and steep rise in BAC. In a relatively brief period, this may lead to loss of consciousness, coma, progressive respiratory depression, and death. Thus, a "chug-a-lug" contest can be a fatal game.

In general, the acute lethal dose of alcohol is considered to be from 5 to 8 mg/kg of body weight—the equivalent of about a fifth to a fifth and a half of 86-proof liquor for the typical 160-pound male. Acute doses of this amount of alcohol can be expected to result in BACs in the range of 0.35 to 0.70. Alcohol overdoses with fatal outcomes are consistently associated with BACs in this range, which is not at all surprising. It is known that a BAC above 0.40 often severely, and all too commonly, lethally depresses respiratory function.

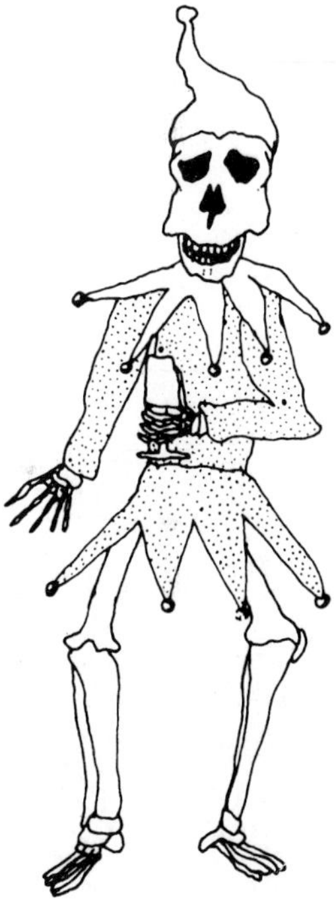

Of course, the exact lethal dose and BAC in any individual will vary with age, sex, general physical health, and degree of tolerance to alcohol. All things being equal, a very large, healthy, young adult male will tolerate a dose of alcohol that might be fatal for a small, medically ill, elderly female. This is true, only more so, for an alcohol-dependent person who has established a high level of tolerance, compared to the alcohol-naive novice drinker.

The alcoholic person may tolerate an acute dose of alcohol that would kill an otherwise comparable nonalcoholic individual. Although chronic heavy drinking and a high tolerance to alcohol may provide the alcoholic individual with some margin of safety, this protection has limits. Even the most severely dependent person may do him- or herself in by consuming enough alcohol in one drinking bout to raise the BAC to the upper end of the lethal range. Therefore, it is probably fair to say that a BAC of 0.70 or higher is virtually certain to be lethal to anyone. The higher the level within the 0.35 to 0.70 range, the greater the risk of death.

DIFFERENCES IN WOMEN

Substitute a 120-pound woman in the previous scenarios, and the weight differential would dramatically speed up the process. A woman and a man who have identical body weights and who both drink the same amount of alcohol will have different blood alcohol levels. Hers will be higher. Women and men differ in their relative amounts of body fat and water. Women have a higher proportion of fat and correspondingly lower amounts of water. This difference is highly relevant, since alcohol is not very fat soluble. Her body contains less water than his within which to dilute the ingested alcohol, which results in her having a higher concentration of alcohol in her blood.

Simply on that basis, let's contrast a 120-pound woman to our hypothetical 160-pound male drinker. With 1 drink in 1 hour, she would have a BAC of 0.04; 2½ drinks, and her BAC would be to slightly over 0.10. By 5 drinks, she'd have a 0.21 reading. Should she make it through 11 drinks, she'd be in a coma with a blood alcohol level of 0.45, and potentially at risk of dying.

Beyond body weight and differences in the proportions of fat and water, there are other important differences between men and women with respect to how they handle alcohol. A body of research that is now somewhat controversial suggested that a woman's menstrual cycle may significantly influence her rate of absorption and/or metabolism of alcohol. This difference is presumed to relate to changes in the balance of sex hormones and appears to be the result of several interacting factors. During the premenstrual phase of her cycle, a woman absorbs alcohol significantly faster than in other phases of the menstrual cycle. So, premenstrually, a woman would get a higher blood alcohol level than she would from drinking an equivalent amount at other times. In practical terms, a woman may find herself getting high or becoming drunk faster right before her menstrual period. Also, evidence exists that women taking birth control pills absorb alcohol faster and consequently may have higher blood alcohol levels. More recent studies have failed to confirm these earlier findings

The differences between men and women in the levels of gastric alcohol dehydrogenase also are significant. Gastric ADH may account for the metabolism of up to 30% of alcohol in males. This means that, for men, nearly one-third of the alcohol consumed will be metabolized in the stomach and never pass into the small intestine to be absorbed into the bloodstream. This is not true for women, who have lower levels of gastric ADH. Because of this, significantly less alcohol is metabolized in the stomach and, consequently, more alcohol is available to enter their circulation when the alcohol passes from the stomach to the small intestine. Therefore, when consuming identical amounts of alcohol, women will have higher blood alcohol concentrations than men, even if one takes into account the differences in weight and relative proportions of body fat and water.

There are also apparent differences in the metabolism of alcohol in both male and female heavy drinkers. In both men and women with a history of heavy drinking, there is less gastric ADH. Since women have less gastric ADH to start with, and because it declines with heavy alcohol use, there is a virtual absence of gastric ADH among women who drink heavily. Thus, for women who have a history of heavy drinking, the amount of alcohol that reaches the bloodstream will be virtually identical to that resulting from a dose of alcohol administered intravenously.

These differences in metabolism and the resulting demands upon the liver to metabolize larger amounts of alcohol may be one of the mechanisms accounting for women's recognized greater vulnerability to liver disease.

Quite possibly, other important biological differences in alcohol's effects may exist between men and women. Most of the older research on the physiological effects of alcohol has been conducted on men, and researchers had assumed that their findings are equally true for women. Though the basic differences between the absorption rates of men and women were reported as early as 1932, they were largely forgotten or ignored until the mid-1970s. The impact of the menstrual cycle was not recognized or reported until 1976! Given these failures to examine the effects of the primary and obvious difference between men and women, who knows what more subtle areas have not yet been considered. Women have gotten short shrift not only in terms of alcohol research, but in all areas of medical investigation. In light of this, the National Institutes of Health is making efforts to promote equal inclusion of women as subjects in biomedical research studies and in clinical trials of new drugs.

Despite individual biological differences, virtually all people react to alcohol in basically the same way. This is true despite the fact that, for a given blood alcohol level, a very heavy drinker who has developed tolerance to alcohol may show somewhat less impairment in function than an inexperienced drinker would. This uniform, well-documented response enables the law to set a specific and standard blood alcohol level for defining intoxication in both for men and women and across all age groups. The blood alcohol level can be easily measured by taking blood samples or a breathalyzer test. The breathalyzer is able to measure blood alcohol levels because, just as carbon dioxide in the blood diffuses across small capillaries in the lungs to be eliminated in exhaled air, so does alcohol. The amount of carbon dioxide in exhaled air is directly proportionate to that circulating in the bloodstream. The same is true for alcohol. The breathalyzer measures the concentration of alcohol in the exhaled air. From that measurement, the exact concentration of alcohol in the blood can be determined.

TOLERANCE

The immediate effects of consumption of alcohol have been described. With continued regular alcohol use over an extended period, predictable changes take place in the body. Tolerance develops, and any drinker, not only the alcohol-dependent individual, can testify to this. The first few times someone tries alcohol, one drink is enough to make someone feel tipsy. With some drinking experience, one drink no longer has that effect. In part this may reflect greater wisdom. The veteran drinker has learned "how to drink" to avoid feeling intoxicated. The experienced drinker has learned to sip, not gulp, a drink and avoids drinking on an empty

"Medical Declarations" on the alcohol question. The third and final English medical declaration written in 1871. "As it is believed that the inconsiderate prescription of large quantities of alcoholic liquids by medical men for their patients has given rise in many instances to the formation of intemperate habits, the undersigned are of the opinion that no medical practitioner should prescribe it without a sense of grave responsibility. They believe that alcohol, in whatever form, should be prescribed with as much care as any powerful drug. The directions for its use should be so framed as not to be interpreted as a sanction for use to excess, or necessarily for the continuance of its use when the occasion is past."

WALTER W. SPOONER

The Cyclopaedia of Temperance and Prohibition, 1891

stomach. The other reason is that, with repeated exposures to alcohol, the central nervous system (CNS) adapts to its presence in increasing amounts. It can tolerate more alcohol and still maintain normal functioning. This is one of the properties that defines alcohol as an addictive drug. Over the long haul the body requires a larger dose to induce the effects previously produced by smaller doses.

Not only does tolerance develop over relatively long spans of time, but there are also rapid adaptive changes in the CNS on each drinking occasion. A drinker is more out of commission when the blood alcohol level is climbing than when it is falling. In a testing situation, if someone is given alcohol to drink and then asked to perform certain tasks, the results are predictable. Impairment is greater on the ascending limb—the rising side of blood alcohol concentration curve, the absorption phase. As the blood alcohol level drops during the elimination phase, the individual, when similarly tested, will be able to function better with the same blood alcohol content. It is as if one learns to function better in the presence of alcohol after "practice." In fact, what probably has happened is that the brain has made some subtle adjustments in the way it functions in the presence of alcohol. Here, too, there are differences between men and women. Both show greater impairment as alcohol levels rise, but there are differences in the kinds of impairment. When intoxicated, women appear to have greater impairment than men for tasks that require motor coordination. Yet, they are superior to men in tasks that require attention. Since driving requires both skills, neither appears the better bet on the highway.

On Tobacco

I do not think that all are equally susceptible of narcotic influence. Novices trying their first cigar, are not all affected in the same degree, nor in the same way. In some, nausea will be the strongest symptoms; in others, intoxication. Some will make successive trials with little diminution of the woes that attend beginners; others seem to be fascinated almost at once. Before one has learned to tolerate use, another is already joined to his idol. I have a suspicion too that to live among smokers, to inhale constantly the strong fumes of tobacco, produces in some cases not only a degree of physical preparation for the use of it, but tends to implant the appetite, and urge with more or less force in the direction of indulgence. The one whose nervous system responds most promptly and fully to the intoxication will soonest be entangled in the meshes of the habit.

J.T. CRANE

Arts of Intoxication, 1870

ALCOHOL AS AN ANESTHETIC

Alcohol is an anesthetic, just as depicted in all the old Western movies. But by modern standards, it is not a very good one. The dose of alcohol required to produce anesthesia is very close to the lethal amount. When the vital centers have been depressed enough by alcohol to produce unconsciousness, it takes only a wee bit more to cause respiratory cessation and put someone permanently to sleep. Sadly, several times a year almost every newspaper obituary column documents a death from alcohol. Usually the tragedy involves young people. It may be chugging a fifth of liquor on a dare or as a prank, or coerced drinking as part of a college fraternity initiation, following which the person passes out and if left alone and unattended, dies in his sleep.

OTHER TYPES OF ALCOHOL

In this discussion of alcohol, it is clear that we have been referring to "booze," "suds," "the sauce," "brew," or any of the other colloquial terms for beverage alcohol. To be scientifically accurate, this kind of alcohol is called ethanol, ethyl alcohol, or grain alcohol. "Alcohol," if one is precise, is a term used to refer to a family of substances. What all alcohols have in common is a particular grouping of carbon, hydrogen, and oxygen atoms arranged in a similar fashion to form the alcohol molecule. They differ only in the number of carbon atoms and associated hydrogen atoms. Each alcohol is named according to the number of carbons it has. Ethanol has 2 carbon atoms.

- *"ol" refers to an alcohol*
- *Methanol is synonymous with methyl alcohol*
- *Ethanol is synonymous with ethyl alcohol*

One other kind of alcohol with which everyone is familiar is methanol, also known as wood alcohol, or methyl alcohol. It has one carbon atom, and is an ingredient of antifreeze, paint thinners, and sterno. Another is rubbing, or isopropyl, alcohol, comprised of 3 carbons. It is a common ingredient in perfumes and after-shave, for example.

Most commonly these types of alcohols are consumed if ethanol is unavailable, often with severe consequences. Due to their different chemical makeup, these other alcohols cause big problems if taken into the body. The difficulty lies in the differences in rates of metabolism and the kinds of by-products formed. For example, it takes 9 times longer for methanol to be eliminated than it does ethanol. Although methanol itself is not especially toxic, when the liver enzyme ADH acts on it, formaldehyde instead of acetaldehyde is formed. Formaldehyde causes tissue damage, especially in the eyes. The formaldehyde is then broken down into formic acid, which is also not as innocent as the acetic acid produced by ethanol metabolism and can cause severe states of acidosis. Ingestion of methyl alcohol can lead to blindness and can be fatal; it requires prompt and vigorous medical attention. In addition to administration of ethanol, treatment may include renal dialysis.

The treatment of acute methanol poisoning is one of a handful of situations in clinical medicine where ethanol has a legitimate and important therapeutic role. Administering ethanol to a methanol-poisoned patient slows the rate of methanol metabolism, which results in a reduction of the levels of toxic by-products formed. Why? Because ethanol successfully competes with methanol for the limited amount of the liver enzyme ADH, which is required for the metabolism of either variety of alcohol. Rapidly administering ethyl alcohol, while at the same time treating acidosis and correcting the body's acid-base imbalance, may ameliorate or even entirely eliminate serious complications. The U.S. Food and Drug Administration has approved a new drug to treat poisoning from ethylene glycol, also known as glycol alcohol, a major constuent of antifreeze. This drug, called Fomepizole, inhibits alcohol dehydrogenase, thereby slowing the ethylene glycol's metabolism.

Poisonings from nonbeverage alcohols don't happen only to those alcohol-dependent persons who in desperation will drink anything. Several years ago there was an Italian wine scandal in which table wines were laced with methanol, resulting in more than 100 deaths. A far more common accident involves the toddler who gets into the medicine cabinet or the teenager or adult who doesn't know that all alcohols are not the same chemically and that some may have very dangerous effects.

THE INFLUENCE OF EXPECTATIONS

The focus in this chapter has been on the pharmacological properties of alcohol. The physical changes described, especially alcohol's effects on the CNS, are directly tied to the amount of alcohol consumed and the rapidity with which it is ingested. Pharmacologists refer to these phenomena as dose- and rate-related effects. However, the human psyche also enters into the equation. Although one's beliefs, wishes, or attitudes cannot negate alcohol's actions, they can have an impact. A person's expectations influence the experience of drinking and how a drinking episode is interpreted. There is increasing literature on this alcohol "expectancy" effect, which examines how beliefs about alcohol's effects influence drinking behavior. Some of these studies involve research situations in which people think they are getting alcohol when, in fact, the drink they consume has none. The explanation for this interaction between pharmacological effects and beliefs is that beliefs are likely to influence what in your surroundings you notice and tune in to when drinking. Thus, the person who expects that drinking makes people more aggressive is likely to see others as "asking" for a fight, whereas the person who thinks that drinking enhances sexuality will be attuned to "invitations" for intimacy.

IN CONCLUSION

Any substance taken into the body may have significant effects, and alcohol is no exception. All too often we have discovered these effects to be more harmful than we had previously thought. Chemical additives, fertilizers, pesticides, antibiotics given to livestock destined for the table, and even coloring agents have been questioned. As more information emerges, many substances are being recognized as less benign than was previously supposed. In some instances the federal Food and Drug Administration (FDA) has outlawed or severely restricted use. Let us hope that caution born of enhanced knowledge with respect to the use of alcohol and other drugs and their potential consequences will become as widespread. Many of the devastating yet largely avoidable problems our society encounters as a result of alcohol use—including accidents, traffic fatalities, domestic violence, suicide, and homicides—may be lessened as uninformed and ill-considered use is replaced by greater knowledge about the effects of the legal drug we drink.

REFERENCES AND FURTHER READING

Abramson S, Singh AK. Treatment of the alcohol intoxications: Ethylene glycol, methanol and isopropanol (review). *Current Opinion in Nephrology and Hypertension* 9(6):695–701, 2000. (32 refs.)

Chamberlain E, Solomon R. The case for a 0.05% criminal law blood alcohol concentration limit for driving (review). *Injury Prevention* 8(Supplement 3):1–17, 2003. (109 refs.)

Eaton DL. Scientific judgment and toxic torts: A primer in toxicology for judges and lawyers. *Journal of Law and Policy* 12:5–42, 2003. (50 refs.)

Editor. Health risks and benefits of alcohol consumption. *Alcohol Research & Health* 24(1):5–11, 2000. (93 refs.)

Editor. Papers on absorption, distribution, and elimination of alcohol in non-alcoholics. *Alcoholism: Clinical and Experimental Research* 24(4):244–257, 2000.

Filmore MT, Blackburn J. Compensating for alcohol-induced impairment: Alcohol expectancies and behavioral disinhibition. *Journal of Studies on Alcohol* 63(2): 237–246, 2002. (31 refs.)

Gibbons B. Alcohol: The legal drug. *National Geographic* 181(Feb):2–35, 1992.

Graham AW, Schultz TK. *Principles of Addiction Medicine,* 3rd ed. Chevy Chase, MD: American Society of Addiction Medicine, 2003.

Lowinson JH, Ruiz P, Millman RB, Langred JG. *Substance Abuse: A Comprehensive Textbook,* 4th ed. Baltimore, MD: Williams and Wilkins, 2005.

Moskowitz H, Burns M. Effects of alcohol on driving performance. *Alcohol Health and Research World* 14(1):12–14, 1990. (24 refs.)

Parlesak A, Billinger MHU, Bode C, Bode C. Gastric alcohol dehydrogenase activity in man: Influence of gender, age, alcohol consumption and smoking in a Caucasian population. *Alcohol and Alcoholism* 37(4):388–393, 2002. (32 refs.)

White AM. What Happened? Alcohol, memory blackouts, and the brain *Alcohol Research & Health* 27(2): 186–196, 2003. (80 refs)

Whitfield JB. Acute reactions to alcohol (review). *Addiction Biology* 2(4):377–386, 1997. (70 refs.)

CHAPTER 4

Alcohol Dependence

Thanks be to God, since my leaving drinking of wine, I do find myself much better, and do my business better, and do spend less money, and less time in idle company.
SAMUEL PEPYS
Diary, January 2, 1662

AND WHAT GIVES YOU THE RIGHT TO CALL ME AN ALCOHOLIC?

DEFINITIONS

The social problems associated with alcohol use were described in Chapter 2. Even if there were not such a phenomenon as alcohol dependence, the mere presence of the beverage alcohol would lead to social disruption and considerable social costs. This is now recognized. For too long the statistics on dented fenders caused by impaired drivers, the dollars lost by industry, or even the percentage of alcohol-related hospital admissions were ignored. Seen merely as the product of many people's single, uninformed encounters with alcohol, they were dismissed as the cost a drinking culture has to pay.

Attitudes, however, have changed dramatically. Those who choose to drink are no longer seen as potentially endangering only themselves. Drinkers no longer are accepted as having a right to get drunk, to unwind, or, from time to time, to indiscriminately "tie one on." Drinkers no longer are viewed as not accountable for things that occur while they are under the influence. Having come to recognize the impact of these individual decisions on the public safety, society has significantly changed its attitudes as to what constitutes acceptable and unacceptable drinking. Though still not universally true, in more and more quarters individuals are *not* considered free to drink in a manner that endangers others. Increasingly, intoxicated behavior is not overlooked, is far less tolerated, and is likely to be met with direct expressions of disapproval.

There are, however, those whose drinking behavior will not be touched by admonitions to drink responsibly. There are those whose behavior will not be altered by TV commercials that urge friends to select a designated driver to see that all return home safely after an evening that includes drinking. There are those whose behavior will not respond to friends' suggestions to "take it easy" or friends' expressions of disapproval. The special problem that besets these 17 million individuals is that, for them, alcohol is no longer the servant, but the master. The chances are quite good that this concern is individualized with the faces of people we know or have known. There are also the estimated 68.2 million family members who live directly in the shadow of someone's dependence on alcohol.

What is alcohol dependence? This question confronts substance abuse clinicians daily. A physician may request assistance in determining if an alcohol problem exists. A client or a spouse may challenge, "Why, she can't be an alcoholic because. . . ." Even in nonworking hours the question crops up during conversation with good friends or casual acquaintances. A number of definitions are available. As a starting point, consider the word "alcoholic." This continues to be the term most commonly used for those with alcohol dependence. The word itself provides some clues. The suffix *-ic* has a special meaning, according to *Webster's New Collegiate Dictionary:*

> ic n suffix: One having the character or nature of; one belonging to or associated with; one exhibiting or affected by.

Attaching *-ic* to alcohol forms a word to denote the person linked with alcohol. That's a start. Clearly, not all drinkers are linked with alcohol, just as all baseball players are not linked with the Boston Red Sox. Why the link, or association? The basis is probably frequency of alcohol use, pattern of use, quantity used, or frequency of indications that the person has been drinking. "Belonging to" has several connotations, including "an individual being possessed by or under the control of." The Chinese have a saying: "The man takes a drink, the drink takes a drink, and then the drink takes the man." This final step closely approximates what the word "alcoholic" means. It offers a good picture of the progression of alcoholism—that is, alcohol dependence.

It is worth noting that the discussion or debate on who is alcohol dependent and what constitutes alcohol dependence is relatively recent. This doesn't mean that society before had not noticed those we now think of as suffering from this. Certainly, those deeply in trouble with alcohol have been recognized for centuries. But their existence was accepted as a fact, without question or any particular thought about the matter. To the extent that there was debate, it centered on the purported cause, as well as how the person should be handled. Essentially two basic approaches prevailed. One was that "obviously" these individuals were morally inferior. The evidence cited was that the vast majority of people who drank did so moderately without presenting problems for themselves or their communities. The other view was that "obviously" such individuals were possessed: would any in their right minds drink like that of their own volition?

With increasing scientific study and understanding of the "drink taking the man" phenomenon, the more complicated the task of definition

Drunkenness is nothing but voluntary madness.
SENECA

became. In addition to the awareness that some people are distinctly different from many who drink moderately, the other clear discovery was that not all those with alcohol dependence are alike. Not all develop DTs (delirium tremens) when they stop drinking. There are big differences in the quantity of alcohol consumed and the number of years of drinking before family problems arise. Many chronic, heavy drinkers develop cirrhosis, but more do not. Given the range of differences among those with alcohol dependence, what is the basic core, the essential features that are common to all? An answer to this question is fundamental to any attempt to define the condition.

Early Definitions

During the latter half of the twentieth century, the view of alcoholism as a disease gradually took hold. This entailed attempts to define the condition. What follows is a cross section of the early definitions that were put forth.

- *1940s, Alcoholics Anonymous.* AA has never had an official definition. The concept of Dr. William Silkworth, one of AA's early friends, is sometimes cited by AA members: ". . . an obsession of the mind and an allergy of the body. The obsession or compulsion guarantees that the sufferer will drink against his own will and interest. The allergy guarantees that the sufferer will either die or go insane." Another operative definition frequently heard among AA members is "an alcoholic is a person who cannot predict with accuracy what will happen when he takes a drink."
- *1946, E.M. Jellinek, a pioneer in modern alcohol studies.* "Alcoholism is any use of alcoholic beverages that causes any damage to the individual or to society or both."
- *1950, World Health Organization (WHO).* The WHO's Alcoholism Subcommittee defined "alcoholism" as "any form of drinking which in extent goes beyond the tradition and customary 'dietary' use, or the ordinary compliance with the social drinking customs of the community concerned, irrespective of etiological factors leading to such behavior, and irrespective also of the extent to which such etiological factors are dependent upon heredity, constitution, or acquired physiopathological and metabolic influences." A first attempt, this initial formulation has since been substantially revised.
- *1960, Mark Keller, former editor of the Journal of Studies on Alcohol.* "Alcoholism is a chronic disease manifested by repeated implicative drinking so as to cause injury to the drinker's health or to his social or economic functioning."
- *1968, American Psychiatric Association, Committee on Nomenclature and Statistics.* "Alcoholism: this category is for patients whose alcohol intake is great enough to damage their physical health, or

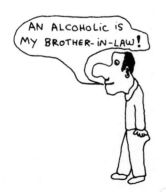

their personal or social functioning, or when it has become a prerequisite to normal functioning." Three types of alcoholism were further identified: episodic excessive drinking, habitual excessive drinking, and alcohol addiction. With the third edition of the association's *Diagnostic and Statistical Manual* (1980) this was significantly expanded.

- *1977, American Medical Association (AMA).* From the *Manual on Alcoholism,* edited by the AMA Panel on Alcoholism: "Alcoholism is an illness characterized by significant impairment that is directly associated with persistent and excessive use of alcohol. Impairment may involve physiological, psychological, or social dysfunction."

One swallow doesn't make a summer but too many swallows make a fall.
G. D. PRENTICE

In examining the early definitions, we find that each, although not necessarily conflicting with the others, tends to have a particular focus. Some are purely descriptive. Others attempt to speak to the origins of the condition. Several concentrate on the unfortunate consequences associated with alcohol use. Others zero in on hallmark signs or symptoms, especially loss of control or frequency of intoxication.

Add to these expert definitions all of the definitions that have been used casually by each of us and our neighbors. These have varied from "alcoholism is an illness," to "it's the number one drug problem," to "when someone's hammered all the time," to "when someone drinks in the morning." Note that, generally, laypeople have had far more permissive criteria and have adopted definitions that would exclude themselves and most they know as candidates for the condition.

one drink is plenty
Two drinks too many
And three not half enough.
W. KNOX HAYNES

Toward Uniformity in Terminology

Actions taken by the World Health Organization in 1977 and the American Psychiatric Association (APA) 3 years later were important in clarifying and promoting greater consensus as to the definition of "alcoholism." The WHO prepares and publishes the *International Classification of Diseases,* known as the *ICD.* It provides a comprehensive list of all injuries, diseases, and disorders and is used worldwide. The APA publishes a manual restricted to mental disorders, known as the *Diagnostic and Statistical Manual.* The changes by the WHO and the APA also increased the consistency across the various drug classes. Ironically, for the sake of clarification, both groups abandoned use of the term "alcoholism." Neither group disputed the existence of the phenomenon of alcoholism; however, for medical and scientific purposes, both the WHO and the APA substituted "alcohol dependence syndrome" for what had been discussed as alcoholism. This was done because of the multiple definitions abounding in the professional community. This change also was necessitated by the general public's widespread, everyday use of "alcoholic" and the variants that were being coined, such as "work-aholic." When the same term is shared, but used differently, by laypeople and medical scientists, confusion is likely. So, paradoxically, it was in part the very success in educating the public about alcoholism as a disease that necessitated the change in terminology.

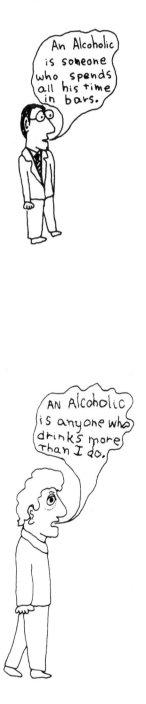

Uniform terminology is essential. When it comes to clinical interactions with colleagues and other professionals, the day is past when each clinician has the luxury of defining the disease according to individual biases and preferences. In the United States, the APA's *Diagnostic and Statistical Manual* provides the approved terminology. The 1980 version of the *Diagnostic and Statistical Manual,* the third edition (*DSM-III*), was noteworthy in several respects. It was the first to distinguish between two separate alcohol-related syndromes: alcohol abuse and alcohol dependence. Both conditions entail impairment in social and occupational functioning. The essential distinguishing feature of dependence was the presence of tolerance and withdrawal. There is always room to quibble with definitions, and that operational definition did have its critics. The major criticism of the definition was that physical dependence is required to make the diagnosis of dependence. This is never a black-and-white situation. There are those who may not show marked physical dependence but whose lives are in utter chaos because of alcohol use. However, this was an instance when living with imperfections was preferable to the alternative, which would have been everyone's continuing to feel free to define the condition for themselves. In subsequent revisions of the manual, the *DSM-III-R* in 1987 and the *DSM-IV* in 1994, changes were made in response to these concerns.

With the growing acceptance of alcoholism as a medical condition, there has been a corresponding drop-off in the number of formal definitions. Attention has turned instead to efforts to specify the conditions which need to be met to make the diagnosis. However, suddenly, what seemingly had been settled—that alcohol dependence is a disease and ought to be treated as such—was called into question. The prospect of health-care reform and the need to make decisions about what would and would not be covered by any mandated health insurance rekindled the debate. It was in this context that, in 1993, the American Society of Addiction Medicine (ASAM), a professional association of physician specialists in the alcohol and other drug field, issued a policy statement defining "alcoholism":

> Alcoholism is a *primary,* chronic *disease* with genetic, psychological and environmental factors influencing its development and manifestations. The disease is often *progressive* and *fatal.* It is characterized by continuous or periodic *impaired control* over drinking, preoccupation with the drug alcohol, use of alcohol despite adverse consequences, and distortions in thinking, most notably *denial* . . .

The statement then proceeds to elaborate on each of the words in italics. Interestingly, ASAM makes an explicit statement about the meaning of the word "disease." It emphasizes that a disease represents an "involuntary disability." However, despite how far we have come, the journey is not ended. There remain discrepancies in how insurance handles substance use and psychiatric illnesses, versus those seen as "physical" illnesses.

A DISEASE?

The remainder of this chapter will be devoted to the evolution of the understanding of alcoholism as a medical condition and the major pieces of work that have led to the present formulation of what alcohol dependence is, its complexity, and how to recognize it. First, we turn to the work of E. M. Jellinek, who has been called the father of alcohol studies, not only in the United States but also internationally. Next discussed are the guidelines established by the Committee of the National Council on Alcoholism and published in 1972. The guidelines represent the first effort to set forth explicit signs and symptoms to be used in diagnosing alcoholism. Following this, in 1980, there was the publication of the APA's first diagnostic criteria for alcohol dependence. Then, in 1983, a landmark study by George Vaillant was published, outlining the natural history of alcoholism and its recovery. Finally, this chapter discusses the most recent revisions to the APA's *Diagnostic and Statistical Manual of Mental Disorders,* with the research and thinking that shaped them.

Anyone who is sufficiently interested in alcohol problems to have read this far is probably accustomed to hearing alcoholism referred to as an illness, a disease, a sickness, or a medical condition. This has not always been the case. Alcoholism—alcohol dependence—has not always been distinguished from drunkenness. Alternatively, it has been categorized as a sin or character defect. The work of Jellinek was largely responsible for the shift from a defect to an illness model. Through his research and writings, in essence he said that, it was mislabeled.

disease *(dĭz-ez) [Eng. dis-priv. + ease]. 1. morbus, illness, sickness; an interruption; cessation; or disordering of body functions, systems, or organs. 2. A pathological entity characterized usually by at least two of these criteria: a recognized etiologic agent(s), an identifiable group of signs and symptoms, or consistent anatomical alterations. See also syndrome.*

syndrome *(sĭn'drom) [G. syn, together, + dromas, a running]. The aggregate of signs and symptoms associated with any morbid process and constituting together the picture of the disease.*

sign *(sin) [L. signum, mark]. 1. Any abnormality indicative of disease, discoverable by examination; an objective symptom of disease. 2. In psychology, any object or artifact that represents a specific thing or conveys a specific idea to the person who perceives it.*

symptom *(sĭmp'tom) [G. symptoma]. Any morbid phenomenon or departure from the normal in function, appearance, or sensation which is experienced by the patient and indicative of disease. See also, sign.*

Source: *Webster's New World/Stedman's Concise Medical Dictionary.* New York: Prentice Hall, 1997.

Implications of Disease Classification

Whether alcoholism is or is not a disease is, to use researchers' terminology, *not* an empirical question. No test or experiment can be conducted to prove or disprove that alcoholism is an illness. But clearly, how we label something is very important. It provides clues about how to feel and think, what to expect, and how to act. For instance, whether a particular bulb is tagged as a tulip or garlic will make a big difference. Depending on which you think it is, you'll either chop and sauté or plant and water. Very different behaviors are associated with each. An error may lead to strangely flavored spaghetti sauce and a less colorful flower bed next spring.

For both laypeople and professionals, the recognition that alcohol dependence belongs properly in the category of disease has had a dramatic impact. Sick people generally are awarded sympathy. The accepted notion is that sick people do not choose to be sick. Being sick is not

"AN Alcoholic" is what all the liberals and do-gooders call A drunkard.

pleasant. It is agreed that care should be provided to restore health. During the period of sickness, people are not expected to fill their usual roles or meet their responsibilities. A special designation is given to them—that of patient. Furthermore, sick people are not to be criticized for manifesting the symptoms of their illness. To demand that a person with the flu stop running a fever would be pointless, as well as unkind. Accompanying the perception of alcoholism as an illness, the individual with the disease—the alcoholic—has come to be viewed as a sufferer and victim. Much of the alcoholic's bizarre behavior has come to be recognized as unwillful and as symptomatic. No longer the object of scorn, the individual with alcoholism is seen as requiring care. The logical place to send the alcoholic is a hospital or rehabilitation facility, instead of jail. Since the 1940s, there has been a gradual shift in public perceptions. Nationwide polls now find that over 80% of the respondents say they believe alcoholism to be an illness.

Although Jellinek's efforts may have triggered this shift, a number of other events added impetus. The National Council on Alcoholism put its efforts into lobbying and public education. The American Medical Association and American Hospital Association published various committee reports. State agencies created treatment programs. Medical societies and other professional associations assumed responsibility for their members' education and addressed the ethical responsibility to treat alcohol problems. It is suspected that the single biggest push came from recovering alcoholics, especially through the work of AA. Virtually everyone today has personal knowledge of an apparently hopeless alcoholic who stopped drinking and now seems a new, different person.

The formulation of alcoholism as a disease opened up possibilities for treatment that were formerly nonexistent. It brought into the helping arena the resources of medicine, nursing, social work, psychology, and other professions that before had no mandate to be involved. The adoption of this viewpoint was also important in reducing the stigma associated with the condition of alcoholism. In turn, this improved the likelihood that individuals and families would seek help rather than be encumbered by shame or burdened by a sense of hopelessness, trying to keep the condition a family secret. Finally, the resources of the federal government were focused on alcohol problems as a major public health issue, and a host of treatment and educational programs were created.

An Alcoholic is someone who drinks in alleyways instead of in bars.

Criticisms of the Disease Concept

The disease concept of alcoholism has had its critics. One criticism arose in academic circles. Over 2 decades ago, a rash of articles were published, setting forth different models, or frameworks, for viewing alcoholism. The various models were described as the moral model, disease model, AA model, learning model, self-medication model, and social model. The writers described these models as if they were mutually exclusive and conflicting, as if an either/or choice were required. Such narrow thinking is now discredited. The current view is that models representing different approaches are not in opposition; they might be compared to the "blind men describing the elephant" phenomenon. They complement one another and merely highlight different aspects. To view alcoholism as a disease does not mean that one discounts the role of learning, disregards the influence of society, or fails to recognize that some drinking is self-medication. In fact, the medical field considers such elements as it explores a range of health concerns. This is described in more detail in Chapter 5. Similarly, the views of AA on alcoholism don't require that one discount alcoholism as a disease. Certainly its members don't.

Another objection to the disease concept arose from a concern that it places too much emphasis on the physician, nurse, and other health professionals. While health-care professionals certainly have a role to play in diagnosis and physical treatment, their training does not necessarily prepare them for the specialized counseling that is part of substance abuse treatment. Even if it does, a physician or nurse working independently does not have available all the time needed to offer counseling, support, and education to both patient and family, yet the disease concept may imply that only a physician or nurse is qualified to provide or direct treatment. Criticism frequently has been leveled at MDs and other health-care workers for being uninterested in or unconcerned with the problem of alcohol dependence. Possibly the misuse of the disease concept fosters unrealistic expectations of, and places undue burdens on, these professionals. It may also fail to recognize the interdisciplinary nature of many health-care teams.

Another criticism with some merit is that the disease label implies the possibility of a cure through the wonders of modern medicine worked on a passive patient. Emphasis on alcohol dependence as a *chronic* illness requiring the active participation of the patient in rehabilitation should remove this reservation. Characteristically, the management of chronic disease involves 5 elements. (1) There is treatment of acute flare-ups. (2) Emotional support is a necessity; after all, no one likes having a chronic illness. (3) Education is needed, so that the individual can be well informed about the illness and can assist in self-care. (4) Rehabilitative measures are initiated to prompt the life changes necessary to live with the limitations imposed by the illness. (5) Family involvement is critical, so that the family can be informed and can deal with the impact that the chronic illness has on their lives, which is a prerequisite for their being supportive. A noteworthy characteristic of a chronic illness is that it tends to develop slowly. Quite conceivably, with an acute illness (such as flu), one can go to bed feeling well and wake up sick the next morning. It literally happens overnight. However, one does not become diabetic, arthritic, or drug dependent overnight. The disease state develops slowly.

'Tis not the drinking that is to be blamed, but the excess.
JOHN SELDON, 1689

In a similar vein, some have expressed discomfort with the slogan adopted by the National Institute on Drug Abuse (NIDA): *Addiction is a brain disease.* Widely featured in the institute's media campaigns this slogan was launched after being approved by a conference of national experts convened in 1995 by NIDA. In large part, the goal was to reduce the stigma associated with addiction. While a noteworthy aim and certainly supported by recent research, nonetheless, some consider this a gross oversimplification, which may have some unintended consequences. For one, there is the possibility that this disproportionately turns attention to the role of drug therapies while ignoring newer behavioral therapies. Also, by locating the problem in diseased brains, it is possible that we can lose sight of the social conditions and environmental factors that foster the use of addicting substances.

Another concern voiced is that the disease concept might be used as an excuse: "Don't look at me; I'm not responsible. I'm sick. Poor me [sigh, sigh]." But this criticism overlooks a significant point: an alcoholic is to be expected to try shooting holes in any definition of "alcoholism." Some who criticize the disease concept on this basis are possibly those who have run headlong into the denial that characterizes alcohol dependence. If denial goes unrecognized as a symptom of the disease, it can only cause frustration. It is impossible to overestimate how sensitive alcohol-dependent individuals are to what will immobilize those around them, so that they can continue drinking undisturbed. As you acquire more information about alcohol dependence, you will begin to recognize these maneuvers—the first step in gaining skill to counter these tactics intended to disarm others.

Another recent variant of this criticism is less concerned with the particular individual who is alcohol dependent than with the larger social setting. People are questioning whether, as a society, we have become too accepting of the notion of disease or victim and too willing to excuse behaviors for which people need to be held accountable. Evidence cited is the proliferation of "recovery literature." In it, everyone is seemingly a victim of some sort, as witnessed by the burgeoning discussion of codependency, adult children of alcoholics, and dysfunctional families. Constructs and terms borrowed from the sphere of "traditional" addictions have been applied to other apparent compulsive or excessive behaviors. Thus, one hears of workaholics, shopping addicts, exercise addiction, sexual addiction, and most recently computer or Internet addiction.[1]

Upon first hearing of the notion of sexual addiction, someone commented, "Whatever happened to bad judgment, immorality, sin, and the

[1]While beyond this discussion, there is ongoing research into the possible biological basis of the newer "addictions," those that do not involve use of alcohol or other drugs. It is hypothesized that changes in the brain's neurochemistry associated with these behaviors are experienced as a high. This in turn invites these behaviors to be repeated.

notion of personal responsibility for choices?" Indeed, such questions do need to be asked. In overextending concepts such as the disease model to areas further afield, there is the danger of trivializing and diminshing the usefulness of the model when it is very much needed.

NATURAL HISTORY

The "natural history" of an illness refers to the typical progression of signs and symptoms as the disease unfolds untreated. Jellinek was one of the first to speak of alcoholism as a disease and of its progression. Thus, he was seeing the condition in what was wholly a new light and considering it from a perspective that was quite different from the views that then prevailed. An appreciation of this early work is important. Those in any profession need to be knowledgeable about its history. As in our personal lives our family history casts a long shadow and partially determines how we see the world, so history molds the thought and theory of our professions and occupations. We may not always be fully aware of the influences in our personal lives; the same is true of our professional practice. Much of how we view alcohol dependence today is clearly derived from the work of Jellinek. Those involved in substance abuse counseling need to be familiar with the work that marked the evolution of the field.

Jellinek's Phases of Alcoholism

How did Jellinek arrive at his disease formulation of alcoholism? A trained biostatistician, he was understandably fascinated by statistics—the pictures they portray and the questions they raise. Much of his work was descriptive, defining the turf of alcoholism: who, when, where. One of his first studies, published in 1952, charted the signs and symptoms associated with alcohol addiction. This work was based on a survey of more than 2,000 members of AA. Although differences certainly existed among persons, to him the similarities were striking. There was a definite pattern to the appearance of the symptoms. Also, there was a progression of the disease in terms of increasing dysfunction. The symptoms and signs tended to cluster together. On the basis of these observations, Jellinek developed the idea of 4 phases of alcohol addiction: prealcoholic, prodromal, crucial, and chronic. Although many in the alcohol field may not be aware of their origins, these phases have been widely used in alcohol treatment as a part of patient education. The 4 phases are portrayed on p. 76.

In the *prealcoholic phase,* according to Jellinek's formulation, the individual's use of alcohol is socially motivated. However, the prospective alcoholic soon experiences psychological relief in the drinking situation. Possibly his or her tensions are greater than other people's, or

Signs of Developing Alcoholism
derived from E. M. Jellinek

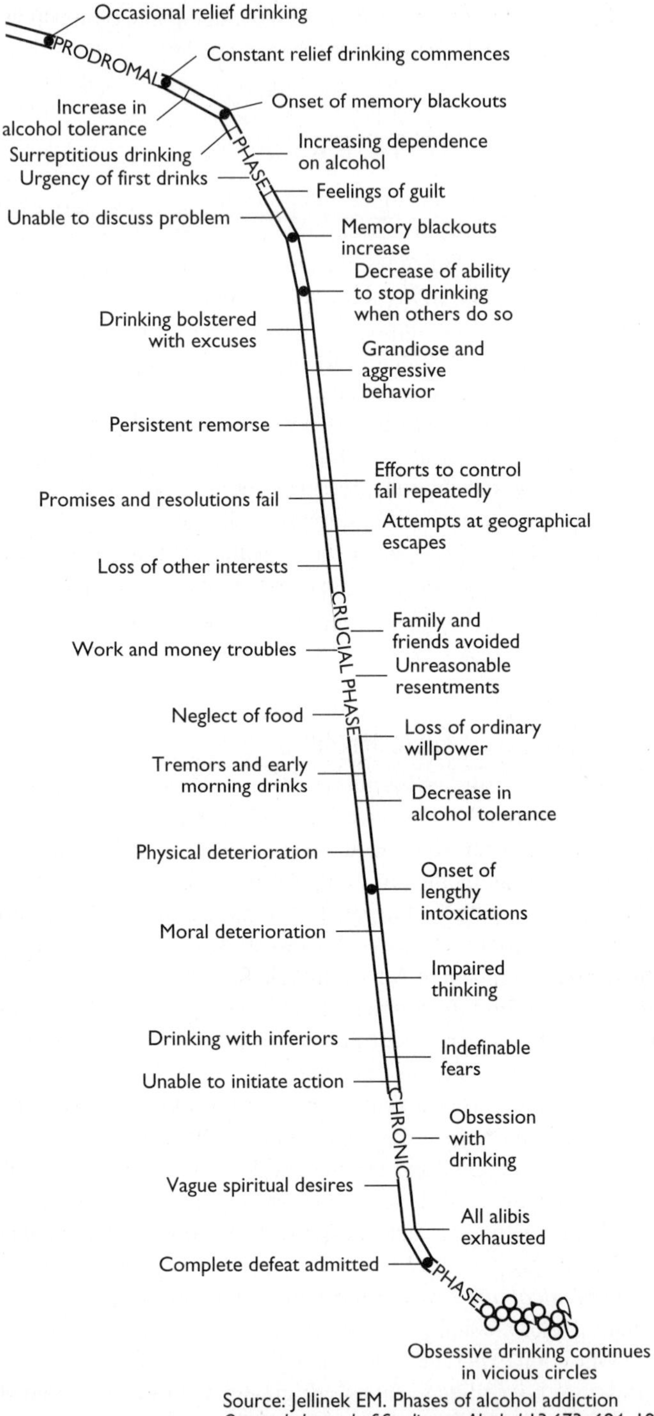

Source: Jellinek EM. Phases of alcohol addiction *Quarterly Journal of Studies on Alcohol* 13:673–684, 1952.

possibly the individual has no other way of handling tensions that arise. It does not matter. Either way, the individual learns to seek out occasions at which drinking will occur. At some point the connection is perceived. Drinking then becomes the standard means of handling stress. But the drinking behavior will not look different to the outsider. This phase can extend from several months to 2 or more years. An increase in tolerance gradually develops.

Prealcoholic

Suddenly the prealcoholic enters the *prodromal phase.* "Prodromal" means warning or signaling disease. According to Jellinek, the behavior that heralds the change is the occurrence of "alcoholic palimpsests," or blackouts.[2] Blackouts are amnesia-like periods during drinking. The person seems to be functioning normally but later has no memory of what happened. Other behaviors emerge during this phase that testify to alcohol's no longer being just a beverage, but a "need." Among these warning signs are sneaking extra drinks before or during parties, gulping the first drink or two, and feeling guilt about the drinking behavior. At this point consumption is heavy but not necessarily conspicuous. To look "okay" requires conscious effort by the drinker. This period can last from 6 months to 4 or 5 years, depending on the drinker's circumstances.

Prodromal

The third phase is the *crucial phase.* The key symptom that ushers in this phase is loss of control. Now taking a drink sets up a chain reaction. The drinker can no longer control the amount consumed after taking the first drink, yet the drinker can control whether or not to take a drink. So it is possible to stop drinking for a time. With loss of control, the drinker's cover-up is blown. The drinking is now clearly different. It requires explanation, so rationalizations begin. Simultaneously, the alcoholic attempts a sequence of strategies to regain control. The alcoholic's thinking goes as follows: "If I just ______, then it will be okay." Tactics alcoholics commonly adopt are deliberate periods of abstinence, changes in drinking patterns, and geographical changes to escape/avoid/be relieved of whatever; similarly, job changes occur. All these attempts are doomed to failure. The alcoholic responds to these failures by being alternately resentful, remorseful, and aggressive. Life has become alcohol centered. Family life and friendships deteriorate. The first alcohol-related hospitalization is now likely to occur. Morning drinking may begin to creep in, foreshadowing the next phase.

Crucial

The final phase in the process as outlined by Jellinek is the *chronic phase.* In the preceding crucial phase, drinkers may have been somewhat successful in maintaining a job and their social footing. Now, as drinking begins earlier in the day, intoxication is an almost daily, day-long phenomenon. "Benders" are more frequent. The individual may also go to dives and drink with persons outside his normal peer group. Not unexpectedly, the alcoholic finds him or herself on the fringes of society.

[2]This is a description of Jellinek's work. A discussion of blackouts and the more recent findings about them appears in Chapter 6.

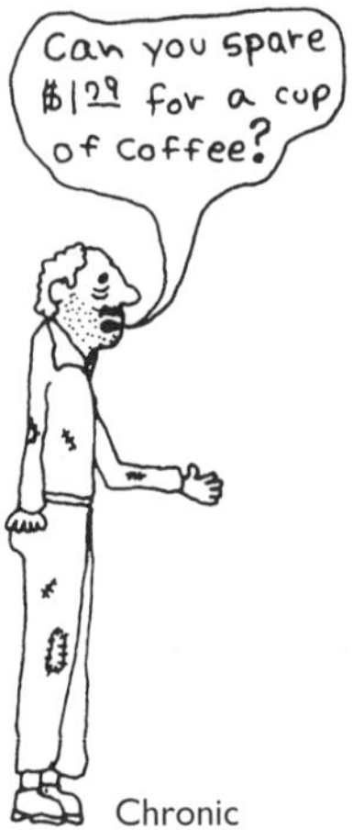

When ethanol is unavailable, poisonous substitutes are the alternative. During this phase, marked physical changes occur. Tolerance for alcohol drops sharply; no longer able to hold the liquor, the alcoholic becomes stuporous after a few drinks. Tremors develop. Many simple tasks are impossible in the sober state. The individual is beset by indefinable fears. Finally, the rationalization system fails. The long-used excuses are revealed as just that—excuses. The alcoholic is seen as spontaneously open to treatment. Often, however, drinking is likely to continue, because the alcoholic can imagine no way out of his or her circumstances. Jellinek did emphasize that alcoholics do not have to go through all 4 phases before successful treatment can occur.

Types of Alcoholism: Jellinek's Species

The pattern just described sets forth the phases in the emergence of alcoholism. Were the same research on which this is based conducted today, people would be quick to point out a number of limitations. For example, all of those studied were members of AA. This would raise the immediate question of whether they were representative of all those with alcoholism. Indeed, Jellinek asked that question. Jellinek continued his study of alcoholism, focusing on alcohol problems in other countries. The differences he found could not be accounted for simply by the phases of alcohol addiction. They seemed to be differences of kind, rather than simply of degree of addiction. This led to his formulation of species, or categories, of alcoholism. He named each species with a Greek letter:

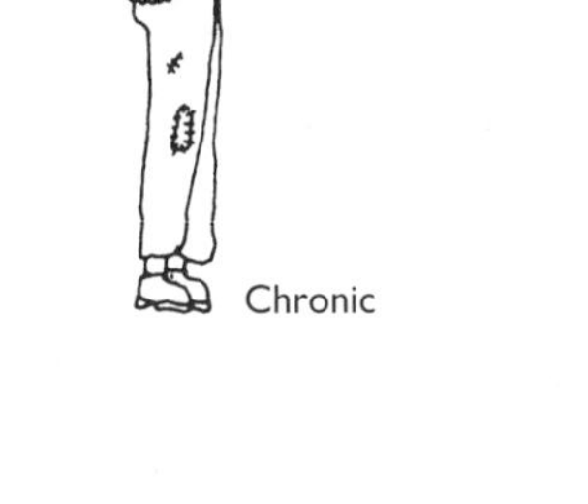

- *Alpha Alcoholism.* This type represents a purely psychological dependence on alcohol. There is neither a loss of control nor an inability to abstain. What is evident is the reliance on alcohol to weather any discomforts or problems in life, which may lead to interpersonal, family, or work problems. A progression is not inevitable. Jellinek noted that other writers may call this species "problem drinking."
- *Beta Alcoholism.* This is present when physical problems, such as cirrhosis or gastritis, develop from alcohol use but the individual is not psychologically or physically dependent. Beta alcoholism is likely to occur in persons from cultures in which there is widespread, heavy drinking and an inadequate diet.
- *Gamma Alcoholism.* This variant is marked by a change in tolerance, physiological changes leading to withdrawal symptoms, and a loss of control. In this species there is a progression from psychological to physical dependence. It is the most devastating species in terms of physical health and social disruption. This is the species Jellinek originally studied. It progresses through the 4 phases discussed: prealcoholic, prodromal, crucial, and chronic. Jellinek considered the gamma alcoholic to be the most prominent type in the United States. This species was the type most common among the AA members

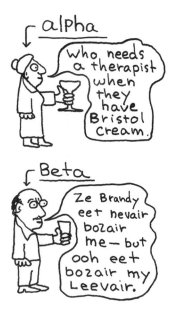

whom Jellinek studied. The characteristics of this species are often seen as synonymous with alcoholism.

- *Delta Alcoholism.* Delta alcoholism is very similar to the gamma species. There is psychological and physical dependence, but there is no loss of control. Therefore, on any occasion the drinker can control the amount consumed. The individual, however, cannot stop drinking for even a day without suffering withdrawal.
- *Epsilon Alcoholism.* While not studied in-depth, this type appeared to be significantly different from the others. Jellinek called this *periodic alcoholism,* a type marked by binge drinking. Though not elaborating, he felt this was a species by itself, not to be confused with relapses of gamma alcoholics.

Having described the various species in *The Disease Concept of Alcoholism,* Jellinek concluded that possibly not all of the species identified are properly categorized as diseases. There was no question in his mind that gamma and delta varieties, each involving physiological changes and a progression of symptoms, are diseases. He speculated that maybe alpha and epsilon varieties are, however, symptoms of other disorders. By more adequately classifying and categorizing the phenomenon of alcoholism, he brought scientific order to a field that formerly had been dominated by beliefs. That was no modest contribution.

Current Thinking

A considerable portion of the research now being undertaken is addressing questions that concerned Jellinek. As noted earlier, although there are common features in alcoholism, there are differences, too. For this reason, alcohol dependence is sometimes described as a heterogeneous disease. Differences need to be explained. They represent factors that may have important implications for treatment, prevention, or early diagnosis. By way of comparison, it is recognized that there are different types of pneumonia, and different types of diabetes. Distinguishing among them is necessary to determine appropriate treatment; in the case of pneumonia, the type dictates the type of antibiotic that will be prescribed.

Since the 1960s there have been efforts to identify different types of alcohol dependence, in effect, updating Jellinek's species. The hope has been that if successful, this would enable us to better tailor treatment. Several subtypes of alcohol dependence have been proposed. In some cases, the typology proposed is based on a single characteristic; in other instances, several factors are included. Among the features used in creating typologies are age of onset, personality traits (such as the presence or absence of impulsiveness), the presence or absence of major psychiatric illness, the presence or absence of antisocial personality disorder and criminality, as well as a positive or negative family history of alcohol dependence. The most serious symptoms and earliest onset tend to be seen in those with the following features: positive family history, history of antisocial personality disorder, personality traits that include impulsivity and risk taking.

As noted, the hope would be that it we can match treatments and types of alcohol dependence for the best outcomes. *Project Match* was a large national multisite clinical research effort sponsored by the NIAAA to explore this very question. To the surprise of many, there was no clear advantage of a particular treatment for a designated type of alcoholism. What this means, however, is unclear. Does this suggest that our psychosocial treatments are not as different and as distinctive as we may think? Or does it suggest that more work is required to identify the significant factors between possible subgroups? Or possibly, the match will prove to be important in the biological arena, and involve medications. A recent preliminary report explored the impact of medication in addition to the usual psychosocial treatments in two subtypes. The results showed that those with Type A alcoholism (which is distinguished by later onset, fewer childhood risk factors, fewer alcohol-related problems, less severe dependence, and less psychiatric illness) had better outcomes when treated by serotonergic drug therapy, compared to a placebo. However, the same pharmacological treatment had no such benefit for Type B alcoholism.

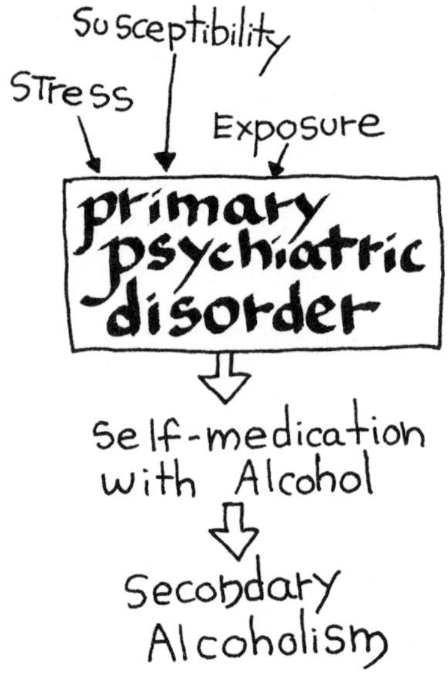

While a number of typologies have be posed, two are most commonly discussed. One is *familial alcoholism,* marked by a positive family history of alcoholism. Compared to the nonfamilial variety, it has an earlier age of onset, it has no increased presence of other psychiatric disorders, and it has more severe symptoms that necessitate early treatment. Interestingly, Jellinek, too, recognized a possible subgroup of alcoholics. In 1940, he proposed a diagnostic category termed "familial alcoholism."

Another set of distinctions sometimes made is between *primary alcoholism* and *secondary,* or *reactive, alcoholism.* The secondary, or reactive, type is seen as alcohol dependence that grows out of or is superimposed on a psychiatric illness or major psychological problem. This is not to imply that such researchers think that this alcoholism need not be treated in its own right. It does mean that, in such cases, the individual probably requires active treatment for more than alcoholism—that is, treatment for the condition(s) that spawned or facilitated its development.

GUIDES FOR DIAGNOSIS

NCA Criteria

Having introduced the perspective of alcoholism as a disease, the next major task was to establish guidelines for diagnosis. The first step was taken in 1972, with the publication of a paper entitled "Criteria for the Diagnosis of Alcoholism." The article was prepared by a committee of the National Council on Alcoholism (NCA) and published in 2 medical journals. The committee's charge was to set forth guidelines to be used by physicians in diagnosing alcoholism. Physicians were provided thereby with an explicit, firm set of standards to use in making a diagnosis. In undertaking this endeavor, the committee collected all the signs and symptoms of alcoholism that could be ascertained through physical examination, medical history, social history, laboratory tests, and clinical observations. These signs and symptoms were then organized into 2 categories, or tracks of data. The first track was called the "physiological and clinical data." Included within that track were the facts a physician can discover through physical examination, laboratory tests, or medical history. The second track was termed the "behavioral, psychological, and attitudinal data." It was composed of information that the patient or family might report about the patient's life situation, the patient's social history, as well as those things the physician can observe directly about the patient's involvement with alcohol.

Alcoholic: Arrested

Within each of the 2 data tracks, the criteria were further divided into subgroups of major or minor criteria. That means exactly what you would expect: major criteria were the "biggies"; the presence of only 1 was sufficient to make the diagnosis. However, several minor criteria were needed to support a diagnosis. Finally, each of the potential signposts was weighted as to whether or not it "definitely," "probably," or "possibly" indicated alcoholism. Table 4.1 summarizes some of the key criteria set forth by the NCA's criteria committee.

Many similarities exist between the symptoms of alcohol addiction developed by Jellinek in 1952 and the criteria published 20 years later. However, Jellinek composed his list based on the self-reports of recovering alcoholics, so the symptoms were from their point of view. A good number of the symptoms Jellinek included involve efforts to deceive and the attempts of the alcoholic individuals to appear normal. This provided little assistance to the physician or helper interviewing an active alcoholic. In those situations, the physician is unable to rely on his or her usual instincts to believe the client. To further complicate the process of making a diagnosis based on Jellinek's list, many of the behaviors included are not the kinds of things a physician can easily detect, so the NCA criteria were a marked improvement.

The committee that developed the criteria for diagnosis also addressed the nature of alcoholism and commented on its treatment. Alcoholism was characterized as a chronic, progressive disease. It was noted that, although alcoholism is incurable, it is highly treatable. Because it is a chronic disease, the diagnosis once made never can be dropped. Therefore, an individual successfully involved in a treatment program would have his or her diagnosis amended to "alcoholism: arrested" or "alcoholism: in remission." Criteria were set forth to determine when this change in diagnosis is appropriate. The committee recommended that factors other than the length of sobriety be taken into account. Among the items listed as signs of recovery are full, active participation in AA;

Alcoholism: Arrested

Table 4.1 NCA Criteria for Diagnosis of Alcoholism

Physiological Data	Diagnostic * Significance
Major Criteria	
Physiological dependence evidenced by withdrawal syndromes when alcohol is interrupted or decreased	1
Evidence of tolerance, blood alcohol level of 0.15 without gross evidence of intoxication or consumption of the equivalent of a fifth of whiskey for more than 1 day by a 180 lb man	1
Alcoholic blackouts	2
Major alcohol-related illnesses in person who drinks regularly:	
Fatty liver	2
Alcoholic hepatitis	1
Cirrhosis	2
Pancreatitis	2
Chronic gastritis	3
Minor Criteria	
Laboratory tests	1*
Blood alcohol level of 0.3 or more at any time	1*
Odor of alcohol on breath at time of medical appointment	2

Behavioral Data	Diagnostic * Significance
Major Criteria	
Continued drinking, despite strong medical contraindications known to patient	1
Drinking despite serious medical problems	1
Patient's complaint of loss of control	2
Minor Criteria **	
*Repeated attempts of abstinence	2
Unexplained changes in family, social, or business relationships	3
Spouse's complaints about drinking	2

*There appears to be some discrepancy between 1 meaning "must diagnose alcoholism" and the committee's statement that more than one minor criterion must be in evidence. This is noted, but no explanation can be provided.

**Similar to Jellinek's symptoms of phases of Alcohol Addiction.

active use of other treatments; use of Antabuse-like preparations; no substitution of other drugs; and a return to work. The committee was primarily interested in diagnosis, not treatment, yet implicit in the standards suggested for diagnosing "alcoholism: arrested" is a view that alcoholism requires a variety of treatment and rehabilitative efforts.

The NCA criteria never had a significant impact on medicine as a whole, and were known primarily to those in the substance abuse field. However, they clearly influenced the thinking of the American Psychiatric Association, and served as a model for the changes adopted by the APA in the following decade.

Diagnostic Criteria of the American Psychiatric Association

DSM-III Criteria

Although definitely on the right track and more useful to clinicians than Jellinek's formulations, the NCA criteria were nonetheless cumbersome. The publication in 1980 of the APA's *Diagnostic and Statistical Manual of Mental Disorders,* third edition, known as the *DSM-III,* was a significant step forward, a milestone not only for alcoholism but for other psychiatric conditions as well. It provided a major departure from previous diagnostic schemes in several ways. For one, the *Manual* set forth very specific diagnostic criteria, explicitly specifying what signs and symptoms must be present to make a diagnosis for a specific condition. The purpose of this was to make the diagnosis of psychiatric conditions more uniform. Thus, diagnosis was no longer based on what the clinician thought was the underlying reason for the condition—for example, whether it was psychological maladjustment or a physiological abnormality.

The third edition of the *Manual* entailed too a significant revision, reorganization, and renaming of major groups of psychiatric illnesses. Thus, for the first time *substance use disorders,* which includes alcohol dependence and alcohol abuse, became a separate major diagnostic category. Previously these different addictions had been assigned to the category of personality disorders. This earlier assignment had reflected the common notion that substance abuse is the result of psychological problems. With the creation of the new category, the manual no longer implied any particular etiology.

The *Diagnostic Manual* and its counterpart, *International Classification of Diseases* (*ICD*), are routinely updated and revised to reflect new knowledge. In response to clinicians' concerns and clinical research, in subsequent editions, some modifications were made in the way alcohol dependence was defined.

One of the criticisms of the third edition had been that alcohol dependence was tied to the presence of physical evidence of addiction, either the presence of tolerance and/or withdrawal symptoms. Thus, in the *DSM-III* formulation, while lives might be in utter disarray due to drinking, if there were not physical manifestations of dependence, a diagnosis of alcohol dependence was not possible. This was the case even though the drinking pattern was not that of a social drinker and though the consequences of drinking were clearly destructive. In response to this concern, modifications were introduced in the revision of the third edition (*DSM-III-R*) and several further modifications made in the fourth edition (*DSM-IV*).

DSM-IV/DSM-IV TR Criteria[3]

Revision of the APA's diagnostic manual is a complex process. It entails convening study groups of experts who not only review the literature but also conduct pilot tests to determine the impact of any changes being considered. In developing the fourth edition there were several issues of particular importance to those involved in preparing the section on substance use. The group felt it was important to devise a single set of criteria that would be applicable to all psychoactive substances. For example, evidence of withdrawal might be a common feature of dependence, even though the symptoms would depend on the particular substance. Another area of concern was the relationship of any proposed criteria to the World Health Organization's classification system, *ICD-10*. Indeed, pilot research showed that there was a high degree of overlap between the two classification systems. If a person is diagnosed as alcohol dependent by one standard, there is a very high likelihood that he or she will be diagnosed as dependent by the other criteria.

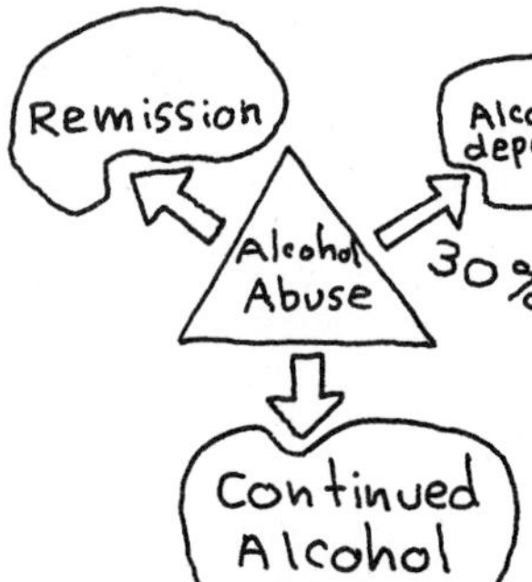

One of the biggest issues with which the task force drafting the *DSM-IV*'s substance-related disorders section struggled was whether to keep or drop the category of abuse. There were those who questioned whether abuse really is a separate condition or whether it is really just "early" dependence. Because some of the same criteria, such as "use despite negative social consequences," were used to diagnose both conditions, the issue was further confused. In making diagnoses, the idea is to find the features that distinguish among illnesses, not the features that are common among them. Here research findings were able to offer some guidance. A follow-up study was conducted of individuals who had been diagnosed with alcohol abuse 4 years previously. The results showed that

[3]The *DSM-IV TR* was published in 2000. This version was issued because the next edition was not going to be published for several years. The changes in the *DSM-IV TR* are primarily limited to updates of the literature review. But there are several instances in which points of confusion have been clarified. Within the section on substance abuse disorders, the only change is to clarify the meaning of the diagnosis Polysubstance Use Disorder. It is to be used *only* when people are using a variety of substances, but do not meet the criteria for abuse or dependence for any of these drugs individually. If criteria are met for abuse or dependence for more than one substance, then there should be multiple diagnoses.

alcohol abuse did not inevitably blossom into dependence. That was true of only 30% of those reexamined. For the remaining 70%, either their problems remitted or a pattern of abuse continued without escalating. Thus, the natural history of alcohol abuse appears to differ from that of alcohol dependence. For the latter, the likelihood that dependence will go away without treatment is very low. The more common pattern is continued and worsening symptoms. The task force decided to retain abuse as a category distinct from dependence. The counterpart to abuse in the ICD-10 schema is "harmful use."

Finally, the task force also was aware that, in some sections, the *DSM-III-R* was not as specific as was desirable. For example, the severity of dependence was to be diagnosed as mild, moderate, or severe. Severe was to be applied when "many criteria" beyond the minimum number required were positive. But what is "many"?

In the *DSM-IV,* the number of criteria for dependence was reduced from 9 to 7, not by deleting items but by combining previously separate items. Beyond the diagnosis, there is other information that clinicians are requested to note in a medical or clinical record. They are asked to indicate if dependence occurs with or without physiological dependence. For those who are alcohol dependent but no longer actively drinking, and in recovery, a description of their current status is important. Several options are provided to denote the extent of recovery, whether there is full or partial remission, and the duration, either early or sustained. The time interval suggested for determining that someone has achieved full, sustained remission is a 12-month period. Other information to be noted in a medical or clinical record is whether the patient is living in a controlled environment, be it a halfway house or a correctional facility, and whether the patient is using specific medications that interfere with or deter intoxication. Such medications are more common in the treatment of narcotics addiction. Disulfiram (Antabuse) and naltrexone (ReVia®) apply for those with alcohol dependence. In both of these last situations, a controlled environment or medication to support abstinence are important because they may well have implications for the patient's ability to maintain sobriety independently.

The criteria used for the diagnosis of abuse do not overlap those for dependence. However, it may seem a fine line to distinguish between continued use that causes physical or psychological problems (dependence) and continued use that leads to social or interpersonal problems (abuse). But there is a difference. Drinking qualifies as abuse if it leads to problems with other people, even if there is no particular distress for the drinking person. The *DSM-IV TR* criteria are presented in Box 4.1.

In addition to standards for diagnosing substance abuse and substance dependence, other substance-related conditions are addressed in the *DSMIV/DSM-IV TR.* These include intoxication and withdrawal, as well as conditions That are substance induced, such as a substance-induced sleep

I do Not drink
More Than
a Sponge. -Rabelais

BOX 4.1

DSM-IV TR Diagnostic Criteria

DSM-IV Criteria for Alcohol Dependence

The *DSM-IV* describes *alcohol dependence* as a maladaptive pattern of use leading to significant impairment or distress, when three or more of the following seven items occur in the same 12-month period:

1. Tolerance can be evidenced either as (a) a need for increased amounts of alcohol to achieve intoxication or the desired effect, or (b) diminished effect with continued use of the same amount.
2. Withdrawal is the presence of characteristic signs for alcohol withdrawal, or the use of the same or closely related substance to relieve or avoid withdrawal.
3. Drinking in larger amounts or over a longer period than was intended.
4. A persistent desire or unsuccessful efforts to cut down or control drinking.
5. Considerable time spent in activities related to drinking, or recovering from drinking episodes.
6. Important social, occupational, or recreational activities given up or reduced due to drinking.
7. Drinking continues even when it is known that physical or psychological problems are caused by or aggravated by continued use.

DSM-IV Criteria for Alcohol Abuse

The *DSM-IV* describes *alcohol abuse* as a maladaptive pattern of use leading to significant impairment or distress, when one or more of the following have occurred in a 12-month period:

1. Recurrent drinking that results in a failure to fulfill major role obligations at work, school, or home.
2. Recurrent drinking when it is physically hazardous, such as while driving, or when involved with risky recreational activities.
3. Recurrent alcohol-related legal problems.
4. Continued drinking despite persistent social or interpersonal problems caused or aggravated by use.

disorder, sexual disorder, or delirium (mental confusion), which otherwise would be handled in other sections of the diagnostic manual. The Focus box highlights substance use disorders, including diagnostic criteria for substance dependence, substance abuse, and intoxication.

Natural History of Alcoholism: Jellinek Revisited

In 1983, George Vaillant published *The Natural History of Alcoholism.* This book set forth the results of several studies that have been invaluable in confirming, and in many instances, amplifying our understanding

FOCUS ON . . .

Diagnostic Criteria: Substance Use Disorders

Diagnostic Criteria for Substance Dependence

A maladaptive pattern of substance use, leading to clinically significant impairment or distress, as manifested by three (or more) of the following, occurring at any time in the same 12-month period.

1. Tolerance, as defined by either of the following:
   a. A need for markedly increased amount of the substance to achieve intoxication or desired effect
   b. Markedly diminished effect with continued use of the same amount of the substance
2. Withdrawal, as manifested by either of the following:
   a. The characteristic withdrawal syndrome for the substance, i.e.
      Amphetamines. Cessation or reduction in amphetamine or a related substance use that has been heavy and prolonged, *and* dysphoric mood and two or more of the following physiological changes within a few hours to days after cessation/reduction: fatigue, vivid unpleasant dreams, insomnia or hypersomnia, increased appetite, psychomotor retardation, or agitation. [Note. Same as cocaine]
      Caffeine. No clinically significant withdrawal phenomena.
      Cannabis. No clinically significant withdrawal phenomena. [NB. Some features have been identified as present with the use of very high doses and suggested as representing a possible withdrawal state—irritability or anxious mood, as well as physiological changes such as tremor, perspiration, nausea, change of appetite, and sleep disturbance—but their clinical significance is unclear.]
      Cocaine. Cessation of (or reduction in) cocaine use that has been heavy and prolonged, *and* dysphoric mood and two or more of the following physiological changes, developing with a few hours to several days after cessation/reduction: fatigue, vivid, unpleasant dreams, insomnia or hypersomnia, increased appetite, psychomotor retardation or agitation. [Note. Same as amphetamines.]
      Hallucinogens. Clinically significant withdrawal has not been well documented.
      Inhalants. No clinically significant withdrawal phenomenon identified.
      Nicotine. Daily use of nicotine for at least several weeks, *and* abrupt cessation or reduction in the amount of nicotine use, followed within 24 hours by four (or more) of the following signs: dysphoric or depressed mood, insomnia, irritability, frustration or anger; anxiety; difficulty concentrating; restlessness; decreased heart rate; increased appetite or weight gain.
      Opiates. Either cessation of (or reduction in) use that has been heavy and prolonged (several weeks or longer) *or* administration of an opioid antagonist after a period of opioid use, *and* three or more of the following developing within minutes to several days after cessation/reduction/antagonist use: dysphoric mood, nausea or vomiting, muscle aches; lacrimation or rhinorrhea; pupillary dilation, piloerection, or sweating; diarrhea; yawning; fever; insomnia.
      Phencyclidine. Neither tolerance nor withdrawal has been clearly demonstrated.
      Sedatives, Hypnotics, or Anxiolytics. Cessation or reduction in use that has been heavy and prolonged, *and* two or more of the following developing within several hours to a few days after cessation/reduction: autonomic hyperactivity; increased hand tremor; insomnia; nausea or vomiting; transient visual, tactile or auditory hallucinations or illusions; psychomotor agitation; anxiety; grand mal seizures. [Note: same as for alcohol]
   b. The same (or closely related) substance is taken to relieve or avoid withdrawal symptoms
3. The substance is often taken in larger amounts or over a longer period than was intended
4. There is a persistent desire or unsuccessful efforts to cut down or control substance use

(continued on the next page)

FOCUS ON . . .

Continued

5. A great deal of time is spent in activities necessary to obtain the substance, use the substance, or recover from its effects
6. Important social, occupational, or recreational activities are given up or are reduced because of substance use
7. The substance use is continued despite knowledge of having a persistent or recurrent physical or psychological problem that is likely to have been caused or exacerbated by the substance

Author's Note: Clear withdrawal syndromes have not identified as occurring with caffeine, cannabis, hallucinogens, or phencyclidine, or inhalants. Thus, a diagnosis of dependence upon these substances will be based primarily on the behavioral features (criteria numbered 3 through 7).

Diagnostic Criteria for Substance Abuse

A. A maladaptive pattern of substance use leading to clinically significant impairment or distress as manifested by one or more of the following, occurring within a 12-month period:
   1. recurrent substance use resulting in a failure to fulfill major role obligations at work, school, or home
   2. recurrent substance use in situation in which it is physically hazardous
   3. recurrent substance-related legal problems
   4. continued use despite having persistent or recurrent social or interpersonal problems caused or exacerbated by the effects of the substance

B. The symptoms have never met the criteria for Substance Dependence for this class of substance

Diagnostic Criteria for Intoxication

The following are the criteria for intoxication for specific drugs/drug classes. In all instances it is presumed that the symptoms are not due to a general medical condition, nor are they better explained by a different psychiatric disorder.

Alcohol Intoxication

A. Recent ingestion of alcohol

B. Clinically significant maladaptive behavior or psychological changes (e.g., inappropriate sexual or aggressive behavior; mood lability; impaired judgment; impaired social or occupational functioning) during or shortly after drinking.

C. One or more of the following signs, developing during, or shortly after, alcohol use:
   - slurred speech
   - unsteady gait
   - impairment in attention or memory
   - incoordination
   - nystagmus (crossed eyes)
   - stupor or coma

Amphetamine Intoxication

A. Recent use of amphetamine or a related substance

B. Clinically significant maladaptive behavioral or psychological changes

C. Two or more of the following signs, developing during, or shortly after use:
   - tachycardia or bradycardia (rapid or slow heart beat)
   - dilation of eye pupils
   - elevated or lowered blood pressure
   - perspiration or chills
   - nausea or vomiting
   - evidence of weight loss
   - psychomotor agitation or retardation; muscular weakness, respiratory depression, chest pain or cardiac arrhythmias (irregular heart beat)
   - confusion, seizures, dyskinesias (difficulty in voluntary movement), dystonias (abnormal muscle tone), or coma

Caffeine Intoxication

A. Recent consumption of caffeine, usually in excess of 250 mg (e.g., more than 2 or 3 cups of brewed coffee)

B. Five or more of the following, developing during or shortly after caffeine use
   - restlessness
   - excitement
   - flushed face
   - gastrointestinal disturbance
   - rambling flow of thought and speech
   - tachycardia or cardiac arrhythmia (rapid or irregular heart beat)
   - nervousness
   - insomnia
   - diuresis (increased urine output)
   - muscle twitching
   - periods of inexhaustibility
   - psychomotor agitation

C. The above symptoms cause distress or impairment in social, occupational, or other important areas of functioning.

Cannabis Intoxication

A. Recent use of cannabis
B. Clinically significant maladaptive behavioral or psychological changes (e.g., impaired motor coordination, euphoria, anxiety, sensation of slowed time, impaired judgment, social withdrawal) that developed during or shortly after cannabis use.
C. Two or more of the following signs, developing within 2 hours of cannabis use:
- conjunctiva injection (bloodshot eyes)
- increased appetite
- dry mouth
- tachycardia (rapid heart beat)

Cocaine Intoxication

A. Recent use of amphetamine or a related substance
B. Clinically significant maladaptive behavioral or psychological changes, (e.g., euphoria or affective blunting, changes in sociability, hypervigilance, interpersonal sensitivity; anxiety, tension, or anger, stereotyped behavior; impaired judgment; or impaired social or occupational functioning)
C. Two or more of the following signs, developing during, or shortly after use:
- tachycardia or bradycardia (rapid or slow heart beat)
- dilation of eye pupils
- elevated or lowered blood pressure
- perspiration or chills
- nausea or vomiting
- evidence of weight loss
- muscular weakness, respiratory depression, chest pain or cardiac arrhythmias
- confusion, seizures, dyskinesias (difficulty in voluntary movement), dystonias (abnormal muscle tone), or coma

Hallucinogen Intoxication

A. Recent use of a hallucinogen
B. Clinically significant maladaptive behavioral or psychological changes (e.g., marked anxiety or depression, ideas of reference, fear of losing one's mind, paranoid ideation, impaired judgment, or impaired social or occupational functioning) that developed during, or shortly after, hallucinogen use
C. Perceptual changes occurring in a state of full wakefulness and alertness (e.g., subjective intensification of perceptions, depersonalization, derealization, illusions, hallucinations, synesthesia) that develop during, or shortly after hallucinogen use
D. Two or more of the following signs developing during, or shortly after, hallucinogen use:
- dilated pupils
- tachycardia (rapid heart beat)
- palpitations
- sweating
- blurring of vision
- incoordination
- tremors

Inhalant Intoxication

A. Recent intentional use of a short-term, high dose exposure to volatile inhalants (excluding anesthetic gases and short-acting vasodilators)
B. Clinically significant maladaptive behavioral or psychological changes (e.g., belligerence, assaultiveness, apathy, impaired judgment, impaired social or occupational functioning after use of volatile inhalants, *or* perceptual changes occurring in a state of full wakefulness and alertness (e.g., subjective intensification of perceptions, depersonalization, derealization, illusions, hallucinations, synesthesia) that develop during, or shortly after hallucinogen use
C. Two or more of the following signs, developing during, or shortly after inhalant use or exposure:
- dizziness
- slurred speech
- lethargy
- psychomotor retardation
- generalized muscle weakness
- blurred vision or diplopia (seeing double)
- nystagmus
- incoordination
- unsteady gait
- depressed reflexes
- tremor
- euphoria
- stupor or coma

Opiate Intoxication

A. Recent use of an opioid
B. Clinically significant maladaptive behavioral or psychological changes (e.g., initial euphoria, followed by apathy, dysphoria, psychomotor agitation or retardation, impaired judgment, or impaired social or occupational functioning) that developed during, or shortly after, opioid use
C. Pupillary constriction (or pupillary dilation due to anoxia for severe overdose) and one or more of the following signs developing during, or shortly after, opioid use:

(continued on the next page)

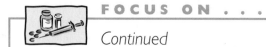

FOCUS ON . . .

Continued

- drowsiness or coma
- impairment in attention or memory
- slurred speech

Phencyclidine Intoxication

A. Recent use of phencyclidine or a related substance
B. Clinically significant maladaptive behavioral changes (e.g., belligerence, assaultiveness, impulsiveness, unpredictability, psychomotor agitation, impaired judgment, or impaired social or occupational functioning) that developed during, or shortly after phencyclidine use
C. Within an hour (less when smoked or snorted, or used intravenously) two or more of the following signs:

- ataxia
- dysarthria (speech difficulty)
- seizures
- hyperacusis (ultra acute hearing)
- hypertension or tachycardia
- muscle rigidity
- vertical or horizontal nystagmus

Sedatives, Hypnotic, or Anxiolytic Intoxication (same as alcohol)

American Psychiatric Association. *Diagnostic and Statistical Manual of Mental Disorders* (*DSM-IV/DSM-IV TR*). Washington, DC: American Psychiatric Association, 2000.

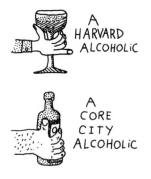

of alcoholism as a disease. This work can be seen as representing an update of the work initiated more than 30 years earlier by Jellinek, when he outlined the phases of alcohol addiction. Vaillant's work is based on 2 groups of men who at that point had been followed for approximately 50 years, from their adolescence into their 60s. The major goal of the research has been to study adult development through the life cycle. There was an interesting side benefit for the alcohol field. Not unexpectedly, during the course of the study, members from both groups developed alcoholism. Thus, for the first time it became possible to begin to separate "the chicken from the egg." The question could be asked, "What are the factors that distinguish those who develop alcoholism from those who do not?"

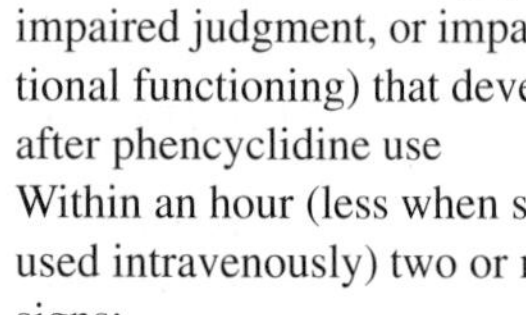

One group in the study, the college sample, was officially described as "students from an Eastern university." In fact, it was composed of Harvard undergraduates from the classes of 1942 to 1944. The other group, referred to as "the core city sample," was comprised of men from high-crime, inner-city neighborhoods. They were initially selected to participate in the study when they were about 14 years old, primarily because they were not known to be seriously delinquent. At the beginning of these studies, members of both groups were extensively interviewed. A variety of psychological tests were administered, detailed family histories were obtained, and measures of the subjects' personal functioning were made. Since that time these men have been periodically recontacted to collect detailed information on the progress of their lives.

In brief, Vaillant determined that those who became alcoholic were not more likely to have had impoverished childhoods or to have had preexisting personality or psychological problems. Therefore, it was his conclusion that such problems, which are often cited as evidence of an "alcoholic personality," do not predate the emergence of the disease. On the contrary, they are the symptoms or consequences of alcohol dependence. As for predictors of alcoholism, the significant determinants were found to be having a family history of alcoholism and having been raised in a culture with a high rate of alcoholism.

Several other findings are worth noting. Vaillant compared the various diagnostic classifications, or diagnostic approaches. He discovered a high overlap between those people diagnosed as alcoholic (using *DSM-III* criteria) and those identified as "problem drinkers" with a high "problem index"—a sociological classification system. The specific negative consequences seemed to be of little importance. However, by the time an individual had experienced 4 or more negative consequences as a result of drinking, it was almost assured that a formal diagnosis of alcohol dependence could be made. Virtually no one had had 4 or more alcohol-related problems through mere "bad luck."

Also, as alcoholism progressed over time, the number of problems tended to increase and the overall life situation—psychological adjustment, economic functioning, social and family relationships—deteriorated. Vaillant observed that studies that point to the contrary usually report on persons who have gone for treatment and been recontacted at a single point. He speculates that these studies have not followed up the individuals for a sufficient length of time. While active alcoholism has a downward course, during the slide, there will be both ups and downs. Presumably, people who enter treatment facilities do so at a low point. Therefore, at follow-up, even if they continue as active alcoholics, it should not be surprising to find their situation somewhat improved. However, if follow-ups were conducted at several times, the full ravages of untreated alcoholism would become apparent. As Vaillant notes, paraphrasing an AA saying, "Alcoholism is baffling, cunning, powerful, . . . and patient."

Vaillant concluded that there is indeed a progression in alcoholism (however, there is not the orderliness in symptoms' emergence that Jellinek had described). As a result of the progression there are only two likely outcomes. The men in the study either died or recovered through abstinence. The proportion who either returned to nonproblematic drinking or whose alcoholism stabilized was very small. Again, over time, with increasing incidence of follow-up, this small middle ground continued to shrink.

In his book *The Disease Concept of Alcoholism,* Jellinek noted that a disease is "simply anything the medical profession agrees to call a disease." By that standard, alcohol dependence has been a disease for some time. However, with the refinement of diagnostic criteria there is now far clearer guidance in identifying those who suffer from it.

RESOURCES AND FURTHER READING

The recommended readings on this resource list might appear out of date. However, the primary, original sources for the major historical pieces of work discussed in this chapter were deliberately selected. Because this chapter reviews the evolution of the disease framework as well as approaches to diagnosis, there is considerable value in examining the original articles. Beyond allowing the authors to speak for themselves, these classic works offer instructive insights into the views of alcoholism that then prevailed.

American Psychiatric Association. *Diagnostic and Statistical Manual of Mental Disorders,* 3rd ed., revised. Washington, DC: American Psychiatric Association, 1987.

American Psychiatric Association. *Diagnostic and Statistical Manual,* 4th ed., TR (text revision). Washington, DC: American Psychiatric Association, 2000.

Basu D, Ball SA, Feinn R, Gelernter J, Kranzler HR. Typologies of drug dependence: Comparative validity of a multivariate and four univariate models. *Drug and Alcohol Dependence* 73(3):289–300, 2004. (57 refs.)

Criteria Committee, National Council on Alcoholism. Criteria for the diagnosis of alcoholism, *American Journal of Psychiatry* 129(2):41–49, 1972.

Dundon W, Lynch KG, Pettinati HM, Lipkin C. Treatment outcomes in type A and B alcohol dependence 6 months after serotonergic pharmacotherapy. *Alcoholism: Clinical and Experimental Research* 28(7):1065–1073, 2004. (33 refs.)

Hasin DS, Grant B, Endicott J. The natural history of alcohol abuse: Implications for definitions of alcohol use disorders. *American Journal of Psychiatry* 147(11):1537–1541, 1990.

Jellinek EM. Phases of alcohol addiction. *Quarterly Journal of Studies on Alcohol* 13:673–684, 1952.

Jellinek EM. *The Disease Concept of Alcoholism.* New Haven, CT: Hill House Press, 1960.

Johnson BA, Cloninger CR, Roache JD, Bordnick PS, Ruiz P. Age of onset as a discriminator between alcoholic subtypes in a treatment-seeking outpatient population. *American Journal on Addictions* 9(1):17–27, 2000. (40 refs.)

Penick EC, Nickel EJ, Powell BJ, Liskow BI, Campbell J, Dale TM, Hassanein RE, et al. The comparative validity of eleven alcoholism typologies. *Journal of Studies on Alcohol* 60(2):188–202, 1999. (75 refs.)

Rinaldi RC, Steindler EM, Wilford BB, Goodwin D. Clarification and standardization of substance abuse terminology. *Journal of the American Medical Association* 259(4):555–557, 1988.

Satel SL. Is drug addiction a brain disease? In Heymann PB, Brownsberger WN, eds. *Drug Addiction and Drug Policy: The Struggle to Control Dependence.* Cambridge MA: Harvard University Press, 2001, pp. 118–143. (35 refs.)

Stepney R. The concept of addiction: Its use and abuse in the media and science. *Human Psychopharmacology* 11(Supplement 1):S15–S20, 1996. (18 refs.)

Vaillant GE. *The Natural History of Alcoholism, Revisited,* Cambridge, MA: Harvard University Press, 1996.

Woody G, Schuckit M, Weinrieb R, Yu E. A review of the substance use disorder section of the DSM-IV. *Psychiatric Clinics of North America* 16(1):21–32, 1993.

CHAPTER 5

Etiology of Alcohol Dependence

What is man, when you come to think upon him, but a minutely set, ingenious machine for turning, with infinite artfulness, the red wine of Shiraz into urine?
ISAK DINESEN, 1934

What are the causes of alcohol dependence? As more knowledge is gained, the answers become more complex. It may be useful to make a comparison to the common cold. Once you have "it," there isn't much question. The sneezing, the runny nose, the stuffed-up feeling that the cold tablet manufacturers describe so well leave little doubt. But why you? Because "it" was going around. Your resistance was down. Others in the family have "it." You became chilled when caught in the rain. You forgot your vitamin C. Everyone has a pet theory and usually chalks it up to a number of factors working in combination against you. Some chance factor does seem to be involved. There are times when we do not catch colds that are going around. Explaining the phenomenon cannot be done with precision. It is more a matter of figuring out the odds and probabilities as the possible contributing factors are considered.

PUBLIC HEALTH MODEL

Members of the public health field have developed a systematic way of tackling the problem of disease, its causes, and the risks of contracting it. First, they look at the agent, the "thing" that causes the disease. Next, they consider the host, the person who has the illness, to find characteristics that may have made him or her a likely target. Finally, the environment is examined, the setting in which the agent and host come together. A thorough look at these three aspects ensures that no major influences are overlooked. This is exactly what occurred in response to the anthrax outbreaks in the weeks following the World Trade Center tragedy. There was discussion of how the anthrax, the agent, had been prepared. How fine was the powder? Had it been treated to make it more likely to be

carried in the air? There was attention to the host. Where did the individual work? What placed that person in a place to have contact with anthrax? Then there was attention to the environment. Was it a closed room, the nature of ventilation systems, the type of envelope, the mail-handling machines?

With respect to alcohol each of these areas is significant. Accordingly, alcohol dependence is often termed a biopsychosocial illness, reflecting the fact that causality is seen as an interplay of *bio*logical, *psycho*logical, and *social* factors. Alcohol dependence qualifies as a public health problem. It is among the leading causes of death in the United States. It afflicts 1 out of every 10 adults. It touches the lives of 1 out of every 8 children. The response to alcohol dependence is, unfortunately, pale, compared with its impact.

From the public health viewpoint the first sphere to be examined as a possible cause is the *agent.* For alcohol dependence the agent is the substance, alcohol. This is such an obvious fact that it might seem silly to dwell on it. No one can be alcohol dependent without an exposure to alcohol. The substance must be used before the possibility of dependence exists. Alcohol is an addictive substance. With sufficient quantities over long enough time, the body undergoes physical changes. When this has occurred and the substance is withdrawn, there is a physiological response, withdrawal. For alcohol there is a well-defined set of symptoms that accompanies cessation of drinking in an addicted person. Any person can be addicted to alcohol, but to use this fact alone to explain alcohol dependence represents untidy thinking. That alcohol is addicting does not explain why anyone would drink enough to reach the point of addiction. Temperance literature had tried to paint a picture of an evil demon in the bottle. Take a sip, and he's got you. This is no longer a convincing metaphor. It is obvious that drinking need not lead inevitably to a life of drunkenness. Let us look at the action of the drug itself. What invites its use and makes it a candidate for use sufficient to cause addiction? Following that, we move to the individual: what is it in the individual's physiological and psychological makeup that may place him or her at risk? For the sake of discussion these two aspects are separated, but in reality they are closely intertwined. Finally, the chapter turns to the larger social scene, the culture, and all of the attitudes, the spoken and unspoken rules about alcohol use and what is okay or not okay, as well as what is and is not legally available.

THE AGENT

We take any number of substances into our bodies, from meats to sweets, as solids or liquids. Although everyone overeats occasionally, considering habitual overeating as a form of "substance abuse," or the associated craving as just as powerful as that associated with drugs, is a very recent concept. A physiological basis for this is only now being explored. However,

Candy is dandy
But liquor is quicker.
OGDEN NASH

in the case of alcohol, the physiological effects themselves suggest some of the reasons it is such a likely candidate for heavy chronic use. First, alcohol is a depressant drug. One of its first effects is on the central nervous system, the "higher" centers related to judgment, inhibition, and the like. What is more important is what this feels like, how it is experienced. With mild intoxication comes relaxation, a more carefree feeling. It is generally experienced as pleasant, a high. Preexisting tensions are relieved. A good mood can be accentuated. Alcohol is experienced as changing mood for the better. This capacity of alcohol is one factor to remember in trying to understand use sufficient for dependence.

A common expression is "I sure would like a drink now." It may be said after a hard day at work, after a round of good physical exercise, or after a period of chaos and emotional stress. This expression certainly includes the awareness that alcohol can influence our emotional state. Equally as important is the word "now." There is a recognition that the effects are immediate. Not only does alcohol make a difference, but it does so very rapidly. If alcohol had a delayed reaction time—say, 3 days, 3 weeks, or even 3 hours—it wouldn't be a useful method to alter mood states. The unpredictability of people's lives makes drinking now for what may happen later seem quite pointless. So its speed in altering emotional states is another characteristic of the drug alcohol that enhances its likelihood for overuse.

Alcohol has another characteristic common to all depressant drugs. With mild inebriation, behavior is less inhibited; there are feelings of relaxation. However, at the same time there is a gradual increase of psychomotor activity. While feeling the initial glow, the drinker is unaware of this. As the warm glow subsides, the increased psychomotor activity becomes apparent, often experienced as a wound-up and edgy feeling, similar to that caused by too many cups of coffee or caffeinated soft drinks. The increase in psychomotor activity builds up gradually. Since it is delayed and its onset is masked, the drinker is not very likely to recognize the feeling as a product of the alcohol use. This phenomenon is akin to a mini-hangover. Possibly some people, including those not dependent on alcohol, have a second or third drink "to relax" and, in fact, to get rid of the very feelings created by the earlier ones.

What is being discussed here is the abuse potential of the drug alcohol. "Abuse potential" refers to the likelihood that individuals will choose to readminister a drug. There are ways of studying the abuse potential of a drug in a laboratory setting. For example, given a choice of 2 substances, both of which have been sampled, which 1 will people choose if given a choice of 1 over the other? If there is a marked preference for drug A, rather than drug B, then A is the one with more likelihood for abuse. Another approach is to compare a new drug with one that has a known level of abuse. Here the question is "Which will people choose?" If people are given 2 choices, with 1 being a drug and the other a placebo—meaning the other is inert, without any psychoactive properties—is there any preference? If the drug is not selected more frequently than the "nondrug" it has a very low abuse potential. In essence people don't feel any different than if they'd taken nothing. Another method is to ask people to rate the effects of a drug: "How does it make you feel? Is it pleasant? Would you want to take it again?" In addition, they can be asked to rate the drug in comparison with other substances. If someone's eyes light up and a smile comes to their face as the person describes his or her response to the drug, watch out. The drug has a greater likelihood of abuse than if the individual is unimpressed by its effects or finds it unpleasant.

The peculiar charm of alcohol lies in the sense of careless well-being and bodily comfort which it creates. It unburdens the individual of his cares and fears. Under such conditions it is easy to laugh or to weep, to love or to hate, not wisely but too well.

DR. HAVEN EMERSON

Alcohol and Man. New York: Macmillan, 1932.

Beyond the immediate effects of the drug there are other related factors that influence abuse potential. As a general rule, the quicker the effects are felt the greater the likelihood of abuse. And at the same time, the more rapidly the drug effects disappear, the greater its abuse potential. Typically the drugs with the highest abuse potential are those whose desired effects are strong and immediate. It's truly magic. The effects of a drug are also related to the way it is taken into the body. The most rapid response occurs with inhaling or injecting, which delivers the drug to the brain quickly. But the speed of delivery is only part of the story. The other factor that influences abuse potential is how rapidly these desired effects fade. If drugs have a dramatic impact but only a short duration, this invites readministration. What further increases the odds of readministration and increases the likelihood of abuse is when the drug has unpleasant effects as it wears off. To use an example from other drugs, in terms of abuse potential, cocaine ranks right up there on all counts. Forget the half hour or so that may be needed to feel alcohol; with the ingestion of cocaine it is literally seconds. This is clearly captured by the language used to describe cocaine's effects. It is described as a "rush," not as a "warm glow" or a "buzz," the phrases heard with alcohol. However, the euphoria fades quickly. The effects dissipate within 10 to 30 minutes, depending on whether the cocaine was snorted or injected. As the effects wane, there is the inevitable "crash," characterized as feelings of dysphoria, a general negative feeling state. Among drinkers, the vast majority are properly described as social drinkers; of those who use cocaine regularly there are proportionately far fewer "social snorters."

THE HOST—GENETIC FACTORS

The belief that alcoholism runs in families has long been a part of the folk wisdom. If not in your childhood then certainly in your parent's, a great-aunt may well have explained away the town drunk with "He's his father's son." No further comment was presumed necessary. The obvious truth was clear: many of life's misfortunes are the result of "bad" genes. Historically just such an understanding of genetics, supported by warped theological views, led to statutes that authorized the sterilization of the feebleminded, the hopelessly insane, as well as the chronically drunk.

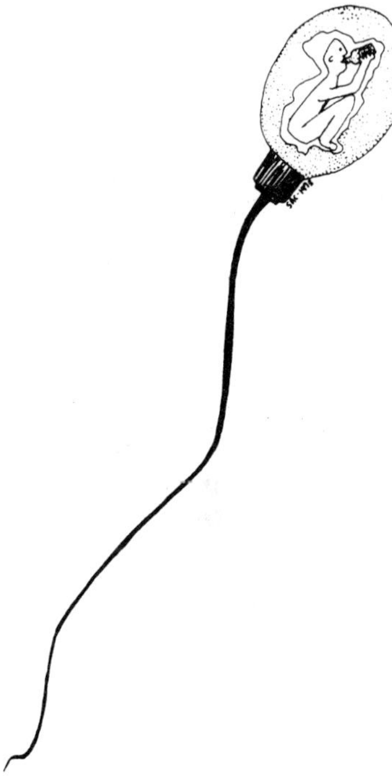

Such an approach has fallen into disrepute. It is now clear that heredity is not as simple as it seemed. Each individual, at the point of conception, receives a unique set of genetic material. This material is like a set of internal instructions, which guide the individual's growth and development. In many instances, the genetic endowment simply sets down limits, or predispositions. The final outcome will depend on the life situation and environment in which the person finds, or places, him- or herself. Thus, some people tend to be slim and some tend to put on weight easily. Such a tendency is probably genetic. In large measure, however, whether people are fat, thin, or just right depends on them.

Nature Versus Nurture

What are the facts about the role of heredity in alcohol dependence? Actually, alcohol dependence does run in families. The child of an alcohol-dependent parent is more likely to become similarly alcohol troubled. One study tracing family trees found that 50% of the descendants of alcoholics were themselves also alcoholic. Though that figure is a bit higher than other similar studies, it is a dramatic example of the typical finding that suggests that the offspring of those who are alcohol dependent have a 4 times greater risk of developing the disease.

The observations of those working in the area of alcohol rehabilitation and treatment lend anecdotal support to the view of a constitutional vulnerability. Some clients report a major alcohol problem very early in life, often by the time of adolescence, which progressed rapidly in the absence of any unique, identifiable psychological stress. Similarly, at AA meetings the remark may be heard, "I was an alcoholic from my first drink." Usually this means that for seemingly idiosyncratic reasons the speaker never drank "normally," as did peers, but used, and was affected by, alcohol differently. Interestingly, back in 1940, Jellinek recognized a possible hereditary factor and suggested a distinguishable familial type of alcoholism. (This is described in Chapter 4.)

we have no idea why little Ebenezer might be having Trouble at School. Everything at home is fine!

However, something running in families is not proof that it is inherited. After all, speaking French runs in families—in France. Separating nature from nurture is a complex but necessary job. Certainly, an alcohol-dependent, actively drinking parent would be expected to have an impact on a growing child. It is not unreasonable to expect that inherent in the family lies the soil of addiction. Yet again, the simple fact that this sounds reasonable does not make it true.

The current understanding is that heredity plays a significant role in the development of alcohol dependence in some people. Research is exploding in this arena. Much has been learned since the early 1970s. There are different types of research which shed light on this question from different angles. These different types of studies are described in the following sections. Ultimately, if heredity is a factor, there must be some basic biochemical differences between those who are prone to develop alcohol dependence and those who are not. But the initial task was simply to establish the extent to which alcohol dependence does or does not run in families.

Twin and Adoption Studies

Heredity. The heredity of form and the heredity of mental traits and character are unquestioned. Inebriety belongs to the same class, and has been recognized as hereditary for all ages. On one of the monuments of Egypt there is a drawing of a drunkard father and several drunken children, and the grouping conveys the idea that the inebriety of the parent was the direct cause of the children's disgrace.
WALTER W. SPOONER

The Cyclopaedia of Temperance and Prohibition. New York: Funk & Wagnalls, 1891.

Methods of scientific investigation using an experimental model are not possible in the task of separating human nature from nurture. We can't ask some families to raise children one way and other families to raise their children differently, so that the differences can be determined. Human research requires locating individuals with particular life experiences or characteristics and then comparing them with those with other backgrounds. Twin studies and adoption studies are the two classical methods of doing this. Donald Goodwin is a clinician-researcher who conducted some of the important initial work on the topic of alcoholism and the role of genetics. Many of his (and others') studies have used data from Scandinavia, because these countries keep very complete records of marriages, births, and so on. This makes tracing families easier.

One early study was based on a large sample of male twins. In each set, 1 twin was alcoholic. The researchers determined whether the twins were identical or fraternal. Then they interviewed the twin of the known alcoholic. The prediction was that, if alcohol dependence has a hereditary basis, the other twin of identical sets would be more likely also to be alcohol dependent than if he were a fraternal twin. This assumption was made because identical twins share the same genetic material. That proved to be the case. However, the hereditary endowment does not act to totally dictate the development of alcohol dependence, because not all the identical twins were both alcoholic. It was further discovered that an apparent predisposition exists toward having, or being spared, the social deterioration associated with dependence. If both twins were alcoholic, the best predictor of the other twin's life situation was not how much or how long he had been drinking. The life situation of the first twin was more reliable. So there appears to be a hereditary predisposition both to alcohol dependence and the social problems associated with it.

An adoption study conducted by Goodwin, using Danish subjects, further supported the influence of heredity. He traced children born to an alcohol-dependent parent. These children had been adopted by the age of 6 weeks. He compared them with adopted children of biological parents without alcohol problems. The adoptive families of both groups were essentially the same. He discovered that those who had a biological parent who was alcoholic were themselves more likely to develop alcohol dependence in adulthood. Thus, dependence cannot be attributed simply to the home environment. While these earliest studies involved only males, subsequent research suggests that there is a similar genetic predisposition among females.

Drunkards beget drunkards.
PLUTARCH

Further studies have helped separate the relative influence of genetic makeup and home environment. These studies have used half-siblings. Of the half-siblings, 1 had an alcoholic parent; the other did not. Thus, 1 of the children had a biological predisposition, while the other did not. These half-brothers and half-sisters were raised together in the same home. In some cases both were reared in a nonalcoholic family. In other cases, both grew up in a home with an alcoholic parent. As expected, those with a genetic background positive for dependence were themselves more likely to develop alcoholism as adults. Of equal significance was the finding that being reared in a home with an active alcoholic did not further increase the chances of developing dependence. This was true for both the biologically at-risk children and their half-brothers and half-sisters who did not have a biological predisposition. This finding has been confirmed by other studies. Growing up in a home with an alcoholic parent does not add to the risk of developing alcoholism. Such findings provided strong support for the importance of the genetic predisposition in some cases of alcoholism.

Studies of Nonalcoholic Blood Relatives

With the presence of a genetic factor established, the next step was to understand the nature of this genetic predisposition. The National Institute on Alcohol Abuse and Alcoholism (NIAAA) established a major research effort, the Collaborative Study on the Genetics of Alcoholism, to explore these questions. Any genetic difference between those biologically prone to alcohol dependence and those who are not will be manifested in some biochemical differences. Efforts are under way to explore what biochemical differences distinguish between these two groups. The major hypotheses are that there are differences in the way our bodies handle alcohol and how our brains experience its effects. The differences could conceivably be differences of metabolism, differences in response to chronic exposure to ethanol, or possibly a unique response to a single dose. For example, those at high risk may experience greater pleasure and those at low risk more discomfort.

What does the research to date show?

- One group of studies has looked at how alcohol's effects are experienced. These studies have used young men who exhibit no symptoms of alcohol dependence but who have an alcoholic blood relative. Those having an alcohol-dependent family member typically describe a lesser response to a single dose of alcohol than do those with no alcoholic blood relative. To translate this—those with a family history of alcohol dependence don't feel as "high" as those who have no family history of dependence. So think about it: if feeling alcohol's effects is a significant part of drinking, then those with a family

history will need to drink more than their peers. This may increase their risks for dependence.

This difference in response to alcohol proved to be important. Follow-up studies 8 years later indicated that those who had a markedly lessened response to alcohol were 4 times more likely to themselves be alcohol dependent. Fifty-six percent of the subjects with a low alcohol response had developed dependence, versus only 14% of those with high levels of sensitivity. Notice that the comparison was no longer on the basis of having or not having an alcohol-dependent relative. The comparison was the response to alcohol's effects. But having alcohol dependence in the family stacked the deck in terms of the chances of being a high or low responder.

- In a similar vein, other studies have explored other responses to alcohol. One such study determined that those with a family history of dependence have greater muscle relaxation with a single dose of alcohol than those without such a family background. After drinking, those at high risk are more likely to have brain alpha-wave activity, as measured by electroencephalogram (EEG). Such brain waves are associated with feelings of relaxation.
- High-risk subjects, those with a family history of alcohol dependence, perform less well on portions of standard neuropsychological tests. Such tests measure a variety of cognitive functions. This finding is noteworthy because it long has been recognized that those who are alcohol dependent do poorly on some of these tests, such as a test for abstracting ability. However, this diminished performance had always been presumed to be the result of brain damage from heavy drinking. Now the question has to be whether or not this condition predates the dependence.
- Finally, there also appears to be a difference in metabolism. In one study, a group of presently nonalcoholic young men with an alcohol-dependent father or brother showed greater acetaldehyde levels during alcohol metabolism than another similar group who did not have an alcohol-dependent family member. Much higher levels of acetaldehyde often accompany drinking in Asians. These higher levels produce a disulfiram-like reaction, which discourages alcohol consumption and thereby provides some protection against the development of alcohol dependence. Paradoxically, though, with a modest increase of acetaldehyde the addiction process may be facilitated.

These differences have often been considered as deficiencies. It is now being recognized that what is inherited may not necessarily be a deficiency but might, paradoxically, be described as a strength. In other words, some people might inherit an ability to handle alcohol too well. They may be more immune to negative physical consequences of drinking, such as nausea and hangovers, or may be able to function better than the average person when alcohol is ingested. If so, those who are at risk for alcohol dependence are deprived of the very cues that, for others, keep drinking in check.

Genetic Markers

Genetics research has become increasingly sophisticated. It is now possible not merely to examine genes directly but also to manipulate them. Techniques have been developed that allow the altering of portions of genes. People speak of "gene therapy" or "genetic engineering." The massive national research program, the Human Genome Project, has succeeded in charting human genetic material. This was a challenge similar in scope to earlier efforts to land a person on the moon or to go to Mars. This has opened the door for treating illnesses that are known to be caused by a specific genetic abnormality. Such genetic-based treatments will be able to go beyond the therapies currently available, because the source of the disease is totally removed.

Early Genetic Research

Step back to what were the dark ages of genetic research in the alcohol field. The earliest genetic marker studies, premolecular biology, were relatively straightforward. They attempted to link alcohol dependence to other traits that were known to be inherited. If such associations could be identified, this would indicate the gene responsible. Some of the characteristics examined for an association with alcohol dependence were blood type, an inherited type of colorblindness, and the ability to taste or not to taste particular chemicals. This work continues. Indeed, a study published in 2001 reexamined data collected earlier, involving more than 12,000 people. It found that those with dark eye color were less likely to abuse alcohol than those with light eye color. Another study found that there were differences in the ability to taste a particular substance, depending on whether there was a family history of alcoholism and depression. Those with alcoholism alone were nontasters, and those with a family history of alcoholism and depression were "super-tasters," finding the substance extremely bitter. The point of comparison were those without a history of either illness, and who were in the middle in terms of tasting. This suggests that there are two types of familial alcohol dependence.

Animal Studies

Animal studies, too, have offered valuable insights. The findings cannot be directly generalized to humans; however, work with chimps, baboons, and rats can shed light on the promising areas for human investigation and can provide clues. Among the more interesting early animal studies was the discovery of "drinking rats." Different strains of rats were given a choice of water or water spiked with alcohol of differing concentrations. Inevitably, they sampled each and usually opted for plain water.

They drank the alcohol-water solution only when it was the sole liquid available. However, several strains of rats were important exceptions. They preferred alcohol and water solutions of around 5%, which translates to 10 proof. These drinking rats could be inbred to produce offspring that preferred even higher alcohol concentrations.

But do these rats develop a condition that appears to resemble alcohol dependence? Seemingly they do—there are some strains that consistently choose to drink alcohol and reach a BAC of 0.5 to 0.20. These rats will work (press a bar in their cages) to obtain alcohol. In addition, the alcohol's attraction is not merely its taste or smell. They select it over other favorite foods or drinks; they will even self-administer alcohol directly into the stomach. These rats seek alcohol for its pharmacological properties. Furthermore there is evidence of tolerance, as well as differences in initial sensitivity to alcohol.

The studies of drinking rats have offered other insights. Other behaviors were noticed among the drinking rats that distinguished them from their nondrinking counterparts. Several of the observed differences seemingly have parallels to human behaviors. Thus, these differences may shed some light on factors that give impetus to drinking. For example, the drinking rats were described as having an innately higher level of activity when presented with a new environment. They are more inclined to explore. They are also described as more anxious. They seemingly have temperaments that are similar to those associated with higher levels of drinking in humans.

While drinking rats indicate that genetics play a role, a more recent animal model allows examining the role of specific genes. So, besides drinking rats, there are now knockout mice. Recent developments in genetic engineering make it possible to turn off (i.e., knock out) individual genes. Differences in behavior that arise when a gene is inactivated allows researchers to identify its impact on function and behavior.

But the basic question remains, what is the inherited "something"? Ultimately the difference lies somewhere in the brain chemistry. This brings to light one area in which alcohol is different from other drugs. There is no one single receptor in the brain that has been identified as uniquely linked to alcohol. By contrast, we know that there are special sites in the brain—such as opiate receptors, nicotine receptors, and benzodiazepine receptors—which are responsible for a significant portion of those drugs' effects. So in the absence of a special alcohol receptor, the assumption is that alcohol must affect or alter the function of a wide range of the usual receptors and neurotransmitters that serve as the communications system for the central nervous system. The area of particular interest is the neurotransmitters—dopamine, serotonin, GABA, and the naturally occurring internal opioid systems.

Here, too, animal studies have been helpful. The drinking and nondrinking rats differ with respect to their brain chemistry. In some instances there are more or lesser amounts of a particular enzyme. Or there can be more or fewer receptors that are available to respond to these chemicals. Also, differences exist in the concentration of these receptors in different parts of the brain. The range of possible factors in combination can boggle the mind. By current count, for serotonin, just one of the many different neurotransmitters, there are 7 variants of receptor cells. Quite conceivably, each could respond differently to the presence of alcohol.

Human Studies

A study published in 1990, involving human subjects, seemed a major breakthrough in understanding the genetic basis of alcohol dependence. The excitement proved to be a bit premature, however. In hindsight it is recognized that possibly we were a bit naive in thinking it could be so easy. That research involved an examination of genetic material in the brain tissue of persons with alcohol dependence, and compared it to the brain tissue of nondependent individuals. Of particular interest was a gene, known as D_2, that is associated with the brain's receptors for dopamine, a neurotransmitter. Dopamine is one of the neurochemicals in the brain that is involved with the sensation of pleasure. The receptor is the site where this neurochemical acts. It was found that there are two forms of this gene. Different forms of a gene are called alleles. As a point for comparison, think of the gene for eye color as having different alleles. One allele corresponds to brown eyes, another to blue eyes, and so on. The researchers discovered that there are two forms of the dopamine receptor gene. In the shorthand that geneticists use, these gene variations are referred to as A_1 and A_2. Of special interest was whether or not dependence is associated with a particular form of the gene. Indeed, that was found to be so. Among those with alcohol dependence, 69% had the A_1 allele. Only 20% of those without dependence had that version. This kind of association suggested that the A_1 gene may increase the susceptibility to dependence. Its presence does not make alcohol dependence inevitable, or one would expect a 100% association. Likewise, its absence does not offer immunity.

We're drinking my friend,
To the end of a brief episode,
Make it one for my baby
And one more for the road.
JOHNNY MERCER
"One for My Baby"

Other researchers had difficulty in reproducing the findings of this 1990 study. This raised the question of whether the first results were just a fluke and a matter of chance. (It's sort of like winning the lottery—statistically improbable, but it does happen.) A decade later, the answer seems to be "No it wasn't, but. . . ." The group of alcoholics in the initial study had very severe forms of alcohol dependence. This is the variety of dependence that is now seen as most likely to have a genetic component. Equally important, the comparison group was carefully selected for the absence of alcohol dependence. This comparison population was described as being "super normal." Because alcohol dependence is so common, unless one makes a clear point of excluding alcoholics, the chances are that within a random assortment of people some will be alcohol dependent. Indeed, later research that also restricted the characteristics of the populations it studied also found associations between the A_1 gene and alcohol dependence.

Research on the D_2 gene has suggested other relationships. It has been found that D_2 plays a role in how alcohol is metabolized. One form of the D_2 gene is associated with the flushing that is common in some Asians in its promotion of faster metabolism of aldehyde dehydrogenase (see Chapter 3). The D_2 gene also seems to be implicated in the differences in cognitive style and neuropsychological functioning that were found in looking at people at risk for alcohol dependence.

What is evident, too, is that, to understand alcohol's effects, one must think in terms of a cascade effect, with one reaction leading to another, which in turns sparks another, which has an impact on something else, and so on. The following excerpt from a scientific article captures this complexity:

> The dopaminergic system, and in particular the dopamine D_2 receptor, has been implicated in reward mechanisms. The net effect of neurotransmitter interaction at the mesolimbic brain region induces "reward" when dopamine is released from the neuron at the nucleus accumbens and interacts with a dopamine D_2 receptor. "The reward cascade" involves the release of serotonin, which in turn at the hypothalamus stimulates enkephalin, which in turn inhibits GABA at the substania nigra, which in turn fine-tunes the amount of dopamine released at the nucleus accumbens or "reward site." It is well known that under normal conditions in the reward site dopamine works to maintain our normal drives. In fact, it has come to be known as the "pleasure molecule" and/or the "antistress molecule." When dopamine is released into the synapse, it stimulates a number of dopamine receptors (D_1–D_5) which results in increased feelings of well-being and stress reduction. A consensus of the literature suggests that when there is a dysfunction in the brain reward cascade, which could be caused by certain genetic variants, especially in the dopamine system causing a hypodopaminergic trait, the brain of that person requires a dopamine fix to feel good. This trait leads to drug-seeking behavior.[1]

The nature of the changes in this process led the researchers to describe addiction as a "reward deficiency syndrome." What is clear too is that different neurotransmitters play a role, some involved in a number of different drugs of abuse, and others specific for a particular drug. (See Chapter 3.)

The current wisdom is that no single gene accounts for the genetic basis for alcohol dependence. What is presumed is that there are a number of genes that may function both independently as well as in concert.

---

[1]Blum K, Braverman ER, Holder JM, Lubar JF, Monastra VJ, Miller D, et al. Reward deficiency syndrome: A biogenetic model for the diagnosis and treatment of impulsive, addictive and compulsive behaviors. *Journal of Psychoactive Drugs* 32(Supplement):1–112 (entire issue), 2000.

Genetics play a role in another way. Genetic makeup seems to determine our susceptibility not just to alcohol dependence but also to organ damage associated with heavy drinking, or the severity of withdrawal, as well as determining our susceptibility to other drug dependencies and some co-occurring psychiatric disorders.

Familial Versus Nonfamilial Alcohol Dependence: So What?

Given the strong evidence for the role of a genetic factor in some cases of alcohol dependence, it is being suggested that we routinely begin to think in terms of at least 2 types of alcohol dependence: familial and nonfamilial. The familial form is believed to be characterized by a positive family history of alcohol dependence, an earlier age of onset, and more destructive symptoms. This necessitates and leads to treatment at a relatively young age. This form involves no increased likelihood of other psychiatric illness. On the other hand, the nonfamilial type is seen as having a later onset. It is also characterized by less virulent symptoms.

With a genetic vulnerability clearly established, how might this information be used clinically? Certainly the issue is relevant to prevention efforts. But how might it also be useful in treating alcohol dependence? In what is clearly a very preliminary and pilot effort, there has been some exploration of the impact of medications that affect dopamine activity. In one study alcoholics with the D_2 gene associated with dopamine deficiency who received such medication reported less craving, less anxiety, and less depression. They were less likely to drop out of treatment. This medication certainly does not cure alcohol dependence. It has the promise to address biochemical problems, which, if attended to, make it possible for people to participate in treatment and decrease the likelihood of relapse.

THE HOST—PERSONALITY AND PSYCHOLOGICAL MAKEUP

It is important to note at the outset of this section that, in the not-too-distant past, psychological factors were seen as the single most important predictors and/or precursors of future dependence. The bio and the social elements in what we now see as a three-fold biopsychosocial illness received far less attention. There are probably several reasons for this. Research on what was then called alcoholism stopped during Prohibition. "No alcohol—no problem" was the short-lived attitude. Much of what we now take as fact and as always having been known was established relatively recently. Until 1953, the DTs were thought to be caused by malnutrition, not by alcohol withdrawal. It was only in 1973 that fetal alcohol syndrome was described in the scientific literature in the United

States. Until 1976, it was thought that cirrhosis of the liver was due wholly to malnutrition. Molecular biology, a field that can help identify the basic mechanisms for a genetic predisposition, is a very new medical science. It wasn't that long ago that cloning sheep, much less humans, was in the realm of science fiction.

Given how little was known about the basic medical facts, it is not surprising that people looked to psychological explanations to understand the origins of alcohol dependence. Particular attention was directed to defining the nature and origins of what was presumed to be the "alcoholic personality."

Psychological Needs

When you stop drinking, you have to deal with this marvelous personality that started you drinking in the first place.
JIMMY BRESLIN

It is now generally recognized that our behavior is at least partially determined by factors of which we are unaware. What are these factors? Our grade school social studies classes usually focused on food, clothing, and shelter as the 3 basic human needs. But there are emotional needs, just as real and important, if people are to survive healthfully and happily. What do we need in this realm?

> What are the emotional foods that every human being must have regardless of age? What are the basic emotional requirements that must come to every small infant, to every growing child, to every adult?
>
> In the first place, there must be affection and a lot of it. Real, down-to-earth, sincere loving. The kind that carries the conviction through body warmth, through touch, through the good mellow ring of the voice, through the fond look that says as clearly as words, "I love you because you are you."
>
> Closely allied with being loved should come the sure knowledge of belonging, of being wanted, the glow of knowing oneself to be a part of some bigger whole. Our town, our school, our work, our family—all bring the sound of togetherness, of being united with others, not isolated or alone.
>
> Every human being also needs to have the nourishment of pleasure that comes through the senses. Color, balanced form and beauty to meet the eye, harmonious sounds to meet the ear. The heady enjoyment of touch and taste and smell. And finally, the realization that the pleasurable sensations of sex can be right and fine and a part of the spirit as well as the body.
>
> Everyone must feel that he is capable of achievement. He needs to develop the ultimate conviction, strong within him, that he can do things, that he is adequate to meet life's demands. He needs also the satisfaction of knowing that he can gain from others recognition for what he does.
>
> And most important, each and every one of us must have acceptance and understanding. We need desperately to be able to share our thoughts and feelings with some other person, or several, who really understand. . . . We yearn for the deep relief of knowing that we can

be ourselves with honest freedom, secure in the knowledge that says, "This person is with me. He accepts how I feel!"[2]

If these needs are not met satisfactorily, the adult is not whole. A useful notion in assessing what has happened is to think of the unmet needs as "holes." Everybody has some holes. They vary in number, size, and pattern. And, too, some holes may prove to be more debilitating than others. What is true for all is that holes are painful. We attempt to cover up, patch over, or camouflage our holes, so that we can feel more whole, less vulnerable, and more presentable.

Early Psychological Approaches

Historically, through the 1960s, a variety of personality theories were applied to the problem of alcoholism. Each represented an attempt to categorize the nature of the "holes," their origins, and the reasons that alcohol is used to cover them up. Although seemingly logical enough at the time, there were several major flaws in these studies. One was that the people being studied were already alcohol dependent. The idea that an alcoholic personality might be a result of the disorder rather than an underlying cause was overlooked. One of the strengths of George Vaillant's work in the 1980s was that he began not with alcohol-dependent people but with individuals *before* their development of alcoholism. In effect, he studied large samples of people over time, beginning in late adolescence. Some of these people later developed dependence, and others did not. Thus, he was able to see what actually were the predictors of the disease.

Personality Theories Applied to Alcohol Dependence

Among the theories of personality that shaped early thinking, the first was the psychoanalytical, based on the work of Sigmund Freud. Freud himself never devoted attention to alcoholism. However, his followers applied his theory to the disease. It is impossible to briefly address the whole of Freud's work. He recognized that psychological development is related to physical growth. He identified stages of development, each with its particular, peculiar hurdles that a child must overcome on the way to being a healthy adult. Tripping over one of the hurdles, he felt, led to difficulties in adulthood. Some of the events of childhood may be especially painful, difficult, and anxiety-producing. They may persist, unrelieved by the environment. This makes the child feel incompetent, resulting in a hole. The child seeks unique ways to patch over the holes.

---

[2] Baruch D. *New Ways of Discipline: You and Your Child Today.* New York: McGraw-Hill, 1949.

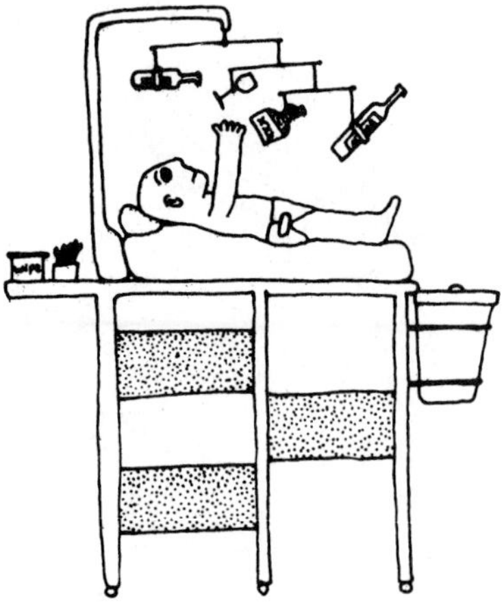

However, the existence of the hole shapes future behavior. It may grow larger, requiring more patchwork. The hole may render the child more vulnerable to future stress and lead to new holes.

There is virtually no one today who would seriously appeal to psychoanalytic theory as a significant factor in explaining alcohol dependence. But in the mid-twentieth century, this was the majority view in psychiatric circles. *Oral fixation* was one construct used to understand alcoholism. This means the holes began in earliest childhood. Observe infants and see how very pleasurable and satisfying nursing and sucking are. Almost any "dis-ease" or discomfort can be soothed this way. Individuals whose most secure life experiences were associated with this period will tend to resort to similar behaviors in times of stress. Thus, according to this theory, alcoholics are likely to be individuals who never fully matured beyond infancy. They are stuck with childlike views of the world and childlike ways of dealing with it. They are easily frustrated, impatient, demanding, wanting what they want when they want it. They have little trust that people can help meet their needs. They are anxious and feel very vulnerable to the world. According to this theory, nursing a drink seems an appropriate way of handling discomforts. Alcohol is doubly attractive because it works quickly: bottled magic.

Another psychoanalytic concept, applied to male alcoholics, was that of *latent homosexuality.* It needs to be pointed out that homosexuality, like alcoholism, is far better understood today. It is no longer considered a disease. Being gay or lesbian is no longer seen as caused by psychological problems. Sexual orientation is seen as genetically established. One does not choose to be homosexual any more than one chooses to be 6 feet tall. While it seems far-fetched to us in the twenty-first century, there was discussion of drinking being prompted by the fact that a bar could provide a socially acceptable format for male companionship.

Other personality theorists focused on different characteristics. Adler latched onto the feelings of dependency. He saw the roots of alcoholism as being planted in the first 5 years of life and tied to feelings of inferiority and pessimism. The feelings of inferiority, or the longing for a sense of power, may require strong proofs of superiority for satisfaction. If continuing into adulthood, as new problems arise and create anxiety, the person may seek a sense of feeling superior rather than really overcoming difficulties. So, theoretically, to the alcoholic, drinking as a solution is intelligent. Alcohol does temporarily reduce the awareness of anxiety and gives relief from feelings of inferiority.

In 1960, William and Joan McCord published *Origins of Alcoholism.* Their studies used extensive data collected on 255 boys throughout their childhoods. What they found negated many of the psychoanalytic theories. Oral tendencies, latent homosexuality, and strong maternal encouragement of dependency were not, in fact, predictors of alcoholism. The McCords' work highlighted the complexity of the social and psychological interactions.

For the most part, the use of psychodynamic personality theories to understand the origins of alcohol dependence has faded away. Interest in personality is no longer tied to the notion of holes or deficiencies that emerge from early childhood experiences. Rather interest in personality has turned to those personality traits, or predispositions, that influence how each of us tends to interact with others in the world. The other branch of psychology important in understanding the origins of alcohol and drug problems is the field of learning theory.

Current Thinking

There is no longer an effort to explain alcoholism exclusively on the basis of individual personality. However, it is recognized that individual factors can and do play a role. The issue now is to better understand how individuals, given their particular genetic and physical makeup, interact with their environment. Probably the field of psychology is one area that is most sensitive to the different contributing factors from these domains. In an earlier edition of this book, we referred to this as "the slot machine approach." To become alcohol dependent requires getting 3 cherries to come up on the slot machine. An individual may be born with 1 cherry, thanks to his or her genetic makeup. The culture in which the individual is raised may provide a second, or a sociological, cherry. And the person's psychological makeup may confer a third cherry. Or there may be some variation: say, two-thirds genetic and one-third psychological. But 1 cherry is not an accurate predictor of who becomes alcoholic.

Learning Theory

Learning is recognized as a major factor in molding our actions. Behavior is a result of learning, which is motivated by an individual's attempt to minimize unpleasantness and maximize pleasure. What is pleasant is a very individual thing. A child might misbehave and be punished, but the punishment, for that child, might be a reward and more pleasant than being ignored. Thus, what is pleasant or rewarding is very much a factor of the individual and his or her unique environment.

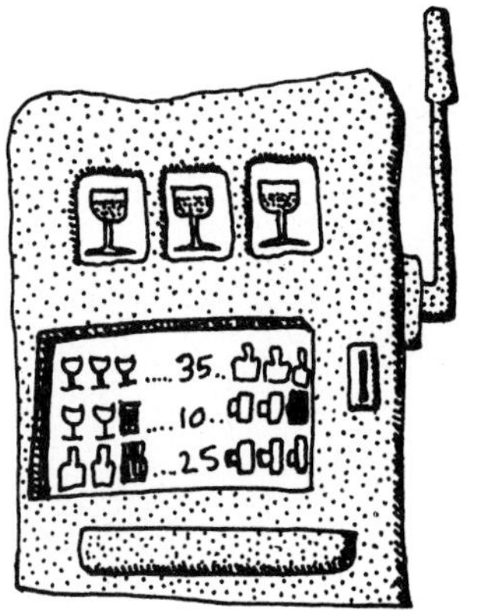

In applying learning theory to alcohol dependence, the view is that drinking has a reward system. Alcohol or its effects are sufficiently reinforcing to cause continuation of drinking by the individual. Behavior most easily learned is that with immediate, positive results. The warm glow and feeling of well-being associated with the first sips are more reinforcing than the negative morning-after hangover. This theory would hold that anyone could become alcoholic if the drinking were sufficiently reinforced. Vernon Johnson, founder of a highly successful treatment program and author of the book *I'll Quit Tomorrow,* gave great emphasis to the importance of learning in explaining drinking. He noted that those who use alcohol have learned from their first drink that alcohol is exceedingly trustworthy: it works every time and it does "good things." This learning is highly successful, being sufficient to set up a lifetime relationship with alcohol. The relationship may alter gradually over time, finally becoming a destructive one, but the original positive reinforcement keeps the person seeking the "good old days" and minimizing the destructive elements. Seen in this light, alcohol-dependent people are not so distant from people who remain in what are now unsatisfactory marriages, jobs, or living situations out of habit or some hope that the original zest will return. Of course, after alcohol dependence is established, continued use isn't primarily prompted by recollections of the good old days. Learning has clearly established that a drink is what will relieve the considerable discomfort of emerging withdrawal.

Rational Addiction

This is a rather new approach, one that has drawn upon the field of economics. Our choices as consumers are seen by economists as quite rational, being guided by our wish to secure the greatest possible happiness from our expenditures. (Economists use the word "utility" rather than happiness.) In making decisions, we balance out an array of pros and cons. We consider our options and are guided by past experiences, and our future expectations. During our usual day, most of this is largely unconscious, it simply happens. If I want a candy bar, the odds are fairly good I'll go with a Hershey bar every time. I don't give it a lot of thought. With a major purchase this process is likely to be far more deliberate and can require a bit of time. Indeed, time is one of the things that we spend to make what we hope to be the right choice. If it's a new car, we may talk to friends, check things out on the Internet, visit different dealerships, compare prices. The final choice will not be governed only by the sticker price. Other things are of value to us. For some, it may be the particular manufacturer, if the car is U.S. or foreign made, its color, the warranty period, gas mileage, the costs of options we really want such as a sun roof, the ease servicing, or later trade-in value." Each of us values these various factors differently: "As long as it's red" versus "As long as it starts." Some of the features may have an immediate value, such as the sound system, and others will only matter in the future, such as trade-in value.

The negative consequences of addiction seem so obvious. Thus, at first glance, addictions seem to be very irrational behavior. Not so, say the economists. There are simply a few quirks. For one, the payoff, the pleasure, or need for (the utility) of drug use at any particular moment, is clearly linked to past use. Generally this is not a factor. How much I enjoy my Hershey bar today can't easily be predicted by how many I've had in the past. In addition for drugs, over time, *more* consumption is required to yield the pleasure that earlier came from a smaller amount. If you like to go to the movies, you don't have to go to a double feature now because you used to go to a single show. Addictive substance behaviors are different. It is a commodity for which past use does predict its value (importance) later on.

Another important characteristic is that active drug users are not future oriented: they need it *now.* To use the economic term, they discount the future costs associated with the decision to use. With drug use there is nothing equivalent to figuring out what a car's future trade-in value is likely to be. The greater the present value of using, which those in the substance abuse field might describe as craving, the more likely the person is to be short-sighted about future costs and negative effects.

The framework of economics, with its array of mathematical formulas, is used to describe not only the addictive process but also some elements of treatment. The models suggest that people will change when the long-term benefits are clearly seen as greater than the short-term costs of forgoing use. Indeed an element of treatment is to assist clients to foresee the future, and to recognize the links between use and negative consequences. To use a phrase heard in AA, "Think through the drink." Rational addiction models also have been used to explain other aspects of addictive behavior, such as binge drinking, and why going cold turkey and abrupt cessation may be more successful than efforts to cut down.

Expectancies

How do beliefs about alcohol—that is, our expectations—determine our response? What are the sources of information that give rise to our beliefs, and how do these change? What is the relative influence of peers versus family? How does the relative weight of these shift as children move from preadolescence through young adulthood? The research suggests that expectancies of alcohol's effects are important in drinking behavior. There are multiple sources of these beliefs. Some come from the larger cultural landscape, including everything from alcohol advertising to the depiction of alcohol use in TV and movies. There is also the culture of the family, how we see alcohol being used, the kinds of occasions in which alcohol is used, the kinds of behavior that occur in the presence of drinking, and the related attitudes.

Research suggests, too, that learning about alcohol occurs in very subtle ways and from a very early age. For example, it has been demonstrated that even in the first year of life infants respond to the smell of alcohol. Infants whose parents drink more heavily mouth an alcohol-beverage-scented toy more frequently than do infants with little or no exposure to alcohol. Something similar also happens for children between the ages of 3½ and 6 years, but with an added twist. Children whose parents drink—in this instance, beer—either like or dislike the odor of beer, depending on how the parents use alcohol. To the extent drinking is escapist—that is, linked to withdrawing from people or creating emotional distance—the children are more likely to describe the odor of beer as unpleasant.

Temperament

The field of psychology has also been examining the issue of temperament—which is similar to but different from personality. Temperament is not thought to be merely or purely the product of life experiences or parenting styles. Rather, temperament represents an innate predisposition that influences one's ways of tackling the world. People seem to have an innate tendency to be risk takers or to avoid risk taking, to welcome novelty or to like things to be more predictable. Whether one is shy or outgoing, adventuresome or cautious, in part seems to be a biological given. Also there seem to be predispositions toward different cognitive styles. These have some bearing on how we tackle problem solving, as well as the degree to which we consider future consequences of actions.

The following traits and behavior patterns have been identified as risk factors for future alcohol or other drug problems. Some of these are seemingly interrelated. It is important to consider each of the following traits as existing on a continuum rather than as their being present or absent.

- *Cognitive structure.* Those who dislike ambiguity and desire to make decisions based on definite knowledge are at reduced risk.
- *Harm avoidance.* Those who dislike exciting activities, especially involving potential physical dangers, are at reduced risk.
- *Impulsivity.* Those who are more willing to act on the spur of the moment, to speak their minds freely, or to not hide their emotions are at higher risk.
- *Playfulness.* Those who describe themselves as liking to do things just for fun or who spend substantial time in games, sports, and social activity are at higher risk.
- *Disinhibition/sensation seeking.* Those who are extroverts, who like to take both social and even physical risks just for the sake of having the experience, and who like spontaneous activities are at higher risk.
- *Stressful life events.* The presence of painful, stressful experiences increase the risk of future substance use problems. Such events include the divorce of parents and other serious life disruptions such as a parent's loss of a job, a serious illness, a death in the family, domestic violence, or physical or sexual abuse.

Such traits are considered lifelong predispositions. While seen as predispositions nonetheless they are modified by experience, learning, and life circumstances. For example, liking novelty at age 63 probably looks far different from what it looked like when the same person was 17 years old, the same with impulsivity.

In addition, there are some psychiatric disorders that are recognized to be correlated with substance abuse problems in adulthood. These include conduct disorders, antisocial personality disorders, and attention deficit hyperactivity disorder. (See Chapter 12 for further discussion.) If or how these might contribute to substance abuse problems is not clear, but what is evident is that they represent risk factors, meaning they signal the greater likelihood of a later substance abuse problem.

The other side of the coin from risk factors is protective factors. It is important to be alert not only to things that might signal a potential problem but also to those that reduce the likelihood of its occurrence. What traits and life experiences shield someone from developing alcohol problems and alcoholism? If one were to boil them all down, it might be said that the basic psychological needs have been met and in some abundance. In brief, those who have positive social bonds to family, to community, to school, or to a religious community are less likely to develop problems later.

THE ENVIRONMENT—SOCIOLOGICAL FACTORS

Cultural Orientation

Statistically the odds of becoming an alcoholic have in the past varied significantly from country to country. This is not a matter of genetic differences. The genetic differences within racial and ethnic groups are greater than the differences between groups. Alcohol consumption varies widely from country to country (see Table 5.1). Equally important are the differences in attitudes and customs that prevail.

Studies in epidemiology once showed that the Irish, French, Chileans, and Americans had a high incidence of alcoholism. The Italians, Chinese, and Portuguese had substantially lower rates. The difference seemed to lie with the country's habits and customs. Indeed, whether someone drinks at all depends as much on culture as it does on individual characteristics. With television, jet travel, and so on, differences among cultural groups are less clear-cut than they once were. However, historically the differences in rates of alcoholism from culture to culture were substantial enough to provoke study and research. Just as genetic and psychological approaches fall short of fully explaining the phenomenon of alcoholism, so do cultural differences. But a review of past studies is useful in considering the ways in which broad cultural attitudes seemingly contribute to high rates of alcoholism or, conversely, in identifying those attitudes that promote moderate use.

Culture includes the unwritten rules and beliefs by which a group of people live. Social customs set the ground rules for behavior. These rules are learned from earliest childhood and are followed later, often without a thought. Many times such social customs account for the things we do "just because . . ." The specific expectations for behavior differ from nation to nation and between separate groups within a country. Differences can be tied to religion, gender, age, and social class. The ground rules

Table 5.1 The Top 10 Chart: International Comparisons of per Capita Alcohol Consumption*

Per Capita Consumption
(Liters of Alcohol, Total Population 2002)

				Beverage Type					
Rank	Country	Total	% Change from 1977	Spirits		Beer		Wine	
1.	Luxembourg	11.9 L	19.6%	1. Russia	6.2 L	1. Czech Rep	155.0 L	1. Luxembourg	59.1 L
2.	Hungary	11.1	21.6%	2. Latvia	5.7	2. Ireland	147.1	2. France	56.0
3.	Ireland	10.8	83.6%	3. Cyprus	4.3	3. Germany	121.5	3. Italy	51.0
4.	Czech Rep	10.8	28.3%	4. Czech Rep	3.7	4. Austria	109.3	4. Portugal	43.0
5.	Germany	10.4	1.7%	5. Slovak Rep	3.5	5. Luxembourg	108.2	5. Switzerland	41.8
6.	France	10.3	−36.3%	6. Hungary	3.4	6. UK	100.6	6. Argentina	36.1
7.	Portugal	9.7	−2.1%	7. Japan	3.3	7. Denmark	96.7	7. Hungary	36.0
8.	Spain	9.6	−17.1%	8. Thailand	3.2	8. Belgium	96.0	8. Greece	33.9
9.	UK	9.6	79.9%	9. China	3.0	9. Australia	92.4	9. Uruguay	32.8
10.	Denmark	9.5	39.1%	10. Ireland	2.5	10. Slovak Rep	92.3	10. Denmark	32.0
>25.	United States	6.6		18. United States	1.9	11. United States	82.0	28. United States	15.0

*Keep in mind, when reviewing this or any similar chart, that international comparisons are always approximations. National consumption data may not reflect actual consumption. Generally any information on consumption is derived from tax revenue, so home-brewed beer or spirits distilled at home, or any alcohol smuggled into a country, all of these escape taxation, and are not represented in the per capita consumption figures.

The northern Scandinavian countries are aware that the official statistics underrepresent actual consumption. Sweden estimates that actual consumption may be as much as 40%–50% higher than official data indicate. This is seen as a result of their high taxes on alcohol which set the price far above other European countries, along with the tradition of home-made vodka and very long unpatrolled coast lines.

Also per capita consumption is based on the entire population, rather than those 15 and older, which is sometimes termed the "drinking population." So if a country has a larger proportion of children than another, that leads to greater underestimates of adult consumption.

Source: Based on *World Drink Trends, 2004.* International Beverage Consumption and Production Trends, Produktschap Voor Gedistilleerde Dranken, NTC Publications Ltd. This and additional information on international comparisons can be found on the website of Alcohol Advisory Council of New Zealand. <www.alcohol.org.nz>

apply to drinking and other drug use as much as to other customs. Cultures vary in attitudes toward substance use, as they differ in the sports they like or what they eat for breakfast.

Virtually all societies have alcohol. At the same time, there are some dramatic differences among societies in terms of attitudes, drinking patterns, and the kinds of problems associated with alcohol use. Several distinctive drinking patterns and related attitudes toward alcohol have been identified. The orientation that predominates in a culture or a cultural subgroup was, and in certain cases still is, thought to be influential in determining that group's rate of alcoholism. One such attitude toward drinking is *total abstinence,* as is seen among Muslims and Mormons. With drinking forbidden, the chances of alcohol dependence are almost nil. Expectedly, these groups as a whole have very low rates of alcoholism. However, there is an interesting twist, as we'll see later, about what happens when members leave their group.

Another cultural attitude toward alcohol promotes *ritual use.* Drinking is primarily connected to religious practice, ceremonies, and special occasions. Any heavy drinking in other contexts is frowned on. When drinking is tied to social occasions, with the emphasis on social solidarity and camaraderie, it is termed *convivial use.* Finally, there is *utilitarian use,* in which the society allows people to drink for their own personal reasons—to meet their own needs—for example, to relax, to forget, or to chase a hangover. Rates of alcohol dependence are highest where utilitarian use is dominant.

Differences among nations are growing less marked. Italy has adopted the cocktail party; America has taken on France's wine habit. Nonetheless, a look at some of the differences between the traditional French and Italian drinking habits which persisted through World War II and the 1950s shows that cultural attitudes toward the use of alcohol can influence the rate of alcohol dependence. Both France and Italy are wine-producing countries—France is first in the world, Italy second. Both earn a substantial part of their revenue from the production and distribution of wine, yet the incidence of alcohol dependence in Italy a generation ago was less than one-fifth that of France.

Traditionally in France there were no controls on excessive drinking. Indeed, there was no such thing as excessive drinking. Wine was publicly advertised as good for the health—credited with promoting gaiety, optimism, and self-assurance. It was seen as a useful or an indispensable part of daily life. Drinking in France was a matter of social obligation; a refusal to drink was met with ridicule, suspicion, and contempt. It was not uncommon for the French to have a little wine with breakfast, to drink small amounts all morning, to have half a bottle with lunch, to sip all afternoon, to have another half bottle with dinner, and to nip until bedtime, consuming 2 liters or more a day. People did get drunk. On this schedule, drunkenness would not always show up in drunken behavior. The body, however, was never entirely free of alcohol. Even people who never showed open drunkenness could have withdrawal symptoms and even DTs when they abstained. The habit, and the social atmosphere that permitted it, seemed to be facilitating factors in the high rate of alcoholism in France.

During the same period Italy, on the other hand, which had the second-highest wine consumption in the world, consumed only half of what was consumed in France. Italy had a low rate of alcoholism on a world scale. The average Italian didn't drink all day, but only with noon and evening meals. One liter a day was the accepted amount, and

FOCUS ON . . .

Alcohol Use in Developing Countries

As noted in the discussion of cultural influences, differences between cultures are not as marked as was once the case. Any number of factors are credited with blurring national boundaries—the emergence of the Internet, Coca-Cola, the rise in international travel, the youth culture and pop music, the formation of the European Union, the film industry, the rise of multinational corporations. A related but little discussed phenomenon is the changes in alcohol use taking place in developing countries. Cultural stress and social change is especially striking in these societies. Nowhere in the world are the changes around alcohol use potentially more disruptive or occurring more rapidly.

By way of background: A 1998 report of the World Bank indicates that globally, 1.3 billion people subsist on less than $1 (U.S.) per day, and this number is growing. Forty-two percent live in south Asia, 16% in Sub-Saharan Africa, and 12% in Latin America. The social disparities between developing and developed countries are growing. While there are considerable differences between developing societies, there are several common features. Typically an elite class governs the country, with the bulk of the population poor and living in slums and shantytowns, or eking out a livelihood in the countryside. Rapid urbanization has led to megacities, urban areas with concentrated poverty, uncontrolled sprawl, congestion, and pollution. Nonetheless, even with the migration to cities, except for Latin America, the bulk of people in developing countries continue to live in rural areas. The percentage is 70% in China, 73% in India, and 69% in sub-Saharan Africa. Everywhere unemployment is high.

The monumental social change inevitably involves changing identities for individuals, families, and communities. With migration, the traditional networks of mutual obligation and traditional customs are strained. Traditional roles, defined by gender, kinship, and age are evolving. Traditional drinking patterns too are changing. These changes are the subject of a major report, *Alcohol in Developing Societies: A Public Health Approach,* undertaken by the Finnish Foundation for Alcohol Studies and sponsored by the World Health Association.

The following are some of the significant findings:

- Most societies have a tradition of alcohol production that extends back in time to before the modern eras. While there is enormous variety in customs, for the most part cultures associate drinking with sociability, with the effects on mood and state of mind probably being the most valued aspects of drinking.
- Traditional beverages typically have had a lower alcohol content than western beverages.
- In general, adults in developing countries are more likely to abstain from drinking than in developed countries. And commonly women are nondrinkers outside of Western societies.

	Lifetime or Last Year Abstainers		Current Drinkers	
Country	% Male	% Female	% Male	% Female
India (1980)	42%	98%	58%	2%
China (1993)	17	74	82	26
Seychelles (1989)	25	71	75	26
Chile (1996)	23	56	77	44
Namibia (1998)	39	53	61	47
Thailand (1992)	30	55	71	46
Bolivia (1993)	42	68	23	52
United States (2000)*	68	41	32	59

- In virtually all traditional cultures, with economic development alcohol ceases being a cottage industry, or a home-produced or communally produced product. It becomes a commodity. Alcohol is sold, rather than being distributed through trade or as a gift.

Source: Room R, Jernigan D, Carlini-Marlott B, Gureje O, Makela K, Marshall M, et al. *Alcohol and the Developing World: A Public Health Perspective.* Hakapaino, Finland: Finnish Foundation for Alcohol Studies, 2002.

*Substance Abuse and Mental Health Services Administration. *National Household Survey on Drug Abuse: Main Findings 2000.* Rockville MD: Substance Abuse and Mental Health Services Administration, 2000.

- Industrially produced beers replace those made in the community, especially in Africa. Commercial beers gain market share on the basis of prestige and promotion, even though they are more expensive. A few examples: In the early 1970s, Carlsberg had 5% of the beer market in Malaysia; by the late 1990s, it had grown to 65%. European-style malt beverages represented 9% of South Africa's market in 1970; by 1996 it had grown to 45%. During the same period, the traditional sorghum beer fell from 50% to 20%.
- Multinational corporations are gaining an increasing share of the beer market. While possibly industrial production is safer, no research has verified this. Breweries are built by the multinationals in the developing country. Large-scale industrial breweries result in employment losses, especially among women, for whom cottage-produced beer was a major source of employment. For governments a major attraction of industrial-produced alcohol is the greater ease of taxing. A major problem associated with industrial style Western production is the increase in consumption which accompanies advertising and promotion.
- Many traditional societies have a drinking pattern that includes episodes of intoxication. However, these tend to be tied to community-wide special occasions that occur infrequently, have understood rules, and might be viewed as sanctioned time out. So for the most part the intoxication is neither disruptive nor causes significant problems for the individual or the community. An illustration from Zimbabwe:

  > Zimbabwean women by tradition brewed a cloudy or opaque beer made from sorghum or maize for ceremonies, spirit-medium celebrations, or the culmination of community efforts like planting and harvesting. Brewing took more than a week, and when it was ready, it had to be drunk promptly, or it would sour to the point of being undrinkable.
  >
  > During a "beer-drink," other tasks were set aside. Drinking to intoxication, but without complete loss of self-control, was a customary pleasure. The community suffered little harm from it, because it happened during a time regulated by tradition, insulated from work and other responsibilities. Made from sorghum, and averaging 3% alcohol, the beer also had some nutritional value.

- Specific, socially defined drinking styles tend to persist even when the circumstances change. The old style is transferred into the new context, which may lead to problems. If intoxication was part of the traditional, festive, or ceremonial use patterns, with increased frequency of drinking occasions, it looks a lot like binge drinking.

Beyond describing the changes taking place in alcohol use, the *Report* also identifies a variety of steps that can be taken in the arena of health and social policy, at the local, regional, national, and international levels.

anything over that was considered excessive. There was no social pressure for drinking, as in France. As Jellinek said, "In France, drinking is a must. In Italy it is a matter of choice." Drunkenness, even mild intoxication, was considered a terrible thing, unacceptable even on holidays or festive occasions. For example, a man with a reputation for boozing would have had a hard time getting along in Italy. He would have had trouble finding a wife. Both she and her parents would have hesitated to consent to a marriage with such a man. His social life would have been hindered, his business put in jeopardy; he would have been cut off from the social interaction necessary for advancement.

Jews historically have had a low rate of alcohol dependence. Jewish drinking patterns are similar to the traditional Italian pattern, bolstered by the restraint of religion. The Irish were more like the French and have had a high incidence of alcohol dependence for many of the same reasons. The Irish had ambivalent feelings toward alcohol and drunkenness, which tended to produce tension and uneasiness. Drinking among the Irish (and other groups with high rates) was largely convivial on the

The Innkeeper loves the drunkard, but not for a Son-in-law.
-Yiddish Proverb

surface, yet purely utilitarian drinking—often lonely, quick, and sneaky—was a tolerated pattern.

What, then, were the specific factors that accounted for the differences? These were obviously not based on abstinence. Among the Italians and Jews, many used alcohol abundantly and yet had a low incidence of dependence. While the attitudes in these cultures have changed over the years, some factors that affect the rates of alcohol dependence still seem to be found in certain groups. Low rates of dependence are found in cultures in which the children are gradually introduced to alcohol in diluted, small amounts, on special occasions, and within a strong, well-integrated family group. Parents who drink a small or moderate amount with meals and who are consistent in their behavior and attitudes set a healthy example. There is strong disapproval of intoxication. It is not socially acceptable, stylish, funny, or tolerated. A positive acceptance of moderate, nondisruptive drinking and a well-established consensus on when, where, and how to drink are evident. Drinking is not viewed as a sign of adulthood or, for men, virility, and abstinence is socially acceptable. It is no more rude to say no to liquor than to a soda. Liquor is viewed as an ordinary thing. No moral importance is attached to drinking or not drinking; it is neither a virtue nor a sin. In addition, alcohol is not seen as the primary focus for an activity; it accompanies, rather than dominates or controls.

High rates of alcohol dependence tend to be associated with the reverse of the patterns just discussed. Wherever there has been little agreement on how to drink and how not to drink, rates of alcohol dependence go up. In the absence of clear, widely agreed-upon rules, whether one is behaving or misbehaving is uncertain. Ambivalence, confusion, and guilt easily can be associated with drinking. Those feelings further compound the problem. Individuals who move from one culture to another are especially vulnerable. Their guidelines may be conflicting, and they are caught without standards to follow. For this reason, individuals who belong to groups that promote abstinence similarly run a very high risk of alcoholism if they do drink. Thus, while Mormons as a group have a low rate of alcoholism, among those raised as Mormons who drink there is a much higher rate.

Again, the research provides insights into the broad determinants for differing rates of alcohol dependence. In many cases the studies traditional practices of specific groups that have changed in the intervening years. For example, French drinking patterns have changed dramatically. Many changes are being attributed to automation and television. The workers in a high tech company are not going to be sipping wine throughout the day, as was the custom of their grandfathers who were manual laborers. The bistro no longer serves as the hub of social life, and the practice of stopping by after work has declined with the advent of television. The French, just like their American counterparts, head home to an evening with the tube—the news, the Monday-night soccer match, the late movies.

Just as cultural differences among groups are becoming less marked, it cannot be assumed that every member of a specific group follows the group norms. Being Jewish is no protection against alcohol problems or alcohol dependence. The historically low rates among Jews may lead to underrecognition and greater stigmatization of those who are alcohol dependent.

Drinking Styles and Alcohol Problems

The focus in this section thus far has been on the effects of culture on alcohol dependence. In addition, attitudes, norms, and drinking patterns are predictive of the occurrence of negative consequences arising from alcohol use. These attitudes, norms, and drinking patterns include the following:

- Solitary drinking
- Overpermissive norms of drinking
- Lack of specific drinking norms
- Tolerance of drunkenness
- Adverse social behavior tolerated when drinking
- Utilitarian use of alcohol to reduce tension with anxiety
- Lack of ritualized and/or ceremonial use of alcohol
- Alcohol use apart from family and social functions with close friends
- Alcohol use separated from overall eating patterns
- Lack of child socialization into drinking patterns
- Drinking with strangers, which increases violence
- Drinking pursued as recreation
- Drinking concentrated in young males
- A cultural milieu that stresses individualism, self-reliance, and high achievement

Influence of Cultural Subgroups

Beyond the influence of broad-based cultural factors, there has been recent interest in the relative influence of cultural subgroups, such as family or peers, as well as the characteristics of the immediate drinking situation. Not surprisingly, much of this research has focused on adolescents and the factors that promote or protect against alcohol use and abuse. Some of these studies have resulted in some interesting findings. However, although considerable research is being conducted, each study is fairly circumscribed and specific. This body of research has yet to be integrated into a theoretical approach to the influences of the smaller social systems in which we live.

Now is the time for drinking [nunc est bibendum], now is the time to make the earth shake with dancing.
HORACE
(Ode I. 37)

For example, among the research findings of interest, in a group of people drinking, the heaviest drinker sets the pace for the others. Thus, how much an individual drinks on a particular occasion is likely to be influenced by the amount consumed by others in the group. Another finding is that adolescent alcohol use increases with perceived access to alcohol and the perceived lack of degree of adult supervision. If one were to extrapolate from the broad cultural norms, one might reasonably suspect that, when alcohol use is introduced in the home, this provides a protective factor. However, some research has not supported that assumption. To the contrary, adolescents who are introduced to alcohol in the home are more likely than other adolescents to use alcohol in unsupervised settings. The researchers note that further study is required to examine whether later unsupervised use is an across-the-board phenomenon or is associated with different ways in which alcohol use is introduced. Having a glass of wine with a family meal may be quite different from a father and daughter each having a beer while watching a televised football game.

Legal Sanctions and Approaches

The focus thus far has been on the unwritten rules that govern drinking behavior and that influence the rates of alcohol problems and alcohol dependence. How about the rules incorporated into law that govern use and availability? The evidence shows that these can play a significant role. Think back to this nation's experience of Prohibition. On one level, Prohibition can only be described as a fiasco. It did little to abolish problems associated with alcohol use, and it is credited with introducing other social problems, which resulted from bootlegging and the illegal market for alcohol. On the other hand, with the lowering of consumption there was a marked reduction in the prevalence of alcoholism. Death from cirrhosis during Prohibition declined.

Short of Prohibition, there are significant ways society can influence the use of alcohol. The common denominator involves laws that limit access to alcohol. A major factor influencing access is price. As the price of alcoholic beverages increases, people drink less. The group that is most responsive to price changes are moderate drinkers, as opposed to light or heavy drinkers. Presumably, light drinkers use alcohol so infrequently that it is not a significant part of the their household budget. Also, for them drinking tends to be tied to special occasions, such as an anniversary dinner, a retirement party, or a family reunion. For example, if you drink only once a month, even if the price doubles that isn't going to have a big impact on your pocketbook. However, for the moderate drinker, as the price of alcohol increases there are occasions when a soda will do just as well, or a cup of coffee becomes a substitute for a beer. Even heavy drinkers, who tend to give up almost anything before sacrificing the alcohol, are not wholly indifferent to price. A significant relationship has been found between the rate of cirrhosis and the level of liquor taxes. The level of taxation has also been found to have a small but significant impact on rates of violent crime. As consumption declines, the rates of rape, assault, and robbery go down.

The Last Straw

New Hampshire's budget woes have not yet set the masses marching in the streets. Warnings that our schoolchildren will be deprived have not done it. Warnings that a student's costs for attending the University of New Hampshire will rise have not done it. Warnings that there will be less treatment for the mentally ill have not done it. Warnings that there will be reduced counseling services for the troubled have not done it. Warnings that there will not be enough manpower to ensure pure water supplies have not done it. Warnings that law enforcement officials may not be able to hold down the crime rate have not done it. But now you better batten down the hatches and keep your riot shields handy. This week there was a headline that said, "LIQUOR STORES THREATENED BY BUDGET." That'll do it.

Editorial that appeared in *The Valley News,* Lebanon, New Hampshire, in September 1977, after the New Hampshire legislature and governor had failed to adopt a budget for the state.

Despite the fact that taxation can be a potent means of influencing alcohol use, and despite the fact that there is a growing concern about the problems associated with alcohol, since the early 1950s, the tax rate on alcohol has been declining. In 1954, the average tax—the total of federal, state, and local taxes—was about 50% of the cost of the alcohol, before taxes were added. By the early 1980s, that tax rate had been halved. In 2000, allowing for inflation the average tax was only one-third of what it was in the 1950s. By way of contrast, in Sweden taxes have historically been imposed according to alcohol content. The tax on vodka is 90% of the retail price. One of the concerns in Sweden is that, as a result of its membership in the European Economic Union, it will no longer be able to independently set taxes on alcohol and keep the price high by taxing imports of alcohol produced in other member countries.

Beyond tax policy, there are other legal approaches to dealing with alcohol issues. One way is to restrict access by restricting sales hours for package stores and corner convenience stores. One example is Alaska's local option laws. Concerned about the high rate of death and injury resulting from alcohol use in native villages, the state allows individual native villages to set their own laws. These cover the sale, importation, and possession of alcohol. Rates of injury, homicide, and suicide have dropped markedly in response to the limitations on access. The same approach has been used in inner-city neighborhoods. Community groups have made efforts to reduce the number of alcohol outlets. Research has demonstrated that, in reducing the availability of alcohol, there is also a reduction in hospitalizations for alcohol-related problems.

Another legal measure that can have an impact on alcohol use is related to regulations on advertising. An interesting effort to reduce advertising was an amendment introduced into the U.S. Senate. It would have disallowed advertising expenses by the alcohol industry as tax deductions. In the words of the sponsor, Senator Robert Byrd of West Virginia, "This is not the introduction of a 'sin tax,' but rather an end to a 'sin subsidy' that has left American taxpayers subsidizing alcohol advertising and picking up the tab for the high costs imposed on society by alcohol consumption."

The party line of the alcohol beverage industry is that advertising does not influence whether or not people drink. Rather, the impact of advertising is seen as influencing the selection of a particular beverage or brand. To use advertising jargon, the goal of advertising is to increase market share; however, research suggests that this is not quite the case. As advertising increases, so does the level of consumption. One question of public policy is how to restrict advertising. It has been suggested that a complete ban will simply lead to other avenues to promote sales. Counteradvertising is suggested as one potential step. This, too, raises some interesting policy questions. The federal government committed $1 billion for a 5-year media blitz that continued through 2002. This campaign was orchestrated by the "Partnership for a Drug-Free America." Other

Gentlemen, our business plan is simple. We're going to develop a wine cooler laced with nicotine and market it on nonsmoking airplane flights.

major partners were the alcohol and tobacco industries. Interestingly, this campaign, in focusing on illicit drugs, ignored the drugs of choice among American teens—alcohol and nicotine. The question needs to be considered if this oversight sends an unintended and unfortunate message—drinking and smoking are not as big a deal. Of course, this $1 billion was only a fraction, about 5%, of the advertising and promotion budget of the alcohol and tobacco industries during the same period.

With all of the attention to "the war on drugs," many in the alcohol and public health fields are appalled by the lack of attention alcohol is receiving, despite the fact that its associated problems dramatically overshadow those associated with illicit drug use. There are those, too, who remember the public's response to the counterculture of the 1960s, when psychoactive drug use and experimentation were accepted by a large segment of the adolescent and young adult population. Alcohol was then viewed as far more benign than other drugs. The refrain of parents when confronted with an adolescent's drinking was purportedly a relieved, "Well, at least he isn't on drugs." As a means of reminding everyone that alcohol is a drug, the federal Center for Substance Abuse Prevention (CSAP) adopted the terminology of "alcohol and other drug use," rather than the phrase "alcohol and substance abuse." That was later changed to "alcohol, tobacco, and other drug use," or the acronym ATOD.

Cross-Cultural Comparisons

Often, questions are raised about what lessons might be learned from the experience of other countries with different laws and drinking practices. Frequently queries deal with adolescents, such as the impact of the legal drinking age. The implication is that knowing the answer will give some guidance as to steps that we might take in our country. But we aren't that lucky. Things are just not that simple. The drinking age, in this example, is embedded in a context of cultural attitudes about what represents appropriate and inappropriate use. In addition, it is only one of many laws that influence drinking, such as limits set on the numbers and locations of alcohol outlets, the taxes that thereby influence price, or the laws that govern drinking and driving.

In Europe the legal age to purchase alcoholic beverages is lower than in the United States—typically, between ages 16 and 18. In addition, in many countries there is not a single legal drinking age. It can vary by the setting, such as stores versus restaurants; by the type of beverages; and by the alcohol content. Table 5.2 lists the legal drinking ages in various countries.

Even when we know the legal age for purchase in a particular country, we need to be cautious regarding quick comparisons. Having a legal age for purchase on the books doesn't mean that it is enforced with the same rigor as occurs in the United States. While hard for Americans to appreciate, legal drinking age simply isn't as important elsewhere as it is in the United States. The differences in language indicate this. In the

Table 5.2 Legal Ages for Purchase of Alcohol

Country	Purchasing Age
Austria	age for drinking in public varies by state
	age 18, spirits (9 states)
	age 16, wine/beer (8 states)
	age 15 (other states)
Belgium	age 16
Denmark	age 15 in shops
	age 18 in restaurants and bars
Finland	age 20, over 2.2% alcohol content
	age 18, = 2.2% alcohol
France	age 16
Germany	age 16, beer and wine
	age 18, spirits
Greece	age 18 for purchase in public places
Ireland	age 18
Italy	age 16
Luxembourg	age 16
Netherlands	age 16, beer and wine
	age 18, spirits
Norway	age 18, wine and beer
	age 20, spirits
Portugal	age 16
Spain	age 16 for most areas
	age 18 in the Basque region
Sweden	age 18 in restaurants and grocery stores ("medium strength")
	age 20 in state-run liquor stores no age restriction for light beer, 2.25% alcohol content
United Kingdom	age 16 in pubs and restaurants with meals
	age 18 for other purchase

Source: EuroCare, an organization comprised of members of the European Union directed to alcohol issues and problems. Compiled by data provided by member nations. See EuroCare's website, which provides alcohol-related data, reports, and policy statements. The website address is www.eurocare.org.

United States we refer to the "legal drinking age"; in Europe the reference is to the "legal age for purchase." Other countries are a bit befuddled at times by the extent to which we in the United States are so caught up with drinking age. While our mind-set may be a mystery to them, the reverse is equally true. The following is a good example. A study was conducted in Switzerland on adolescents' ability to purchase alcoholic beverages in bars and restaurants. In 4 out of 5 attempts, 13- and 15-year-old boys were able to purchase beer or pastis, an aniseed-flavored aperitif. In Switzerland the minimum age to purchase beer is 16 and for pastis is 18. Researchers who were observing these transactions noted that "the time needed to refuse orders appeared to be a big factor in making these sales." This seemed to them a reasonable explanation. This demonstrates how much culture influences how we understand the "facts." In the United States, there would be few researchers and even fewer state liquor control board investigators who would consider "being busy" an acceptable reason not to card people. There was another part of the paper that was telling for the purpose of this discussion. Follow-up interviews with the bar and tavern owners and personnel found that only 17% knew the correct minimum legal ages for purchasing and consuming alcoholic beverages. For those of us who live in a country where seemingly every teen, every parent, and every bartender knows the legal drinking age, the more casual, from our point of view, attitude of the Swiss is difficult to imagine.

Any perceived casual attitude of the people in European countries regarding age for purchase is offset by very strict laws in other areas. The most dramatic difference is around drinking and driving. In most European countries a BAC of 0.05 is the cut-off for driving while intoxicated; penalties tend to be more harsh than in the United States. Take Sweden, for example. In 1990, Sweden lowered its level for impaired driving from 0.05 to 0.02. (This is the same level as is being promoted in the United States for those under age 21, a level referred to as "zero tolerance"—no alcohol use if driving.) The penalties for drinking and driving in Sweden are linked to the BAC. Lesser offenses are for BACs of between 0.02 and 0.10; more serious offenses are for BACs above 0.10. Lesser offenses lead to fines and license suspensions lasting anywhere from 6 months to 1 year. The driver also has to see a physician and have a liver enzyme test, which provides some indication of a history of heavy use. A physician visit and laboratory tests are required when a driver applies for license restoration. Restoration of the license is conditional, with further medical evaluations required, in 6 and 12 months. Any evidence of heavy drinking results in either a continued revocation of driving privileges or rerevocation. For more serious offenses, a BAC above 0.10, there are prison terms as well as fines in about half of all cases. (Prior to 1990, prison terms were virtually routine for all serious offenses. The changes in the law were made in part to reduce prison costs.) For serious offenders, regaining one's driving license is likely to be accompanied by a number of restrictions, as well as the required medical evaluation. Driving may be limited to essential purposes, such as transportation to work, or may be allowed only on weekdays, or no driving may be allowed after 9 P.M.

Barrow, in northern Alaska with 4,000 residents, over half of whom are Inuit, has a high rate of alcohol-related problems. Over a several year period, a series of local votes were held to decide whether to ban the importation and possession of alcoholic beverages. In the 12 months starting November 1993, the year prior to the first ban, 90 of the approximately 2,000 outpatient visits per month to the local hospital were documented in the patient encounter as alcohol-related. After alcohol intoxication/detoxification, the most common diagnoses in this group of alcohol-related diagnoses were trauma, medical/gastrointestinal problems, withdrawal, suicide attempts, and family violence.

The alcohol ban was repealed in October 1995, but reimposed six months later in March 1996. Changes in the availability of alcohol have had an immediate impact on health care utilization. The alcohol-related outpatient visits to the hospital fell from 90 per month before the first ban to 15 during the first ban. When the ban was repealed the rate rose to 60 per month, and fell again to 17 per month after the ban was reimposed. Admissions to the local detoxification facility also fell dramatically during the two bans. While the number of women seeking help for violence at a women's shelter did not appear to be changed during the bans, there was a decrease in the severity of domestic violence.

From: Room R, Jernigan D, Carlini-Marlatt B, Gureje O, Makela K, Marshall M, et al. *Alcohol and the Developing World: A Public Health Perspective.* Hakapaino, Finland: Finnish Foundation for Alcohol Studies, 2002. p. 200.

Table 5.3 The Social Impact of Alcohol Policy Changes

Country/Date/Policy Change	Change in Total Consumption in Next Year	Change in Alcohol Problems Indicators: Indicator	Change in Consumption
Denmark, 1917	−76%	Cases of DTs	−93%
Huge increase in taxes on spirits, some increase in beer taxes		Chronic alcoholism deaths	−83
Sweden, 1955			
Abolition of *motbok* (alcohol rationing)	+25	Cases of DTs	+438
Finland, 1969			
Beer sold in grocery stores	+46	Deaths from alcohol-specific causes	+58
Russia, 1985–1988			
Multipronged effort to reduce availability	−34	Deaths from alcohol-specific causes, an estimated 1.5 million lives saved*	−54

Source: Room R. Alcohol Policy Effectiveness in: *Strategic Task Force on Alcohol.* Department of Health & Children, Dublin, Ireland, 2000.
*Newstov AV. Alcohol-related human losses in Russia in the 1980s and 1990s. *Addiction* 97(11):1413–1425, 2002. (42 refs.)

Do these laws have an impact? In 1996, Sweden, with a population of slightly over 8 million, had a total of 30 alcohol-related fatalities. Alcohol is implicated in only 4.8% of all driving fatalities, a rate about 7 times less than in the United States. But here, too, there are other differences. For young Swedes, beer is the most popular alcoholic beverage, as is true in the United States. But it is estimated that 60% of the beer is consumed as part of meals, rather than at parties, or outings, or, to use the American phrase, when "going out drinking."

There are a few natural occasions when it is possible to gain some insights into the impact of a particular legal approach. These occur at a time when there is an important shift in public policy or social circumstances. Several examples are presented in Table 5.3.

In our country, such opportunities were provided with the advent of the rise in drinking age. One can compare the differences in drinking among different age groups and the differences in associated problems, such as DWI, before and after the law change. Yes, there was less drinking and there were fewer accidents when the legal age was raised. Even here other factors are at work. For example, changes in laws are generally accompanied by publicity, stricter enforcement, and more visible law enforcement. As a consequence, there is less inclination to think that one might "get away with it."

The most dramatic and recent examples of the impact of legal changes on drinking practices and associated problems are from the former Soviet

Union and Soviet-bloc countries during the 1980s and 1990s. For example, in the early 1980s, when martial law was established in Poland, vodka was rationed, leading to a decline in drinking and alcohol problems. Not many years later, between 1988 and 1991, the import taxes were abolished and millions of liters of very cheap alcohol were imported in what was known in Poland as "the schnapps-gate affair." Consumption quickly matched earlier levels. In the Soviet Union in the mid-1980s, Gorbachev implemented a far-ranging anti-alcohol campaign. Almost overnight, breweries were converted into manufacturing plants for fruit juices. One innovation was the introduction of replaceable caps for vodka bottles. Previous to that, fifths of vodka produced for domestic consumption had only a foil cover, which was peeled off. Why would one need a cap that could be replaced on a bottle? Typically, a fifth of vodka would be consumed at one sitting. With this array of reforms, there was a marked decline in drinking and its related problems. Between 1985 and 1988, there was a 34% decline in consumption, and deaths from alcohol-specific causes decreased by over half, by 54%.

The decline in consumption was short-lived. By the 1991 breakup of the Soviet Union, alcohol production, both legally and through black-market/private initiatives, and consumption levels had returned to their earlier levels. Several years later, due to an overproduction of alcohol, there was a new development—vodka was being sold in paper cups from kiosks on the street. The heavier drinking, combined with the social upheaval that accompanied the dissolution of the Soviet Union, with the accompanying loss of jobs, the loss of pensions, and a decline in health care system, resulted in a dramatic decline in life expectancy. From 1992 to 1994, there was a 4.4-year decline in life expectancy for men, and 2.6 year decline among women. The decline in the expected life span was most significant for those in midlife, the very group with the highest drop and subsequent rise in drinking. And, life expectancy continues downward. The rate of suicide has skyrocketed, to one of the highest in the world. Between 1990 and 1999, the homicide rate increased 82%, to a rate that is 20% higher than in western Europe. Alcohol is implicated in all of this. Of those convicted of homicide, 80% were intoxicated at the time of the crime. Victims too are usually intoxicated. Add to this the rapidly rising opiate problem and an AIDS rate that may soon approximate the highest rates in Africa. The net result: the Russian population is shrinking by 750,000 annually.

An examination of the Soviet-Russian anti-alcohol initiatives also demonstrates the potential for unintended and unanticipated consequences. When alcohol availability was limited by Gorbachev, there was a sudden shortage of sugar, presumably arising from the home production of distilled spirits. This is certainly consistent with the American experiment with Prohibition. But there were also reforms with unforeseen consequences. One strategy to reduce the consumption of vodka—the most popular drink—was to introduce wines and other beverages with a lower alcohol content. Vodka had never been a woman's drink. With the introduction of other alcoholic beverages, drinking among women rose markedly. Along with that, there was a corresponding sharp rise in fetal alcohol syndrome (FAS). Women had tended not to drink vodka, and certainly not in the traditional Russian drinking style. The common drinking pattern in all of Eastern Europe, including Russia and Finland, is very heavy drinking at one sitting. We would term it "binge drinking." There it has no special name; it is simply drinking. To the extent that women not only increased consumption but also adopted the standard drinking patterns, the risk of FAS rose accordingly. Recall that the risks to the fetus increase with the number of incidents of heavy drinking. So even with the same level of total consumption, more moderate drinking on more occasions poses less danger to the fetus than fewer drinking occasions but with greater intake per occasion.

Cultural Influences on Recovery

A classic essay, "The Cybernetics of 'Self': A Theory of Alcoholism," while not addressing the causes of alcoholism per se, provides an interesting hypothesis on the potential impact of cultural orientation on recovery. It provides an insight into the cultural reasons that abandoning alcohol is so difficult for the alcohol dependent.

The essay's author, Gregory Bateson, points out that Western and Eastern cultures differ significantly in the way they view the world. Western societies focus on the individual. The tendency of Eastern cultures is to consider the individual in terms of the group or in terms of one's relationships. To point out this difference, consider how you might respond to the question "Who is that?" The Western way to answer is to respond with the person's name, "That's Eric Jones." The Eastern response might be "That's my neighbor's oldest son." The latter answer highlights the relationship among several persons.

One of the results of Westerners' zeroing in on the individual is an inflation of the sense of "I." We think of ourselves as wholly separable and independent. Also, we may not recognize our relationships to other persons and things and the effects of our interactions. According to Bateson, this can lead to problems. One example he cites is our relationship to the physical environment. If nothing else, the ecology movement has taught us that the old rallying cry of "man against nature" does not make sense. We cannot beat nature. We win—that is, we survive—only if we allow nature to win some rounds, too.

How does this fit in with alcohol? The same kind of thinking is evident. The individual who drinks expects, and is expected, to be the master of alcohol. If problems develop, the individual can count on hearing "Get it together." The person is supposed to fight the alcohol and win. There's a challenge. Who can stand losing to a "thing"? So the person tries various tactics to gain the upper hand. Even if the individual quits

drinking for a while, the competition is on: the person versus it. To prove who's in charge, sooner or later the drinker will have "just one." If disaster doesn't strike then, the challenge continues to have "just one more." Sooner or later, the pattern of heavy drinking is reinstated.

Bateson asserts that successful recovery requires a change of world view by the person in trouble with alcohol. The Western tendency to see the self (the I) as separate and distinct from, and often in combat with, alcohol (or anything else) has to be abandoned. The alcoholic must learn the paradox of winning through losing, the limitations of the I and its interdependence with the rest of the world. He continues with examples of the numerous ways in which AA fosters just this change of orientation.

In the Twenty-First Century

In terms of social policy, in our country, we cannot expect to have all of the approaches described earlier implemented as one piece of legislation. American society tackles policy concerns in a more incremental fashion. A variety of steps have been taken that reflect efforts to moderate drinking patterns.

In the United States, for the most part, the laws regulating alcohol use are set by the states. This includes defining by law what constitutes intoxication, as well as setting the legal drinking age. States vary, as well, on when, where, and what a citizen may drink within their borders. And some states even vary from county to county—in Texas, for example. Laws range from dry, to beer only, to anything at all but only in private clubs, to sitting down but not walking with drink in hand, ad infinitum. States also provide a role for communities in establishing local ordinances, such as those governing the location, number, and hours of operation of alcohol retail outlets and bars.

The differences between states have significantly narrowed in response to the federal government's use of financial incentives, as well as changes in public perceptions. The uniform increase of the drinking age to 21 years was championed by many. The hope was that it would be an effective measure to reduce alcohol-related highway fatalities among young people. But it was also resisted on several grounds. Some cited the fact that the age of majority is 18 years. College administrators, despite their recognition of problem drinking on campus, were concerned about living with a law that was so out of sync with the behavior of their students. Ultimately the states' changes in drinking age laws were in no small part prompted by a federal incentive—the tying of federal highway funds to a state's enactment of a 21-year-old drinking age. States are similarly being encouraged to lower the standard for legal intoxication to a BAC of 0.08. Beyond this, states have begun to enact zero tolerance laws. For those under age 21, these laws establish a very low BAC, from 0.0 or 0.02, as the level for defining driving under the influence. In addition, all states have established BAC limits for operating motor boats, and some have extended these to other recreational vehicles such as snowmobiles.

There have been other governmental initiatives that would have been highly improbable a generation ago, such as the requirement that alcohol beverages have warning labels. This was accomplished despite the presence of a highly organized and well-financed alcohol beverage industry lobby. Such steps require broad public support rather than advocacy by a small, highly vocal minority. Regulatory agencies at the state level are having a major influence. Again, sparked by a receipt of federal monies, efforts to monitor the ability of underage people to purchase alcohol and cigarettes are being monitored. Both the failure to ask for proof of legal age and the sale of products to minors have consequences ranging from fines to suspension of licenses. Our society is far beyond not bothering to check for infractions or simply providing a slap on the wrist if a violation occurs.

With respect to drinking and driving, the changes are being maintained. Driving fatalities attributable to alcohol continue to decline and have been more than cut in half from the high in 1977. The efforts of community- and state-level organizations—such as MADD (Mothers Against Drunk Driving) and its derivative, SADD (Students Against Drunk Driving)—continue. In addition, community-level coalitions have emerged, sparked by federal and state funding of prevention programs. Lobbying for stricter penalties for drinking and driving offenses has continued. The concept of the designated driver clearly has taken hold. Advertising campaigns to combat drinking and driving are now commonplace, at least at holiday times. All of this has had an impact.

The legal system also has both spurred and reflected changes in society. One influence has been the issue of legal liability and the suits that can be filed for compensation when death or injury occurs as a result of drinking. There long have been Dram Shop laws, which hold a tavern owner or barkeeper liable for serving an obviously intoxicated customer. Until relatively recently these were rarely invoked, but this is no longer the case. Liability also has been extended to hosts and to those who might allow an intoxicated person to use their car. The issue of liability, particularly in light of higher legal drinking ages, has prompted college campuses to pay attention to issues of alcohol use. Similarly, parents and other adults are being held accountable for serving alcohol to minors at private parties.

Concern about liability has touched the workplace as well. Companies have abandoned hosting parties where the alcohol flows freely, particularly on company time. If drinking takes place at work-sponsored activities, during the time for which an employee is being paid, any alcohol-impaired employee injured on the way home is a candidate for worker's compensation. In addition, the company can anticipate a lawsuit. Other changes in business practices have resulted from a small change in the Internal Revenue Code. The 3-martini lunch went by the boards when the IRS no longer allowed companies to write off the purchase of alcohol as a legitimate business expense. This is a good example of how social change occurs. Small changes, such as alteration of the

tax code, affect behavior, which in turn modifies perceptions or allows alternative views to be expressed. The 3-martini lunch not only does not qualify as a business expense; it no longer is viewed as a requisite for doing business and, in most quarters, is considered inappropriate.

As changes have been prompted by governmental action, they have been reinforced and mirrored by the actions of private groups who also have the capacity to influence patterns of alcohol use. For example, in professional and collegiate sports, drunken fans were long seen as an inevitable part of the game. At professional sports events, drinking in the stands is spurred by beer sales at the concession stand, not an insignificant source of revenue for professional teams. Now professional teams have made efforts to sharply curtail drinking. In some instances drinking has been entirely banned in stadiums. In both professional and college stadiums there are now blocks of family seats, where no alcohol consumption is allowed. In addition, advertising at sports events is now being called into question. Back in 1990, the NCAA limited the amount of advertising by beer companies during television broadcasts of its games.

Attitudes toward alcohol use continue to be varied. In some quarters, it is quite "in," and sophisticated to drink. In others, people truly can take it or leave it. In others, it is frowned on. Despite the considerable changes in laws and public policy, our contradictory and ambiguous views toward alcohol remain embodied in our liquor laws. Regardless of concern about adolescent use, the law implies that on that magical twenty-first birthday, individuals are treated as if they suddenly know how to handle alcohol appropriately. As the rhetoric of "just say no" is applied to alcohol, as it has been in federally funded campus prevention efforts and the growing prevention efforts among teens, it skirts the issue of alcohol's legal status for those 21 and over. There's no mention of when or under what circumstances it is okay to "say yes."

An approach well established in other countries has barely taken hold in the United States. This is the concept of *harm reduction.* From this perspective the issue is less about whether individuals use or do not use alcohol or other drugs than it is focused on reducing problems associated with use. With respect to intravenous drug use, for example, the emphasis is on taking steps to reduce needle sharing and other activities that will increase the risk of AIDS. In terms of alcohol, examples of harm reduction are efforts to promote designated drivers and efforts to teach teens to recognize alcohol poisonings. In the view of those involved in harm reduction, such efforts should not be seen as condoning IV drug use or as condoning adolescent drinking. What such policies try to reflect is the reality that risky behavior *does* occur. And in light of that reality a harm reduction perspective maintains that it is possible and important to reduce associated risks, even as one simultaneously tries to curb the behavior.

Interestingly there are technologies available that could be viewed as harm reduction at a societal level, rather than as reduction of individual harm. For example, interlock devices can be installed on the cars of those arrested for DWI to prevent the car from being driven. Clearly, these do nothing to alter the individual's drinking pattern, but they do protect the public safety. Another technology available involves skin patches that can detect the presence of any alcohol or other drug use. That isn't all. They can be wired to a small device, similar to a pager, that can electronically transmit a signal to a police station, for example. Thus, there is the potential for identifying anyone convicted of DWI who takes a drink. Strangely, while available and relatively low-cost, these are little used. An important question is why, but the answer is unclear.

As a society we ideally want alcohol without the associated problems. As individuals, what inconveniences and costs are we willing to assume? Will we accept further steps to limit access to alcohol? Would we, for example, accept a ban on package sales after 10 P.M. on the assumption that folks who want to buy alcohol at that hour don't need it? Or how willing are each of us to intervene if confronted by a possible use that presents a threat to public safety? If driving on an interstate highway and witnessing an erratic driver, does it occur to us to telephone the police on a cell phone? Would we make such a call if it required pulling to a rest area to use a pay phone? How likely are we to make the call if it requires exiting the highway to locate a public telephone?

Interestingly, recent surveys show that there is far more support for controls on alcohol use than our current laws suggest. Over 80% of the general public support restrictions on alcohol use in public places, such as parks, beaches, concert venues, and college campuses. Eighty-two percent support increased alcohol taxes, provided the funds are used for treatment or prevention programs. Over 60% support alcohol advertising and promotion restrictions, such as banning billboard advertising, banning promotion at sporting events, and banning liquor and beer advertising on television.

Collectively, will we allocate a reasonable share of the alcohol tax dollar to help the inevitable percentage who get into trouble with the drug? Will treatment of alcohol and other drug problems, in fact, be covered by health insurance in the same fashion as other medical conditions? Will health insurance treat substance abuse in a fashion equivalent to other medical conditions? In light of concern about cost, the question has been raised as to why those who don't need such benefits should be forced to purchase the coverage and be required through their insurance payments to subsidize the treatment of others. Can we resist the "we" versus "they" attitude such discussion implies? It suggests a belief that those with alcohol and/or other drug problems brought on their difficulties themselves. For all the discussion of addictions as a disease, seemingly just below the surface continues to lurk the perception of addictions as immoral, "bad" behavior. The fate of parity bills may be one of the most telling statements of how far we have or have not come in our national understanding of this public health issue.

RESOURCES AND FURTHER READING

Several of these references may appear dated. However, those included are original primary sources—that is, the articles in which the ideas or findings set forth were first introduced in the scientific literature.

Alcohol Epidemiology Program, Wagenaar AC. *Alcohol Policies in the United States: Highlights from the 50 States.* Minneapolis, MN: University of Minnesota, 2000. (40 refs.)

Bales R. Cultural differences in rates of alcoholism. *Quarterly Journal of Studies on Alcohol* 6:489–499, 1946.

Bassett JF, Dabbs JM Jr. Eye color predicts alcohol use in two archival samples. *Personality and Individual Differences* 31(4):535–539, 2001. (12 refs.)

Bateson G. The cybernetics of "self": A theory of alcoholism. *American Journal of Psychiatry* 34:1–18, 1971.

Berman M, Hull T, May P. Alcohol control and injury death in Alaska native communities: Wet, damp and dry under Alaska's local option law. *Journal of Studies on Alcohol* 61(2):311–319, 2000. (24 refs.)

Bierut LJ, Dinwiddie SH, Begleiter H, Crowe RR, Hesselbrock V, Nurnberger JI Jr., et al. Familial transmission of substance dependence: Alcohol, marijuana, cocaine, and habitual smoking: A report from the Collaborative Study on the Genetics of Alcoholism. *Archive of General Psychiatry* 55(11):982–988, 1998. (28 refs.)

Blum K, Braverman ER, Holder JM, Lubar JF, Monastra VJ, Miller D, et al. Reward deficiency syndrome: A biogenetic model for the diagnosis and treatment of impulsive, addictive and compulsive behaviors. *Journal of Psychoactive Drugs* 32(Supplement):1–112 (entire issue), 2000. (636 refs.)

Bowers BJ. Applications of transgenic and knockout mice in alcohol research. *Alcohol Research & Health* 24(3): 175–184, 2000. (38 refs.)

DiCarlo ST, Powers AS. Propylthiouracil tasting as a possible genetic association marker for two types of alcoholism. *Physiology and Behavior* 64(2):147–152, 1998. (40 refs.)

Elster J, Skog OJ, eds. *Getting Hooked: Rationality and Addiction.* Cambridge, England: Cambridge University Press, 1999. (Chapter refs.)

Ferguson RA, Goldberg DM. Genetic markers of alcohol abuse (review). *Clinical Chimica Acta* 257(2):199–250, 1997. (232 refs.)

Finn PR, Justus A. Physiological responses in sons of alcoholics. *Alcohol Health and Research World* 21(3):227–231, 1997. (15 refs.)

Giesbrecht N, Greenfield TK. Public opinions on alcohol policy issues: A comparison of American and Canadian surveys. *Addiction* 94(4):521–531, 1999. (30 refs.)

Goodwin DW. Is alcoholism hereditary? *Archives of General Psychiatry* 25:545–549, 1971.

Gruber J, Koszegi B. Is addiction "rational"? Theory and evidence. *Quarterly Journal of Economics* 116(4): 1261–1303, 2001. (40 refs.)

Helzer JE, Canino GJ, eds. *Alcoholism in North America, Europe, and Asia.* New York: Oxford University Press, 1992. (chapter refs.)

Heyman G. An economic approach to animal models of alcoholism. *Alcohol Research & Health* 24(2):132–139, 2000. (29 refs.)

Holder HD, Giesbrecht N, Horverak O, Nordlund S, Norstrom Olsson O, et al. Potential consequences from possible changes to Nordic retail alcohol monopolies resulting from European Union membership. *Addiction* 90(12):1603–1618, 1996. (44 refs.)

Johnson V. *I'll Quit Tomorrow* (rev. ed.). New York: Harper & Row, 1980.

Li T-K, McBride WJ. Pharmacogenetic models of alcoholism (review). *Clinical Neuroscience* 3(3):182–188, 1995. (81 refs.)

Marques PR, Voas RB, Tippetts AS, Beirness DJ. Behavioral monitoring of DUI offenders with the alcohol ignition interlock recorder. *Addiction* 94(12):1861–1870, 1999. (14 refs.)

Maryniak I. Death in Russia. *Index on Censorship* 31(2): 24–29, 2002. (1 ref.)

McCord W, McCord J. Some current theories of alcoholism: A longitudinal evaluation. *Quarterly Journal of Studies on Alcohol* 20:727–749, 1959.

Mennella JA, Garcia PL. Children's hedonic response to the smell of alcohol: Effects of parental drinking habits. *Alcoholism: Clinical and Experimental Research* 24(8):1167–1171, 2000. (28 refs.)

Nemtsov AV. Alcohol-related human losses in Russia in the 1980s and 1990s. *Addiction* 97(11):1413–1425. 2002. (42 refs.)

NIAAA. The genetics of alcoholism. *Alcohol Health and Research World.* 19(3):161–256 (entire issue), 1995.

Noble EP. The D-2 receptor gene: A review of association studies in alcoholism and phenotypes. *Alcohol* 16(1):33–45, 1998. (119 refs.)

Pittman DJ, White HR, eds. *Society, Culture, and Drinking Patterns Reexamined.* New Brunswick, NJ: Rutgers Center of Alcohol Studies, 1991.

Prescott CA, Aggen SH, Kendler KS. Sex differences in the sources of genetic liability to alcohol abuse and dependence in a population-based sample of US twins. *Alcoholism: Clinical and Experimental Research* 23(7):1136–1144, 1999. (63 refs.)

Room R. Alcohol Policy Effectiveness. *Strategic Task Force on Alcohol, May 2002.* Department of Health and Children. Dublin, Ireland, 2000.

Schuckit MA, Edenberg HJ, Kalmijn J, Flury L, Smith TL, Reich T, Bierut L, Goate A, Foroud T. A genome-wide search for genes that relate to a low level of response to alcohol. *Alcoholism: Clinical and Experimental Research* 25(3):323–329, 2001. (32 refs.)

Tatlow JR, Clapp JD, Hohman MM. The relationship between the geographic density of alcohol outlets and alcohol-related hospital admissions in San Diego County. *Journal of Community Health* 25(1):79–88, 2000.

Vaillant G. *The Natural History of Alcoholism, Revisited.* Cambridge, MA: Harvard University Press, 1995.

Wagenaar AC, Harwood EM, Toomey TL, Denk CE, Zander KM. Public opinion on alcohol policies in the United States: Results from a national survey. *Journal of Public Policy* 21(3):303–327, 2000. (47 refs.)

CHAPTER 6

Medical Complications

PART I. ADVICE FOR THE MODERATE DRINKER

Regular alcohol use in moderation, which means no more than 1 to 2 drinks per day, has been shown to have beneficial preventive effects in relation to a number of medical illnesses. These include coronary artery disease and ischemic heart disease; stroke; the development of gallstones and associated gallbladder disease; Type II diabetes; chronic bronchitis; certain types of lymphoma; hypercholestecolemia; and benign prostatic hypertrophy. Accompanying this is the fact that light to moderate drinkers have lower mortality than others in their age group who are either teetotalers or heavy drinkers.

In considering these reported benefits of regular moderate alcohol use, it is important to emphasize the importance of the operative word, "moderate." There are some other caveats. For one, this doesn't mean an average of 1 to 2 drinks and thus saving up several days' quota for a blowout on a Saturday night. Equally important, this beneficial effect is not universal, either. While it probably comes as no great surprise that excessive use of alcohol over a long period can lead to serious problems, what is unfortunately less recognized and appreciated is that, even in moderate amounts, alcohol use can present substantial medical risks for some individuals. There is no set "dose" of alcohol that reliably can be considered safe for people in general or even for any single individual throughout his or her life.

Contraindications to Moderate Use

For some people, in some circumstances, at particular times, what is usually considered moderate alcohol use is too much. The most striking example is the caution against alcohol use during pregnancy. It is becoming more widely appreciated that drinking during pregnancy can cause abnormalities in the infant, a condition called *fetal alcohol syndrome (FAS),* or a less severe condition termed *fetal alcohol effects (FAE).* A woman wishing to conceive should be thoughtful about her drinking. Since many pregnancies are not confirmed until the middle of the first trimester, she might ingest harmful levels of alcohol before being aware of her pregnancy. There are other possible adverse consequences of alcohol use during pregnancy. Moderate alcohol use has been linked to an increase in spontaneous abortions. Drinking as little as 1 drink per day, for a total of 1 ounce of alcohol per day, doubles the risk of spontaneous abortion during the second trimester. Nursing mothers, too, are advised to refrain from alcohol use because alcohol can pass to the infant through breast milk. Though maternal alcohol use while nursing does not appear to affect mental development, infants whose mothers consumed 1 or more drinks per day have been found to have slower rates of motor development.

Even relatively modest alcohol use can create problems for those with cardiac and circulatory problems, such as coronary artery disease and/or congestive heart failure, as well as hypertension. High blood pressure in up to 10% of all cases is believed to be the direct result of alcohol use. For those with established hypertension, alcohol use can make the management and adequate control of blood pressure more difficult. It may also increase the risk for stroke. Moderate drinking also has been found to elevate the level of certain blood fats in individuals (those with Type IV hyperlipoproteinemia).

Others for whom moderate drinking may be unwise include individuals with seizure disorders, diabetes mellitus, gout, osteoporosis, and various skin conditions, including psoriasis, as well as those with gastric and duodenal ulcers. The ways in which alcohol may aggravate these conditions are discussed in Part II of this chapter. Although none of these medical conditions may constitute an absolute contraindication to using alcohol, all fall into the category of relative contraindications. A glass of wine with meals once or twice a week may present no problem, but several drinks before dinner plus wine with the meal or an evening on the town is ill advised. As a general rule, anyone being treated for an acute medical condition ought to inquire about the need to modify temporarily what may be very moderate drinking. In addition to the possibility of alcohol's complicating medical conditions, there is the possibility of it interacting with the medications prescribed to treat them.

Alcohol-Drug Interactions

Alcohol-drug interactions may be the area in which the moderate drinker is potentially most vulnerable to medical problems arising from alcohol use. Alcohol is a drug. When alcohol is taken in combination with many prescribed medications, or over-the-counter or alternative/herbal preparations, there can be undesirable and quite possibly dangerous alcohol-drug interactions. Though these interactions can vary from individual to individual, they depend primarily on the amount of alcohol and type of medication consumed, as well as the person's drinking history. The moderate drinker who has not developed tolerance to alcohol will have a very different response from that of the habitual heavier drinker. In fact, the consequences may be far more serious.

The Basis of Alcohol-Drug Interactions

Two basic mechanisms can explain virtually all alcohol-drug interactions. One is that the presence of alcohol alters the liver's capacity to metabolize other drugs. In the moderate drinker, this system, which metabolizes a variety of other drugs as well as alcohol (see Chapter 3), may be significantly inhibited, or slowed down, in the presence of alcohol. Therefore, drugs ordinarily metabolized by the liver's cytochrome P450 system (known in the past as the microsomal ethanol oxidation system [MEOS]) will not be removed as rapidly or as completely as usual. The result is that these medications will then be present in the body in higher than expected levels. This can result in unexpected toxic effects.

On the other hand, for those with a long history of heavy drinking, alcohol has the opposite effect on the cytochrome P450 system. The activation of this system is enhanced, or speeded up, through a process known as enzyme induction. Thus, certain drugs are removed, or metabolized, more quickly. The medication is removed more rapidly, so its levels in the body are lower than expected or desired. The net effect is that the individual is very likely not receiving the intended therapeutic effects of a given dose of the drug. To compensate for this, it may be necessary to increase the dose of the drug administered to achieve the intended therapeutic effect.

The other major source of difficulty results from so-called additive and/or synergistic effects. Alcohol is a CNS depressant. Other medications may also depress CNS functions. When two depressant drugs are present simultaneously, their combined effects may be equal to or often far greater than would be expected with the sum of the two. It is important to be aware that drugs and alcohol are not metabolized instantaneously. Recall that it takes the body approximately 1 hour to handle one drink (whether the drink is a 12-ounce bottle of beer or a mixed drink with a shot of 80-proof liquor). Therefore, if someone has had several drinks, an hour or two later alcohol will still be in the system. As long as alcohol remains in the body, the potential exists for significant additive effects, even though the other depressant drugs are taken several hours later, or vice versa.

Common Interactions of Medications and Alcohol

Many of the potential interactions of alcohol with some commonly prescribed medications are outlined in Appendix B, although the table in the

FOCUS ON DRUGS

More Than the Sum of the Parts: Alcohol and Cocaine

The combination of alcohol and cocaine is popular among drug users. Those using both drugs report more intense feelings of being high than occur with the use of either alone. In a laboratory setting, there is increased "liking" reported for cocaine when combined with alcohol, even when the actual level of cocaine in the blood is the same. In tandem with this, people feel less impaired than they feel with an equivalent blood alcohol but without cocaine present. They also find that with alcohol present, the coming down from a cocaine high is less uncomfortable. So the combination of the two substances enhances the high, while easing some of the negative aspects of both the cocaine and the alcohol.

At least two physiological factors are at play here: First, in the presence of alcohol, cocaine levels increase by as much as 30%. Presumably this is due to both alcohol and cocaine competing for a finite supply of some of the enzymes required for metabolism. (If the cocaine is taken a half hour after drinking, there is no such effect.) Second, alcohol does not merely delay the metabolism of cocaine, it actually alters the process. In the presence of alcohol, approximately 20% of the cocaine—rather than being metabolized into inert products that are removed from the body—is diverted and transformed into a substance called cocaethylene.[1]

The significance of cocaethylene as a metabolic by-product is that for all practical purposes, cocaethylene is essentially a variant of cocaine. It has the same psychoactive effects. Equally significant, it has a much longer half-life, meaning it remains in the body longer. For the user, the cocaethylene high is indistinguishable from a pure cocaine high. The pleasurable effects associated with cocaine persist, due to the continuing presence of cocaethylene, even after the cocaine itself has been eliminated. From the user's perspective, alcohol acts as an enhancer of the effects of cocaine. It is possible too that cocaethylene binds more strongly to brain receptors, which may contribute to its perceived more pleasurable effect.

Cocaine and alcohol interact in other ways. Among the most significant is the increase in heart rate and blood pressure that occurs with the combination of alcohol and cocaine. And the impact is proportionately greater with higher levels of cocaine. These effects persist for up to two hours. Cocaine and alcohol independently increase heart rate and blood pressure. In turn, the by-product cocaethylene has an even greater effect on heart rate. Cardiac problems are a known complication of acute cocaine use. These are not problems that only accompany long-term cocaine use. It has been estimated that up to 65,000 patients annually are evaluated in hospital emergency rooms for possible heart attacks in the wake of cocaine use. The risk of sudden death is greater among those using alcohol with cocaine than those taking just cocaine. It has been reported that the risk of sudden death is 20 times greater for alcohol and cocaine taken in combination than cocaine alone.

This isn't all. The concurrent use of cocaine and alcohol is also associated with greater levels of violence—whether from severe beatings, to thoughts of homicide or homicidal plans, to threatening others with weapons—than is present with either cocaine or alcohol alone. The combination of the two drugs also seems to increase thoughts of suicide. The basis for this is unclear but is possibly related to the increased impulsivity that accompanies the inhibition of the brain centers that help us keep the lid on. Similarly there is increased incidence

(continued on the next page)

[1]**Metabolism of cocaine.** In the absence of alcohol, cocaine is broken down into two major products. Two versions of the enzyme carboxylesterase accomplish this. One of the metabolic products is benzoylecogine and other is ecgonine methyl ester. These in turn are excreted by the kidneys. The enzymes involved in this process are not exclusively devoted to the metabolism of cocaine. Rather they are involved in the metabolism of a family of compounds known as esters, which are chemically distinguished by the presence of an R-OH in their chemical structure. The carboxylesterase enzymes are found in a number of tissues—heart, stomach, kidney, and colon—but most abundantly in the liver. They are involved in the metabolism of an array of esters; they can be considered as providing the body protection by assisting in the elimination of a variety of foreign substances taken in through the diet or other routes.

In the presence of alcohol, rather than just these two byproducts, an additional byproduct very similar to cocaine itself is produced, cocaethylene. It too remains in the circulation and will need to be metabolized by the carboxylesterase enzymes. (By analogy, cocaine's transformation into cocaethylene is a bit like the person who is recycling at home, throwing a portion of stuff gathered up back into the recycling bin, which means only having to rehandle it later.)

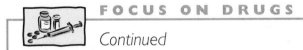

FOCUS ON DRUGS

Continued

of risky sexual activity when both cocaine and alcohol are present, again at a rate greater than for either drug alone.

Polysubstance use is quite common. Of note is that joint cocaine/alcohol dependencies are virtually twice as common as joint opiate-alcohol dependencies. Their respective rates are 62% and 35%. It is presumed that this isn't accidental but due in part to the pharmacological effects of alcohol and cocaine when administered together. While much remains to be learned, it has been questioned whether some of the medical problems that have been attributed to cocaine alone are in fact due to the simultaneous use of alcohol with cocaine. Possibly the alcohol element in the cocaine picture has been ignored for too long, and the fact that at least two-thirds of cocaine users are also abusing alcohol, even if not qualifying for a diagnosis of alcohol dependence, is likely not mere coincidence.

Bailey DN. Cocaethylene: A novel cocaine homolog. *Western Journal of Medicine* 167(1):38–39, 1997. (3 refs.)

Bolla KI, Funderburk FR, Cadet JL. Differential effects of cocaine and cocaine plus alcohol on neurocognitive performance. *Neurology* 54(12): 2285–2292, 2000. (34 refs.)

Harris DS, Everhart ET, Mendelson J, Jones RT. The pharmacology of cocaethylene in humans following cocaine and ethanol administration. *Drug and Alcohol Dependence* 72(2):169–182, 2003. (41 refs.)

Laizure SC, Mandrell T, Gades NM, Parker RB. Cocaethylene metabolism and interaction with cocaine and ethanol: Role of carboxylesterases. *Drug Metabolism and Disposition* 31(1):16–20, 2003. (26 refs.)

McCance-Katz EF, Kosten TR, Jatlow P. Concurrent use of cocaine and alcohol is more potent and potentially more toxic than use of either alone: A multiple-dose study. *Biological Psychiatry* 44(4):250–259, 1998. (42 refs.)

Pennings EJM, Leccese AP, de Wolf FA. Effects of concurrent use of alcohol and cocaine. (review). *Addiction* 97(7):773–783, 2002. (81 refs.)

appendix is not all-inclusive. If a drug is not listed, don't assume that it has no interaction with alcohol. Anyone who uses alcohol and is taking other medications is advised to ask his or her physician or pharmacist specifically about potential alcohol-drug and drug-drug interactions.

Problems Associated with Drinking and Intoxication

Accidents and Injury

Along with alcohol-drug interactions, the other common medical problems associated with alcohol use are accidents and injuries. These are more likely to occur during an intoxicated state because of the nature of alcohol-induced impairment. Judgment is impaired, placing individuals in situations that invite danger. Diminished judgment, along with decreased reaction and response time and poorer coordination and motor skills, leads to a lessened ability to cope with whatever may occur. In addition to injuries' being more common with intoxication, their severity has also been found to rise with the level of impairment. Similarly, other psychoactive substances that affect judgment and motor skills can be contributing factors in alcohol-related accidents.

HIV/AIDS

In the minds of the general public as well as health-care and substance abuse professionals, AIDS is clearly linked with those who use drugs intravenously, a group for whom AIDS is becoming virtually endemic. The dramatic rise of AIDS among intravenous drug users is not based primarily on the pharmacological properties of the drugs but, rather, on the route of administration. Among intravenous drug users, HIV infection is readily transmitted by the common and dangerous practice of sharing needles. Given the multiple problems that accompany chronic drug use, those who are actively using drugs are difficult to influence by informational and preventive efforts.

Within the rapidly growing body of research on AIDS, the relationship of alcohol use and AIDS has also been examined. The ability of chronic alcohol use to suppress the immune system has been clearly established. Even the effects of acute use among those who generally drink moderately have become evident. Pilot experiments with healthy volunteers suggest that a single administration of alcohol equivalent to 0.7 to 3.1 liters of beer (two to eight 12-ounce cans) can have a negative impact on the immune system. Furthermore, these effects may persist for up to 4 days after ingestion. The question this raises is whether casual alcohol consumption can either increase the vulnerability to infection or enhance the progression of latent HIV infection. On behavioral grounds alone, there is a link between intoxication and an increased risk of HIV infection. With intoxication, sexual activity is likely to be more casual and less considered, with sexual partners determined by their availability rather than with the presence of an emotional relationship, and be less likely to involve contraception or safe-sex practices to reduce the risk of sexually transmitted diseases, including HIV infection.

Unexpected and Sudden Natural Deaths

The association between intoxication and unnatural causes of death, such as accident, suicide, and homicide, is described in Chapter 2. Equally as significant is the recent finding of the high prevalence of positive BACs among people who have died suddenly and unexpectedly from natural causes. This finding is based on the determination of the blood alcohol concentration as part of medicolegal autopsies conducted for all natural out-of-hospital deaths occurring during a 1-year period in a large Finnish metropolitan area. For this group of sudden and unexpected deaths, 36% of males and 15% of females had positive blood alcohol levels. The blood alcohol concentration for approximately half of these men and women was 0.15 or greater. Acute consumption of alcohol in nonalcoholics was certified as being a significant contributor in 23% of male and 8% of female sudden, unexpected deaths. For men, acute alcohol use was a contributing factor for 11% of deaths from coronary artery disease, 40% of other heart disease, and 7% for all other diseases. For both sexes the most vulnerable individuals are those in middle age.

Alcohol Use and Exercise

With the increasing interest in fitness and exercise, what are the recommendations for drinking in relation to sports and exercise? Alcohol can affect performance and be the source of potential problems if used immediately before, during, or immediately after exercise. Athletes who release pregame tension with a "few beers" before competition to take care of the jitters may slow reaction time and impair coordination, thus reducing their performance and increasing the risk of injury. Before competition, endurance athletes sometimes "carbohydrate load"—that is, eat extra carbohydrates to increase the glycogen stored in muscles, that serves as a source of energy. They may include beer as part of their precompetition meal. However, beer is a poor source of carbohydrates compared to juices or soda. As for calories, two-thirds of the calories in beer come from the alcohol. Thus they represent "empty calories" with little nutritional value and therefore are a poor energy source. These calories are used as heat and are not available for energy. Besides being a poor source of nutritionally useful carbohydrates, the alcohol can affect heat tolerance and lead to dehydration because of alcohol's inhibition of antidiuretic hormone. Athletes who consume alcohol before a performance are at risk for significant fluid loss. Cardiac arrhythmias, including atrial fibrillation (described below) have been reported in otherwise healthy athletes following consumption of unusually large amounts of alcohol. Hence, the recommendation of sports physicians is not to consume alcohol for 24 hours before competition.

PART II. MEDICAL COMPLICATIONS OF CHRONIC HEAVY ALCOHOL USE

Alcohol dependence is one of the most common chronic diseases in the United States. The prevalence is 10% in the population at large. Untreated, its natural history is a predictable, gradually progressive downhill course. The observable early symptoms and manifestations of the primary disease, alcohol dependence, are largely behavioral and nonphysical. Later in its course, it causes a broad spectrum of secondary medical morbidities and complications involving numerous organ systems. These are associated with a host of physical signs and symptoms. These medical problems have a markedly negative impact on the overall quality of life. In fact, studies have shown that those with long-standing alcohol dependence have a worse quality of life than that reported by a variety of cancer patients.

It is important to emphasize the distinction between the primary disease of alcohol dependence and its later secondary medical complications. Alcohol dependence is one of the most highly treatable of chronic illnesses. If recognized and treated early—before major medical complications have occurred—it may be entirely arrested, and without any

There is this to be said in favor of drinking, that it takes the drunkard first out of society, then out of the world.
EMERSON, 1866

significant long-term sequelae. Successfully treated individuals can function quite normally. Their only long-term limitation is that they cannot use alcohol. Its complications, on the other hand, may be progressive, irreversible, and have a fatal outcome if the underlying alcohol dependence goes untreated.

This section focuses on the later secondary medical complications of alcohol dependence. Because virtually every organ system is affected, an acquaintance with the medical complications of chronic heavy alcohol use constitutes familiarity with an exceedingly broad array of medical disorders. In the past, in view of the protean and multisystem manifestations of both tuberculosis and syphilis, it was often said that "to know TB or syphilis is to know medicine." The same could be said of alcohol dependence—to know alcohol dependence and its secondary complications is to know a great deal about medicine.

We will now touch briefly, in a systems-oriented fashion, on many of the major medical problems related to long-term alcohol use and abuse. First, however, let us take a look at a composite picture of a person manifesting the visible signs of chronic heavy drinking.

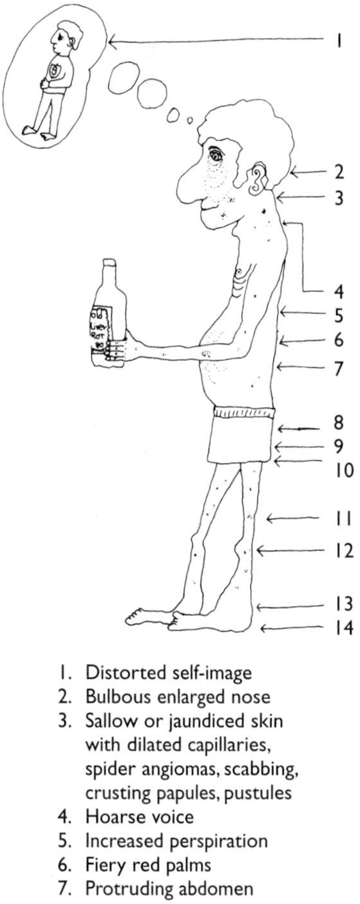

1. Distorted self-image
2. Bulbous enlarged nose
3. Sallow or jaundiced skin with dilated capillaries, spider angiomas, scabbing, crusting papules, pustules
4. Hoarse voice
5. Increased perspiration
6. Fiery red palms
7. Protruding abdomen
8. Pubic hair thinned or lost
9. Shrunken testicles
10. Hemorrhoids
11. Thin
12. Multiple bruises
13. Swollen ankles
14. Unsteady walk with broad-based gait

Visible Signs and Symptoms of Chronic Heavy Drinking

Statistically, the typical alcoholic is male; thus, we will use "he" in our examples. However, female alcoholics can and do show virtually all the same signs and symptoms of chronic heavy alcohol use, except those involving the reproductive organs. Indeed, among women medical complications may appear sooner and be more severe earlier in the drinking career. Bearing in mind that any given alcohol-dependent person may have many or only a few of these visible manifestations, let us examine a hypothetical chronic drinker who has most of them.

He is typically a thin, but occasionally somewhat bloated-appearing, middle-aged individual. He may appear anxious and/or depressed. Hyperpigmented, sallow, or jaundiced skin accentuates his wasted, chronically fatigued, and weakened overall appearance. He walks haltingly and unsteadily with a broad-based gait (*ataxia*). Multiple bruises are evident. He perspires heavily. His voice is hoarse and croaking, punctuated by occasional hiccups, and he carries an odor of alcohol on his breath. His dental problems are obvious. There are teeth missing, others have caries. There is serious periodontal disease and halitosis (bad breath).

His abdomen protrudes, and on closer examination it reveals the *caput medusae*—a prominent superficial abdominal vein pattern which looks like the snakes that were Medusa's hair in Greek mythology. There is marked *edema,* or ankle swelling, and he has hemorrhoids. His breasts may be enlarged; his testicles may be shrunken; and his chest, axillary, and/or pubic hair may be entirely lost or thinned. Close inspection of the face reveals dilated capillaries and acnelike lesions. His nose is enlarged

There are more old drunkards than old physicians.
RABELAIS

and bulbous, a condition called *rhinophyma.* On his extremities there is scabbing and crusting secondary to generalized itching. On the upper half of his body he has "spider angiomas." These are small red skin lesions that blanch with light pressure applied to their centers and spread into a spidery pattern with release of pressure. His palms may be a fiery red (liver palms). He may have "paper money" skin, so-called because abnormally dilated capillaries, appearing much like the tiny, red-colored fibers in a new dollar bill, are distinctly visible. In colder climates, there may be evidence of repeated frostbite. The fingernails are likely to be affected. They may have either transverse, white-colored bands (*Muehrcke's lines*) or transverse furrows (*Beau's lines*), or they may be totally opaque without half-moons showing at the base of the nail. He may have difficulty fully extending the third, fourth, and fifth fingers on either or both hands because of a flexion deformity called *Dupuytren's contracture.* A swelling of the parotid glands in the cheeks, giving him the appearance of having the mumps, is known as "chipmunk fascies." Finally, a close look at the whites of his eyes reveals small blood vessels with a corkscrew shape.

With this as a picture of what is externally visible, let us look inside the body at the underlying diseased organ systems that account for these visible changes.

Gastrointestinal System

Many a man keeps on drinking till he hasn't a coat to either his back or stomach.
GEORGE PRENTICE

Alcohol affects the gastrointestinal (GI) system in a variety of ways. This system is the route by which alcohol enters the body and is absorbed. It is where the first steps of metabolism take place. Moderate amounts of alcohol can disturb the normal functioning of this system. Chronic heavy use of alcohol often raises havoc. Alcohol can have both direct and indirect effects. Direct effects are any changes that occur in response to the presence of alcohol. Indirect effects are whatever occur as a consequence of the initial, direct effects.

Irritation, Bleeding, and Malabsorption

Both acute and chronic use of alcohol stimulates the stomach lining's secretion of hydrochloric acid and irritates the lining of the gut in general. It also inhibits the muscular contractions, called peristalsis, that move food through the intestines, and may interfere with the absorption of nutrients and vitamins. In combination, these effects often cause a generalized irritation of the mucous membranes lining the gut, especially in the stomach. Chronic heavy drinkers often complain of frequent belching, loss of appetite, alternating diarrhea and constipation, morning nausea, and vomiting. Some of theses symptoms may be due to slowed gastric emptying which occurs more frequently with wine or beer as compared to liquor.

Pouring to achieve a large "head" on the beer enhances the bouquet and allows less carbonation to reach the stomach.

Alcohol-induced irritation is not found throughout the entire GI system but, rather, more often is localized to particular portions of it. For instance, if the esophagus is irritated, esophagitis results—experienced as midchest pain and pain when swallowing. Acute and chronic stomach irritation by alcohol results in gastritis, which involves inflammation, abdominal pain, and maybe even bleeding. Chronic alcohol use can certainly aggravate, if not cause, ulcers of the stomach or duodenum (the first section of the small intestine). Bleeding can occur at any of the irritated sites. This represents a potentially serious medical problem. Bleeding from the GI tract can be either slow or massive. Either way, it is serious. Frequently, the alcoholic's blood clots less rapidly, so the body's built-in defenses to stop bleeding are weakened. Surgery may even be required to stop the bleeding. Although alcohol may aggravate ulcers through direct irritant effects, it may also have a counterbalancing beneficial effect as it kills *Heliobactor pylori,* the stomach bacterium that plays an important role in causing ulcers.

There are also other causes of GI bleeding. The irritation of the stomach lining, not unexpectedly, upsets the stomach. With that can come prolonged nausea, violent vomiting, and retching. This may be so severe as to cause mechanical tears in the esophageal lining and bring on massive bleeding. Another cause of massive and often fatal upper GI bleeding is ruptured, dilated veins along the esophagus (esophageal varices). The distention and dilation of these veins occurs as a result of chronic liver disease and cirrhosis.

Chronic heavy alcohol use increases the severity of periodontal disease and thus contributes to tooth loss. Heavy alcohol use facilitates the development of gastroesophageal reflux disease (GERD) and chronic esophogitis. This is due to relaxation of the sphincter in the lower part of the esophagus, the muscle that prevents the contents of the stomach from moving into the esophagus, and reduced motility in the esophagus. Chronic irritation of the esophagus by a combination of long-standing heavy alcohol consumption, especially liquor (distilled beverages), along with cigarette smoking significantly increases the risk for esophageal cancer. The result of chronic, excessive use of alcohol on small intestinal function can lead to abnormal absorption of a variety of foods, vitamins, and other nutrients. No specific diseases of the large intestine are caused by alcohol use; however, diarrhea frequently occurs in alcoholics. This results because absorption of sodium and water is inhibited due to alcohol's effects on the gut. Hemorrhoids, a by-product of liver disease and cirrhosis, also are more common in alcoholics.

Pancreatitis

Alcohol is frequently the culprit in acute inflammation of the pancreas. This is known as acute pancreatitis. The pancreas is a gland tucked away behind the stomach and small intestine. It makes digestive juices, which are needed to break down starches, fat, and proteins. These juices are

A drunkard is like a whiskey bottle, all neck and belly and no head.
AUSTIN O'MALLEY

secreted into the duodenum through the pancreatic duct, in response to alcohol as well as other foodstuffs. The pancreatic secretions are alkaline and thus are important in neutralizing the acid contents of the stomach, thereby helping protect the intestinal lining. The pancreas also houses the islets of Langerhans, which secrete the hormone insulin, needed to regulate sugar levels in the blood.

Currently there are two major theories as to how alcohol causes acute pancreatitis. The first, which is less favored, suggests that the pancreatic duct opening into the duodenum, the first part of the small intestine, can become swollen if the small intestine is irritated by alcohol. As the pancreatic duct swells, pancreatic digestive juices cannot pass through it freely; they are obstructed or "stopped up." In addition, it has been suggested that bile from the bile duct, which opens into the pancreatic duct, may "back up" into the pancreatic duct and enter the pancreas itself. The pancreas then becomes inflamed. Because the bile and digestive juices cannot freely escape, in effect, autodigestion of the pancreas occurs.

The second theory holds that some of the excess fats in the bloodstream caused by excessive drinking are deposited in the pancreas. These fats are then digested by pancreatic enzymes, whose usual task is breaking down dietary fats. In turn, the products of this process, free fatty acids, cause cell injury in the pancreas, which results in further release of fat-digesting enzymes, thus creating a vicious cycle.

The symptoms of acute pancreatitis include nausea, vomiting, diarrhea, and severe upper abdominal pain radiating through to the back. Chronic inflammation of the pancreas can lead to calcifications, which are visible on abdominal X-rays. This is chronic pancreatitis, a relapsing illness that occurs in long-term heavy drinkers who are genetically predisposed to developing it. Chronic pancreatitis is now believed to result from the cumulative effects of repeated acute illness episodes. These repeated incidents of acute illness lead to the destruction of cells and subsequent scarring which cause the digestive and hormonal abnormalities associated with the chronic form of the illness. Recent research shows that certain pancreas cells contain alcohol dehydrogenase and aldehyde dehydrogenase and thus are capable of metabolizing alcohol. The alcohol produced may have direct toxic effects on pancreatic cells. Diabetes can result from decreased capacity of the pancreas to produce and release insulin as a result of chronic cell damage involving the islets of Langerhans.

Gallbladder Disease

Moderate alcohol use decreases the risk of developing gallstones and gallbladder disease.

Liver Disease

The liver is a fascinating organ. Recall that it is the liver enzyme alcohol dehydrogenase (ADH) that begins the process of breaking down alcohol.

The liver is also responsible for a host of other tasks. It breaks down nutrients, toxins, and medications. It manufactures essential blood components, including clotting factors. It stores certain vitamins, such as B-12, which is essential for red blood cells. It helps regulate blood sugar (glucose) levels, a critical task because glucose is the only food the brain can use. Liver disease occurs because alcohol disturbs the metabolic machinery of the liver. Metabolizing alcohol is always a very high-priority function of the liver. Therefore, whenever alcohol is present, the liver is "distracted" from attending to normal and necessary functions. For the heavy drinker, this can be a good part of the time.

As you may know, liver disease is one of the physical illnesses most commonly associated with alcoholism. Three major forms of liver disease are associated with heavy alcohol use: acute fatty liver, alcoholic hepatitis, and alcoholic cirrhosis. Acute fatty liver may develop in anyone who has been drinking heavily, even for relatively brief periods of time. Fatty liver gets its name from the deposits of fat that build up in normal liver cells. This occurs because of a decrease in the breakdown of fatty acids and an increase in the manufacture of fats by the liver. The latter is a result of the "distracting" metabolic effects of alcohol (see Chapter 3). Acute fatty liver occurs whenever 30% to 50% or more of someone's dietary calories are in the form of alcohol. This is true even if the diet is otherwise adequate. Acute fatty liver is a reversible condition if alcohol use is stopped.

Alcoholic hepatitis is a more serious form of liver disease, and it often follows a severe or prolonged bout of heavy drinking. (Alcoholic hepatitis is not related to infectious hepatitis [hepatitis A], serum hepatitis [hepatitis B], or non-A, non-B hepatitis, known as hepatitis C.) Although more commonly seen in alcoholics, hepatitis, like acute fatty liver, may occur in nonalcoholics as well. In hepatitis, there is actual inflammation of the liver and variable damage to liver cells. One may also find associated evidence of acute fatty liver changes. Frequently liver metabolism is seriously disturbed. Jaundice is a usual sign of hepatitis. Jaundice is a yellowish cast to the skin and whites of the eyes. The yellow color comes from the pigment found in bile, a digestive juice made by the liver. The bile is being handled improperly in the liver, and therefore excessive amounts circulate in the bloodstream. Other symptoms of alcoholic hepatitis may include weakness; itching or welts, which are a variety of hives; tiring easily, loss of appetite, nausea and vomiting, low-grade fever, weight loss, increasing ascites (fluid collecting in the abdomen), dark urine, and light stools.

In some patients, alcohol-induced hepatitis is completely reversible with abstinence from alcohol. In others, alcoholic hepatitis may be fatal or go on to become a smoldering, chronic form of liver disease. Among patients with alcoholic hepatitis who stop drinking, only one in five will go on to develop alcoholic cirrhosis. For those who continue to drink, 50% to 80% develop cirrhosis. For many, alcoholic hepatitis is clearly a

forerunner of alcoholic cirrhosis, but it is thought that alcoholic cirrhosis can also develop without the prior occurrence of alcoholic hepatitis.

The liver has a remarkable ability to heal itself and regenerate, but there are limits. Cirrhosis is a condition in which there is widespread, permanent destruction of liver cells. These cells are replaced by non-functioning scar tissue. In fact, the word "cirrhosis" simply means scarring. There are many types and causes of cirrhosis. However, in the United States, long-term heavy alcohol use is the cause in the majority (80%) of cases. About 1 in 10 long-term heavy drinkers eventually develops alcoholic cirrhosis. Given the nature of the disease, it is accompanied by very serious and often relatively irreversible metabolic and physiological abnormalities, which is very bad news. In fact, more than half of the patients who continue to drink after a diagnosis of alcoholic cirrhosis has been made are dead within 5 years.

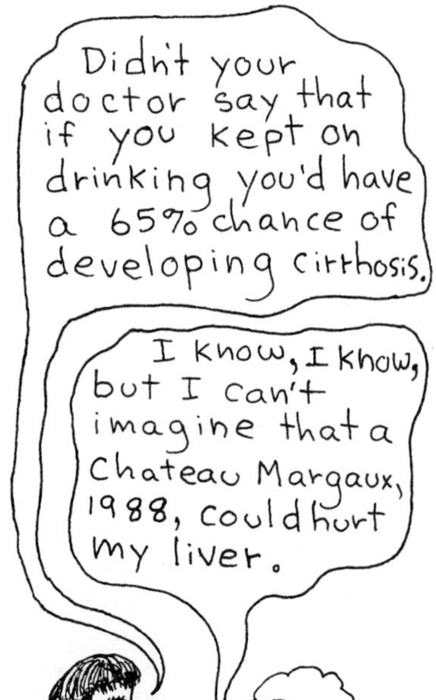

In alcoholic cirrhosis, the liver is simply unable to perform its work properly. Toxic substances, normally removed by the liver, accumulate and circulate in the bloodstream, creating problems elsewhere in the body. This is particularly true of the brain. The liver normally handles the majority of the blood from the intestinal tract as it returns to the heart. The cirrhotic liver, a mass of scar tissue, is unable to handle the usual blood flow. The blood, unable to move through the portal vein (the normal route from the blood vessels around the intestines to the liver), is forced to seek alternative return routes to the heart. This leads to pressure and "backup" in these alternative vessels. This condition is called portal hypertension. It is this pressure that causes the veins in the esophagus, which are part of this alternative return route to become enlarged, producing esophageal varices and inviting hemorrhaging. The same pressure accounts for hemorrhoids and *caput medusae.*

Another phenomenon associated with cirrhosis is ascites. As a result of back pressure, the fluid in the tissues of the liver "weeps" directly from the liver into the abdominal cavity. This fluid would normally be taken up and transported back to the heart by the hepatic veins and lymph system. Large amounts of fluid can collect and distend the abdomen; a woman with ascites, for example, can look very pregnant. If you were to gently tap the side of a person with ascites, you would see a wavelike motion in response, as fluid sloshes around.

Another result of alcoholic liver disease is diminished ability of the liver to store glycogen, the body's usual storage form of sugar. There is also less ability to produce glucose from other nutrients, such as proteins. This can lead to low blood sugar levels (see Chapter 3). This is an important fact when it comes to treating an alcoholic diabetic, since insulin also lowers the blood sugar. Another situation in which this is important is in treating coma in any alcoholic. Insufficient amounts of blood sugar may cause coma, essentially because the brain does not have enough of its usual fuel supply to function normally. Intravenous glucose may be necessary to prevent irreversible brain damage in these patients. On the other hand, alcohol and alcoholic liver damage may also lead to states of diabetes-like, higher than normal blood glucose levels. This occurs in large part because of both the effects of liver disease and the effects of alcohol on the hormones that regulate glucose.

Hepatic encephalopathy or coma can be one result of cirrhosis. In this case, the damage comes from toxins circulating in the bloodstream. In essence, the brain is poisoned by these toxins. Its ability to function is seriously impaired, leading to progressive neurological and behavioral changes and eventually coma. Cancer of the liver is also a complication of long-standing cirrhosis. Another source of bad news is that as many as 50% of those with cirrhosis also have pancreatitis. These persons have two serious medical conditions. Still other complications may include GI bleeding, salt and water retention, and kidney failure. The main elements of the treatment for cirrhosis are abstinence from alcohol, multivitamins, a nutritionally balanced diet, and bed rest. Even with such treatment, however, the prognosis for cirrhosis is not good, and many of the complications just described may occur.

The different forms of alcohol-related liver disease result from specific alcohol-induced changes in liver cells. Unfortunately, there is no neat and consistent relationship between a specific liver abnormality and the particular constellation of symptoms that develops. Although laboratory tests indicate liver damage, they cannot pinpoint the specific kind of alcohol-related liver disease. Therefore, some authorities believe that a liver biopsy, which involves direct examination of a liver tissue sample, is essential to evaluate the situation properly.

Until the early 1970s, it was not recognized that the liver damage common in alcoholism is a direct result of the alcohol. Rather, it was believed that the damage was caused by poor nutrition. It has since become clear that alcohol itself plays the major, direct role. Even in the presence of adequate nutrition, liver damage can occur when excessive amounts of alcohol are consumed.

In addition, in recent years it has been established that heavy alcohol consumption increases oxidative stress. This leads to a worsening of hepatic fibrosis in individuals who have hepatitis C.

Gastrointestinal Cancers

Chronic heavy alcohol use, especially in the presence of co-occurring tobacco use, facilitates the development of cancers throughout the gastrointestinal system—of the pharynx, esophogus, stomach, colon, and liver. However, it appears that wine is less of a carcinogen than other forms of alcoholic beverages.

Hematological System

The blood, known as the hematological system, is the body's major internal transportation system. Blood carries oxygen to tissues. It takes up waste products from cell metabolism and carts them off to the lungs and kidneys for removal. It carries nutrients, minerals, and hormones to the cells. The blood also protects the body through the anti-infection agents it carries. Although the blood is a fluid, it also contains "formed elements" (solid components). These formed elements include red blood cells, white blood cells, and platelets. They are all suspended in the serum, the liquid part of the blood. Each of the formed elements of the blood is profoundly affected by alcohol abuse. Whenever there is a disturbance of these essential blood components, problems arise.

Red Blood Cells

The most common problem involving the red blood cells is anemia—too few red blood cells. Anemia is a general term, like "fever." It simply means insufficient function or number of red blood cells. Logically one can imagine this coming about in a number of ways. Too few red blood cells can be manufactured if there is a shortage of nutrients to produce them or if toxins interfere with their production. Even if they are produced in adequate amounts, they can be defective. Or they can be lost—for example, through bleeding. Or they actually can be destroyed. Alcohol contributes to anemia in each of these ways.

How does alcohol abuse relate to the first situation, inadequate production? The most likely culprit is inadequate nutrition. Red blood cells cannot be manufactured if the bone marrow does not have the necessary ingredients to do so. Iron is a key ingredient. Alcohol, or some of its metabolic products, such as acetaldehyde, are thought to interfere with the bone marrow's ability to use iron in making hemoglobin, the essential, oxygen-carrying part of the blood. Even if there is enough iron in the system, it "Just passes on by." On the other hand, poor diet, common among those who are alcohol dependent, may mean insufficient iron intake and thus too little iron in the system. Chronic GI bleeding may also result from chronic alcohol abuse. If so, the iron in the red blood cells is lost and not available for normal recycling. This type of anemia is called *iron deficiency anemia.* Another variety, *sideroblastic anemia,* is also related to nutritional deficiencies. This comes from too little pyridoxal phosphate (a substance that facilitates the production of vitamin B6 related cofactor). This substance is also needed by the bone marrow cells to produce hemoglobin.

These two varieties of anemia account for the inadequate production of red blood cells. Another variety, *megaloblastic anemia,* is also related to nutritional deficiencies. There is too little folate. This happens because folate is not in the diet in sufficient quantities and/or the small intestine is unable to absorb it properly because of other problems due to chronic alcohol abuse. What results then is defective red blood cell production. Without folic acid, red blood cells cannot mature. They are released from the bone marrow in primitive, less functional forms that are larger than normal.

Chronic loss of blood from the gut—GI bleeding—can also lead to anemia. The bone marrow simply cannot make enough new cells to keep up with those that have been lost. The body normally destroys and "recycles" components of old red blood cells through a process called hemolysis. The abnormally rapid hemolysis that may occur with chronic heavy alcohol use can shorten the life span of red cells by up to 50%. One cause of abnormal hemolysis is hypersplenism, which results from chronic liver disease—the spleen, enlarged and not working properly, destroys perfectly good red blood cells as well as the old, worn-out ones. Toxic factors in the blood serum are also thought to be responsible for 3 other varieties of accelerated hemolysis. *Stomatocytosis* is a transient, relatively benign form of anemia related to binge drinking but unrelated to severe alcoholic liver disease. *Spur cell anemia,* on the other hand, is associated with severe, often end-stage, chronic alcoholic liver disease. The name comes from the shape of the red cell, which, when seen under the microscope, has jagged protrusions. *Zieve's syndrome* is the simultaneous occurrence, in an alcoholic patient, of jaundice, transient hemolytic anemia, elevated cholesterol levels, and acute fatty liver disease without enlargement of the spleen.

In France, other changes in red blood cells have been reported in those who drink at least 2 to 3 quarts of wine each day. These are changes typically seen with lead poisoning. (Lead, even in low concentrations, can mean trouble.) Excessive intake of wine in France is thought to be a significant source of dietary lead. In the United States, there are periodic reports of lead poisoning connected with alcohol use, but the circumstances are different. The beverage has not been wine but moonshine. In these cases, old car radiators were being used in the distilling process.

White Blood Cells

White blood cells are one of the body's main defenses against infection. The chronic use of alcohol affects white cells. It contributes to increased susceptibility to and frequency of severe infections, especially of the respiratory tract, in those with alcohol dependence. Alcohol has a direct toxic effect on white blood cell reserves. This leads to a reduced number of two types of white cells that fight infection—granulocytes and T lymphocytes (T-cells). *Chemotaxis,* or white cell mobilization, is diminished by alcohol. In other words, although the white cells' ability to kill the bacteria is not affected, they have difficulty reaching the site of infection in adequate numbers. Alcohol also interferes with white cell adherence to bacteria, which is one of the body's defensive inflammatory reactions. As a result, under the influence of alcohol, white cells may have a diminished ability to ingest bacteria.

Platelets

Alcoholics are frequently subject to bleeding disorders. Bleeding can occur in the GI tract, the nose, the gums, and many other places. That is why heavy drinkers bruise easily. This is largely explained by the effect of alcohol on decreasing the number of platelets. Platelets are a major component of the body's clotting system and act as a patch on a leak. Alcohol has a direct, toxic effect on the bone marrow's production of platelets. Thus, 1 out of every 4 alcoholic patients will have abnormally low platelet counts. Within 1 to 3 days of stopping drinking, the count will begin to rise. Recall that severe liver disease can cause hypersplenism. This can cause abnormally rapid destruction of platelets, as well as red blood cells, thereby contributing to the low platelet counts often seen in those with alcohol dependence.

Clotting Factors and DIC

When the liver's metabolic processes are disrupted by the effects of chronic alcohol use, there is often a decrease in the production of some of the necessary clotting factors. Thirteen to 15 such substances are needed to make a normal blood clot. Of these, 5 are liver-produced. Hence, liver disease may contribute to bleeding problems in alcoholics, due to lowered levels of clotting factors.

Severe liver damage can also contribute to the occurrence of *disseminated intravascular coagulation (DIC).* This is a life-threatening state of diffuse, abnormally accelerated coagulation. This coagulation consumes large quantities of clotting factors, as well as platelets, and leads to dangerously lowered levels of both, which in turn can result in excessive and uncontrolled bleeding and death.

Immune System

Another area of research has been examining ways in which the immune system may be altered by alcohol. Actually the body has two immune systems. One includes immune factors circulating freely in the blood system. These include several components, such as antibodies, complement, and immunoglobulins. The other is associated with antibodies attached to individual cells. Changes in both systems can occur with chronic alcohol use. The ability of serum (the unformed elements of the blood) to kill gram-negative bacteria is impaired by alcohol. This may be related to the diseased liver's lowered ability to produce complement, an important agent in the body's inflammatory response. Many immune and defensive responses depend on adequate levels of complement.

Although not clearly established, the effects of alcohol on certain kinds of lymphocytes (B-cells) may lead to decreased production of circulating antibodies, which normally fight bacterial infections. Alcohol has also been shown to decrease the numbers of the other major type of lymphocytes (T-cells) which mediate cellular immunity. Moreover, alcohol inhibits their responsiveness to stimuli that ordinarily activate their functioning. These factors are believed to be major contributors to increased susceptibility to infections in heavy, long-term drinkers. Immune suppression may also be secondary to malnutrition and chronic liver damage.

Research has suggested that alcohol-induced changes in other types of white cells, together with changes in the cell-based immune system, may lead to an increased production of certain types of fibrous tissues, which are characteristic of cirrhosis. A current question is whether the scar tissue in cirrhosis is at least in part due to the white cell changes and alterations in immune response that are induced by chronic alcohol use. Similar questions are also being raised in relation to the identified anti-inflammatory cardioprotective effects of moderate alcohol use (discussed below).

Even though the hematological complications of chronic heavy alcohol use are many and potentially quite serious, in general they are totally reversible with abstinence. But the liver disease that caused some of them may be so severe as to preclude this. The speed with which these complications improve is often dependent on improvement in the underlying liver disease. Reversal can be enhanced in many instances by administering essential vitamins and minerals, such as folate, pyridoxine, and iron, that are deficient in addition to restoring a fully adequate diet. Still, cessation of alcohol is the most important factor.

Cardiovascular System

A specific form of heart muscle disease is thought to result from long-term heavy alcohol use. Known in the past as alcoholic cardiomyopathy, it is now referred to as *alcoholic heart muscle disease (AHMD).* This occurs in a clinically apparent form in 2% of alcoholics. However, it is estimated that 80% have similar, though less severe and therefore subclinical, forms of alcohol-related heart muscle abnormalities. When clinically apparent, AHMD is a severe condition characterized by low-output heart failure (meaning the heart doesn't pump the volume of blood needed to meet the body's demands), as well as shortness of breath with the least exertion, and dramatic enlargement of the heart. This is due to weakness in the pumping action of the heart muscle. Most commonly, AHMD occurs in middle-aged men who have been drinking heavily for 10 or more years. It often responds well to discontinuing alcohol, plus long-term bed rest. As some have noted, "abstinence makes the heart grow stronger." Other standard medical treatments for congestive heart failure may also be helpful as adjuncts in the treatment of AHMD.

Another form of alcoholic heart disease, high-output congestive heart failure, is known as *beriberi heart disease.* High-output heart failure is a form of secondary heart failure. It occurs when an otherwise normal heart fails because it can't keep up with the abnormally high metabolic needs of the body. For reasons that are unclear, it results from a deficiency of vitamin B-1, thiamine. It may respond dramatically to correction of the thiamine deficiency and replacement of thiamine in the diet.

Finally a rather unusual and specific type of severe cardiac disease occurred in the past among drinkers of a particular type of Canadian beer. It was caused not by alcohol per se but, rather, by the noxious effects of small amounts of cobalt. The cobalt had been added to the beer to maintain its "head." These cases occurred in the mid- to late 1960s and had a mortality rate of 50% to 60%. Fortunately, the cause was identified, and this cobalt-induced heart disease no longer occurs. An earlier similar epidemic of congestive heart failure because of arsenic-contaminated beer occurred around the turn of the twentieth century in England. These examples demonstrate the potential problems of additives.

A variety of abnormalities in cardiac rhythm have been associated with alcohol. In fact, nearly the entire spectrum of such abnormalities may be caused by acute and chronic alcohol intake. Speeding up of the normal heartbeats is called *sinus tachycardia,* which may be associated with palpitations. This is thought to occur because of the effects of alcohol and its metabolite, acetaldehyde, in releasing norepinephrine. The sinus node is the normal pacemaker of the heart. Its rate of firing can be speeded up by increasing the amount of circulating epinephrine and norepinephrine. Abnormal beating of the heart, or *arrhythmias,* may affect either the upper (atrial) or lower (ventricular) portions of the heart. The upper chambers of the heart are like the primers for the lower parts, which are the pumps. Thus, ventricular rhythm irregularities that interfere with the heart's pumping action tend to be more serious. *Atrial fibrillation* and *atrial flutter* occur in the atrial heart muscles and produce ineffective atrial beats, which diminishes the pumping efficiency of the ventricular beats that follow. Atrial fibrillation can also be a significant risk factor for strokes.

Another alcohol-induced rhythm disturbance involving the upper part of the heart is *paroxysmal atrial tachycardia.* This involves a different and more rapid than usual kind of heartbeat. There are also abnormal heartbeats involving the lower part of the heart. These can be dangerous. If these irregular heartbeats occur in a particular pattern, which may be induced by alcohol, they can cause sudden death. In fact, studies have shown an increased incidence of sudden death in alcoholic populations. Alcohol also causes an increase in the frequency of *premature ventricular contractions.* These, along with atrial flutter and fibrillation, are the most common alcohol-induced arrhythmias. Atrial fibrillation has also been reported to occur after heavy drinking episodes. It does not appear to be associated with long-term moderate use.

Seasonal alcohol-induced, arrhythmia-related syndromes have been reported. They go by the name *holiday heart syndrome.* As you might expect from the name, such arrhythmias occur after heavy alcohol intake, around holidays, and may also occur on Mondays after heavy weekend drinking. The syndrome involves palpitations and arrhythmias but no evidence of cardiomyopathy or congestive heart failure. The signs and symptoms generally clear completely after a few days of abstinence.

Even in moderate amounts, alcohol exacerbates certain abnormalities of blood fats (specifically Type IV hyperlipoproteinemia) but not in normal persons who don't have this condition. In such patients, alcohol elevates fat levels of a particular kind believed to increase the rate of development of arteriosclerosis (hardening of the arteries). As a result, the coronary arteries become increasingly narrowed and may eventually become blocked, leading to premature heart attacks. Even small amounts of alcohol can significantly affect this disorder in individuals at risk.

Alcohol is also well known for causing dilation of superficial skin blood vessels and capillaries. It does not seem to have a similar effect on the coronary arteries. Therefore, despite its use in treating angina in the past, alcohol is not currently considered helpful. In fact, current research indicates that, in persons with angina, alcohol decreases exercise tolerance. In conjunction with vigorous physical activity, alcohol use by persons with angina may be especially dangerous.

Research findings suggest that moderate amounts of alcohol may provide a protective effect against the development of arteriosclerotic coronary artery disease. The research indicates that the equivalent of 1 drink per day may have roughly the same effect on serum cholesterol as the average lipid-lowering diet or regular vigorous exercise. The cardioprotective effect of alcohol appears to be greatest when alcohol is taken in the form of red wine although white wine too may be helpful. Moderate alcohol intake is known to increase levels of HDL cholesterol and decrease levels of LDL cholesterol. Higher and lower levels of these substances, respectively, are associated with lower risks of heart attacks, so moderate daily use of alcohol may be desirable from the heart's point of view. In addition to its effects on cholesterol metabolism, alcohol itself, in moderate amounts, and the antioxidants present in wine may have an anti-inflammatory effect in the endothelial cells that line the coronary arteries. These cells are involved in the development of the plaques which play a key role in causing the blockage of vessels that results in heart attacks. Studies have shown that this reduced tendency of platelets and other cells to adhere to the endothelial cells is because of changes within the endothelial cells themselves which promote this adherence. While this cardioprotective effect occurs with moderate use of alcohol, higher doses of alcohol cause inflammation, which promotes adherence and therefore makes heart attacks more likely.

Research has shown a definite link between heavy drinking and hypertension. Heavy drinkers have elevated systolic and diastolic blood pressures. This is true even when weight, age, serum cholesterol level, and smoking are controlled. Although this relationship seems well established, the specific role alcohol plays in the development of atherosclerosis (the process by which hardening of the arteries occurs) is much less clear, especially in view of the multiple factors that cause atherosclerosis. The potential importance of alcohol in causing strokes has been recognized, probably as a result of alcohol's effects on blood pressure. (See the section "Nervous System.") It is well established that the cessation of heavy alcohol use reduces both systolic and diastolic blood pressures.

Genitourinary System

Urinary Tract

Almost uniquely, the kidneys are not negatively affected by alcohol to any great extent. What happens in the kidneys generally is the result of disordered function elsewhere in the body. For example, alcohol promotes the production of urine through its ability to inhibit the production and output of *antidiuretic hormone (ADH)* by the hypothalamic-pituitary region of the brain. Normally blood goes to the kidneys for filtering, and water and wastes are separated from the blood and then excreted through the bladder. Usually during this process, ADH causes water to be reabsorbed by the kidneys to maintain the body's fluid balance. When this hormone's levels are suppressed, the kidneys' capacity to reabsorb water is diminished, and it is eliminated from the body. Alcohol inhibits this hormone's production when the blood alcohol level is rising. This is so after consuming as little as 2 ounces of pure alcohol. When the blood alcohol level is steady or falling, there is no such effect. In fact, the opposite may be true; excess body water may be retained. Alcohol can also lead to acute urinary retention and the recurrence and exacerbation of urinary tract infections and/or prostatitis. This is due to alcohol's ability to cause spasm and congestion in diseased prostate glands, as well as in the tissues surrounding previously existing urethral strictures, a narrowing of tubes that carry urine from the bladder.

It has recently been found that patients with alcoholic cirrhosis occasionally have abnormalities involving the glomeruli, the filtration units in the kidneys. The glomeruli are tiny structures at the extreme "upstream end" of the kidney's major functional unit, the nephron. They act somewhat as sieves, filtering excess fluid and wastes from the blood, while retaining the red and white blood cells, platelets, serum proteins, and other elements that are to be returned to general circulation. There are two main types of glomerular abnormalities that are related to alcohol use. The first, a benign type of *glomerulosclerosis,* is the more common and rarely causes significant problems. The second, *cirrhotic glomerulonephritis,* fortunately far less common, interferes with the filtration process and the elimination of metabolic wastes produced by the kidney. Cirrhosis may also cause other troubles. It can cause retention of sodium, which may play a significant role in the ascites and edema seen with cirrhosis, the abnormal handling of other substances, and an inability to excrete excess water normally. The complex causes of all these functional renal abnormalities are not fully understood and are very likely caused by a number of factors in combination.

A nearly always fatal but fortunately uncommon consequence of chronic heavy alcohol use is *hepatorenal syndrome.* This is thought to be caused by a toxic serum factor or factors produced by severe alcoholic liver disease. These factors cause shifts in kidney blood flow and impede effective filtration of the blood by the kidney. Unless the underlying liver disease is reversed, irreversible kidney failure can occur. Interestingly, there appears to be nothing intrinsically wrong with the kidneys themselves. They can be transplanted into patients without underlying liver disease and will perform normally. Likewise, liver transplantation in such patients will restore normal kidney function. Thus, the kidney failure is thought to be due to some circulating toxic factor or factors presumably resulting from the associated liver disease.

Reproductive System and Pregnancy

Chronic heavy alcohol use adversely affects the reproductive system in both men and women. In women there may be decreased fertility and skipped menstrual periods; in men diminished libido, impotence, and occasionally sterility may result. In addition to its many other functions, the liver plays an important role in the balance of sex hormones, so when liver function is impaired, an imbalance of sex hormones results. This can play havoc with normal reproductive function in both men and women.

Both male and female sex hormones are normally present in both sexes, only in different proportions. Increased levels of female hormones in alcoholic men, caused by decreased liver metabolism of these hormones, can lead to "feminization" of features. Breasts can enlarge, testicles can shrink, and a loss or thinning of body hair can occur. Sex-hormone alterations in males can also result from alcohol's direct inhibitory action on the testes, decreasing the production of testosterone, the main male sex hormone. Chronic heavy intake of alcohol also may speed up the liver's metabolism of testosterone, thereby further decreasing its levels. Testosterone levels may also be lowered in other ways, such as by alcohol's direct inhibiting effect on the brain centers involved in the production and release of luteinizing hormone (LH), which normally stimulates the production and release of testosterone by the testicles. When alcohol diminishes LH levels, the net effect is decreased circulatory testosterone levels. This brain-mediated inhibitory effect of alcohol is a direct one, independent of any liver or nutritional factors.

Sex-hormone alterations in women are not as well understood. In part, this is because the female reproductive system, located within the body, is less accessible to study and research. However, it is also because the effects of the use of alcohol by women as a distinct area of inquiry is a fairly recent development. Nonetheless, there is some evidence that alcohol, paralleling its effects on men, may have direct toxic effects on the ovaries and the pituitary gland. In addition, as with men, indirect endocrine effects due to liver disease may play a role. Women with abnormal liver metabolism may increase testosterone levels, causing a loss of female sexual characteristics, thus interfering with normal sexual functioning. These effects play an important role in the menstrual and fertility changes in female alcoholics.

Wine prepares the heart for love, unless you take too much.
OVID

Finally, although sexual interests and pursuits may be heightened by alcohol's relaxation of inhibitions, ability to perform sexually can be impaired. For example, in men there may be either relative or absolute impotency, despite alcohol-fueled increased desire. Centuries ago, Shakespeare in *Macbeth* (Act II, Scene 1) described these paradoxical effects of alcohol:

> **Macduff:** What three things does drink especially provoke?
> **Porter:** Merry sir, nose-painting, sleep, and urine. Lechery, sir, it provokes, and unprovokes; it provokes the desire, but it takes away the performance.

Abstinence from alcohol, improvement in liver disease, and an adequate diet will significantly improve, though often not reverse completely, the alcohol-induced changes in sexual and reproductive functions. Some males who are testosterone deficient may benefit from testosterone replacement therapy.

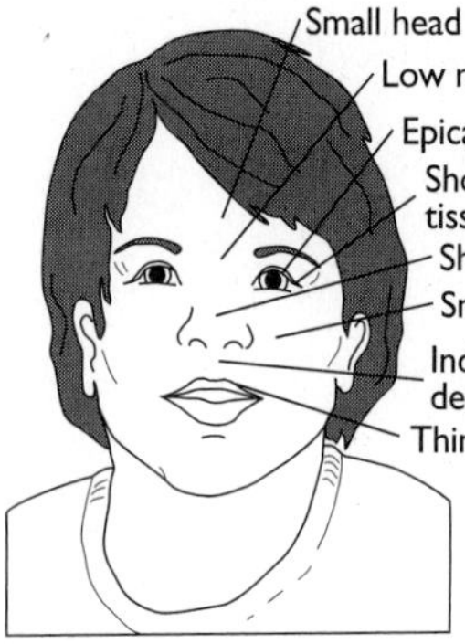

Fetal Alcohol Syndrome and Fetal Alcohol Effects Since the 1970s, considerable attention has been directed toward the effects of chronic alcohol use during pregnancy. It was in 1971 that a researcher first reported his observations of infants born to alcoholic mothers. The constellation of features observed has since been termed *fetal alcohol syndrome (FAS).* Alcohol can pass through the placenta to affect the developing fetus and interfere with normal prenatal development. At birth, infants with FAS are smaller than normal, both in weight and length. The head size is smaller, probably as a result of arrested brain growth. These infants also have a "dysmorphic facial appearance"—that is, they appear "different," although the differences are not easily described. The features include an overall small head, flat cheeks, small eyes, and a thin upper lip. At birth these infants are jittery and tremulous. Whether this jitteriness is the result of nervous system impairment from the long-term exposure to alcohol and/or mini-withdrawal is unclear. There have been reports of newborn infants having the odor of alcohol on their breath. Cardiac problems and mental retardation are also associated with FAS in almost half of the cases (46%). FAS, in combination with fetal alcohol effects (FAE), has been established as a leading cause of mental retardation and developmental disabilities in the United States—and the most preventable one. (See Chapter 8 for further discussion of the effects of maternal drinking on children.)

It is now well established that a mother does not have to be an alcoholic to expose her unborn baby to the harmful effects of alcohol during pregnancy. Nor do alcohol's effects on the fetus have to occur as full-blown fetal alcohol syndrome. They can occur with variable degrees of severity. When less severe, they are referred to as *fetal alcohol effects (FAE).*

Perhaps even more worrisome than the classical FAS are the reports documenting the potential adverse effects on unborn babies of any pregnant woman drinking more than 1 drink (½ ounce of pure alcohol) on even a single occasion. Drinking more than 1 drink per day invites increased risk of abnormalities. As the amount of alcohol consumed on any given day rises, the risk of congenital abnormalities also increases. The following figures are not a numerical average but, rather, refer to the amount of alcohol consumed on any single day by a pregnant woman:

Less than 1 drink	Very little risk
Two drinks	Threshold for risk
Two to 4 drinks	10% risk for abnormalities
Ten drinks	50% risk for abnormalities
More than 10 drinks	75% risk for abnormalities

Clearly, FAE is not restricted to the children of women who are alcoholics. Not unexpectedly, given similar findings with other drugs, the teratogenic effects of alcohol are greater in the first three months of pregnancy than they are in the fourth through ninth months. Based on this information, in the summer of 1977, the NIAAA issued a health warning advising expectant mothers not to have more than 2 drinks a day. In 1981, a much stronger warning was issued. The U.S. Surgeon General (the nation's highest public health official) advised that women wishing to become pregnant, as well as women who are pregnant, consume no alcohol. More recent research confirms that this advisory was well advised.

Current research suggests that there are both dose-related and threshold effects. "Dose-related" means that, the more alcohol consumed, the greater the likelihood of damage to the unborn child. "Threshold" refers to a particular level when the effects of drinking "kick in." Amounts below the threshold seemingly have no impact, but when drinking exceeds the threshold amount, there is a risk of alcohol-induced problems. The current research suggests that the threshold is around 1 drink per day, during the second trimester. Drinking 1 to 2 drinks per day, for a total of 1 ounce of alcohol per day, doubles the risk of spontaneous abortions during the second trimester. Also, the age of the mother may play a role. One study found that, even with the same levels and patterns of drinking, older mothers, those over age 30, were 2 to 5 times more likely to have children with functional impairment than were mothers under age 30.

The basis for alcohol's role in fetal alcohol syndrome and fetal alcohol effects (FAS/FAE) is becoming more clear. It now appears that the presence of alcohol—even in fairly small amounts—alters neurotransmission (specifically the GABA and glutamate neurotransmitters), which suppresses and disrupts nerve cell activity. This effect interferes with the timing and sequence of normal fetal nerve development, with large numbers of neural cells receiving signals, literally, to commit suicide through a process known as apoptosis. Millions of brain cells are lost through this process. This is believed to be responsible for the reduced brain size and permanent neurobehavioral disturbance that are the central features of FAS.

Heredity. There are on record many instances of inebriety in children conceived soon after marriage (when the parents drank wine), although children born to the same parents later in life (when the parents abstained) were temperate. If the parent is intoxicated at the time of conception, the child is likely to be a victim to insanity, inebriety and idiosy. Mothers who indulge in intoxicants freely before the birth and during the lactation of their children impart to them impulses toward inebriety.

WALTER W. SPOONER

The Cyclopaedia of Temperance and Prohibition, 1891

How alcohol interferes with normal prenatal growth is not fully understood. Research with animals suggests that alcohol crosses the placenta freely and diffuses throughout fetal tissues in much the same fashion as it does in adult tissues. As a toxin, alcohol seems to disrupt the normal growth sequence; the developing fetus cannot later "make up" for these disruptions. In fact, research has shown that parental alcohol exposure causes persistent, long-term growth impairment, which has been shown to be present in 10-year-old children. The particular abnormalities seen are directly related to the critical developments that were occurring when alcohol was present.

Preliminary research suggests, too, that the alcohol level of some of the fetal tissues may be higher than that of the mother. If this is the case, the reason has not been clearly identified. One would predict that the alcohol, because it can pass freely through the placenta to the fetus, should be able to exit just as easily. Therefore, both mother and fetus would be expected to have equivalent blood alcohol levels. Case reports of women who drank alcohol during labor, and in whom blood alcohol level studies were done, indicate that the newborn baby's blood alcohol and tissue alcohol levels do not drop as fast as the mother's. The reason, presumably, is that the infant has an immature liver. Newborns do not have the fully developed enzyme systems (such as alcohol dehydrogenase) necessary to metabolize and eliminate alcohol as rapidly as their mothers do. Thus, for a given maternal blood alcohol level, the fetus may have a higher blood and tissue alcohol concentration for a longer period of time than the mother.

During the years since FAS and FAE were first recognized, there has been an opportunity to follow affected individuals into adolescence and young adulthood. The nature and extent of impairments found to be associated with FAS and FAE can only be characterized as devastating. Mental retardation is a common part of the picture. In one large group of FAS and FAE individuals, it was found that their average IQs were 68 and 73, respectively. (Typically an IQ of 100 is considered average.) In the study group, the range of IQs extended from 20 (severely retarded) to 105 (the normal range). No FAS patient had an IQ of 90 or greater at follow-up. Thus, there is considerable variation, and it is impossible to predict the severity of intellectual deficits that may be present in individual cases.

What is evident is that individuals with FAE as well as FAS are at very high risk for diminished intellectual and adaptive functioning. In the study just noted, the average chronological age was 16.5 years, but in terms of general functioning and ability to get along in the world, the general level of functioning was estimated to be equivalent to normal children of 7.5 years of age. Impulsiveness, lack of social inhibition, and social naïveté are often problems as well. Attention deficit hyperactivity disorder (ADHD) is one of the more common behavioral deficits found in children with FAS. Also, ADHD in these individuals is commonly less responsive to treatment with stimulant medications than is ADHD in children without FAS/FAE. In the study, 95% of the children had been in special education classes at some point during their school experience.

People with FAS often behave in ways that cause them problems because their behavior is inappropriate and potentially dangerous, or it invites being exploited by others. Inappropriate sexual behavior is common. Behavior that as children or preteens may have been seen by others as being very "friendly," involving touching and being physically close to others, becomes socially less acceptable as they grow older. Among adolescents and in adulthood, such behavior can result in social problems and legal encounters. A recently recognized problem is the presence of FAS/FAE among persons in the criminal justice system.

Most significantly, there is no improvement with age—in IQ, achievement, or ability to cope with everyday tasks. Within one large study of adults with FAS, only 5% lived alone and none were fully self-sufficient. The special needs of children with FAS/FAE persist through life. This means that protective services and special structures are necessary for these children throughout their lives. Clinical research has been directed to identifying what kinds of supportive services within schools and the community, as well as behavioral therapies, can best assist these children as they enter school and move into adulthood.

Respiratory System

Alcohol affects normal breathing. Low to moderate doses of alcohol increase the respiratory rate; presumably this is due to the direct effect of alcohol on the respiration center in the brain. In larger, anesthetic, and/or toxic doses, the respiration rate is decreased. This latter effect may contribute to respiratory insufficiency in persons with chronic obstructive pulmonary disease who drink heavily, or it may cause death in cases of acute alcohol poisoning.

In the past, it was thought that for the most part alcohol spared the lungs as far as direct harmful effects were concerned. This is apparently not the case. In recent years such effects have been recognized and investigated. Alcohol can interfere with a variety of important pulmonary defenses at the cellular level, both mechanical and metabolic. These impaired defenses can contribute importantly to chronic air flow obstruction and possibly produce bronchospasm in some individuals. The direct effects of alcohol on the lungs may have significant consequences for individuals with emphysema, chronic obstructive pulmonary disease, chronic bronchitis, and asthma. With the high association of smoking and heavy drinking, lung cancer is more common among those with alcohol dependence. Clinical research in recent years has established that chronic heavy alcohol use is a clear risk factor for the development of the acute lung injury and respiratory distress syndromes that have high levels of morbidity and mortality. Possible factors explaining this relationship include frequency of pulmonary infections, trauma, and

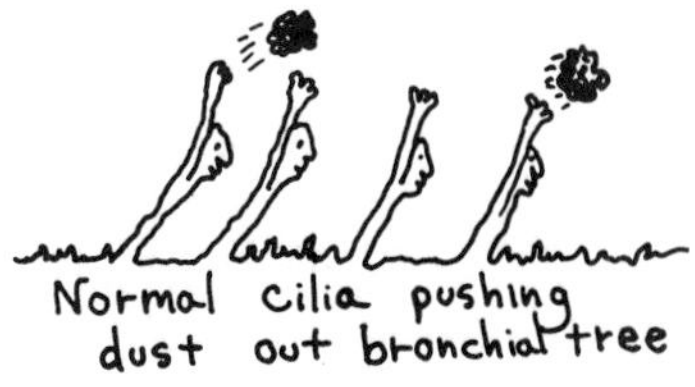

aspiration, as well as disruption of a number of normal cellular processes that protect the lungs.

There also are a number of noxious effects of alcohol that can affect the lungs in an indirect fashion. The combination of stuporousness, or unconsciousness, and vomiting as a result of excessive alcohol use can lead to aspiration of mouth and nose secretions or gastric contents. This can lead to bacterial infections and/or aspiration pneumonia. Because of alcohol-induced diminished defenses against infection, pulmonary infections, especially with pneumococci and gram-negative bacteria, occur more frequently and severely in those with alcohol dependence than in others. Also because of diminished defenses against infection, there is a higher incidence of tuberculosis. Thus, any heavy drinker with a newly positive skin test for tuberculosis should be considered for treatment to prevent possible active tuberculosis.

Endocrine System

The endocrine system is composed of the glands of the body and their secretions, the hormones. Hormones can be thought of as chemical messengers, released by the glands into the bloodstream. They are vital in regulating countless body processes. There is a very complex and involved interaction between hormonal activity and body functioning.

Although there are many glands in the body, the pituitary gland, located in the brain, can be thought of as the master gland. Many of its hormonal secretions are involved in regulating the other glands. This is through the so-called hypothalamic-pituitary-adrenal (HPA) axis. Alcohol can affect the endocrine system in three major ways. First, alcohol can alter the function of the pituitary gland. If this happens, the other glands are unable to function properly because they are not receiving the proper "hormonal instructions." It is believed that chronic heavy alcohol use may lead to premature aging through alcohol's chronic activation of the HPA axis. Second, alcohol can affect other glands directly. Despite other glands' receiving the correct instructions from the pituitary, alcohol can impede their ability to respond appropriately. Third, interference with normal endocrine function can result from alcohol-induced liver damage. One of the functions of the liver is to metabolize hormones, thereby removing them from the system. Liver disease diminishes this capacity, and hormonal imbalances can result.

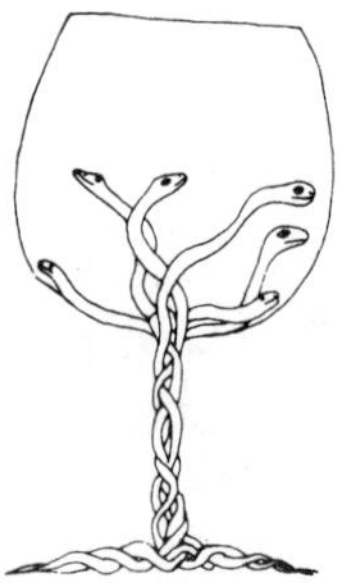

As previously described, the level of testosterone, the male sex hormone, is lowered by alcohol in a number of ways. First, it is lowered by the direct action of alcohol on the testes and, second, through alcohol's inhibitory action on the pituitary gland and its subsequent failure to secrete LH, the hormone that stimulates the testes' secretion of testosterone. Another factor is that the liver's clearance of testosterone may be decreased in the alcoholic. This may lead to abnormal function in males.

Finally, malnutrition, which frequently occurs in those with alcohol dependence, may inhibit the function of the hypothalamic-pituitary-adrenal axis at all levels.

Serious liver disease reduces the liver's ability to break down another of the pituitary's hormones, melanocyte-stimulating hormone (MSH). This may result in increased levels of MSH, which leads to a deepening of skin pigmentation and frequently a "dirty tan" skin color. With increased levels of other hormones that stimulate the activity of other cells, the question arises whether such increased hormone levels have a potential role in the development of various cancers.

The adrenal glands are also affected by alcohol. The adrenal glands produce several hormones and thus serve multiple functions. One function known to all of us comes from the release of adrenaline (epinephrine) when we are frightened or fearful. This charge of adrenaline, with its associated rapid heartbeat and sweating, causes the fight-or-flight response. Heavy intake of or withdrawal from alcohol prompts increased release of catecholamines, such as epinephrine, by the adrenals. This may be partly responsible for the rapid heartbeat and hypertension that occur during withdrawal. Another adrenal hormone, aldosterone, which plays a major role in regulating the body's salt and water levels, increases both with heavy use and during alcohol withdrawal. Increased aldosterone levels often lead to significant and potentially serious salt and water imbalances, visible clinically as swelling (edema). Increased aldosterone levels are frequently seen in patients with cirrhosis with ascites. This is thought to be, in part, the cause of the peripheral edema that is also seen with this condition. In some alcoholics the adrenals secrete excess cortisol. The excess cortisol causes a condition clinically indistinguishable from a condition known as Cushing's disease, except that it clears rapidly with abstinence from alcohol.

Animal research is raising several interesting questions about alcohol's effects on the endocrine system. In animals, heavy alcohol intake increases the levels of norepinephrine in the heart. This raises the question of whether increased levels of norepinephrine might contribute to the development of alcoholic heart muscle disease.

Carbohydrate metabolism, which is regulated by the hormone insulin, can be affected by chronic alcohol intake. Heavy drinking may lead to abnormally high levels of glucose similar to those seen in diabetics. This condition is referred to as *hyperglycemia.* Usually all that is needed to correct this is abstinence from alcohol and an improved, well-balanced diet. Long-term excessive alcohol intake as well as short-term heavy drinking binges can, on the other hand, lead to low blood sugar levels, known as *hypoglycemia.* This abnormality has two endocrine system-related causes. First, because of poor diet and liver dysfunction, the liver has less glycogen, the body's stored form of glucose that is usually available for conversion into circulating glucose. Second, the liver is less able to convert proteins and amino acids into glucose. Hypoglycemia can cause coma and, if severe and prolonged, can result in irreversible brain damage. This is a medical emergency and must be treated as rapidly as possible with glucose administration.

Recent studies have shown that moderate alcohol intake is associated with a reduced incidence of diabetes and diabetes-related coronary artery disease. However, the reverse seems to be true of chronic, heavy drinking.

The increased NADH to NAD^+ ratio is also a major function in causing two dangerous forms of metabolic acidosis frequently seen in alcoholics. The first is known as *alcoholic ketoacidosis,* which occurs when the altered cofactor ratio leads to the production not of carbon dioxide and water, as alcohol is metabolized, but ketones, which are organic acids. This disorder may be fatal. The second form, called *lactic acidosis,* also occurs because of the altered ratio of NADH to NAD^+. In this case, there is an increased production of lactate. Both types of acidosis are dangerous and must be treated with intravenous fluids and sodium bicarbonate.

Cancer

Research is being conducted to explore whether alcohol's effect on the endocrine system contributes to the development of different types of cancer. Heavy drinkers are known to have a higher incidence of skin, thyroid, laryneal, oral, head and neck, esophageal, stomach, liver, lung, colon, prostate, and breast cancers. Recall that the pituitary gland is the body's master control gland. It influences the activity of various other glandular tissues through the hormones it secretes. Alcohol inhibits the breakdown of pituitary MSH. It may also play a role in the release of hormones that promote thyroid activity and milk production by the breast. These three hormones have one thing in common: they affect their target tissues—the skin, thyroid gland, and breast—by causing these tissues to increase their metabolic activity. So, the pieces may be falling into place. Cancer, simply put, occurs when there is uncontrolled or abnormal cellular metabolic activity and growth and inadequate immune defenses, which normally would eliminate cancerous cells that develop. It is possible that alcohol's presence over long periods of time produces so many hormonal messages to the skin, thyroid, and breast tissues that, in certain at-risk patients, in some as yet undetermined fashion, malignant cells are produced at these sites.

Recent research has established that acetaldehyde, a carcinogen and mutagenic product of alcohol metabolism, is probably responsible for the increased incidence of cancer with heavy drinking. Because alcohol may also impair the function of the body's protective immune surveillance system, malignant cells are not eliminated by the body. In fact, recent research suggests that alcohol plays an important role, not only in carcingogensis but also in the promotion of cell invasion into healthy tissue.

Skin

Chronic alcohol use affects the skin both directly and indirectly. Its most pronounced direct effect is dilation of the vessels of the skin. A variety of pathological effects on other systems are reflected by the appearance of the skin. For example, a chronic flushed appearance, itching, jaundice, thinning of the skin, acne, changes in hair distribution, the presence of spider angiomas, a grayish cast to the skin, and fingernail changes all may reflect significant liver dysfunction. Bruising, paleness, and skin infections may reflect major abnormalities in the hematological and immune systems.

Skin changes may also suggest the presence of nutritional deficiencies in alcoholism. These include vitamin B deficiency, especially of niacin, which causes pellagra, and vitamin C and zinc deficiencies. Skin manifestations often reflect the chaotic life situations of many with alcohol dependence. There may be evidence of accidents, such as bruises, abrasions, lacerations, and multiple old scars. In colder climates there may be evidence of frostbite. Nicotine stains and/or cigarette burns may be present. Heavy and chronic alcohol use, among other causes, precipitates or aggravates a skin condition known as *rosacea* in predisposed persons. This condition includes flushing and inflammation, especially of the nose and middle portion of the face. Particularly striking is the excessive growth of the subcutaneous tissue of the nose, a condition called *rhinophyma* or "rum nose." Another skin condition associated with chronic alcoholism and alcoholic liver disease is *porphyria cutanea tarda.* This includes increased pigmentation, hair growth, and blistering in sun-exposed areas. It has been thought by some that there may be a causal link between other important skin diseases, such as psoriasis, eczema, and scleroderma, and heavy alcohol use. Others feel that it is more likely that these conditions are simply much harder to manage and therefore seem to be more severe in alcoholics because of their concurrent multiple medical problems, nutritional inadequacy, and generally poor treatment compliance.

Skeletal System

Chronic alcohol use affects the skeletal system in several significant ways. First, at least four types of arthritis are linked to heavy alcohol use. *Gouty arthritis* results from increased uric acid levels, which can occur in two ways. One is as a result of the increased levels of organic acids that accompany the altered ratio of NADH to NAD^+. In this instance the kidneys try unsuccessfully to secrete both uric acid and these other organic acids, so excess amounts of uric acid accumulate. The other cause of gouty arthritis, called *saturnine gout,* in alcoholics is from consuming lead-contaminated moonshine. The lead can damage the kidneys, which leads to increased uric acid levels. In both cases, abstinence and specific treatment for gouty arthritis may prove beneficial.

Arthritis occurs, too, in conjunction with alcoholic pancreatitis. This is believed to be caused by the direct or indirect damage to joints by the enzymes that are circulating in the bloodstream as a result of damage to the pancreas. *Degenerative arthritis,* also known as "old age" arthritis or osteoarthritis, occurs more frequently with chronic heavy alcohol use. This probably comes from the higher frequency of falls, injuries, and bone fractures in alcoholics. *Septic arthritis* (acute infection in a joint space) also is seen more frequently in those who drink heavily. This is probably a result of several factors in combination. *Osteoarthritis* is more common in alcoholics and involves roughened joint surfaces, where bloodborne infectious agents may be more likely to settle. Alcohol-dependent persons are likely to have a higher incidence of bloodborne bacterial infections for a number of reasons, including more frequent infections of all types, more frequent injuries, and less attention to personal hygiene. Again, the alcoholic's defenses against such infections are diminished. Interestingly, alcohol use/abuse does not appear to have either positive or negative effects on autoimmune disorders.

Osteoporosis, a generalized thinning or demineralization of the bones most typically occurring in the elderly, is accelerated by heavy alcohol use. This condition can lead to a 25% decrease in bone mass, which in turn can frequently lead to fractures. Fractures of the hip (especially the neck of the femur), the wrist, the upper arm bone or humerus, and the vertebral bodies in the spinal column are the most common. Rib fractures are also quite common in heavy drinkers, but they are probably caused by an increased frequency of falls and trauma, rather than as a result of intrinsic changes in the bone. Many factors contribute to the occurrence of osteoporosis in alcoholics. They include alcohol-induced loss of calcium and/or magnesium due to excess excretion by the kidneys, decreased absorption of calcium and/or vitamin D by the small intestine with a diminished capacity for absorption, and the demineralizing effects of excessive adrenal corticosteroid hormones, due to the stimulating effects of alcohol on the adrenal glands. Recent research has highlighted malnutrition as a major cause of the bone thinning seen among those with heavy excessive alcohol use.

Aseptic necrosis, a form of bone death, especially of the head of the femur, caused by inadequate blood supply, is another condition especially frequent in alcoholic men. In fact, as many as 50% of all people with this condition (of whom two-thirds are men) have a history of heavy alcohol use. Deformity of the hip joint often results from this and can lead to severe arthritis, which can be disabling and may eventually require total hip joint replacement. The cause is unknown but is postulated to be related to fat deposits, which are thought to be caused by pancreatitis or alcohol-induced abnormalities in the liver's metabolism of fats (see Chapter 3). These fatty deposits are believed to lodge in the small arterial vessels supplying the femoral head and cut off blood flow, resulting in bone death.

Nervous System

The central nervous system (CNS), of all the major organ systems, is perhaps most profoundly affected by the effects of acute and chronic alcohol use. Over time, with sufficient quantities of alcohol, the CNS becomes adapted to its presence. This adaptation is what addictive states are all about. Drinking a quart of liquor daily for as little as 1 week can create a state of physical dependence.

Dependence, Tolerance, Craving, and Withdrawal

"Physical dependence" is defined by the presence of tolerance with increasing intake of alcohol and withdrawal with its cessation. "Tolerance" refers to physiological changes that occur as a result of repeated exposure to alcohol. Tolerance represents the nervous system's efforts to adapt and function more or less normally despite the presence of alcohol. These changes include alterations in how the body handles alcohol (metabolic tolerance) as well as changes in alcohol's effects on the nervous system (functional, or behavioral tolerance). After repeated exposures, there is both an increased rate of metabolism of alcohol and a decrease in behavioral impairment at a particular blood alcohol level. Consequently, the person requires increasing amounts of alcohol to get the effects previously produced by lower doses and to ward off withdrawal symptoms.

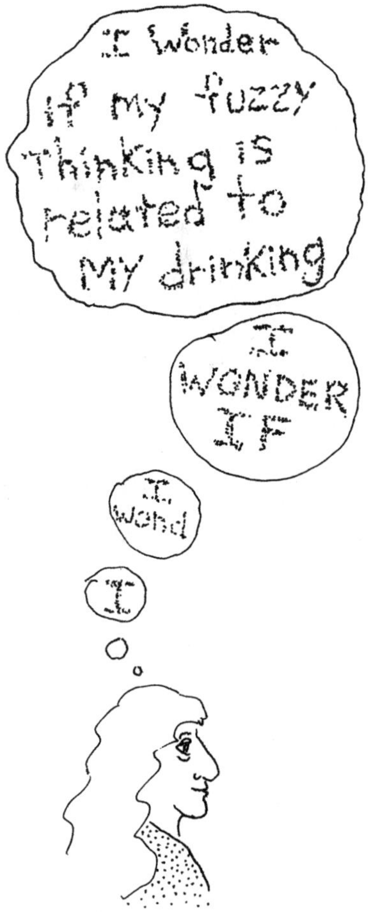

Once physical dependence has been established, if consumption is curtailed there are characteristic symptoms. These symptoms constitute the so-called *abstinence,* or *withdrawal, syndrome.* One sure way to terminate an abstinence syndrome is to administer more of the addictive drug. The withdrawal symptoms for any drug are generally the reverse of the effects induced by the drug itself. Alcohol belongs to the depressant class of drugs. Therefore, the alcohol abstinence syndrome is characterized by symptoms that are indicative of an activated state. The hangover, a kind of mini-withdrawal, testifies to this. The well-known symptoms of withdrawal—jumpiness, edginess, irritability, and hyperactivity—are exactly the opposite of those resulting from alcohol's depressant effects.

Individuals who have regularly used large quantities of alcohol—that is, they have developed tolerance to that amount—will have withdrawal symptoms whenever there is a relative absence of alcohol. This means that, although they may still be drinking, withdrawal symptoms will appear if the amount consumed is less than usual and therefore the blood alcohol level is lowered. The symptoms include intention tremors (tremors occurring when the person is trying to do something), which are rapid and coarse and involve the head, tongue, and limbs. These are the basis for the morning shakes, in a heavy drinker whose last drink was the night before.

If the chronic heavy drinker does not consume more alcohol, he or she is likely to develop more serious symptoms of withdrawal. These are thought to represent a kind of rebound effect. In the absence of alcohol and its chronic suppressant effects, certain regions of the brain become overactive. The severity of the symptoms of withdrawal can vary widely, depending on the length of time of heavy drinking and the amount of alcohol consumed during that period, plus individual metabolic differences among people. The symptoms of withdrawal include tremulousness, fever, tachycardia, hypertension, agitation, seizures, and hallucinations. These will be discussed in detail later in this chapter.

Craving is also associated with addiction and results from changes in the central nervous system. With alcohol, craving is that deep desire, that virtually irresistible impulse, that strong "need" to have a drink. When it strikes, it is difficult to ignore it. Craving is different from withdrawal, although the state of abstinence may trigger it. In fact, multiple factors may be triggers—the situation, a song on the radio played at a favorite bar, certain foods, particular friends, or one's mood. These urges arise from physical changes in the brain, particularly changes in certain neurotransmitter systems.

Alcohol Idiosyncratic Intoxication (Pathological Intoxication)

Aside from withdrawal symptoms, other important CNS disorders are related to alcohol use. A relatively unusual manifestation is a condition previously called pathological intoxication. In the APA's *Diagnostic and Statistical Manual (DSM) III-R* it was renamed "alcohol idiosyncratic intoxication." The fourth edition, the *DSM IV TR* subsequently relegated the condition to an "other" category: "alcohol related disorders not otherwise specified." This seems to qualify as an awkward and not very descriptive label. Some susceptible persons, for reasons unknown, have a dramatic change of personality when they drink even small amounts of alcohol. It is a transient, delirium-like state with a very rapid onset. The individual becomes confused and disoriented; may have visual hallucinations; and may be very aggressive, anxious, impulsive, and enraged. In this state the person may carry out senseless, violent acts against others or him- or herself. The state can last for only a few minutes or for several hours; then the person lapses into a profound sleep and has amnesia for the episode. If interviewed later, the person might be very docile, not at all the raging mad person present during the episode. Most likely the person would report, "I don't know what happened; I just went bananas," and would be remorseful about the harm caused during the episode. It is unclear whether there is a relationship between this syndrome and other organic impulse disorders. However, some experts believe it to be a seizurelike state triggered by alcohol.

Organic Brain Disease

Chronic heavy alcohol use can also lead to varying degrees of dementia, or organic brain disease. The particular type of brain disease, its name and associated impairment, is determined by the portion of the brain involved. *Wernicke's syndrome* and *Korsakoff's psychosis* are two such syndromes closely tied to alcoholism. Sometimes they are discussed as two separate disorders; other times people lump them together as the Wernicke-Korsakoff syndrome. Both are caused by nutritional deficiencies, especially thiamine, vitamin B-1, in combination with whatever direct toxic effects alcohol has on nerve cells in the brain. Chronic heavy drinking is associated with decreased dietary intake of thiamine and its decreased absorption from the small intestine, as well as diminished utilization of the available thiamine. In addition, recent evidence suggests that a genetic factor in the form of an inherited lack of an enzyme (transketolase) may play an important role in the development of Wernicke-Korsakoff syndrome in susceptible people.

The difference between these syndromes in terms of pathology is that Wernicke's syndrome involves injury to the midbrain, cerebellum, and areas near the third and fourth ventricles of the brain. Korsakoff's psychosis results from damage to areas of the brain important to memory and executive functions and is often associated with damage to peripheral nerve tissue as well. Prognostically Wernicke's syndrome has a brighter picture. When recognized and treated early, it often responds very rapidly to thiamine therapy. Korsakoff's psychosis is much slower to respond to treatment and is less likely to improve significantly. Patients with Korsakoff's psychosis often eventually require nursing home or custodial care.

Clinically a person with Wernicke's syndrome is apt to be confused, delirious, and apprehensive. There is a characteristic dysfunction called *nystagmus* (abnormal, rapid lateral eye movements) and/or paralysis of the eye muscles that control particular eye movements, also known as *gaze paralysis.* Nystagmus and other eye abnormalities are among the first symptoms to appear and, following treatment, the first to disappear. Difficulty with walking (ataxia) and balance are also a typical part of Wernicke's syndrome. This can lead to unsteadiness and gait disturbances. Both are caused by peripheral nerve damage in conjunction with cerebellar damage.

Korsakoff's psychosis presents a somewhat different picture. There is severe memory loss and confabulation. *Confabulation*—that is, making up tales, talking fluently without regard to facts—is the hallmark. It occurs in an individual who is otherwise alert, responsive, and able to attend to and comprehend the written and spoken word. Thus the memory impairment is greatly out of proportion to other cognitive dysfunctions. Because of the severe damage to areas of the brain crucial to memory, the person simply cannot process and store new information. In order to fill in the memory gaps, he or she makes up stories. These are not deliberate lies: trickery would require more memory and intent than someone with Korsakoff's psychosis could muster. For example, were you to ask someone with this disorder if he or she had met you before, the response might be a long, involved story about the last time you had been together. It would be pure fantasy, having no basis in reality. This is the phenomenon of confabulation. Memory for things that happened both recently and long ago is variably but usually severely impaired. Things simply are not able to be stored for recall, and the person cannot remember events even 5 minutes after they occur. With Korsakoff's psychosis, ataxia may also be present. Ataxia causes a characteristic awkward manner of walking, with feet spread apart to prevent falls. Korsakoff's psychosis and Wernicke's syndrome can both have sudden, rapid onset. Frequently Korsakoff's psychosis follows a bout of delirium tremens (the DTs).

Cerebral atrophy (generalized loss of brain tissue), or "brain shrinkage," often occurs with chronic heavy alcohol use. Research has shown that these basic changes are due in large part to the direct toxic effects of alcohol, which particularly seem to affect the frontal and prefrontal areas of the brain. Most often this is seen in people in their 50s and 60s. Another name for this disorder is *alcoholic dementia* or, in current parlance, *alcohol-induced persisting dementia* (*AIPD*). Some combination of factors common in alcohol dependence is thought to cause the condition—such as malnutrition and the accompanying vitamin deficiencies, long-term exposure to the direct toxic effects of alcohol, or a history of previous head traumas. Interesting recent research has shown that for some with AIPD, a drug called Rivastigmise, used with Alzheimer's patients, may be beneficial. As distinct from Alzheimer's, which has a progressive deterioration, individuals with AIPD are stabilized with abstinence from alcohol.

Treatment of organic brain disease typically includes administration of thiamine and a well-balanced diet. Discontinuing alcohol is imperative. Treatment is more successful in reversing the signs and symptoms of Wernicke's syndrome. Only about 20% of persons with Korsakoff's psychosis recover completely. The recovery process is slow, often taking as long as 6 to 12 months. The mortality rate of the combined disorder is approximately 15%. The dementia associated with cerebral atrophy is irreversible. However, with abstinence and adequate nutrition it may not progress further.

Alcoholic cerebellar degeneration is a late complication of chronic heavy alcohol use in combination with nutritional deficiencies. It is more likely to occur in men, typically after 10 to 20 or more years of heavy drinking. Patients gradually develop a slow, broad-based, lurching gait, as if they were about to fall over. This results from the fact that the cerebellum, the area of the brain that is damaged, is the part of the brain that coordinates complex motor activity, such as walking. There is no associated cognitive dysfunction because the portions of the brain governing such activities are not usually affected, but signs of peripheral neuropathy and malnutrition may be present.

Two forms of organic brain dysfunction are a direct result of severe alcoholic liver disease. These are acute and chronic *hepatic* or *portosystemic-encephalopathy (PSE)*. They are caused by the diseased liver's diminished ability to prevent naturally occurring toxic substances from getting into the general body circulation. (These toxins include ammonia and glutamine, which are normally confined to the blood vessels flowing from the small intestines into the liver, where they are usually completely metabolized.) This wreaks havoc with the central nervous system. In both the acute and chronic forms of PSE there may be severe cognitive and memory disturbances; anxiety and depressive symptoms; sleep disturbances; changes in levels of consciousness, with the extreme being the *hepatic coma,* which can be fatal; a flapping-like movement disorder called asterixis; and a foul, musty odor to the breath. In the acute form, which is much less common, there is no evidence of the chronic liver disease that is almost always present in the chronic form. Along with abstinence from alcohol to allow the liver to recover as much normal function as possible, aggressive, multipronged medical management must be instituted. The goal of treatment is to reduce the body's production of toxic nitrogen-containing substances.

A particularly severe variant of chronic PSE is known as chronic *hepatocerebral disease.* This is a complication of long-standing liver disease, in which the brain has been harmed by toxins chronically circulating in the bloodstream. As a result, the brain has areas of cell death and a proliferation of scarlike CNS cells. Mirroring these, there is a corresponding loss of brain function, with dementia, ataxia, speech impairment (dysarthria), and sometimes bizarre movements. Scarred or damaged brain tissue cannot be repaired, so any such losses are permanent. Patients with this condition often require chronic nursing-care facilities.

Two other organic brain diseases, which are quite uncommon but serious when they occur, are also related to alcohol abuse and nutritional deficiencies. First, *central pontine myelinolysis* involves a part of the brainstem known as the pons. This disease can vary in intensity from very mild to fatal over a 2- to 3-week period. The pons controls respiration, among other things. As the degeneration of the pons progresses, coma and finally death occur from respiratory failure. Second, *Marchiafava-Bignami disease,* also exceedingly uncommon, involves the nerve tracts connecting the frontal areas on both sides of the brain. Their degeneration leads to diminished language and motor skills, confusion, gait disorders, incontinence, seizures, dementia, hallucinations, and frequently death.

Nerve and Muscle Tissue Damage

Nerve cells in other parts of the body can also be damaged by chronic heavy alcohol use. The most common disturbance is *alcoholic polyneuropathy* resulting from nutritional deficiencies. This disorder has a gradual onset, progresses slowly, and can vary in severity. Recovery is often slow and generally incomplete, taking weeks to months after the discontinuation of alcohol ingestion and the administration of appropriate vitamins. Most commonly the distal nerves (those farthest from the body

trunk) are affected first. The damage to these nerves seems to be caused primarily by nutritional deficiencies, though direct toxic effects of alcohol may also be involved. Typically someone with polyneuropathy has a painful, burning feeling in the soles of the feet. Yet there is an absence of normal touch and position. Because there is sensory impairment, the individual doesn't have the necessary feedback to the brain to tell him or her how the body is positioned in space. This loss of position sense may lead to an unsteady, slapping style of walking because the person is uncertain where the feet and legs are in relation to the ground.

Muscle damage occurs in 40% to 60% of all chronic heavy drinkers. It often occurs in tandem with alcohol-caused nerve damage. Therefore, muscle tissue is usually wasted in the same areas that are affected by nerve damage. Other forms of muscle damage and degeneration have been reported even in the absence of neuropathy. One form involves acute muscle pain, swelling, weakness, and the destruction of muscle tissue in the aftermath of acute binges and is referred to as *acute alcoholic myopathy.* Another form seen in chronic heavy drinkers is *chronic alcoholic myopathy,* which involves weakness, decreased muscle mass, muscle cramps, and muscle pain in the proximal muscles (those nearer the body trunk). This type of alcohol-induced muscle disease is believed to be due to long-term exposure to large amounts of alcohol and its effects on cell membranes. Only one type of muscle fiber appears affected (Type II, white glycolytes). Improvement in muscle weakness occurs with decreased alcohol consumption.

Yet another type of muscle damage may result when a person is intoxicated, passes out, and lies unconscious in the same position for a long period. With the constant pressure of body weight on the same muscles, pressure necrosis can result, leading to muscle degeneration. Like any other acute myopathies, abnormally large amounts of certain muscle proteins (myoglobins) are released into the bloodstream. If these muscle protein levels become high enough, kidney failure can occur. Potassium is also a product of such muscle tissue breakdown. An increase in the level of potassium in the blood can disturb mineral balance throughout the body. For reasons that are currently unclear, heavy drinkers are known to be very prone to muscle cramps.

Finally, a condition known as *alcohol-tobacco amblyopia* (diminished vision) is another nervous system disorder. As the name implies, it is associated with chronic, excessive drinking and smoking. It is characterized by the slow onset of blurred, dim vision with pain behind the eyes. There is difficulty reading, intolerance of bright light, and loss of central color vision. Although blind spots can occur, total blindness is uncommon. The cause is thought to be a vitamin deficiency coupled with the direct neurotoxic effects of alcohol. Treatment includes B-complex vitamins plus abstinence, which are usually effective in reversing the eye symptoms. Typically recovery is slow and unfortunately often only partial.

Subdural Hematomas

An indirect result of chronic alcoholism is the increased frequency of *subdural hematomas.* These can be the result of falling down and striking the head, being assaulted, or being in an auto accident, all of which are more likely to occur when intoxicated. Any such injury to the head can cause tearing of the vessels of the brain lining, the dura, with bleeding as a result. The skull is a rigid box, so any bleeding inside this closed space exerts pressure on the brain. This type of bleeding can be very serious, even life-threatening, and often goes unrecognized. The signs and symptoms vary widely, although fluctuating states of consciousness (that is, drifting in and out of consciousness) are often associated with this. Treatment involves surgical removal of the blood clot.

Miscellaneous CNS Disturbances

Other neurological conditions occur with increased frequency in alcoholics. These include *bacterial meningitis, seizures following head trauma,* and *concussive syndromes. Strokes* (cerebrovascular accidents) and *brain* and *sub-arachniod hemorrhages* seem to occur with increased frequency during acute alcohol intoxication. They are more common as well with chronic heavy use. These are thought to be due to the hypertensive effect of alcohol and may be aggravated by alcohol's interfering with the normal clotting mechanisms. Recent research has shown that chronic heavy drinking is associated with abnormal central olfactory processing. Its severity appears to be related to the duration of drinking and may contribute to the apparent lack of interest in food that is seen in many heavy drinkers.

Neuropsychological Impairment

Personality changes have long been regarded as a prominent feature of chronic alcohol use. Historically this was chalked up to serious underlying psychological problems. Then the emphasis shifted to viewing the "alcoholic personality" as an adaptive behavior style that the alcoholic develops to rationalize his or her alcohol problems and to justify the continuation of drinking. There was little systematic research to explore a physiological basis, if any, for these behaviors. This has changed in the past several decades. Neuropsychological research, using formal psychometric testing, has uncovered specific impairments associated with alcohol abuse.

Overall intellectual deterioration is generally not seen until very late in the course of alcoholism. The IQ of most alcoholics, especially verbal IQ, remains relatively intact and in the normal range. Nonetheless, other specific deficits frequently occur, including diminished ability to solve problems, to perform complex psychomotor tasks, and to use abstract concepts, as well as memory impairment. The drinking history is the

major factor determining the severity of these impairments. How much alcohol has been consumed and for how long are the critical questions to be asked. Recent research suggests that genetic susceptibility may be involved. (This is suspected to involve the apolipoprotein [apo E] allele, an established risk factor for dementia.) Neurological deficits tend to improve with abstinence. The first 2 to 3 weeks of abstinence bring the most dramatic improvement. After that, further improvement occurs gradually over the next 6 to 12 months. It is important to realize that improvement, although substantial, is not necessarily complete.

The areas of the brain that seem to be the most affected are the frontal lobes and the right hemisphere; hence, the frequent presence of executive dysfunction, the so-called dysexecutive syndrome, and nonverbal functional impairments. This may also help explain the profound personality changes associated with chronic alcohol use. In fact, some of the behaviors accompanying dependence, such as an inability to abstain and loss of control, may in part be a result of organic brain dysfunction. Most of the impairments in functioning are subtle and not readily apparent to the casual observer. In fact, many of the subjects in clinical studies documenting neuropsychological impairment appeared "normal." They were often described with terms such as "young, intelligent, and looking much like any other citizen." That should alert us to the possibility that such alcohol-related brain damage and associated neuropsychological impairment may be more widespread than previously thought. Of course, memory difficulties are a prominent feature of many alcohol-related CNS disorders. This implies adverse effects on regions of the brain involved with normal memory. In the past it was believed that no new nerve cells could be produced in adulthood. We now know that this is not the case. Neural stem cells give rise to new neurons throughout life. This process is called neurogenesis. Experimental data indicate that high doses of alcohol can disrupt neurogenesis in a number of ways. Some of these may well in part account for the damaging effects alcohol can have on the brain.

Miscellaneous Effects

Chronic alcohol use is also related to a variety of other signs, symptoms, and conditions that do not fit neatly into a discussion of any particular organ system.

Hodgkin's disease is a form of lymphatic cancer that, although certainly very serious, is becoming more and more treatable. Many persons with Hodgkin's disease who drink may experience pain in the lymph nodes that are affected by the disease. Alcohol abuse may also be associated with *Dercum's disease,* which is characterized by symmetrical and painful deposits of fat around the body and limbs. This is often seen in association with liver disease, diabetes, elevated serum lipids, peripheral neuropathy, and consumption of large amounts of alcohol. Painless parotid gland enlargement, which looks very much like mumps and is called "chipmunk fascies," may be seen in as many as 25% of patients with cirrhosis.

An interesting property of alcohol is its ability to alleviate dramatically tremor in persons with familial tremor. As suggested by the name, this condition runs in families. It may occur in relatively young persons, although it is more common in the elderly. The cause is unknown. To account for the heavier than expected drinking seen in many patients with this condition, it has been hypothesized that they might be self-medicating their tremor by drinking, thereby inviting the eventual development of dependence. Fortunately, other drugs are as effective as, or more effective than, alcohol for this condition and are much safer. Alcohol is also very potent in relieving symptoms of social anxiety/phobia, a highly disabling psychiatric disorder. Interestingly individuals with chronic fatigue syndrome (CFS) find that drinking causes a number of adverse effects, such as increased tiredness, as well as causing nausea, hangovers, and insomnia. The impact of alcohol is evident to these individuals, and sufficiently unpleasant so that in a sample of CFS patients, two-thirds reduced the amount of alcohol use and one-third stopped drinking completely.

Chronic alcoholism accounts for 30% of postoperative complications.
Who are the chronic alcoholics? The patients or the surgeons?

Chronic heavy alcohol use is associated with a variety of metabolic disorders, including the following:

- *Hyperuricemia* (elevated uric acid levels in the blood), causing a number of medical complications (see the section "Skeletal System")
- *Diminished potassium levels* (hypokalemia), caused by excess mineral-regulating hormone (aldosterone), associated with cirrhosis and ascites; this may cause dangerous cardiac rhythm problems
- *Decreased magnesium levels* in the blood, probably from alcohol's enhancement of the kidney's excretion of magnesium, along with decreased oral intake of and increased loss of magnesium through the GI system
- *Metabolic acidosis,* an increase of hydrogen ion concentration in the blood, resulting from altered liver metabolism
- *Decreased levels of calcium and phosphate,* possibly due to increased neural excretion of calcium, decreased vitamin D levels, and/or lowered intestinal absorption of calcium, which in turn may contribute to alcohol-induced osteoporosis
- *Increased postoperative complications,* which are more common among heavy drinkers than moderate drinkers, a rate 3 times greater; these include postoperative infections, cardiopulmonary problems, excessive bleeding, and they are presumed to be due to a combination of depressed immune function, alcohol-related cardiac problems, and compromised clotting factors; it has been found that one month of abstinence before surgery significantly reduces the number of postop complications

What is being described are the many medical complications frequently associated with chronic heavy drinking and/or alcoholism. It is important, however, to realize that health problems can arise from any alcohol use. One does not have to be an alcoholic or a problem drinker. Increasingly, alcohol use is being considered a risk factor for the development of a variety of common illnesses. The earlier general notion that alcohol poses a health hazard "only if you really drink a lot" is going by the wayside.

Sleep and Sleep Disturbances in Alcoholics

Many people say they can't sleep unless they have a drink or two before bedtime "to relax." Actually, alcohol interferes with sound sleep. To understand this, consider how people sleep, how alcohol affects normal sleep, and what can be done for clients who cannot sleep after they have stopped drinking.

Scientists have studied sleep by recording the brain waves of sleeping subjects on an EEG. Everyone sleeps in basically the same way. There are four stages of sleep: stage 1, stage 2, delta sleep, and rapid eye movement (REM) sleep. Each stage has characteristic brain-wave patterns. These stages occur in a fairly predictable sequence throughout the night.

Sleep Stages

Before we can fall asleep, we need to relax. This is a fairly individualized affair—what might relax one person might stimulate someone else. Some relax best in a dark, quiet bedroom; others need a loudspeaker blasting rock music before they can let go. In either case, as soon as one becomes drowsy, the brain will emit alpha waves, as shown on an EEG. Next comes the transition period, a time when one is half asleep and half awake. This is called stage 1. One still feels awake but does not attend to input from the environment. Brief dream fragments or images may occur at this time. Stage 1 sleep lasts anywhere from 2 to 10 minutes in normal sleepers, but it can last all night in some recovering alcoholics. Finally, there comes the real thing—sleep. The average, nondreaming sleep is called stage 2, and we spend about 50% to 60% of our sleep in this stage. Stage 2 is a medium-deep and restful sleep, and the first episode of it lasts about 20 to 45 minutes.

Gradually sleep deepens until we are in the most sound sleep of the night—delta sleep. The length of time one spends in delta sleep depends on age, ranging from up to several hours in children to little or no time in older age groups. Delta sleep is concentrated mainly in the early part of the night and rarely occurs after approximately the first 3 hours of sleep. After delta sleep, we return to stage 2 sleep for a while. Then, about 60 to 90 minutes after falling asleep, the most exciting sleep begins. This is rapid eye movement, or REM, sleep. The brain waves now resemble a waking pattern. The eyes are moving rapidly under closed eyelids, but the body is completely relaxed (in fact, paralyzed, except for the diaphragm and respiratory muscles). During REM sleep we dream. The first dream of the night lasts about 5 minutes. Following it, there is a return to stage 2, and possibly some delta sleep again, but it is not quite as deep as the first time. The second dream sleep of the night occurs about 3 hours after sleep onset and lasts about 10 minutes.

The cycle of alternating nondreaming (stage 2) and dreaming (REM) sleep continues throughout the night. Dreams occur about every 90 minutes. As the night goes on, nondreaming sleep becomes shorter, and dreaming (REM) sleep becomes longer. You can see that we are guaranteed about 4 dreams in 6 hours of sleep. In fact, we dream for about 20% of an average night. During dreaming, part of the brain is awake but part is not. For example, the long-range memory part of the brain does not function during dreaming. So, to remember a dream, we have to wake up from it and think about the dream immediately after we awaken. (Because dreaming is a light state of sleep, we often wake up from it.) Someone who reports dreaming a lot either is not sleeping very well, and therefore wakes up a lot, or thinks about the dreams a lot just after waking. Someone who claims never to dream is probably a reasonably sound sleeper, with few awakenings. That person probably also jumps right out of bed on waking and therefore forgets the dreams. Someone who claims to be dreaming "more" lately has either become more interested in him- or herself and thinks more about the dreams or is waking up more due to poorer sleep.

Sleep seems to be good for both body and mind. Stage 2 and especially delta sleep are thought to be mainly body-recovery sleep. When this sleep functions well, the body feels refreshed on awakening in the morning. Dreaming sleep, on the other hand, has something to do with psychological recovery. People do not go crazy if they are deprived of dreams, as was originally believed, but they lose some psychological stability. Someone who is usually very reliable, stable, and punctual may become irresponsible, irritable, and impulsive if deprived of REM sleep. How much sleep does someone need? The old 7 to 8 hours rule is useless. It depends on the individual. Some people do perfectly well with only 2 or 3 hours; 12 hours are necessary for others.

Sleep Disturbances

Why do we need sleep? Take it away and see what happens. Despite what most of us think, an occasional sleepless night is not all that devastating. Although we might feel awful and irritable, total loss of sleep for 1 or 2 nights has surprisingly little effect on normal performance and functioning. Two exceptions are very boring tasks, such as watching radar blips or driving long distances, and very creative tasks, such as writing an essay. These are affected by even 1 night of very little sleep.

On the other hand, for most jobs of average interest and difficulty, if we really try to do so, we can draw on our reserves and rally to the task even after 2 to 4 totally sleepless nights.

Three brain systems regulate sleep: the awake, or arousal, system (the reticular activating system); the sleep system; and the REM (dreaming) system. There is a continual struggle among these each one trying to dominate the others. These systems have different anatomical bases in the brain and apparently run on different neurotransmitters. If you influence these neurochemicals, you disturb the balance among the 3 systems. This is the basis for alcohol's impact on sleep.

It is not too difficult to disturb the balance between the waking and the sleeping systems for a few days. Stress and stimulants, such as coffee and Dexedrine®, will strengthen the waking system; sleeping pills will help the sleeping system. However, after just a few days or weeks, the brain chemistry compensates for the chemically induced imbalance, and these agents become ineffective. Therefore, after just 1 month on sleeping pills, an insomniac's sleep will be as poor as ever. There is even some evidence that the continued use of sleeping pills in itself causes poor sleep. Furthermore, when the sleeping pill is withdrawn, sleep will become extremely poor for a few days or weeks because the brain's chemical balance is now disturbed in the opposite direction. Many people stay on sleeping pills for decades, even though the pills do not really help them because of this "rebound insomnia" when they try to sleep without drugs. Because one sleeps so poorly for a while when withdrawing from the chronic use of sleeping pills, caution should be used, cutting down on the use of sleeping pills in very gradual doses over a period of weeks. Abrupt withdrawal from some sleeping pills can be dangerous and can even cause seizures.

In addition, practically all sleeping pills, contrary to advertising, suppress dreaming sleep. After someone stops taking the pills, dreaming sleep increases in proportion to its former suppression. It then can occupy from 40% to 50% of the night. Dreaming sleep, too, takes 10 days or so to get back to normal. During these days there is very little time for deep sleep because dreaming takes up most of the night. One feels exhausted in the morning because there was very little time for body recovery. Nonetheless, people who have taken heavy doses of sleeping pills for a long time often sleep better after being withdrawn than they did while taking them. It is all right to take a sleeping pill on rare occasions—say, before an important interview or after 3 to 4 nights of very poor sleep. However, it rarely makes any sense to take sleeping pills regularly for more than a week or so.

Insomnia

Insomnia can be based on either an overly active waking system or a weak sleeping system. On rare occasions insomnia can have an organic or a genetic basis. Some people have a defective sleep system from birth;

however, most insomnias are based on psychological factors. Any stress, depression, or tension will naturally arouse the waking system. When this is the case, the cure obviously involves helping the person deal with the psychological stress.

Surprisingly, poor sleep is often little more than a bad habit. Say you went through a stressful life situation a few years back and, quite naturally, couldn't sleep for a few nights because of it. Being very tired during the day after a few bad nights, you needed sleep more and more. So you tried harder and harder to get to sleep, but the harder you tried, the less you could fall asleep. Soon a vicious cycle developed. Everything surrounding sleep became emotionally charged with immense frustration, and the frustration alone kept you awake.

How can this cycle be broken? The treatment is simple and effective, provided you stick with it. The first step is to recognize you are misusing the bed by lying in it awake and frustrated. The specific rules for treatment are as follows:

1. Whenever you can't fall asleep relatively quickly, get up, because you are misusing the bed. You can do your "frustrating" somewhere else, but not in the bedroom.
2. As soon as you are tired enough and think you might fall asleep quickly, go to bed. If you can't fall asleep quickly, get up again. This step is to be repeated as often as necessary, until you fall asleep quickly.
3. No matter how little sleep you get on a given night, you have to get up in the morning at the usual time.
4. No daytime naps!

If you stick to this regimen for a few weeks, your body will again become used to falling asleep quickly. Therapists trained in this type of behavioral treatment may be of considerable help and support.

Shortening the time spent in bed is also crucial to many insomniacs. Because they haven't slept during the night, many insomniacs stay in bed for half the morning. They want to catch a few daytime naps, or they feel too tired and sick to get up after not sleeping. Pretty soon they lie in bed routinely for 12, 14, even 20 hours. They sleep their days away while complaining of insomnia. It is important that one maintain a regular day/night rhythm, with at least 14 to 16 hours out of bed, even if the nights are marred by insomnia. In some individuals, undiagnosed medical disorders or physical disturbances during sleep may give rise to insomnia. If insomnia problems persist for months or years, it is a good idea to consult with a doctor or a specialist in sleep disorders.

Alcohol's Effects on Sleep

How does alcohol affect sleep? Many find that a nightcap "fogs up" an overly active waking system. No question, some people can fall asleep faster with a drink. However, alcohol depresses REM (dreaming) sleep and causes more awakenings later at night. The drinker frequently wakes many times throughout the night, which results in a lack of recovery during sleep (i.e., fully refreshing sleep). These effects continue in chronic drinkers. In addition, the pressure to dream becomes stronger the longer it is suppressed. The dreaming sleep system will finally demand its due. Thus, after a binge there is a tremendous recovery need for dreaming. It is thought that part of the DTs and the hallucinations of alcohol withdrawal can be explained by a lack of sleep (many awakenings) and a pressure to dream (lack of REM). The great fragmentation of sleep and lack of delta and REM sleep in chronic alcoholics is a serious problem. Even though they think they sleep well, there is little or no recovery value in it. This very poor sleep makes people want to sleep longer in the morning and during the day, which adds to the usual problem of coping.

Another sleep problem of major concern to alcoholics is that of sleep apnea, a relatively common breathing disturbance in which a person's air passages become obstructed during sleep. It is especially common in older individuals and those who are overweight. Alcohol, by causing edema in the upper respiratory passages, can markedly worsen sleep apnea and put the affected individual at serious risk for medical complications that can be life-threatening. Frequent, loud snoring is often a good indicator of this problem.

What happens to sleep when an alcohol-dependent person ceases alcohol use? First, there is the rebound of dreaming. Increased dreaming can last up to 10 days before subsiding. Often there are nightmares because dreaming is so intense. The sleep fragmentation lasts longer. A loss of delta sleep can go on for as long as 2 years after drinking ceases. Even in sobriety, those with alcohol dependence, as a group, still have more sleep disturbances than others. The reasons are unknown. It could be due to chronic damage to the nervous system during binges, as has been produced in alcoholic rats, or it could be that some alcoholics were poor sleepers to start with. Of note, insomnia is associated with a higher rate of relapse following treatment. In any case, it appears that, the longer one refrains from drinking, the more sleep will improve.

Blackouts

Having covered a multitude of physical disorders associated with alcohol abuse, it would seem that there is nothing left to go wrong! However, there remains one more phenomenon associated with alcohol use that is highly distinctive: the blackout. Contrary to what the name may imply, it does not mean passing out or losing consciousness. Nor does it mean psychological blocking out of events, or repression. A blackout is an amnesia-like period, which is often associated with heavy drinking. Someone who is or has been drinking may appear to be perfectly normal. He or she seems to function quite normally with the task at hand, yet later the person has no memory of what transpired. A better term might be "blank out." The blank spaces in the memory may be total or partial.

A person who has been drinking and who experiences a "blank out" will not be able to recall how the party ended, how he got home, how she landed the 747, how he did open-heart surgery, or how the important decisions at a business lunch were made. As can be imagined, this spotty memory can cause severe distress and anxiety, to say nothing of being dangerous in certain circumstances.

What causes blackouts? The exact mechanisms are not fully understood, but apparently, during a blackout, recent memory function is severely and selectively impaired by alcohol, while virtually all other spheres of affect—cognition, behavior, remote memory, and brain function—remain relatively intact. Up to one-third of all alcohol-dependent people report never having had a blackout. Others have blackouts frequently. Then there are others who experience them only occasionally. Recent research indicates that blackouts occur in nondependent individuals who have drunk more heavily than they usually do and to the point of intoxication. However, blackouts have usually been associated with fairly advanced alcohol dependence and thus are thought to be generally dose-dependent and dose-related. As a general rule, the greater the severity of the alcoholism (the heavier the drinking and the greater the number of years over which it has occurred), the more likely the occurrence of blackouts. There is also a positive relationship between the occurrence of blackouts and the extent and duration of alcohol consumption during any given drinking episode. Several other factors also correlate with the occurrence of blackouts in alcoholics: poor diet, high tolerance, a previous head injury, and the tendency to gulp drinks.

We were to do more business after dinner; but after dinner is after dinner—an old saying and a true, "much drinking, little thinking."
JONATHAN SWIFT, 1768

The current research findings on blackouts differ in significant respects from the frequently quoted early alcohol research, done in the 1950s by E. M. Jellinek, which was described in Chapter 4. In considering the progression of alcoholism, Jellinek focused on blackouts as being an early manifestation of the disease or as a warning sign for those at risk for developing it. He felt that blackouts had a high degree of specificity in predicting eventual alcoholism. Thinking has now changed. Studies done more recently have found that 30% to 40% of young to middle-aged, light-to-moderate (social) drinkers have at least one alcohol-induced blackout. Typically it occurs on one of the few occasions when they are truly inebriated. In fact, among these individuals, blackouts seem to be most frequent among those who generally are light drinkers.

How are the disparities between the old and new research findings reconciled? One possibility is that individuals vary in their susceptibility to blackouts. Accordingly those people who experience the blackout-producing effect of alcohol may find no memory of events so frightening and/or unpleasant that they are strongly motivated to drink only in moderation in the future. Others, possibly with a genetic predisposition to alcoholism, may have a naturally high tolerance for blackouts. Consequently they do not experience blackouts until relatively late in their drinking careers, after the disease of alcoholism has been established. In effect, those who become alcoholics, not having experienced blackouts earlier, may have been deprived of an important physiological and behavioral warning signal.

What is evident, despite the still limited research, is that, for some reason in some people alcohol selectively interferes with the mechanisms of memory, a complex process that in general is still not fully understood. We can recall and report what happened to us 5 minutes ago. Similarly, many events of yesterday or a week ago can be recalled. In many cases, our memories can extend back many years—indeed, decades. Psychological and neuropsychological research has identified different types of memory, categorizing them into immediate, short-term (recent), and long-term memory. All these types of memory involve the brain's capacity to receive, process, and store information.

According to one popular theory of memory function, the brain has at least two kinds of "filing systems" for information. Immediate memory is stored electrochemically for very short periods. Long-term memory involves a biochemical storage system that is relatively stable over long periods. Short-term, or recent, memory is a way station somewhere between these two that is thought to involve the process of converting electrochemical brain activity into stable changes in neuronal cells involving proteins at the molecular level. It is hypothesized that this is the point at which alcohol exerts its influence to impair memory function. It is suspected that this occurs because alcohol interferes with the metabolic production of proteins by certain neuronal cells. This in turn inhibits the brain's ability to move short-term memories into longer-term storage.

Although alcohol interferes with the conversion process, it does not seem to interfere directly with the electrochemical basis of immediate memory (memory for the events occurring during the blackout itself) or for events from before the blackout (those already stored in long-term memory as stable protein macromolecules). This could account for the seemingly normal appearance and function of the person in a blackout, even with respect to relatively complicated tasks.

The amnesia that occurs during a blackout is typically one of two types. It may be sudden in onset, complete, and permanent, or it can lack a definite onset and be something that the person is unaware of until he or she is reminded of or spontaneously recalls the forgotten event. In the latter instance, recall is usually dim and incomplete. Interestingly, in such cases recall may be enhanced by the use of alcohol. This facilitation of recall by alcohol is thought to reflect the phenomenon of state-dependent learning, in which whatever has been learned is best recalled when the person is in the same state or condition that existed at the time of the original learning.

Interestingly, there has been discussion of blackouts being used as a defense in criminal proceedings. Although a novel approach, it appears that there is no evidence to support the contention that a blackout alters judgment or behavior at the time of its occurrence. The only deficiency appears to be in later recalling what occurred during the blackout. Of course, having no memory of an event would make it difficult to prepare a case or to decide from one's own knowledge whether to plead guilty or innocent. It is hoped that more will be learned about blackouts. Research, however, is difficult because it depends almost entirely on anecdotal self-report. Thus far, no one has found a predictable way to produce blackouts experimentally. Nor can one know for sure when a spontaneous blackout is occurring. Thus, to date it has not been possible to use any of the new, highly sophisticated, noninvasive, neurodiagnostic imaging techniques that might shed light on the neurophysiological basis of blackouts.

Withdrawal Syndromes

The physiological basis of withdrawal is hypothesized to be related to alcohol's depressant effects on the CNS. With regular heavy use of alcohol, the activity of the CNS is chronically depressed. With abstinence, this chronic depressant effect is removed. There follows a period of rebound hyperactivity. An area of the CNS particularly affected is the reticular activating system, which modulates or regulates the general level of CNS arousal and activity. The duration of the withdrawal syndrome is determined by the time required for this rebound overactivity to be played out and a normal baseline level of neurophysiological functioning to be reestablished. Studies of CNS activity with EEGs during heavy drinking, abstinence, and withdrawal support this. Interestingly, volumetric MRI studies have shown that during withdrawal the white matter volume in the brain increases by as much as 20%.

Not everyone physically dependent on alcohol who stops drinking has the same symptoms. In part, the severity of the withdrawal state is a function of how long someone has been drinking and how much. Another big factor is the drinker's physical health plus his or her unique physiological characteristics. Therefore, accurately predicting the difficulties with withdrawal is impossible. Despite the phrase "abstinence syndrome," withdrawal can occur even while someone continues to drink. The key factor is a relative lowering of the blood alcohol level. Thus, relative abstinence is the condition that triggers withdrawal. This phenomenon often prompts the alcoholic's morning drink. He or she is treating withdrawal symptoms.

Four major withdrawal syndromes have been described in conjunction with alcohol. These include a state of *hyperarousal, alcoholic hallucinosis, convulsive seizures,* and *delirium tremens* (*DTs*). Although they can be distinguished for the purpose of discussion, clinically the distinctions are not so neat. In reality, these syndromes often blend together.

Hyperarousal The earliest and most common sign of acute alcohol withdrawal is a generalized state of *hyperarousal.* This can include anxiety, irritability, insomnia, loss of appetite, rapid heartbeat (tachycardia), and

I figure when I can't Pop the Pop Top it's time to stop.

tremulousness (the "shakes"). Avoiding this state often is what motivates the actively drinking alcoholic to have a morning or midday drink. Recall that, with increasing tolerance, increasing amounts of an addictive drug are necessary to ward off withdrawal symptoms, and only a relatively lowered blood alcohol concentration (BAC) is necessary to induce withdrawal. An alcoholic who is used to drinking heavily in the evenings will eventually feel shaky the next morning. The BAC will have fallen from the level of the night before. A drink, by raising the BAC, will take this discomfort and edginess away. With time, further boosts of booze during the course of the day may be necessary to maintain a BAC sufficient to prevent the shakes. As tends to be the case with all addicting drugs, users will consume progressively increasing amounts, not for their positive effects but as a means of dealing with withdrawal symptoms.

If the physically dependent person abstains completely, there will be a marked increase in symptoms. The appearance will be one of stimulation. The alcoholic will startle easily, feel irritable, and in general be revved up in a very unpleasant way. He or she will have a fast pulse, increased temperature, elevated blood pressure, sweating, dilated pupils, a flushed face, and trouble sleeping. Usually these symptoms subside over 2 or 3 days. The shakes will disappear, and the vital signs will return to normal. However, feeling awful, being irritable, and having difficulty sleeping can persist for 2 to 3 weeks or even longer. Although the judicious use of medication (primarily the benzodiazepines) may make the withdrawal process more tolerable by lessening the severity of symptoms, this acute withdrawal syndrome by itself often does not require medical treatment. But it is important that the person not be left alone and be carefully observed for the occurrence of seizures or signs of incipient DTs. When the acute stage passes, the probability of developing DTs is greatly lowered. However, if the acute symptoms do not resolve or if they worsen, the person should be evaluated by a physician because such symptoms indicate that the progression to DTs is likely.

Alcoholic Hallucinosis This is another syndrome of alcoholic withdrawal. This condition occurs in about 25% of those withdrawing from alcohol. It is usually seen early, within the first 24 hours of withdrawal. It includes true hallucinations, both auditory and visual. It also includes illusions, the misperception or misinterpretation of real environmental stimuli. However, the individual with hallucinosis is oriented to person, place, and time. Very bad nightmares often accompany this withdrawal syndrome. It is believed that the nightmares are due to REM rebound following the release from alcohol's long suppression of dreaming sleep. This rebound effect usually clears by the end of the first week of withdrawal. In a small number of cases, however, a chronic and persistent form of the syndrome may develop and continue for weeks to months. Acute alcoholic hallucinosis is not dangerous in itself and does not require specific medical treatment. It is important, however, to recognize it as a relatively common withdrawal phenomenon and to not be misled into thinking that the hallucinations are indicative of an underlying primary psychiatric disorder.

The chronic form of alcoholic hallucinosis accompanying alcohol withdrawal is often thought of as a separate syndrome. It is characterized primarily by persistent, frightening auditory hallucinations. Usually the hallucinations have a distinctly paranoid flavor and are of voices familiar to the patient, often of relatives or acquaintances. In the early stages they are threatening or demeaning, or they arouse guilt. Because they are true hallucinations, the person believes they are real and acts on them as if they were. This can lead to the person's harming him- or herself or others. When the hallucinations persist over time, they become less frightening and may be tolerated with greater equanimity. Some patients with chronic hallucinosis develop a schizophrenia-like condition and require treatment with antipsychotic medications. However, in most instances alcoholic hallucinosis does not indicate an underlying psychiatric problem but simply represents the CNS's response to the acute absence of alcohol. Appropriate treatment entails observing someone in an environment in which he or she will be safe, plus the possible use of mild sedation. Alcoholic hallucinosis, unless very severe, probably should not be treated with antipsychotic medications during the first 2 to 4 days of withdrawal. During that period there is an increased risk for seizures, and such drugs can lower the seizure threshold.

Convulsive Seizures This third withdrawal syndrome, sometimes referred to as "rum fits," can occur in association with acute alcohol withdrawal. These seizures are almost always generalized, grand mal, major motor seizures, in which the eyes roll back in the head; the body muscles contract, relax, and extend rhythmically and violently; and there is loss of consciousness. In fact, these seizures are so common that the occurrence of any other type of seizure should raise concern about causes other than simply alcohol withdrawal. After the seizure, which typically lasts a minute or two, the person may be stuporous and groggy for as long as 6 to 8 hours. Although very frightening to watch, convulsive seizures in and of themselves are not usually dangerous. Any treatment during a seizure is limited to protecting the person's airway and to preventing injury from the seizure-induced muscle activity.

A serious complication of an isolated seizure is the development of *status epilepticus,* in which seizures follow one another with virtually no intervening seizure-free periods. Usually only one or two seizures occur with acute alcohol withdrawal. Status epilepticus is very uncommon with alcohol withdrawal. If present, it suggests causes other than the alcohol withdrawal. The only long-term treatment of alcohol withdrawal seizures is to prevent them through abstinence. Unless a person in withdrawal has a history of seizures, anticonvulsant drugs are not routinely prescribed. If they are used for seizures clearly attributable to acute alcohol withdrawal, they should be discontinued before discharge, because further seizures would not be expected after withdrawal. It is critical, though, to rule out any other possible cause of the seizures and not merely to assume that alcohol withdrawal is responsible. Infections, electrolyte disturbances, and falls with associated head trauma or subdural hematoma, to which the alcoholic is prone, can be causes. Seizures are most likely to occur between 12 and 48 hours after stopping alcohol use, but they can occur up to 1 week after the last drink. Alcohol withdrawal seizures indicate a moderate to severe withdrawal problem. Up to one-third of persons who have withdrawal seizures go on to develop DTs.

Withdrawal seizures are also thought to be caused by rebound CNS hyperexcitability. Alcohol has an anticonvulsant effect acutely in that it raises the seizure threshold. With abstinence, however, the seizure threshold is correspondingly lowered. (This has been postulated as the basis for the increased seizures in epileptics who drink, because these seizures tend to occur the morning after, when the blood alcohol level has fallen.)

Delirium Tremens Also known as the DTs, this is the most serious form of alcohol withdrawal syndrome. In the past, mortality rates as high as 15% to 20% were reported. As many as 1 of every 5 persons who went into DTs died. Even with modern treatment, there is a 1% to 2% mortality rate. The name indicates the two major components of this withdrawal state, and either of these components can predominate. "Delirium" refers to hallucinations, confusion, and disorientation. "Tremens" refers to heightened autonomic nervous activity, marked tremulousness and agitation, fast pulse, elevated blood pressure, and fever. Someone who eventually develops the DTs initially has all the symptoms of early withdrawal. However, instead of clearing by the second or third day, the symptoms continue and, in fact, get worse. In addition to increased shakiness, profuse sweating, fast pulse, hypertension, and fever, there are mounting periods of confusion and anxiety attacks. In full-blown DTs, there are delusions and hallucinations, generally visual and tactile. The terrifying nature of the hallucinations and delusions is captured by the slang phrase for DTs, "the horrors." Seeing bugs on the walls and feeling insects crawling all over the body naturally heighten the anxiety and emotional responses. In this physical and emotional state of agitation and heightened arousal, infections, respiratory problems, fluid loss, and physical exhaustion can create further difficulties. These complications contribute substantially to the mortality rate. The acute phase of DTs can last from 1 day to 1 week. In 15% of cases it is over in 25 hours; in 80%, within 3 days. The person will then often fall into a profound sleep and, on awakening, feel better, though still weak. Usually he or she will have little memory of what has happened.

Since there is no specific cure for DTs, treatment is aimed at providing supportive medical care while it runs its course. Vital signs are monitored closely to spot any developing problems. Efforts are made to reduce the agitation, conserve energy, and prevent exhaustion. This involves administering sedatives. Despite arguments to the contrary, there is no specific single regimen that is clearly superior. Amounts and type of medications are determined by the patient's physical condition. One of the concerns is liver function. The liver, possibly damaged by alcohol, is the organ needed to metabolize virtually any drug given. If the liver is not up to the task, drugs are not as speedily removed from the body, a situation that can lead to further problems. The benzodiazepines (Ativan®, Librium®, Valium®, Serax®) are often the first choices in drugs. They have been shown to be as effective as other agents, have a wider margin of safety and less toxicity than some of the alternative drugs, and happen to contribute a significant anticonvulsant effect. The specific benzodiazepine chosen depends on a number of pharmacological considerations and the adequacy of the individual's liver function. As symptoms abate, the dose is decreased gradually over time to avoid cumulative unwanted sedation. Paraldehyde, an old, time-tested, and effective agent, has over time become less popular. Paraldehyde is metabolized by the liver and consequently must be used with care when significant liver disease is present. It also must be carefully stored in sealed brown bottles to prevent its breakdown into acetaldehyde. Last, it imparts an objectionable odor to the breath that is unavoidable because it is extensively excreted by the lungs. The typical major tranquilizers, or antipsychotic agents, are also somewhat less desirable. Although they may have sedative and tranquilizing properties, they also lower the seizure threshold, which is already a problem for withdrawing alcoholics. This latter drawback is less of a problem with the newer atypical antipsychotic agents, which may be helpful. Whatever medication is used, the purpose is to diminish the severity of the acute symptoms accompanying the DTs, not to introduce long-term drug treatment for the alcoholism.

Although predictions cannot be made about who will go into DTs, those who fit the following description are the most likely candidates. A daily drinker who has consumed over a fifth a day or more for at least a week prior to abstinence and who has been a heavy drinker for 10 years or more is statistically very susceptible. The occurrence of withdrawal seizures, or the persistence and worsening rather than improving over time of the acute early withdrawal symptoms, should indicate that the DTs are more likely to occur. If in a prior period of acute abstinence the person had convulsions, extreme agitation, marked confusion, disorientation, or DTs, he or she is also more likely to have them again. Another ominous sign is recent abuse of other sedatives, especially barbiturates, which also have serious withdrawal syndromes much like those seen with alcohol. Abuse of multiple drugs complicates withdrawal management. If there is evidence of physical dependence on more than one drug, generally simultaneous withdrawal will not be attempted. Serial withdrawal is the preferred approach.

Delirium Tremens. Delirium tremens, or mania a potu, is a nervous disorder caused by the habitual use of alcoholic stimulants, and in regard to its pathological tendency may be defined as nature's ultimate protest against the continuance of the alcohol vice. The first remonstrance comes in the form of nausea, langor and sick headache-symptoms familiar in the experience of every incipient toper. Loss of appetite and general disinclination to active exercise are the penalties of intemperance in its more advanced stages of development, and those injunctions remaining unheeded, nature's ultimatum is expressed in the incomparable distress of nervous delirium.

WALTER W. SPOONER

The *Cyclopaedia of Temperance and Prohibition,* 1891

Late Withdrawal Phenomenon

The so-called late withdrawal phenomenon is a less than tidy concept. It refers to withdrawal-like symptoms that occur after the period normally associated with withdrawal. Two different situations are covered by this phrase. Sometimes the phrase is used when there is an unexpected reemergence of withdrawal symptoms. While not common, this situation is more likely to occur in instances of dependence on several drugs. Thus, different withdrawal syndromes may be occurring simultaneously, each of which has a different timetable. If high doses of benzodiazepines are used to treat the symptoms of acute alcohol withdrawal, and these are abruptly discontinued, there may be a reemergence of withdrawal symptoms. So this may be a sedative-hypnotic withdrawal syndrome caused by discontinuing the benzodiazepines and may not be a delayed alcohol withdrawal. It can be treated by reintroducing the benzodiazepines and then discontinuing them more gradually.

Another way the phrase is used is in reference to a protracted abstinence syndrome—characterized by persistence over a variable but prolonged period (several weeks to months) of symptoms suggestive of the acute stages of alcohol withdrawal. These can include variable cognitive and memory disturbances, anxiety and irritability, insomnia, tremulousness, depressive symptoms, and an intense desire to drink. Neither the basis for this syndrome nor the frequency of its occurrence is known. The suspicion is that comorbid psychiatric conditions may play a role, and that what becomes apparent are emerging symptoms of depression, anxiety disorders, or panic disorders that may have been previously masked by the alcohol. Unfortunately, alcohol provides prompt relief for this often intensely uncomfortable state.

Some Cautions

Often those who experience withdrawal symptoms certainly don't intend to! Withdrawal occurs in a physically dependent person whenever a drug is reduced or terminated, so circumstances may play their part and catch some people unaware. Dependent individuals who enter hospitals for surgery, thereby having to curtail their usual consumption, may, to their surgeon's (and even their own) amazement, develop acute withdrawal symptoms. Another circumstance is family vacations. When the secretly drinking homemaker who has been denying a problem intends to just "sweat it out," grit her teeth, and get along without her usual alcohol intake, she can wind up with more than she bargained for.

By definition, any clinician working with alcohol-dependent persons works with people who do want to loosen their grip. Giving up alcohol can be tough on the body as well as the emotions. In making any clinical assessment of an alcohol problem, the therapist has to be concerned about the possibility of physical dependence and the likelihood of withdrawal. In all cases, medical evaluation is essential. Withdrawal needs to be medically supervised and carefully monitored. Not every withdrawing patient requires hospitalization. In fact, the vast majority of patients—up to 90%, in some studies—who do not have serious medical complications can be safely and effectively withdrawn from alcohol on an outpatient basis.

Overall treatment planning has to include arrangements for care during the process of physical withdrawal. No person should be alone, unattended. Family members need to know what to be alert for, so that the necessary medical treatment can be sought when and if indicated. A simple rule of thumb is that, if there is any significant likelihood of serious withdrawal, seek hospitalization. Virtually everyone who is alcohol dependent has stopped drinking for a day or so at some point, so he or she has a sense of what happened then. Any client with a history of previous difficulty during withdrawal is at increased risk in the future. Even when there is no history of difficulty during withdrawal, if current symptoms are worse, one should seek medical treatment immediately. At every step along the way it is imperative that alcohol-dependent persons receive lots of TLC. They need repeated reassurance and support. They need their questions answered and all procedures explained. Anything that can be done to reduce anxiety and fear is vitally important. Surprisingly such support may help clients through alcohol withdrawal without the use of sedative-hypnotic medications.

RESOURCES AND FURTHER READING

Alcohol Health and Research World. 21(1):entire issue, 1997.

Alcohol Health and Research World. 21(2):entire issue, 1997.

Al-Jarallah KF, Shehab DK, Buchanan WW. Rheumatic complications of alcohol abuse (review). *Seminars in Arthritis and Rheumatism* 22(3):162–171, 1992.

Apte MV, Wilson JS. Alcohol-induced pancreatic injury (review). *Best Practice & Research. Clinical Gastroenterology* 17(4):593–612, 2003. (140 refs.)

Ashley MJ, Rehm J, Bondy S, Single E, Rankin J. Beyond ischemic heart disease: Are there other health benefits from drinking alcohol? *Contemporary Drug Problems* 27(4):735–777, 2000. (208 refs.)

Bates ME, Bowden SC, Barry D. Neurocognitive impairment associated with alcohol use disorders: Implications for treatment (review). *Experimental and Clinical Psychopharmacology* 10(3):193–212, 2002. (200 refs.)

Beatty WW, Tivis R, Stott HD, Nixon SJ, Parsons OA. Neuropsychological deficits in sober alcoholics: Influences of chronicity and recent alcohol consumption. *Alcoholism: Clinical and Experimental Research* 24(2):149–154, 2000. (29 refs.)

Bujanda L. The effects of alcohol consumption upon the gastrointestinal tract (review). *American Journal of Gastroenterology* 95(12):3374–3382, 2000. (84 refs.)

Chen W-JA, Maier SE, Parnell SE, West JR. Alcohol and the developing brain: Neuroanatomical studies. *Alcohol Research & Health* 27(2):174–180, 2003. (48 refs.)

Chick J. Safety issues concerning the use of disulfiram in treating alcohol dependence (review). *Drug Safety* 20(5):427–435, 1999. (50 refs.)

Chikritzhs TN, Jonas HA, Stockwell TR, Heale PF, Dietze PM. Mortality and life-years lost due to alcohol: A comparison of acute and chronic causes. *Medical Journal of Australia* 174(6):281–284, 2001. (15 refs.)

Chiriboga CA. Fetal alcohol and drug effects (review). *Neurologist* 9(6):267–279, 2003. 130 refs.)

Cohen AD, Halevy S. Alcohol intake, immune response, and the skin. *Clinics in Dermatology* 17(4):411–412, 1999. (28 refs.)

Crews FT, Nixon K. Alcohol, neural stem cells, and adult neurogenesis. *Alcohol Research & Health* 27(2): 197–204, 2003, (25 refs.)

Diaz LE, Montero A, Gonzalez-Gross M, Vallejo AI, Romeo J, Marcos A. Influence of alcohol consumption on immunological status: A review. *European Journal of Clinical Nutrition* 56(Supplement): S50–S53, 2002. (16 refs.)

Editor. Medical consequences of alcohol abuse. *Alcohol Research and Health* 24(1):27–31, 2000. (3 refs.)

Griffiths HJ, Parantainen H, Olson P. Alcohol and bone disorders. *Alcohol Health and Research World* 17(4):299–304, 1993. (18 refs.)

Gutjahr E, Gmel G, Rehm J. Relation between average alcohol consumption and disease: An overview (review). *European Addiction Research* 7(3):117–127, 2001. (161 refs.)

Halsted CH. Nutrition and alcoholic liver disease (review). *Seminars in Liver Disease* 24(3):289–304. (137 refs.)

Henry JA. Metabolic consequences of drug misuse. *British Journal of Anaesthesia* 85(1):136–142, 2000. (49 refs.)

Kosten TR, O'Connor PG. Management of drug and alcohol withdrawal (review). *New England Journal of Medicine* 348(18):1786–1795. (67 refs)

Levitsky J, Mailliard ME. Diagnosis and therapy of alcoholic liver disease (review). *Seminars in Liver Disease* 24(3):233–247, 2004. (173 refs.)

McLellan AT. Is addiction an illness: Can it be treated? (review). *Substance Abuse* 23(3 Supplement):67–94, 2002. (199 refs.)

Meister K, Whelan E, Kava R. The health effects of moderate alcohol intake in humans: An epidemiologic review. *Critical Reviews in Clinical Laboratory Sciences* 37(3):261–296, 2000. (193 refs.)

Meng Q, Gao B, Goldberg ID, Rosen EM, Fan SJ. Stimulation of cell invasion and migration by alcohol in breast cancer cells. *Biochemical and Biophysical Research Communications* 273(2):448–453, 2000. (30 refs.)

National Institute on Alcohol Abuse and Alcoholism. *Tenth Special Report to the U.S. Congress on Alcohol and Health.* Rockville, MD: National Institute on Alcohol Abuse and Alcoholism, 2000.

Nordstrom-Klee B, Delaney-Black V, Covington C, Ager J, Sokol R. Growth from birth onwards of children prenatally exposed to drugs: A literature review. *Neurotoxicology and Teratology* 24(4):481–488, 2002. (47 refs.)

Oscar-Berman M, Marinkovic K. Alcoholism and the brain: An overview. *Alcohol Research & Health* 27(2): 125–133, 2003. (28 refs)

Parekh RS, Klag MJ. Alcohol: Role in the development of hypertension and end-stage renal disease (review). *Current Opinion in Nephrology and Hypertension* 10(3):385–390, 2001. (96 refs.)

Poschl G, Seitz HK. Alcohol and cancer (review). *Alcohol and Alcoholism* 39(3):155–165, 2004. (139 refs.)

Regev A, Jeffers LJ. Hepatitis C and alcohol. *Alcoholism: Clinical and Experimental Research* 23(9):1543–1551, 1999. (63 refs.)

Rehm J, Gmel G, Sempos CT, Trevisan M. Alcohol-related morbidity and mortality. *Alcohol Research & Health* 27(1):39–51, 2003. (106 refs)

Standridge JB, Zylstra RG, Adams SM. Alcohol consumption: An overview of benefits and risks (review). *Southern Medical Journal* 97(7):664–672, 2004. (73 refs)

Streissguth A, Kanter J, eds. *The Challenge of Fetal Alcohol Syndrome: Overcoming Secondary Disabilities.* Seattle, WA: University of Washington Press, 1997. (208 refs.)

White AM. What happened? Alcohol memory blackouts, and the brain. *Alcohol Research & Health* 27(2): 186–196, 2003. (80 refs.)

CHAPTER 7

The Behavior of Dependence

There are some striking similarities in the behavioral "look" of those who are alcohol dependent. This is true whether the person is male or female, age 17 or 57. From these similarities a general profile can be drawn. Although it will not apply totally to all, this profile will cause signal bells to ring when seen by someone familiar with substance use disorders. Indeed, it was this pattern of similarities among those with alcohol dependence that in part prompted the futile pursuit for "the alcoholic personality."

A BEHAVIORAL COMPOSITE

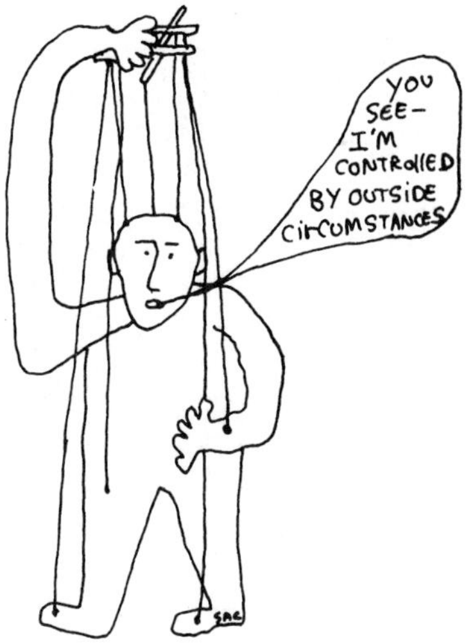

Those who are alcohol dependent create confusion for those around them. They are constantly sending out mixed messages: "Come closer; understand." "Don't you dare question me!" The moods and behaviors can be very volatile: jubilant and expansive, then secretive, angry, suspicious. Laughing or crying—tense, worried, and confused, she quickly changes to a relaxed, "Everything's fine." Anxious over unpaid bills one day, the alcohol-troubled person is financially irresponsible the next. He buys expensive toys for the kids while the rent goes unpaid. She may be easygoing or fight like a caged tiger over a "slight." His telling unnecessary lies and having them come to light is not uncommon.

A considerable amount of time is spent justifying and explaining why she does things. She is constantly minimizing any unpleasant consequences of drinking. He is hard to keep on track. There is always a list of complaints about any number of people, places, and things. She considers herself the victim of fate and of a large number of people who "have it in for her." He has thousands of reasons why he really needs and deserves a drink. She is exuberant over a minor success, only to decline rapidly into "I'm a failure because of . . ." He is elusive and is almost never where he says he'll be when he says he'll be there. She is absolutely rigid about her schedule, especially her drinking times.

The mood swings are phenomenal. The circular thinking never quite makes sense to others. The denial can cause a lot of exasperation. Now and then the thought surfaces in the drinker's awareness that he or she might have a psychiatric problem. Those around the drinker also can wonder if that is where the problem lies. She is a perfectionist at some times and a slob at others. Though occasionally cooperative, he's often a stone wall. Her life is full of broken commitments, promises, and dates, which she often doesn't remember making.

Most of all, the behavior denotes guilt. Extreme defensiveness accompanies alcohol dependence. This seems to be one of the key behaviors that is picked up on early and is seen, but not understood, by others: "What's up with Andy? He's so touchy!" Sometimes behavior that can only be described as that of a drunken slob is obvious. But often the really heavy drinking is secretive and carefully hidden.

It would be easier to pin down the problem if the behaviors occurred only with a drink in hand. This is rarely the case. The behaviors are sometimes more pronounced when the individual has stopped drinking or is working very hard at controlling the drinking. The confusion, anger, frustration, and depression are omnipresent until a radical change occurs in the relationship with alcohol.

Woe unto them that rise up early in the morning, that they may follow strong drink.
ISAIAH 5:11

HOW, IF NOT WHY?

The profile in the preceeding section is a fair description of the behavior that accompanies alcohol and, for that matter, other drug dependence. This behavior is part of the disease syndrome, which develops slowly. The many changes in personality occur gradually, making them less discernible either to the individual or to those around him or her, so the slow, insidious personality change is almost immune to recognition as it occurs. In addition, the disturbed behavior is interspersed with behavior that seems entirely normal and appropriate. This, too, is confusing.

This kind of behavior not only is an issue for family members, friends, or colleagues at work. It also represents a problem for those in the helping professions, be they social workers, physicians, clergy, or counselors. The behavior of those with alcohol dependence does not invite a warm response from others. For the most part such behavior is exactly what we try to avoid. It is irritating, distasteful, annoying, and at the least poor manners. These are *not* the patients that instinctively invite their helpers to go the extra mile. These clients can leave those trying to help them feeling frustrated, unappreciated, and questioning if the energy they are expending is worth the effort.

Those in the helping professions may recognize such responses to clients or patients as inappropriate. This is not how one is supposed to feel or wants to feel. But that doesn't make things okay. Lecturing oneself, gritting one's teeth, or forcing a smile just doesn't do it. Ultimately, to be able to work with alcohol-dependent clients requires a framework to make sense of this behavior. This framework has to provide a way of seeing this behavior as normal for one with alcohol dependence, as symptoms of the condition. In the course of working with clients an important part of treatment is communicating this insight to patients. They often find themselves as confused as others. This behavior not only is usually a source of confusion but also induces guilt and shame.

Despite the fact that a host of physical problems has long been known to accompany long-term heavy drinking, medical researchers are only now charting the physiological basis for the behaviors seen (see Chapter 6). Despite the inability to provide the exact cause of personality changes, there is a useful model for viewing the transformation that occurs. Vernon Johnson, in his book *I'll Quit Tomorrow,* set forth a process to explain the personality changes that mark alcohol dependence. Johnson's model in effect described what emerging alcohol dependence feels like from the inside out. This becomes a basis for empathy among potential helpers.

Wine in excess keeps neither secrets nor promises.
CERVANTES, DON QUIXOTE

Johnson's model, introduced in the 1970s, represented a *paradigm shift* in the alcohol field. This phrase refers to the adoption of a new way of thinking that makes previous views feel out of date or wrong. The conventional wisdom at that time was that alcoholics could not be successfully treated until they "hit bottom." It was as if those in the treatment community sat around, waiting for persons to request treatment. Indeed, some of the policies then in place seem punitive and virtual malpractice by the standards of the twenty-first century. For example, an inpatient program, then the norm, would require that someone not drink for the 24 hours prior to admission. This was supposed to demonstrate motivation and a "real" desire for treatment. That this might be virtually impossible or dangerous seemed not to be taken into account.

What is the progression in Johnson's framework? Alcohol dependence requires the use of alcohol—an obvious fact. Another obvious fact is that, for whatever reasons, drinking becomes an important activity in the life of the problem drinker. The individual develops a relationship with alcohol. The relationship, with all that word implies, is as real and important a bond as the bond with friends, a partner, or the long-time family pet. Accordingly, energy is expended to maintain the relationship. The bond may be thought of as a love affair. Long after the good times, the pleasure, and the thrill are gone, all kinds of mental gymnastics are used to maintain the myth that it's still great.

How does this progression occur? The first step is quite simple. It applies to all who use alcohol. The individual destined for later trouble is seemingly no different from anyone else in the beginning. For anyone who uses alcohol, the first important experience is *learning the mood*

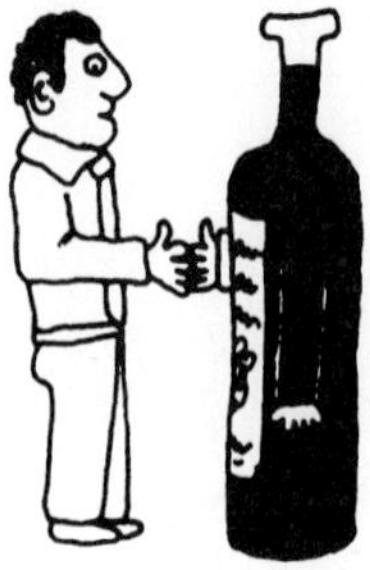

swing. This learning has a physiological basis. Alcohol is a drug with acute effects. It makes us feel good. At any time, our moods could be plotted on a graph representing a continuum. One end represents pain, and the other end represents euphoria. Before drinking, if our mood falls in the middle or normal range, the effect of the drink is to shift our mood toward the euphoric end. When the effects of the alcohol wear off, we're back where we started.

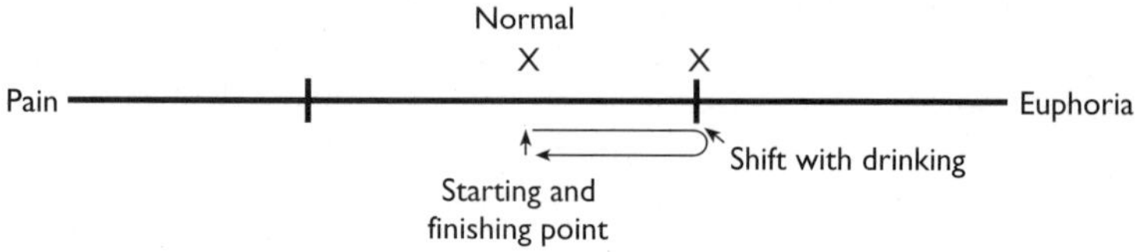

Learning the Mood Swing

Anyone who drinks learns this pharmacological effect of alcohol. As important, individuals learn that it happens consistently. Alcohol is a drug that can be depended on. Reflect back on the discussion of alcohol's acute effects in Chapter 3; you'll recall that a number of things make this learning potent. You do not have to wait very long to experience what alcohol does. The effects of the drug can be felt almost immediately. For the new drinker, who has not acquired any tolerance to alcohol's effects, the change can be dramatic.

The primary payoff for drug use is generally thought of as the physiological effects. But there are other factors at work. Consider nicotine. The first-time smoker does not find smoking pleasant. There is dizziness, feelings of nausea, and an unpleasant taste. One would have a hard time explaining continued smoking on the basis of the initial physiological effects. Rather, the positive feeling state that accompanies smoking is what smoking *means* to the person, not what the nicotine does. The attraction may be that smoking is considered to be sophisticated, or denotes independence from parental or social norms. In the beginning, smoking occurs despite the immediate physical experience. However, the nicotine that accompanies the smoke quickly plays a role in perpetuating use. The same can be true with alcohol. The novice drinker may not like the taste. But there can be a social as well as drug-induced payoff.

The second stage in the developmental process is termed *seeking the mood swing*. This happens after someone learns that alcohol can be counted on to enhance or improve mood. Now drinking can have a particular purpose. Anyone who drinks occasionally does so to make things better. Whatever the occasion—an especially hard day at work, a family reunion, a promotion, or recovery from a trying day of hassling kids—the expectation is that alcohol will do something nice. In essence the person has a contract with alcohol. True to its promise, alcohol keeps its side of the bargain. Furthermore, by altering the dose the person can control

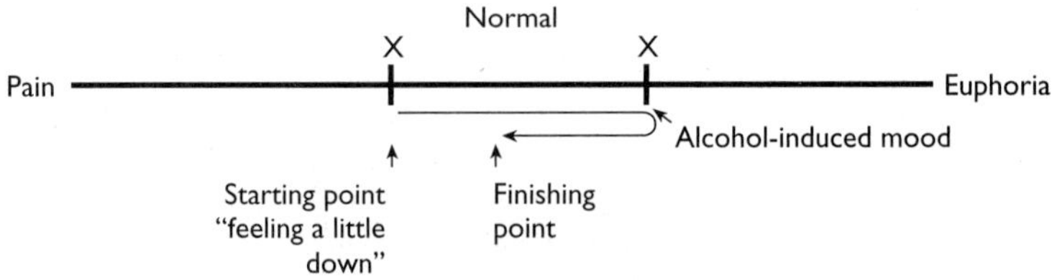

Seeking the Mood Swing

the degree of mood change. Again there are no problems. Nothing up to this point suggests that alcohol use can be anything but pleasurable.

Somewhere along the line, predictably, most people who use alcohol will have a negative drinking experience. This may happen early in someone's drinking career. The unpleasant event can be the discomfort of a hangover or it can be the sensation of closing one's eyes and feeling the world spin. It need not be the physical aftermath of intoxication but the behavior that took place then. What occurred when drinking can make the person squirm at its recollection. At any rate, most people are quite clear that alcohol was the significant factor. They tell themselves, "No way, never again," and that's that. Possibly described as sadder but wiser as a result of what has happened, they alter their pattern of use in the future. That in turn markedly reduces the likelihood of future problems. For a minority of drinkers, this scenario will have a different outcome. These are the people for whom alcohol use becomes an emerging problem. In Johnson's schema, these people have crossed a thin, invisible line, that separates the second and third stages. The third phase is *harmful use*. Suddenly alcohol use has a boomerang effect. Alcohol, which previously had only a beneficial, positive effect, now has some negative consequences. Sketched out on the pain-euphoria continuum, initially the mood changes in the desired direction and achieves the drinker's purpose. But then something new occurs: the mood swings back, "dropping off" the person with less comfortable feelings than prior to the drinking.

Who hath woe?
Who hath sorrow?
Who hath contentions?
Who hath babbling?
Who hath wounds without cause?
Who hath redness of eyes?
They that tarry long at the wine.
Proverbs 28:31–32

No man ever repented that he arose from the table sober, healthful, and with his wits about him.
JEREMY TAYLOR
The Marriage Ring, 1653

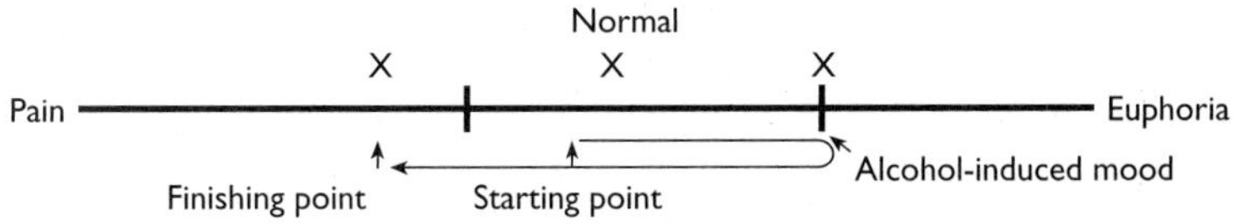

Harmful Use

Reaching the stage of harmful use has important consequences. From this point, to continue drinking in the same fashion will exact emotional costs. For whatever reasons, unwilling to abandon the use of alcohol as a means of altering their moods, some are willing to pay the price and accept whatever the negative consequences may be. This decision to accept the consequences isn't a conscious one. Emotionally they remain loyal to their relationship with the drug, alcohol. It is here that denial enters the picture. There is also a revamping of priorities, which is needed to maintain the relationship with alcohol, to allow the relationship to go unexamined.

The most significant costs are psychological. Drinking and the drug-induced behavior and its consequences are inconsistent with the individual's fundamental values and self-image. To deal with this contradiction, continued use requires the individual to make personality adjustments. The normal psychological devices are used to distort reality just enough to explain away the costs. These psychological defenses are the same ones each of us uses virtually daily to some degree. If you're walking down the street, say hello to a friend, and get no response, your feelings are momentarily hurt. Almost automatically, you tell yourself, "She must not have seen or heard me." So you shut off the hurt feelings with an explanation that may or may not be true. You pick an explanation that allows you to turn off the unpleasant feelings the situation has evoked. Another time, if you're ill-tempered, a complete grouch, and behaving in a fashion that you don't really like, you become uncomfortable with yourself. In such circumstances, you could say, "Yep, I sure am being a real pain in the neck to anyone near me." More likely the internal conversation will come out: "I've not been myself. The pressure of work must have gotten to me." In this way, we all attempt to control our discomfort and maintain psychic harmony. In doing so, we often overlook the obvious and adjust our experience just enough to take off the painful, rough emotional edges.

One of the disadvantages of wine is that it makes a man mistake words for thoughts.
SAMUEL JOHNSON

The person with a budding alcohol problem uses these kinds of defenses to maintain harmony and equilibrium in the relationship with their drug of choice. One way to accomplish this and explain away the costs is to *suppress emotions.* As negative emotions arise, the individual strives to keep them at bay: "I just won't think about it." So the fellow who made a fool of himself at last night's party tries to ignore the whole thing: "Hey, these things happen sometimes. There's no sense in worrying about it." However, pretending emotions aren't there doesn't make them disappear. They simply crop up somewhere else. Because suppression doesn't work totally, other psychological devices need to be used. *Rationalization* is a common device—seizing an explanation that inevitably stays clear of alcohol itself: "I really got hammered last night but . . ." or " I wouldn't have been plastered if Dylan hadn't been pushing the drinks." In this latter example, *projection* is at work as well. The reason for whatever occurred and the accompanying emotional discomfort was that the drinks were stiff and it's Dylan's fault. No responsibility is accepted by the drinker or blame laid on alcohol.

A number of rationalizations are so frequently used that they might almost qualify as warning signals of alcohol dependence—for example: "I can't be alcoholic because I *never* drink in the morning. *I'm* too young, too old, too smart, etc. I can quit *whenever* I want to. *Everyone* I know drinks the same way I do. I drink *only* beer. I drink only wine spritzers. I never miss work." Casual drinkers do not consider such explanations necessary.

Several factors allow such distortions to go unchallenged. One is attributable to the action of the drug. Alcohol warps perceptions. The only firsthand memory anyone will have of a drinking event is the one that was laid down in a drugged state. So if someone under a haze of alcohol perceives herself as being clever and witty, sobering up in the morning is not going to be sufficient to make her realize that she was loud, coarse, and vulgar. This "rosy memory" is termed by Johnson as *euphoric recall.* Until recently, with the advent of greater public awareness of alcohol problems, it was unlikely that other people would take it upon themselves to let the drinker know what really transpired. There might not be any problems if these distortions were only occasional, but they aren't. And what proves to be even more destructive is that with continued, heavy drinking, the discrepancy becomes greater and greater between what the individual expects to happen and what does happen. Proportionately, the need for further distortion to explain this discrepancy grows.

Drinking is supposed to improve the mood, but as dependence emerges, more and more frequently the opposite proves to be the case. To illustrate this on the mood continuum, after a drinking occasion the emotional state is one of greater discomfort than it was before the drinking. As alcohol's effects wear off, the individual is finding him- or herself being dropped off further down toward the pain end of the spectrum. The result of alcohol use is not an enhanced but a diminished sense of well-being.

A vicious cycle is developing. The psychological mechanisms used to minimize the discomfort simultaneously prevent a recognition of what is really happening. None of the defenses, even in combination, are completely foolproof. At times, individuals feel remorse about their behavior. At those times it doesn't matter where the blame lies—on someone else, on themselves, on alcohol—drinkers regret what's happening, so a negative self-image develops.

For the most part, the drinker truly believes the reality created by his or her projections and rationalizations. Understandably this begins to erode relationships with others. There are continual hassles over whose version of an event is accurate. This introduces additional tensions, and problems arise with friends, family, and coworkers. Self-esteem shrinks. The load of negative feelings expands. Ironically there is more and more reliance on the old relationship with alcohol. Drinking is deliberately structured into life patterns. Drinking is anticipated. The possibilities of drinking may well determine which invitations are accepted, where business meetings are held, and other activities. Gradually all leisure time is set up to include drinking.

The stage is set for the last developmental phase in the emergence of clear-cut dependence. The individual now *drinks to feel normal.* This is

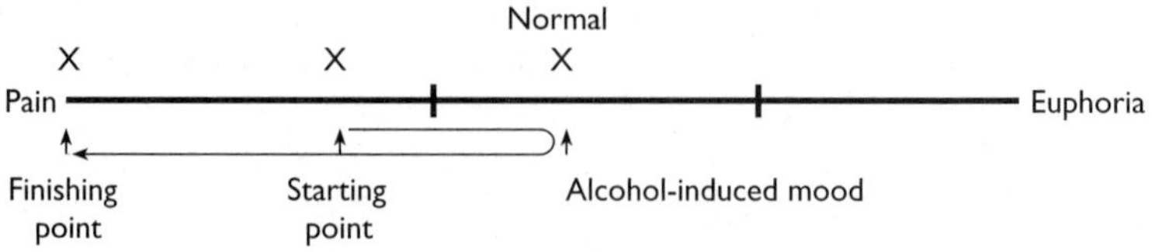

Drinking to Feel Normal

often wholly unappreciated by those for whom drinking is not a problem. Others assume, erroneously, that the alcohol-dependent person is drinking to feel good and have fun. By this point the idea of drinking to feel euphoric has long since gone. Alcohol has become essential, just to achieve a normal feeling state.

In addition to offering a normal feeling state, alcohol may assist normal functioning in other respects. Psychologists have documented the phenomenon of "state-dependent learning." Things learned in a particular context are most readily recalled under similar circumstances. Thus, things learned when sober are best recalled later in a sober state. Similarly, information learned while drinking is also more available for recall later when the person is again (or still) consuming alcohol. Thus, the heavy drinker may have a repertoire of behavior, coping mechanisms, social skills, and even information that, if learned during drinking, is less accessible when sober. In fact, drinking may be necessary to tap a reservoir of knowledge. This fact is what sometimes explains the inability to find liquor stashes that were hidden when drinking. Another way in which alcohol may be essential to normalize function is to ward off withdrawal symptoms if the drinker has become physically dependent.

Boundless intemperance
In nature is a tyranny; it hath been
Th'untimely emptying of the happy throne
And fall of many kings.
SHAKESPEARE
Macbeth

Memory distortions are not uncommon at this point. Blackouts may mean the absence of memory for some events. Repression is a psychological mechanism that also blocks out memory. Further havoc continues to be raised by "euphoric recall." The memories are only of the good times and the sense of relief associated with drinking. The problems and difficulties seemingly don't penetrate.

DETERIORATING FUNCTIONING

Because of the transformation of thinking, distorted view of reality, and ebbing self-esteem, the alcohol-dependent person's functioning deteriorates. Each of us is expected to fulfill various roles in life. For each slot in which we find ourselves, there is an accompanying set of expectations about appropriate behavior. Some of the typical roles are parent, spouse or partner, employee, citizen, or friend. Others may be more transient, such as scout leader, committee chair, patient, Rotary Club member, soccer coach, or Sunday school teacher. No matter what the role, with alcohol or other drug dependence, performance usually suffers. There are expectations that others have of us in a particular role. The alcohol-dependent

If God wanted us high,
He would have given us wings.
ARSENIO HALL

individual does not reliably meet them. Behavior is inconsistent. The individual is undependable—sometimes doing what is expected and doing it beautifully; the next time, it's "no show" followed by the flimsiest excuse. To add insult to injury, he or she gets furious at others for being disappointed, for being annoyed, or for not understanding.

Unreliable behavior has a profound impact on the people around the alcohol- or other drug-dependent person. Since these people have the normal insecurities of all humans, they think it might or must be their fault. Unwittingly they accept the rationalizations and projections. Some find themselves confused and often feel left out. They sense and fear the loss of an important relationship, one that has been nourishing to them. In turn, their own behavior can become distorted. Now, in addition to whatever problems are directly attributable to alcohol or drug use, interpersonal relationships are impaired. This fuels the tension.

Wine makes a man better pleased with himself; I do not say that it makes him more pleasing to others.
SAMUEL JOHNSON

FAMILY AND FRIENDS

Focus for a moment on family, close relationships, and friends. Applying behavioral learning terms, the dependent person has people in his or her life on a variable interval reinforcement schedule. There they are, busily trying to accommodate. They feel that, somehow, if they behave differently, do the "right thing," the alcohol-dependent person will respond. One time they're harsh; the next time they try an understanding approach. Then another time they might try to ignore the situation. But nothing works. The dependent person does not respond in any predictable way to others' behavior. If he happens to be a "good boy" or she's been a "perfect lady" on occasion, it really has no connection to what the family has or has not done. The others, in fact, are accommodating themselves to the alcohol-dependent individual. Never sure why some times go better, they persist in trying—and trying some more. Meanwhile, the inconsistency and unpredictability remain.

Eventually families or partners, as well as close friends, give up and try to live around the situation. Alternately the drinker is ignored or driving them crazy, yet, out of love and loyalty, for all too long others provide protection from the consequences of the drinking. Johnson introduced the term "enabling behavior" to describe this dynamic. (Enabling is discussed further in Chapter 8.) In a marriage or intimate relationship, if one partner has a major substance use problem, the other gradually assumes the accustomed functions of the impaired partner. Even though she may be the regular cook in the household, he may have contingency plans for supper in case it isn't ready that night. If he is the one who usually helps with the kids with homework or attends their sports events, she may consider herself on call to fill in. In case he is up to it, fine; if not, a ready excuse is hauled out and she fills in. Such interactions can lead to resentments in everyone. The person carrying the load feels burdened; the drinker feels deprived and ashamed.

With alcohol dependence present, sexual problems in intimate relationships are likely. Sexual functioning is not merely a physical activity; it also has strong psychological components. How someone feels about him- or herself and a partner is bound to show up in bed. Any alcohol use can disturb physiological capacity for sex. Shakespeare said it most succinctly: "alcohol provokes the desire but takes away the performance." In the male, alcohol interferes with erection—popularly referred to as "brewer's droop." The psychological realm has as strong an impact. Satisfying sexual relationships require an emotional relationship, a bond of love and affection. In a relationship with alcohol as the third member, neither partner is able to trust that bond; there are doubts on both sides. Problems result in many ways. Intoxication invites revulsion and rejection. Any qualities of love have, for the moment, been washed away by the alcohol. Sexual intimacy can become a weapon, too. One of the partners can try the tactic of emotional blackmail used in the ancient Greek play *Lysistrata:* refusing sex unless the partner changes his or her behavior. On the other hand, both partners can approach intercourse as the magic panacea. If they can still make love, they can minimize the importance of everything else lacking in the relationship.

In the earlier stages of an alcohol problem, friends, especially close ones, will offer the same kind of excuses for the individual that family members do. But as time goes on, and problems mount as behavior deteriorates, friendships disappear in inverse relationship to their closeness. In the later stages of alcohol dependence there may be "drinking buddies" but few true friends. The reasons are fairly obvious. Casual acquaintances are unlikely to be interested in becoming friends after a few examples of erratic behavior. It's simply not worth it. Close friends who have begun to see a problem emerging will probably try to help by talking to the drinker. In the early stages of an alcohol problem this may well be effective in prompting treatment. However, defenses grow in proportion to the magnitude of the alcohol problem. In the later stages the alcohol-dependent person may tell friends to mind their business, thus immobilizing them. The relationship with the bottle takes precedence over all others.

The exceptions only highlight the problem. One type of friend who may remain a companion is one who drinks in the same fashion and can be counted on to share the six-packs on the way home from work or to enjoy hitting the bars on the weekend. Another kind of friend will remain in loose touch, ready to lend a hand when needed. This person, often a recovering person, knows the friendship cannot be maintained or profitably cultivated while the drinking continues, but he or she will often stay in touch, poised to be of assistance and support, should the drinker show evidence of wishing to face the problem and stop. On the other hand, when faced with an alcohol problem in someone close to them, recovering individuals—and treatment professionals, for that matter—

BOX 7.1

Alcohol and the Workplace, in South Korea

In 1999, a series of scandals in the public prosecutor's offices shed light on drinking customs on the job in South Korea. The *Korea Herald* (1999) reported that "a prosecutor, intoxicated after several glasses of a beer-whiskey cocktail during lunch, dropped in at the press-room for a chat with reporters. There [the prosecutor] touched the breast of a female reporter." This was reported in the press and the ensuing public protest led to a ban on prosecutors' daytime drinking. A few months later there was another episode. A farewell lunch held in the prosecutor's office dining room included the ritual of *poktanju* (boilermakers). This practice involves "continuously passing, to all at the table, glasses of beer with a shot glass of whiskey, placed inside." Shortly after the lunch, "Still under the influence of five glasses of this peculiar cocktail," a prosecutor met with reporters back at his office. In his ramblings, he mentioned an operation launched several months earlier that had been intended to provoke a strike by government workers. This admission sparked outrage, protests, and led to an investigation. In the wake of all this, the government issued a 10-point code of conduct for public servants that included restrictions on drinking in connection with official business.

New code of conduct [editorial]. *Korea Herald.* June 15, 1999.

From: Room R, Jernigan D; Carlini-Marlatt B, Gureje O, Makela K, Marshall M, Medina-Mora M, et al. *Alcohol and the Developing World: A Public Health Perspective.* Helsinki, Finland: Finnish Foundation for Alcohol Studies, 2002.

often don't have an edge on anyone else. They, too, can be overwhelmed by the chaos that can ripple out from an alcohol-dependent person. They may also show denial, wanting the problem to be "anything but."

WORK

Often, although alcohol or drug-dependent people are deeply mired in deteriorating social and family relationships and suffering physical problems, they still may be able to function at work. The work arena seems to be the last part of the drinker's life to be affected. The job is often the status symbol for both the dependent employee and the partner. With more families counting on two paychecks, maintaining the income of both members is necessary. He or she might think or say: "There's nothing wrong with me. I'm still bringing in a good paycheck!" The other is likely to make excuses to the drinker's supervisor to protect the family livelihood.

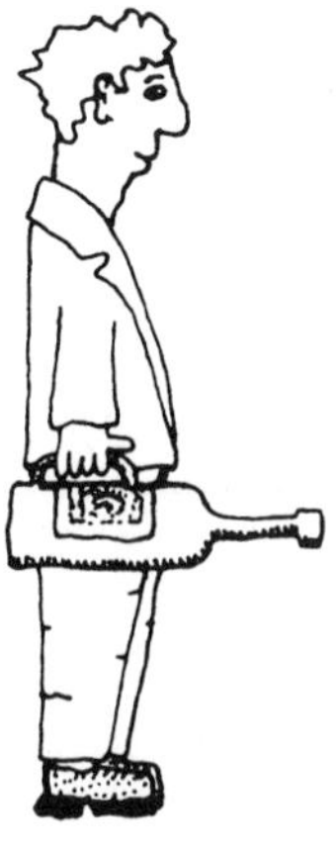

Intervention at the workplace is, of course, possible at even the earliest signs. Much effort is being made to alert employers to the early signs of alcohol and other drug use problems and to acquaint them with rehabilitation possibilities. The employer is in a unique position to effect treatment at a relatively early stage. A recommendation that someone go for treatment may well be a precipitating factor in a recovery. The fact that the employer sees the problem and is willing to acknowledge it can go far in breaking down the denial system. Keeping a job may be sufficient motivation for an employee to face the problem. (Employee assistance programs and their impact on earlier intervention and treatment are described further in Chapter 11.)

Those in serious trouble with alcohol generally believe that their public cover-up is successful. The behavior of those about them, too, often does little to challenge this misconception. Deteriorating functioning is covered up by other workers. Absences with the "flu" are ignored, and a gradual decline in their work is put down to "problems at home" or another such excuse. Most people, finding that it is not easy to confront someone with a drinking problem, wait until ignoring it is no longer possible. Over 20 years ago a study found that persons other than family members had noticed drinking problems on an average of 7 years before the impaired person first sought help. Vaillant's work confirmed this, too. He found although 4 or more alcohol-related problems were virtually sufficient to guarantee a diagnosis of alcohol dependence, it wasn't, in fact, until 11 separate such incidents had occurred that people entered treatment.

OTHER DRUGS OF ABUSE

How might other drug use alter the scenario sketched here? Much of this model would seem to be applicable to drugs other than alcohol. However, a drug's illicit status may introduce a bit more complexity. Johnson's schema was created to describe the progression of alcohol use. The first two stages Johnson sketches out are seen as applying to anyone who uses alcohol; that is, first learning what alcohol does and then in the second stage seeking its effects. Nothing happens during the first two stages to suggest that possibly drinking isn't such a great idea.

Central to Johnson's formulation is the fact that alcohol use in America is widely accepted. Unlike a Muslim country in which any drinking is frowned upon and any drinking that occurs is far more private, drinking in our American culture is not hidden. Nonproblematic drinking is essentially a public behavior. On any run-of-the-mill day, alcohol is part of what we see around us. It is so common that it often doesn't even register. For example, we are not shocked when the evening news includes a video clip of our president toasting a foreign dignitary at a formal state dinner. The number and variety of beer logos on baseball caps we pass as we walk down the street barely register. In America, seeking the mood swing is perfectly okay in a multitude of situations.

That's not the case when it comes to illicit drugs. From virtually the start of any illicit drug use, the user can't be so casual. According to Johnson's formulation, the equation is straightforward—the drinker compares how he or she feels before and on the heels of drinking. As long as the positives outweigh any negatives there is no reason to think any further about alcohol use.

The illicit drug user has to put something else into the mix. Simply put, the use of illicit drugs requires something else be weighed, the trade-

FOCUS ON DRUGS

Buying Drugs on the Internet

The National Center on Addiction and Substance Abuse at Columbia University (CASA) is conducting a study on the diversion and abuse of prescription medications. In the process, information came to light that was so alarming the center took the unusual step of preparing a white paper to publish separately what researchers had discovered: the utter ease with which anyone can purchase drugs over the Internet.

During a week in January 2004, CASA research staff identified almost 500 Web sites offering scheduled drugs for sale. Of these a number were portal sites that simply funnel the traffic to an anchor site, a transfer that may not be evident to the viewer. So the actual sales operations were fewer. In its final analysis, 157 sales sites were included in the study. Not all online pharmacies sold all of the prescription drugs. Here's the breakdown for the major drug classes: Opioids (codeine, Fentanyl, OxyContin, Percodan) were available on 103 sites; depressants (benzodiazepines such as Valium and Xanex as well as barbiturates such as Seconal) could be purchased on 144 sites; and stimulants (such as Ritalin and Adderall) were offered on 47 sites.

As laid out in the white paper, "Anyone—including children—can easily obtain highly addictive controlled substance online with a prescription. All they need is a credit card." Among the major points:

- Fully 90% of sites providing controlled drugs did not require a prescription. This includes the 41% of online prescription pharmacies that stated no prescription was required and 49% that offered an online consultation. The consultation most commonly asked the supposed patient to complete a health questionnaire online. In some cases a consultation fee was charged.
- 4% required that a prescription be faxed.
- 2% required that a prescription be mailed.
- 4% made no mention of prescriptions.
- Regarding the origins of the drugs, 28% of the sites indicated that the medications would be shipped from within the United States. For 47%, the source was identified as a foreign country. In some instances that is all that was noted; in others a specific country was named; and for still others, simply a region, such as Europe or Latin America was noted as the source. For the remaining 25% of the sites no mention was made of the drugs' origins.

Several case examples involve efforts by law enforcement personnel to purchase drugs. In one case, OxyContin was purchased without a prescription. The online form required the purchaser to check a box indicating that the purchaser would forward medical records. Nonetheless, the online pharmacy billed the credit card and shipped the drugs, without such information ever being sent. One month later, the online pharmacy automatically charged the same credit card and shipped out an unrequested refill.

The sale of drugs on the Internet is a fairly new phenomenon and the laws and regulations have yet to catch up. Essentially this activity is wholly unregulated. Licensing and regulation of pharmacies occurs at the state level. These cyber-pharmacies transcend state laws. There are multiple federal agencies with a potential stake in this. However, current law and procedures are ill-suited to handle a situation that could not have been imagined when these laws and regulations were drafted.

From: Foster S., *"You've Got Drugs!" Prescription Drug Pushers on the Internet.* A CASA White Paper. New York: National Center on Addiction and Substance Abuse at Columbia University, February 2004.

off of the anticipated pleasures in light of the possible problems. It is unlikely that this will be particularly conscious. No one sits down with paper and pencil and makes a list of the pros and cons. But in effect, that mental calculation is being made. For example, we might factor in the ease of getting a drug, the likelihood of getting caught, what is required to lower the risk of that, and what those consequences would be. The decision to use on any particular occasion will be determined by how this personal cost-benefit analysis turns out. So, before seeking the mood swing the possible user is answering the question: Is the mood swing worth it?" The relative weight will determine the behavior.

One can imagine any number of things that would cause different people to weigh the same factors differently, leading to two opposite responses to the question they ask themselves: "Is drug use now worth it?"

The hallmark of *harmful use* is when drinking continues despite the fact that the drinker's mood state is less positive after than it was before drinking. Recall, this is the point at which Johnson says psychological devices are required to distort reality, at least enough to explain away the costs. A variety of psychological mechanisms is available. With illicit drug use these psychological defenses have to be used earlier in the game. Before the state of harmful use, at the point of *seeking the mood swing,* illicit drug users have to justify to themselves *any* use. The list of potential explanations is almost limitless: "It's no big deal," or "I'm not hurting anyone," to "It's nobody else's business," or "The laws are totally stupid." For the discussion here, the issue isn't whether these arguments are or are not valid. For this discussion, the significant factor is simply that they are required at all. The question this raises is whether the need for mental gymnastics—something not required to allow/justify seeking the mood swing with drinking—has a ripple effect down the line. If a user repeatedly answers "Yes" to the question of "Is use worth it?" what does it take to begin responding "No"? If there haven't been any particular negative consequences from the user's perspective, does the "Yes" come easier? Learning theory would suggest so. Also, drug effects must be factored in. The more a user *really* likes a drug's effects, the more serious the negative consequences need to be to tip the balance.

Beyond any possible modifications to the Johnson schema, with illicit drug use there are other factors worth noting. Regular use of other drugs entails time and effort merely to assure a reliable supply. There isn't the option of dashing out quickly to the nearest convenience store and picking up a bag of heroin along with the half gallon of milk for the kids. There isn't the equivalent of the neighborhood bar, where you can stop on the way home from work to order up a line of cocaine instead of a beer. Depending on who your friends are, you can't count on going to a wine and cheese event and finding joints rolled up, attractively displayed next to the veggies and dip. Illicit drug use entails hustling. Part of the hustle is the unending series of choices that entail not so good options. Do you take the kids along when you go out to score, thinking "After all they'll probably just fall asleep in the car"? Or do you leave them alone at home, thinking "After all, it's their bedtime, and they hardly ever wake up at night, and I wouldn't be gone *that* long"?

Alcohol-dependent persons may find themselves going with a cheap wine instead of the expensive foreign, vintage bottle. But there's no question it's ethanol. With many illicit drugs, who knows? Depending on the substance, a question that surfaces with illicit drugs has to do with possible contaminants or substitutes. Another factor that research has shown is part of illicit drug use is the greater likelihood of encounters with the law and higher rates of crime.

A few thoughts on adolescents. Adolescent substance use is addressed in detail in Chapter 11, so the comments here are limited. In the face of possible alcohol or drug use, parents' behavior can look a lot like what is described here for family members generally. Under the best of circumstances, adolescents' behavior can be fairly erratic. With the usual ups and downs, how do you know if or which parts of the roller coaster ride can be attributed to drug use or drinking?

Parents don't always *really* want to know. What are they going to do? And the kids generally have any number of reasons to keep it hidden. Even if use is suspected, parents may be quite happy and relieved to hear their kid claim it isn't so. And teens can be very imaginative. One good tactic adolescents use to counter suspicion is doing a few things to demonstrate how mature, responsible, and thoughtful they are—even if it's only hanging up the backpack rather than leaving it in the middle of the floor. If the parents were to bring up a concern about possible alcohol or drugs, adolescents are capable of performances that would warrant Academy Awards. They can act hurt, outraged, insulted, and incredulous, as if the parent's mere thought that they'd be doing drugs has to rank up there as about *the* most stupid thing the parent has *ever* done. And the merry-go-round continues.

A FINAL THOUGHT

Often alcohol- or drug-impaired persons have no idea how obvious their difficulties are to so many other people. When they are finally confronted, it can be a great shock to find out how much of their behavior that they thought was hidden was, in fact, observed. The rationalization and denial systems actually convince the alcohol-impaired person that no one on the job or in the community knows about the drinking problem.

The behavior that accompanies alcohol or drug dependence causes pain and confusion for all—the individual and those around him or her. Unfortunately, most of the family's and friends' efforts to alter the situation don't work. Regardless of good will, alcohol dependence rarely responds to the more common maneuvers of concerned friends or family. Affecting these destructive patterns takes a special knowledge of the dynamics of the disease, its effects on others, and treatment approaches, with the clinical skills of a disinterested, but not an uninterested, participant.

RESOURCES AND FURTHER READING

In this chapter the attempt has been to convey what dependence feels like for the individual with the disease and for those whose lives are closely touched by it. Tackling the scientific writings, with their reports of controlled studies, tables of data, and reams of footnotes, is unlikely to be a useful avenue for further exploration. Instead, it is suggested you turn to literature. An autobiography of someone with alcohol or other drug dependence can provide insight into and understanding of the behavior and feelings that characterize the disease. Consider the plays of Eugene O'Neill: *Long Day's Journey into Night* powerfully captures the family beset by addiction.

Identify a recovering individual with whom you can just talk. Don't consider this a formal interview; consider it a conversation initiated by an interested person who wants to know what another's life is like. Take as a guide the conversation you might have with a close friend who has returned from a long-anticipated trip of a lifetime. Through your questioning and listening, by asking that person to "relive" the trip, you become a companion on the adventure.

Attend an open meeting of AA or NA. As members tell their "stories," as they speak about "what it was like, what happened, and what things are like now" the behavior and the emotional life of alcohol and drug dependence are powerfully conveyed.

Johnson V. *I'll Quit Tomorrow,* rev. edition. New York: Harper & Row, 1983.

Schuckit MA, Smith TL, Anthenelli R, et al. Clinical course of alcoholism in 636 male inpatients. *American Journal of Psychiatry* 150(5):786–792, 1993.

CHAPTER 8

Effects of Alcohol Problems on the Family

THE "FAMILY ILLNESS"

In the early 1980s, a review of 2 books purporting to be comprehensive works on alcoholism noted the scanty attention paid to the impact of alcohol on the family. The reviewer plaintively asked, "Why is so much written about the effects of alcoholism upon a patient's liver enzymes and so little written about the effects of parental alcoholism on the children?" Fortunately, that question no longer has the same ring of truth to it.

One of the major developments in the alcohol field during the 1980s was the vastly increased attention to the plight of the family. This is evidenced particularly by the involvement of families in alcohol treatment. In addition, there were efforts to reach out to family members, even if the alcohol-dependent person was not in treatment. As part of the attention to the family, one began to hear alcohol dependence described as a "family illness." This refers to the tremendous impact those with active alcohol dependence have on those around them. There is no way the family members can escape or ignore the alcohol-troubled member. In a Gallup poll conducted in 2000, 35% of the respondents said alcohol had been a cause of trouble in their families. The majority of the impairments symptomatic of alcohol dependence are behavioral. So in the day-to-day interactions of family life, the family members are confronted with the behaviors symptomatic of alcohol dependence, although the behaviors initially may appear to have little connection to the drinking. Over time, the family can become as functionally impaired as the alcohol-dependent member.

Since the reviewer's lament, the issues of the family have caught the attention of the alcohol research community. However, there is always a lag time between an issue's gaining the attention of the researchers and the point at which the research is conducted, the data are analyzed, the results are published, and the findings are translated into practice. In the meantime, clinicians are forced to do the best they can, drawing on their clinical observations and using the information that is available.

Inevitably, the approaches during such transitional periods will later be recognized as a combination of fact and fiction. As research findings become available, the challenge is to refine our practice to incorporate the new knowledge, and, as required, lay aside our earlier formulations. That in many respects is where we are now. We can no longer continue discussing the problems of alcohol and the family simply by drawing on the best guesses of yesterday. We are being forced to recognize there is far more variety in family life today than there was several generations ago. Families today come in many forms. They include traditional families—statistically described as husband, wife, 2.2 children, and a dog—to single-parent families, unmarried couples, same-sex couples, and blended families, which include children from prior marriages or relationships. Variations on the traditional theme inevitably introduce new twists for families. While there may be common issues, there may be differences posed by the particular family structure.

The Family's Response

The earliest attention to alcohol and the family can be traced to a classic monograph published by Joan Jackson in 1954, "Alcoholism and the Family." It endeavored to describe the stages that occur as a family comes to grips with alcoholism. Her work paralleled that of E. M. Jellinek, who only 8 years before had studied members of AA to identify the stages of alcohol addiction (see Chapter 4). Jackson's work was conducted through her attending meetings and speaking with members of a group known as the AA Auxiliary. Later, the Auxiliary became what we know as Al-Anon Family Groups. Given the era in which her research was conducted, the stages she identified are based on the family in which the husband and father was the alcoholic and when alcoholism was considered a disease of middle age, taking hold between the ages of 35 and 50. The 6 stages Jackson sketched out are described in the following sections in the order in which, in her sample, they typically unfold.

Denial

Occasional episodes of excessive drinking at first are explained away by both partners. Early in the emergence of alcoholism, drinking because of tiredness, worry, nervousness, or a bad day is not unbelievable. The assumption is that the episode is an isolated instance and therefore no problem. If the couple is part of a group in which heavy drinking is acceptable, this provides a handy cover for developing dependency. A cocktail before dinner easily becomes 2 or 3, and wine with the meal and brandy afterward also pass without much notice.

Attempts to Eliminate the Problem

In this stage, the alcoholic's partner recognizes that the drinking is not normal and tries to pressure him or her to quit, to be more careful, or to cut down: "If you would only pull yourself together," "If you would only use a little willpower," or "If you really love me, you won't do this any more." Simultaneously, the alcoholic's partner tries to hide the problem from the outside and keep up a good front. At the same time the alcoholic probably sneaks drinks or drinks outside the home, in an attempt to hide the amount he or she is drinking. Children in the family may start having problems in response to the family stress.

Years after Jackson's article, Vernon Johnson pointed out, in *I'll Quit Tomorrow,* that these early attempts to eliminate the problem may be successful. In such cases, formal treatment or AA involvement is unlikely. Indeed, it may not be needed. Historically the danger for families at this point was that they might enter some general counseling—whether with clergy, a psychologist, or a social worker—that failed to address the problem drinking head on. In such cases, couples or individual therapy easily became a part of the denial. It could be a way for the affected person to continue drinking and for both partners to pretend to be doing something about it. Helping professionals are far more knowledgeable about substance abuse today, so the chances of alcohol problems going undetected are less likely.

Disorganization and Chaos

The family equilibrium has now broken down. The alcoholic's spouse can no longer pretend everything is okay and spends most of the time going from crisis to crisis. Financial troubles are common. Under a great deal of stress, possibly questioning her own emotional health, the spouse may seek outside help. In general, women are more likely than men to use outside assistance. Too often, spouses may seek help from friends who know no more than they do about what to do. Similarly, they may seek out a member of the clergy who has no training in dealing with alcoholism. Or they may turn to the family physician, who in the past may have prescribed some "nerve" pills when confronted by their distraught condition. If at this stage the nonalcoholic partner seeks assistance from alcohol professionals and/or becomes involved with Al-Anon, the process will probably take a different course altogether.

Somebody PUT TOO MUCH ice IN MY DRINK!!

Reorganization in Spite of the Problem

The spouse's coping abilities have been strengthened. He or she gradually assumes the larger share of responsibility for the family unit. This may mean getting a job, or taking over the finances. The major focus of energy is no longer directed toward getting the alcoholic partner to shape up. Instead, the spouse takes charge. The spouse fosters family life, despite the alcoholism. It has since been recognized that the degree to

FOCUS ON DRUGS

Marijuana Toxicoses in Dogs

Marijuana (Cannabis sativa) is a commonly used recreational drug among humans; animals may be exposed following ingestion or accidental inhalation of smoke. From January 1998 to January 2002, 213 incidences were recorded of dogs that developed clinical signs following oral exposure to marijuana, with 99% having neurologic signs, and 30% exhibiting gastrointestinal signs. The marijuana ingested ranged from 1/2 to 90 g. The lowest dose at which signs occurred was 84.7 mg/kg and the highest reported dose was 26.8 g/kg. Onset of signs ranged from 5 min to 96 h, with most signs occurring within 1 to 3 h after ingestion. The signs lasted from 30 min to 96 h. Management consisted of decontamination, sedation (with diazepam as drug of choice), fluid therapy, thermoregulation and general supportive care. All animals made full recoveries. Copyright 2004, Comparative Toxicology Laboratory.

Janczyk P, Donaldson CW, Gwaltney S. Two hundred and thirteen cases of marijuana toxicoses in dogs. *Veterinary and Human Toxicology* 46(1):19–21, 2004. (9 refs.)

which a stable family life can be established and maintained, even if the alcoholic remains in the home, can have important implications for the welfare of children in the family. Children fare far better in families in which the family rituals are maintained, whether these are celebrations, such as Christmas or birthdays; or regular family meal times; or family vacations, or any of the other things, large or small, that "we always do."

Efforts to Escape

Separation or divorce may be attempted. If the family unit remains intact, the family continues living around the alcoholic member.

Family Reorganization

In the case of separation, family reorganization occurs without the alcoholic partner and parent. If the alcoholic achieves sobriety, a reconciliation may take place. Either path will require both partners to realign roles and make new adjustments.

Further Thoughts

Jackson's formulations are focused on the family in which the husband is alcohol dependent. An important difference is found in marriage outcomes depending on which partner has the alcohol problem. Among those with alcohol dependence, the female alcohol-dependent member is much more likely to be divorced than is her male counterpart. In the past, those trying to account for this difference speculated that women who marry someone with alcohol dependence have unconscious, neurotic needs to be married to weak, inadequate males. The implication was that, because of this need, they stay married and get psychological strokes for doing so. That view no longer has much credence. Given economic realities, it is not unexpected that the nonalcoholic wife stays in her marriage longer than the nonalcoholic husband. She may feel a need for the husband's financial support to maintain the family. Indeed, following a divorce, the economic situation for the majority of women and their children declines. On the other side, men in general are less likely to seek outside help for any kind of problem—no matter what. Therefore, the husband of an alcoholic may see no alternative to divorce to save himself, as well as the children.

Research on marriage has identified some reasons that partners choose each other. For all persons, it is generally recognized that finding one's "true love" and the choice of a marriage partner is not a random event. People tend to select marriage partners with similarities to their parents. There are women who marry men with alcohol problems who themselves had fathers with alcohol dependence. For them, a situation that appears to others as stressful and painful may simply be what they expect in a marriage. Those involved in alcohol treatment are struck by the fact that some women marry or live with a succession of alcohol-dependent men.

Jackson's formulations may be useful in considering the situation of a family and its efforts to cope. Although this model provides a useful general framework, do not expect all families to experience these stages in the textbook fashion. Some families might get bogged down in different stages. Some never move beyond denial. Some may seem trapped in an endless cycle of chaos and crisis. And some go through a painful succession of attempts to escape from the situation, reconciliations, followed by later attempts again to escape. Our understanding of the factors that account for these differences is limited. One factor that may make a difference is when the problem drinking emerges. Those who have studied alcoholic marriages suggest that wives most able to help themselves and their families are those who were married before their husbands became problem drinkers.

THE FAMILY SYSTEM

A common dimension of virtually all approaches to the family with an alcohol-dependent member is viewing the family as a system. This is a very common perspective within the larger field of family therapy. Central to this is the belief that changes in any part of the system (any family member) affect all of the others. The other members, in response, also make changes in an attempt to maintain the family equilibrium. The metaphor that captures this close interdependence is that of a circus family specializing in a high-wire balancing act. All members of the act climb up to the top of the tent. In turn, they step out onto the thin wire to begin an intricate set of maneuvers to build a human pyramid high above the audience. Timing and balance are critical; the mutual interdependence is obvious. Each is sensitive to even the tiniest movement of the

Harry's idea of being romantic and tender is opening my beer cans for me.

others. All of the family members in the troupe continually adjust and readjust their balance, which is necessary to maintain the routine. If only one fails to do the expected, the entire routine fails.

In essence, families with an impaired member function in a very similar fashion. The behavior that accompanies alcohol dependence begins to invade the family routine. Everyone attempts to compensate, with the goal of restoring the equilibrium to the family. Most families make precarious, and usually unhealthy, adjustments to the presence of drinking. They expend energy to maintain the status quo. The family's behavior is designed to avoid doing anything that might further upset the delicate balance that prevails, which to their minds would prompt further deterioration of the family's situation. And after having adjusted to a problem, the family would be required to make significant readjustments if the impaired member were to seek treatment.

In terms of the kinds of accommodations that families make, there can be a range of responses. At one extreme, the drinking member is almost like a boarder in the family's household. The family isolates the alcohol-dependent member. They expect little. They give little. In this way, they maintain some stability and continuity for themselves. At the other extreme, all of family life is alcohol centered, responding to the crisis of the moment. In addition, families can vacillate between patterns of accommodating the impaired member, depending on whether the person is drinking or not drinking.

Recent research has identified 3 approaches family members use in living with an alcoholic: (1) keeping out of the way of the drinker and managing one's own life; (2) caregiving, counseling, and controlling; and (3) resigning and maintaining a facade. While all are used at various times, there may be a "usual approach," and the approach most commonly chosen differs by gender and between spouse and children. Most commonly the spouse is involved with caregiving, counseling, and controlling. Children of problem drinkers, on the other hand, are more likely to opt for keeping out of the way of the drinker and managing their own lives. Men more than women are more likely to adopt resignation, while women are likely to selectively keep out of the way while also engaged in caregiving.

Enabling

No family member has ever caused alcohol dependence, despite what the dependent member may claim. However, family members can, despite their best intentions, behave in a way that allows the drinking to continue. They may protect the alcohol-dependent member, make excuses or accept the explanations, and endeavor in a variety of ways to cover up. They call the employer, pretending the absenteeism is due to "the flu." Or they cover a bad check or retain a good lawyer to beat a DWI charge.

The alcohol-impaired member's actions are bound to create stresses and increase the family's anxiety level. This in turn may provoke more drinking to relieve the dependent person's own anxiety, which raises the family's anxiety even higher, and the family members react by simply doing more of what they were already doing. The pattern escalates on both sides until a crisis occurs. The family is no better able to cope with the disease in its midst than is the impaired member; thus, involvement in treatment is essential.

Vernon Johnson, in his observations of families, noticed how common such behaviors are and their unintended results. While attempting to live with and around the illness and to reduce the level of pain for themselves, the family's behavior often unwittingly allows the drinking to continue. This is occurring whenever the family's actions protect the alcohol-dependent member from the consequences of drinking. By removing the costs that result from drinking, the family takes away the major impetus for change. This phenomenon Johnson termed "enabling." Enabling behavior can be "white lies," the explanations provided to others that take the person off the hook. Enabling can consist of "overlooking," or not commenting on, the most outrageous behavior. Often it entails active intervention on the individual's behalf. It is happening whenever others scurry around to raise bail money and then follow up with a call to the local newspaper requesting that the arrest be kept out of the paper. It is happening when parents cover the cost of an adolescent son's car repairs plus the added insurance premiums resulting from a DWI. Enabling can be cleaning up your college roommate when she comes in drunk and throws up on herself, the rug, the bed, and your sweater, which she is wearing.

Ironically, while sparing the alcohol-dependent person from experiencing the consequences and thus the associated pain, the family members absorb the pain themselves. The behavior considered as enabling may be viewed as necessary because "I care," "These things happen," "I just can't take any more," "I'm afraid of what will happen to me (to the children) if I don't," "Someone has to assume some responsibility," and on and on. Nonetheless, it often involves actions that are distasteful or feel wrong. Enabling behaviors can evoke twinges of guilt, anger, despair, frustration, and shame. To draw upon a metaphor from a family systems approach commonly used in psychotherapy, the enabler and alcoholic are in an "escalating equilibrium." This means that the behavior of each reinforces and maintains the other, while also raising the costs and emotional consequences for both.

Co-dependency

A term commonly used to describe the effects of alcohol problems on family members is "co-dependency," and "co-dependent" is the term

used for the affected family member(s). There has never been a single consistent definition for these terms. In some instances, these are used as a label—a shorthand means to refer to affected family members. At the other end of the spectrum, co-dependence has been proposed as a personality disorder, a distinct psychiatric condition warranting inclusion in the American Psychiatric Association's *Diagnostic and Statistical Manual.* This view has received little support.

Timmen Cermak, M.D., one of the major advocates for naming co-dependency as a new psychiatric disorder, suggested the following criteria for making the diagnosis:

1. Continued investment of one's self-esteem in the ability to control oneself and others in the face of serious adverse consequences
2. Assumption of responsibility for meeting others' needs to the exclusion of one's own
3. Anxiety and boundary distortions with respect to intimacy and separation
4. Enmeshment in relationships with personality-disordered, chemically dependent, other co-dependent, and/or impulse-disordered individuals
5. Three or more of the following: excessive reliance on denial; constriction of emotions; repression; hypervigilance; compulsions; anxiety; substance abuse; an experience of being the victim of past or current physical or sexual abuse; stress-related medical illnesses; remaining in a primary relationship with an active substance abuser for at least 2 years without seeking help.

Research has not provided support for the notion of family members' sharing a set of symptoms that represent a discrete psychiatric condition.

The widespread adoption of the terms "co-dependency" and "co-dependent" has been the source of considerable discomfort for many in the alcohol and substance abuse fields. Since its initial introduction, the concept has been widely adopted by self-help groups and has spread into the popular culture. Witness the book *Co-dependent No More,* which topped the *New York Times* best-seller list for nearly a year. Such a widespread popular acceptance of an idea that is without scientific support represents a dilemma for clinicians. The notion of co-dependency has hit a responsive chord. This fact should remind us of the pain that family members experience in response to problems in their midst, the sense of impotence these can evoke, and their felt need for assistance in making changes. However, in discussions with clients, it is important to draw on its utility as a metaphor, without implying it is or acting as if it were a proven scientific concept. If we treat it as more than a metaphor, we are in danger of providing poor clinical care. No one would dispute the effects of alcohol dependence on family members, or the fact that these family members are statistically more likely to encounter many problems and in greater numbers than their counterparts in the general population. However, to award labels indiscriminately and to presume that every family member shares the constellation of symptoms is a grave disservice to clients. Assumptions based simply on family status cannot substitute for a careful assessment and evaluation. There is a danger, too, that the strengths of families and family members are overlooked when one assumes pathology.

Current Thinking

I get no kick from champagne,
Mere alcohol doesn't thrill me at all,
So tell me why should it be true
that I get a kick out of you?
COLE PORTER
"I Get a Kick Out of You," 1934

The research on families touched by alcohol and other substance abuse is growing. What has become clear is that not all families are affected by alcohol dependence in a uniform manner. Thus, there are few universal statements that can be made about families facing substance abuse or dependence. Furthermore, it is now recognized that the features originally seen as distinctive to the alcohol-troubled family are also seen in other families confronted by stress. The response to stress seemingly is the common denominator. It doesn't matter whether it is the result of alcohol or other substance use, serious mental illness, or family disruptions due to job loss or death.

Among the questions now being considered are the factors that are associated with differing levels of family dysfunction, the factors that are associated with stable recoveries in families following treatment, and the indications for different types of family treatment. Attention is also being directed to a family's protective factors, those family attributes that seem to reduce the disruption that can accompany substance abuse. Interestingly, much of the current research is directed to the types of factors in the family that may promote or protect children from later alcohol problems, rather than looking for a general psychological profile. For the child of an alcohol-dependent parent, the single major problem resulting from parental alcohol dependence is the child's own increased risk of alcoholism, due to genetic endowment.

The earliest examination of the impact of alcohol on the family zeroed in on its psychological impact and the impact on personality, self-esteem, and identity. Attention has now turned to other factors and their costs to family members. Domestic violence is more common in the home with alcoholism. Psychiatric illness may also be present. Members of the family themselves have greater levels of physical illness, especially of stress-related illnesses. Family members are more vulnerable to gastrointestinal disease, migraine headaches, hypertension, anxiety, and depression. A comparison of health-care costs for family units both before and after alcohol treatment of a family member bears this out. Before treatment of the alcohol-impaired individual, others in the family have significantly more medical problems than do the general population. After treatment, this difference disappears.

CHILDREN OF ALCOHOLICS

Children in the Home

It is estimated that, in the United States, 25% of children under the age of 18 are living in a family with a parent in need of alcohol or other substance abuse treatment. These children deserve special attention. In an atmosphere of conflict, tension, and uncertainty, their needs for warmth, security, and even physical care may be inadequately met. In a family in which adult roles are inconsistently and inadequately filled, children lack good models to form their own identities. It is more likely that such children will have a harder time than will their peers as they enter into relationships outside the home, at school, or with playmates. A troubled child may be the signal of an alcohol problem in a family.

It cannot be emphasized too strongly how much remains unknown about the impact of alcohol problems on children. In the following discussion of children's coping styles and the impact that continues into adulthood, it must be emphasized that these formulations are not based on unbiased scientific research. Much of what has been attributed to children of alcoholics originated in self-help groups of adults who grew up in alcohol-troubled homes. Or the information has come from children of parents with alcohol dependence who have sought treatment. Although their wounds are real, one must ask how far one can safely generalize from their experiences. They may represent a minority of children in alcohol-troubled homes. Or they may be speaking primarily for another generation—when alcohol treatment was less common, when family treatment was almost unheard of, and when alcohol dependence was more of a stigma. In any case, it must be remembered that being a child in an alcohol-troubled family does not confer an automatic sentence of lifelong problems.

Without question, growing up with an alcohol-dependent parent is far from ideal. At the same time, the experiences of children in these families vary greatly. There are different patterns of drinking and different behaviors associated with drinking. Children are various ages, as are their parents, when the drinking problem becomes apparent, or when loss of control occurs. Furthermore, there are differences in the coping styles of the nonalcohol-dependent parent, which can moderate the impact of the drinking on family life. All these factors influence how a parent's drinking affects the child. The specific problems of particular children will vary. Furthermore, a child's own natural resilience may be buttressed by the nurturing of extended family, scout leaders, coaches, teachers and neighbors, or parents of peers. Thus, a child's experience may be less impoverished than it might appear. Furthermore, many of the problems encountered are not exclusive to the alcoholic home. Many of the characteristics attributed to alcoholic families may be generally true of any dysfunctional family. Nonetheless, in thinking of children it is hard not to think in terms of the dramatic.

Take 5 minutes to imagine what life might be like for a child with a parent who is alcohol dependent:

- *As a preschooler.* What is it like to lie in bed, listening to your parents fight? Or to have Daddy disappear for periods of time unexpectedly? Or to be spanked really hard and sent away from dinner just because your milk spilled? Or to have a succession of sitters because Mommy works two jobs? Or to get lots of attention one moment and be in the way the next instant?
- *As an elementary school child.* What is it like when Mom forgets to give you lunch money? Or to wait and wait after soccer practice for a ride, long after the other kids have been picked up? Or for Dad to cancel out on the scout hike because he is sick? Or to not be allowed to bring friends home to play? Or to have your friends' mothers not let them ride in your car? Or to be scared to tell Mom you need a white shirt to be a pilgrim in the class Thanksgiving play?
- *As an early adolescent.* What is it like if you can't participate in school functions because you must get home to care for your younger brothers and sisters? Or if the money you made mowing lawns is missing from your room? Or if Dad's name is regularly featured in the court column? Or if Mother asks you to telephone her boss because she has a black eye from falling down? Or if there's no one from your family to go to the athletic awards banquet?
- *As an older adolescent.* What do you imagine awaits you after high school? Do you really want to enlist in the service or just to get away? Or what if your dad doesn't fill out the college financial aid forms on time? Or if your Mom borrowed your car and did in the fender while trying to park?

In considering the impact of such behaviors, it is helpful to consider the normal developmental tasks that confront children of different ages and consider how these may be impeded by a parental alcohol problem. Those who have studied the process of emotional development see very early childhood as the period in life in which the major emotional tasks center on developing a sense of security and an ability to trust the environment. This is the time that children should learn that they are able to interact with others to have basic needs met. For the children of alcohol-dependent parents, these basic conditions may not be met. For preadolescent children, a major emotional task is developing a sense of autonomy and an ability to use rules to cope with life events. For adolescents, the emotional tasks center around separating from the family and developing the ability to function independently in the world.

The problems may have begun before birth. As discussed in Chapter 6, maternal alcohol use can influence fetal development. At its most extreme, this is expressed as fetal alcohol syndrome. In addition to the direct impact of the drug, behaviors associated with heavy drinking may affect fetal development. Physical trauma, including falls, malnutrition, or abnormalities of glucose metabolism are not uncommon. Any of these can have an impact on a developing baby.

The emotional state of the expectant mother is presumed to influence fetal development. It certainly has an influence on the course of labor and delivery. The emotional state of the alcohol-dependent expectant mother might differ dramatically from that of a normal, healthy, nondrinking expectant mother and may be a source of problems. An alcohol-troubled expectant father may exert some indirect prenatal influences. If he is abusive or provides little emotional and financial support, this can cause anxiety in the mother. Lack of support and consequent anxiety during pregnancy are associated with more difficult deliveries. In turn, these difficulties are related to developmental disorders in children. In a similar vein, stress at certain times during pregnancy increases fetal activity. This, in turn, is linked to colicky babies. No specific data are available on labor and delivery for either female alcoholics or wives of male alcoholics.

Another crucial time in any infant's life comes shortly after delivery. The very early interactions between mother and infant are important influences in the mother-child relationship. Medications that may be required for a difficult delivery can make the bonding more difficult. Both the mother and the infant, under the effects of the medication, are less able to respond to each other.

A new mother needs emotional and physical support to help her deal with the presence of the baby in her life. At a minimum, the baby requires food, warmth, physical comfort, and consistency of response from the mother. In the case of a family with an active alcohol-dependent member, one cannot automatically assume that everything is going smoothly.

Children's Coping Styles

Some children of alcoholics may be having quite apparent and obvious problems. Yet given the potential for a chaotic environment in the alcoholic family, it is sometimes striking how well children cope with the presence of alcohol dependence. About two decades ago, drawing on a family systems approach to the alcoholic family, clinicians working in the alcohol field postulated several distinctive coping styles that children adopt in response to parental alcoholism. These are described in the following paragraphs. These coping styles were also seen to be tied to problems in later life.

Children's alleged coping styles are widely discussed. Efforts to verify these behavior patterns have generally been unsuccessful. At best they can only be used as a metaphor, as a way of outlining the kinds of adjustments children might make. To encourage a family or for you yourself to put a family under a microscope to identify a child's role in the alcoholic family is unwarranted.

What are these supposed coping styles? One formulation includes 3 roles that children may adopt. One is to be the *responsible one*. This role is seen as usually falling to the only child or the oldest child, especially the oldest daughter. The child may assume considerable responsibility, not only for him- or herself but also for younger brothers and sisters—taking over chores and keeping track of what needs to be done. In general, this child compensates as much as possible for the instability and inconsistency introduced by the parental alcoholism. A second coping response is that of the *adjuster.* This child doesn't take on the responsibilities of managing. Instead, the child follows directions and easily accommodates to whatever comes along. This child is remarkable for how much he or she takes in stride. The third proposed style is to be the *placater.* This role involves managing not the physical affairs, as the responsible one does, but the emotional affairs. This child is ever attuned to being concerned and sensitive to others. It may include being sympathetic to the alcoholic and alternately to the nonalcoholic parent, always trying to soothe ruffled feathers.

The common denominator to these roles is that each in its own way is an attempt to survive, a coping strategy. These roles are seen as providing the child with support and approval from persons outside the home. For example, the responsible one probably is a good student, is Mommy's little helper, and gets praise for both. The danger to a child is becoming frozen in the adopted role. The role can become a lifetime pattern. What is helpful in childhood can be detrimental for an adult. Thus, the responsible one can become an adult who needs always to be on top of things, in control, destined to experience the stress of attempting to be a lifetime superachiever. The flexible one (the adjuster) may be so tentative, so unable to trust as to be unable to make the long-term commitments that are required to succeed in a career or intimate adult personal relationships, such as that of spouse or parent. Likely as not, the adjuster adults, so attuned to accommodating others, allow themselves to be manipulated. An ever present option for the adult adjuster would be to marry someone with a problem, such as alcohol dependence, which allows continuation of the adjuster role. The adult placaters are seen as continually caring for others, often at the price of being unaware of their own needs or being unable to meet them. This can lead to large measures of guilt and anger, neither of which a placater can handle easily.

A different but similar typology of the roles that children adopt includes the *family hero,* the *lost child,* the family *mascot,* and the *scapegoat.* The first 3 have much in common with the 3 styles just discussed: the responsible one, the adapter, and the placater. Most of these coping styles would not elicit external attention or invite intervention. The exception is the scapegoat, who is the one most likely to be in trouble in school or with the authorities. This is the one who, usually acting angry and deviant, may be the only child clearly seen as having a problem. If the child is a teenager, the trouble may take the form of drug or alcohol abuse. (This is discussed in the section on adolescents in Chapter 11.) Frequently, through the attention focused on this child by outsiders or the

Dear, you've got to stop bringing home so much work from the office.

family, the family alcohol problem may first surface. Of course, initially the family will see the child as the central problem. And the scapegoat's behavior takes the focus off the parental alcohol problem. Having a common problem to tackle may help keep a fragile family intact. Often the family creates the myth that the drinking is the parent's coping response to the child's behavior. Alternately, the child may be held responsible for aggravating the parent's drinking.

It is suggested that, in adulthood, these coping styles could be translated into skills. The placater's sensitivity and ability to be sympathetic and understanding may be assets in helping professions, such as social work, psychiatry, and counseling. So, too, the responsible ones may have acquired skills that can serve them in good stead, through their diligence as students and their continued sense of responsibility. The challenge for both is to appreciate the origins and to be attuned to the pitfalls.

Adult Children of Alcoholics

Another aspect of the attention directed to the issues of the family was the emergence in the mid-1980s of adult children of alcoholics (ACoA) as a group warranting special attention. This may be seen as a logical outcome of the attention then being directed to younger children, who were living in a home with an alcohol-troubled parent. Why not expect that these children would carry behavior patterns into adulthood?

Based on clinical observations and anecdotal reports, a set of characteristics was identified as purportedly common to adult children of alcoholics. These characteristics included fear of losing control, fear of feelings, fear of conflict, an overdeveloped sense of responsibility, feelings of guilt when standing up for oneself, an inability to relax or to have fun, harsh self-criticism, the tendency to live in a world of denial, difficulties with intimate relationships, adopting the victim stance, the tendency to be more comfortable with chaos than with security, the tendency to confuse love and pity, the tendency under pressure to assume a black-and-white perspective, a backlog of delayed grief, a tendency to react rather than to act, and an ability to survive. The source of these traits was seen as lying in the dynamics of the alcohol-troubled family and as sparked by the behavior of an alcohol-dependent parent.

Because attention and help for alcohol dependence was then such a recent phenomena, that era's adult children had been reared in homes where the parental alcohol problem received no treatment and they, as children, received no help. Whether the alcoholic parent died from the disease, left the home, or recovered, those adult children saw themselves as experiencing difficulties that developed from these earlier experiences.

With hindsight, the interest in adult children was a bit of a fad. Some research initially supported the notion of a distinctive set of traits shared by adult children of alcoholics. But these early studies were flawed. They studied those who were involved in treatment or in self-help groups. In any kind of psychological research, there is the possibility that individuals involved in treatment are not representative of those who don't feel a need to seek help. Subsequent research following more stringent designs has not supported the notion of a distinct set of personality traits for adult children of alcoholics. The current thinking is that the problems adult children of alcoholics may experience are not unique to the alcoholic family. In fact, they are also found among adults who have grown up in families with considerable stress and serious problems, such as mental illness or domestic violence. Even here, not everyone who has grown up in families with such problems has these traits.

If there is no scientific support for these childhood roles, or for the set of symptoms ascribed to adult children of alcoholics, why have they not faded from discussion? Note how these characteristics are dependent on a lot of "coulds," "mights," and "tends to." In effect, a logical sequence is postulated that "could" be true. But there is more to it. An article entitled "Psychological Characteristics of Children of Alcoholics," authored by Ken Sher Ph.D. in a 1997 issue of NIAAA's *Alcohol and Research World,* addressed this question. Sher reported that over 40 years ago it was recognized that people are likely to accept a personality description as valid merely because it is "so vague, double-headed, socially desirable, or widely occurring in the general population that it is difficult to refute." These types of descriptions are termed "Barnum" statements. This is in honor of noted showman P. T. Barnum, whose recipe for a successful circus was "making sure there's a little something for everyone."

Sher points out how many of the descriptors of children of alcoholics have all of the features of classic Barnum statements—for example,

Barnum Characteristic	**Statement**
Vague	Children of alcoholics have difficulty in determining what normal is.
Double-header	Children of alcoholics are either super-responsible or super-irresponsible.
Socially desirable traits	Children of alcoholics are sensitive to others' needs.
Common in general population	Children of alcoholics are uncomfortable when they are the center of attention.

Indeed, two researchers tested the idea that many of the traits attributed to children of alcoholics are such Barnum statements. They administered a supposed personality inventory that people were told would generate a "profile" for them, based on their individual responses. The profile actually presented, which was identical for all individuals, consisted of generalizations drawn from the literature on adult children of alcoholics. How did people respond to "their" profiles? All of the subjects rated the adult child of alcoholics profile as highly descriptive of themselves. This was equally true of those from nonalcohol-troubled or nonproblem families as it was of actual children of alcoholics. In addition, people saw these descriptions as particular to themselves and more accurate for them than for people in general.

Someone has used another analogy for this phenomenon, making a comparison to the daily newspaper's astrology horoscopes. Most of the statements that are given in such columns are the kind of things that a large number of people can identify with. After all, if they only applied to a handful of people, who would read them? So you read "You often are not as tidy as you would like to be" or "You like to have your accomplishments recognized but hate to be the center of attention." These statements work because they sound familiar to all of us.

It cannot be assumed that all children who grew up or are now growing up in an alcoholic home share a single set of personality characteristics. Nor can it be assumed that all problems encountered in adult life can be attributed to being a child of an alcoholic. Nonetheless, the adult-children-of-alcoholics framework may well be useful to those suffering from problems, of whatever origins, who need to find some way out of an impasse and to make needed changes.

Resiliency

Unfortunately, with the attention directed to the problems that the alcoholic family poses for children, what was too long overlooked was the fact that children are not inevitably destined to problems in later life. An important piece of research that did not get the attention it deserved examined this very question. The research was conducted by Emmy Werner. It compared the offspring of alcoholics who had and those who had not developed serious coping problems by age 18. The study examined the characteristics of the children and the caregiving environment in which they were raised. Those studied were members of a multiracial cohort of approximately 700 children born in 1955 on the Hawaiian island of Kauai. Follow-up studies were conducted at ages 1, 2, 10, and 18. Of this entire group, approximately 14% had either a mother or a father who had alcoholism. Children of alcoholics who had not developed serious coping problems by age 18 were distinguished from those who had, in terms of their personal characteristics and their early environment. Those without serious problems had a belief in taking care of themselves, an orientation toward achievement, a positive self-concept, and an internal locus of control (meaning that their behavior was prompted more by their own feelings and beliefs than its being a response to others). In terms of the environment, in the first 2 years of life they received a high level of attention from the primary caregiver and experienced fewer stressful events that disrupted the family unit. Thus, Werner found it was not the presence or absence of alcoholism per se that predicted difficulties but, rather, the interaction of the child and the environment. Werner also identified some differences depending on the sex of the alcoholic parent and the child. Boys had higher rates of psychosocial problems in childhood and adolescence than did girls. Also, the children of alcoholic mothers had higher rates of problems in childhood and adolescence than did offspring of alcoholic fathers.

These findings have been found in subsequent studies. The view now is to think in terms of risk and protective factors. Risk factors are those things that are associated with the presence of an alcohol or other substance use problem. Protective factors are those things that seem to shield or reduce the chance of a problem. These factors can reside in the individual or the environment. In addition, it is necessary to also consider *mediating variables.* These are the circumstances or conditions which influence the impact a risk or protective factor may have. By analogy, a radio may be turned on, but the mediating variable is the volume control; its setting determines what comes through. For example, stress may be a risk factor for alcohol problems; however, also important is the individual's coping skills. With good coping skills and the person's belief that he or she can do something to alter the situation, heavy drinking is less likely.

Extended family are often an underappreciated source of support for children. A study conducted in Scotland focused upon their role in protecting children from the negative effects of drug use. The extended family often provides both psychological support and practical assistance. This ranges from providing meals, to faithfully attending school functions, to providing child care or actually taking children into their homes. These relationships not only can be a buffer for children but also widen the net of those caught up in living around and with drug dependence. Extended family may at times feel overwhelmed by the responsibility and obligations to the child. They may feel besieged by feelings of anxiety, worry, anger, and disappointment over the parent's drug problem and its impact. There is the potential that the arrangements may break down and leave the already vulnerable children exposed to further ruptured relationships and instability.

Home is the place where,
when you have to go there,
They have to take you in.
ROBERT FROST
"The Death of a Hired Man," 1914

Genetic Vulnerability

The single most important way in which the child of an alcoholic is vulnerable to alcohol dependence is in terms of genetic endowment. Children of alcoholics are considered at risk for development of the disease in an approximate 4:1 ratio to those without an alcohol-dependent parent. Research has suggested that gender can also be a significant factor influencing later life problems. Boys of alcoholic parents are more likely to suffer from attention deficit hyperactivity disorder than are children of parents without alcohol dependence. On the other hand, girls are more likely than their brothers to encounter eating disorders or depression in later life.

Compared to alcohol dependence, with one exception, far less is known about the genetic vulnerability in respect to other drugs. That exception is nicotine. There is a clear genetic component for the development of nicotine dependence. In addition, there seems to be a separate, additional genetic component which influences the severity of withdrawal symptoms. This influences the relative difficulty in smoking cessation.

Alcohol Dependence in Other Family Members

Alcohol dependence is obviously not limited to the parental generation. It may occur in adolescents, or it may occur in grandparents. The effects on the family are still powerful, even if less dramatic. Substance abuse problems in adolescents and the elderly are discussed in Chapter 11. However, it is important to realize that, regardless of the family member affected, the effects of alcoholism are not limited to the individual alone. The problems of the family are now seen as requiring intervention. Also, they are increasingly the focus of prevention efforts. In addition, family issues are now a central part of any alcohol treatment. Treatment approaches to the alcoholic family are discussed in Chapter 10.

Other Substance Use and Its Impact on the Family

While clearly recognized that drug use other than alcohol also touches the family, the research in this area is quite limited. One recent paper by Clifton Hudson and colleagues describes it as sparse and notes that most of what is said about drug use and the family is generalized from research in the alcohol field, even though it is recognized that there are differences. The research findings available on drug use problems and the family might be thought of as similar to a stack of snapshots that have not yet been sorted, culled, and placed into an album. Going through a stack of unorganized photos provides useful and interesting information, but the burden is on the viewer to put the larger picture together.

Typically family research in the substance use field focuses on the impact down the family tree, that is, the impact of the parental use on children. Isn't this what comes to mind upon hearing the phrase "impact on the family"? The lack of research on the impact of other drug use on the family may partially be attributable to the age groups in which various drug use is most common. When it comes to inhalants, or the so-called club drugs, for example, the odds are that it is not the parent who is in trouble. If the problem is ecstasy, the chances are that it isn't Mom or Dad who is the one headed out to the raves. The work by Hudson and colleagues on the social adjustment of significant others and family members is among *the* first to examine the impact on those within the drug user's family, including parents. What was found is that substance use in a spouse creates more problems and stress than does substance use in a child. This greater toll is not simply due to the loss of emotional support. This is primarily due to the fact that a spouse's substance abuse threatens the family's financial stability. While a child's substance use problem is clearly stressful, a parent's resources to deal with it haven't been diminished. The impact of an adolescent's or young adult's alcohol or drug problem on the larger family unit will likely be moderated by the age of the child, whether still living in the home or off at college, or living independently. The presence of other children in the home will also play a role in molding the family's response.

Given the limited research to date, what else can be said? There are two things worth noting: The first is that parents, vis-à-vis a child's substance use, are not that different from the typical spouse in failing to recognize what is going on. In responding to surveys, parents consistently underestimate the reality of the drug scene that confronts most adolescents, including their own. Parents almost universally underestimate the level of their adolescents' alcohol and other drug use, along with the relatively easy access their children have to a variety of drugs. Second, what is underappreciated is the impact of older siblings on the alcohol and drug use of their younger brothers and sisters. Just as parents are role models, so are older children in the family. When it comes to nicotine, the smoking or nonsmoking of older siblings has as great an impact as does the smoking status of parents. The protective value of nonsmoking parents can be offset by an older sister or brother who smokes. Parents have a greater influence during early adolescence; in later adolescence it is siblings who have the greater influence for other children in the family.

Casualty of the War on Drugs

Involvement with the criminal justice system is more likely with drug use than with alcohol. As noted in Chapter 2, the prison population is burgeoning in response to the war on drugs. People of color and the poor are disproportionately incarcerated. In a substantial number of cases, this is for simple possession or low-level involvement in the drug trade. A recent article entitled "Counting the Drug War's Female Casualties" begins with a haunting illustration. It cites the case of a woman who, though only having had a minor involvement in her boyfriend's drug transactions, has been sentenced to 34 years in federal prison.

Commonly the family as a whole is affected. The impact on family was poignantly brought to my attention in a casual conversation with a friend, on the use of computers in the schools. The friend teaches in a midwestern inner-city middle school. In that school, which website is the one most frequently accessed? It is the state's criminal justice system website! With a parent who is incarcerated, that is where children turn for basic information about addresses, or information on visiting days and visiting hours. The removal of parent from the home has deep impacts for the family that are cross generational. A drug arrest can make the family ineligible for student financial aid, can lead to evictions and

FOCUS ON...

Passive Smoking

Of the many drugs of abuse, whether licit or illicit, nicotine has the greatest impact on other members of the family. At the least, smoking has an impact on the family's economic situation. For the person with a one-pack-a-day habit at $5.25 per pack—the going price in a Vermont small town general store—that represents more than $1,900 a year literally going up in smoke. That's more than the family's annual cost for fuel oil, which also goes up in smoke but at least provides warmth in the process. Of course, it isn't simply the financial cost, or the smell of tobacco smoke that permeates the household and clings to everyone's clothes. The health consequences for nonsmokers living or working with smokers are considerable. When a smoker smokes, everyone in the area smokes as well. This is referred to as *passive smoking, environmental smoking,* or *secondhand smoke,* terms that are essentially synonymous.

A variety of laboratory tests are available to detect nicotine. Both urine and saliva samples can be used to test for recent use. Unlike alcohol, neither nicotine nor a major by-product of metabolism, cotinine, is rapidly removed from the body. These by-products are retained in the body for extended periods, including their becoming part of the structure of hair, fingernails, and toenails. In essence hair provides a smoking history, whether personal smoking or secondhand smoke. Based on known estimates of the rate of hair growth, it is possible to determine when exposure occurred. Testing hair samples is the major way of measuring past nicotine exposure in smokers and nonsmokers, from adults to newborns. By comparing nicotine levels in various family members, depending on their own personal smoking habits, it is possible to distinguish the portion of nicotine exposure that comes from passive smoking versus someone's own smoking.

Exposure to nicotine can occur before birth. A major cause of underweight in newborns in maternal smoking. When smoking, the pregnant woman is sharing the nicotine with the developing fetus. Equally important, nicotine is transferred to the fetus, by a nonsmoking woman's exposure to secondhand smoke. The pregnant woman is simply the vehicle for delivering other's nicotine to the unborn child. This secondhand—or more properly thirdhand—smoke isn't limited to exposure in the home and family members' smoking. The workplace can be a significant source of passive smoking. Low birth weight is not the only impact on the developing fetus. In addition there is a 4 times greater risk for overall smaller size at birth, for in utero nicotine-exposed infants. The level of prenatal nicotine exposure is proportional to the level of smoking by the mother and her exposure to environmental smoke. Smoking during pregnancy is also associated with higher levels of lead in blood of newborns, with a 15% increase for each 10 cigarettes smoked. Other problems have been linked to prenatal nicotine exposure. There is evidence that smoking during pregnancy is related to children's later behavioral problems. A careful research study suggests that a quarter of behavior problems seen at age 5, especially aggression, can be attributed to prenatal nicotine exposure during early pregnancy. The hypothesis is that exposure to nicotine alters fetal brain development. Preliminary work suggests that paternal smoking even *prior* to conception may have negative consequences. One study indicates that the equivalent of 5 pack-years of smoking prior to pregnancy is linked to a higher rate of childhood cancers.

Nicotine contributes to an array of health problems throughout childhood. These range from an increased incidence of sudden infant death syndrome, to higher rates of asthma and more asthma attacks requiring medical intervention or hospitalization. Secondhand smoke is also a determinant of the rates of coughs, pneumonia, bronchitis, frequency of middle ear infections, and tonsillectomies and/or adenoidectomies. Children with diabetes also have more complications if exposed to secondhand smoke. And each year children die in home fires caused by careless smoking. Also of note, parents significantly underreport exposure to secondhand smoke, and the only reliable measure is through laboratory tests of the child.

Media campaigns, along with schools and pediatricians and family physicians, are aimed at smoking cessation among parents. If smoking cessation doesn't succeed, the goal is to at least have the home and car be smoke free zones. The success of such initiatives to restrict smoking vary, depending on how many other adults in the household or coworkers smoke, on whether there are children in the home, the level of the smoker's dependence, plus the level of recognition by the smoker of the dangers of secondhand smoke. While useful and to be encouraged, these bans are not 100% effective.

The impact of secondhand smoke continues throughout life. While acute respiratory problems are seen in children, chronic respiratory problems are more common among adults. For example, while smokers are at the greatest risk for lung cancer, nonsmokers too are at risk through secondhand smoke. One study of women with lung cancer found that among those who had never smoked, there was nonetheless an average of 27 years of exposure from a smoking spouse, an average of 19 years of exposure from parents, and 15 years of exposure from coworkers.

The clear evidence that secondhand smoke has a major negative impact on others' health was a major factor in bans on smoking in the workplace. For nonsmoking adults, historically the workplace has presented twice the risk of nicotine exposure than in the home. One of the first occupational groups to lobby for a ban on smoking in the workplace was airline flight attendants. Another group of employees at high risk are those who work in what one researcher calls the 5 Bs—bars, bowling alleys, billiard halls, betting establishments, and bingo parlors. These settings were found to have nicotine levels from 2.5 to 18.5 times higher than offices or homes. At those levels of exposure to secondhand smoke, it is estimated that lung cancer rates will increase from at least 3 to as much as 13 times.

The public health impact of environmental smoke has prompted changes in perceptions and public policy. The law has been used in a variety of ways to reduce harms associated with tobacco: These include mandating warning labels on nicotine products, the introduction of smoking bans in the workplace and in public places, and the more recent tobacco industry settlements requiring further regulation of advertising and marketing to youth. Family courts also incorporate research findings on environmental smoking. As one jurist noted, "A family court that does not issue court orders restraining persons from smoking in the presence of children under the court's care fails those children whom the law has entrusted to its care." Accordingly to ensure the best interest of the child, it is both appropriate and necessary to consider exposure to smoking as a factor in awarding child custody, or determining visitation.

thereby up the odds for homelessness, and can exclude them from public housing for life, all due to the conduct of a single family member. When drug use places someone in the criminal justice system, it is not uncommon that women and children are pressed more deeply into poverty, in turn creating greater public health problems, more desperation, and arguably more crime. While more prisons and jails are providing treatment programs for inmates with alcohol and drug problems, they remain far too few and arguably are provided too late in the criminal justice process.

Pack-years is used as a measure of exposure to nicotine. 1 pack-year is equivalent to smoking a pack per day for a year. Note: a half pack per day for two years equals 1 pack-year.

Families in Their Communities

Finally, in considering the impact of substance use on the family, it needs to be appreciated that families too are touched by their environments. Families live in communities, in neighborhoods. The nature of that community makes a difference. With alcohol the concentration of outlets for sales makes a difference in the levels of drinking and crime. The poorest communities have the highest concentration of alcohol sales outlets. Communities vary too on the levels of public drug use, access to drugs, acceptance of drug use, and presence of drug-related crime. While an economically depressed community may present special risk factors, economically advantaged communities are hardly immune; neither are rural communities. In all communities, there are programs that are protective factors and assist family members, be they recreational programs, church and religious groups, or youth and neighborhood organizations.

RESOURCES AND FURTHER READING

Alcohol Health and Research World. Special issue on children of alcoholics 21(3):entire issue, 1997.

Avenevoli S, Merikangas KR. Familial influences on adolescent smoking (review). *Addiction* 98 (Supplement): 1–20, 2003. (152 refs.)

Barnard M. Between a rock and a hard place: The role of relatives in protecting children from the effects of parental drug problems. *Child & Family Social Work* 8(4):291–299, 2003.

Batra V, Patkar AA, Berrettini, WH, Weinstein, SP, Leone FT. The genetic determinants of smoking. *Chest* 123(5): 1730–1739, 2003. (92 refs.)

Beidler RJ. Adult children of alcoholics: Is it really a separate field of study? *Drugs and Society* 3(3/4):133–141, 1989.

Cermak TL. *Diagnosing and Treating Co-dependence: A Guide for Professionals Who Work with Chemical Dependents, Their Spouses and Children.* Minneapolis MN: Johnson Institute Books, 1986.

Fuller JA, Warner RM. Family stressors as predictors of codependency. *Genetic, Social, and General Psychology Monographs* 126(1):5–22, 2000. (41 refs.)

George WH, La Marr J, Barrett K, McKinnon T. Alcoholic parentage, self-labeling, and endorsement of ACOA-codependent traits. *Psychology of Addictive Behaviors* 13(1):39–48, 1999. (50 refs.)

Goldfarb B. Counting the drug war's female casualties. *The Journal of Gender, Race & Justice* 6(Fall):227+, 2002. (177 refs.)

Harrington CM, Metzler AE. Are adult children of dysfunctional families with alcoholism different from adult children of dysfunctional families without alcoholism? A look at committed, intimate relationships. *Journal of Counseling Psychology* 44(1):102–107, 1997.

Harter SL. Psychosocial adjustment of adult children of alcoholics: A review of the recent empirical literature. *Clinical Psychology Review* 20(3):311–337, 2000. (120 refs.)

Hudson CR, Kirby KC, Firely ML, Festinger DS, Marlowe DB. Social adjustment of family members and significant others (FSOs) of drug users. *Journal of Substance Abuse Treatment* 23(3):171–181, 2003. (48 refs.)

Hunt ME. A comparison of family of origin factors between children of alcoholics and children of non-alcoholics in a longitudinal panel. *American Journal of Drug and Alcohol Abuse* 23(4):597–613, 1997. (43 refs.)

Hussong AM, Chassin L. Parent alcoholism and the leaving home transition. *Development and Psychopathology* 14(1):139–157, 2002 (44 refs.)

Jackson JK. The adjustment of the family to the crisis of alcoholism. *Quarterly Journal of Studies on Alcohol* 15(4):562–586, 1954.

Johnson V. *I'll Quit Tomorrow,* rev. ed. New York: Harper & Row, 1980.

Kreek MJ, Nielsen DA, LaForge KS. Genes associated with addiction: Alcoholism, opiate, and cocaine addiction (review). *Neuromolecular Medicine* 5(1):85–108, 2004. (172 refs.)

Melchert TP. Clarifying the effects of parental substance abuse, child sexual abuse, and parental caregiving on adult adjustment. *Professional Psychology: Research and Practice* 31(1):64–69, 2000. (39 refs.)

Menees MM, Segrin C. The specificity of disrupted processes in families of adult children of alcoholics. *Alcohol and Alcoholism* 35(4):361–367, 2000. (46 refs.)

Rotunda RJ, Scherer DG, Imm PS. Family systems and alcohol misuse: Research on the effects of alcoholism on family functioning and effective family interventions (review). *Professional Psychology: Research and Practice* 26(1):95–104, 1995. (106 refs.)

Tyndale RF. Genetics of alcohol and tobacco use in humans (review). *Annals of Medicine* 35(2):94–121, 2003. (352 refs.)

Vail MO, Protinsky H, Prouty A. Sampling issues in research on adult children of alcoholics: Adolescence and beyond. *Adolescence* 35(137):113–119, 2000. (19 refs.)

Vink JM, Willemsen G, Engels RCME, Boomsma DI. Smoking status of parents, siblings and friends: Predictors of regular smoking? Findings from a longitudinal twin-family study. *Twin Research* 6(3):209–217, 2003. (38 refs.)

Walker JP, Lee RE. Uncovering strengths of children of alcoholic parents (review). *Contemporary Family Therapy* 20(4):521–538, 1998.

Werner EE. Resilient offspring of alcoholics: A longitudinal study from birth to age 18. *Journal of Studies on Alcohol* 47(1):34–40, 1986.

Woititz J. *Adult children of alcoholics.* Hollywood, FL: Health Communications, 1983.

Wolstein J, Rosinger C, Gastpar M. Children and families in substance misuse. *Current Opinion in Psychiatry* 11(3):279–283, 1998. (45 refs.)

Xian H, Scherrer JF, Madden PAF, Lyons MJ, Tsuang M, True WR, et al. The heritability of failed smoking cessation and nicotine withdrawal in twins who smoked and attempted to quit. *Nicotine & Tobacco Research* 5(2): 245–254, 2003. (49 refs.)

CHAPTER 9

Evaluation and Treatment Overview

When one is acutely aware of alcohol or other drug problems, the question arises, "How can they be treated?" Perhaps your question is more personal, "How can I help?" As a prelude to this, it is essential to consider how people recover and what treatment or intervention is about.

At this juncture in earlier editions of this book, the focus was almost exclusively on alcohol dependence. After making a principled plea for early intervention, backing that up with the reminder that this approach is indicated for any chronic disease process, then acknowledging that this represented an ideal, which was infrequently reflected in actual practice, the book launched into treatment of alcohol dependence. There was virtually no mention of evaluation, diagnostic assessment, or treatment approaches to problems associated with alcohol use. Indeed, even 10 years ago many substance abuse clinicians had very little need for or opportunity to use those skills. The diagnosis of dependence, for all practical purposes, had occurred before a client's arrival in the clinician's office. Very few individuals came into contact with substance abuse treatment facilities by mistake. Then the chief practical use for informing substance abuse professionals of diagnostic criteria was to enable them to educate other human service professionals, thereby facilitating identification and referrals of those whose problems were going undetected. This information was also helpful in providing client education. Similarly, the major role of the substance use history was in developing treatment plans, rather than its being a prerequisite for diagnosis.

get the Alcoholic out OF The Bottle

In days past, those who would now be diagnosed as having alcohol abuse were treated as "early-stage" alcoholics. Accordingly they were provided the standard treatment for alcohol dependence. Their life situations often were reminiscent of the typical alcohol client's circumstances

As muse or creative companion, alcohol can be devastating. In memoriam to some of those who did battle with this 2-faced spirit:
John Barrymore
Mickey Mantle
Truman Capote
Tennessee Williams
John Berryman
Robert Young
John Cheever
Lillian Roth
Ulysses S. Grant
O. Henry (William Sydney Porter)
Eugene O'Neill
Stephen Crane
Hart Crane
F. Scott Fitzgerald
Edna St. Vincent Millay
Jack London
Ernest Hemingway
Dylan Thomas
Diana Barrymore
Isadora Duncan
Sinclair Lewis
Kenneth Roberts
Judy Garland
Willem de Kooning
Robert Benchley
Edgar Allan Poe
Jim Thorpe
Charles Jackson
Dame May Whitty
Sarah Churchill
Jackson Pollock
W. C. Fields
Audie Murphy
Henri de Toulouse-Lautrec
Janis Joplin
Baudelaire
Brendan Behan
Ring Lardner
Robert Lowell
Jimi Hendrix
Alexander the Great

10 to 20 years before treatment. Remember, an average of 7 years elapsed from the point of the disease being clearly present to the point of entering treatment. That fact was used to "sell" the diagnosis and attempt to have the client accept it, hopefully with gratitude! Treatment professionals obviously recognized that such individuals were different from the usual client. It was recognized that providing full-blown treatment for dependence might be a bit drastic. However, it was viewed as the prudent, cautious approach. Even if the diagnosis of dependence was incorrect, initiating treatment seemed preferable to the alternative, which would be allowing the condition to go unaddressed and presumably progress. The two choices were then perceived as either loss of drinking "privileges" or potential loss of life. Equally important was the fact that, back then, the clinician could offer the problem drinker no other treatment options. Another pitfall occurs when conceptualizing all alcohol problems in terms of the progression of the alcohol dependence. It is related to the temptation to treat all alcohol problems as emerging dependence and therefore offer dependence treatment. This can cause clients to balk or bolt. This can also set up barriers when dealing with other professionals. Such an approach can give the impression of clinicians not as therapists, but as technicians, always ready to apply their treatment formula indiscriminately.

The situation now is dramatically different. Along with alcohol use, other drug use is common. Those with alcohol dependency continue to represent the majority of those who come into contact with treatment programs, but at the same time there is an ever increasing proportion of referrals for other kinds of alcohol-related problems. One can no longer assume that any alcohol problem is synonymous with dependence. The problem may be abuse. The referral may have followed on the heels of a drinking incident. There are self-referrals of individuals who are concerned about a family member, a friend, or their own alcohol use. Similarly, treatment personnel are called on more and more by other helping professionals—school counselors, social workers, physicians, and clergy—to provide consultation.

With clients now reflecting the spectrum of substance use problems, there is increasing demand on therapists to provide a thoughtful assessment and to match clients to appropriate treatment. Assessment, evaluation, and diagnostic skills have become more central in this era of managed care. It has been a long time since insurance companies, state regulatory agencies, HMOs, or for that matter clients, their families, or employers unquestioningly accepted 28 days of residential treatment—once the norm—as the treatment of choice.

THEORETICAL PERSPECTIVES

It may have been far simpler when the major and exclusive concern for the clinician was alcohol dependence. Knowing how to treat the person sitting in the office was rarely a difficulty. The real challenge and major frustration was in getting those who needed care across the threshold. As the clinical concerns broaden to encompass a range of substance use problems, life becomes more complicated for the clinician. The information in this chapter is intended to provide a framework and offer orientation.

In terms of alcohol, if treatment programs are oriented primarily toward treating alcoholism, ironically that orientation serves as a set of blinders preventing recognition of other kinds of substance use problems. This is reminiscent of the old adage "If the only tool you have is a hammer, every problem tends to look like a nail." In thinking about alcoholism, we have tended to think of a progression, moving from alcohol use, to alcohol problems, to alcohol abuse, to alcoholism. In such a framework, severity depends on where the client falls on that continuum. This thinking contains some pitfalls. The necessity for action or intervention is understandably associated with what is perceived as the seriousness of the situation. Thus, the person with the alcohol problem may be seen as being in less danger. This is not necessarily the case.

PROBLEMS OF USE

Alcohol problems are not restricted to alcohol dependence. Nor are they restricted to alcohol use at intoxicating levels. For example, the danger of alcohol use by the individual who is depressed is not dependence—it is suicidal thoughts being "loosened" by the person's impaired state and diminished capacity. Therefore, those who are in treatment for depression should be counseled to abstain from alcohol.

Adolescents provide some of the most dramatic examples of the dangers of alcohol use. For teenagers, the primary danger of alcohol use isn't dependence, although it certainly does occur. The leading causes of death in this age group are accidents, suicide, and homicide, all of which are clearly linked to alcohol use. The net and tragic result is that the age group from 16 to 24 years has all too recently been the only group in our country with a declining life expectancy. Alcohol use may also have more subtle dangers for adolescents, such as impeding emotional and social maturation. In addition, there are the problems related to sexuality, unwanted pregnancies, and HIV infection. Any drinker is at some risk for alcohol problems. Alcohol is a potent pharmacological agent. Negative consequences can follow on the heels of a single drinking episode. These would represent problems of acute use. Negative consequences can also result from the pattern of use. This represents a chronic problem. Evaluation and assessment need to explore both possibilities.

What is a "safe" dose of alcohol or a low-risk pattern of alcohol use? This varies from individual to individual. What is judicious use similarly varies for a single individual throughout his or her life span. For the pregnant woman, no alcohol is the safest alternative. Alcohol use is a health issue in the broadest sense. Treatment professionals are unlikely to see an individual until a problem becomes evident. Therefore, much of the burden of prevention and identification of individuals at risk falls to those outside the clinical arena.

Chronic Disease Framework

The model for managing chronic disease is very useful. When considering the spectrum of substance use problems, it offers an approach that ensures that acute problems are effectively addressed. At the same time, it ensures that dependence will not develop unnoticed. All acute problems are seen as requiring attention in their own right, as well as being a potential warning of a possible long-term problem. The following example may help demonstrate this approach.

In the general medical management of any chronic disease, among the most significant actions are those taken before the clear onset of the full-blown disease process. Consider heart disease. A young man comes to his physician's office. He is overweight, both smokes and drinks, consumes a cholesterol-laden diet, never exercises, and has a family history of males who die before the age of 50 of coronary disease. From his physician's perspective, he is a walking time bomb. To feel comfortable intervening, the physician does not have to be convinced that this individual will be true to his genes. It is sufficient to know that statistically this individual is at risk. Even if the client is wholly asymptomatic—that is, has no elevation of blood pressure—the physician will feel perfectly comfortable urging rather drastic changes to reduce risk. (These changes for our hypothetical young man are equivalent to the changes associated with abstinence.) If the physician were really on top of it, she would refer this client to several groups, load him down with pamphlets, and through continuing contacts monitor compliance and provide encouragement and support. This model is the optimal approach to the management of alcohol problems. In this framework, with respect to alcohol problems, the most relevant question is no longer "Is this person alcoholic?" The central question instead becomes "If this person continues with the current alcohol use pattern, is he or she at risk for becoming alcohol dependent or developing other alcohol-related problems?"

Using the framework of chronic disease, many of the questions that now plague caregivers are circumvented. In this discussion, the assumption is that alcohol dependence is a condition like heart disease. As a chronic disease, alcohol dependence has well-demonstrated warning signs. It develops slowly over time. For this reason, it would probably be impossible to pinpoint an exact time at which a nonalcoholic "turns" alcoholic. No one wakes up in the morning having come down with a case of alcohol dependence overnight. Remember, the time when it is most critical to act is before the disease process is firmly established, when the individual is in that "gray" area, so it is useful to think in terms of whether someone is developing dependence. If so, then intervention is appropriate.

Such an approach makes it clear that any alcohol problem is sufficiently serious to warrant continuing attention. It has become widely recognized that alcohol dependence isn't cured and that ongoing efforts will be needed to maintain abstinence. Similarly, an alcohol problem shouldn't be assumed to be "fixed" by a single encounter with a clinician or participation in an alcohol education class. An ongoing relationship is appropriately established to monitor the client's status. Over time, there needs to be the opportunity to assess the efforts to moderate risks and alter dangerous drinking patterns. If these efforts prove to be unsuccessful, then further intervention is required.

Consider the changes that have occurred over the past 25 years regarding tobacco use. Questions about smoking are now a standard part of any medical history. Probably very few smokers are unaware that smoking may cause or aggravate medical problems. A smoker who sees a physician expects to be asked questions about smoking and awaits the associated comments that smoking is ill-advised. Beyond that there is the increasing likelihood that a referral will be made to a smoking cessation program. Also the attitudes of the general public have changed. People no longer silently put up with secondhand smoke. There are concerned family members and friends of smokers, who express their concerns directly to the smoker. The regulation of smoking in public places has become the norm. Restaurants generally must provide nonsmoking accommodations, and more and more are smoke-free. Beyond protecting nonsmokers, these regulations certainly cramp a smoker's style and prompt him or her to consider the inconvenience as well as the problems that result from smoking. We may well be on the brink of a similar revolution with alcohol use.

Now alcohol is more commonly viewed as a drug. Drunkenness is far less tolerated. Intoxication is becoming less socially acceptable in more and more circles and circumstances. The possibility that an intoxicated person puts others in jeopardy is an issue of public concern. Reinforcing this is the general public's heightened interest in a variety of efforts to promote health—diet, exercise, and other self-care measures. This has provided a moderating influence upon alcohol use. So along with less red meat, fewer animal fats, jogging, and personal trainers, there's more bottled water. Coupled with all these changes are the improvements that have taken place in the professional training of physicians, clergy, nurses, social workers, and teachers about alcohol, alcohol problems, and alcohol abuse and dependence, compared with the previous generation.

At the same time, there is still some way to go. In the abstract, a person can be well informed about alcohol or other drug problems, but when they pop up in real life, it can be a different matter. All too often, along with the realization that there is a possible alcohol problem comes a lot of hand-wringing and waiting. The family, friends, physician, and clergy—all those involved—can be immobilized. They can often wait until the possible problem has progressed to the point where it is unequivocally and unquestionably the real thing.

Challenges of Problems Associated with Use

Also an issue is the fact that the professional treatment community internally has not yet reached a clear consensus as to what constitutes appropriate treatment for those who are in trouble with alcohol but who are not alcohol dependent. This should not be a surprise. The rank-and-file clinicians in the substance abuse field have not had the similar collective experience in approaching alcohol problems that they have had with dependence. These are not the patients that the formal treatment system historically has seen. The legacy of some of the earliest approaches to treatment of alcohol dependence, too, may continue to cast a shadow. This refers to efforts many years ago to institute controlled drinking among clients with dependence, an approach that has been discarded. However, what was ineffective with that population in many instances is exactly the approach called for in the treatment of alcohol abuse, when abstinence is not an essential goal in treatment.

While the formal treatment community may not have experience, nor its clinicians particular skill in handling the range of problems associated with alcohol use, this doesn't mean that there is nothing to be done. The AUDIT screening test, was developed through a collaborative effort of the World Health Organization (WHO) for primary health-care settings. Another part of that WHO collaboration was examining efforts that might be taken by the physician to short-circuit an emerging alcohol problem. At the time the WHO study was initiated it was realized that, even though it didn't seem to make sense, nonetheless, for some patients brief advice or counseling was effective in addressing their alcohol problems. In fact, such *brief interventions* could be as successful as formal treatment. It was this realization that helped spark the WHO study. Now such physician-based efforts are called either brief interventions or *brief treatments.* There isn't a single, standard format. Some of these brief interventions consist of a single, 5-minute session of advice, and others have used a single, hour-long counseling session, However, those that have been found to be successful share common features. Unfortunately, as these interventions are implemented largely outside of the formal alcohol treatment system, alcohol program staff may not be familiar with these approaches. While understandable, this really isn't acceptable. By comparison, it would be like oncologists, those who treat cancer, being unfamiliar with prevention or steps to treat cancer prior to its having spread and requiring dramatic, invasive treatment efforts. Brief interventions are discussed in more detail later in the chapter.

SCREENING AND EVALUATION

Screening efforts for any health-care problem can be undertaken at various levels. They can be applied routinely to everyone, or they can be targeted, administered only to those in higher-risk groups. Broad-based screening efforts, meaning routine use of a screening tool in a range of settings, is desirable when the condition is common. Otherwise, checking everyone makes no sense. But to justify doing so, it is also important that a condition be treatable. The common cold may warrant routine screening on the basis of its being commonplace. But inasmuch as there is very little to be done to alter its course, and the serious long-term consequences are rare, screening would be a waste of time. It is also necessary that screening efforts be practical—that the available tools be both inexpensive and easily administered. Finally, the instrument used has to be well "tuned." It needs to cast a sufficiently broad net so as not to miss many people but at the same time not to falsely include too many people who don't have the condition. Using these criteria, screening for alcohol problems is clearly warranted. The condition is common and treatable. A failure to treat carries serious consequences, and screening can be done easily and inexpensively in any setting.

Laboratory Tests

Presently there is no laboratory test that is recommended for screening. All of the screening tests described in the following section are based on interviews. There has been considerable exploration of laboratory tests that might be able to identify heavy drinkers. Until the mid-1990s, the most sensitive laboratory test was the GGT (gamma-glutamyl transferase), and it missed up to two-thirds of the excessive drinkers or those who were alcohol dependent. At best, laboratory measures were able to detect the presence of medical complications that resulted from heavy drinking.

Since then several other markers have been identified. CDT (carbohydrate-deficient transferrin) is the most promising for clinical use in the near future. Transferrin, produced by the liver, is a protein that is responsible for transporting iron in the blood. It is very sensitive to the amount of alcohol consumed. Having the equivalent of 4 beers a day causes increased levels of CDT, so it is sensitive to actual drinking rather than being tied to liver disease that results from the drinking. Research shows it likely to be *the* laboratory test for assessing alcohol use. However, there are some questions that remain to be answered to fully understand the lab results. What is the effect of age? What are the male-female differences? What other medical conditions might be associated with increased levels of CDT? (Seemingly there are very, very few.) What is the best way to measure CDT, by the absolute amount or as a percentage of the total transferrin in the blood sample? Also, is the reliability for detecting heavy drinking improved if the CDT value is combined with the results of other common lab tests? Since it does measure recent drinking levels, it has potential for use in aftercare and detection of relapse. Two other newly identified markers similarly are sensitive to recent alcohol consumption. One is based on the changes alcohol causes in the normal breakdown product of serotonin metabolism (5-hydroxytryptophol). The other is a product of alcohol metabolism, ethyl glucuronide, which remains up to 80 hours after drinking. It is unlikely that any of these laboratory measures will replace interview formats for broad-based screening. No laboratory test can be as inexpensive as asking several questions. However, one of these tests may prove useful in confirming a diagnosis.

Screening Instruments

A number of screening tests are available that are effective in identifying those with a high likelihood of having alcohol dependence or other alcohol problems. As their name indicates, they are screening instruments, not diagnostic instruments. Screening instruments do not provide sufficient information to allow formulation of a treatment plan, although there are other standardized instruments to assist with that. These screening tests, if routinely administered, can assist in identifying those for whom a closer examination is appropriate. In this instance the goal is to identify those whose alcohol or other drug use warrants closer scrutiny. These screening tests are basic tools for any human service worker's repertoire. Screening for alcohol problems should be routine in any counseling or health-care setting. In the process of screening for alcohol use there is also the possibility to screen for other drug use as well.

These tests may have less immediate utility in a setting that deals exclusively with alcohol and/or other drug problems. Something has already occurred to suggest a problem exists. Otherwise, the client would not be sitting in a clinician's office. However, familiarity with these tools is important on several counts. Referrals to alcohol treatment services may include a report with the results of screening tests. Also, training of other professionals may well be a part of the clinician's work. This is core information to be passed on to other helping professionals.

The major screening tests are described in the following sections. First, a word is in order to those who are suspicious of screening instruments and their ability to detect a problem, especially given that prominent symptoms of dependence include minimizing, denial, repression, plus distortions of memory and perception. Part of developing such instruments is to compare the results obtained by the test with the results of an assessment by a trained substance abuse clinician. The purpose of a screening instrument is, after all, to approximate the judgment that would be made by professionals were they to undertake a systematic evaluation. Indeed, for the instruments described here, those who answer the indicated number of questions positively are those whom the clinicians would agree had the syndrome (dependence or abuse) that the instruments are designed to detect.

If you remain leery, reflect back to the description of the behavior that is symptomatic of alcohol dependence in Chapter 7. The client's candor, or absence of distortion, is possibly not so unexpected. What the

FOCUS ON DRUGS

Screening for Drug Problems

Drug Abuse Screening Test (DAST)

1.	Have you used drugs other than those required for medical reasons?	**Yes**	No
2.	Have you abused prescription drugs?	**Yes**	No
3.	Do you abuse more than one drug at a time?	**Yes**	No
4.	Can you get through the week without using drugs (other than those required for medical reasons)?	Yes	**No**
5.	Are you always able to stop using drugs when you want to?	Yes	**No**
6.	Do you abuse drugs on a continuous basis?	**Yes**	No
7.	Do you try to limit your drug use to certain situations?	**Yes**	No
8.	Have you had "blackouts" or "flashbacks" as a result of drug use?	**Yes**	No
9.	Do you ever feel bad about your drug abuse?	**Yes**	No
10.	Does your spouse (or parents) ever complain about your involvement with drugs?	**Yes**	No
11.	Do your friends or relatives know or suspect you abuse drugs?	**Yes**	No
12.	Has drug abuse ever created problems between you and your spouse?	**Yes**	No
13.	Has any family member ever sought help for problems related to your drug use?	**Yes**	No
14.	Have you ever lost friends because of your use of drugs?	**Yes**	No
15.	Have you ever neglected your family or missed work because of your use of drugs?	**Yes**	No
16.	Have you ever been in trouble at work because of drug abuse?	**Yes**	No
17.	Have you ever lost a job because of drug abuse?	**Yes**	No
18.	Have you gotten into fights when under the influence of drugs?	**Yes**	No
19.	Have you ever been arrested because of unusual behavior while under the influence of drugs?	**Yes**	No
20.	Have you ever been arrested for driving while under the influence of drugs?	**Yes**	No
21.	Have you engaged in illegal activities to obtain drugs?	**Yes**	No
22.	Have you ever been arrested for possession of illegal drugs?	**Yes**	No
23.	Have you ever experienced withdrawal symptoms as a result of heavy drug intake?	**Yes**	No
24.	Have you had medical problems as a result of your drug use (e.g., memory loss, hepatitis, convulsions, or bleeding)?	**Yes**	No
25.	Have you ever gone to anyone for help for a drug problem?	**Yes**	No
26.	Have you ever been in hospital for medical problems related to your drug use?	**Yes**	No
27.	Have you ever been involved in a treatment program specifically related to drug use?	**Yes**	No
28.	Have you been treated as an outpatient for problems related to drug abuse?	**Yes**	No

Scoring: Each item in bold = 1 point
6 or more = substance use problem (abuse or dependence)

Reference: Gavin DR, Ross HE, Skinner HA. Diagnostic validity of the Drug Abuse Screening Test in the assessment of DSM-III drug disorders. *British Journal of Addiction* 84(3):301–307, 1989. (23 refs.)

alcohol-troubled client often strongly disagrees with is not the facts, but their interpretation. Thus, the alcohol-dependent individual might very readily acknowledge that a family member has expressed concern about drinking. What he or she would be likely to dispute is whether the concern is justified. The client may well provide the interviewer a very lengthy and unsolicited rebuttal of the family's concern and offer justifications for the drinking.

CUT DOWN
I'm cutting down— I'm only getting Two six-packs Tonite.
ANNOYED
Love me, Love my beer! Goodbye!
GUILTY
I Hope No ONE saw me here last night.
EYE OPENER
I wonder if the state liquor store is open yet?

CAGE

Since its introduction in 1970, the CAGE, developed by Ewing and Rouse, has become recognized as one of the most efficient and effective screening devices for alcohol dependence. The CAGE is both easy to administer as well as less intimidating than some of the other screening instruments. It consists of the following 4 questions:

"Have you ever felt you should	**C**ut down on your drinking?"
"Have people	**A**nnoyed you by criticizing your drinking?"
"Have you ever felt bad or	**G**uilty about your drinking?"
"Have you ever had an	**E**ye-opener first thing in the morning to steady nerves or get rid of a hangover?"

Scoring 2 or 3 affirmative answers should create a high index of suspicion of the presence of alcohol dependence. Four positive responses are seen as equivalent to a diagnosis of alcohol dependence. The CAGE is not intended to screen for other alcohol problems (that is, a score of a 1 or 2 does not indicate alcohol abuse).

For those concerned about being overly inclusive and thus falsely identifying as possibly alcoholic those who are not, the CAGE holds little danger. It is very reliable in providing an initial way of sorting those who may be alcohol dependent from those who are not. Of those with a CAGE score of 1, only 20% are nonalcoholics. As the number of positive responses increases, the nonalcoholic individuals who would be incorrectly labeled drops markedly. Only 11% of those who score 2 are, in fact, nonalcoholics. For 3 positive responses, the proportion of nonalcoholics drops to 1%; for 4 affirmative responses, the percentage is 0.

Trauma Index

Recognizing how commonly trauma is associated with excessive alcohol use, several Canadian researchers developed a 5-question scale to identify early-stage problem drinkers, among both men and women, in an outpatient setting. The questions are as follows:
Since your 18th birthday, have you

1. had any fractures or dislocations to bones or joints?
2. been injured in a traffic accident?
3. had a head injury?
4. been injured in an assault or a fight?
5. been injured after drinking?

Two or more positive responses are indicative of excessive drinking or alcohol abuse. Though not as sensitive as the CAGE or the MAST, it will identify slightly over two-thirds of problem drinkers.

Michigan Alcohol Screening Test (MAST)

The MAST is another of the most widely used screening tools. The original MAST, first published in 1971 by Selzer and associates, was a 25-item yes or no questionnaire (see page 238). It was designed for use either within a structured interview or for self-administration. The questions touch on medical, interpersonal, and legal problems resulting from alcohol use. Since its introduction, the reliability and validity of the MAST have been established in multiple populations. Several variations have since been developed. The Brief MAST uses 10 of the MAST items. The Short MAST (SMAST) was specifically created to be self-administered and uses 13 items found to be as effective as the entire MAST for screening.

The CAGE, MAST, and Trauma Index have several limitations. One is that they look at lifetime problems. Typically the wording is "have you ever. . . ." Thus, someone in middle age who hasn't had a problem for a decade could still come out with a positive score. Presumably, a few follow-up questions could pick this up rather quickly. While a potential nuisance, this is hardly an insurmountable problem. Furthermore, knowing there is a past history of alcohol problems is important. A more serious concern is how effective these instruments are in identifying alcohol problems among women and members of racial/ethnic minority groups. Almost universally these tests were developed using white, middle-aged males. As a general rule, these tests have performed less well with women. Where this is a particular issue is in obstetric settings, where alcohol use is a special concern, and the need to intervene is so important. That is the reason for the creation of the following instrument.

TWEAK

This 5-item scale was initially developed to meet the need for a sensitive, easy to administer screening test for pregnant women. It draws on existing tools, with the researchers eliminating or rewording questions that didn't seem to work as well with women, while retaining those that did. While designed for women, it has since been examined for use in other populations as well. TWEAK is an acronym that stands for **T**olerance, **W**orry about drinking, **E**ye-opener, **A**mnesia (blackouts), and **K/Cut** down. The questions and scoring are as follows:

1A. How many drinks does it take before you begin to feel the first effect of alcohol? (Tolerance)	3 or more drinks = (2 points)
or	
1B. How many drinks does it take before the alcohol makes you fall asleep or pass out? Or, if you never pass out, what is the largest number of drinks that you have? (Tolerance)	5 or more drinks = (2 points)
2. Have your friends or relatives worried about your drinking in the past year?	Yes = 1 point

BOX 9.2 MAST (Michigan Alcoholism Screening Test)

Points		
2	(*1.)	Do you feel you are a normal drinker?
2	2.	Have you ever awakened the morning after some drinking the night before and found that you could not remember part of the evening before?
1	3.	Does your wife, husband (or parents) ever worry or complain about your drinking?
2	*4.	Can you stop drinking without a struggle after 1 or 2 drinks?
1	5.	Do you ever feel bad about your drinking?
2	(*6.)	Do friends or relatives think you are a normal drinker?
0	7.	Do you ever try to limit your drinking to certain times of the day or to certain places?
2	*8.	Are you always able to stop drinking when you want to?
5	(9.)	Have you ever attended a meeting of Alcoholics Anonymous (AA)?
1	10.	Have you gotten into fights when drinking?
2	11.	Has drinking ever created problems with you and your wife, husband?
2	12.	Has your wife, husband (or other family member) ever gone to anyone for help about your drinking?
2	(13.)	Have you ever lost friends or girlfriends/boyfriends because of your drinking?
2	(14.)	Have you ever gotten into trouble at work because of drinking?
2	15.	Have you ever lost a job because of drinking?
2	(16.)	Have you ever neglected your obligations, your family, or your work for 2 or more days in a row because you were drinking?
1	17.	Do you ever drink before noon?
2	18.	Have you ever been told you have liver trouble? Cirrhosis?
2	(19.)	Have you ever had delirium tremens (DTs), severe shaking, after heavy drinking?
5	(20.)	Have you ever gone to anyone for help about your drinking?
5	(21.)	Have you ever been in a hospital because of your drinking?
2	22.	Have you ever been a patient in a psychiatric hospital or on a psychiatric ward of a general hospital where drinking was part of the problem?
2	23.	Have you ever been seen at a psychiatric or mental health clinic or gone to a doctor, social worker, or clergy for help with an emotional problem in which drinking has played a part?
2	24.	Have you ever been arrested, even for a few hours, because of drunk behavior?
2	(25.)	Have you ever been arrested for drunk driving or driving after drinking?

*Negative responses are alcoholic responses.

Note: Parentheses indicate questions included in the Brief MAST. Parentheses and underlines indicate questions included in the shortMAST (SMAST).

Scoring: A score of 3 points or less is considered nonalcoholic, 4 points is suggestive of alcoholism, and a score of 5 points or more indicates alcoholism.

3. Do you sometimes take a drink in the morning, when you first get up? (Eye-opener) — Yes = 1 point
4. Are there times when you drink and afterwards can't remember what you said or did? (Amnesia) — Yes = 1 point
5. Do you sometimes feel the need to cut down on your drinking (K or C, Cut down) — Yes = 1 point

A total score of 3 or more is considered positive for either version of the TWEAK.

Alcohol Use Disorders Identification Test (AUDIT)

The AUDIT was developed through the efforts of the World Health Organization (WHO). The goal was to create a screening tool that would meet several criteria. First, it had to identify high-risk alcohol use, those whose alcohol use warranted closer examination, not simply alcohol dependence. Second, the screening instrument needed to be effective in different cultures, in both developing and developed countries. Third, it had to be suitable for use by an array of health-care workers. The project was initiated in 1982 with the active collaboration of alcohol specialists in many countries. The AUDIT on page 240 consists of 10 questions. It has been tested in a variety of populations. At this time, it is the most widely accepted screening instrument. Literally hundreds of studies have examined its use with people from different countries, from different age groups, or different languages.

CRAFFT

The CRAFFT is a screening tool developed for use with adolescents. While drawing upon adult instruments the questions have been rephrased to incorporate situations suited to teens. It consists of 6 questions.

1. Have you ever ridden in a **C**ar driven by someone (including yourself) who was high or had been using alcohol or drugs?
2. Do you ever use alcohol or drugs to **R**elax, feel better about yourself, or fit in?
3. Do you ever use alcohol or drugs while you are by yourself **A**lone?
4. Do you ever **F**orget things you did while using alcohol or drugs?
5. Do your **F**amily or **F**riends ever tell you that you should cut down on your drinking or drug use?
6. Have you ever gotten into **T**rouble while you were using alcohol or drugs?

Two or more positive responses suggest the need for further evaluation.

Dartmouth Assessment of Lifestyle Instrument (DALI)

Most screening instruments do not work as well for those with serious mental illness. These existing instruments rely on questions that tap into physical dependence, such as the need for an "eye-opener" (both the CAGE and TWEAK). For those with serious mental illness, problems may appear far before physical signs and symptoms are present. The life situations of those with serious mental illness are often tenuous. Problems can occur in the presence of alcohol or other drug use far before there is the appearance of tolerance or withdrawal. Alcohol or other drug use can also make management of the psychiatric condition more difficult. This instrument was developed for this population. The DALI consists of questions to assess both alcohol and other drug use problems

BOX 9.3 AUDIT—*Alcohol Use Disorders Identification Test*

1. How often do you have a drink containing alcohol?

Never	(0)
Monthly or less	(1)
Two to four times a month	(2)
Two to four times a week	(3)
Four or more times a week	(4)

2. How many drinks containing alcohol do you have on a typical day when you are drinking?

1 or 2	(0)
3 or 4	(1)
5 or 6	(2)
7 to 9	(3)
10 or more	(4)

3. How often do you have six or more drinks on one occasion?

Never	(0)
Less than monthly	(1)
Monthly	(2)
Weekly	(3)
Daily or almost daily	(4)

4. How often during the last year have you found that you were not able to stop drinking once you had started?

Never	(0)
Less than monthly	(1)
Monthly	(2)
Weekly	(3)
Daily or almost daily	(4)

5. How often during the last year have you failed to do what was normally expected from you because of drinking?

Never	(0)
Less than monthly	(1)
Monthly	(2)
Weekly	(3)
Daily or almost daily	(4)

6. How often during the last year have you needed a first drink in the morning to get yourself going after a heavy drinking session?

Never	(0)
Less than monthly	(1)
Monthly	(2)
Weekly	(3)
Daily or almost daily	(4)

7. How often during the last year have you had a feeling of guilt or remorse after drink?

Never	(0)
Less than monthly	(1)
Monthly	(2)
Weekly	(3)
Daily or almost daily	(4)

8. How often during the last year have you been unable to remember what happened the night before because you had been drinking?

Never	(0)
Less than monthly	(1)
Monthly	(2)
Weekly	(3)
Daily or almost daily	(4)

9. Have you or someone else been injured as a result of your drinking?

No	(0)
Yes, but not in the last year	(2)
Yes, during the last year	(4)

10. Has a relative or friend, or a doctor or other health worker been concerned about your drinking or suggested you cut down?

No	(0)
Yes, but not in the last year	(2)
Yes, during the last year	(4)

SCORING: Questions 1–8 are scored 0, 1, 2, 3, or 4
Questions 9 & 10 are scored 0, 2, or 4 only.
The minimum score (for nondrinkers) is 0 and the maximum possible score is 40.
A score of 8 or more indicates a strong likelihood of hazardous or harmful alcohol consumption.

From: Saunders JB, Aasland OG, Babor TF, de la Fuente JR, Grant M. Development of the Alcohol Use Disorders Identification Test (AUDIT): WHO Collaborative Project on Early Detection of Persons with Harmful Alcohol Consumption II. *Addiction* 88(6):791–804, 1993.

BOX 9.4 DALI—*Dartmouth Assessment of Lifestyle Instrument*

Question	*Scoring* *Alcohol Score*
1. Do you wear seatbelts while riding in a car? Yes = 0, No = 1, refused or don't know = .4	________
2. How many cigarettes do you smoke? (not scored)	
3. Have you tried to stop smoking cigarettes? (not scored)	
4. Do you control your diet for total calories? (not scored)	
5. How much would you say you spent during the past six months on alcohol? \$0–\$49 = 0, > \$49 = 1, ref/DK = 1, > \$49 = −1*	________
6. How many drinks can you hold without passing out? If patient does not know, ask "how many do you think it would take?" 0 = 0, 1–5 = 1, ref/KD = 1.6	________
7. Have friends or relatives worried or complained about your drinking in the past 6 months? Yes = 0, No = −1, ref/DK = .5	________
8. Have you ever attended a meeting of AA because of your drinking? Yes = 0, No = −1, ref/DK = −.8	________
9. Do you sometimes take a drink in the morning when you first get up? Yes = 0, No = −1, *ref/DK = −.8*	________
10. How long was your last period of voluntary abstinence? Or most recent period when you chose not to drink?† > or = 60 mo = 0, 0–59 mo = 1, ref/DK = .4	________
11. How many months ago did this abstinence end? or When did you start drinking again? 0 months = 0, > 0 months = 1, ref/DK = .4	________
	Drug Score
12. Have you used marijuana in the past 6 months? Yes = 0, No = −1*, ref/DK = .7	________
13. Have you lost a job because of marijuana use? Yes = 0, No = −1*, ref/DK = .9	________
14. How much would you say you spent in the past 6 months on marijuana? 0\$ = 0, > 0\$ = 1, ref/DK = 1	________
15. How troubled or bothered have you been in the past 6 months by marijuana problems? not at all = 1, slightly = 2, moderately = 3, considerably = 4, extremely = 5, ref/DK = 1	________
16. Has cocaine abuse created problems between you and your spouse or parents? Yes = 0, No = −1*, ref/DK = −.8	________
17. How long was your longest period or voluntary period when you chose not to use cocaine?† 0–59 months = 1, > 59 months = 0, not applicable = 0	________
18. Do you ever use cocaine when you're in a bad mood? Yes = 0, No = 1, ref/DK = 0	________

Total ________ + ________ = ________
alcohol drug alcohol & drug

Scoring: The total score can range from −4 to +6. Alcohol scale: Scores between +2 and +6 indicate a high risk of a current alcohol use problem. Drug scale: A score above −1 indicates a high risk for cocaine or marijuana problems.

*a minus value.

†NB. 2 or more wks = a month; exclude periods of incarceration or hospitalization.

among those with chronic mental illness. This questionnaire has 18 questions. Three of the first 4 are unscored and are included to set the tone for the inventory. The inventory was developed to be administered by computer and thus is scored automatically. (Hand scoring is a bit cumbersome, but doable.) Interestingly, virtually all patients are able to complete a computer version and enjoy doing so, and the information elicited is as reliable as that secured through an interview.

Initial Follow-Up Questions

When screening is positive, what next? William Clark of Harvard Medical School, and formerly the chief of medicine at Cambridge City Hospital, authored some of the earliest material on alcohol diagnosis directed to physicians. Although his comments are concerned with the medical interview, they would be useful in any counseling situation. He has 3 basic rules: (1) ask about the person, not about the alcohol; he is a firm believer in routinely using the CAGE questions; (2) use the laboratory sparingly; that's easy for nonphysicians to follow; (3) be prepared with some follow-up questions for use when the CAGE is positive. He suggests a series of follow-up questions to get at the client's preoccupation with alcohol. To help remember them, he uses 2 mnemonics, HALT and BUMP.

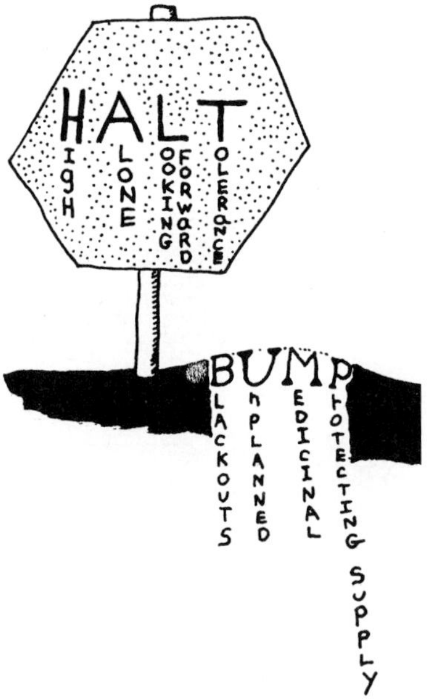

"Do you usually drink to get	**H**igh?"
"Do you sometimes drink	**A**lone?"
"Have you found yourself	**L**ooking forward to drinking?"
"Have you noticed an increased	**T**olerance for alcohol?"

"Do you have	**B**lackouts?"
"Have you found yourself using alcohol in an	**U**nplanned way?"
"Do you drink for	**M**edicinal reasons?"
"Do you work at	**P**rotecting your supply of alcohol?"

To get at the common problems associated with alcohol use, Clark suggests another series of questions. The device for remembering this is FATAL DTs: **F**amily history of alcohol problems, **A**lcoholics Anonymous attendance, **T**houghts of having alcoholism, **A**ttempts or thoughts of suicide, **L**egal problems, **D**riving while intoxicated, **T**ranquilizer or disulfiram use.

Identifying Situations Requiring Medical Attention

While there is no suggestion that a counselor attempt to deliver medical care, there are situations in which being informed about medical issues is important. When screening is positive, medical information is part of the additional information required. Counselors need to evaluate withdrawal risks and to be aware of situations where medical attention is indicated. Every counselor needs to have someone to turn to as a medical backup.

Some general questions about health status that should be asked include the following:

- Have you ever been hospitalized and, if so, for what?
- Do you have a history of accidents or injuries, or have you been in any fights that required medical attention? Did any of these occur when you were drinking or using drugs?
- Have you been seeing a doctor recently or thought that you should have seen one?
- When was the last time you were seen by a physician?

Assessing Withdrawal Risk

For clients who are drinking or using other drugs, or who have recently stopped, there is the potential for withdrawal. To assess withdrawal risks, the following information should be secured for any patient for whom there has been a decrease in regular use or a recent cessation of use.

- *The type and amounts of drugs used during the past week.* Try to elicit specific details and quantifiable amounts. When the amount is essentially unknown to the individual, make efforts to infer levels of use. The following questions may be necessary:
  —"How often do you go to the liquor store?"
  —"How much do you purchase?"
  —"How long does this amount last?"
  For prescription drug abuse, the question to ask is "How long does a prescription last?"
  "How many sources do you have for the prescription?"
  For illicit drugs, the key aspects are "How often do you use cocaine or crack? Daily? Weekends? How often do you purchase drugs?"
- *Level of tolerance.* "What is the amount of the alcohol/drug you require to feel the effects?"
- *The interval since the last alcohol or drug use and the current physical status.* This information provides a valuable means of assessing tolerance. It indicates the symptoms of withdrawal with a declining blood level. In response to this, what objective signs are there of the presence of withdrawal? Tremulousness? Agitation? Sweating? Confusion? Hypervigilance? Rapid pulse?
- *Current or past medical problems, allergies.*
- *Prior experience of either decreasing or stopping drinking or drug use.* Prior clinical status during withdrawal is significant, especially when prior withdrawal was problematic. This is not to be limited to formal detoxification. Many individuals have had periods of relative or absolute abstinence dictated by circumstances such as conscious

efforts to curtail or limit use, or hospitalizations or vacation periods, which disrupt their usual drinking pattern.

When it comes to drugs other than alcohol, regardless of training clinicians will ever be as knowledgeable as some of their clients regarding various drug actions and the desired effects. Do not trip yourself up as a result of your lack of knowledge by pretending to be informed. Sometimes clients refer to drugs by their street names, which you may not recognize, or talk about drug effects using street slang. Ask the client to define these terms. Ask what a drug does for him or her; ask how it is administered, the duration of the effects, and what it feels like as the effects wear off. There may be some disbelief about your naïveté, but generally clients will appreciate that you bothered to ask and were sufficiently well informed to ask the right questions.

Indications for Immediate Medical Evaluation

Many medical emergencies will be clearly recognizable. In these situations, use emergency transportation, police, or rescue squads. This is especially important if the client needs life support. This is evidenced by shallow, uneven breathing; rapid pulse; or fluctuating levels of consciousness. Another emergency situation is when there is a threat of danger to others or harm to self. When an individual is transported for emergency care, inform the emergency department of the patient's imminent arrival. Any information that can be provided to emergency staff is helpful, including current status; names of family or friends who may be with the patient and can provide information; diagnostic impressions; and relevant medical history.

The following indications for immediate medical evaluation may not appear to be immediately life-threatening; however, prompt medical attention should be arranged. Without an adequate evaluation, serious problems could occur.

- Recent substance intake at levels that risk developing toxicity, poisoning, or organ damage even if the patient is asymptomatic
- Ingestion of unknown quantities and substances
- Hallucinations, marked paranoia
- Confusion or delirium
- Severe agitation; efforts to quiet the patient are unsuccessful
- Severe tremors
- Tachycardia (heart rate 110 per minute)
- Fever (38.0°C)
- History or evidence of trauma, especially head trauma
- Patient is semiconscious and able to be aroused briefly but falls asleep when stimulus is removed

For individuals who have recently stopped drinking or have reduced their consumption significantly or intend to, the following suggest a significant risk for serious withdrawal:

- History of a difficult withdrawal
- Seizures or history of seizures
- Dependence on multiple substances

There are also situations that, while not medical emergencies, still warrant a patient's arranging for a checkup. These include all clients with heavy, extended alcohol or other drug use who have not had a recent checkup, anyone reporting a history of bleeding, and those who have a history of chronic medical illness, such as high blood pressure, who are not under a doctor's care.

SUBSTANCE USE HISTORY

Beyond attending to immediate medical problems, when routine screening provides evidence of an alcohol or other drug problem, then a more detailed use history is always indicated. Similarly an alcohol/drug use history should be an integral part of an interview with any troubled person, whether the person has gone to a physician or hospital with a physical problem or to a social worker, psychiatrist, psychologist, or clergy member concerning an emotional or a life adjustment problem. The reasons for this should now be clear. This is a drinking society; most people drink at least some alcohol. Alcohol is a chemical and not as benign as previously thought. It simply cannot be ignored as a possible factor in whatever brings a person to a caregiver of any kind. Again, do not limit your attention to dependence alone. The purpose of the alcohol use history is simply to get as clear a picture of alcohol use as you would of other medical aspects, family situation, job difficulties, or mood. It is part of the information-gathering process, which is later added up to give you an idea of what is going on in the person's life and how best to proceed.

Clinical Style

Many sample drinking history forms are floating around—for physicians, nurses, and other health-care providers. Whatever the actual form, the attitude of the questioner is as important, if not more important, than the list of questions. If asking about drinking strikes you as an invasion of privacy, a waste of time, or of little use because the presenting problem is clearly not alcohol- or other drug-related, then you are going to be uncomfortable asking and will probably get less reliable answers from an uncomfortable client. If your bias is the opposite and you see alcohol or other drugs lurking in the corner of every problem, again discomfort and unreliable answers will probably be your lot. Somehow you need to begin with an objective stance. Alcohol might or might not be a factor, just as any other aspect of the client's life might or might not be of concern.

Motivation

For too long, the tendency has been to lay the blame for treatment failure on the client's shoulder. He or she was "in denial," wasn't ready to change, was unmotivated, hadn't "hit bottom." A growing body of research shows that clinical style can make a difference in terms of treatment outcome. Tied to this is the recognition that there is a series of discrete stages that accompanies any behavioral change. A significant contribution of learning psychologists active in the alcohol and substance abuse fields has been in clarifying the concept of motivation. In the past, motivation was seen as a characteristic of a client, as something that was either absent or present. Motivated clients were perceived as having good outcomes; conversely, treatment failures were often chalked up to a client's lack of motivation. William Miller, Ph.D., a psychologist, drawing on work done in other areas, has introduced the alcohol and substance abuse treatment field to a very different view of motivation. In his formulation, motivation is a dynamic process, with discrete stages that parallel the stages occurring whenever anyone makes significant life changes. Specific clinical interventions are either well suited or to be avoided, depending on where the client is in the change process. The stages outlined by Miller are as follows:

1. *Precontemplation.* This is the point when the individual is not even considering change. There is no perceived need to. Instead, a problem is recognized by someone else, such as a family member, physician, clergy, or coworker. In this stage, the important clinical task is to help the individual gain awareness of the dangers involved in his or her present behaviors.
2. *Contemplation.* Now the individual is more ambivalent. There is a mixture of favoring and resisting change. As change is considered, the person perceives both pluses and minuses. In this stage if confronted with arguments on one side, the client's likely response is to defend the opposite side. So it is helpful for the clinician to address the negative effects of the alcohol use, the features the client considers pluses, and the potential benefits of change. It is not uncommon for those with alcohol problems to find themselves in situations where there is a lot at stake. There is the person arrested for DWI at risk of losing driving privileges. There is the woman who risks the loss of her children due to neglect. There is the nurse who is threatened with the loss of her license. Several studies show that people will be far more likely to make changes to avoid losing something than to make changes in response to losses. How does this finding fit into this view of motivation? The prospect of loss gets the individual's attention. When weighing the negative factors associated with not doing anything, against the benefits associated with making changes, the deck is stacked in favor of the latter. Thus, the balance is in favor of making changes. The person is posed from moving

from the stage of contemplation to the next stage. But if the loss has already occurred, and there is no longer anything to be gained by making changes, the individual is likely to move from contemplation back to precontemplation.

3. *Determination.* In this stage there is less ambivalence. The client often "sounds" different and can acknowledge a situation warranting change. Efforts are actively being made to consider alternatives. For the patient at this stage, rapid, immediate intervention is important. If too much time passes, the individual reverts to the stage of contemplation. Thus, a potential opportunity for change has been lost. In this stage the client needs the professional's assistance in selecting an optimal strategy for making changes, plus lots of support for the resolve to follow through.
4. *Action.* At this point the client is engaged in implementing a plan, which may be formal treatment. So the clinical task is providing assistance and direction as the client carries out the plan.
5. *Maintenance.* When significant changes in behavior have been made, then maintenance of the change is what becomes important. Maintenance of change is seen as being sustained by continuing action. Interestingly, the process of making change is, in and of itself, reinforcing. It encourages the desire to make other needed changes and demonstrates that change is possible.

If relapse occurs, then it is necessary to once again go through the stage of initiating change, again starting with contemplation.

Rather than motivation being considered a "thing" that one does or doesn't have, this formulation considers motivation as a process. It is a process that can be helped or hindered by the clinician's efforts. Different clinical approaches are considered to be particularly helpful at particular stages in prompting change. These are outlined in Table 9.1.

Table 9.1 Stages of Motivation

Stages of Change	Clinician Efforts to Promote Motivation
Precontemplation	Raise doubts. Prompt the client to consider the risks and problems with the current situation.
Contemplation	Here the client is ambivalent; try to tip the balance. Have the client consider the benefits of change and risks of the situation continuing as is.
Determination	Focus on specific actions the individual can take.
Action	Facilitate the steps outlined above.
Maintenance	Identify factors that may prompt a relapse and develop strategies to counter this.

Tailoring the clinical approaches to the stage of change is a process that has been termed *motivational interviewing*. Miller has been involved, too, in articulating this approach.

History Taking

When to Ask

It takes practice to take a reliable alcohol/drug history. It also takes recognition of timing and a good look at what is in front of you. It may seem redundant to say, but an intoxicated or withdrawing client cannot give you good information. You wouldn't expect accurate information from someone going under or coming out of anesthesia. Unfortunately, some of the forms designed to be filled out at intake show little recognition of this fact. Use your common sense. Try to ask the questions you need to at a time when the person is at least relatively comfortable, both emotionally and physically. Ask them matter-of-factly. Remember that your own drinking pattern is no yardstick for others. For example, when someone responds to the question "How much do you usually drink on a typical occasion?" with "About 4 or 5 drinks or so," don't stare, open-mouthed.

What to Ask

The information needed about alcohol consumption includes what the client drinks, how much, how often, when, where, and is it causing, or has it caused, a problem in any area of life, including physical problems. These questions can be phrased in different ways. A more informal approach may be better than simply sitting there, filling out a form and asking each question in order. An issue that is too often excluded is the question of what the drinking does for the client. Questions such as "How do you feel when you drink?" "What does alcohol do for you?" and "When do you most often want a drink?" can supply a lot of information.

How to Ask

If the questions are asked conversationally along with other questions regarding general health, social aspects, and other use of prescribed drugs or medications, most people will answer them. The less threatened you are by the process, the more comfortable the individual being questioned will be.

Following questions about alcohol use, queries should be directed to other drug use. You could ask a question such as "Have you used drugs other than those required for medical reasons?" If the answer is positive, the follow-up questions would be what substances, under what circumstances, with what kinds of accompanying problems, and is there concern by either the individual or others.

Recording the Data in the Record

Alcohol use should be adequately described in the client's chart or medical record, so that changes in drinking patterns can be detected over time. If there is no evidence of alcohol being a problem, that, too, should be noted. Notes in the chart should include sufficient objective detail to provide meaningful data to other clinicians. Avoid one-word descriptions, such as "socially" or "occasionally." If the agency does not have a prescribed format, the following should be included for all clients: drinking pattern, problems related to alcohol use, expression of concern by family or friends, the MAST or CAGE score, and the presence or absence of other drug use.

Additional information may be desired for the counselor's own records. The worksheet on pages 250–251 is one means of summarizing the data elicited. It helps assemble information that is pertinent to making a diagnosis of alcohol abuse or dependence.

WHAT NEXT?

Making a Referral

Having identified an alcohol or another drug problem, the clinician who isn't primarily a substance abuse professional is faced with referring the client to a treatment program. This may be either for further evaluation or for treatment. Drawing on motivational interviewing, the following are key: removing barriers, practical as well as attitudinal; giving clear direction; actively helping; providing feedback; and reinforcing and supporting the client's efforts to effect change.

To make this concrete, keep several things in mind. First, you cannot enthusiastically recommend the unfamiliar. Therefore, you need to know about various facilities, their programs, and their personnel. Second, in making any referral, there's always a danger of clients falling through the cracks. Therefore, you need to be actively involved in the referral. Don't just give an agency name and phone number, with instructions for the client to call. You make the appointment with a specific individual, at a specific time. With this active helping, the likelihood of the individual's following through virtually doubles, jumping from under 40% if the client is given only a phone number and told to call to over 80% when the counselor sets up the appointment. Inform the family or significant others of the actions being taken and why. Third, if you've had an ongoing relationship with the client, a referral may feel like abandonment. If appropriate, continue the contact and let the client know that you are both in this together.

In large measure the ability to effect a successful referral lies in conveying a sense of concern and hope. It also depends on assisting the client to see the difficulties in a new light, that there may be a disease

DSM-IV Diagnostic Worksheet

Client Name

	Symptoms			Diagnostic Criteria *Alcohol Abuse:* A definite diagnosis of abuse is made when *one* of A is "yes," and both B & C are also "yes."	Yes ☐	No ☐
A1	__Missing school/work __Lost job	__Intoxicated at home __Use at work or school __Other	__Lost time from work __Child care neglected	A) 1 Recurring failure to meet social, family, work responsibilities due to use.	____	____
2	__Driving under the influence __Reckless driving __Serious injury	__Arrests __Physical fights or property damage	__Increased tolerance __Past heavy drinking pattern __Other ____________	2 Recurrent use when this is physically hazardous.	____	____
3	__DWI __Domestic disputes	__Arrests __License suspension	__Unpaid child support __Other ____________	3 Recurring legal problems.	____	____
4	__Friends/family express concern __Guilty about use __Arguments about drinking	__Alcohol related arrests __Blackouts __Physical health harmed by use	Drinking causes life problems: __relationship __legal__job __Other ____________	4 Continued use despite negative consequences or recurring problems due to use.	____	____
				B) These symptoms have occurred repeatedly during a 12-month period.	____	____
				C) Never having met the criteria for Dependence. The pattern is consistent with a diagnosis of abuse.	____	____

				Alcohol Dependence A definite diagnosis of dependence is made when any three of A *and* B are "yes."	Yes	No
1	__Consumed as much as 1 case beer, 1 gallon wine, 1/5 hard liquor at one time __4+ drinks/sitting	__Less use required to achieve intoxication	__Other	A) 1 Marked tolerance (50%) increase) to achieve effect.	____	____
2	__Morning hand tremor __Night sweats __Morning drinking __Drinking before work	__Morning nausea __Headache __Use of substitutes to self-medicate withdrawal symptoms	__Hallucinations __Other __________	2 Withdrawal symptoms or use to avoid withdrawal symptoms.	____	____
3	__Not a social drinker __Drinks more than intended	__More frequently __Greater quantity	__Experiences difficulty cutting down __Other __________	3 Drinking more or for longer periods than intended.	____	____
4	__Thoughts about cutting down __Guilty about use	__Sees self as problem drinker __Annoyed with concerns of others	__Periods of abstinence __Relief drinking __Other	4 A persistent desire, or one or more unsuccessful efforts to control use.	____	____
5	__Daily drinking __Binge drinking	__Hidden alcohol __Preoccupation with alcohol	__Drinking alone __Needs drink __Other __________	5 Considerable time spent obtaining alcohol, or drinking it, or recovering from its effects.	____	____
6	__Lost friends __Arguments about drinking	__Physical fights or property damage under the influence __Increased isolation	__Other __________	6 Important activities (social, occupational, recreational) given up or reduced because of drinking.	____	____
7	__Prior DWI __Other arrests __Lost job due to alcohol __Other __________	__Told drinking harming liver __Told by MD to decrease use __Blackouts __Health would be better without alcohol/drug use	After drinking: __rowdy/noisy __courage/self-confidence __angry/quarrelsome	7 Continued drinking despite knowledge of persistent social, psychological, or physical problems due to use.	____	____
				B) These symptoms have occurred repeatedly during a 12-month period. The pattern is consistent with a diagnosis of dependence. If Substance Dependence: with__or without__physiological dependence	____	____

causing these difficulties, and that it's not a question of who is at fault. In presenting the need for referral, remember that someone can absorb only so much information at one time. Consider for a moment the woman whose physician discovers a lump in her breast. The physician's next step is making a referral to a surgeon for a biopsy and possibly to an oncologist. This is not the time to discuss the relative merits of radical mastectomy and/or chemotherapy in terms of 5-year survival. Nor is it the time to talk of side effects from chemotherapy. Such presentations would be likely to cause the woman to run because she abandons hope, or it might cause her to retreat into denial. The important messages to convey initially are (1) the situation is serious enough to warrant further investigation, (2) the patient is being referred to someone who can be trusted, and (3) both of you are in this together. The same concern is what one is attempting to convey when making a referral for substance abuse problems.

Evaluation in a Substance Abuse Treatment Setting

For those working in a designated substance abuse program, the situation is a bit different. The person may be referred or come in with a good idea that alcohol is a problem. The person may, however, want to prove that it isn't. Because of the alcohol treatment designation, the questions about substance use can be more forthright and in depth. Consequently the client's responses may be more guarded—particularly responses to how much and how often. However, those are not the most helpful questions anyway. Indeed, some suggest never asking these questions, at least in an initial encounter. The reason is that they are the questions most likely to trigger the client's defenses. It is probably the topic that has caused the most friction with family. If asked, the responses around alcohol can range all the way from a gruff "A few and just socially" to a bragging "A whole case of beer whenever I feel like it." The prospective client will usually need to feel somewhat comfortable about seeing the clinician before more candor is possible. And there is always the possibility that the client doesn't know exactly how much or how often. Remember the maxim "Ask about the person not about his or her drinking (or other drug use)." The key thing for the clinician is to get as much reasonably reliable information as possible to develop appropriate treatment plans or initiate an appropriate referral. Information about quantity and frequency is not necessary to diagnose dependence. It can be useful in gauging the level of physical dependence and assessing possible withdrawal problems; however, tolerance can be gleaned indirectly by other means, such as "How many drinks does it take to feel the effect?"

Another point to consider is that you do not always have to get all the history immediately. If a client comes to a treatment facility smelling of alcohol, clearly uncomfortable, and somewhat shaky, you need to know immediately how much alcohol has been consumed, for over what period, and when the last drink was taken. You also need to know about other physical problems and what happened on other occasions when drinking was stopped. These questions are necessary to determine if the client needs immediate attention from a physician. If the client is not in crisis, the evaluation may occur over several outpatient visits.

Initial Interview

The initial interview is intended to get a general picture. As a result of the initial interview, the alcohol clinician will want to be able to answer the following questions:

1. What is the problem the client sees?
2. What does the client want?
3. What brings the client for help now?
4. What is going on in the individual's life—that is, what are the facts of the family situation, social problems, medical problems, alcohol use (how much, for how long), and other drug use?
5. Is there a medical or psychiatric emergency?
6. What are the recommendations?

Certainly, much other information could be elicited. But the answers to the foregoing questions make up the essential core for making decisions about how to proceed. Counseling is an art, not a science. No series of rules can be mechanically followed. However, one guideline is in order for an initial interview; it is especially apt in situations in which someone is first reaching out for help: don't let the interview end without adopting a definite plan for the next step. Why? People with alcohol or other problems are ambivalent. They approach and back off from help. Remember the stages of change. The contemplation stage is probably the most common at this point, preceding determination and adopting a plan of action. The person who comes in, saying, "I'm an alcoholic and want help" is rare. You are more likely to meet the following: "I think I may have a problem with alcohol, sort of, but it's really . . ." The concrete plan adopted at the close of the interview may be very simple, nothing more than agreeing to meet a couple more times, so that you can get a better idea of what's going on. Set a definite time. Leaving future meetings up in the air is like waving good-bye. It is not uncommon for the individual to try to get off the hook by flattering the therapist: "Gee, you've really helped me. Why don't I call you if things don't improve? Why, I feel better already, just talking to you."

Client's view of world

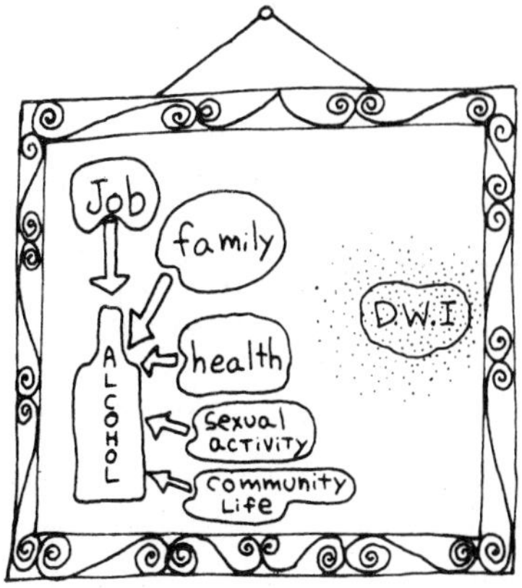

Despite the title of substance abuse therapist, clients first going to an agency are not going to have a clinician do "his or her treatment routine" on them. Possibly what they really want is a clean bill of health. They want to figure out why their drinking isn't "working" anymore. The only thing that may be clear is the presence of drinking. Clients are often unaware of its relationship to the problems in their life. As clients paint a picture of what is going on in their lives, the therapist will certainly see things the clients are missing or ignoring. You can see, for example, that the

Counselor's view of client's world

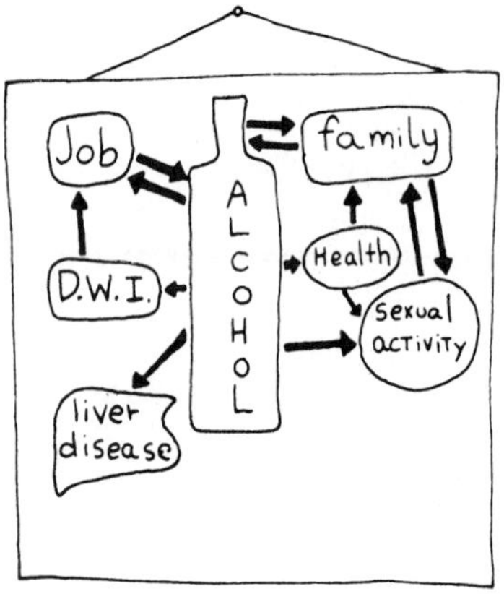

client is alcohol dependent. In your opinion, the client may unquestionably need some intensive treatment. However, at the moment, the client is unable to use the treatment. To begin, it is necessary to make a few critical connections—that is, get the arrows pointed in the right direction.

Standardized Assessment Tools

The substance abuse field is increasingly using standardized instruments to promote treatment planning as well as to provide a yardstick for measuring treatment effectiveness. The most widely used tool for both of these purposes is the *Addiction Severity Index (ASI).* It was first introduced in the early 1980s and has been widely adopted. The ASI is a semi-structured interview that collects data from 7 areas: medical, employment, legal, alcohol, other drug use, family-social functioning, and psychological status. For each of these areas, there is a score indicating the severity of the problems in that area. Everyone in the substance use field should acquire skill in using the Addiction Severity Index. Training programs to introduce the ASI to clinicians have been developed, some including videotape vignettes that help you learn to use the index smoothly.

Family Involvement

Participation of family in the evaluation is very desirable and becoming the norm. This is so vital that it's hard to imagine why family involvement was not always the case. In some instances family members are the more reliable historians. In any case their perspective on the problem is essential. By including family members, the clinician can assess first-hand their needs and their ability to provide support, as well as engage them as partners in treatment.

Manual-Guided Treatments

Increasingly, agencies are likely to draw upon manual-guided treatment approaches. These manuals grew out of efforts to compare different treatment approaches. This requires standardization across facilities and clinicians. It is essential that treatment A be the same, regardless of who is providing it. In counseling research, there is also the matter of standardizing the dose or amount of treatment provided. Project MATCH created treatment manuals, now available through the NIAAA; these set forth the number of sessions, the goals for each session, and the topics to be addressed. (See Chapter 10 for further discussion of specific manual-based approaches.)

Treatment Planning and Treatment Settings

An evaluation may take several sessions. In essence, the goal of the evaluation is to understand the client's situation and, based on that, to develop a plan that will offer the client the optimal chance of acquiring the skills and resources needed to maintain abstinence. The treatment plan may use many of the treatment techniques discussed in Chapter 10.

Criteria for Selecting Treatment Services

What is the appropriate treatment setting? One wants to avoid either undertreatment or overtreatment. The American Society of Addiction Medicine (ASAM) has developed *patient placement criteria* to guide decisions about the appropriate treatment setting. Six factors—or, using ASAM terminology, "dimensions"—have been identified as germane to determining the type of care required. These dimensions are outlined in the following list, along with some of the key questions to consider to assess each:

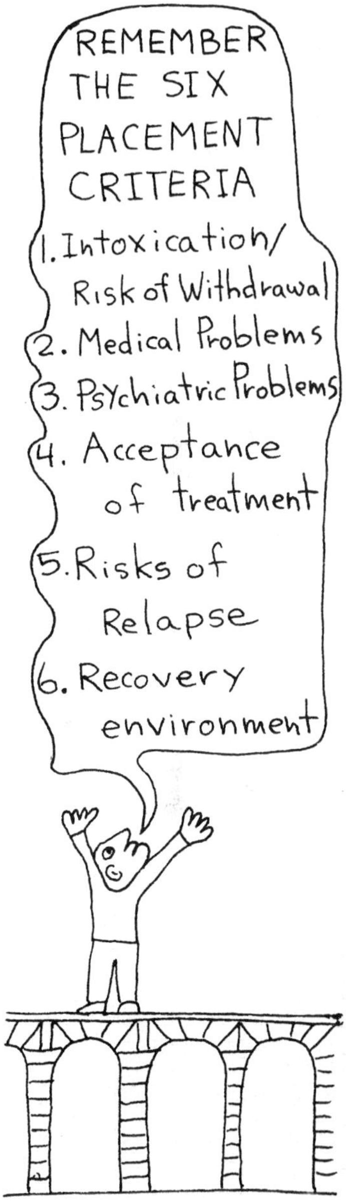
REMEMBER THE SIX PLACEMENT CRITERIA
1. Intoxication/ Risk of Withdrawal
2. Medical Problems
3. Psychiatric Problems
4. Acceptance of treatment
5. Risks of Relapse
6. Recovery environment

- *Dimension 1: Acute intoxication and/or likelihood of withdrawal syndromes.* Is the patient currently intoxicated? Does the level of intoxication represent a potentially life-threatening situation? Is there evidence of physical dependence? Is withdrawal likely? If so, are there factors that may complicate detoxification, such as the presence of other medical problems or a history of serious withdrawal? If withdrawal could be accomplished without medical supervision, are there family or friends available to provide support and identify any emerging problems were these to arise?
- *Dimension 2: Biomedical conditions and complications.* Are there any serious medical problems that may complicate treatment or chronic conditions that need to be monitored?
- *Dimension 3: Emotional-behavioral conditions.* Are there apparent psychiatric issues? Are they an expected part of the addictive disorder, or do they appear to be a separate disorder?
- *Dimension 4: Acceptance of need for treatment.* Does the patient recognize the need for treatment? Is the patient indicating a desire for treatment versus resisting treatment? Is the patient feeling pressured or coerced to enter treatment? To what extent is entry into treatment prompted by internal motivation, and to what degree is it the result of external pressures?
- *Dimension 5: Relapse or likelihood of continued use.* What are the apparent immediate risks if the patient does not enter treatment at this time? What are the longer-term risks associated with continuing to drink or use drugs? What kind of skills and supports does the patient have both to stop alcohol or drug use and to maintain abstinence?
- *Dimension 6: Recovery environment.* This refers to the client's social situation. What kind of family and social supports are present? What is the client's employment status, educational status, and financial situation? What community resources are needed and available—vocational counseling, social service agencies, and so on? Is the client confronted by a situation in which family members' or friends' drug or alcohol use would invite relapse or threaten participation in treatment?

Taking into account the results of the assessments of these domains, 5 levels of patient care have been identified. These specify the kind of care that is required, given the client's status. These levels of care are as follows:

- *Level 0.5: Early intervention.* This level of care was added when the criteria were reviewed and subsequently revised. So as not to introduce confusion by renumbering the existing levels, this was made 0.5 (one-half), to place it before Level I.
- *Level I: Outpatient services*
- *Level II: Intensive outpatient and partial hospitalization services*
- *Level III: Inpatient/residential services*
- *Level IV: Medically managed intensive inpatient services*

To help clinicians incorporate the data, ASAM has devised a table, in the form of a grid. For each type or level of care, the relevant factors are reviewed for each domain. In some instances, there is a single dimension that is *the* deciding factor in specifying what kind of care should be provided. For example, if there is apt to be serious withdrawal in a medically ill patient, medically managed intensive inpatient care is indicated. In that circumstance, other domains, such as the recovery environment or degree of family support, are irrelevant. These come into play after the medical status is stabilized. They will then be considered to determine whether the client is discharged to outpatient care or a residential program. Not only do the criteria state what kind of care is required, given the patient's status in each of the 6 areas, but they also indicate when discharge from a particular level of care is appropriate.

Treatment Planning for Those Previously Treated

A few comments are warranted with respect to treatment planning for the client who was in treatment previously. A portion of the evaluation needs to focus on prior treatment. What was the treatment? Did the client have a period of stable sobriety? If so, what contributed to its maintenance? To what do the family and the client attribute the resumption of drinking or drug use? These perceptions may be either insightful or way off base. However, they are important beliefs that will need to be either supported or challenged. If a stable sobriety or abstinence was never achieved, what are their hypotheses as to what went wrong? Is there evidence to suggest a psychiatric disorder that has gone undiagnosed? Is there multiple drug use? In light of what is known about matching patients to particular treatments, is there a particular treatment approach that is indicated? Also, is this individual a good candidate for drug therapies?

The client who has been through treatment a number of times and has not achieved abstinence is often termed a "treatment failure." This is unfortunate. This categorization fails to recognize that relapse is not uncommon. Also, this is obviously a very loaded label for the client and the family (if they are still in the client's life), as well as the treatment staff. It is never possible to predict when treatment will be successful. Nonetheless, simply one more exposure to the same treatment is possibly not the best clinical decision. The comparison might be made to someone with an infection that does not respond to a particular drug. Simply increasing the dose probably won't work. One of the things treatment repeaters do have going for them is a knowledge of what doesn't work. To the extent possible, the client should be actively engaged in treatment planning and committing to it—for example, agreeing ahead of time to attend more AA meetings, seeking an AA sponsor, entering a halfway house after inpatient care, and continuing in aftercare. A sense of self-efficacy is an important factor, too. This refers to the individual's belief in his or her ability to effect change. Efforts to help clients focus on what they have learned and how this can be useful are important.

Another difficulty commonly encountered with these clients is that they show up in the midst of a serious crisis—for example, a medical illness requiring hospitalization, family turmoil, or legal problems. This can lead to a situation in which the person, willing to comply (or at least not to resist), in essence finds him- or herself entered into a program. Although one may need to respond to the crisis, it is imperative to engage the client as soon as possible in planning treatment after the crisis is stabilized.

If someone comes to an agency with a history of multiple unsuccessful treatment attempts in that agency's program, the question needs to be asked whether a referral to another facility might be indicated. It is important this not be done as "punishment." Instead, it should be a clinical decision based on the possibility that entry into treatment elsewhere may increase the odds in favor of a different outcome because that staff will not have been involved in the previous efforts and see the client as a failure.

TREATMENT OF ALCOHOL PROBLEMS AND ALCOHOL ABUSE

Within the professional community there is reasonable consensus about what constitutes the standard of treatment for alcohol dependence. However, there are no universally accepted standards of care for the treatment of other types of alcohol problems. Nonetheless, some guidelines are presented here to serve as a conservative approach until the time when a body of clinical experience with treatment of alcohol problems emerges, similar to that which has been acquired around alcohol dependence.

Alcohol Incidents

Alcohol incidents are negative consequences that result from an individual's drinking. This may be an injury or a fight leading to police involvement. However, a thorough clinical evaluation indicates no pattern of recurring problems to indicate abuse or dependence.

The "Thou Shall Nots"

If it is a small sacrifice to discontinue the use of wine, do it for the sake of others: if it is a great sacrifice, do it for your own sake.
S. J. MAY

Don't presume that the incident has been enough to teach someone a lesson and guarantee that there will be no future difficulties. It's easy to assume that the embarrassment, guilt, discomfort, or anxiety that resulted was sufficient. It may even seem almost cruel to discuss it further. Others may mistakenly think that the polite, kind thing to do is "just not mention it." Especially with younger people, who may be those most likely to experience an alcohol-related problem, the incident may be treated by peers as a joke. What is required? All those who may have contact—be it emergency room personnel, a school counselor, the police, or the family—need to acknowledge the role of alcohol in what occurred. The actual or potential seriousness needs to be made clear. If you recall the progression of alcohol dependence in the framework set forth by Johnson (described in Chapter 7), the absence of feedback by others in the face of alcohol-related incidents is, in part, what allows a chronic alcohol problem to blossom. In fact, a second such incident should be a clear tip-off that a problem is emerging. One DWI "might" just happen, but a second should sound the warning signal that the person is continuing in a destructive pattern, despite prior negative consequences.

In the face of an incident involving alcohol, basic education is essential. This should not be cursory and superficial, but detailed and personalized. Alcohol has to be explained as a drug to the individual in light of what has occurred. What does BAC mean? How is it that alcohol can induce poor choices? What happens when someone chugs drinks? What are the mechanisms for alcohol-drug interactions?

The underlying message is that, if people are going to use the drug alcohol, they need to be fully informed about it. Don't assume that people, however bright and sophisticated, are sufficiently knowledgeable about alcohol and its actions to figure out what the risks are. Thus, the evaluation should also include an inventory of drinking practices, a review of settings in which drinking takes place, behaviors associated with drinking, and family history of alcohol problems or medical conditions that may be adversely influenced by alcohol use. The question to be answered is this: "Are there circumstances that are likely to place the individual at risk?" If so, specific steps should be discussed to address these. What might the person who is faced with being a passenger in a car with an intoxicated driver do? For the person who takes allergy medications, what are the implications for drinking? Identify potential problems and help the client think through—ahead of time—what should be done. One finding from the substance abuse prevention research is pertinent. One of the techniques in reducing teenage drug use is literally to have the kids practice how to say no. Adequate information alone isn't enough, nor are exhortations to "just say NO." They need some practice doing it. What is required are tips for applying this knowledge. This is very important, too, in the event that future problems with alcohol use occur. If a problem is handled in the fashion being suggested, later it could be safely assumed that the individual, from that point on, was fully informed. A subsequent problem indicates that a serious ongoing problem with alcohol is emerging and that alcohol dependence may be unfolding.

It is important that an alcohol incident not be treated as a secret. With the client's consent the situation should be brought to the attention of the client's family, friends, or spouse. The family needs to be informed in order to be aware and supportive of what is recommended. Although in an ideal world at least one follow-up visit might be scheduled just to check in with the individual, it is more likely that this will not happen. The family physician, often an untapped ally, is in a position to monitor how things are going in the future. The family physician is in a position to inquire routinely about alcohol use and therefore may be in the best position to spot any future difficulties. Because one of the most useful factors in spotting an alcohol problem early is detecting changes that occur over time, getting the occurrence of an alcohol problem into the individual's medical record is important. A brief communication with the physician will accomplish that. For the person at risk for developing alcohol dependence, the signs and symptoms that should trigger a need for further evaluation should be understood by all.

Brief Interventions

Alcohol incidents may bring someone to the attention of an alcohol treatment program. It is more likely that these individuals will come to the attention of other helping professions.

Consistently, brief interventions have been shown to reduce drinking as well as reducing the most risky drinking patterns. Such interventions have an impact, too, on the use of health-care services. Michael Fleming, M.D., a family practitioner who has long been interested in the role of family physicians in handling alcohol and other drug issues explored this. He along with colleagues conducted a large study of community-based primary-care practices. Over the study period, more than 17,000 patients were routinely screened to identify problem drinking. From this group, about 700 patients with patterns of harmful use were selected to participate in the study. Half received a brief treatment that entailed two 10- to 15-minute counseling sessions. These were provided by the doctor, using a "script" and involved advice, education, and a contract detailing what the patient would do. Twelve months later the results were significant. The amount of alcohol consumed had been reduced; the number of days on which people drank 5 or more drinks (binge drinking) declined. There was also a decline in the days of heavy drinking. Furthermore, those who received the intervention had fewer emergency room visits, fewer motor vehicle accidents, and less use of health-care services.

The effectiveness of brief interventions has been seen with prescription drug use as well. For example, one study examined efforts to reduce the use of benzodiazepines (drugs such as Valium and Librium) among patients who were taking more than was medically indicated. All the intervention entailed was the physician's sending a letter instructing the patient to cut down, advising on how to do this gradually, and suggesting that perhaps in time use could be stopped. Six months later, the group as a whole had reduced this prescription drug use by a third. One out of 5 had ceased use entirely. All of this was the result of a single letter!

In addition to brief interventions in the doctor's office, this technique has also been introduced into other medical settings. These initiatives have been successful in emergency departments, among pregnant women, among hospitalized patients, and even in the medical clinics in the workplace. Efforts are also under way to explore the use of new technologies, particularly the use of the Internet. The Addiction and Mental Health Foundation (Canada) has posted a self-assessment instrument on its website, http://notes.camh.net/efeed.nsf/newform. Persons can complete the questionnaire, and then immediately get personalized feedback based on their responses. This feedback includes a comparison of the person's drinking to the population at large, the risk for alcohol-related problems, an estimate of the amount of money spent annually, and also even how much time the person spends intoxicated.

Such brief or minimal interventions do not work with everyone. For these individuals, this can be one route into more formal, traditional treatment. Such a process is sometimes referred to as *stepped care.* Stepped care is a way of thinking about providing treatment. The basic philosophy is that the first treatment provided should be the least intensive, and least expensive, option that is anticipated to work. The phrase "anticipated to work" is important. People should not blindly be referred for the least intensive, least costly option. But where there is a reasonable expectation that either of two treatments may be effective, start with the less intensive. Thus, intensive outpatient treatment would be selected over residential care. In such cases, if people do not respond to the treatment provided, then move to the more intensive treatment. This approach is common in many areas of medicine. For example, it is similar to the way in which antibiotics are prescribed. The most powerful, newer drugs are not those routinely prescribed. They are reserved for those who do not improve with the standard, more common medications. In terms of alcohol or other drug problems, the absence of change after a brief intervention can be the basis for a health-care professional's decision to make a referral to substance abuse professionals.

In reviewing articles on brief treatments that have been described in the scientific literature, William Miller identified 6 features that appear to be common to all. These elements can be remembered by the acronym FRAMES: Feedback, Responsibility, Advice, a Menu of options presented to the patient, Empathy, and Self-efficacy.

- ***F**eedback about patients' personal risk.* Typically health professionals delivering brief intervention give feedback on the risky aspects associated with the patient's drinking. This includes things such as current health problems aggravated by drinking or those caused by drinking, as well as other problems in their lives that appear to be related to their alcohol use.
- ***R**esponsibility of the patient.* Research has consistently shown that people are more likely to make changes if they feel their own behavior can make a difference, so brief interventions generally emphasize the patient's role and responsibility for making decisions. For example, a doctor or nurse may tell patients, "No one can make you change or make you decide to change. What you do about your drinking is up to you."
- ***A**dvice to change.* Health professionals can give explicit advice to reduce or stop drinking. This can be done in the same way that they would give advice to a diabetic about diet or would give specific advice about exercise.
- ***M**enu of ways to reduce drinking.* Consistent with the idea that responsibility lies with the patient, individuals can be offered a variety of ways they can change their drinking. This can include identifying and reducing high-risk situations, or finding other ways to cope with stressful situations. There are patient education and some self-help manuals.
- ***E**mpathetic counseling style.* A warm, reflective, and understanding style of delivering brief intervention is more effective than an aggressive, confrontational, or coercive style. In comparing these styles, one study found that there was a 77% reduction in drinking when an empathetic style was used, as opposed to only 5% when a confrontational approach was used.
- ***S**elf-efficacy or optimism of the patient.* Self-efficacy is the individual's belief that he or she can do things that will make a difference. In studies of treatment generally, patients who don't feel powerless do better, so efforts in brief treatment are directed to empowering patients and helping them feel optimistic about their ability to make changes.

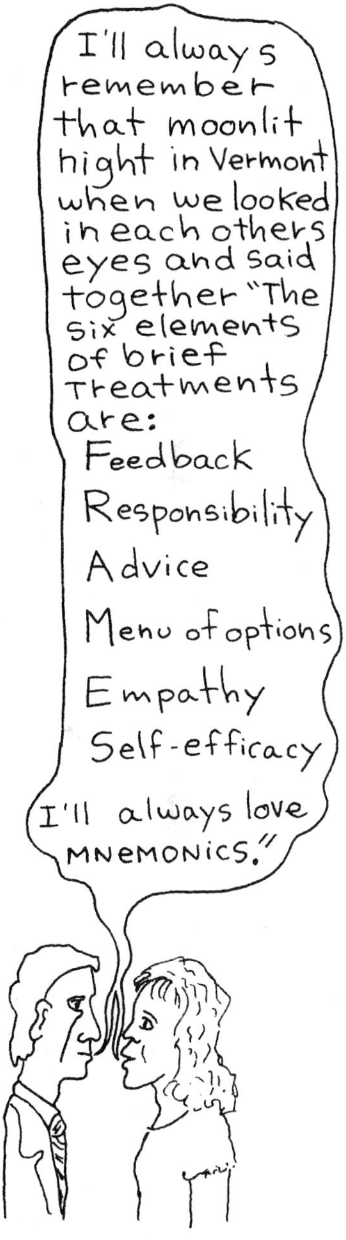

In considering what makes brief treatments work, the role of the physician cannot be ignored. Doctors are generally seen as acting on their patient's behalf, of having specialized knowledge, and as being objective. While people may be suspicious of a spouse's motives, that isn't usually the response to their doctors. Even if people don't follow a doctor's advice, at least they will listen! One interesting insight comes from a study that was never conducted. Prior to the emergence of brief, office-based interventions, Michael Fleming, MD, was a member of a group of family doctors who wished to study the use of a Johnson-style intervention. (The details of these techniques are described in Chapter 10.) This was a process recognized as a technique family members could use as a means of moving people into treatment. In brief, the family intervention, led by an alcohol professional, uses a family meeting in which family members mention specific behaviors that are seen as evidence of an alcohol problem and expressed their concern for the person. In the study that never happened, a group of physicians were trained to conduct such interventions; however, they never got to conduct the intervention. In each instance when the physician brought up the need for treatment, the patient agreed, and no such family meeting was required. Seemingly the authority of the physician and the way he or she expressed concern for the patient were all that was needed.

Finally, studies of spontaneous remission suggest factors that explain the impact of brief interventions. "Spontaneous remission" is a term borrowed from the general medical field. It refers to the fact that sometimes, without treatment, patients recover for reasons that are not understood. In reference to alcohol problems, this refers to those with serious alcohol problems and alcohol dependence who stop drinking on their own. Those who have studied this are always careful to point out that the remissions were virtually never spontaneous or true remissions. Typically something happened that sparked these people to make changes. Nor were they true remissions, in the sense that the individuals resumed nonproblemmatic drinking. When questioned about the things that prompted them to stop drinking, several factors were commonly mentioned. The following were identified, along with the percentage each was mentioned: illness or accident (33%); extraordinary events, such as humiliation, suicide attempts, or pregnancy (29%); religious or conversion experience (26%); alcohol-caused financial problems (22%); intervention by immediate family (18%); alcohol-related death or illness of a friend (14%); education about alcoholism (12%); and alcohol-related legal problem (8%).

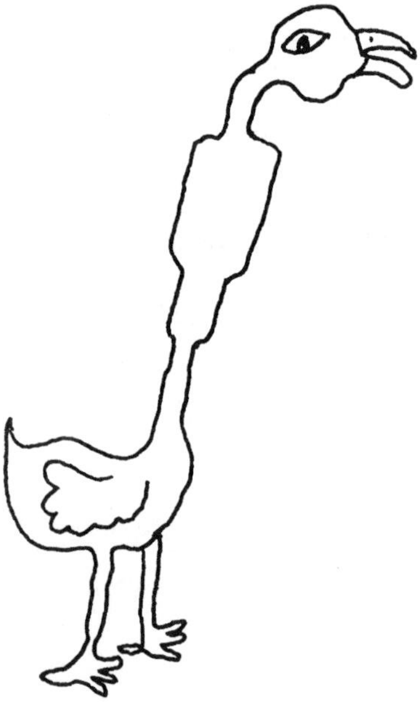

Alcohol Abuse

Unlike an alcohol incident, which is an acute problem, a diagnosis of alcohol abuse reflects a chronic problem. Alcohol abuse is diagnosed where there is a pattern of use that is physically hazardous, that interferes with the ability to fill major obligations—at home, work, or school—or that causes major problems with other people. Practically speaking, alcohol abuse can be considered to be present when there is a pattern of alcohol problems and there's the sense that dependence is "just around the corner." If there is not physical dependence or loss of control then, from a physiological standpoint, the moderation of drinking practices is possible. Interestingly, for a substantial portion of clients who are using alcohol in a risky fashion it is not always easy to determine if there is a loss of control. This is because these individuals have never made an effort to control their alcohol use. They are in social situations where almost anything goes. Even if dependence is not present, for some, moderating alcohol use may still represent a monumental feat. Consider the college student who is in a heavy-drinking fraternity. Changing drinking patterns will require changes in the student's circle of friends, daily routine, and choices of recreational activities. To achieve this magnitude of change will require that the client be engaged in more than a supportive chat.

Intervening requires that the individual be engaged in a formal treatment effort, involving education, individual counseling, and possibly participation in a group with others in the same situation. Monitoring efforts to moderate alcohol use and avoid future problems is imperative. Through this process, in a number of cases, evidence may mount that there is loss of control or preoccupation with drinking, indicating that abstinence and treatment for alcohol dependence are now needed. In essence, if efforts to address alcohol abuse are unsuccessful, the diagnosis of dependence can now be made.

TREATMENT OF ALCOHOL DEPENDENCE

Treatment of dependence is nothing more (or less) than the interventions designed to short-circuit the disease process and provide an introduction to an alcohol-free existence. Alcohol dependence is among the leading causes of death in the United States. It shouldn't be. In comparison with other chronic diseases, it is significantly more treatable. Virtually any alcohol-troubled person who seeks assistance and is willing to participate actively in rehabilitation efforts can expect to lead a happy, productive life. The same may not be true for a victim of cancer, heart disease, or emphysema. The realization that this is treatable is becoming more widespread. The public efforts of prominent individuals who are recovering has contributed to this acceptance. Both professional treatment programs and AA are discovering that clients today are often younger and in the early or middle stages of the disease when they seek help. It is imperative for the helping professions to keep firmly in mind the hope that surrounds treatment.

Just as people initially become involved with alcohol for a variety of reasons, so is there similar variety in what prompts treatment. For every person who wends his or her way into alcohol dependence, there is also an exit route. This exit is most easily accomplished with professional help. The role of the professional is to serve as a guide, to share knowledge of the terrain, to be a support as the alcoholic regains footing, and to provide encouragement. The therapist cannot make the trip for the client but can only point the way. The therapist's goal for treatment, the destination of the journey, is to assist the alcohol-dependent individual in becoming at ease in the world, able to handle life situations. This will require stopping alcohol use. Experience demonstrates that those drinking

There are two things that will be believed of any man whosoever, and one of them is that he has taken to drink.
BOOTH TARKINGTON

who are alcohol dependent cannot be happy, at peace with themselves, or alive in any way that makes sense to them. The question for the professional is never "How can I make him or her stop?" The only productive focus for the therapist is "How can I create an atmosphere in which he or she is better able to choose abstinence for him- or herself and gain the tools to accomplish this?"

In this discussion, abstinence is presumed to be required for the treatment of alcohol dependence. Vaillant, when questioned as to an alcoholic's ability to resume social drinking, called on an interesting analogy. He posed the situation of a motorist who decides to remove the spare tire from the car trunk. The disastrous consequences of that action may not strike until the next day, or the next week, or even within the month, but sooner or later. . . . In addition, the seriousness of the consequences cannot be predicted. The disaster may be only a flat tire in one's driveway, or it may be a blowout on a busy freeway during rush hour. It may represent an inconvenience, or it may entail serious consequences. Sooo . . . why get rid of the spare?

Abstinence as a requisite for recovery is viewed as having a solid physiological basis. Tolerance, once established, remains, even in the absence of further alcohol use. Were someone who has been abstinent for a considerable period to resume drinking, the person would very quickly be capable of drinking amounts consistent with the highest levels previously consumed. Drinking isn't resumed with a physiologically clean slate. It may have taken a drinking career of 10 or more years for the alcohol-dependent person to reach consumption levels of a fifth a day. However, with tolerance established, even after a decade of sobriety, literally within days it would be possible to be back to the same level. The rapid reinstatement of tolerance is recognized in medical circles as one of the hallmark signs of dependence, or what was formerly described as addiction. For those clients who ask, "Is total abstinence really necessary?" one stock response is "Your body will always remember it has developed dependence, even if you forget."

Obstacles to Treatment

If alcohol dependence is so highly treatable, what has been going wrong? Why aren't more people receiving help? The obstacles require examination. Historically, one big handicap has been society's attitude toward alcohol and its use. To describe someone as alcoholic feels more like an accusation than a diagnosis. Despite all the public information and education, the notion remains that talking about someone's drinking is in bad taste. It seems too private, none of anyone's business. Most of us have a good feel for the taboo topics—sexual behavior or people's way of handling their children. The way someone drinks has long been a strong taboo. We have not yet reached the point at which to comment on what is perceived as unwise, dangerous, or inappropriate. Alcohol use is a wholly neutral topic, much less a topic on which we can universally assume anyone would welcome another's observations. The notion of heavy drinking as a moral issue still remains a situation for which willpower is the presumed solution. The person with the alcohol problem believes that as firmly as anyone and expends considerable energy at trying not to drink so much.

Another obstacle is the confusion introduced by the very nature of the symptoms. One common characteristic of alcohol-dependent behavior is the extreme variation, the lack of consistency—sometimes good mood, sometimes foul mood, sometimes plastered, sometimes sober. This inconsistency prompts a host of explanations. Further, this inconsistency allows the individual, family, and friends to hope things will get better if left alone. It permits them to delay seeking assistance. It almost seems to be human nature to want—and wait for—things to improve on their own. Consider for a moment a simple toothache. If the toothache comes and goes, you probably will delay a trip to the dentist. After all, maybe it was something hot you ate. Maybe it was caused by something cold. On the other hand, if the pain is constant, if it is clearly getting worse, if you can remember wicked toothaches in the past, you'll probably call immediately for an emergency appointment with your dentist. The total time you are actually in pain in the latter case may be much less than what you would have put up with in the former example, but you are spurred into action because it doesn't appear it will improve by itself.

Another obstacle can be the lack of treatment resources or lack of access. This is particularly true for women as well as adolescents. In the wake of managed care, treatment is less accessible to many. Residential stays are largely limited to detoxification. However, the length of time patients are in detox may be insufficient to help them understand the need for ongoing treatment and get them engaged in the process of rehabilitation. Often the patient, even though physically present, may be little able to absorb information or engage in much reflective thought, given the disturbances in cognitive function that are part of withdrawal.

Factors in Successful Treatment

Having alluded to failure and some sense of what to avoid, let us proceed to success. The likelihood of success is greatly enhanced if treatment is tailored to the characteristics of the disease being treated. The following factors, always present, should guide both the planning and process of treatment.

1. Dysfunctional life patterns. The individual's life has been centered around alcohol or other drugs. If this is not immediately evident, it is because the client has done a better than average job of disguising the fact. Thus, the clinician cannot expect a repertoire of healthy behaviors that come automatically. Treatment will help the individual build new behaviors, as well as rediscover behaviors from the past

to replace the warped alcohol-induced responses. This at times is what makes intensive treatment, whether inpatient or outpatient, desirable. Besides cutting down the number of easy drinking opportunities, it provides some room to make a new, fresh beginning.

2. Alcohol or other drugs as a constant companion. Alcohol or other drugs are used to anticipate, get through, and then get over stressful times. These individuals, to their knowledge, do not have effective tools for handling problems. In planning treatment, the clinician should be alert to what may be stressful for a particular client and provide supports. In the process, the therapist can tap skills the client can turn to instead of the bottle or the drug of choice.
3. Psychological wounds. Any drug, including alcohol, can be both a best friend and a worst enemy. The prospect of life without the drug seems either impossible or so unattractive as to be unworthwhile. The dependent individual feels lost, fragile, vulnerable, and fearful. No matter how well put together the client can appear or how much strength or potential the clinician can see, the client by and large is unable to get beyond those feelings of impotence, nakedness, and nothingness. Even when being firm and directive, the therapist has to have an awareness of this.
4. Physical dysfunctions. Chronic alcohol or other drug use often takes its toll on the body. Even if spared the more obvious physical illnesses, other subtle disturbances of physical functioning are often present. For example, with alcohol, sleep disturbance can last up to 2 years. Similarly, a thought impairment sometimes occurs on cessation of drinking. In the initial stage of recovery, difficulty in maintaining attention is commonplace. There will be diminution of adaptive abilities. During treatment, education about the drug alcohol and its effects can help allay fears, instructing always that the most important ingredient in treatment is time away from the drug. Reminding the client of this and helping him or her see that improvement will come with more drug-free time is an important factor.

Do you really Think I drink like a fish?

5. Chronic nature of dependence. A chronic disease requires continuing treatment and vigilance regarding the conditions that can prompt a relapse. This continued self-monitoring is essential to success in treatment.
6. Deterioration in family function. As described in Chapter 8, the family needs as much help as the family member who is the identified patient. Better outcomes result when the family has a treatment program independent of the addicted member's treatment.

Recovery Process

Recall how the progression of alcohol or other drug dependence can be sketched out. Similarly, recovery is a process that does not happen all at once. Gradually, in steps, the client becomes better able to manage his or her life. In the discussion in this section, recovery is similarly seen as having different phases: the preliminary or introductory phase, active initial treatment, and the continuing maintenance of recovery. There is no clear-cut beginning or end point, yet each phase has its observable hallmarks.

Others, too, have sketched out the stages or progression of recovery. Stephanie Brown has titled these stages of recovery as (1) drinking, (2) the transition from drinking to abstinence, (3) the early stages of recovery, and (4) ongoing recovery. The terminology may differ slightly, but the common denominator of these perspectives is to approach recovery as a dynamic process. It occurs over time, with the client addressing different tasks at different points. The clinician needs to have a repertoire of skills to be able to intervene appropriately.

Preliminary or Introductory Phase

The preliminary or introductory phase begins when the problem of alcohol comes to the foreground. This happens when those nagging suspicions that there is something wrong with the drinking are permitted to surface. On personal initiative, there might be some initial inquiries, which may be directed to friends and associates: "You know, Jane was really mad at me for getting tight when we went out last Friday night. You were there. I don't see anything wrong with letting go after a long hard week, do you? She's always on my back about something these days." Often others may not recognize these queries as a disguised or tentative cry for help. This is equivalent to precontemplation and contemplation in the stages of change framework.

Ideally the friend, coworker, or colleague who is the recipient of these initial queries listens carefully and avoids the trap of offering false reassurance or reinforcing denial with a comment such as "Oh, you're just imagining it." Ideally the listener will share the information that people can get in trouble with alcohol and that alcohol use can be a significant health problem. That person will then urge the seeking of a professional opinion and do whatever is necessary to see that the alcohol troubled person gets there. Instead, the first overture may be made by a member of the clergy, a family member, a friend, or a perceptive physician—someone who is sufficiently concerned to speak up and take the risk of being accused of meddling. Suspecting an alcohol problem, any one of them might request that an alcohol expert be sought to explore the possibility. On the other hand, a court may sentence an individual convicted of DWI to an education and assessment program. Increasingly common, too, is that the spouse seeks assistance as a result of living with alcohol-induced chaos or the employer notices developing problems and intervenes.

At this point the alcohol-dependent person is nibbling at the bait. He moves close and backs off. She wants to know, but she doesn't. Sharing the societal view of the stigma against those with alcohol problems, individuals will do or say anything to avoid being labeled as one of "them." Of course, the drinking causes problems, but he or she doesn't want or is scared to stop. What someone in this state really wants to learn is how to drink minus the problems. In the process of the evaluation, a major task of the therapist is helping the client come to grips with the impossibility of this hope. Treatment is doomed if the counselor is seduced into playing the "patsy" or, on the other hand, if the clinician tries to seduce the client by being the "rescuer." Having a coworker with whom to discuss cases and their frustrations can help keep the objectives in sight.

For a long time it was thought that alcohol dependence was a disease that required the client to make a self-diagnosis for successful treatment to occur. Treatment, full-steam ahead, was considered impossible until the alcohol-dependent client, inside him- or herself, attached that label to cover all that was transpiring. An intellectual understanding was thought to be inadequate; it had to come from the heart. The whole thing could be confusing. He or she didn't have to be happy about the diagnosis, simply needing to know it was true. Then without hope of his or her own, the client borrowed the therapist's belief that things can change. This thinking has now been brought into question. Within the stages of change model, the critical moment is when the client comes to see that the balance has been tipped in favor of the need to change versus going with the status quo. When this occurs, the client goes from contemplation to determination. Whatever words one uses to describe this, there seemingly is a moment when the client decides to take a leap of faith, when the risk of the unknown and the possibility of something better is preferable to what is.

Active Treatment Phase

At the point of acknowledging a desire to change, clients by themselves often are at a dead end. If they knew what to do, they would have done it. In essence, they turn the steering of their lives over to the therapist. The clinician, in turn, must respond by providing clear, concrete, and simple stage directions. A rehabilitative regimen needs to be set forth. The environment must be simplified. The number of decisions to be confronted must be pared down. There is little ability to deal with anything more than "How am I going to get through this day (or hour) without a drink?" Effort needs to be centered on doing whatever is necessary to buy sober time. To quote the old maxim, "Nothing succeeds like success." A day sober turns on the light a little. It has become something that is possible. In the face of alcohol dependence, this is an achievement. It does not guarantee continued sobriety, but it demonstrates the possibility. In the sober and straight time, the individual in treatment is gaining skills. Behavior is discovered that can be of assistance in handling those events that previously would have prompted drinking or drug use.

Professionals in the substance abuse field have long believed that clients who become involved in AA or other 12-step programs have a much better chance of recovery. Research of treatment outcomes

confirms this impression. These programs combine key ingredients considered essential for recovery. They provide support; they embody hope. They provide concrete suggestions without cajoling. They provide a haven, a place which ensures contact with other sober alcoholics or straight addicts. Their slogans are the simple guideposts needed to reorder a life. And their purpose is never lost. George Vaillant, in *The National History of Alcoholism,* discussed four factors that his research identified as associated with recovery. All are embodied in AA affiliation. AA offers a source of *hope.* Attendance at meetings and associations with members provides the needed *external reminders* to prevent the fading from memory of one's being alcohol dependent. It offers the opportunity for *new relationships,* in which one starts out with a clean slate and can enjoy relationships not encumbered by the emotional baggage of the heavy drinking. AA also offers *support.*

The necessity for a direct and uncluttered approach cannot be overstressed. In early treatment, clients are not capable of handling anything else. This is one of several reasons for the belief that substance abuse has to be the priority item on any treatment agenda. The only exceptions are life-threatening or serious medical problems. To work actively and successfully on a list of difficulties is overwhelming. Interestingly enough, when treatment is undertaken, other life problems often resolve. Furthermore, waiting to treat the dependent until some other matter is settled invites ambivalence. This waiting feeds the voice that says, "Well, maybe it isn't so bad after all," or "I'll wait and see how it goes." In essence one allows the client to move from the stage of action and determination back to precontemplation. Furthermore, other matters are unsolvable as long as drinking is in the picture; the individual has no resources to tackle anything. He or she is drugged.

Focusing on alcohol as a priority, achieving the client's acceptance of this, and providing room and skills to experience sobriety make up the meat of therapy. As this takes place, the individual is able to assume responsibility for managing his or her life, using the tools acquired. With this, the working relationship between clinician and client shifts. They collaborate in a different way. The clinician may be alert to potential problematic situations, but the client increasingly takes responsibility for identifying them and selecting ways to deal with them. Rather than being a guide, the therapist is a resource, someone with whom the client can check things out. At this point, continuing treatment has begun.

Continuing Treatment Phase

The alcohol-dependent person learns, as do others with a chronic disease, the importance of being able to identify situations and their responses to them that may signal a flare-up. With dependence this entails maintaining a continuing awareness of that status if abstinence is to be maintained. The client isn't going to be seeing the therapist for a lifetime as a reminder of the need to be vigilant. Each person will need to cultivate resources to help support sobriety. Within treatment programs, explicit attention is directed to relapse prevention. This may involve stress reduction efforts, focusing on specific things to be used when faced with the urge at drink, or efforts directed at enhancing general coping strategies. The thinking is that the skills that are needed to maintain sobriety may be different from those needed earlier in treatment. Relapse is seen as being triggered by things going on within the individual, internal events, as well as external events. Important internal factors boil down to thoughts, attitudes, and feelings. Negative feelings can include anger, feelings of frustration, guilt, and helplessness. The thoughts and feelings that can get people in trouble are the little phrases that so often seem to play across the mind's screen automatically: "Just one drink wouldn't matter." "I won't be able to ________, without a drink." The fill-in-the-blank can include everything from "have fun," to "relax," to "concentrate," to "survive the stress of this weekend." Coupled with this is the expectation that having a drink is a positive thing in the short run. The long-term effects don't make it into the equation. There is a saying in AA, "Think through the drink." It addresses this issue.

A client's hope for change often must be sparked by the clinician's belief in that possibility. Your attitudes about your clients and their potential for health exerts a powerful influence. This doesn't mean you cannot and will not become frustrated, impatient, or angry at times. Whether therapy can proceed depends on what you do with these feelings. You can carry them only so long before the discomfort becomes unbearable. Then you will either pretend they aren't there or unload them on the client. Either way, your thinking can become "She can never change," "This guy is hopeless," or "She's just not ready." When that happens, therapy is not possible, even if the people continue meeting. A better approach is to find a coworker with whom you can discuss these feelings of impotence and frustration. Clients have a remarkable way of bringing to light your own rough edges. If an impasse in working with a particular client isn't broken through, the client should be referred to a coworker.

Treatment is a process involving people. People have their ups and downs, good days and bad days. Some that you think will make it won't. Some that you are sure don't have a chance will surprise you. There will be days when you will wonder why you ever got into this line of work. On others it will seem a pretty good thing to be doing. Remembering that it is an unpredictable process may help you keep your balance.

Common Themes in Treatment

Early Issues

Early in the recovery process, many clients have a tendency to become quite upset over very small matters. They look well, feel well, and sound well—but they really aren't quite there yet. This can be very trying for the clinician, the client, and the family. Reminding them of how sick they have recently been makes their upsets less threatening. The steps after any major illness seem slow and tedious. There are occasional setbacks, yet eventually all is well. It works that way with substance abuse, too. It is simply harder to accept because there are no bandages to remove, scars to point to, or clear signs of healing to check on. It cannot be emphasized enough that it takes time.

During the early phase of treatment, one point often overlooked is the client's inability to function on a simple daily basis. It is almost inconceivable to therapists (or anyone, else for that matter) that a person who seems reasonably intelligent, looks fairly healthy after detoxification, and is over 21 can have problems with when to get up in the morning or what to do after getting up. Along with family, work, and the social deterioration caused by alcohol dependence, the simple things have gotten messed up, too. He may have gargled, brushed his teeth, and chewed mints continually while drinking in an effort to cover up the smell of alcohol. He may, on the other hand, have skipped most mealtimes and eaten only sporadically with no thought to his nutritional needs. Also, as we have seen in Chapter 5, sleep is likely to be disturbed. Getting dressed without trying to choke down some alcohol to quell the shakes may be a novel experience. It may have been years since he has performed the standard daily tasks in a totally drug-free state.

Clients are rather like Rip Van Winkle during the early weeks of their recovery. Everything they do is likely to feel strange. The face looking back at them from the mirror may even seem like a stranger's. They became used to the blurred perceptions they experienced while drinking. It is terribly disconcerting to find virtually every task one faces as a whole new thing. Whereas it used to take 2 very careful days to prepare Thanksgiving dinner, it now requires only a few hours. The accompanying wine for the cook, trips back to the store for forgotten items (and, by the way, a little more booze), the self-pity over having to do it, the naps necessary to combat the fatigue of the ordeal, the incredible energy devoted to controlling the drinking enough to get everything done—all these steps are eliminated.

The newly sober individual is faced with the novelty of time—either having too much time or not having enough time. He or she also may panic over the problem of what to do next. Many clients will need help scheduling their time. After years of getting by on the bottle, they have to regain a sense of how much time it really takes to accomplish some tasks. The individual may plan to paint the entire house in two days or, conversely, decide that he or she can't possibly fit a dental appointment, a luncheon engagement, and a sales call into one day. The perception of time is as distorted as other areas of perception. Reassurance that this is a common state of affairs, along with assistance in setting realistic daily goals, is greatly needed. This is one reason newcomers to 12-step programs find the slogans "Keep it simple" and "First things first" so helpful.

Another aspect of reorienting the client to reality involves the misperception of events. The faulty memories caused by the drugged state will have to be reexamined. One cannot always wait for some sudden insight to clear things up. For example, he is talking to you about difficulties he has had with his wife. He remembers her as a nag, on his back about a "few little drinks." You might remind him that, on the occasion in question, he was picked up for driving while impaired with a blood alcohol content of 0.20—clearly not just a few drinks. Then you point out that, because he has misperceived the amount he was drinking to such an extent, he may have misperceived his wife's behavior. The opportunity is there, if indicated, to educate the client briefly on the distortions produced by the drug or alcohol and to suggest that sober observations of his wife's behavior are more valid. You might, instead, suggest a couple's meeting, but keep clearly in front the issue of the alcohol use.

Another easy trap to fall into is to expect the same course of recovery for most clients. They don't get sick at the same rate, and neither do they get well at the same rate. One will be up and at 'em and lookin' good in very short order; another will seem to be stuck, barely hanging on, forever; and there will be those in between. What is difficult for one is easy for another. Don't assume that you know what is going to be a problem for any particular person.

These are some of the common difficulties, but there are lots of surprises. There are simply no formulas or easy prescriptions that will work every time. There is no substitute for knowing and dealing with the person sitting before you.

A Bit Later

After about 3 months and achieving some level of comfort with the new state of affairs, the focus of treatment can shift. Until then, attention is mainly on the mechanics of daily living. With that out of the way, or reasonably under control, the focus can become sorting out the client's stance in the world, feelings, and relationships. Though 3 months is an arbitrary designation, it is not wholly so. Recall the subacute withdrawal syndrome (see Chapter 6). With alcohol, the acute withdrawal period may pass within 5 days, but a longer period is required to regain the ability to concentrate, for example. Thus, there is a physical basis for what the alcohol-dependent client in early recovery can work on productively. This does not mean that all the problems previously discussed are totally resolved or that work is not continuing on some of them. It simply means that other concerns may now be surfacing. It is also at this point that an assessment should be made as to whether to refer the client to other professionals if the present caregiver is not equipped to handle this work.

Some issues are fairly common, and one must be alert to them. Most basically require finding a balance between 2 extremes of behavior that are equally dangerous. John Wallace, Ph.D., a psychologist with long experience in the field, has compared these extremes to rocks and whirlpools, which must be avoided in the recovery voyage.

- *Denial.* One of the first difficulties entails denial. The tendency for clinicians new to alcohol treatment, when faced with a massive rejection of reality, is to want to force these clients to face all the facts right now. The trouble with this approach is that self-knowledge is often bought at the price of anxiety, and anxiety is a drinking trigger. What to do? Provide lots of support to counteract the initial anxiety caused by the acceptance of the reality of the drinking itself. Then, gradually, keep supporting the small increments in awareness that occur in the sober experience.

  There is always the temptation to take denial personally, to think the client is "lying." Remind yourself that the person has adopted this defense as protection against the massive pain that would accompany facing the cold, hard facts. Its function is to deceive or protect the self, not others. It is difficult, but necessary, to remember that the denial of a particular issue is serving a useful purpose at the time, keeping overwhelming pain and anxiety at bay until more strength is available. The therapist must decide how much of either the client can tolerate. The therapeutic issue is whether the denial is still necessary or whether it has become counterproductive, blocking further progress.

- *Guilt.* The presence of denial, the function of which is to protect against emotional pain, is evidence that the behavior is not congruent with the individual's core values and internal image. (The phrase used in psychotherapy for this phenomenon is "ego dystonic"—that is, being out of harmony with one's real self.) Thus, where there is denial, the issues of guilt and its fraternal twin, self-blame, cannot be far behind. It is clearly desirable to mitigate the degree of both. It is simultaneously necessary to avoid the pitfalls of their opposites, rejecting social values and blaming others. Although excessive guilt leads to the guilt-drinking spiral, some degree of conscience and sense of responsibility is necessary to function in society. The therapist needs to be clear on this issue. The clinician must be able to point out unnecessary burdensome guilt on the one hand and yet allow honest guilt to be expressed. Dealing with both kinds of guilt appropriately is essential. On the blame issue, help is needed in accepting personal responsibility where necessary. Often it can be helpful to point out that the disease itself, rather than oneself or others, may be the true cause of some of the difficulties, while gently reminding clients that they are responsible for what happens now.
- *Compliance versus rebellion.* Two other unhealthy extremes are often seen, particularly early in treatment: compliance and rebellion. In either case, strong confrontation is not a good strategy to choose. It seems simply to produce more of either. The compliant client becomes a more model client; the rebellious one says, "Aha! I was right. You are all against me," and then drinks. Moderation is again the key. The aim is to help clients acknowledge their alcohol dependence and accept the facts of their situation.

- *Emotions.* Emotions, and what to do about them, are another obstacle to be faced. Newly sober persons are likely to repress their feelings entirely. They do this to counteract their all too uncontrolled expression during the drinking experiences. Respect for this need to repress the emotions should prevail in the initial stages of recovery. But the eventual goal is to assist the client to recognize emotions and deal with them appropriately. Clients need to learn (or relearn) that feelings need not be repressed altogether, or conversely, wildly acted out. Instead, a recognition and acceptance of them can lead to better solutions. These are by no means the only examples of extremes for which the therapist needs to be alert. The therapist needs to be wary when dealing with any extreme behavior or reaction to avoid having the client plunge into the opposite danger. Some of these problems are continuing ones and may require different tactics at different stages in the recovery process.
- *Dependency and intimacy.* Many articles, and, indeed, whole books, have been written about dependency and alcoholism. Historically, the alcohol-dependent individual was depicted as a particularly emotionally dependent type who had resolved conflicts inappropriately by using alcohol. This is basically another variant of the earlier mistake of confusing the symptoms of alcohol dependence with the individual's personality before its onset. Nonetheless, it is crucial to address issues of dependency throughout treatment. One long-term worker in the field, LeClair Bissel, MD, has summed up the whole of treatment as "the task of helping people to become dependent upon people rather than booze." Be alert during treatment to clients' characteristic all or none approaches. There is the vacillation between stubborn independence and indiscriminate dependence.

  During the early months of recovery the individual may need to poll everyone he or she knows to make a decision on some seemingly inconsequential matter. However, when a major decision comes along, no advice is solicited. As individuals discover their need for others, this can lead to discomfort and confusion. On one hand, there is the potentially mistaken notion that turning to others is evidence of weakness, and a voice within says, "I should be able to do this myself." On the other hand, having little recent history of good judgment and little reason to trust one's own capacities—and feeling there may not be much margin for error—one can see a tendency to turn to others for almost everything. One of the long-term tasks of recovery is not only to recognize the need for dependence but also to become more discriminating in handling it. The basic questions the client will be addressing in this process are "Whom should I and can I be dependent on? For what? At what cost? For what gain?"

  Closely tied to the issue of dependency is that of intimacy. Intimacy is the capacity for closeness, for allowing oneself to be vulnerable to another. One of the tasks in early recovery is becoming reacquainted with oneself while growing emotionally. To be rediscovering oneself while also establishing relationships with others is not an insignificant undertaking. One of the features of AA that contributes to recovery is that AA provides a community in which the traditions of the fellowship provide safeguards and limits for all its members as the issues of dependency and intimacy in relationships get sorted out. It is also a setting in which one discovers that people are all interdependent to some degree.

Left to their own devices, those in recovery seem to have an uncanny capacity for finding persons with whom they forge destructive relationships. There are always those around who would rescue them and be willing to assume the role of their perpetual caretakers.

Another issue may be encountered by single persons or those caught in unhappy marriages. It is not uncommon for them to find themselves suddenly involved in an affair or an extramarital relationship. With a little bit of sobriety, they are very ripe to fall in love. This may have several roots. They may be questioning their sexuality, and the attentions of another may well provide some affirmation of attractiveness. Also possible is that with sobriety comes a sense of being alive again. There is a reawakening of a host of feelings that have long been dormant, including sexual feelings. In this sense, it may be like the bloom and intensity of adolescence. A romantic involvement may follow very naturally. Unfortunately, it can lead to disaster if followed with abandonment. A counselor needs to be alert to this general possibility, as well as the possibility of being the object of the crush.

"Why Do I Drink?"

This is the recurrent theme of many active alcoholics and those beginning active treatment. Generally it is of little value to focus on this question, even when it seems most pressing to the client. It takes the client off the hook. It looks to the past and to external causes. The more important question addresses the present moment: "What can be done now?"

If there is a time to deal with the "whys," it comes during the continuing treatment phase. Don't misunderstand. Even then, long hours spent studying what went wrong, way back, are never helpful. On the other hand, the "whens" can be very instructive. The question "When do I want a drink?" points out the areas in which work can be done to prevent relapse. Typically some clues can be discerned from the present, daily life events, on those occasions when taking a drink is most tempting. Examining such situations can provide clients with a wealth of practical information about themselves for their immediate use and can allow them to develop strategies to address these situations in other ways. Dealing with the present is of vital importance. Newly recovering individuals, who have spent their recent lives in a drugged state, have had less experience than most of us in attending to the present. The automatic tendency is to analyze the distant past or to worry about the future. The only part of life that any of us can hope to handle effectively is the present.

Getting Stuck

Speaking of dependency, anyone working with alcohol-troubled people is bound to hear this remark sometime: "Sending someone to AA just creates another dependency." The implication of this is that you are simply moving the dependency from the bottle to AA and ducking the "real" issue. That the dependency shifts from alcohol to AA, to a clinician, or to a treatment program for the newcomer is probably true. This should be viewed as a plus. Also, no one should get stuck in a life that is just as alcohol centered as before, with the focus merely shifting to not drinking instead of how to continue drinking. Granted, physical health is less threatened, traumatic events are less frequent, and maybe even job and family stability have been established. Nonetheless, it is a recovery rut.

The fact that some do get stuck is true. Many factors probably account for this. One might be an "I never had it so good, so I won't rock the boat" feeling, a fear of letting go of the life preserver, even when safely ashore. Another factor is that some people in recovery, particularly those who began drinking as teenagers, have spent the bulk of their adult lives actively drinking. Therefore, they have no baseline of adult healthy behaviors to return to. They are confronted with gaining sobriety, growing up, and functioning as adults simultaneously. This is a tall order, which can be overwhelming. To make the task more manageable, it may well be tempting for these people to keep their world narrowed down to recovery. The only thing they now feel really competent to do, the only area where they have had support and a positive sense of self, is in getting sober. Giving up the status of newcomer to be replaced by that of sober, responsible adult may be scary, so a relapse or drinking episode may ensue. They then can justify and ensure that they can keep doing the only thing they feel they do well, which is being a client, an AA newcomer, and a recovering person.

It would take 14,931,430 six-packs of 12-oz cans to float a battleship.
NATHAN COBB
Boston Globe

Another factor that may cause the newcomer to get stuck might be that some clinicians (and some 12-step members) are better equipped to deal with the crisis period of getting sober than with the later issues of growth. Time constraints too can be the cause of the clinician's inability to encourage the letting go, or stretching, phase. They are often overwhelmed with the numbers of clients truly in crisis. They simply have no time or energy to help the clients who are getting along okay. Those who are not content with their clients' just getting by could aid the process by referring them to different types of therapy and groups that deal with specific issues. The adjunctive treatments are not substitutes for substance abuse therapy. Instead, they supplement whatever has worked thus far, whether it is self-help, individual therapy, or some other regimen.

Relapse

Any individual with a chronic disease is subject to relapse. For those with alcohol dependence, relapse means the resumption of drinking.

Why does this occur? The reasons are numerous. For the newly sober person it may boil down to a gross underestimation of the seriousness and severity of the disease. For these individuals, there has been a failure to really come to grips with their own impotence to deal with it single-handedly. Hence, while perhaps going through the motions of treatment, they may have a lingering notion that, although others in recovery may need to do this or that, somehow they are exempt. This may show up in very simple ways, such as the failure to address the little things that are likely to make drinking easier than not drinking: "Hell, I've always ridden home in the bar car; after 20 years that's where my friends are." "What would people say if ________?" "There's a lot going on in my life; getting to the couples group simply isn't possible on a regular basis." If families and close friends are not well informed about treatment and are not willing to make adjustments, they can unwittingly support and even invite this dangerous behavior.

For the recovering individual with more substantial sobriety, relapse is commonly tied to two things. Relapse may be triggered by the recovery rut. On the other hand, if things have been going well in the recovering alcoholic's life, there is the trap of considering alcohol dependence to be a closed chapter. There is a preference for the phrase "recovering alcoholic" rather than "recovered." The use of "recovering" serves as a reminder that one is not cured of alcohol dependence.

An observation frequently made when considering the treatment of addictions is reminiscent of Mark Twain's comment about having stopped smoking—"I've done it many times." The more difficult task for clients is not necessarily stopping the drinking or substance use but maintaining abstinence. Treatment programs are focusing on this issue in a more formal fashion. In the past the temptation for treatment professionals, as they contemplated relapse, was simply to add more and more components to the original treatment regimen, as if engaged in a search for the missing ingredient. The popular view now is that the maintenance of sobriety entails different tasks for the client from those necessary for ceasing initial use and that one can teach skills that will enhance a client's ability to maintain sobriety. Formal relapse prevention components have become part of some treatment centers' standard programs.

It is recommended that how a drinking episode is to be handled, were it to occur, be discussed and incorporated into the continuing treatment plan. After all, relapse occurs. It is far better for the client, family, and clinician to openly discuss how it will be handled beforehand. In the midst of the crisis of relapse, neither the family nor the client can do their most creative and clear-headed problem solving. Also, having gotten this taboo subject out in the open, it may be easier for all to attend to the work at hand, rather than worry about "what if." Any plan for responding to a relapse should be very explicit and concrete; for example, the family will contact the therapist and the client will agree to do A, B, and C. "Relapse" has been used to refer to any drinking. However, it is important to recognize that while any drinking is a source of concern, there can be significant differences, depending on the response. Some drinking episodes may be better described as a break in sobriety, but not relapse in the sense that the individual resumes drinking as if the period of sobriety had never occurred.

Seasoned clinicians often say that the most dangerous thing for a recovering alcoholic is a "successful drink." By this, they refer to the recovering individual who has a drink, does not mention it to anyone, and suffers no apparent ill effects. It wasn't such a big deal. A couple of evenings later it isn't a big deal, either. Almost inevitably, if this continues, the individual is drinking regularly, is drinking more, and is on the threshold of being reunited with all the problems and consequences of alcohol dependence. The danger, of course, is that, the longer the drinking continues, the less able the individual is to recognize the need for help or to reach out for it. Someone who had a difficult withdrawal in the past may also be terrified of the prospect of stopping again. It may be wise for you to make an agreement with the client that if he or she has a drink—or a near encounter—this has to be discussed.

The crucial question Mr. Jones is whether we are dealing with a lapse, a prelapse, a relapse or a collapse.

With some substantial sobriety, reentering treatment after a relapse may be especially difficult. Among a host of other feelings there is embarrassment, remorse, guilt, and a sense of letting others down. Recognition that alcohol dependence is a chronic disease and that it can involve relapses may ease this. However, refrain from giving the impression that relapse is inevitable. Following a relapse, it is necessary to look closely at what led up to it, what facilitated its occurrence. The client can gain some valuable information about what is critical to maintaining his or her own sobriety. That is another reason it is so important to deal with a relapse openly. You must also be sensitive to the issues that a relapse may evoke in the family.

For the moment, the family also may be thrown back into functioning just as it did during the old days of active drinking. The old emotions of hurt, anger, righteous indignation, and the attitude of "to hell with it all" may spring up as strongly as before. This is true even if—or especially if—the family's functioning has vastly changed and improved. All of that progress suddenly evaporates. There also may be the old embarrassment, guilt, and wish to pretend it isn't so.

Longer-Term Change

The client's best insurance against relapse is continuing to make changes and addressing the inevitable rough spots. Although contacts may be less frequent, don't be casual with follow-up. Be sure that a client is given the opportunity to discuss the problems he or she is having. Appreciate that clients may be reluctant to talk about their problems. They may feel they should be able to handle things alone, or they may feel they are letting you down. It isn't as if you don't know the person you are seeing. Bring up issues that have been problematic in the past, such as work or family issues. Find out how things are going now. If there were particular concerns the last time you met, be sure to find out how things turned out. Identifying successes is every bit as important as identifying difficulties. Notes made in the clinical record may be especially important to help you keep track of what has been discussed and to identify any recurrent themes. Be sure to review your notes before seeing a client; it's easy to lose track of what happened, when, and sometimes even to whom.

Pay attention to the things that are known to be stress points for any person. These may include job changes, even when it's a promotion; entrances and exits from the family, whether it's a birth, death, divorce, or the children leaving home for the military, college, or even kindergarten; illness in the family; or changes in economic circumstances, whether due to retirement, a family member's entering or leaving the work force, or even winning the lottery. Don't forget holidays. These supposedly joyous occasions are often stressful. Preholiday tension is often followed by postholiday blues.

At the point of concluding formal counseling, it is important to keep the door open. It is not uncommon that people will from time to time return to see a clinician for a brief series of sessions. At these points issues related to drinking or efforts to avoid drinking may no longer be in the foreground. Rather, these sessions are likely to address the broader issues that enhance sobriety and that are part of the process of change and growth that was initiated on entry into alcohol treatment.

The reason for emphasizing treatment over a fairly long period is simple. It might be said that recovery requires becoming "weller than well." To maintain sobriety and avoid developing alternate harmful dependencies, the client needs to learn a range of healthy alternative behaviors to deal with tensions arising from problems that accompany living. Nonaddicted members of society may quite safely from time to time alleviate such tensions with a drink or two. Because living, problems, and tensions go hand in hand, being truly helpful implies efforts to assist the client to become healthier than might be necessary for the general population.

Treatment Outcome

A common question is "Does treatment work?" A review published in 2001 examined this question. It examined the results from 7 large, multisite centers. These included outpatient and inpatient programs, programs with a broad spectrum of clients. The findings showed that, a year after entering treatment, 1 in 4 clients was continuously abstinent. (This figure does not tell who was abstinent at 1 year, just those continuously abstinent. So someone who had a brief lapse in the beginning of treatment wasn't included in this figure, despite the fact that most clinicians would consider the individual as doing well.) In addition, 1 in 10 was using alcohol moderately and without problems. For the remaining individuals (about two-thirds), alcohol consumption had decreased by

87%, and alcohol problems were also decreased by 60%. This may be discouraging to some.

In discussing these results, the authors make several important points. First, they suggest a comparison with other chronic illnesses. If 1 year later, 98% were alive, of whom one-third were totally symptom-free, and the remaining people improved by an average of 57% to 87%, everyone would be thrilled. Frequently, too, success is measured by a single variable, drinking or not drinking. It is argued that other factors need be considered, such as the lower rates of problems, which has a social benefit beyond any benefits to the individual. Very important is that these figures describe the result of *a single treatment* episode. These figures represent a simple snapshot of treatment effectiveness. Also of significance is that one finds even higher rates of abstinence following treatment for particular populations. For example, there are those who are pushed into treatment and have to participate actively in aftercare in order to keep their jobs and/or professional licenses. This includes those in the military, physicians, nurses, and pilots. In these situations, up to 80% are abstinent at 1 year.

Factors Influencing Treatment Outcome

The most significant factor influencing treatment outcome is the characteristics of clients' pretreatment. Those who are still employed, whose families are intact, and who have social supports do better. The findings of Project MATCH suggest that, in terms of treatment outcome, the type of program plays less of a role in treatment outcome than do the client's characteristics.

And, yes, the clinician plays a role in determining the effectiveness of treatment. A variety of studies have looked at client outcome in terms of clinician characteristics. Of interest was whether there were differences in rates of clients' dropping out of treatment and in rates of abstinence at follow-up. A variety of clinician characteristics have been examined. There are the obvious ones, such as age, education, gender, race and ethnicity, and personal experience with alcohol or other drug abuse. Also examined are how clinicians interact with clients. This includes the clinician's emotional responses to clients and the therapeutic alliance—the bond between client and therapist—personality traits, beliefs about substance use disorders, and finally, if there is a specified treatment format, how well the clinician sticks to the prescribed format sometimes called manualized therapies.

Among all of the factors studied, which do not predict a client's outcome? While it may be surprising, age, gender, professional training, and the therapist's recovery status were *not* associated with how well clients fared. Factors that were related to clients' outcome included the following:

1. *Clients' evaluation of their counselor's competence.* These evaluations were based on the client's ratings of his or her clinician's helpfulness, self-confidence, knowledge, and organizational skills.

2. *Clinicians' emotional responses.* By listening to tapes of therapy sessions, clinicians can be rated by their level of anxiety, anger, and positive or negative connections with patients. As anticipated, the clinicians with the most positive interactions had better outcomes.
3. *Therapeutic alliance.* The therapeutic alliance isn't determined solely by the clinician's behavior. Studies suggest that both clients' and therapists' ratings of this aspect predict treatment effectiveness and clients' remaining in treatment.
4. *Degree of adherence to manualized approaches.* Differences between individual therapists fade when they follow procedures set forth in manualized therapies. This suggests that, if counselors are trained to use standard approaches and follow these, there is less likelihood that there will be differences in patients' progress, depending on the particular counselor they have.
5. *Clinicians' interpersonal styles.* Empathy is a factor that has been regularly reported as a factor that influences the client's response to treatment. Among one group of clinicians studied, the least effective therapist in an alcohol program had a 25% rate of successful outcomes. The most successful had a 100% rate of successful client outcomes. The major factor explaining the difference in outcome was the therapists' degree of empathy. Along with empathy, other related factors that have been identified as important are being genuine, respectful, and concrete. Similarly, the patients of clinicians with a confrontative style do less well than do the patients of clinicians with a supportive style.

With this information as a backdrop, Chapter 10 turns to various treatment approaches, from individual counseling, to group work, to family counseling and self-help.

RESOURCES AND FURTHER READING

Screening

Allen JP, Litten RZ, Fertig JB, Babor T. A review of research on the Alcohol Use Disorders Identification Test (AUDIT). *Alcoholism: Clinical and Experimental Research* 21(4):613–619, 1997.

Allen JP, Wilson VB, eds. *Assessing Alcohol Problems. A Guide for Clinicians and Researchers,* 2nd ed. Bethesda, MD: NIAAA, 2003.

Ewing JA. Detecting alcoholism, the CAGE questionnaire. *Journal of the American Medical Association* 252(14):1905–1907, 1984.

Rosenberg SD, Drake RE, Wolford GL, Mueser KT, Oxman TE, Vidaver RM, et al. Dartmouth Assessment of Lifestyle Instrument (DALI): A substance use disorder screen for people with severe mental illness. *American Journal of Psychiatry* 155(2):232–238, 1998. (48 refs.)

Schorling JB, Buchsbaum DG. Screening for alcohol and drug abuse (review). *Medical Clinics of North America* 81(4):845–865, 1997. (97 refs.)

Selzer M. The Michigan Alcoholism Screening Test: The quest for a new diagnostic instrument. *American Journal of Psychiatry* 127(12):1653–1658, 1971.

Sillanaukee P, Massot N, Jousilahti P, Vartiainen E, Sundvall J, Olsson U, et al. Dose response of laboratory markers to alcohol consumption in a general population. *American Journal of Epidemiology* 152(8):747–751, 2000.

Skinner HA: The Drug Abuse Screening Test. *Addictive Behavior* 7(4):363–371, 1982.

Skinner HA, Holt S, Schuller R, Roy J, Israel Y. Identification of alcohol abuse using laboratory tests and a history of trauma. *Annals of Internal Medicine* 101(6):847–851, 1984.

Assessment

Carey KB, Teitelbaum LM. Goals and methods of alcohol assessment. *Professional Psychology: Research and Practice* 27(5):460–466, 1996. (63 refs.)

Clark WD. Alcoholism: Blocks to diagnosis and treatment. *American Journal of Medicine* (71):275, 1981.

Clark WD. The medical interview: Focus on alcohol problems. *Hospital Practice* 20(11):59–68, 1985.

Juhnke TA, Vace NA, Curtis RC, Coll KM, Paredis, DM. Assessment instruments used by addiction counselors. *Journal of Addiction & Offender Counseling* 23(6):66–72, 2003. (22 refs.)

Lordan EJ, Kelley JM, Peters CP, Siegfried RJ. Treatment placement decisions: How substance abuse professionals assess and place clients. *Evaluation and Program Planning* 20(2):137–149, 1997. (35 refs.)

McLellan TA. *Guide to the Addiction Severity Index: Background, Administration and Field Testing Results.* Rockville, MD: National Institute on Drug Abuse, 1988.

Motivation

Britt E, Blampied NM, Hudson SM. Motivational Interviewing: A review. *Australian Psychologist* 38(3):193–201, 2003. (103 refs.)

Downey L, Rosengren DB, Donovan DM. To thine own self be true: Self-concept and motivation for abstinence among substance abusers. *Addictive Behaviors* 25(5):743–757, 2000. (46 refs.)

Krampen G. Motivation in the treatment of alcoholism. *Addictive Behaviors* 14(2):197–200, 1989.

Miller WR. *Enhancing Motivation for Change in Substance Abuse Treatment. Treatment Improvement Protocol (TIP) Series 35.* Rockville, MD: Center for Substance Abuse Treatment, 1999. (285 refs.)

Miller WR, Rollnick S. *Motivational Interviewing: Preparing People to Change Addictive Behavior.* New York: Guilford Press, 1991. (299 refs.)

Shen Q, McLellan AT, Merrill J. Client's perceived need for treatment and its impact on outcome. *Substance Abuse* 21(3):179–192, 2000. (64 refs.)

Clinical Care

Barry KL. *Brief Interventions and Brief Therapies for Substance Abuse. Treatment Improvement Protocol (TIP) Series 34.* Rockville, MD: Center for Substance Abuse Treatment, 1999. (540 refs.)

Beck O, Helander, A. 5-Hydoxytryptophol as a marker for recent alcohol intake. *Addiction* 98(Supplement 2): 63–72, 2003. (68 refs.)

Cunningham JA, Humphreys K, Koski-Jannes A. Providing personalized assessment feedback for problem drinking on the Internet: A pilot project. *Journal of Studies on Alcohol* 61(6):794–798, 2000. (25 refs.)

Dennis M, Scott CK, Tuck R. An experimental evaluation of recovery management checkups (RMC) for people with chronic substance use disorders (review). *Evaluation and Program Planning* 26(3):339–352, 2003. (105 refs.)

Isaacson JH, Collins GB. New strategies for detecting and treating problem drinking. *Cleveland Clinic Journal of Medicine* 65(1):14–17, 1998. (5 refs.)

Maist SA, Saitz R. Alcohol use disorders screening and diagnosis. *American Journal on Addictions* 12(Special): 512–525, 2003. (71 refs.)

Miller WR, Walters ST, Bennett ME. How effective is alcoholism treatment in the United States? *Journal of Studies on Alcohol* 62(2):211–220, 2000. (41 refs.)

O'Connor PG, Schottenfeld RS. Patients with alcohol problems (review). *New England Journal of Medicine* 338(9):592–602, 1998. (112 refs.)

Schwan R, Albuisson E, Malet L, Loiseaux MN, Reynaud M, Schellenberg F, et al. The use of biological laboratory markers in the diagnosis of alcohol misuse: an evidence-based approach. *Drug and Alcohol Dependence* 74(3):272–279, 2004. (412 refs)

Schwarz MJ, Domke I, Helander A, Janssens PMW, van Pelt J, Springer B, et al. Multicentre evaluation of a new assay for determination of carbohydrate-deficient transferrin. *Alcohol and Alcoholism* 38(3):270–275, 2003. (30 refs.)

Swift R. Direct measurement of alcohol and its metabolites. (review). *Addiction.* 98(Supplement 2):73–80, 2003. (34 refs.)

Wurst FM, Skipper GE, Weinmann W. Ethyl glucuronide the direct ethanol metabolite on the threshold from science to routine use. *Addiction* 98 (Supplement 2): S1–62, 2003. (58 refs.)

CHAPTER 10

Treatment Techniques and Approaches

INDIVIDUAL COUNSELING

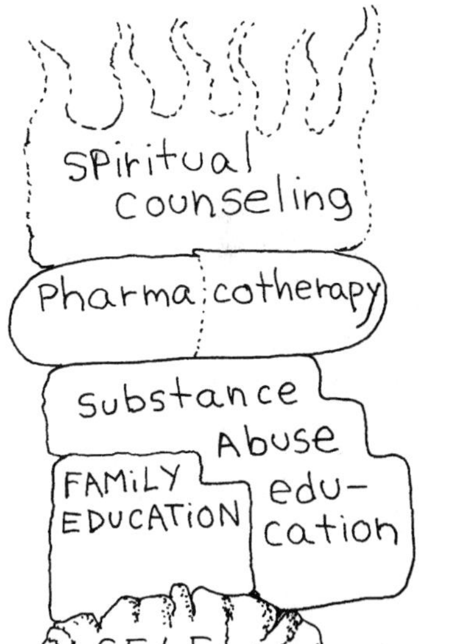

Treatment can be defined as all the interventions intended to short-circuit the process of abuse or dependence and to introduce the individual to effective sobriety. This can be put in equation form as follows:

> Treatment = individual counseling +/or family therapy
> +/or family education +/or client education
> +/or group therapy +/or medical care +/or self-help
> +/or pharmacotherapy +/or vocational counseling
> +/or activities therapy +/or spiritual counseling. . . .

As can be seen, individual counseling is only a small part of the many things that treatment can involve. So what is it? A very simple way to think of individual counseling is as the time, place, and space in which the rest of the treatment is organized, planned, and processed. One-to-one counseling is a series of interviews. During these sessions the therapist and client work together to define problems, explore possible solutions, and identify resources, with the therapist providing support, encouragement, and feedback to the client as he or she takes action.

One of the difficulties in thinking about, discussing, or writing about counseling is knowing where to begin. It can seem a bit overwhelming. One of the problems is that most of us have never seen a counselor at work. We have all seen police officers, telephone line workers, carpenters, or teachers, busy on the job. So we have some sense of what is involved in those lines of work and can imagine what such work entails. The clinician's job is different. It is private and not readily observable. Unfortunately, most of our ideas come from books and television. It doesn't take too much television viewing to get some notion that a good

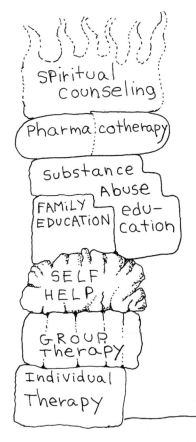

counselor is almost a magician, relying on uncanny instincts to divine the darkest, deepest secrets of the client's mind. You can't help thinking the therapist must have a T-shirt with a big letter "S" underneath the button-down collar. Television does an excellent job of teaching us that things are not always as they seem, yet, remember, in real life they often—indeed, usually—are. Everyone is quite adept at figuring out what is going on.

Observation

Each day we process vast amounts of information without much thought. Our behavior is almost automatic. Without the benefit of a clock, we can make a reasonable estimate of the time. When shopping, we can, without too much trouble, distinguish the clerk from fellow customers. Sometimes, though, we cannot find a person who seems to be the clerk. Take a couple of minutes to think about the clues you use in separating the clerk from the customer. One of the clues might be dress. Clerks may wear a special outfit, such as a smock, an apron, or a shirt with the store's logo. In colder weather, customers off the street will be wearing or carrying their coats. Another clue is behavior. The clerks stand behind counters and cash registers, the customers in front. Customers stroll about, casually looking at merchandise, whereas clerks systematically arrange displays. Another clue might be the person's companions. Clerks are usually alone, not hauling their children or browsing with a friend. Although we have all had some experience with guessing incorrectly, it rarely happens. In essence, this is *the good guys wear white hats* principle. A person's appearance provides us with useful, reliable information about them. Before a word of conversation is spoken, our observations provide us with some basic data to guide our interactions.

Presumably you are convinced everyone has observational powers. Usually, people simply do not think about these skills. The only difference between the clinician and others is that the therapist will cultivate these observational capacities, listen carefully, and attend to how something is said and not merely what is said. The counselor will ask him- or herself: "What is the client's mood? Is the mood appropriate to what is being said? What kinds of shifts take place during the interview? What nonverbal clues, or signs, does the client give to portray how she feels?" So, in a counseling session, from time to time, momentarily tune out the words and take a good look. What do you "see"? Reverse that. Turn off the picture and focus on the sound.

One important thing to note is that the questions you ask yourself (or the client) are not "why" questions. They are "what" and "how" questions that attempt to determine what is going on. Strangely enough, in substance abuse treatment, successful outcomes can occur without ever tackling a "why." Ignoring what or how issues, however, may mean you'll never even get into the ball park.

So what is the importance of observation? It provides data for making hypotheses. A question continually before the therapist is "What's going on with this person?" What you see provides clues. You do not pretend to be a mind reader. Despite occasional lapses, you do not equate observations, or hunches, with ultimate truth. Observations, coupled with a knowledge of alcohol and drugs and their impact on people, suggest where attention might be focused. For example, a client whose coloring is poor and who has a distended abdomen and a number of bruises will alert the counselor to the possibility of serious medical problems. The client may try to explain this all away by "just having tripped over the phone cord," but the therapist will urge the client to see a physician.

You do your work by observing, listening, and asking the client (and yourself) questions to gain a picture of the client's situation. The image of a picture being sketched and painted is quite apt to capture the therapeutic process. The space below is the canvas. The total area includes everything that is going on in the individual's life. As the client speaks with the therapist, this space is filled in. Now the therapist is getting a picture of the client's situation. Not only do you have the "facts" as the client sees them, but also you can see the client, and his or her mood and feelings, and get a sense of what the world and picture feels like to the client as well. As this happens, the space gets filled in and begins to look like this:

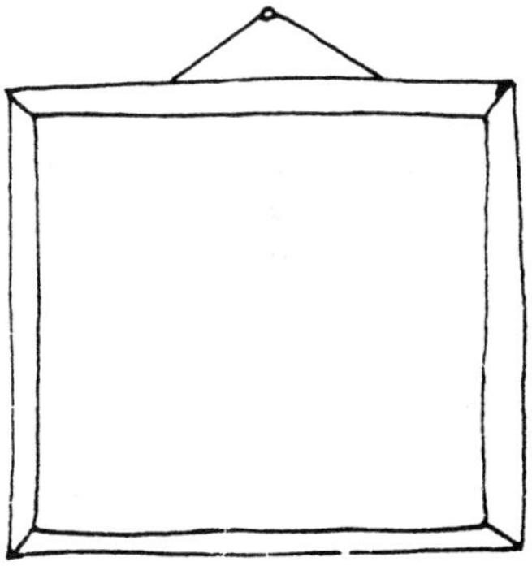

You have a notion of the various areas that make up the client's life: family, physical health, work, economic situation, community life, how the person feels about him- or herself, and so on. You are also aware of how substance use may affect these areas. As you find it necessary, you will guide the conversation to ensure that you have a total picture of the client's life. You are also aware that if the client is having a problem, it means that the pieces are not fitting together in a way that feels comfortable. Maybe some parts have very rough edges. Maybe one part is exerting undue influence on the others. So you must also attempt to see the relationship and interaction between the parts.

Feedback

In assisting the client to "see" what is going on, the therapist's observation skills pay off. A common feature of alcohol dependence, for example, is a markedly warped perception of reality. The ability of the therapist to provide accurate feedback to the client, giving specific descriptions of behavior and of what the client is doing, is very valuable. The alcohol-dependent person has lost the ability for self-assessment. It is quite likely that any feedback from family members or friends has also been warped and laced with threats so that it has become useless. In the counseling session, it may go like this: "Well, you say things are going fine. Yet as I look at you, I see you fidgeting in your chair, your voice is quivering, and your eyes are cast down toward the floor. For me, that

Table 10.1 Sample Feedback Sheet

1. Based on the information I obtained during the assessment, I calculated the number of standard drinks you consumed each day and have summarized three important indicators of your drinking:

   Total number of standard drinks per week ________

   Average number of standard drinks per drinking day ________

   Highest consumption in a day ________

2. When we look at everyone who drinks in the United States, you have been drinking more than approximately ________ percent of the population of women/men in the country.

3. I also estimated your highest and average blood alcohol level (BAL) in the past month. Your BAL is based on how many standard drinks you consume, the length of time over which you drink that much, whether you are a man or a woman, and how much you weigh. So,

   Your average peak BAL in an average week was ________

   Your estimated average BAL in an average week was ________

   This is a measure of how intoxicated you typically become. In the United States the legal intoxication limit is 0.08.

4. You have experienced negative consequences from drinking. Here are some of the most important:

________________	________________
________________	________________
________________	________________
________________	________________
________________	________________
________________	________________

From: Roberts LJ, McCrady BS. *Alcohol Problems in Intimate Relationships: Identification and Intervention*. Bethesda, MD: National Institute on Alcohol Abuse and Alcoholism, 2003.

doesn't go along with someone who's feeling fine." Period. The therapist simply reports the observations. There is no deep interpretation. There is no attempt to ferret out unconscious dynamics. The client is not labeled a "liar." The therapist's willingness and ability to simply describe what is observed is a potent therapeutic weapon. Feedback too includes the efforts to help the drinker recognize discrepancies between his or her current circumstances and personal and family goals and hopes. Also it can include information that allows the drinker to see how her drinking compares to that of others (see Table 10.1). The client can begin to learn how he or she comes across, how others see him or her. Thus, the use of observation can educate clients about themselves.

Education

Clients also need education about alcohol as a drug, about other drugs, and about the disease of addiction. Provide facts and data (see Tables 10.2 and 10.3). A host of pamphlets are available from state alcohol agencies, medical societies, the federal alcohol and drug institutes, insurance companies, and self-help groups. Everybody likes to understand what is happening to them. This is becoming increasingly apparent in all areas of medicine. Some institutions have hired patient educators. Patient education sessions on diabetes, heart disease, cancer, and care of newborns are commonplace. Education about alcohol and other drug problems is

Table 10.2 Alcohol Consumption Norms for U.S. Adults (%)

Note: The numbers in this table are cumulative percentages—i.e., the percentage of the population that drinks at or below each drinking level.

Drinks per Week	Men	Women	Total	Drinks per Week	Men	Women	Total
0	29	41	35	21	88	96	92
1	46	68	58	22	88	97	92
2	54	77	66	23–24	88	97	93
3	57	78	68	25	89	98	93
4	61	82	71	26–27	89	98	94
5	67	86	77	28	90	98	94
6	68	87	78	29	91	98	95
7	70	89	80	30–33	92	98	95
8	71	89	81	34–35	93	98	95
9	73	90	82	36	93	98	96
10	75	91	83	37–39	94	98	96
11	75	91	84	40	94	99	96
12	77	92	85	41–46	95	99	97
13	77	93	86	47–48	96	99	97
14	79	94	87	49–50	97	99	98
15	80	94	87	51–62	97	99	98
16	81	94	88	63–64	97	>99.5	99
17	82	95	89	65–84	98	>99.6	99
18	84	96	90	85–101	99	>99.9	99
19	85	96	91	102–159	99	>99.9	>99.5
20	86	96	91	160+	>99.5	>99.9	>99.8

Source: Roberts LA, McCrady BS. *Alcohol Problems in Intimate Relationships: Identification and Intervention. A Guide for Marriage and Family Therapists.* Rockville, MD: National Institute on Alcohol Abuse and Alcoholism, 2003, page 30.

Table 10.3 Blood Alcohol Level Estimation Charts

Men—Approximate Blood Alcohol Percentage

Body Weight in Pounds

Drinks	100	120	140	160	180	200	220	240	Sample Behavioral Effects
0	.00	.00	.00	.00	.00	.00	.00	.00	Only Completely Safe Limit
1	.04	.03	.03	.02	.02	.02	.02	.02	Impairment Begins
2	.08	.06	.05	.05	.04	.04	.03	.03	Driving Skills Significantly Affected; Information Processing Altered
3	.11	.09	.08	.07	.06	.06	.05	.05	
4	.15	.12	.11	.09	.08	.08	.07	.06	
5	.19	.16	.13	.12	.11	.09	.09	.08	
6	.23	.19	.16	.14	.13	.11	.10	.09	Legally Intoxicated; Criminal Penalties; Reaction Time Slowed; Loss of Balance; Impaired Movement; Slurred Speech
7	.26	.22	.19	.16	.15	.13	.12	.11	
8	.30	.25	.21	.19	.17	.15	.14	.13	
9	.34	.28	.24	.21	.19	.17	.15	.14	
10	.38	.31	.27	.23	.21	.19	.17	.16	

One drink is 1.5 oz. shot of hard liquor, 12 oz. of beer, or 5 oz. of table wine.

Women—Approximate Blood Alcohol Percentage

Body Weight in Pounds

Drinks	90	100	120	140	160	180	200	220	240	Sample Behavioral Effects
0	.00	.00	.00	.00	.00	.00	.00	.00	.00	Only Completely Safe Limit
1	.05	.05	.04	.03	.03	.03	.02	.02	.02	Impairment Begins
2	.10	.09	.08	.07	.06	.05	.05	.04	.04	Driving Skills Significantly Affected; Information Processing Altered
3	.15	.14	.11	.10	.09	.08	.07	.06	.06	
4	.20	.18	.15	.13	.11	.10	.09	.08	.08	
5	.25	.23	.19	.16	.14	.13	.11	.10	.09	
6	.30	.27	.23	.19	.17	.15	.14	.12	.11	Legally Intoxicated; Criminal Penalties; Reaction Time Slowed; Loss of Balance; Impaired Movement; Slurred Speech
7	.35	.32	.27	.23	.20	.18	.16	.14	.13	
8	.40	.36	.30	.26	.23	.20	.18	.17	.15	
9	.45	.41	.34	.29	.26	.23	.20	.19	.17	
10	.51	.45	.38	.32	.28	.25	.23	.21	.19	

One drink is 1.5 oz. shot of hard liquor, 12 oz. of beer, or 5 oz. of table wine.

Subtract .015 for each hour that you take to consume the number of drinks listed in the table. For example, if you are a 160 pound woman, and have two drinks in two hours, your BAC would be $.06 - (2 \times .015) = .03$

NOTE: Blood Alcohol Level (BAL) charts do not take into consideration a wide range of additional variables that contribute to the determination of BAL's achieved and the behavioral effects experienced at a given BAL. These additional variables include: age, water to body mass ratio, ethanol metabolism, tolerance level, drugs or medications taken, amount and type of food in the stomach during consumption, speed of consumption, and general physical condition. ***Thus, BAL charts only provide extremely rough estimates and should never be used alone to determine any individual's safe level of drinking.***

Source: Roberts LA, McCrady BS. *Alcohol Problems in Intimate Relationships: Identification and Intervention. A Guide for Marriage and Family Therapists.* Rockville, MD: National Institute on Alcohol Abuse and Alcoholism, 2003, page 32.

important for two reasons. The first is to help instill new attitudes toward alcohol dependence—that it is a treatable disease, with recognizable signs. The hope is to elicit the client's support in helping manage and treat the problem.

The other reason for education is to help the client handle feelings of guilt and low self-esteem. The chances are pretty good that the client's behavior has been looked at as downright crazy—and not just to others; it has also been inexplicable to the individual. The fact that he or she has been denying a problem confirms this. There is no need to deny something unless it is so painful and so inconsistent with values that it cannot be tolerated. Learning the facts can be a big relief. Suddenly, things make sense. All the bizarre behavior becomes understandable. That makes a significant difference. Successful recovery appears to be related to a client's acceptance of this framework of disease as the basis for what has been occurring. Energy now can be applied to figuring out how one can live successfully around the illness. The individual is relieved of the need to hash around, in the past to uncover causes, to figure out what went wrong. There is no need to dwell on the pattern of harmful, senseless behavior; it becomes merely a symptom, one that the individual isn't doomed to reexperience if efforts are made to maintain sobriety and to live drug-free.

Self-Disclosure

At this juncture it seems appropriate to add some cautionary word about the technique of *self-disclosure.* This is a counseling technique. As such, it requires the same thoughtful evaluation of its usefulness as any other counseling tool. It is important to recognize that self-disclosure is not limited to sharing information of one's own problems with alcohol. "Self-disclosure" in counseling or therapy refers to sharing not only the facts of one's life but also one's feelings and values. This is in contrast to the style of the early psychoanalyst, who never revealed personal information nor in any way presented him- or herself as an individual to clients. Counselors are self-disclosing when they express empathy or when they note that the client's concerns are those with which other clients have also struggled.

The concept of self-disclosure, however, has special meaning in the alcohol and substance abuse field. The clinician may be a recovering alcoholic and may be involved in AA, where self-disclosure is appropriate and part of the clinician's own self-help regimen. But professional counseling is a different story. In the early stages of the client's treatment or in the assessment process, it may seem natural to allay some of the client's nervousness or resistance with the news that a clinician, too, has "been there," knows how he or she feels, and furthermore can testify to the possibility of a successful recovery. What seems natural may, however, be totally inappropriate as well as countertherapeutic. It is just as likely that the client may become suspicious and wonder if you are guilty of seeing substance use problems everywhere. Therapists need to remember that their professionalism is important to the client, particularly in the early days of treatment. That professionalism is comforting. The patient in an intensive cardiac care unit is interested in the physician's medical assessment of his or her condition, what the next recommended steps are, and the possible outcome. That patient is not interested in hearing the physician's personal story of his or her own heart attack.

This is not to imply that self-disclosure should never be used or that it is ineffective. But the technique too often is used as a matter of course without proper thought given to the possible ramifications in a particular instance. Because it is a powerful clinical tool, it needs to be used thoughtfully. It should never be used to make the therapist feel more comfortable by "getting everything out in the open" or as a substitute for professional skills.

When is self-disclosure therapeutic? There may be times when the behavior that has resulted from alcoholism or drug use creates an overwhelming sense of worthlessness, isolation, and pervasive hopelessness. In such circumstances, self-disclosure may be useful. It may provide a desperately needed human connection, helping relieve feelings of utter despair, and may spark just a glimmer of hope and a recognition that maybe, just maybe, things can be different. In a group setting, it may be preferable that such efforts to reach out come from group members. But there are times, certainly in individual sessions, when this falls to the clinician.

Client Responsibility

The therapist expects the client to assume responsibility for his or her actions. You do not accept the client's view of himself as either a pawn of fate or a helpless victim. An ironic twist is present. You make it clear that you see the client as an adult who is accountable for his or her choices. Simultaneously you are aware that those dependent on alcohol, when drinking, abdicate control to a drug. Recall the definition of the alcoholic as one who cannot predict what will transpire after a drink. Therefore, being responsible ultimately means that the attempt to manage alcohol use must be abandoned. Here again, facts about the drug alcohol and the disease of alcohol dependence are important. A large chunk of the client's work will be to examine the facts of his or her own life in light of this information.

The client's need to have an alibi, to rationalize, and to otherwise explain away the obvious varies. But the therapist consistently holds up the mirror of reality, playing the client's story back to him or her. The therapist shares his or her observations, and in this way the client is enabled to move toward the first step of recovery—acknowledging the inability to control alcohol.

Possible Mis-steps

Those with alcohol dependence are sometimes described as being manipulative or as con artists. These kinds of descriptions may capture what alcoholic behavior feels like to others, whether family or friends. But if that is how the counselor feels, there is a problem. These are angry terms. If this is how clinicians feel, the view will trip them up. For one, the client may be representing the reality as he or she experiences it. Equally important, the individual is far more interested in deceiving him- or herself than in deceiving you. So you flatter yourself if you take it personally. To the extent a client deliberately misrepresents events, it's not that dissimilar to young children's whistling in the dark to chase away monsters. This is a way of clients not being overwhelmed by feelings and a way of keeping fear at bay. These clients are likely to be overwhelmed by a sense of desperation. Their lives are in chaos; their efforts to handle things have been unsuccessful. There is little hope that things can be different. Yes, there is magical thinking, too. Just as a woman hopes a lump in her breast is benign, so, too, the problem drinker wants to find a way to make the craziness of his or her life understandable, avoid the label of alcoholic, and not have to stop drinking completely.

To continue drinking, in spite of the consequences, requires alcohol-dependent persons to adopt behaviors and perceptions of the world that can make their drinking feel and appear rational. This habit does not disappear with the first prod, push, or pull toward treatment. With alcohol dependence, the habit of protecting the right to drink (even to death) is a long-standing one. When a client discovers that a counselor is probably not going to hand out a simple "3-step way to drink socially" and thus allow the drinking to continue, the client may be tempted to bolt. From the client's perspective, he or she may try to do so gracefully:

"Gee, you've really helped me to see exactly what I have to do. I'll do __________ and __________ and everything will be just fine. Thanks so much. You've made my life so much better already."

"I can't imagine why Sarah says what she does about my drinking. She really needs to get a life! After all, I only have a couple of beers with the guys after work."

Many individuals can be very convincing, adding tears, a charming smile, or bruises from a beating. If they are not falling down, slurring their words, throwing up, or being very argumentative, it is hard not to believe them. There they sit, full of confidence, hopeful, and very friendly. Again, this isn't a charade for your benefit but desperate efforts to hold on to the picture they paint. Experience has shown that, were these individuals not to enter counseling, at some point you or your counterpart elsewhere would see, hear from, or hear about them. Their situations would have gone downhill. They don't know how familiar their stories are—to themselves, the stories are unique. These people are trying to hang on to the only help they feel they have—the bottle. You may be able to help them loosen the grip by not allowing these pat replies to go unchallenged. However, truth can be absorbed only in small doses. And in the beginning, the most important step is to buy time.

There is a trap worth mentioning. It is one to which the least experienced clinician is most vulnerable. What some clinicians may try to do, although perhaps not consciously, is to seduce the client into treatment. Possibly aware of prior treatment failures, and sensitive to the alcohol-dependent person's distrust, apprehension, and isolation from others, these counselors are *very* understanding; they avoid anything that might cause the individual to bolt. Their compassion, understanding, and empathy are intended to win the client over. But no therapeutic relationship, no matter how good—can ever compete with the alcohol-dependent person's primary relationship, the one with alcohol. The therapist cannot be available on demand, on call 24 hours a day, or be guaranteed to make the person feel better, dissolve fears, and wash away concerns. If the counselor isn't aware of this, the client certainly is.

I've heard him renounce wine a hundred times a day, but then it has been between as many glasses.
DOUGLAS JERROLD

Problem Identification and Problem Solving

In therapy, problem identification and problem solving constitute a recurring process. No matter what the problem, two kinds of forces are always at work: some factors help perpetuate the problem; other factors encourage change. These can be sketched out in a diagram. Suppose the problem is "I don't like my job." The line going across represents the current situation. The arrows pointing upward stand for the factors that ease or lighten the problem. The arrows pointing downward represent the factors aggravating the problem.

If the individual's goal is to be more content at work, this might happen in several ways. The positive forces can be strengthened or others added, or attempts can be made to diminish the negative ones. A similar sketch might be made for the drinking. This kind of chart can help you decide what factors might be tackled to disturb the present equilibrium.

Left to his or her own devices, the client could avoid discomfort for years. For the clinician to allow such discomfort to surface can be the most helpful thing to do for years. The fact that he or she is sitting in front of you indicates that something has happened to jiggle the equilibrium. This is significant. Take advantage of it. Jiggle the equilibrium further. In the previous illustration, to take away the family denial or coworker cover-up would blow the whole act. It is becoming widely acknowledged.

The Therapeutic Relationship

Whole volumes have been written on the nature and components of the therapeutic relationship. This book cannot even begin to summarize what has been set forth. Some of the attributes of the helping relationship were alluded to at the beginning of Chapter 9. The therapist is a guide. The therapist cannot do the work but can only attempt to bring the client's attention to the work that needs to be done. The therapist may provide some "how to" suggestions but will proportionally provide more support as the client does the actual work.

Although an exposition of the therapeutic relationship is beyond the scope of this book, several items are common points of confusion. First, whatever the unique nature of the client-clinician relationship, it is not a friendship. It is not based on liking one another. The value of the therapist to the client is paradoxically that the counselor is *not* a friend; the therapist does not need or exact anything from the client. Indeed, if that sneaks into the equation, then the potential value of the therapist accordingly has been diminished. Beyond being someone with a knowledge of alcohol/drugs and their effects, the therapist is someone who can be trusted to be candid and open and who strives for objectivity. He or she can be counted on to say what needs to be said and trusted to hear the difficult things a client must say without scolding or judging. Although it may initially sound demeaning, in fact, the therapist is most effective with clients when the relationship is just part of the job.

With the client-therapist relationship outside the realm of friendship, several potentially difficult situations for the clinician are more easily avoided. Some predictably difficult situations are when the client becomes angry, threatens to drop out of counseling, claims you are taking someone else's side, or insists that you don't care or understand. It's very tempting and so easy to experience such situations as personally (and undeservedly) directed toward you. So first take a deep breath. Second, remind yourself it isn't you who's being attacked. This is not an occasion for either reminding the client of "everything you've done for him," or just how experienced you are, even if the client doesn't appreciate it. As quietly and calmly as possible, discuss what's going on, which includes acknowledging the feelings the client is experiencing. Resist trying to make the patient feel better or talk him or her out of those feelings. Expression of negative emotion is something to be anticipated. Indeed, if it never occurs, it may mean that the therapist is sending signals that it is not permitted. Allowing negative feelings to be expressed doesn't mean being a sponge for everything, or not setting limits, not stating a different perspective if you have one. One of the most important lessons the client may need to learn during treatment is that negative emotions can be expressed and the world doesn't fall apart. Nor will other people immediately try to placate or run away.

The other side of the "emotions coin" can present a different trap. It is difficult not to respond to "You are so wonderful," "You are the only person who really understands," or "You are the only person I can say this to." Beyond the danger of inflating the therapist's ego, there is the danger for the client that all the power is invested in the therapist. In the process of treatment, it is important that the client experience, and take credit for, the therapeutic work that is being done. So, for example, in responding to "You are the only person who really understands," a gentle reminder of the client's share of the work is appropriate. You might ask if there are other relationships, too, in which the client wishes to be able to share more and then help decide how to attempt to do that.

Case Management and Administrative Tasks

An inevitable and necessary part of a therapist's work is administrative—writing notes in charts, contacting agencies or counselors for previous records, dictating discharge summaries, and contacting the referring party or others to whom a client will be referred. This is often perceived as a pain in the neck and the portion of one's job most likely to get short shrift. However, attending to these details is an important part of good clinical care. Treatment is rarely a solo act, but a team effort. How effectively the team functions often depends on the clinical personnel who orchestrate and coordinate the various efforts.

The client's chart or medical record is one very important vehicle for communicating information. This is especially true in a residential facility, with multiple staff working different shifts. There are often questions as to what should and shouldn't go in a chart. Although not wishing to take lightly the concern for confidentiality, it can be a red herring. In thinking about what to include in the chart, ask yourself, "What do others need to know to respond therapeutically?" Rarely does this have anything to do with "deep, dark secrets." More often it has to do with the everyday nuts and bolts—worrying over a date for discharge, preoccupation with an upcoming court appearance, or a strained family meeting. The chart is not the place for verbatim accounts of individual sessions. But notation of any general themes, plus any modification of treatment plans, is needed. It also falls to the client's primary therapist or case managers to present cases at team planning meetings. On such occasions, a little preliminary thought helps. Are there special questions you have that you'd like to discuss with others? Along with these formal routes of communication, there are also informal channels. Take the opportunity to brief others.

Beyond orchestrating the activities of an agency treatment team, it falls to the case manager to be a liaison, and often an advocate, with external groups, such as employers, vocational counselors, social service workers, or the courts. Many clients have a wide range of need for supportive services. In these situations, you must always have the client's permission before acting. Also, it is important not to do for clients what they can do for themselves. Generally, it is more therapeutic to do a lot of hand holding as clients take care of business, rather than doing it yourself in the interest of efficiency. This can be very time-consuming, but this work should never be dismissed as less important than other aspects of treatment.

GROUP WORK

Group as Therapy

Being part of a group can promote some powerful therapeutic work. Some have described group therapy as the treatment of choice for addictions. Several reasons are set forth. One researcher has noted that "in the group setting, the 'cost' of character traits is illuminated." A pioneer in group therapy, Irving Yalom, M.D., in commenting on groups for alcohol problems, notes that there is power in groups—"the power to counter prevailing pressures to drink, to provide support, to offer role models, and to harness the power of peer pressure."

Membership in a group can also provide individuals with important information about themselves. Each of us has characteristics and traits that are visible to others but that are unknown to us, as illustrated by the following diagram, which is called a Johari Window.

	Not Known to Self	**Known to Self**
Known to Others	• reactions of others • mannerisms	• age • height • gender
Not Known to Others	• unconscious	• occupation • feelings • family history

Through the group process, the size of the "unknown" areas become smaller.

In a group setting, an individual's character traits can be illuminated for the individual. This news isn't always welcome. What the individual sees, or realizes others can see, may create discomfort. It can evoke shame and guilt. In the past, such feelings have been drowned in alcohol, so surviving these without drinking can in itself be a powerful experience. In a group, where the members feel safe, new behaviors can be explored. Historically the phrase *tiger land* was used by alcohol-dependent persons to describe the world. That's a fairly telling phrase. Through group treatment, ideally the client will reexperience the world differently. The whole thing need not be a jungle—other people can be a source of safety and strength.

Another bonus from a group experience is derived from individuals' opportunities to become reacquainted with themselves—not their drinking selves, but the selves that have been submerged by the drinking. A group provides its members a chance to learn who they are, their capabilities, and their impact on and importance to others. Interacting candidly and openly provides an opportunity to adjust and correct their mental pictures of themselves. They get feedback. Group treatment of those in a similar situation reduces the sense of isolation. Those with active alcohol dependence tend to view themselves very negatively and have an overwhelming sense of shame over their behavior. Coming together with others proves that one is not uniquely awful.

Mere confession is not therapeutic, however. Something else must happen for healing to occur. Just as absolution occurs in the context of a church, in a group that functions therapeutically the members act as priests to one another. Members hear one another's confession and say, in essence, "You are forgiven; go and sin no more." That is to say, group members can see one another apart from the behavior that accompanies the drinking. They can also often see a potential that is unknown to the individual. This is readily verified in our own lives. Solutions to other people's problems are so obvious, but not so to solutions of our own. Members of the group can see that people need not be destined to continue their old behaviors. Old "sins" need not be repeated. Thus, they instill hope in one another.

Interestingly enough, one often finds that people are more gentle with others than they are with themselves. In this regard, the group experience has a beneficial boomerang effect. In the process of being kind to and understanding of others, the members are in turn forced to accord themselves similar treatment.

When you ask one friend to dine,
Give him your best wine!
When you ask two,
The second best will do!
LONGFELLOW

What has been discussed in this section is the potential benefit that can be gleaned from a group exposure. The ways in which this group experience takes place can vary widely. Group therapy comes in many styles and can occur in many contexts. Being a resident in a halfway house puts one in a group, just as is the person who participates in outpatient group therapy. Group therapy means the use of any group experience to promote change in the members. Under the direction of a skilled leader, the power of the group process is harnessed for therapeutic purposes.

Types of Groups

In contemplating group work for those with alcohol or other drug problems, the leader needs to consider several basic issues. What is the purpose of the group? What are the goals for the individual members? Where will the group meet? How often? What will the rules be? The first question is the key. The purpose of the group must be clear in the leader's mind. There are many possible legitimate purposes. Experience shows that not all can be met simultaneously. It is far better to have different types of groups available, with members participating in several, than to lump everything into one group and accomplish nothing. Some of the most common types of groups are psychoeducational, support, problem-solving, and activity.

Psychoeducational groups. Are the most common type of group in alcohol treatment programs. Typically these groups are organized around a lecture, film, or presentation by a specialist in the substance abuse field, followed by a group discussion. Topics may include alcohol's effects on the body, symptoms of addiction, and the role of drinking in generating problems with others. In the discussion, members are encouraged to explore their own personal experience to identify the way the information presented applies personally to them. There is a complex relationship among knowledge, feelings, and behavior. Correct facts and information do not stop serious problematic drinking, but they can be important in breaking down denial, which protects the drinking or drug use. Information provides an invaluable framework for understanding what has happened and what treatment is about. In a psychoeducational group, clients acquire some cognitive tools to participate more successfully in their own treatment.

That is a treacherous friend against whom you must always be on your guard. Such a friend is wine.
C. N. Bovee

There are also **support groups.** A primary function of these groups is to promote self-awareness. The group function is to support abstinence and to identify the characteristic ways in which people sabotage themselves. In these groups, the emphasis is on the here and now. The participants are expected to deal with feelings as well as facts. The goal is not for members to achieve an intellectual understanding of why things have occurred or are occurring. Rather, the goal is to have members discover how they feel and learn how feelings are translated into behavior. Then they can choose how they would prefer to behave and try it on for size.

Problem-solving group. These are directed at tackling specific problems or stressful areas in the group members' lives. Discussion, role play, or a combination may be used. For example, how to say no to an offer to have a beer, how to handle an upcoming job interview, or how to get through the upcoming holidays can be an appropriate subject. The goals are to develop an awareness of potential stressful situations; to identify the old, habitual response patterns; to recognize how these patterns have created problems; and then to try new behaviors. These sessions thus provide practice for more effective coping behaviors.

Activity groups. These are those least likely to resemble the stereotype of group therapy. In these groups an activity or a project is undertaken, such as planning for a picnic. The emphasis is on more than the apparent task. The task is also a sample of real life. Thus, it provides an arena for the clients to identify areas of strength and weakness in interpersonal relationships. Here, too, is a safe place to practice new behaviors.

Group Functions

No matter what the kind of group, a number of functions will have to be performed. For any group to work effectively, there are some essential tasks, regardless of the goal. Initially the leader may have to be primarily responsible for filling these roles:

- *Initiating:* suggesting ideas for the group to consider, getting the ball rolling

- *Elaborating or clarifying:* clearing up confusion, giving examples, expanding on the contributions of group members
- *Summarizing:* pulling together loose ends, restating ideas
- *Facilitating:* encouraging others' participation by asking questions, showing interest
- *Expressing group feelings:* recognizing moods and relationships within the group
- *Giving feedback:* sharing responses to what is happening in the group
- *Seeking feedback:* asking for others' responses about what you, a member, are doing

As time goes on, the leader teaches the group members to share the responsibility for these functions. These represent skills, too, that have application to a variety of interactions and settings.

Different types of group therapy can be useful at different times during recovery. During the course of a residential stay or intensive outpatient treatment, a client might well attend a psychoeducational group, a relapse prevention group, and a couples group. In addition, the person could attend outside self-help meetings. In this example, the client would be participating in four types of groups. On discharge the person may return for a weekly group and with a spouse continue in a couples group. None of these group experiences is intended to substitute for self-help groups. The most effective treatment plans will prescribe self-help plus substance abuse–related group therapy. Being treated for diabetes clearly wouldn't exclude one from AA or group therapy. They have different purposes. So too self-help involvement (AA) doesn't preclude formal group therapy. Here too these groups have different purposes, and are neither in conflict with one another nor substitutes for each other.

Sunday night I go to a parent support group. Monday night I have my NA meeting Tuesday night is my Overeaters Anonymous meeting Wednesday night is my children of alcoholics group Thursday there's a single mother's support group Friday is my emotions anonymous group And Saturday nights I stay home and watch television. I love Saturday nights.

Groups as a Diversion

For a while group experiences, for the general population, became something of a fad. In the 1960s and 1970s, there were many kinds of groups—marathon, encounter, TA, gestalt, sensitivity, EST. They were seemingly offered everywhere: schools, churches, workplaces, by women's clubs, community centers. There was a whirlwind of activity around the use of groups for "personal growth." While these variants of groups directed to personal growth may sound a bit passé, the group phenomenon remains, having simply changed focus. Groups directed at personal growth were supplanted by an ever burgeoning number of self-help groups. The earliest self-help groups were modeled after AA—Narcotics Anonymous (NA), Cocaine Anonymous (CA), Gamblers Anonymous, and Overeaters Anonymous. On the heels of these were groups for adult children of alcoholics; victims of incest, rape, and child abuse; co-dependency; those with sexual addictions; plus those who have been batterers or have engaged in or are concerned about their potential for child abuse.

The emphasis placed on groups in this section does not imply that those with a serious drinking or drug problem should ride the group therapy circuit. To the contrary, those seeking and requiring substance abuse treatment in a group not restricted to those with alcohol problems is likely to waste their own and other people's time. Until one has taken some steps to combat one's substance use, there is little likelihood of working on other problems successfully. Inevitably the still drinking group member will raise havoc in a nonalcohol-focused group. They will have others running in circles, figuring out the whys, providing sympathy, and they will remain unchanged. Eventually others in the group will wear out, end up treating the alcohol-dependent member just as the family does, and experience all the same frustrations. However, in a group with others in trouble with alcohol and a leader familiar with the dynamics of alcohol dependence or alcohol abuse, it's a different story. The opportunity to divert others' attention from the role of alcohol is diminished to virtually zero because everyone knows the game thoroughly. The agenda, in this latter instance, clearly is how to break out of that pattern.

WORKING WITH FAMILIES

Historically, and for too long, family members of those being treated for alcohol problems were shortchanged. In the past, if a family member contacted a treatment agency about an alcohol problem in the family, what was likely to happen? He or she may have been told to have the troubled person call on his or her own behalf or may have heard a sympathetic "Yes, it's awful" and be told to call Al-Anon. It was unusual that family members were invited to come in as clients in their own right. In instances in which the alcohol-troubled person was seeking help, the family may have been called in by a clinician only to provide some background information and was then subsequently ignored. Any further attention family members got came only if a problem arose or if the counselor believed that family members weren't being supportive. Treatment efforts did not routinely take into account the problems the family faced and their own, independent need for treatment. Although these events may still occur, nonetheless very few in the field would claim that the approach is adequate. By definition, treatment that ignores the family has come to be seen as second-rate care. Although larger treatment programs now have staff whose specialty is family work, every clinician needs to have some basic understanding of the issues that confront families, of whatever composition, and needs to develop some basic skills for working with family members.

Too often, any family that doesn't match the traditional mold is invisible. The importance of the extended family as a support system can go unrecognized. The special problems of single mothers, the difficulties that confront blended families, or tension in intergenerational households can be overlooked. The poet Robert Frost defined "home" as the place where, "when you have to go there, they have to take you in." Calling on this definition, "family" includes all those in the "home." This is the model to keep in mind.

Members of the family may need treatment as much as the dependent person. More and more often they are coming to this conclusion themselves and seeking help. Clinicians are likely to find that more and more of their clients are, in fact, family members. The most important thing the clinician needs to keep in mind is that the client being treated is the person in the office—in this case, the family member. The big temptation, and what was once seen as the appropriate stance, was to try treating the alcohol-dependent family member in absentia. This may be the family members' wish, too, but it would be futile to attempt it.

Family Members Troubled by Another's Alcohol Use

Robert's father is willing to drive us here, but he won't come inside. He prefers to stay in the car with his bottle of bourbon.

What does the family or support system need? One important need is for education about the nature of alcohol and other drugs in the picture and the problems that evolve with chronic heavy use and dependence. The family also needs education on how the symptoms of the disease affect the family. Another area in which assistance is required is in sorting out the family's behavior to see how it fits into or even perpetuates the substance use. They need also to sort out their feelings and realistically come to grips with the true dimensions of the problem and the toll being exacted from them. Accompanying all this is the need to examine their options, given what is facing them. Most important, the family members require support to live their own lives despite the alcohol problem in their midst. Paradoxically, by doing this, the actual chances of short-circuiting the process of addiction are enhanced.

Just as all those with dependence do not display the identical symptoms or have the same degree of chronicity and extent of impairment, so is the same true of family members. In the assessment process, many of the same questions the therapist asks in dealing with the individual should be considered. What has caused the family member to seek help now? What is the family's understanding of the problem? What supports do they have? What is the economic, social, and family situation like? What coping devices do they use? What are their fears? What do they want from the clinician? Where the clinician goes in working with the family will depend on the answers to these questions. Treatment plans for family members might include individual counseling, support groups, and services from other community agencies.

In the discussion in this section, "families" and "family members" have been used interchangeably. Contact with a helping person is typically made by an individual. Efforts to include the other members of the family may be resisted. This may result from that individual's sense of isolation from the feeling that he or she is carrying the burden alone, and that no one else in the family cares. Or it may arise out of fear that other family members will disapprove of his or her having spilled the beans about the family's situation. With support from the counselor, the individual family member may later elect to involve other members.

Family Interventions

The initial focus has to be working with the family members on their own problems. Nonetheless, the indisputable fact is that the dependence is a central problem and that the family would like to see the alcohol-dependent member receive help. It is important to recognize that, ineffective as their efforts may have been, still much of a family's energy has gone into "helping." Now, as a result of education about the disease, and after assistance with sorting out their own situation, they in essence have become equipped to act more effectively in relation to the alcohol-dependent family member. At the very least, the family has been helped to abandon those well-intentioned behaviors that ironically allowed the drinking to continue.

It is now recognized that more is possible. In the early 1970s, a time when the alcohol field believed that treatment could not be successful unless the alcohol-dependent individual had hit bottom and requested help, a new clinical technique came along. It was introduced by the Johnson Institute in Minneapolis and proved otherwise. This clinical approach is known as an *intervention.* It consists of involving the family and other significant people in the person's life to promote the alcohol-dependent member's entry into treatment. This intervention technique and its supporting rationale were first described in *I'll Quit Tomorrow.*

The introduction of the intervention dramatically changed the treatment field. It forced clinicians and the recovering community—all concerned about those with alcohol dependence—to rethink some of the earlier assumptions about what was necessary for successful outcomes. Family and clinicians no longer had to sit around helplessly, waiting and praying for some magic insight to prompt the request for help. Whether described as "raising the bottom," "early intervention," or "confrontation," clinicians now had a therapeutic tool that could help move sick people into care.

With the introduction of the intervention technique, it has become increasingly apparent, too, that successful treatment can occur in a number of situations in which the initial entry into treatment might be considered "coercive." Among the programs with the best treatment outcomes are those in which the stakes are quite clear, such as EAPs (employee assistance programs), programs conducted by the military, court-mandated treatment, or treatment offered to professionals where there is close monitoring post-treatment, such as occurs for example with airline pilots, physicians, and nurses. In such instances, while the individual may not be highly motivated to enter treatment, entry into care is clearly preferable to the alternative. Recall that diagram on page 292 depicting forces promoting or negating change. External circumstances often play a role in sparking change. With hindsight it is now apparent that the early treatment field did not appreciate how common ambivalence is.

The Johnson-Style Intervention

The intervention process involves a meeting of family, other concerned persons, and the affected individual, conducted under the direction of a trained clinician. In that meeting the family members confront the troubled family member. Each family member, in turn, reading from a prepared list, would present specific incidents related to drinking that have caused him or her concern. Each person also expresses the hope that the person will enter treatment. The term "confrontation" has taken on a meaning quite different from that when introduced by Vernon Johnson. Now it too often can be an aggressive, even hostile form of "tough love," with the emphasis on the tough, not the love. It is associated with boot camp–style drug programs, or Synanon therapeutic communities. As originally used, "confrontation" did *not* equal attack. According to Webster's, to confront means "to cause to meet: bring face to face." In Johnson's mind, the alcoholic truly did not see the situation as others did, hence the need to convey exactly what transpired during different drinking incidents. Johnson also realized that, for the alcohol-dependent person to hear anything, family members needed to speak with genuine concern for his or her welfare. To use the language of motivation and stages of change, the intervention can be seen as moving someone from precontemplation to contemplation to determination. By force-feeding the painful facts, the intervention process cuts a wedge in the denial and can be viewed as precipitating a crisis.

It should be clear that conducting an intervention is not something one does on the spur of the moment. It is not something to be done impromptu, just because the family is together. Nor is it something you describe to the family and suggest they do on their own, after supper some evening.

And now, before we have dessert, I think we should all tell Pappa how we feel about his drinking.

The effectiveness of intervention depends on the participants' ability to voice a genuine concern and describe incidents that have caused concern in an objective, straightforward manner. This takes briefing and preparation. Part of the preparation is emotional, unloading and dealing with the host of negative feelings that beset family members. Typically this will entail several meetings. The idea is not to prepare a complete inventory of everything that ever happened. Instead, each person selects an incident or two that vividly demonstrates the problems associated with use, and demonstrates behavior that all recognize as at odds with the person's values. The participants also need to discuss what treatment options are to be presented and the actions they will take if the person does not seek help. Is the spouse ready to ask for a separation? Is the grown daughter ready to say she will not be comfortable allowing Mom to babysit for the grandchildren anymore? Are the parents ready to make continuation of college tuition payments contingent on their son's entering treatment? A successful intervention also requires that the therapist be supportive to all present, equally, and deflect the affected member's anxiety and fears, which may surface as anger.

There have been relatively few formal studies on this Johnson-style intervention process. As described in Chapter 9, when family physicians were trained to conduct these interventions, they never had the opportunity to do so. Every patient, out of 25 patients approached, agreed to treatment without a formal intervention. So there are no results from that study. More recently, several styles of intervention intended to engage a family member into treatment were compared. They found that, in a Johnson-style intervention group, over half of the family members decided not to proceed. However, of those who did, 75% of the family members entered treatment.

Current Approaches

The formal Johnson-style intervention described above is less commonly used. However, many of its elements have become standard approaches in work with families. A recently published guide by the NIAAA for marriage and family counselors highlights key ingredients. Indeed, it reflects many elements of the Johnson intervention. This guide introduces one other important component. Given the recognition that violence is more common when alcohol and other drug use are present, the immediate priority is seen as ensuring the safety of family members. The NIAAA guide emphasizes that attention needs to be paid to specific aggressive behaviors, such as throwing objects, grabbing a family member roughly, slapping, pushing, hitting, or threatening harm, and the presence of guns or weapons in the home. If violence is present, steps to ensure the safety of the family are essential. Work with family members may be needed to convey the fact that violence is *not* normal.

In addition to ensuring family safety, other tasks include:

- Changing the consequences of drinking. This includes addressing issues of covering up, hiding feelings about drinking, and mopping up after the dependent family member.
- Providing feedback to the drinking member.
- Providing support for change.

In addition, emphasis is placed upon the family member's needs for self-care, whether through professional care or participation in self-help groups.

Community Reinforcement and Family Training (CRAFT)

A different format for family intervention has been developed. It is called Community Reinforcement and Family Training, known as CRAFT. This approach uses cognitive-behavioral methods to teach the family and significant others how to use behavioral principles to reduce the alcohol-troubled person's drinking and to help motivate the drinker to seek treatment. Simultaneously it focuses on the family members' own needs and seeks to find ways to reduce stress, to ensure safety for family members, and to build meaningful and positive elements into their lives. This is a manual-guided effort, meaning that there is specific training for clinicians in using the technique and there are guidelines for what is to be accomplished in sessions.

Research has compared the CRAFT approach with the Johnson intervention technique and with Al-Anon. All three approaches were seen as leading to similar benefits for family members. However, the CRAFT approach resulted in higher rates of entry into treatment for the alcohol-troubled family member. With CRAFT, the rate of entry into treatment was 67%, compared with 30% for the Johnson intervention (although the majority of families elected not to proceed with the intervention) and 13% for Al-Anon.

Family Treatment in Conjunction with Alcohol Treatment

By whatever process and point at which individuals enter formal treatment, involvement of the family is critical. The family should be included as early as possible. Family involvement is far from being elective or a nice touch; it is vital to securing an adequate database for treatment planning.

Say alcohol dependence is clearly evident—it has progressed to the stage at which it could be diagnosed by anyone. In this circumstance, the family may be the only reliable source of even the most basic information, such as how much alcohol is being consumed, medical history, and prior alcohol treatment. The individual's judgment may be so severely impaired that others need to make key decisions about care.

SAC
I drink
when I have
occasion, and
sometimes
when I have
no occasion.
-Cervantes

The family members' views of what the problem is, their understanding of alcoholism as a disease, their ability to provide support, and their willingness to engage in the treatment will have a bearing on the treatment plans for the individual. The family may be in pure chaos, where concern for the alcohol-dependent member is lost under feelings of anger and frustration. In this case inpatient care may be far preferable to outpatient treatment. On the other hand, the family may have already been involved in treatment for themselves and thus be able to be supportive and to marshal their collective resources.

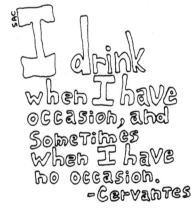

Many substance abuse clinicians find themselves with clients referred from other sources. To point out the obvious, for them the individual and his or her family are new patients. Even the best crafted letter of referral or prior telephone contact only imparts basic information. These data need to be supplemented by working with the patient and family to develop treatment plans. Even more important, while a medical record or chart can be used to pass along a client from one clinician to another, therapists cannot pass along or be the recipient of another's therapeutic relationship. Each clinician needs to establish this for him- or herself.

For these reasons a family meeting is becoming a routine part of the intake and assessment process. At this time, the clinician will seek the family members' view of what is happening. In initial contacts with the family, the clinician doesn't go into a family therapy routine. It is data-collecting time. For a newly involved clinician, the task is to understand how the family sees and deals with the substance abuse in its midst. In joint meetings, be prepared to provide the structure and lay the ground rules. For example, explain that people often see things differently and that you want to know from each of those present what has been going on. If need be, reassure them that everyone gets equal time, but no interruptions by other family members.

During the individual's treatment, the family may become involved in regularly scheduled family counseling sessions or participate in a special group for family members or couples, in addition to attending Al-Anon. Some residential treatment programs are beginning to hold family weekends. In these programs the families of patients are in residence and participate in a specially structured program of education, group discussion, and family counseling.

Suggestions for Working with Families During Treatment

The data gathering completed, the task turns to helping the family make the readjustments necessary to establish a new balance. Following are some concrete suggestions for dealing with families at this treatment stage. The clinician is the most objective person present; therefore, it is up to him or her to evaluate and guide the process.

- Concentrate on the interaction, not on the content. Don't become the referee in a family digression.
- Teach them how to check things out. People tend to guess at other people's meanings and motivations. They then respond as though the guesses were accurate. This causes all kinds of confusion and misunderstandings and can lead to mutual recriminations. Put a stop to these mind-reading games and point out what is going on.
- Be alert to scapegoating. A common human tendency is to lay blame on someone else. This is true whatever the problem. The family with an alcohol-dependent person tends to blame the drinker for all the family's troubles. They thereby can neatly avoid any responsibility for their own actions. Help them see this as a no-no.
- Stress acceptance of each person's right to his or her own feelings. Any good therapy stresses acceptance of each person's right to his or her own feelings. One reason for this is that good feelings get

blocked by unexpressed bad feelings. One of the tasks of a therapist is to bring out the family's strengths. The focus has been on the problems for so long that they have lost sight of the good points.

- Be alert to avoidance transactions. Avoidance transactions include such things as digressing to Christmas three years ago in the midst of a heated discussion of Dad's drinking. Point this out to the family and get them back on track. In a similar vein, to "speak the unspeakable" to bring out in the open the obvious, but unmentioned, facts.
- Guide them into problem-solving techniques as options. Make functional and dysfunctional patterns clear to the family. Help them begin to use the healthy techniques in therapy, with an eye to teaching the family to use the techniques on their own.

Family Issues

The client's entry into treatment may impose immediate problems for a family. The spouse may be concerned about even more unpaid bills, problems of child care, fears of yet more broken promises, and so on. In the face of these immediate concerns, the possibility of long-range benefits may offer little consolation. Attention must be paid to helping the family deal with the details of everyday living. Just as the alcohol-troubled individual in early treatment requires a lot of structure and guidance, so does the family. Another issue for the family is to develop realistic expectations for treatment. On one hand, they may think everything will be rosy, that their troubles are over. On the other, they may be exceedingly pessimistic. Commonly they will bounce back and forth between these two extremes.

The family members at some point will need to have the affected member "really hear," at an emotional level, what it has been like for them. If there has been an intervention, it stressed objective, factual recounting of events and sympathy for the affected member. Although a presentation of the family's emotional reality is not appropriate at the time of any intervention, it must take place at some point. If the family is to be reintegrated into a functioning unit, it is going to require that both "sides" gain some appreciation of what the disease has felt like for the other. How this occurs will vary. Within a series of family sessions there may be a session specifically devoted to feelings, led by skilled family therapists. These can be highly charged, "tell-it-like-it-is" cathartic sessions. To do this successfully requires considerable skill on the therapist's part, as well as a structure that provides a lot of support for the family members. For the individual, the pain, remorse, and shame of his or her drinking or drug use can be devastating. For the family, witnessing the remorse and shame can, in turn, invoke guilt and remorse in themselves. These responses must be addressed; a session cannot be stopped with the participants left in those emotional states. More commonly this material will be dealt with over time, in smaller doses. It may occur within family sessions and frequently within the context of working a 12-step program. Again, the important issue is to recognize this as a family task that must be dealt with in some way at some time. Otherwise, the family has a closet full of secrets that will haunt them, come between them, and interfere with their regaining a healthy new balance.[1]

Pregnancy

You may recall some of the particular family problems that relate to pregnancy and the presence of young children in the family. A few specific words should be said about these potential problematic areas. Contraceptive counseling is important. Pregnancy is not a cure for alcohol problems in either partner. In a couple in which one or both partners are actively drinking, they should be advised to make provisions for the prevention of pregnancy until abstinence is well established. It is important to remember that birth control methods adequate for a sober couple may be inadequate when alcohol is present. Methods that require planning or delay of gratification are likely to fail. Rhythm, foam, diaphragms, and prophylactics are not wise choices if one partner is drinking. A woman who is actively drinking is not advised to use the pill. So the alternatives are few. In the event of an unwanted pregnancy, the possibilities of placement or abortion are difficult options that may need to be considered. At the moment, no amniotic fluid assay test exists that can establish the presence of fetal alcohol syndrome.

Should pregnancy occur and a decision be made to have the baby, intensive intervention is required. If the expectant mother is drinking heavily, every effort should be made to initiate treatment. Even if abstinence is not achieved, a reduction in drinking is important. Regular prenatal care is also important. If alcohol is present, counseling and supporting both parents is essential to handle the stresses that accompany any pregnancy. If the prospective father is alcohol dependent, it is important to provide additional supports for the mother.

Pregnancy is always a stress for any couple or family system. Contraceptive counseling should also be considered for persons in early recovery. At that point, the family unit is busy coping with sobriety and establishing a solid recovery.

Children in the Family

A few words on behalf of older children in the family are in order. In many cases, children's problems are related to their parents' stress. Children may easily become weapons in parental battles. With alcohol or other drug dependence, children may think their behavior is causing the

---

[1]For the alcoholic, dealing with the effects of the alcoholic's drinking on the family may be part of taking an inventory (step 4) and part of making amends (step 8). See the 12 Steps of AA on pages 315–317.

problem. A child needs to be told that this is not the case. In instances where the clinician knows that physical or significant emotional abuse has occurred, child welfare authorities must be notified. In working with the family, additional parenting persons may be brought into the picture. Going to a nursery school or day-care center may help the child from a chaotic home.

What cannot be emphasized too strongly is that children must not be forgotten or left out of treatment. Sometimes parents consider a child too young to understand or feel the children need to be protected. What this can easily lead to is the child's feeling even more isolated, vulnerable, and frightened. Children in family sessions tend to define an appropriate level of participation for themselves. Sometimes the presence of children is problematic for adults, not because they won't understand but because of their uncanny ability to see things exactly as they are. For example, without self-consciousness, the child may say what the rest are only hinting at. Or the child may ask the most provocative questions. Along the same line, while a parent is actively drinking or using, the inevitable concerns and questions of the child must be addressed. Children may not need all the details, but the pretense effected by adults that everything is okay is destructive.

Another area in which it is critically important to address children's concerns is when the parent or caregiver has a serious medical problem, such as HIV/AIDS or hepatitis C, that may require hospital stays and that has a poor prognosis. Often information is withheld from the children, in the interest of preventing worry. What is going on does not escape them. The big questions for them are "What will become of me?" and "Who will take care of me?" Making arrangements for children may be very hard for a sick parent; discussing them with a child can be even harder. Research suggests that the absence of this information and the uncertainty are far more troubling than the facts, including an open discussion of plans for custody.

When initially involving the family, consider the children's needs in building a treatment plan. Many child welfare agencies and mental health centers conduct group sessions for children around issues of concern to children, such as a death in the family, divorce, or substance abuse problems. Usually these groups are set up for children of roughly the same age and run for a set period, such as 6 weeks. The goal is to provide basic information, support, and the chance to express feelings the child is uncomfortable with or cannot bring up at home. The subliminal message of such groups is that the parents' problems are not the child's fault, and talking about it is okay. In family sessions, you can make the message clear, too. You can provide time for the child to ask questions and provide children with pamphlets that may be helpful for them.

Occasionally a child may seem to be doing well. In fact, the child may reject efforts by others to be involved in discussion groups or treatment efforts. If the parent who is alcohol dependent is actively drinking, the child's resistance may be part of the child's way of coping. Seeing you may be perceived by the child as taking sides; it may force the child to look at things he or she is trying to pretend are not there. Resistance also may surface to joining the family treatment during early sobriety for many of the same reasons. Listen to the child's objections for clues to his or her concerns. What is important here is not to let a child's assertion that "everything is fine" pass without some additional questioning.

On the other hand, beware of embarking on a witch hunt to ferret out the unspoken problems of children. Children cannot be expected to function as adults. While they can be amazingly insightful at times, don't presume that those who do not voice "the unspeakable" are therefore hiding something. It is important to appreciate the defenses that children do have. Defenses are never to be viewed as good or bad but as fostering or impeding functioning. Children's defenses may be quite important for them. In dealing with children, if you have any questions or are concerned you are in danger of getting in over your head, seek advice from a child therapist.

Recovery and the Family

A common mistake when working with the family is to assume that, once the drinking stops, things will get better, yet with abstinence the family again faces a crisis and time of transition. Such crises can lead to growth and positive changes, but not automatically or inevitably. For the family who has lived with alcohol, there has been a long period of storing up anger and of mistrust and miscommunication. This may have been the children's only experience of family life. At times, children who previously were well behaved may begin acting out when a parent becomes sober. Children may feel that earlier their parent loved alcohol more than them and that now their parent loves AA more. The parent may have stopped drinking, but in the children's eyes they're still in second place.

Recovering families have a number of tasks to accomplish before they return to healthy functioning. They must strengthen generational boundaries. They must resume age- and sex-appropriate roles in the family. They must learn to communicate in direct and forthright ways with one another. They must learn to trust one another. And finally they must learn to express both anger and love appropriately. It might be expected, if one considers the family as a unit, that there are stages or patterns of a family's recovery. This has not yet been adequately studied. No one has developed a "valley chart" that plots family disintegration and recovery. Those professionals who have had considerable involvement with families of members in recovery are now beginning to discuss some common themes of the family's recovery.

It has been suggested that the family unit may experience some of the same kinds of issues that confront the alcohol- or other drug-dependent individual. It has long been a part of folk wisdom in the alcohol field that the alcohol-dependent individual's psychological and

emotional growth ceases when the heavy drinking begins. So with sobriety, the individual is going to have to face some issues that the drinking once prevented attending to. In the family system, what may be the equivalent of this Rip Van Winkle experience? Consider an example of a family in which the father is the alcohol-dependent individual, whose heavy drinking occurred during his children's adolescence and whose recovery begins just as the children are entering adulthood. If he was basically "out of it" during their teenage years, they grew up as best they could, without very much fathering from him. When he "comes to," they are no longer children but adults. In effect, he was deprived of an important chunk of family life. There may be regrets. There may be unrealistic expectations on the father's part about his present relationship with his children. There may be inappropriate attempts by him to regain the missing part. Depending on the situation, his therapist may need to help him grieve. There may be the need to help him recognize that his expectations are not in keeping with his children's adult status. He may be able to find other outlets to experience a parenting role or reestablish and enjoy appropriate contacts with his children.

Divorce or Separation

George Vaillant, in examining the course of recovery from alcoholism, found that quite commonly those men who recovered "acquired a new love object." Among several other factors, one that differentiated those who recovered from those who did not was having found someone to love and be loved by. This "someone" had not been part of his life during the period of active alcoholism. This cannot be used as evidence that family treatment is not warranted because there has been too much water over the dam, too much pain, and too much guilt. The men in Vaillant's study were those who were treated before the time in which family involvement in treatment was commonplace. So who knows what the outcome would have been had attention been directed to family members as well. Early intervention was not the rule then. His sample consisted of men with long-established cases of dependence. However, it does remind us of an important fact. Not all families will come through alcohol treatment intact. Divorce is common in our society. Even if alcohol-troubled individuals had a divorce rate similar to that of nonalcoholics, it would still mean a substantial number of divorces during or following treatment. Therefore, for some families, the work of family counseling will be to achieve a separation with the least pain possible and in the least destructive manner for both partners and their children.

Issues of family relationships are not important for only the client whose family is intact. For those who enter treatment divorced and/or estranged from their families, the task during the early treatment phase will be to help them make it without family supports. Their family members may well have come to the conclusion long ago that cutting off contact was necessary for their own welfare. Even if contacted at the point of treatment, they may refuse to have anything to do with the client and his or her treatment. However, with many months or years of sobriety, the issue of broken family ties may emerge. Recovering individuals may desire a restoration of family contacts and have the emotional and personal stability to attempt it, be it with parents, siblings, or their own children. If the client remains in follow-up treatment at this point, the clinician ought to be alert to his or her attempts to reconcile with the family. If the individual is successful, it will still involve stress; very likely many old wounds will be opened. If the attempt is unsuccessful, the therapist will be able to provide support and help the person adjust to the reality of those unfulfilled hopes. As family treatment becomes an integral part of treatment for alcohol problems, the hope is that fewer families will experience a total disruption of communications. It is hoped that a more widespread knowledge of the symptoms of alcohol dependence may facilitate reconciliation of previously estranged families.

After some success, when things seem to be going better, there may be some resistance to continuing therapy. In some instances, the family fears a setback and wants to stop while they're ahead. Simply point this out to them. They can try for something better or terminate. In other instances, the family, simply put, may need some time out, an opportunity to consolidate the work that has been done. In either case, leave the door open. Whatever the reasons for termination, the family may return in the future if it hits rough spots.

Couples Therapy

Couples therapy can be considered a variant of family therapy. Of note is the considerable work that has been done in integrating behavioral methods into couples therapy. Research consistently shows that involvement in behavioral-oriented couples therapy leads to reduced drinking and greater satisfaction with the marriage (or other relationship). Equally significant is that behavioral couples therapy has been found to have even better outcomes than does individual-based treatment. "Better" means greater reductions in drinking and greater levels of abstinence, less domestic violence, and fewer separations and divorce. Behavioral-oriented couples therapy strives to eliminate positive reinforcement for drinking and to enhance positive reinforcement for sobriety. It focuses on identifying discrete behaviors that can be altered.

Self-Help for Families

Al-Anon

Long before alcoholism was widely accepted as a disease, much less one that also affects family members, the wives of the early members of AA

recognized disturbances in their own behavior. They also encountered problems living with their alcoholic spouses, whether they were sober or still drinking. They saw that a structured program based on self-knowledge, reparation of wrongs, and growth in a supportive group helped promote the individual's recovery, so why shouldn't there be a similar program for spouses and other family members? In its earliest days, what became Al-Anon was known instead as the AA Auxiliary. Then in the mid-1950s, Al-Anon was officially formed and soon became a thriving program in its own right. The founders were quick to recognize that patterns of scapegoating the alcohol-dependent person and attempts to manipulate the drinking were nonproductive. Instead, they based their program on the premise that the only person one can change or control is oneself. Family members in Al-Anon are encouraged to explore and adopt patterns of living that can nourish them, regardless of the actions of the alcoholic individual in their midst.

Using the 12 steps of AA (described in detail on pp. 315–317) as a starting point, the program also incorporated the AA slogans and meeting formats. The major difference is in Al-Anon members' powerlessness being over others' alcohol use, rather than over their own alcohol use. Effort is directed at gaining an understanding of their habitual responses to situations that are dysfunctional and evoke pain and at substituting behaviors that will promote health and well-being. They are encouraged to accept responsibility for themselves by abandoning their focus on the alcoholic family member as "the problem." Instead, they can see by shared example the effectiveness of changing themselves, of "detaching with love" from the drinker.

Many people have found support and hope in the Al-Anon program. It can promote personal change and growth. This occurs through education about the disease and its impact on families, as well as through sharing experiences with others who have also lived with the shame and grief that are a part of living with the disease of alcoholism. Although no promises are made that this will have an impact on a still-drinking alcoholic, there are many examples of just such an outcome. At the very least, when family members stop the behaviors that tend to perpetuate the drinking, not only will their lives be better, but the odds are increased for a breakthrough in the pervasive denial characteristic of alcohol dependence.

Alateen

Alateen is an outgrowth of Al-Anon set up for teenagers with an alcohol-dependent parent. Their issues are different from those of adult family members, especially the partner. Accordingly they need a group specifically to deal with their problems. Under the sponsorship of an adult Al-Anon or AA member, they are taught to deal with their problems in much the same manner as the other programs teach.

Even with the currently widespread information about alcohol dependence, families still feel stigmatized. Most of them feel completely alone. It is such a hush-hush issue that those in its clutches think they are unique in their suffering. The statistics about the percentage of the population with alcohol problems provides no solace. It is very painful to have a problem about which you are afraid to talk because of the shame of being different. One of the greatest benefits of both Al-Anon and Alateen is the lessening of this shame and isolation. Hard as it may be to attend the first meeting, once there, people find many others who share their problems and pain. This can begin a therapeutic process.

Although Al-Anon and Alateen can be of tremendous assistance to the family, the clinician needs to point out what Al-Anon and Alateen are not designed to do. Frequently confusion is introduced because all family treatment efforts may be erroneously referred to as "Al-Anon." Al-Anon is a self-help group. It is not a professional therapeutic program whose members are trained family therapists, any more than AA members are professional clinicians. However, Al-Anon participation can nicely complement other family treatment efforts. Referral to Al-Anon or Alateen is widely recommended as a part of the treatment regimen for families.

SELF-HELP

Alcoholics Anonymous (AA)

Alcoholics Anonymous is the best known and largest self-help program and has been the model for other 12-step programs. Volumes have been written about the phenomenon of AA. It has been investigated, explained, challenged, and defended by laypeople, newspapers, writers, magazines, psychologists, psychiatrists, physicians, sociologists, anthropologists, and clergy. Each has brought a set of underlying assumptions and a particular vocabulary and professional or lay framework to the task.

In this discussion there are a few underlying assumptions. One is that experience is the best teacher. To learn about AA this text will be relatively unhelpful, compared with attending some AA meetings and watching and talking with people in the process of recovery actively using the AA program. Another assumption is that AA works for a variety of people caught up in the disease and for this reason deserves attention. Alcoholics Anonymous has been described as "the single most effective treatment for alcoholism." The exact whys and hows of its workings are not of paramount importance, but some understanding of it is necessary to genuinely recommend it. Presenting AA to a client with such statements as "AA worked for me; it's the only way," or conversely, "I've done all I can for you; you might as well try AA," are unlikely to be received with enthusiasm.

History

Alcoholics Anonymous began in 1935 in Akron, Ohio, with the meeting of two alcoholics. One, "Bill W.," about a year before had had a spiritual

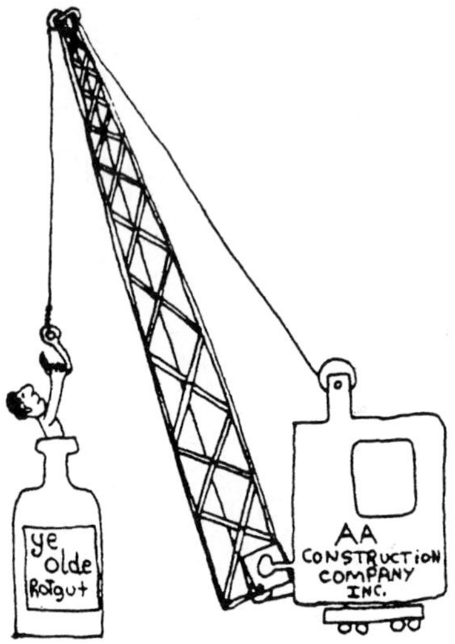

experience that was the major precipitating event in his becoming abstinent. Then, on a business trip to Akron after about a year of sobriety, he was overtaken by a strong desire to drink. He hit on the idea of seeking out and talking with another suffering alcoholic as an alternative to taking that first drink. He made contact with some people who led him to "Dr. Bob," and the whole thing began with their first meeting. The fascinating story of AA's origins and early history is told in the book *AA Comes of Age.* The idea of alcoholics helping each other spread slowly in geometric fashion until 1939. At that point, a group of about a hundred sober members realized they had something to offer the thus far "hopeless alcoholics." They wrote and published *Alcoholics Anonymous,* now known as the Big Book. It was based on a retrospective view of what they had done that had kept them sober. The past tense is used almost entirely in the Big Book. It was compiled by a group of people who, over time, working together, had found something that worked. Their task was to present this in a useful framework to others who might try it for themselves. This story is also covered in *AA Comes of Age.* However, it was in 1941 that AA was thrust into the public eye, as the result of an article published in a widely read national magazine, *The Saturday Evening Post.*[2] The article was entitled "Freed Slaves of Drink, Now They Free Others." In the year following publication, membership quadrupled, growing from 2,000 members to 8,000. In 1999, there were an estimated 1.9 million active members worldwide.

Goals

Alcoholics Anonymous stresses abstinence and contends that nothing can really happen until "the cork is in the bottle." Many other helping professionals tend to agree. A drugged person—and an alcoholic person is drugged—simply cannot comprehend, or use successfully, other forms of treatment. First, the drug has to go. The goals of each individual within AA vary widely: simple abstinence to adopting a whole new way of life are the ends of the continuum. Typically personal goals, too, will change over time. That any one organization can accommodate such diversity is in itself quite remarkable. AA now includes many with drug as well alcohol problems. With people entering AA at a younger age, drug use of some kind often accompanies the alcohol. References to alcohol in the following sections do not exclude the use of other substances.

In AA the words "sober" and "dry" denote quite different states. A dry person is simply not drinking at the moment. Sobriety means a more basic, all-pervasive change in the person. Sobriety does not come as

---

[2]Reading the article by Jack Alexander is highly recommended. This gives a firsthand view of alcohol problems in that era and what is was like for the early members of AA (*Saturday Evening Post,* March 1, 1941). It graphically depicts what confronted the early members of AA and the views of alcoholism in that era, and it is a useful point of reference for anyone in the field.

quickly as dryness and requires a desire for, and an attempt to work toward, a contented, productive life without reliance on mood-altering drugs. The 12 steps provide a framework for achieving this state.

An important piece of advice a newcomer to AA receives is the importance of getting a sponsor. A sponsor is a person with substantial sobriety with whom the newcomer feels comfortable. "Comfortable" does not primarily mean being of similar backgrounds, social class, ethnicity, or any of those things, although it is suggested that a sponsor be of the same sex. It refers to someone the newcomer respects and therefore can speak with and, most important, listen to and hear. The role of the sponsor is to be a mentor and a guide and to assist the newcomer in working the program. "Working the program" refers to efforts to use the 12 steps in making life changes. Much of this occurs outside of formal meetings. The sponsor is a person who will keep an eye out for the newcomer, leading him or her through difficult times and helping out in situations that are better dealt with outside the context of meetings. Sponsors can also help the newcomer focus on the basic principles and not get sidetracked by extraneous, secondary issues. The sponsor is one of the most valuable resources a newcomer can have.

The 12 Steps

The 12 steps function as the therapeutic framework of AA. They were not devised by a group of social scientists, nor are they derived from a theoretical view of alcoholism. Rather, the 12 steps of AA grew out of the practical experience of the earliest members, based on what they had done to gain sobriety. They do, indeed, require action. AA is not a passive process.

The initial undrugged view of the devastation can, and often does, drive the dry alcoholic back to the bottle. However, the 12 steps of AA, as experienced by its sober members, offer hope for another road out of the maze:

Step 1. "We admitted we were powerless over alcohol—that our lives had become unmanageable."
In this step, the individual acknowledges the true culprit, alcohol, and the scope of the problem, the whole life.

Step 2. "Came to believe that a Power greater than ourselves could restore us to sanity."
This step recognizes the insanity of the drinking behavior and allows for the gradual reliance on an external agent (e.g., God, another spiritual concept, the AA group, the therapist, or a combination) to aid an about-face.

Step 3. "Made a decision to turn our will and our lives over to the care of God as we understood Him."
This enables the person to let go of the previous life preserver, the bottle, and accept an outside influence to provide direction. It has

now become clear that, as a life preserver, the bottle was a dud, but free floating cannot go on forever, either. The search outside the self for direction has now begun.

Step 4. "Made a searching and fearless moral inventory of ourselves."
This step provokes a close look at the basic errors in perceiving the world and at behaviors that were part of the drinking debacle. This is the step that begins the process of teaching alcohol-dependent people about their own responsibility during the drinking days. This step also includes space for the positive attributes that can be enhanced in the sober state. An inventory is, after all, a balance sheet.

Step 5. "Admitted to God, to ourselves, and to another human being the exact nature of our wrongs."
This provides a method of cleaning the slate, admitting just how painful and destructive it all was, and getting the guilt-provoking behavior out in the open instead of destructively "bottled up."

Step 6. "Were entirely ready to have God remove all these defects of character."

Step 7. "Humbly asked Him to remove our shortcomings."
Steps 6 and 7 continue the "mopping-up" process. Step 6 makes the individual aware of his or her tendency to cling to old behaviors, even unhealthy ones. Step 7 takes care of the fear of repeated errors, again instilling hope that personality change is possible. (Remember, at this stage in the process, the recently sober person is likely to be very short on self-esteem.)

Step 8. "Made a list of all persons we had harmed and became willing to make amends to them all."

Step 9. "Made direct amends to such people wherever possible, except when to do so would injure them or others."
Steps 8 and 9 are a clear guide to sorting out actual injury done to others and deciding how best to deal with it. They serve other purposes, too. First, they force the person to confront the habit of blaming others for life's difficulties. To make an amend—that is, to attempt to atone for a wrong committed—does not require the forgiveness of the receiver. The recovering person's part is to make the effort to apologize, pay back money, or do whatever is necessary to try to balance the scales. This is not predicated on a positive response by the other. The individual is simply making whatever efforts he or she can to clean up his or her side of the street. Of course, such attempts provide a possibility for repairing presently strained relationships and hope of alleviating some of the overwhelming guilt that is common with initial sobriety. These steps clearly relate to the importance of acknowledging and owning up to events that have occurred.

Step 10. "Continued to take personal inventory and when we were wrong promptly admitted it."
Step 10, along with steps 11 and 12, promotes the maintenance of sobriety and the continuation of the process of change that has already begun. Step 10 ensures that the alcoholic person need not

slip back from the hard-won gains. Diligence in focusing on one's own behavior and not making excuses keeps the record straight.

Step 11. "Sought through prayer and meditation to improve our conscious contact with God as we understood Him, praying only for knowledge of His will for us and the power to carry that out."
This fosters continued spiritual development.

Step 12. "Having had a spiritual awakening as a result of these Steps, we tried to carry this message to alcoholics and to practice these principles in all our affairs."
This points the way to sharing the process with others. This is one of the vital keys Bill W. discovered to maintain his sobriety. It also implies that a continued practice of the new principles is vital to the sober life.

A word must be said here about "two steppers." This phrase is used to describe a few individuals in AA who enter AA, announce they are alcoholics, dry out, and set out to rescue others. However, it is often said in AA that "you can't give away what you don't have." This refers to a quality of sobriety that comes after some long and serious effort, applying all the 12 steps to one's life. It is interesting to note that "carrying the message" is not mentioned until step 12. Once that point is reached, however, it is important that the member reach out to others—repaying a debt, so to speak—and in the process experience feelings of usefulness again.

No AA member who is serious about the program and sober for some time would ever imply that the steps are a one-shot deal. They are an ongoing process, which evolves over time—a great deal of it—into ever widening applications. When approached with serious intent, the steps enable a great change in the individual. That they are effective is testified to not only by great numbers of recovering persons in the fellowship but also by their adoption as a basis for such organizations as Overeaters Anonymous, Narcotics Anonymous, and Gamblers Anonymous. These other fellowships simply substitute their own addiction for the word "alcohol" in step 1.

A therapist, counselor, or friend should be alert to the balance required in this process of working the program. The newcomer who wants to tackle all 12 steps the first week should be counseled with one of AA's slogans: "Easy does it." The member hopelessly anguished by step 4, for instance, could be advised that perfection is not the goal and a stab at it the first time through is quite sufficient. The agnostic having difficulty with "the God bit" can be told about using the group or anything else suitable for the time being as the external agent to rely on. After all, the spiritual awakening doesn't turn up until step 12, either.

The 12 Traditions

AA has very little structure as an organization. It describes itself as a fellowship and functions around the 12 steps and 12 traditions. The 12 traditions cover the organization as a whole, setting forth the purpose of the

fellowship, which is to carry its message to the still-suffering alcoholic. They also define principles of conduct; for example, that AA does not affiliate with other groups or lend its name and that it should not be organized and should remain forever nonprofessional. Individual AA groups are autonomous and decline outside contributions. Thus, all care is taken not to obscure or lose sight of the organization's purpose. The individual groups function in accord with these principles. Their focus is on sobriety, anonymity, and individual application of the program, which includes meetings, attempts to work the 12 steps, and service to other alcoholics.

Anonymity is of particular importance. Alcoholics Anonymous's tradition 12 reads as follows: "Anonymity is the spiritual foundation of all our traditions, ever reminding us to place principles before personalities." This concept evolved out of the growth pains of the organization. Early members admitted candidly that fear of exposure of their problem was their original motivation for remaining anonymous: the need "to hide from public distrust and contempt." However, the principle of anonymity, which was introduced into the fellowship on the basis of fear, soon demonstrated evidence of its value on a totally different level. The same process tends to occur for most individual members of AA. At first, the promise of anonymity is viewed as a safeguard against exposure. The stigma attached to alcoholism has not yet disappeared. Added to this are the alcohol-dependent person's own guilt, sense of failure, and low self-esteem. It is vital to maintain the promise of anonymity to encourage fearful newcomers to try out the program while assuring them of complete confidentiality. As individuals gain sobriety, fear gives way to the deeper understanding revealed in the practice. To be simply Joe or Mary, one alcoholic among many, has a therapeutic value.

In practice, anonymity takes the form of the use of first names only during the meetings, not identifying oneself through the media as a member of AA, and being careful not to reveal anyone else's attendance at meetings. Some meetings end with the reminder "Who you see here and what is said here stays here." It is important that this principle of anonymity be respected for AA to be able to continue its mission to assist other alcoholics.

Meetings Plus

There are open meetings—open to any spouses, friends, interested parties, and so on—and closed meetings—with only professed alcoholics attending. Both types can be speaker or discussion meetings. Speaker meetings have one to three speakers, who tell what it was like drinking (for the purpose of allowing newcomers to identify), what happened to change this, and what their sober life is now like. A discussion meeting is usually smaller. The leader may or may not tell his or her story briefly (or "qualify," in AA jargon). The focus of the meeting is a discussion of a particular step, topic, or problem with alcohol, with the leader taking the role of facilitator.

Attendance at meetings is not all there is to AA. The AA meeting is like a patient's visit to a doctor's office. The office visit doesn't constitute the whole of therapy. It is a good start, but how closely the patient follows the advice and recommendations and acts on what is prescribed makes the difference. Sitting in the doctor's office doesn't do it. The person who is seriously trying to use AA as a means of achieving sobriety will be doing a lot more than attending meetings. Those successful in AA will spend time talking to and being with other, more experienced members. Part of this time will be spent getting practical tips on how to maintain sobriety. Time and effort go into learning and substituting other behaviors for the all-pervasive drinking behavior. Alcoholics Anonymous contacts will also be a valuable resource for relaxation. It is a place a newly recovering alcoholic will feel accepted. It is also a space in which the drinking possibilities are greatly minimized. A new member of AA may spend a couple of hours a day phoning, having coffee with, or being in the company of other AA members. Although it is strongly recommended that new members seek sponsors, newcomers will be in touch with a larger circle of people. Frequent contact with AA members is encouraged, not only to pass on useful information but also to make it easier for the new members to reach out in times of stress, when picking up a drink would be so easy and instinctive. Often a new member's contacting a fellow AA member when a crunch time comes makes the difference between recovery and relapse.

Slogans

Slowly the new member's life is being restructured around not drinking, and usually the slogans are the basis for this: "One day at a time," "Easy does it," "Keep it simple," "Live and let live," "Let go and let God" are just a few. Although they can sound trite and somewhat corny, remember the description of the confused, guilt-ridden, anxious product of alcohol dependence. Anyone in such a condition can greatly benefit from a simple, organized, easily understood schedule of priorities. A kind of behavior modification is taking place so that changes may begin. Some new members feel so overwhelmed by the idea of a day without a drink that their sponsor and/or others will help them literally plan every step of the first few weeks. They keep in almost hourly touch with older members. Phone calls at any hour of the day or night are encouraged as a way to relieve anxiety.

View of Recovery

One thing assumed in AA is that recovery is a serious, lifelong venture. Safety does not exist, and some kind of long-term support is necessary. Everyone has a selective memory. For those with alcohol dependence, the danger is that, after periods of dryness, only *the relief* of drinking is recalled, not the consequences. A reminder of reality seems to be necessary. Any alcoholic with long-term sobriety will be able to tell about the sudden desire to drink popping up out of nowhere. Those who do not succumb are grateful to some aspect of their AA life in getting through. No one knows exactly why these moments occur, but one thing is certain: they are personally frightening and upsetting. They can reduce the reasonably well-adjusted recovering person to a state similar to very early sobriety. The feelings can be compared to the feelings after a particularly vivid nightmare. Whatever the reason for the phenomenon, these unexpected urges to drink do spring up. This is one reason continued participation in AA is suggested. Another is the emphasis (somewhat underplayed from time to time) on a continued growth in sobriety. Certainly, groups will rally around newcomers and help them learn the basics. In discussion meetings with a group of veterans, however, the focus will be on personal growth within the context of the 12 steps. Alcoholics Anonymous may advertise itself as a "simple program for complicated people," but an understanding of it is far from a simple matter. Its simplicity is deceptive and on the order of "Love thy neighbor as thyself"—simple, yet learning to do so could easily take a lifetime.

Referral

Simply telling someone to go to AA probably won't work. On the other hand, it is noteworthy how many people do refer themselves to AA. In most areas of the country, AA has an answering service, listed in the phone book under AA. Daily AA gets calls from those who want to know where a meeting will be held that day or how to speak to a member. Preferably the clinician will do more than hand over the phone book and will play a more active role in the referral. Alcoholics Anonymous is a self-help group. What AA can do and offer is by far best explained and demonstrated by its members. The clinician can assist by making arrangements for a client to speak to a member of AA or can arrange for the client to be taken to a meeting. Helping professionals, whether dealing exclusively with addiction or not, have compiled a list of AA members who have agreed to do this. Even if the clinician is an AA member, a separate AA contact is advisable. It is less confusing to the client if AA is seen as distinct from, although compatible with, other therapy. The therapist need not defend, proselytize, or try to sell AA. Alcoholics Anonymous speaks eloquently for itself. You do your part well when you persuade clients to attend, listen with an open mind, and stay long enough to make their own assessments.

A standard part of many treatment programs is an introduction and orientation to AA or other 12-step programs. This seems very important because treatment programs are an ever growing source of referrals. Many residential treatment programs or intensive outpatient programs include AA and/or NA meetings that are held at the facility. They may also make arrangements to transport clients to outside meetings. It is not unusual for presentations to be included in an educational series or for references to be made to AA in individual counseling or group therapy. Some programs encourage—indeed, some push—clients to work on steps 1 through 5 while they are actively involved in treatment. The hope is that this will give clients added insight into AA and increase the chances of their continuing involvement.

As a growing source of referrals to AA, treatment programs are challenged in several respects. Although wishing to be supportive of AA, treatment programs need to respect the boundaries between AA and treatment. One challenge to treatment programs is to help clients distinguish between formal treatment and AA. Nowhere may this be more important than in terms of aftercare. It must be pointed out that attending a treatment program's alumni group is not the same as going to AA. Nor for that matter is a chat with a sponsor necessarily a substitute for an aftercare session. Conversely, having a therapist should not be allowed to be seen as a substitute for having an AA sponsor. Other challenges for programs is not to appropriate AA through overly lengthy intellectual presentations on the nature of AA. Similarly treatment programs should not use the language of AA and its slogans to mislead clients into thinking such discussions and their treatment are the same as AA involvement. There is a danger of clients' becoming pseudosophisticates with respect to AA. They can use the jargon properly, can make reference to the slogans and the steps, but have very limited firsthand experience of the AA fellowship.

12-Step Facilitation Counseling

The alcohol treatment community has developed an outpatient clinical approach to promote involvement in Alcoholics Anonymous. Known as *12-step facilitation therapy* it consists of 12 to 15 one-hour individual sessions. The therapist actively encourages clients to attend meetings, get a sponsor, examine the first steps, and read AA material as well as learn to use AA resources in times of crisis. A manual has been developed that outlines the material for each of the sessions as well as presenting strategies for handling common clinical problems.

While initially designed for use with individual counseling, there have been subsequent adaptations for use in a group format and for use with drug problems other than alcohol. For those with drug abuse, the major change recommended is increasing to at least twice weekly the frequency of contact during the first three weeks. With the use of 12-step facilitation it is recommended that the initial focus be on establishing sobriety and delaying treatment of other related problems. The exceptions are the presence of major psychiatric conditions such as debilitating depression.

Resistance

Some clients and their families may be resistant to AA. A therapist often finds they may agree to anything, as long as it isn't AA. This resistance probably has a number of sources. It may be based on erroneous information and myths about AA. For some it is embarrassment, plain and simple. The client may have been notorious at the neighborhood bar, appeared regularly in the newspaper for drinking and driving offenses, or

Is this the Alcoholics Anonymous meeting?

almost single-handedly kept the neighborhood general store solvent with beer purchases. But heaven forbid the individual should be seen entering a building where an AA meeting is held. Also, going to an AA meeting represents, if not a public admission, at least a private one that alcohol is a problem. Seeing a therapist, even one clearly specializing in alcohol and substance abuse, may allow the alcohol-troubled client multiple interpretations, at least for a while. Going to AA is clear-cut, not open to ambiguity, and in that respect it is a big step. In dealing with this resistance, education is useful. Also required is a quiet insistence that going at least for a reasonable "experimental" period is expected of the client, so that he or she can get firsthand knowledge.

Sometimes clients will have had some limited prior exposure to AA, which they use as the basis for their objections. Commonly they may recount that their best drinking buddies have had similarly negative experiences and agree with them that AA doesn't work. Such clients say they "tried it once," but it wasn't for them, and they didn't like it. Any examination of what was going on in their lives often reveals that at best this was a very halfhearted "try." More important, liking or not liking AA is not an issue. Usually it matters little if people like any other prescribed treatments as long as the treatment produces positive results. No one likes braces or casts on broken limbs or hospital stays for any reason, but they are accepted as necessary to produce a desired result. It is the results that are important.

Professional resistance toward AA is certainly far less than it once was, but it has not wholly disappeared. Some professionals in the general helping professions are uncomfortable in routinely expecting their clients to use AA. At times one gets the sense that AA is not considered a "real" treatment, or it is considered less sophisticated. Why do these feelings exist? Probably a number of reasons lie behind such attitudes. One is that anyone who deals with alcohol-troubled people will periodically lose touch with what the disease of alcoholism is really like. The literal hell that is the life of the active alcoholic is forgotten. That person is who AA is for, yet at times the primary purpose of AA, to help people escape their hell, is forgotten. Then it is easy to criticize AA for not doing other things, be it provide psychologically oriented therapy group or handle marital problems.

Another point of possible professional resistance is taking clients' objections too seriously. Unwittingly clinicians can buy their criticisms of AA. They accept clients' dislike of AA as a valid reason for their not going. With alcohol problems being addressed at earlier and earlier stages, there may be a tendency for helping professionals outside of the substance abuse field to consider that AA involvement is only for those whose disease has been long-standing and who have many highly visible problems that resulted from drinking. In other words, some people's alcohol dependence isn't seen as bad enough to warrant prescribing AA.

For some, another point of friction is that AA does not build termination into the program. Although more could be said about this, for now it is sufficient to remember that any chronic disease is terminated only by death. For chronic illnesses, even when the disease is under control, regular checkups are routine practice. Finally, professionals sometimes have mistakenly gotten the impression that AA, as an organization, holds AA to be incompatible with other therapies. This is not true. Nothing in the AA program supports this premise. Certainly, an occasional client will give this impression, in which case as a therapist you can help clear up this misconception.

Membership

Since 1968, the General Service Office of AA has conducted a triennial survey of its members. The most recent survey, conducted in 2001, provides a profile of the members. Ages run the gamut; a prior survey indicated the age range to be 12 to 85.

The most recent survey (2001) shows the average age is 46. Two-thirds are under age 50. The following is the breakdown by demographic characteristics:

Age Groups:		*Marital Status*	
under 21	2%	married	37%
21–30	9	single	31
31–40	24	divorced	24
41–50	31	widowed	5
over 50	34	separated	3

Gender:		*Racial/Ethnic Groups*	
Men	67%	White	88%
Women	33	African American	5
those under age 30		Hispanic	4
women	40	Native American	2
		Hispanic & other	1

Men in AA outnumber women by about a 2-to-1 ratio: of all members, 67% are men and 33% women. But the proportion of women is higher in the younger age groups. For those under age 30, 40% are women. In terms of marital status, 37% are married, 31% single, 24% divorced, 5% widowed, and 3% separated. The composition by racial and ethnic groups shows that 88% are white, 14% African Americans, 5% Hispanics, and 2% Native Americans.

What are the paths to AA? Of those surveyed in 2001, a third of members were introduced to AA through treatment facilities, 14% by court order or correctional facility, and 15% by a counseling agency or health-care provider. Before going to AA, 61% of members received some type of treatment or counseling, and 74% of those members said it played an important part in directing them to AA. After going to AA, 64% of members received some type of treatment or counseling, and 85% of those said it was important to recovery. As in the past several surveys, about three-quarters report that their doctors know they are in AA.

Of all those going into AA, about 40% acknowledge a treatment program as a significant factor. That is twice the number since 1977.

In terms of length of sobriety, 48% of members have been sober over 5 years, 22% have been sober between 1 and 5 years, and 30% represent newcomers, those sober less than 1 year. The average length of sobriety is more than 7 years. A prior triennial survey (1992) focused on multiple substance use, 38% of all members reported a history of multiple substance abuse. This was particularly true of younger members. For those under age 21, 79% reported a history of other substance abuse; the proportion for those under age 31 was 60%.

In closing, you are strongly urged to attend a variety of AA meetings; also speak at some length with veteran members. So much has been written about AA—in some respects it is so understandable an approach—that people assume they know what it's about without firsthand knowledge. Just as you would visit treatment programs or community agencies to see personally what they are about, so, too, go to AA.

Other Self-Help Efforts

12-Step and Non-12-Step Groups

A number of other self-help groups have sprung up, some modeling themselves after AA. These include Narcotics Anonymous, Cocaine Anonymous, Nicotine Anonymous, Overeaters Anonymous, and Gamblers Anonymous. Collectively they are referred to as 12-step programs. In brief, they have adopted the 12 steps of AA and simply substitute the name of another substance for alcohol.

In the alcohol field, other self-help groups have emerged that are intended as alternatives to AA. These programs explicitly reject the 12-step approach and several basic tenets of AA, particularly the emphasis on spirituality, the notion of disease, and views of the individual as powerless, as set forth in the first step of AA. In exchange, these alternatives generally emphasize a capacity for change and the ability to make choices. (In some instances, these differences might be viewed as a discussion of whether the glass is half empty or half full.)

These alternative self-help programs include Women for Sobriety, Rational Recovery, Secular Organizations for Sobriety, SMART Recovery (Self Management And Recovery Training), and Moderation Management. One of the first of these alternatives was *Women for Sobriety,* founded in 1976 and obviously for women. Its founding coincided with the emergence of the women's movement, and it was established at a time when women were in a distinct minority in AA. Women for Sobriety places emphasis on the need and ability to make choices. Rather than the 12 steps, Women for Sobriety is based on 13 principles, which it describes as "encouraging personal and emotional growth" (See Box 10.1). These principles are called the "New Life Program."

Web Sites

Rational Recovery
www.rational.org/
Women for Sobriety
www.womenforsobriety.org/
Moderation Management
www.moderation.org/
Alcoholics Anonymous
www.AA.org/
Secular Organizations for Sobriety
www.secularhumanism.org/sos/
SMART Recovery
www.smartrecovery.org/

BOX 10.1 13 Principles of the New Life Program of Women for Sobriety

1. *I have a life-threatening problem that once had me.*
   I now take charge of my life. I accept the responsibility.
2. *Negative thoughts destroy only myself.*
   My first conscious act must be to remove negativity from my life.
3. *Happiness is a habit I will develop.*
   Happiness is created, not waited for.
4. *Problems bother me only to the degree I permit them to.*
   I now better understand my problems and do not permit problems to overwhelm me.
5. *I am what I think.*
   I am a capable, competent, caring, compassionate woman.
6. *Life can be ordinary or it can be great.*
   Greatness is mine by a conscious effort.
7. *Love can change the course of my world.*
   Caring becomes all important.
8. *The fundamental object of life is emotional and spiritual growth.*
   Daily I put my life into a proper order, knowing which are the priorities.
9. *The past is gone forever.*
   No longer will I be victimized by the past; I am a new person.
10. *All love given returns.*
    I will learn to know that others love me.
11. *Enthusiasm is my daily exercise.*
    I treasure all moments of my new life.
12. *I am a competent woman and have much to give life.*
    This is what I am and I shall know it always.
13. *I am responsible for myself and for my actions.*
    I am in charge of my mind, my thoughts, and my life.

Another program, founded in 1985, is *Rational Recovery.* It openly identifies itself as an alternative to those who are turned off by AA. While AA members refer to one of AA's key publications as the Big Book, Rational Recovery dubbed its publication *The Little Book.* It also repudiates the concept of powerlessness; in contrast it emphasizes the perspective that individuals are capable of making the choice not to drink and can take charge of their lives. Rational Recovery advocates the use of a technique it refers to as *addictive voice recognition technique* (AVRT) to help people recognize the automatic thoughts that support continued drinking. These automatic thoughts are described as the voice of "the beast," the metaphor used to describe the part of the self that seeks instant pleasure without regard for the consequences.

A newer self-help group is *Moderation Management (MM),* founded in 1994. It differs from the others in that abstinence is not seen as a requisite goal. Not intended for those with alcoholism/alcohol dependence, it is intended, instead for problem drinkers who have experienced mild to moderate alcohol-related problems. MM has explicit guidelines and limits for moderate drinking. These are presented in Box 10.2.

No one can quibble with the fact that the MM guidelines are consistent with low-risk drinking. But what is going on with people who feel the need of a self-help group to do what most drinkers do automatically? If there is a client who is involved in MM, this suggests that monitoring or follow-up is warranted. Consider contracting with that client about

BOX 10.2 MM Suggested Guidelines and Limits for Moderate Drinking

A moderate drinker

- Considers an occasional drink to be a small, though enjoyable, part of life.
- Has hobbies, interests, and other ways to relax and enjoy life that do not involve alcohol.
- Usually has friends who are moderate drinkers or nondrinkers.
- Generally has something to eat before, during, or soon after drinking.
- Usually does not drink for longer than an hour or two on any particular occasion.
- Usually does not drink faster than 1 drink per half-hour.
- Usually does not exceed the .055% BAC moderate drinking limit (see the note that follows the lists).
- Feels comfortable with his or her use of alcohol (never drinks secretly and does not spend a lot of time thinking about drinking or planning to drink).

The MM Limits

- Never drive while under the influence of alcohol.
- Do not drink in situations that would endanger yourself or others.
- Do not drink every day. MM suggests that you abstain from drinking alcohol at least 3 or 4 days per week.
- For women: do not drink more than 3 drinks on any day, and no more than 9 drinks per week. (See the following note about a "standard drink.")
- For men: do not drink more than 4 drinks on any day, and no more than 14 drinks per week. (See the following note about a "standard drink.")

Note: A standard drink is one 12 oz beer (5% alcohol), one 5 oz glass of wine (12% alcohol), 1½ oz of 80-proof liquor (40% alcohol).

what steps will be taken if he or she finds that the MM guidelines are not being followed. This also requires thought be given to what will be considered evidence and how much, if any, failure to follow these is acceptable. The literature of Moderation Management notes that about 30% of its members move on to join an abstinence-based group, such as AA. Thus, for some it becomes one route to abstinence.

Any clinician whose client reports having used MM in the past should take careful note of that fact. It shows that there were serious concerns about drinking. and significant efforts were made to control use in the past. If he or she is now in the office of a substance abuse counselor, this suggests efforts at moderation have not been successful and points to a diagnosis of dependence.[3]

Electronic Communications and Self-Help

E-mail, the Web, discussion groups, chat rooms—electronic communications has become a part of everyday life. There are websites with tests one can take to determine the presence of an alcohol problem or to

[3]Moderation Management found itself in the news in the spring of 2000. Its founder and the author of *Moderate Drinking: The Moderation Management Guide for People Who Want to Reduce Their Drinking,* used by the group, was arrested for an accident that occurred driving with a BAC of 0.26. She had headed the wrong way on an interstate and had crashed into another car, killing 2 people. Newspaper accounts noted that she had had an alcohol problem since high school and had been in treatment multiple times. She was immediately admitted to an alcohol treatment program. She pleaded guilty to the charge and issued a statement about having ceased involvement in MM and having joined a 12-step program.

identify high-risk drinking. These are part of the self-help terrain, too. Self-help groups have websites that are a source of general information about the groups, a source of literature, and provide a list of meetings. They also include chat rooms. In some instances there are even meetings online. To date there is little information on how these new forums are used, by whom, and how effective they are in what situations. But they are proliferating. This use of technology isn't totally new. In the early days of AA, when meetings were less available and people had to travel long distances, it was not uncommon for people to record meetings, using the old-fashioned reel-to-reel tape recorders. These tapes were then circulated among members. For those on merchant ships or in the Navy or those living in isolated spots, these tapes were how some "attended" AA meetings.

Which Self-Help Approach?

For the clinician, deciding whether to refer a client to a traditional self-help group, such as AA or NA, versus Rational Recovery or Women for Sobriety may not be the big issue it might appear at first glance. Setting aside whatever biases the clinician may have, there are several practical matters. Which groups are present in the client's community? AA is available almost everywhere, while other groups may not be. On the other hand, if a client tries AA and even after a reasonable exposure vigorously resists and is having problems making a connection, then a referral to an alternative program is warranted. Whatever the biases of the counselor, if it works, it works. Remember, what is important is the destination, not necessarily the route.

OTHER APPROACHES

Spiritual Counseling

There is increasing effort to educate and inform clergy members about alcohol abuse, alcoholism, and other drug problems. The goal is to equip pastors, priests, rabbis, ministers, and chaplains to recognize these problems, assist in early identification of the disease, and facilitate entry into the appropriate treatment.

Presumably the merits of this effort are self-evident. There is plenty of room in the alcohol field for many kinds of care providers. This section on spiritual counseling is not about the educational outreach to clergy members. Instead, discussion centers on the contribution that clergy members may make to the recovery process in their pastoral roles. Those with alcohol problems may have a need for pastoring, "shepherding," or spiritual counseling, as do other members of the population. In fact, their needs in this area may be especially acute. Attention to these needs is a critical part of recovery.

It is not easy to discuss spiritual matters. The medical, social work, psychology, or rehabilitation textbook with a chapter on spiritual issues in patient care is the exception. Crisply defining what is encompassed by spiritual issues is not easy; it's easier to say what it is not. "Spiritual" does not mean organized religions and churches. Religions can be thought of as organized groups and institutions that have arisen to meet spiritual needs. The spiritual concern is more basic than religion. That civilizations have developed religions throughout history can be evidence of a spiritual dimension. There are also experiences, difficult to describe, that hint at another dimension different from but as real as our physical nature. They might be called "intimations of immortality," and they occur among sufficient numbers of people to give more evidence for the spiritual nature of humankind.

Over the past several decades there has been a renewed interest in spiritual concerns in contemporary America. Whether it has been transcendental meditation, the teaching of Eastern gurus, fundamentalism, mysticism, the golden era of television evangelists, or the more traditional Judeo-Christian Western religions, Buddhist traditions, or Muslim traditions, people have been flocking to them. They are attempting to follow these teachings and precepts in the hope of filling a void in their lives. It is being recognized that the bottom line may not be adequately calculated in terms of status, education, career, and material wealth. The culturally defined evidence of achievement and success can still leave someone feeling that there is something missing. This "something" is thought by many to be of a spiritual nature. This missing piece has been described as a "God-shaped hole."

Sociologists have observed that the apparent renewed interest in religion and increased church attendance in the mainline denominations can be explained by sheer demographics. It may not be attributable to a societal perception of a spiritual vacuum. Church attendance historically has always been lowest among adolescents and young adults. Consequently with the baby boomers marching through middle age, this large segment of the population has reached the age at which religious interests have always arisen. These two viewpoints are not mutually exclusive. With maturity and some life experiences, a part of adult development is to reassess values, reexamine one's priorities in life, and redefine what is important. An offhand comment seems to capture this well: "No one on a death bed ever expressed regret that he or she hadn't spent more time on work."

Alcohol Dependence as a Spiritual Search

How do spiritual concerns fit in with alcohol use and the disease of alcohol dependence? First, it is worth reflecting on the fact that the word most commonly used for alcohol is "spirits." This is surely no accident. Indeed, consider how alcohol is used. Often it is in the hope it will provide that missing something or at least turn off a gnawing ache. From bottled spirits, a drinker may seek a solution to life's problems, a release from pain, an escape from circumstances. For a while it may do the job, but eventually it fails. To use spiritual language, you can even think of alcohol dependence as a pilgrimage that dead-ends. Alcohol can be thought of as a false god, or, to paraphrase the New Testament, as not being "living water."

If this is the case and alcohol use has been prompted in part by spiritual thirst, the thirst remains even though drinking ceases. Part of the recovery process must be aimed at quenching the thirst. Alcoholics Anonymous has recognized this fact. It speaks of alcoholism as a threefold disease with physical, mental, and spiritual components. Part of the AA program is intended to help members by focusing on their spiritual needs. It is also worth noting that AA makes a clear distinction between spiritual growth and religion.

Working with Clergy

How can the clergy be of assistance? Ideally clergy are society's designated experts on spiritual matters. Notice the word "ideally." The realities of religious institutions may have forced some to be fund-raisers, social directors, community consciences, almost everything but spiritual mentors, yet there are those who do, and maybe many more who long to, act as spiritual counselors and advisors. One way the clergy may be of potential assistance is to help those seeking recovery deal with sin[4] and feelings of guilt, worthlessness, and hopelessness. Many of those with alcohol dependence, along with the public at large, are walking around as adults with virtually the same notions of God they had as 5-year-olds. God has a white beard, sits on a throne on a cloud, checks up on everything we do, keeps a ledger of our behavior, and punishes us if we aren't "good." This is certainly a caricature but possibly not that far from how some feel, if they really think about it.

Those just getting sober feel remorseful, guilt-ridden, worthless, endowed with a host of negative qualities, and devoid of good. In their minds, they certainly do not fit the picture of someone God would like to befriend. On the contrary, they probably believe that, if God isn't punishing them He ought to be. So these persons may need some assistance in updating their concept of God. There's a good chance some of their ideas will have to be revised. There's the idea that the church, and therefore (to them) God, is only for the "good" people. A glance at the New Testament and Christian traditions doesn't support this view, even if some parishes or congregations may act that way. Jesus of Nazareth didn't travel with the "in crowd." He was found in the company of fishermen, prostitutes,

The sway of alcohol over mankind is unquestionably due to its power to stimulate the mystical faculties of human nature, usually crushed to earth by the cold facts and dry criticisms of the sober hour. Sobriety diminishes, discriminates, and says no; drunkenness expands, unites, and says yes.

WILLIAM JAMES

The Varieties of Religious Experience, 1902

[4]The word "sin" comes from the Greek, and its meaning had nothing to do with morality or with someone being "bad." It means "to miss the mark." The word was used in archery practice. Someone stood by the target and shouted back to the archer whether or not he had hit the target or had missed the mark—that is, had sinned—thus allowing the archer to make corrections.

It is hard to believe in God, but it is far harder to disbelieve in Him.
EMERSON

lepers, and tax collectors. Or consider the Judaic tradition as reflected in the Torah or Old Testament. The chosen of God were constantly whining, complaining, going astray, and breaking as much of the Law as they followed. Nonetheless, God refused to give up on them. Virtually all spiritual traditions have taken human frailty as a given. Whether a new perspective on God or a Higher Power leads to re-involvement with a church, assists in affiliation with AA, or helps lessen the burden of guilt doesn't matter. Whichever it does, it is a key factor in recovery.

Again, to use spiritual language, recovery from alcoholism involves a *conversion experience.* The meaning of "conversion" is very simple—"to turn around" or "to transform." Comparing the sober life with the previous drinking certainly testifies to such a transformation. A conversion experience doesn't necessarily imply blinding lights, visions, or a dramatic turning point—although it might. Indeed, if it does involve a startling experience, the newly sober individual will need some substantial aid in understanding and assimilating this experience.

Carl Jung

Interestingly, an eminent psychiatrist recognized the spiritual dimension of alcoholism and recovery back in the days when alcoholism was considered hopeless by the medical profession. The physician was Carl Jung. A man named Roland H. had been through the treatment route for alcoholism before seeking out Jung in 1931. He admired Jung greatly, saw him as the court of last resort, and remained in therapy with him for about a year. Shortly after terminating therapy, Roland lapsed back into drinking. Because of this unfortunate development, he returned to Jung. On his return, Jung told Roland his condition was hopeless as far as psychiatry and medicine of that day were concerned. Very desperate and willing to grab at any straw, Roland asked if there was any hope at all. Jung replied that there might be, provided Roland could have a spiritual or religious experience—a genuine conversion experience. Although comparatively rare, this had been known to lead to recovery from alcoholism. So Jung advised Roland to place himself in a religious atmosphere and hope (pray) for the best. The "best," in fact, occurred. The details of the story can be found in an exchange of letters between Bill W. and Jung, published in the AA magazine *The Grapevine.*

In recounting this story many years later, Jung observed that unrecognized spiritual needs can lead people into great difficulty and distress. He wrote that either "real religious insight or the protective wall of human community is essential to protect man from this." In talking specifically of Roland H., Jung wrote: "His craving for alcohol was the equivalent, on a low level, of the spiritual thirst of our being for wholeness, expressed in medieval language; the union with God."

Such concepts are largely foreign in contemporary American society. Take a survey of those in a few bars—be it the neighborhood tavern or a high-class hotel. How many drinkers do you expect to find who equate their use of alcohol with a search for God? Yet an objective examination of their use of alcohol may reveal otherwise. Alcohol is viewed as a magical potion, with the drinker expecting it to do the miraculous. The problem is that for a time it does, by alleviating shyness or awkwardness, or simply by turning off painful feelings. The backlash occurs later.

The Clinician's Role

If convinced that a spiritual dimension may be touched by both alcoholism and recovery, what do you as a therapist do? First, cultivate some members of the clergy in your area. It seems that many communities have at least one member of the clergy who has stumbled into the alcohol field. It was often not a deliberate, intellectual decision. It may have occurred through a troubled parishioner who has gotten well or one whom the clergy member couldn't tolerate watching drink him- or herself to death any longer and so blundered through an intervention. The pastor may have aided a parishioner with an alcohol problem and then found more and more people with alcohol problems showing up on his or her doorstep for help. Or the clergy may themselves be in recovery and thus drawn into helping others. At any rate, this is the one you want. If you cannot find him or her, find one with whom you are comfortable talking about spiritual or religious issues. That means one with whom you don't feel silly or awkward and, equally important, who doesn't squirm in his or her seat, either, at talk of spiritual issues. (Discussion of God and spiritual concerns can make people, including some clergy, as uncomfortable as does talk of drinking.)

Every form of addiction is bad, no matter whether the narcotic be alcohol or morphine or idealism.
CARL JUNG
Memories, Dreams, and Reflections, 1962

Once you find a resource person, it is an easy matter to provide your client with an opportunity to talk with that person. One way to make the contact is simply to suggest that the client sit down and talk with Joe Smith, who happens to be a Catholic priest, or a rabbi, or something else. It may also be worth pointing out to the client that the topic of concern is important and that the individual mentioned may be helpful in sorting it out. Set up the appointment, and let the clergy member take it from there. Some residential programs include a chaplain as a resource person. This person may simply be available to counsel clients or may take part in the formal program—for example, by providing a lecture in the educational series. What is important is that the presence and availability of this person give the message to clients that matters of the spirit are, indeed, important.

How do you recognize the person for whom spiritual counseling may be useful? First, let us assume you have found a clergy member who doesn't wag a finger, deliver hellfire and brimstone lectures, or pass out religious tracts at the drop of a hat. Rather, you have found a warm, caring, accepting, and supportive individual. A chat with someone like that isn't going to hurt anyone. So don't worry about inappropriate referrals. Nonetheless, for some clients the contact may be particularly meaningful. Among these are individuals who have a spiritual or religious background and are not experiencing it as a source of support but, rather, as a condemnation. Others may, in their course of sobriety, be conscientiously attempting to work the program but have a problem that is hanging them up. Jewish people are another group who may experience difficulty. The belief that "everyone knows Jews don't become alcoholics" presents a problem for those who do. It has been said that there is double the amount of denial and consequent guilt for them. Because the Jewish religion is practiced within the context of a community, there may also be a doubled sense of estrangement. A contact with a rabbi may be very important. It is worth pointing out that someone can be culturally or ethnically Jewish but not have been religiously Jewish. The intrusion of an alcohol problem may well provide the push to the Jewish alcoholic to explore his or her spiritual heritage. Another group for whom spiritual issues may be of particular importance are Native Americans, as spiritual issues are integral to traditional culture. They, too, may need special help in reconnecting with their spiritual heritage and incorporating it into their recovery. The clinician is advised to be sensitive to this, as well as supportive.

But What Is Spirituality?

A recent review of the medical and psychological academic literature documents the burgeoning interest in spirituality. From the early 1920s through the 1970s, there were 26 papers with spirituality as a major topic. From 1981 through 2001, the total number was over 3,200. The bulk of those deal with addictions, about one-third specifically alcohol, about substance abuse generally, and the others deal with a variety of other topics, including those with a relationship to addictions, such as children of alcoholics and co-dependents. While there is clearly a growing interest in spirituality, exactly what this means is not clear. In reviewing the publications, efforts were made to categorize a particular perspective on spirituality, a difficult task. In some cases, the emphasis was placed on what it does not mean—for example, that it is not synonymous with religious groups or formal church involvement. However, 12 conceptualizations of spirituality were identified. These different definitions and points of focus included:

- *Relatedness*: interpersonal relationships
- *Transcendence*: recognition of a transcendent dimension to life
- *Humanity*: the distinctiveness of humanity
- *Core/force/soul*: the inner "core," "force," or "soul" of a person
- *Meaning/purpose*: meaning and purpose in life
- *Authenticity/truth*: authenticity and truth
- *Values*: values, importance, and worth
- *Non-materiality*: opposition of the spiritual to the material
- *Non-religiousness*: opposition of spirituality to, or identity with, religion
- *Wholeness*: holistic wellness, wholeness, or health
- *Self-knowledge*: self-knowledge and self-actualization
- *Creativity*: creativity of the human agent

There is increasing interest in the spiritual dimension in medicine generally. This is reflected by the growing number of studies published in medical journals that examine the spiritual domain in respect to healing. It has long been recognized that those with religious affiliations or who express a belief in God often do better medically. Generally these findings are explained in terms of natural as opposed to supernatural phenomena. Thus, there is discussion of the possible psychological benefits associated with religion, such as the presence of support systems, stress reduction, and the placebo effect. (The placebo effect is the benefit associated with hope or expectations, as seen in improvements that occur when people think they are taking a medication when, in fact, it is a sugar pill.) One recent study took a different stance. This study, reported in *Archives of Internal Medicine* in 1999, involved more than 900 patients admitted to a coronary care unit. It examined the impact of intercessory prayers offered daily by individuals unknown to the patients or physicians and who were geographically at a distance. This was a double-blind controlled study so that neither the patients nor the physicians were aware of which patients were receiving intercessory prayer. Those for whom prayers were offered did better than patients for whom prayers were not offered.

The clinician, as an individual, may or may not consider spiritual issues personally important. What the caregiver needs is an awareness of the possibility (even probability) of this dimension's importance to a client, as well as a willingness to provide the client with a referral to an appropriate individual. Current research findings indicate that an active spiritual or religious involvement reduces the risk of alcohol or other drug abuse. The risk for alcohol dependency is 60% higher among drinkers with no religious affiliation, compared with members of conservative Protestant denominations. Religiously involved individuals are consistently less likely to use alcohol and other drugs and, when they do so, are less likely to engage in heavy use and suffer its adverse consequences. Research has shown that recovering individuals involved in working the 12 steps of Alcoholics Anonymous are more likely to remain abstinent, showing significantly better outcomes than those treated with two other types of psychological therapy without a spiritual component.

Spiritual Issues Versus Faith-Based Initiatives

As discussed here, spirituality is seen as different from affiliation with a particular religious tradition or specific religious group. This distinction is important. Unfortunately, some of the efforts under way at the federal level are not as clear on this. There have been moves to increase public support for "faith-based programs." This includes faith-based substance abuse treatment, particularly in the correctional system. For many years, a variety of social service programs have been sponsored by religious groups. However, in many cases this sponsorship does not dictate the nature of the treatment or services provided. Rather they play a major role in making treatment available for those without financial resources. However, when it comes to substance abuse treatment, not to mince words, a central ingredient in the programs is adoption of a particularly religious view and practices, particularly with a fundamentalist Christian orientation. For example, in these instances, core elements of the faith-based programs are Bible study and worship services.

These programs have not been systematically studied. The chances are greater of finding information about them on the Internet than in the research literature. Some of the claims made for them, such as 80% success rates, are unsupported. Clearly such initiatives may work for some; after all, it is clear that some people recover without any treatment. There is discomfort with the role of religious proselytizing within treatment programs, as well as some of the special handling these programs are requesting, such as being exempted by state licensing regulations.[5]

Meditation

Meditation is frequently suggested as an aid in achieving and maintaining sobriety. It is increasingly being used in many areas of medicine. Any number of approaches are available to those wishing to try it, and many treatment centers include an introduction to one or more of these methods. Meditation classes are now widely available through hospitals, community centers, and churches. Although meditation has different results depending on the type practiced, reaching a meditative state is somewhat similar to practicing relaxation. A fairly relaxed state is necessary before meditation can begin. Some schools of meditation use techniques quite similar to relaxation methods as a lead-in to the meditation period. In yoga, physical exercises are coupled with suggested mental images as a precursor. Studies have shown that altered physiological states accompany meditation and deep relaxation. Altered breathing patterns and different brainwave patterns are examples. These changes are independent of the type of meditation practiced. The real physical response, in part, accounts for the feelings of well-being after meditation periods. Those who practice meditation find it, on the whole, a rewarding experience. Many also find in the experience some form of inspiration or spiritual help.

What is a meditation?

> Perhaps a meditation is a daydream, a daydream of the soul as the beloved and God, the lover, their meeting in the tryst of prayer, their yearning for one another after parting; a daydream of their being united again.
>
> Or perhaps a meditation is the becoming aware of the human soul of its loneliness and the anticipation of its being united with the

[5]See the website for the National Center for Neighborhood Enterprise, www.ncne.com, which sets forth goals and objectives for faith-based substance abuse treatment.

One who transcends the All and is able to come past one's own defenses.

Or perhaps again it is a standing back with the whole of the cosmos before one's mind's eye as one's heart is being filled with the sheer joy of seeing the balances of the All and one's own self as part of it.

Or, perhaps a searching into one's own motives, values, and wishes with the light of the Torah against the background of the past.

Or perhaps . . .[6]

Activities Therapy

Activities therapy has been a mainstay of inpatient psychiatric treatment for a long time. It includes recreational and occupational therapy. To those unfamiliar with this field, the activities that are encompassed may look like "recreation" or diversionary activities, not real treatment. For the activities therapist, the event—such as a picnic, with the associated menu planning, food preparation, setup, and cleanup afterwards—is of far less importance than the process of organizing the activity.

Recall that the alcohol-dependent person's repertoire of social skills has been depleted. Plus, it may have been a long time since there have been social interactions without alcohol, tasks completed, or responsibilities assumed and fulfilled. In addition, many clients have come to think of drinking not only as part of relaxation or leisure time but also as necessary to get some time out from responsibilities, to turn off tensions, or to get into some diversions. Then, too, during treatment the client can spend only so many hours a day involved in individual counseling, attending group therapy sessions, or listening to lectures and films. Activities therapy programs can be the forum in which the client has the opportunity, with support and guidance, to try out some of the new behaviors that may have been discussed elsewhere and will be necessary in sobriety. Activities therapy may be the portion of the therapeutic program that will most closely approximate real life.

A common dilemma for those in recovery is how to fill the time that they used to spend drinking. A part of the activity therapist's task will be to identify past interests or activities that can be reawakened and resumed, not only to fill time but also to provide a sense of accomplishment and belonging. The activities therapist will be sensitive to the client's limitations. The person who used to have a half-acre garden and is now going to make up for lost time by plowing up another half-acre can be cautioned to take it easy. One or two tomato plants plus a few lettuce and radish plants may be the place to start.

---

[6]From Siegel R, Strassfeld M, Strassfeld S. *The Jewish Catalogue.* Philadelphia: The Jewish Publication Society of America, 1973.

One of the more imaginative adaptations of activities therapy in alcohol treatment has been the use of Outward Bound programs. Outward Bound grew out of training measures adopted by the British Merchant Navy in World War II. It was discovered that, among the merchant marines who were stranded at sea, those who survived were not the youngest or those who were most physically fit. Rather, it was their older, "life-seasoned" comrades. From that observation, an attempt was made to provide a training experience that incorporated physically challenging and psychologically demanding tasks to demonstrate to people their capacities.

Outward Bound was introduced in the United States in 1961. Since that time, its programs have been conducted in a range of settings from rehabilitation programs for people with disabilities to training programs for corporate executives. The programs can be a day, several days, or a week in length. Typically an Outward Bound experience combines group exercises, such as a group being given the task of getting all of its members over a 10-foot wall, with individual activities, such as rock climbing. Within alcohol treatment programs, Outward Bound has been made available to individual clients and clients with their families, and it has been used particularly with adolescents. The staff often includes a professional alcohol clinician, as well as the Outward Bound instructors. Integral to Outward Bound is discussing and processing what transpires during each exercise. Alcoholics Anonymous adages such as "One step (day) at a time" and "Easy does it" might be the topic of a group meeting. These take on a new meaning to someone who has been involved in scaling a cliff or negotiating a ropes course 20 feet off the ground.

Recreation and Fun

A family beset by alcohol problems usually has lived a lopsided life. There's probably been little time, energy, or capacity for dealing with anything except crises or for holding one's breath, waiting for the next incident. Any sense of fun or true recreation has long since disappeared in a sea of alcohol. Despite what alcohol-trouble people may claim, being drunk is not fun, and neither are the clenched-teeth efforts to control drinking. Witnessing either of these behaviors is no fun, either. Even small children in the home where alcohol problems are present may have become so inhibited by the tension or so hypervigilant that there is too little opportunity for true play.

A common complaint from the person entering treatment is "Everyone drinks! How can I have any fun if I'm the only one who isn't?" Lots of others in recovery seem to manage, however. Despite the fact that this is often a last gasp effort to discount the need for treatment, it does point to a problem down the line—how to have fun without alcohol or, for some, how to have fun at all. What is the clinician to say? There may be little to be said at the point the question is raised, when the more significant question is "Is life fun now?" But it is an issue that has to be taken seriously.

In planning treatment, the issue of leisure needs to be addressed. Fun ultimately is not what we do but how we experience what we do. It is not an event but an experience. The word "recreation," thus, may be more apt to capture the phenomenon. It flows from the activities in life that refresh us, renew us, and offer us the sorely needed counterpoint to the hectic, busy lives we live. One person's recreation is another's work. Recreation can encompass active pursuits, such as a brisk walk or a pick-up game of softball on the empty neighborhood lot. Recreation can be individual, a private activity with some solitary time for reading a book, writing a letter, or tending a garden. Recreation may be group activity. It may be spontaneous or planned. An essential characteristic of recreation is that it is wholly engaging. When we are living in the present, we can neither worry about tomorrow nor relive yesterday.

Initial treatment, whether in a residential or an outpatient setting, is going to be highly regimented and entail a well-structured schedule. The idea is not to schedule assigned time slots in which clients are instructed to have fun. They would be at a total loss. To relax or have fun does not usually occur on command, either. For those in recovery, it is a capacity that will need to be evoked and rediscovered. For many, the initial moments of relaxation may go unrecognized. They may be quite unspectacular moments. A game of cards, a conversation, or a movie—recreation can encompass anything that pushes alcohol from the foreground and turns off a preoccupation with oneself and one's plight. It is important to assist clients to recognize these moments and to not discount the enjoyment. It is more important, too, to incorporate events that up the odds of these moments' occurring. During later recovery, recreation is no less an issue. At this point it may be considered as a part of the task that confronts us all. It can be put under the rubric of taking care of ourselves. Recreation is a necessary self-indulgence.

Fitness and Well-Being

Activities that center around fitness and sports are becoming a more important element in many individuals' efforts to take care of themselves. Within treatment programs, efforts to address general fitness and well-being are now more common. In residential settings, without conscious effort to have it be otherwise, the day would be filled almost exclusively with sedentary activities. The link between emotional well-being and physical well-being is being appreciated. The treatment of alcohol abuse can simultaneously address larger issues of general well-being, without diverting attention from the focus of alcohol abuse as the paramount concern. Regular exercise and good nutrition do have a significant impact on how people feel. This in turn can set in motion a positive cycle—one of change promoting further change. Feeling better and being proud of efforts that contributed to this leads to an improved sense of competence, reinforces expectations that things can improve, and opens up new possibilities for activities that are rewarding and enhance self-worth.

In keeping with a self-care orientation, many alcohol treatment programs have become "smoke free," do not allow smoking, and promote or require smoking cessation as well as abstinence from alcohol use. The case for not allowing nicotine use can be made on many grounds: (1) smoking is viewed as a health issue and medical concern, as serious as chronic alcohol use; (2) smoking is seen as a behavior that often accompanies drinking, so that if not discontinued it will be a ready cue to take a drink; (3) nicotine is viewed as a drug that is as addictive as or more addictive than alcohol or other substances; or (4) all of the above. As a practical point, the physical and emotional discomfort of withdrawal from alcohol is not compounded by the simultaneous withdrawal of nicotine. Residential programs that have initiated such policies have reported a relatively infrequent number of client complaints in respect to giving up nicotine as well.

Behavioral Approaches

Behavioral therapy and behavior modification have long been a part of substance abuse treatment. For a long time, the terms were used so casually and so imprecisely that what was being discussed was often unclear. Historically several treatment approaches based on behavioral therapy and techniques went against the grain of the treatment field and aroused considerable controversy. One unfortunate result was to make clinicians skeptical of any mention of behavioral approaches. As the substance abuse field has matured, so has the use of behavioral techniques. It is not an exaggeration to say that they are now among the most useful tools available.

Early Approaches

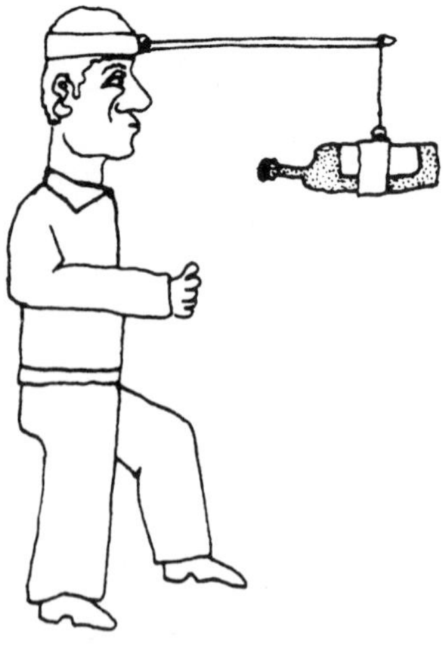

Obviously any therapy has behavior modification as its goal. However, behavioral therapy is the clinical application of the principles psychologists have discovered about how people learn. The basic idea is that, if a behavior can be learned, it can also be unlearned, or changed. This can be done in several ways. To put it very simply, one way is to introduce new and competing behavior in place of the old or unwanted behavior. By using learning principles, the new behavior is reinforced, meaning that the person experiences positive results and the old behavior is in effect "squeezed out." Another technique is to negatively reinforce or punish the unwanted behavior; therefore, it becomes less frequent. Recall the discussion of Johnson's model for the development of drinking behavior in Chapter 7. That explanation was based on learning principles. People learn what alcohol can do; alcohol can be counted on in anyone's early drinking career to have dependable consequences. Therefore, drinking is reinforced and the behavior continues.

Behavioral therapy is a field of psychology that rose to prominence in the early 1950s. Its techniques were then applied to the treatment of

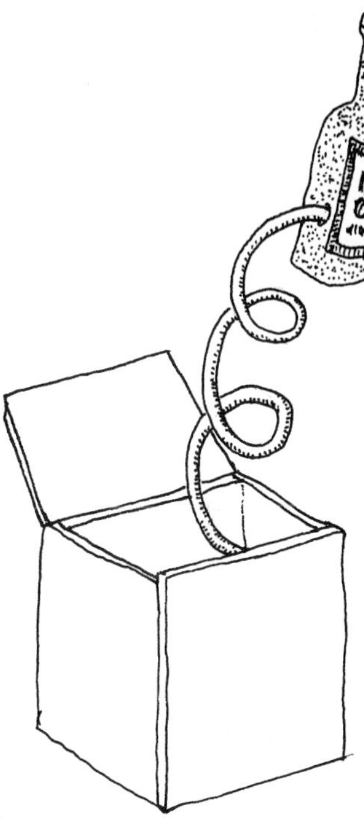

alcoholism. However, the early behavioral approaches fared no better than did other psychological approaches, which also were unable to offer, by themselves, a complete guide to treatment. Historically, one of the first behavioral methods to be used in alcohol treatment was aversion therapy. Electric shock and chemicals were the primary tools. The alcoholic person was given something to drink, and as he or she swallowed the alcohol, a shock was administered. Alternatively, a drug similar to disulfiram (Antabuse® is the trade name) induced sickness when one drank alcohol. The procedure was repeated periodically until it was felt that the drinking was so thoroughly associated with unpleasantness in the subject's mind that the person would be unlikely to continue drinking alcohol. Although short-term success was ensured, those results were not maintained over the long haul. Aversion therapy of this form is virtually never used today.

In the 1970s, there was considerable controversy in the wake of a research program based on behavioral principles. It involved efforts to "teach" controlled drinking to those with alcohol dependence. Given what is now known about the biological basis of dependence, the outcome is not surprising. Over the short haul, the results were promising, but over time virtually no patients were able to maintain nonproblematic drinking. Ironically, while controlled drinking did not prove to have been a viable goal for the treatment of alcohol dependence, many of the approaches used have since been successfully adopted in treating a different population of persons, those whose diagnosis is alcohol abuse. In those cases, abstinence may not be a requisite treatment goal; what is required is a change in drinking patterns to reduce the risk of future dependence or to reduce the likelihood of acute problems. Such approaches have been used, for example, with the college-age population, to reduce dangerous drinking practices. In this context, the phrase "controlled drinking" is less often used than the phrase "moderate use" or "efforts to reduce harm associated with drinking."

Current Behavioral Approaches

Few treatment programs are now exclusively based on behavioral methods. What is now far more common is the use of behavioral methods to treat particular aspects of an alcohol problem in the context of a multipronged clinical approach. But behavioral approaches are a significant ingredient. Indeed, research has shown that behavioral methods are among those with the best outcomes. Some of the approaches that have emerged from behavioral methods and learning theory are described in the following sections.

Relaxation Therapy In recovery the client is likely to face a multitude of problems. One of these may be a high level of anxiety. It can be temporary, the initial discomfort with the nondrinking life, or more chronic if one is the "nervous" type. Whether temporary or chronic, it is an uncomfortable state, and the client has a very low tolerance for it. Those dependent on alcohol, for example, have become accustomed to using alcohol for the quick, if temporary, relief of anxiety. What is later remembered (and longed for) is the almost instant relief of a large swig of booze. When alcohol or drugs are no longer an option, the recovering individual has the problem of how to deal with anxiety. Many simply "sweat it out"; others relapse.

Some positive things can be done to alleviate recovering persons' anxiety. One is relaxation therapy. It is based on the fact that, if the body and breathing are relaxed, it is impossible to feel anxious. The mind rejects the paradox of a relaxed body and a tense mind. Working with this fact, some techniques have evolved to counter anxiety with relaxation. Generally the therapist vocally guides a person through a progressive tensing and relaxing of the various body parts. The relaxing can start with the toes and work up or with the scalp and work down. The process involves first tensing the muscles, then relaxing them at the direction of the therapist. These directions are generally given in a modulated, soft voice. When the client is quite relaxed, it is suggested that a soothing picture be held in the mind. The client is then given a tape of the process to take home, with instructions on its use, as an aid in learning the relaxation. With practice, the relaxed state is achieved more easily and quickly. In some cases, the client may finally learn to relax totally with just the thought of the "picture." Once thoroughly learned, the relaxation response can be substituted for anxiety at will. This response can be used by the recovering alcoholic to deal with those situations in which taking a drink might be almost second nature.

Cognitive-Behavioral Therapy The premise that underlies cognitive-behavioral therapy is that behaviors associated with addictive behaviors are related to a person's basic beliefs and automatic thoughts about drinking. At the most basic level, this can be seen in the immediate response that people have to the idea of a drink. They picture the cold beer, and that leads automatically to their picturing themselves pulling the tab, opening the can, tasting the first sip, and feeling relaxed. Cognitive-behavioral therapies help people recognize these automatic thoughts and replace them with different visions. As part of Project MATCH, a federally funded program to explore how best to match clients with specific treatment approaches, a manual was devised that sketches out the application of this approach over a set number of sessions.

Systematic Desensitization Another behavioral approach to deal with anxiety, systematic desensitization, builds on the relaxation response. This technique has been found quite useful in treating people with phobias. This is an appropriate approach for recovering individuals who may feel panic at the mere thought of a particular situation—that is, even the idea of a specific event gets them so tense that the temptation to drink may be overwhelming.

In this process, with the aid of a therapist, the individual imagines the events that lead to the situation that causes anxiety. As the anxiety builds up, the person is directed to use relaxation techniques he or she has learned. Gradually, going step by step, relaxation is used to turn off the anxiety, and eventually the situation itself becomes much less anxiety-provoking. In alcohol treatment, this approach has been used for persons whose drinking has been partially prompted by stressful, anxiety-producing situations. Given another option, they are better equipped to avoid drinking when such situations arise.

Life Skills Training This is another technique based on behavioral methods. One very simple example of its application is in teaching problem-solving skills. It can also be used to help people recognize high-risk situations and anticipate ways they can say no to situations that threaten sobriety.

Recordkeeping Not uncommonly, in recovery some clients report finding themselves, with some regularity, "suddenly" in the midst of a troubling situation (such as an argument with a spouse), with no idea of what led up to it. There may, instead, be periods of inexplicable despondency. Often there is a pattern, but the key elements may not be apparent. Keeping a personal log or diary of one's daily routine sometimes is used to help identify the precursors that lead up to difficult moments. Recovery requires all kinds of readjustments to routines. By keeping a daily log, over time, one may have a far better sense of what areas need attention.

Contingency Management Introduced initially in drug treatment programs, this approach is becoming more widely used in a variety of settings. An important aspect of programs are contracts with clients. Based on learning theory, goals are set with clients or are set by the program and agreed to by clients. Rewards are built in for meeting these goals. In drug programs, rewards are earned for clean urines at drug testing. In this instance, the rewards are also increased with increased time being drug-free, so the longer someone stays clean, the greater the reward. Clients can earn either money or vouchers that can be redeemed at local stores. There is a considerable body of research indicating the success of this approach.

Relapse Prevention Behavioral techniques are the mainstays of relapse prevention. Relapse prevention efforts are increasingly a standard component of care. Alan Marlatt and colleagues from the University of Washington were among the first to tackle this issue in a systematic fashion and sketch ways in which this can be incorporated into care. A variety of relapse prevention curricula have been developed. These consist of defining the content and approaches to use in a series of counseling sessions. They can include homework assignments, worksheets, skills training, role play, interactive videotapes, and lifestyle interventions, such as exercise, stress management, and relaxation techniques. Prior to that, the substance abuse field tended to avoid any mention of relapse in working with clients. The topic was taboo, as if in acknowledging relapse as a possibility either one was giving permission to clients to resume drinking or suggesting it was inevitable.

FOCUS ON DRUGS

Driving

The effects of alcohol use on driving performance are well-known. How about other drugs?

Marijuana. Marijuana when taken alone has a moderate effect on driving performance. However, in the presence of even small amounts of alcohol, the impairment is dramatically greater. With a BAC of 0.04, in the presence of marijuana, impairment becomes severe. A BAC of 0.04, with marijuana also present, impairs driving performance equivalent to that found with a BAC twice as high. Behaviors that are impaired in actual driving conditions include the ability to stay in one lane, ability to maintain a constant speed, and reaction time.

Stimulants. The most commonly used stimulant is caffeine. Caffeine is considered to benefit driving performance. This is certainly the popular notion, as witnessed by people who are driving long distances or at night, and fuel up with a cup of coffee as well as gasoline. Laboratory tests show that caffeine increases attention and alertness. In terms of driving skills, after caffeine persons who were sleepy will steer more steadily, and are less likely to make jerky movements and stray out of their lanes.

What is the impact of caffeine in combination with alcohol? In *some* respects caffeine *appears* to counter the effects of alcohol. The critical words are "some" and "appears." In simulated driving tests, at a BAC of 0.08 (the legal definition of driving while intoxicated) the presence of caffeine reduced subjects' ratings of how dizzy, or "high" they were, and increased their ratings of "being alert." It also reduced alcohol's impairment of braking time. However, despite feeling less impaired, the caffeine did not fully counter the alcohol-caused impairment in reaction time, and enhance the ability to choose between two possible actions. It might be said that caffeine along with alcohol essentially provides a more awake impaired driver.

There is very little information on the impact of either cocaine or amphetamines on driving ability. However, there is some information on their presence in those involved in traffic accidents. Persons with positive tests for either were more likely to be deemed culpable for the accident, clearly suggesting that they impair driving ability.

Benzodiazepines. The benzodiazepines, having depressant properties, have effects similar to those of alcohol. Combined with alcohol, the effects are additive and increase the level of impairment.

Opiates. Concern about the impact of driving after using opiates arises not only due to illicit use. The question about the impact on driving ability also has arisen in the context of treatment of chronic pain and the use of substitution therapies, such as methadone. Multiple studies over a number of years have examined the impact of medically prescribed opiates. Studies over many years show chronic methadone use produces minimal functional impairment. For chronic pain patients, indeed, opiates may actually improve driving ability, as the presence of pain can be a significant distraction. A recent review confirms that there is no impairment of perception, coordination or reaction time, key skills in driving, there appear to be other areas in which an impact is seen. It was also noted there has been strong, consistent evidence for no greater incidence in motor vehicle violations/ motor vehicle accidents versus comparable controls of opioid-maintained patients; no evidence of impairment as measured in driving simulators among opioid-maintained patients. Another recent study, while confirming this, did note that there may be a reduced ability to follow directions and possibly increased impulsivity.

The question of driving under the influence of opiates outside of those medically prescribed raises an additional set of questions. The impairments in those situations may be due less to the pharmacology of opiates, than to the contexts of use. For example, a study conducted in Australia observed that illicit opiate users commonly drive to pick up their drugs. Furthermore, they often use the drugs inside their cars after scoring. These opiate users recognize that shortly after use they may feel more drowsy and that this may represent an accident risk. Also, with illicit use of opiates, there is an increased likelihood of other drug or alcohol use. In terms of alcohol and opiate combinations, the impairments seen are largely those expected of alcohol alone.

Ecstasy. There has been virtually no research on the impact of MDMA (ecstasy) on driving ability. One exploratory study tested a group of young people on a driving simulator, after having taken ecstasy as they were about to attend a rave (party) and then tested again at the point of leaving the party, after having taken ecstasy as well as other drugs. In brief, with ecstasy alone, many of the skills related to driving were not greatly affected. However, ecstasy did increase risk taking and thereby was seen as increasing the risk of an accident. Driving with ecstasy and other drugs, the post-rave scenario, was characterized as being extremely dangerous. There was impairment in driving related skills, an even further rise in risk taking, in combination these were seen as increasing the risk a full 150% above those who hadn't used any drugs.

Dimension of the Drugged Driving Problem

In 2002, it was estimated that about 35 million people 12 years of age or older used illicit drugs in the past year. Of these about 31% report having driven after illicit drug use. This represents about 5% of the total population. Drugged driving increases with age, peaking at age 21, when the percentage is 18% of all 21-year-old drivers. The rates for males are about twice that of females. In respect to racial and ethnic groups, the highest proportion is among Native Americans (6.3%), followed by whites (5%), blacks (4.5%), Hispanics (3.7%), Native Hawaiians (3.1%), and the lowest, Asian Americans (1.3%)

Drugged driving is most common in the West (5.5%) and Midwest (5.2%), and among those living in metropolitan areas. In respect to education, drugged driving is more common among full-time college students (18%) than their age mates not attending college (14%). Among those over age 26, there are differences by education. Those with less than a high school education is 5%, versus a rate of 6% of those with some college or high school diploma, and 4% among college graduates. Full and part-time workers have a rate of drugged driving that is about 40% lower than those who are unemployed.

There is no U.S. national data on the role of drugged driving and traffic accidents in the United States. A study from Australia examined, over a 9-year period, the role of alcohol and other drugs in traffic fatalities in 3 Australian states. This provides some clues as to the nature of the problem. Alcohol was detected in 30% of all car fatalities. Drugs other than alcohol were present in a quarter of the cases. Marijuana was the drug most commonly present (13.5%), followed by opiates (4.9%); stimulants, which included methamphetamine, MDMA, cocaine, and the ephedrines, (4.1%); and benzodiazepines (4.1%). Over this period, the proportion of fatalities involving drugs increased, with increased marijuana and opiates. At the same time the number of alcohol-related fatalities declined. Of interest was finding that there were differences in drugs involved in fatalities with different types of vehicles. Marijuana was more common among fatalities involving motorcycles (22%). Stimulants were most common in fatalities involving trucks. (23%).

Commercial Tractor-Trailer Drivers

Operation Trucker Check was conducted to determine the extent to which commercial tractor-trailer drivers were impaired by drugs, as well as to assess the trucks for equipment violations. The study included over 1,000 drivers and involved the voluntary collection of anonymous urine specimens, although there was a 19% refusal rate. Of those tested, 21% were positive for an illicit, prescription, or over-the-counter medication. Excluding nicotine and caffeine, the greatest proportion of positive results were for stimulants—methamphetamine, amphetamine, ephedrine, and cocaine. The percentage for marijuana was about half that for stimulants (4.3%). Only 1.3% of the drivers were positive for alcohol. Nonetheless, in light of the patterns of positive results, of those stopped, a handful, about 1.3%, were charged with driving under the influence. It ought to be noted that the trucking industry has mandatory drug testing.

Brookhuis KA, de Waard D, Samyn N. Effects of MDMA (ecstasy), and multiple drugs use on (simulated) driving performance and traffic safety. *Psychopharmacology* 173(3–4):440–445, 2004. (30 refs.)

Couper FJ, Pemberton M, Jarvis A, Hughes M, Logan BK. Prevalence of drug use in commercial tractor-trailer drivers. *Journal of Forensic Sciences* 47(3):562–567, 2002. (10 refs.)

Drummer OH, Gerostamoulos J, Batziris H, Chu M, Caplehorn JRM, Robertson MD, Swann P. The incidence of drugs in drivers killed in Australian road traffic crashes. *Forensic Science International* (134) 2/3:154–162, 2003. (38 refs.)

Fishbain DA, Cutler RB, Rosomoff HL, Rosomoff RS. Are opioid-dependent/tolerant patients impaired in driving-related skills? A structured evidence-based review (review). *Journal of Pain and Symptom Management* 25(6):559–577. (72 refs.)

Lenné MG, Dietze P, Rumbold GR, Redman JR, Triggs TJ. The effects of the opioid pharmacotherapies methadone, LAAM, and buprenorphine, alone and in combination with alcohol, on simulated driving. *Drug and Alcohol Dependence* 72(3):271–278, 2003. (42 refs.)

Office of Applied Studies. Drugged Driving. *The NSDUH Report.* September 16, 2003. A periodic newsletter published by the Office of Applied Studies, Substance Abuse and Mental Health Services. Available online, www.oad.samhsa.gov.

Raymon LP, Steele BW, Walls HC. Benzodiazepines in Miami-Dade County, Florida, driving under the influence (DUI) cases (1995–1998) with emphasis on Rohypnol (R): GC-MS confirmation, patterns of use, psychomotor impairment, and results of Florida legislation. *Journal of Analytical Toxicology* 23(6):490–499, 1999. (52 refs.)

Vainio A, Oillila J, Matikainen E, et al. Driving ability in cancer patients receiving long-term morphine analgesia. *Lancet* 346:667–670, 1995.

The following are common elements of relapse prevention:

- *Identifying high-risk relapse situations and developing strategies to deal with them.* Beyond providing people with essential skills, such efforts also increase the sense of competency. Having been provided a set of tools, there are things that clients can do. They aren't left feeling vulnerable with nothing to do but "keep a stiff upper lip" when problematic situations arise. In this, as well as all of the following instances, the effort is not for the counselor to identify the high-risk situation but for the client to do so.
- *Seeing relapse as a process, not as an event.* Relapse doesn't just come out of the blue. Often one can see a series of things, a chain of events, that precedes a relapse, be it experiencing stress or negative feelings or finding oneself (or placing oneself) in a vulnerable situation, such as going to a favorite old haunt, "just for the music." From this perspective there are any number of steps that can be taken to avoid the accumulation of things that lead to relapse.
- *Dealing with drug and alcohol cues and cravings.* Cues are the little things that can trigger craving. There are many possible cues, or reminders. Clients need to identify their own special package of things that set the ball rolling. It may be a morning cup of coffee for those hooked on cigarettes. It may be a particular setting or social situation, such as the Friday night after-work stop at a tavern with coworkers. In some instances people can avoid the situations that trigger the cravings. In other instances they may think through where the triggering event leads, and create a new competing and negative association.
- *Facing social pressures.* Social pressures include situations in which someone can feel that not drinking or using will make them feel conspicuous, or out of place. This is as common as outright comments of others or offers of a drink. When such offers occur, they often are not motivated by someone out "to get" the client but may be offered quite innocently. A waiter at a restaurant does not know that a customer is a nondrinker, or is trying to be.
- *Creating and nurturing a supportive social network.* Clients need to be able to recognize the supports that are available to them and, in turn, consider ways to use them. This includes families, friends, and self-help programs.
- *Developing skills to handle negative emotional states.* One of the most common triggers for a drink is, simply put, "feeling bad." A variety of very different clinical techniques may be used, depending on the nature of the bad feeling to avoid this. If there is someone who is very passive, never stating his or her views, assertiveness training may be useful. Or if the demon is frustration, finding alternative means of handling this is required.
- *Correcting errors in thinking.* Cognitive distortions—that is, automatic ways of thinking that don't really mesh with reality—can be a

problem. For example, there is the person who sees disaster around every corner, or the one who jumps to conclusions. Efforts to correct these erroneous assumptions are sometimes termed "cognitive therapy." Essentially this is a form of behavioral therapy that considers thoughts, the internal tapes we carry about and listen to without reflection. A variety of exercises have been devised to identify these internal voices, to examine the errors, and to draft new scripts to replace those old ones.

- *Developing a healthy and balanced lifestyle.* Much of the emphasis needs to be on balance. Working hard and accumulating stresses need to be balanced by relaxation, time-outs, and activities undertaken for no better reason than that they are enjoyable. It is also important to consider the role of exercise in providing a sense of well-being.

PHARMACOTHERAPY

Increasing knowledge about the biological factors that are a part of abuse and dependence has opened the doors for the development of drug therapies that may be useful in the treatment of addictive disorders. There is better understanding of the changes in the central nervous system that accompany abuse and dependence that has set the stage for the development of pharmacological agents. The substance abuse field has had some resistance to the use of drug therapies. While risking oversimplifcation, the objections at the core seem essentially punitive and moralistic. For some, pharmacological intervention is seen as offering dependent individuals an easy way out. Closely aligned with this is the notion that the use of drugs to treat addiction may be a "slippery slope." To some, this may send a mixed message and suggest that drugs can be used to solve problems or imply that sobriety or a drug-free life isn't really necessary. Some, too, have described drug therapy as a crutch. This doesn't seem out of place when one's legs are impaired. To the contrary, one might think of drug therapies as vital aids. For the alcohol-dependent person, drug therapy can buy sober time until the legs are steadier and other healthy supports are developed. The supports may be available already, but the individual has to be able to use them successfully.

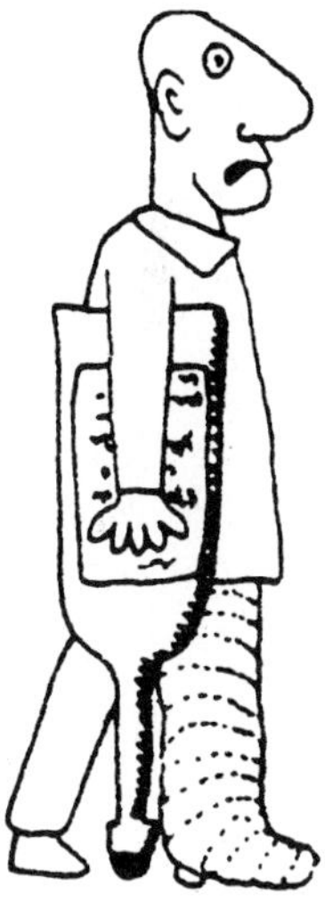

Disulfiram (Antabuse®)

Disulfiram has been available for over 50 years. It was discovered in the late 1940s, through a series of accidents. A group of Danish scientists found that the drug, disulfiram, they were testing for other purposes led to a marked reaction when the researchers who had been working with it had a drink. Disulfiram alters the metabolism of alcohol by blocking out an enzyme necessary for the breakdown of acetaldehyde, an intermediate product of alcohol metabolism. Acetaldehyde is normally present in the body in small amounts, in somewhat larger ones when alcohol is ingested, and in toxic amounts when alcohol is taken into the body after disulfiram medication. Thus, the basis for disulfiram's effects is its effect on metabolism, not its influence in the brain.

This adverse physical reaction is characterized by throbbing in the head and neck, flushing, breathing difficulty, nausea, vomiting, sweating, tachycardia (rapid heartbeat), weakness, and vertigo (dizziness). The intensity of the reaction varies from person to person and varies with the amount of disulfiram present and the amount of alcohol taken in. Disulfiram is excreted slowly from the body, so the possibility of a reaction is present for 4 to 5 days after the last dose and, in some cases, longer. Because of this reaction, Antabuse® has been widely used in the treatment of alcoholism.

Over the years since disulfiram's discovery, trial and error and research have led to some suggestions for its prescription, administration, and use in alcohol treatment. Disulfiram is not a cure. At best, it can postpone the drink. If the recovering client chooses to use disulfiram as an adjunct to AA, psychotherapy, group therapy, and so forth, it can be most useful in helping someone not have the impulsive drink. Because disulfiram stays in the system for such a long time, whatever caused the impulsive desire for a drink can be examined during the 5-day grace period.

Anyone who wishes to use disulfiram should be allowed to do so, provided they are physically and mentally able. The client should first be thoroughly examined by a physician to determine physical status. Some conditions contraindicate disulfiram usage. There is still some debate about the need for such caution with lower doses, but only the client's physician can decide this point. In some cases, physicians consider the risks of a disulfiram reaction not as dire as continued drinking certainly would be. When disulfiram is prescribed, generally 1 tablet (0.5 gm) is given daily for 5 days, and half a tablet daily thereafter. During the initial 5 days the client is carefully monitored for side effects. Once the client is receiving the maintenance dose, the client can continue for as long as it is beneficial. There are those who suggest that administration should be supervised for at least a short time. Preferably the spouse should not be the one expected to do this. Rather, this can be done through a visit to an outpatient clinic or an employee health clinic. Disulfiram should be used in combination with other supportive therapies.

The client taking disulfiram must be thoroughly informed of the dangers of a possible reaction. A variety of substances (such as cough syrup, wine sauces, and paint fumes) that contain some alcohol can cause a reaction. Clients taking disulfiram should be provided a list of such substances. Carrying a card or wearing a "Med-Alert disk," stating they are taking disulfiram, may be wise. Some medications given to accident victims or in emergency situations could cause a disulfiram reaction, compounding whatever else is wrong. There is no way to tell if an unconscious person has been taking disulfiram without such a warning.

Disulfiram can free the client from the constant battle against the bottle. When someone decides to take the pill on a given day, that person has made one choice that will postpone that drink for at least 4 or 5 days. If continuing to take it daily, that fourth or fifth day is always well out ahead. This allows time to begin acquiring or relearning behaviors other than drinking behaviors, and the habits of sobriety can take hold.

Medications Containing Alcohol

Alcohol, in its many forms, was for centuries virtually the only pharmacological agent available to physicians. In the twentieth century, alcohol had rather limited medicinal uses. Now, in addition to being used externally as an antiseptic (e.g., to wash the skin before giving an injection or taking a blood sample, except when this sample is being obtained to measure blood alcohol levels), its only other major use is as an "inert" medium or carrier for liquid medications. Alcohol is an almost universal ingredient of cough medicines and liquid cold preparations sold over the counter or by prescription. Furthermore, the percentage of alcohol in such preparations can be substantial. NyQuil, for example, contains 25% alcohol. That's 50 proof. Alcohol is also an ingredient in a variety of other kinds of commonly used liquid medications. Recovering individuals may be advised to avoid alcohol-containing preparations. For those taking disulfiram, it is imperative. Increasingly, there are preparations available for coughs and colds that do not contain alcohol. A pharmacist is always the most knowledgeable person to provide information on alcohol content of over-the-counter drugs and the availability of alternative preparations.

Anticraving Agents

While potentially triggered by events, feelings, and situations, craving has a physiological basis. The increased knowledge of brain chemistry and the various neurotransmitter systems that play a role in dependence opens a large array of possibilities for the development of drugs that can aid treatment. One drug, naltrexone, first used in the treatment of opiate addiction, has been found to be helpful as well in the treatment of alcohol dependence. In clinical trials it was found that those taking naltrexone, reported fewer episodes of craving. In addition, they reported less of a response to alcohol and drinking smaller amounts if drinking occurred. These early reports in treatment settings were particularly encouraging because the patients taking naltrexone were the "treatment failures"—those who had been in treatment several times and had never achieved sustained sobriety. Naltrexone was approved for alcohol treatment in 1995 and is marketed as Revia®. In the summer of 2004, acamprosate, marketed as Camporal®, was approved for use in the United States. It had been available in Europe for a number of years. Exactly how it works is unclear; unlike disulfiram, it doesn't interfere with alcohol metabolism and induce nausea. Unlike naltrexone, it doesn't appear to block the high associated with alcohol. However, it does act on one of the major neurotransmitter systems (GABA). It appears to reduce craving. Both of these drugs, like disulfiram, can be useful in opening a window of opportunity for clients, by buying time. By addressing the acute, short-term pressures, there is the chance to gain the tools needed to maintain sobriety and to make the needed long-term changes.

TREATMENT MATCHING

With such a variety of treatment approaches, the important question becomes "What works for whom?" Is it simply a matter of taste and clinician preference? Are some treatment approaches better suited for some clients? Is it possible to match patients to treatments that represent a better fit and yield better outcomes? It was this question that promoted the NIAAA to launch a major, multisite research effort, known as Project MATCH. Three treatment approaches were examined, selected because research had shown them to be effective in treating alcohol-dependence. So the natural follow-up question was "Are there some patients who would do better using one approach over the others?" The three approaches were (1) 12-step facilitation, (2) motivational enhancement therapy, and (3) cognitive-behavioral therapy. These were all provided as outpatient treatment. However, for some patients this outpatient treatment followed an inpatient stay, and thus represented aftercare.

The 1,700 clients who participated in the study were alcohol dependent. Each client agreed to an initial assessment and then to accept assignment to one of the treatment approaches. The initial assessment took about 8 hours. The goal was to measure 21 client characteristics that prior research had shown were related to treatment outcome. These included gender; drinking pattern; cognitive impairment; severity of alcohol dependence; prior AA involvement; self-efficacy (level of confidence that one can take action versus feeling immobilized); level of social functioning; presence of any psychiatric problem, and if present what type and its severity; religiosity; readiness to change; social support for abstinence; level of anger; and alcoholism type. There was follow-up of patients at 1 year and again at 3 years.

With only a few exceptions, clients, whatever their characteristics, did equally well in each of the treatment approaches. There were 4 patient characteristics that were significant. Those with these attributes did better or worse in their assigned treatment approaches:

1. *Presence of any psychiatric problem.* For those without any prior inpatient care, and no psychiatric illness, 12-step facilitation led to the best outcomes.

2. *Severity of alcohol dependence.* Those with more severe alcohol dependence who were receiving the assigned treatment (as aftercare) following inpatient care did better with 12-step facilitation.
3. *Level of anger.* Motivational enhancement therapy worked best for people who had high levels of anger and had not had inpatient treatment immediately prior to this therapy.
4. *Social support for abstinence.* Twelve-step facilitation therapy worked best for those with little family support. In effect, the members in 12-step programs became a substitute supportive family for these people.

Possibly the most useful immediate concrete result of this research initiative is not the findings. Instead, it may be the manuals that were developed as part of Project MATCH. They were used to train the clinicians participating in the study. For such research to have any validity, it is necessary that any treatment provided by clinician A is essentially the same as that offered by clinician B or C. To ensure that this was the case, training manuals were developed outlining how each treatment was to be provided. These manuals are very detailed, outlining goals for each session, how time should be allocated within sessions, and so forth. In the current environment in which health insurance will pay for a limited number of sessions, these manuals can be useful tools for any clinician.

In conclusion, all of the therapies presented in this chapter can be used together or in almost any combination that is deemed by the therapist to suit the client's situation. They can be considered as a set of tools, which the therapist and other treatment staff use as appropriate to the circumstances, in any particular combination, to get the job done.

RESOURCES AND FURTHER READING

The reports and treatment-related series available from various federal institutes are valuable tools. In addition to the NIAAA's *Alcohol Alert and Alcohol Health and Research World,* there are also the publications of NIDA, such as *NIDA Notes.* In addition, there are 2 series worth mentioning: The "TAP (Technical Assistance Protocols) Series" and the "TIP (Treatment Improvement Protocols) Series."

Technical Assistance Protocols

TAP 1. Fleisch B. *Approaches in the Treatment of Adolescents with Emotional and Substance Abuse Problems, Technical Assistance Publication (TAP) Series 1.* Rockville, MD: Office for Treatment Improvement, 1991. (42 refs.)

TAP 4. Baker F. *Coordination of Alcohol, Drug Abuse, and Mental Health Services, Technical Assistance Publication (TAP) Series 4.* Rockville, MD: Office for Treatment Improvement, 1991. (95 refs.)

TAP 5. Molloy JP. *Self-run, Self-supported Houses for More Effective Recovery from Alcohol and Drug Addiction, Technical Assistance Publication (TAP) Series 5.* Rockville, MD: Office for Treatment Improvement, 1992. (0 refs.)

TAP 14. Weber EM, Cowie R, eds. *Siting Drug and Alcohol Treatment Programs: Legal Challenges to the NIMBY Syndrome, Technical Assistance Publication (TAP) Series 14.* Rockville, MD: Substance Abuse and Mental Health Services Administration, 1995. (Chapter refs.)

TAP 17. Center for Substance Abuse Treatment. *Treating Alcohol and Other Drug Abusers in Rural and Frontier*

Areas, Technical Assistance Publication (TAP) Series 17. Rockville, MD: Center for Substance Abuse Treatment, 1995. (Chapter refs.)

TAP 18. Legal Action Center. *Checklist for Monitoring Alcohol and Other Drug Confidentiality Compliance, Technical Assistance Publication (TAP) Series 18.* Rockville, MD: Substance Abuse and Mental Health Services Administration, 1996. (0 refs.)

TAP 19. Gorski TT, Kelley JM. *Counselor's Manual for Relapse Prevention with Chemically Dependent Criminal Offenders, Technical Assistance Publication (TAP) Series 19.* Criminal Justice Subseries, Volume II. Rockville, MD: Office for Treatment Improvement, 1996. (0 refs.)

TAP 21. Center for Substance Abuse Treatment, Addiction Technology Transfer Centers Curriculum Committee, Deitch DA. *Addiction Counseling Competencies: The Knowledge, Skills, and Attitudes of Professional Practice, Technical Assistance Publication (TAP) Series 21.* Rockville, MD: Center for Substance Abuse Treatment, 1997. (Chapter refs.)

Treatment Improvement Protocols

TIP 2. Mitchell JL. *Pregnant, Substance-Using Women, Treatment Improvement Protocol (TIP) Series 2.* Rockville, MD: Center for Substance Abuse Treatment, 1993. (92 refs.)

TIP 3. McLellan AT, Dembo R. *Screening and Assessment of Alcohol- and Other Drug-Abusing Adolescents, Treatment Improvement Protocol (TIP) Series 3.* Rockville, MD: Center for Substance Abuse Treatment, 1993. (Chapter refs.)

TIP 6. Barthwell AG, Gibert CL. *Screening for Infectious Diseases Among Substance Abusers, Treatment Improvement Protocol (TIP) Series 6.* Rockville, MD: Center for Substance Abuse Treatment, 1993. (Chapter refs.)

TIP 7. Center for Substance Abuse Treatment. *Screening and Assessment for Alcohol and Other Drug Abuse Among Adults in the Criminal Justice System, Treatment Improvement Protocol (TIP) Series 7.* Rockville, MD: Center for Substance Abuse Treatment, 1994. (41 refs.)

TIP 8. Nagy PD. *Intensive Outpatient Treatment for Alcohol and Other Drug Abuse, Treatment Improvement Protocol (TIP) Series 8.* Rockville, MD: Center for Substance Abuse Treatment, 1994. (39 refs.)

TIP 9. Center for Substance Abuse Treatment. *Assessment and Treatment of Patients with Coexisting Mental Illness and Alcohol and Other Drug Abuse, Treatment Improvement Protocol (TIP) Series 9.* Rockville, MD: Center for Substance Abuse Treatment, 1994. (105 refs.)

TIP 11. Center for Substance Abuse Treatment. *Simple Screening Instruments for Outreach for Alcohol and Other Drug Abuse and Infectious Diseases, Treatment Improvement Protocol Series (TIP) Series 11.* Rockville, MD: Center for Substance Abuse Treatment, 1994. (7 refs.)

TIP 12. Davis C, Henderson R. *Combining Substance Abuse Treatment with Intermediate Sanctions for Adults in the Criminal Justice System, Treatment Improvement Protocol (TIP) Series 12.* Rockville, MD: Center for Substance Abuse Treatment, 1994. (16 refs.)

TIP 13. Gartner L, Mee-Lee D. *The Role and Current Status of Patient Placement Criteria in the Treatment of Substance Use Disorders, Treatment Improvement Protocol (TIP) Series 13.* Rockville, MD: Center for Substance Abuse Treatment, 1995. (35 refs.)

TIP 15. Selwyn PA, Batki SL, eds. *Treatment for HIV-Infected Alcohol and Other Drug Abusers, Treatment Improvement Protocol (TIP) Series 15.* Rockville, MD: Center for Substance Abuse Treatment, 1995. (84 refs.)

TIP 16. Rostenberg PO. *Alcohol and Other Drug Screening of Hospitalized Trauma Patients, Treatment Improvement Protocol (TIP) Series 16.* Rockville, MD: Center for Substance Abuse Treatment, 1995. (165 refs.)

TIP 17. Vigdal GL, ed. *Planning for Alcohol and Other Drug Abuse Treatment for Adults in the Criminal Justice System, Treatment Improvement Protocol (TIP) Series 17.* Rockville, MD: Center for Substance Abuse Treatment, 1995. (171 refs.)

TIP 19. Wesson DR, ed. *Detoxification from Alcohol and Other Drugs, Treatment Improvement Protocol (TIP) Series 19.* Rockville, MD: Substance Abuse and Mental Health Services Administration, 1995. (151 refs.)

TIP 23. Center for Substance Abuse Treatment; Shuman D, Henderson R, Shilton M, Sevick JR, Davis C, Heard J, Vitzthum V. *Treatment Drug Courts: Integrating Substance Abuse Treatment with Legal Case Processing. Treatment Improvement Protocol (TIP) Series 23.* Rockville, MD: Center for Substance Abuse Treatment, 1996.

TIP 24. Sullivan E, Fleming M. *A Guide to Substance Abuse Services for Primary Care Clinicians, Treatment Improvement Protocol (TIP) Series 24.* Rockville, MD: Substance Abuse and Mental Health Services Administration, 1997. (198 refs.)

TIP 25. Fazzone PA, Hotlin JK, Reed BG. *Substance Abuse Treatment and Domestic Violence, Treatment Improvement Protocol (TIP) Series 25.* Rockville, MD: Substance Abuse and Mental Health Services Administration, 1997. (208 refs.)

TIP 26. Blow FC. *Substance Abuse Among Older Adults, Treatment Improvement Protocol (TIP) Series 26.* Rockville, MD: Center for Substance Abuse Treatment, 1998. (418 book refs.)

TIP 27. Siegal HA, ed. *Substance Abuse Treatment and Case Management, Treatment Improvement Protocol (TIP) Series 27.* Rockville, MD: Center for Substance Abuse Treatment, 1998. (174 refs.)

TIP 28. O'Malley S. *Naltrexone and Alcoholism Treatment, Treatment Improvement Protocol (TIP) Series 28.* Rockville, MD: Center for Substance Abuse Treatment, 1998. (138 refs.)

TIP 29. Moore D. *Substance Use Disorder Treatment for People with Physical and Cognitive Disabilities, Treatment Improvement Protocol (TIP) Series 29.* Rockville, MD: Center for Substance Abuse Treatment, 1998. (86 refs.)

TIP 30. Field G. *Continuity of Offender Treatment for Substance Abuse Disorders from Institution to Community, Treatment Improvement Protocol (TIP) Series 30.* Rockville, MD: Center for Substance Abuse Treatment, 1998. (134 book refs.)

TIP 31. Winters KC. *Screening and Assessing Adolescents for Substance Use Disorders, Treatment Improvement Protocol (TIP) Series 31.* Rockville, MD: Center for Substance Abuse Treatment, 1999. (104 book refs.)

TIP 32. Winters KC. *Treatment of Adolescents with Substance Abuse Disorders, Treatment Improvement Protocol (TIP) Series 32.* Rockville, MD: Center for Substance Abuse Treatment, 1999. (122 book refs.)

TIP 33. Rawson RA. *Treatment for Stimulant Use Disorders. Treatment Improvement Protocol (TIP) Series 33.* Rockville, MD: Center for Substance Abuse Treatment, 1999. (226 refs.)

TIP 34. Barry KL. *Brief Interventions and Brief Therapies for Substance Abuse, Treatment Improvement Protocol (TIP) Series 34.* Rockville, MD: Center for Substance Abuse Treatment, 1999. (540 refs.)

TIP 35. Miller WR. *Enhancing Motivation for Change in Substance Abuse Treatment, Treatment Improvement Protocol (TIP) Series 35.* Rockville, MD: Center for Substance Abuse Treatment, 1999. (285 refs.)

TIP 36. Howard J. *Substance Abuse Treatment for Persons with Child Abuse and Neglect Issues, Treatment Improvement Protocol (TIP) Series 36.* Rockville, MD: Center for Substance Abuse Treatment, 2000. (476 refs.)

TIP 37. Batki SL, Selyn PA. *Substance Abuse Treatment for Persons with HIV/AIDS (TIP) Series 37.* Rockville, MD: Center for Substance Abuse Treatment, 2000. (342 refs.)

TIP 38. Young NK. *Integrating Substance Abuse Treatment and Vocational Services, Treatment Improvement Protocol (TIP) Series 38.* Rockville, MD: Center for Substance Abuse Treatment, 2000. (476 refs.)

TIP 40. McNichols L. *Clinical Guidelines for the Use of Buprenorphine in the Treatment of Opioid Addiction. Treatment Improvement Protocol (TIP) Series 40.* Rockville, MD: Center for Substance Abuse Treatment, 2004. (Chapter refs.)

TIP 41. Flores JM. *Substance Abuse Treatment: Group Therapy. Treatment Improvement Protocol (TIP) Series 41.* Rockville, MD: Center for Substance Abuse Treatment, 2005. (Chapter refs.)

Tip 42. Sacks S, Ries RK. *Substance Abuse Treatment for Persons with Co-Occurring Disorders. A Treatment Improvement Protocol (TIP) Series 42.* Rockville, MD: Center for Substance Abuse Treatment, 2005. (Chapter refs.)

Other Research and Resources

Aguilar TE, Munson WW. Leisure education and counseling as intervention components in drug and alcohol treatment for adolescents. *Journal of Alcohol and Drug Education* 37(3):23–34, 1992.

Anton RF, Swift RM. Current pharmacotherapies of alcoholism: A U.S. perspective. *American Journal on Addictions* 12(Special):S53–S68, 2003. (89 refs.)

Bouza C, Angeles M, Ana M, Maria AJ. Efficacy and safety of naltrexone and acamprosate in the treatment of alcohol dependence: A systematic review. *Addiction* 99(7):811–828, 2004. (75 refs.)

Brewer C, Meyers RJ, Johnsen J. Does disulfiram help to prevent relapse in alcohol abuse? *CNS Drugs* 14(5):329–341, 2000. (62 refs.)

Cook CCH. Addiction and spirituality. *Addiction* 99(6): 539–551, 2004. (31 refs.)

Cunningham JA, Humphreys K, Koski-Jannes A. Providing personalized assessment feedback for problem drinking on the Internet: A pilot project. *Journal of Studies on Alcohol* 61(6):794–798, 2000. (25 refs.)

Fals-Stewart W, Birchler GR. A national survey of the use of couples therapy in substance abuse treatment. *Journal of Substance Abuse Treatment* 20(4):277–283, 2001. (22 refs.)

Galanter M, Brook D. Network therapy for addiction: Bringing family and peer support into office practice. *International Journal of Group Psychotherapy* 51(1):101–122, 2001. (67 refs.)

Gossop M, Harris J, Best D, Man LH, Manning V, Marshall J, Strang J. Is attendance at Alcoholics Anonymous meetings after inpatient treatment related to improved outcomes? A 6-month follow-up study. *Alcohol and Alcoholism* 38(3):421–426, 2003. (43 refs.)

Harris WS, Gowda M, Kolb J, Strychacz CP, Vacek JL, Jones PG, et al. A randomized, controlled trial of the effects of remote, intercessory prayer on outcomes in patients admitted to the coronary care unit. *Archives of Internal Medicine* 159(19):2273–2278, 1999. (26 refs.)

Humphreys K, Moos R. Can encouraging substance abuse patients to participate in self-help groups reduce demand for health care? A quasi-experimental study. *Alcoholism: Clinical and Experimental Research* 25(5):711–716, 2001. (19 refs.)

Humphreys K, Wing S, McCartry D, Chappel J, Gallant L, Haberle B, et al. Self-help organizations for alcohol and drug problems: Toward evidence-based practice and policy. *Journal of Substance Abuse Treatment* 26:151–158, 2004. (25 refs.)

International Journal of Group Psychotherapy 51(1):1–122 (entire issue), 2001.

Kaskutas LA, Turk N, Bond J, Weisner C. The role of religion, spirituality and Alcoholics Anonymous in sustained sobriety. *Alcoholism Treatment Quarterly* 21(1):1–16, 2003 (26 refs.)

Klaw E, Humphreys K. Life stories of moderation management mutual help group members. *Contemporary Drug Problems* 27(4):779–804, 2000. (31 refs.)

Mann K. Pharmacotherapy of alcohol dependence: A review of the clinical data (review). *CNS Drugs* 18(8):485–504, 2004. (118 refs.)

McIntire D. How well does A.A. work? Analysis of published A.A. surveys (1968–1996) and related analyses/comments. *Alcoholism Treatment Quarterly* 18(4):1–18, 2000. (13 refs.)

Moak DH. Assessing the efficacy of medical treatments for alcohol use disorders (review). *Expert Opinion on Pharmacotherapy* 5(10):2075–2089, 2004. (132 refs.)

Moos RH, Moos BS. Long-term influence of duration and frequency of participation in Alcoholics Anonymous on individuals with alcohol use disorders. *Journal of Consulting and Clinical Psychology* 72(1):81–90, 2004. (46 refs.)

Myric H, Brady KT, Malcolm R. New developments in the pharmacotherapy of alcohol dependence. *American Journal on Addictions* 10(Supplement):3–15, 2001. (82 refs.)

O'Farrell TJ, Fals-Stewart W. Behavioral couples therapy for alcoholism and drug abuse. *Journal of Substance Abuse Treatment* 18(1):51–54, 2000. (22 refs.)

Overman GP, Teter CJ, Guthrie SK. Acamprosate for the adjunctive treatment of alcohol dependence. *Annals of Pharmacotherapy* 37(7/8):1090–1099, 2003. (62 refs.)

Panasa L, Caspib Y, Fournierc E, McCarty D. Performance measures for outpatient substance abuse services: Group versus individual counseling. *Journal of Substance Abuse Treatment* 25(4):271–278, 2003. (46 refs.)

Pardini DA, Plante TG, Sherman A, Stump JE. Religious faith and spirituality in substance abuse recovery: Determining the mental health benefits. *Journal of Substance Abuse Treatment* 19(4):347–354, 2000. (50 refs.)

Pendery ML, Maltzman IM, West LJ. Controlled drinking by alcoholics? New findings and a reevaluation of a major affirmative study. *Science* 217(4555):169–175, 1982.

Taskforce of College on Problems of Drug Dependence, Stitzer ML, Owen PL, Hall SM, Rawson RA, Petry NM. Standards for drug abuse treatment providers. *Drug and Alcohol Dependence* 71(2):213–215, 2003.
Note: This policy statement was adopted in the wake of discussion of funding faith-based programs. The issue for the College is not sponsorship of treatment by religious organizations, but the need, in all settings, for evidence-based clinical approaches to ensure that quality care is provided.

Tiebout HM. Surrender versus compliance in therapy, with special reference to alcoholism. *Quarterly Journal of Studies on Alcohol* 14:58–68, 1953.

Timko C, Moos RH, Finney JW, Lesar MD. Long-term outcomes of alcohol use disorders: Comparing untreated individuals with those in Alcoholics Anonymous and formal treatment. *Journal of Studies on Alcohol* 61(4):529–540, 2000. (41 refs.)

Wakefield PJ, Williams RE, Yost EB, Patterson KM. *Couple Therapy for Alcoholism: A Cognitive-Behavioral Treatment Manual.* New York: Guilford Press, 1996. (136 book refs.)

Zemore SE, Kaskutas LA, Ammon LN. In 12-step groups, helping helps the helper. *Addiction* 99(8):1015–1023, 2004. (46 refs.)

CHAPTER 11

Special Populations

There may be remarkable similarities between the 15-year-old alcohol abuser who also dabbles with cocaine and the 72-year-old retired schoolteacher who never drank anything stronger than a nice white wine. But that should not blind us to the equally significant differences. In this chapter, the focus is on the distinctive characteristics of special populations, particularly adolescents, college students, the elderly, women, and those in the workplace. Of course, there is no segment of the population untouched by alcohol or other drug problems. The chapter concludes with some suggested ways to identify the needs and issues of groups not discussed in this chapter. The groups selected for attention here are those that cut across all segments of society.

Much work has been done in respect to special population groups. This presentation just begins to skim the surface. Also, space does not allow equal discussion of racial and ethnic groups, or other groups with special issues, such as gays and lesbians. This textbook cannot begin to acquaint you with the characteristics and issues to bear in mind when working with clients from any particular ethnic, racial, or religious group. You are urged to speak with more experienced colleagues, as well as to turn to the ever-increasing body of literature on minorities, racial and ethnic, and special populations groups—African-Americans, Native Americans, Asian-Americans, Hispanics, migrant workers, the disabled. However, in thinking about the special considerations of the groups that are discussed, one of the hopes is to make you more sensitive to the characteristics of any client.

ADOLESCENTS

Adolescence is indeed a special period of life. It lies at the backdoor of childhood yet at the very doorstep of adulthood. At no comparable time

There is no time like the old time, when you and I were young.
OLIVER WENDELL HOLMES
"No Time Like the Old Time" c. 1858

in life do more physical and emotional changes take place in such a narrow span of time. "Adolescence" as a term is less than 150 years old. Before then, one grew straight from childhood into adulthood. The needs of family and culture demanded earlier work and community responsibilities. Survival depended on it. With increasing industrialization, children left the factories and fields to spend more time in school, play, and idle time. Society became increasingly aware of the presence of teenagers as a group who had, and still have, fairly undefinable roles and rights. Most texts define "adolescence" as the period from 12 to 21 years of age. Physical and legal determinants would suggest otherwise. Physical changes indicative of the beginning of adolescence may begin as early as age 7 and not end until the mid-20s. Voting age and draft registration requirements both at 18 have clouded the definition.

Developmental Issues

Physical Changes

The most striking aspect of adolescence is the rapid physical growth. These changes are mediated by the sex hormones. The accompanying rough charts indicate that the first recognizable change in the male is caused by a fat increase dictated by a small but gradual increase in estrogen. Every boy gains weight at the expense of height during these years. Some boys due to become tall and muscular men are quite chubby during these early adolescent years. The next body part to grow is the feet,

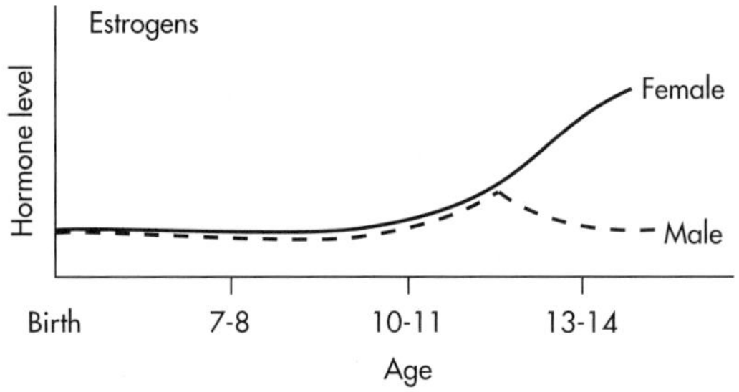

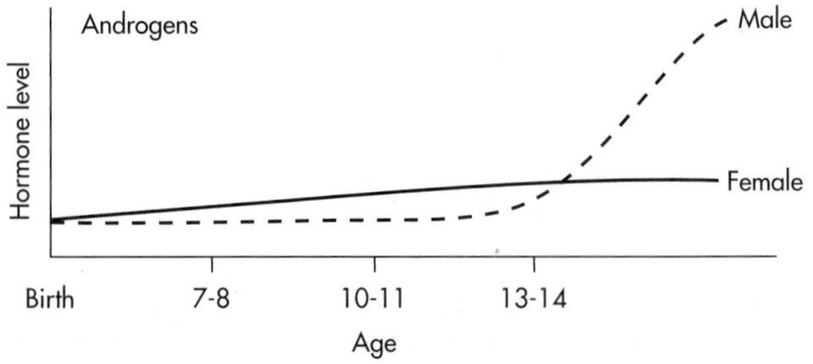

then the thighs, making him appear shortwaisted and gawky. This slows, allowing the rest of the body to catch up. Androgen influence appears later, with pigment changes in the scrotal sac, then enlargement of the testes and penis, the beginning of pubic hair, and early voice changes. The first nocturnal emission, or "wet dream," may occur as early as age 10 or as late as age 15. Even so, the majority of boys remain "relatively sterile" until age 15. The major male growth spurt appears at age 14½ and is due primarily to growth in the backbone. This averages 4 to 4½ inches over an 18-month period. Some boys shoot up 8 to 10 more inches during this time. Axillary and facial hair soon follow. Facial hair may develop entirely in 1 year. Other boys, equally normal but with different genes, may not complete the facial and body-hair growth until their mid- to late 20s.

A girl's first hormonal response is around age 7 or 8, with a normal vaginal discharge called leukorrhea. The feet then grow, but this is rarely as noticeable a change as in the male. A breast "button" begins about age 11 under the skin of one breast first, to be followed in weeks or months under the other breast. The breasts develop into adult breasts over a span of 4 to 5 years. Pubic hair begins approximately 6 months after the breast button stage. The hips widen, and the backbone gains 3 to 4 inches before she is ready for her menses. Although a critical body weight is not the only initiator, the body is influenced by this. If other criteria are met, such as developing breasts, pubic hair, widened hips, and growth spurt, a sample of American girls will begin their menses when weighing from 100 to 105 pounds. Nutrition has a great deal to do with the menarche (first menses); girls in countries with poor nutritional standards begin their menses 2 to 3 years later. The mean age for menarche in the United States is 12. (Pilgrim girls, who suffered from many nutritional deprivations, often had menarche delayed until age 17.) A regular menstrual cycle is not established immediately. Quite commonly a girl will have anovulatory (no egg) periods for 6 to 18 months before having ovulatory periods. This change may bring an increased weight gain, breast tenderness, occasional emotional lability, and cramps at the midcycle. These are consequences of progesterone, a hormone secreted by the ovary at the time of ovulation. An adult pattern in ovulation will not be completed until the early 20s.

We are indeed taller than our ancestors, which can be shown from historical evidence. Clothing, doorways, and furniture were made for shorter men and women. Better nutrition is mainly responsible for the changes seen.

Wine is a mocker, strong drink a brawler, and whoever is led astray by it is not wise.
Proverbs 20:1

Until puberty, boys and girls are equal in muscle strength (if corrected for height and weight). Total body fat increases in girls by 50% from ages 12 to 18, whereas a similar decrease occurs in boys. Muscle cell size and number increase in boys; muscle cell size alone increases in girls. Internal organs, such as the heart, double in size. Blood pressure increases with demands of growth. Pulse rate decreases, and the ability to

break down fatigue metabolites in muscle prepares the male, especially, for the role of hunter and runner which was so important for survival centuries ago.

Marked fatigue coupled with overwhelming strength is often difficult to fully appreciate. An adolescent may wolf down several quarts of milk, a full meal or two, play many hours of active sports, and yet complain bitterly of being tired at all times. This human metabolic furnace needs the food and rest as well as the drive to have the machine function and test itself out. These bodily inconsistencies often show in mood swings and unpredictable demands for self-satisfaction and physical expression.

The rapidity of these changes tends to produce an almost physiological confusion in many adolescents. Quite commonly they become preoccupied with themselves. This can lead to an overconcern with their health. In some instances it is almost hypochondriacal. Adolescents may complain of things that to an adult appear very minor. The thing to remember is that their concern is very real and deep. Attention should be paid to their concerns. Remembering the rapid rate of physical changes that confront adolescents makes their preoccupation with their bodies understandable.

Characteristics

Characteristically adolescence is an extremely healthy time of life. In general, adolescents do not die from the kinds of things that strike the rest of us, such as heart disease. The major causes of adolescent deaths are accidents, suicide, and homicide. Due to this healthiness, adults tend to assume that adolescents with problems are not really sick and thus do not give their complaints the attention they deserve. Furthermore, teens themselves may not perceive their health risk behaviors as dangerous or may be unable to articulate their concerns.

Another characteristic of adolescence is a tremendous need to conform to their peers. There is the need to dress alike, wear the same hairstyle, listen to the same music, and even think alike. A perpetual concern of the adolescent is that he or she is different. Although the sequence of physical development is the same, there is still variation in the age of onset and the rate of development. This can be a big concern for adolescents, whether the teenager is ahead, behind, or just on the norm. Worry about being different is a particular concern for the adolescent who may want or need professional help. The adolescent will not go unless it is "peer acceptable." Kids often stay away from caregivers out of fear. A big fear is that, if they go, sure enough, something really wrong will be found. This, to their minds, would officially certify them as different. They cannot tolerate that. They also fear that counselors will not respect confidentiality and will serve as parent surrogates, rather than working with the teen in a true counselor-client relationship.

Also characteristic of adolescence is wildly fluctuating behavior. It frequently alternates between wild, agitated periods and times of quiescence. A flurry of even psychotic-type thinking is not uncommon. This does not mean that adolescents are psychotic for a time and then get over it. There are just some periods when their thinking makes sense only to themselves and possibly to their friends. For example, if not selected for the play cast, he may be sure that it proves he will be a failure his entire life. If she is denied the use of the family car on Friday, she may overreact. With a perfectly straight face, she may accuse her parents of never letting her have the car, even as she stands there with the car keys, ready to drive off.

Adolescence is very much a time of two steps forward and one step back, with an occasional jog to one side or the other. Despite the ups and downs, it is usually a continuing, if uneven, upward trip to maturity.

Youth's the season made for joys.
ALEXANDER POPE
An Essay on Criticism, 1711

An important fact is that in early adolescence, girls are developmentally ahead of boys. At the onset of puberty, girls are physically about 2 years ahead. This makes a difference in social functioning because social development takes place in tandem with physical development. This can cause problems in social interactions for boys and girls of the same age. Their ideas of what makes a good party or what is appropriate behavior may differ considerably. The girls may consider their male peers "total dweebs." The boys, aware of the girls' assessments, may be shaken up, while the girls feel dislocated, too. With the uneven development of boys and girls during early adolescence, girls may be a year ahead of boys. There is a catching-up period later, but in dealing with younger adolescents, keep this disparity in mind.

Developmental Stages

Some speak about stages of adolescence as a framework for thinking about this intense period of life. *Early adolescence* is seen as extending from age 10 to 14, when teens are just beginning to confront puberty, when ties with parents tend to remain strong. In this stage, adolescents tend to be cooperative both with parents and other adults, and also to have strong anti–substance use attitudes. *Middle adolescence* is seen as encompassing those 15–17. This is when peers come center stage, with adolescents exerting greater influence in one another's life than was true earlier. This is the period when rejection and rebellion become more common. In terms of substance use, it is suggested that in this mid-stage, adolescents may tend to misperceive their peers' substance use as well as the attendant potential health risks. *Late adolescence,* assigned to those ages 18–20 is seen as marking the transition to adulthood. While more self-reliant, adolescents do seek adult guidance and also have a better appreciation of the health and emotional consequences of their choices.

A problem with dividing adolescence into a sequence of stages is that it suggests things are more orderly than is the case. Another way to consider the adolescent period is not in terms of calendar years, but in terms of development issues. There are fairly clear-cut signs that mark the beginning of the adolescent period. But when does adolescence end?

Clearly there is more to adolescence than just physical maturation. Defining the end can lead to philosophical discussions of "maturity." Doesn't everyone know a 45-year-old or 65-year-old "adolescent"? There is more to assigning an end point than just considering a numerical age. One way of thinking about the adolescent period is to assign to it four developmental tasks. From this point of view, once the tasks have been reasonably accomplished, the person is launched into adulthood. These tasks are not tackled in any neat order or sequence. It is not like the consistent pattern of physical development. They are more like four interwoven themes, the dominant issues of adolescence.

After wine, out comes the truth.
Chinese proverb

Developmental Tasks

The first task of adolescence is *acceptance of the biological role.* This means acquiring some degree of comfort with one's identity as either male or female. It is an intellectual effort that has nothing to do with sexuality or experimentation with sexuality.

The second task is the *struggle to become comfortable with one's sexuality.* This does not mean struggling with the question of "how to make out at the drive-in." It is much more the important question: "Who am I as a sexual person, and how do I get along with those to whom I am actually or potentially sexually attracted?" Before adolescence, children are far more casual with each other. With adolescence, those days are over. Simply to walk by someone that one could be sexually attracted to and say, "Hi," without blushing, giggling, or throwing up can be a problem. To become a person capable of sexual and emotional intimacy—able to carry on all manner of social and eventually sexual activities with another person—does not come easily. It is fraught with insecurity and considerable self-consciousness. If you force yourself to remember your own adolescence, some memories of awkwardness and uncertainty come to the fore. Thus, there is the adolescent who does not ask for a date because of the anticipated no. Being dateless is much more tolerable than hearing a no.

The third task is the *choice of an occupational and social identity.* It becomes important to find an answer to "What am I going to do (be)?" As important as a specific occupational niche are the values and attributes that are seen as a part of it. There are usually several false starts to this one. Think of the 5-year-old who wants to be a fireman. He probably never will be, but he gets a lot of mileage for a while just thinking he is. It is not so different for adolescents. It is not helpful to pooh-pooh the first ideas they come up with. Nor is handing over an inheritance and saying, "Go to it," recommended. They need some time to work it out in their heads. A fair amount of indecision, plus some "crazy" ideas, are to be expected.

The fourth task is the *struggle toward independence.* This is a major conflict. There is the internal push to break away from home and parents and, at the same time, the desire to remain comfortably cared for. The conflict shows up in rebellion, because there are not many ways to feel independent when living at home, being fed, checked on, prodded, and examined by parents. Rebellion of some type is common during this period, especially among male adolescents. However, the rebellion need not be over major issues, and may be relatively invisible and untraumatic for both adolescent and parent, if the parents can avoid being drawn into power struggles.

There are many roadblocks to the completion of these four basic tasks. One results from a social paradox. Adolescents are physically ready for adult roles long before our society allows this. Studies of other societies and cultures point this out. In some societies adolescence doesn't cover a decade or more; young people leave school, for example, at earlier ages to go to work or into apprenticeships. Our society dictates, instead, that people stay in an adolescent position for a long time: middle school, high school, college, graduate school. Another social paradox comes from the mixed messages: on the one hand, it's "Be heterosexual, get a date," "Get a job," "Be grown up." On the other hand, it's "Be back by 1 a.m.," "Save the money for college," and "Don't argue with me." The confusion of "Grow up, but stay under my control" can introduce tensions. Another roadblock can be posed by alcohol and other drug use. Of all groups, adolescents are those most likely to be involved with drugs other than alcohol. In considering adolescents, it is imperative to think broadly, in terms of substance use, and problems associated with use, not just in terms of alcohol and alcohol abuse/dependence.

Hide our ignorance as we will, an evening of wine soon reveals it.

HERACLEITUS
c. 500 B.C.

Rebellion

Rebellion can be seen in such things as manner of dress and appearance. It is usually the opposite of what the parents' generation accepts. Little ways of testing out parents crop up in being late from a date, buying something without permission, or arguing with parents over just about anything. The kids are aware of their dependence, and they don't like it. There is even some shame over being in such a position. It is important that parents recognize the rebellion and respond to it. As if following the edict of "Be friends with your kids," some well-meaning parents may accept any behavior from their kids. For example, if the kids, for the sake of rebellion, took home some marijuana to smoke, their parents might just light up, too. Often the kids will do whatever they can just to get their parents angry. They are often reminded by others of how much they look or act like their father or mother, and they don't want that. Adolescents want to be themselves. They do not want to be simply younger copies of their parents, whom they probably don't like much at the moment. Going out and drinking with the gang, doing something weird to their hair that Mom and Dad will hate, not cleaning their rooms, or helping the neighbors but not their parents are all fairly common ways of testing out and attempting to assert independence.

Hi, Dear, why don't you invite your friends in, and we can all sit around and smoke some joints.

Destructive rebellion can occur when the parents either do not recognize the rebellion or do not respond to it. It can take many forms, such

Drink not the third glass,
which thou can't tame
When once it is within thee.
GEORGE HERBERT
"The Church Porch," 1633

as running out of the house after an argument and driving off at 80 miles per hour, getting really drunk, running away, or, for girls, getting pregnant despite frequent warnings from their perhaps overly restrictive parents to avoid all sexual activities.

Alcohol and Other Drug Use

Alcohol and other drug use is common in adolescence. According to *Monitoring the Future,* the regular federal survey of adolescent alcohol and other drug use, in 2003, among eighth graders, 47% had tried alcohol. By the twelfth grade, the percentage who had ever used alcohol increased to 78%. About half of high school seniors are considered current drinkers, having had a drink in the past month. Of seniors who are drinkers, over half report having been drunk in the past month.

In terms of illicit drugs, 23% report having used a drug by grade 8, with that number rising to 51% by twelfth grade. See Table 11.1.

Illicit drug use had been increasing through the 1990s, until 1998 when it began to decline. The majority of the decline in illicit drug use, beginning in 1998, can be attributed to a reduction in marijuana use. But stimulant use too has shown a similar decline. The situation with alcohol is essentially the same. There has been a decline in past year's drinking for all three age groups, as well as a similar downward trend among drinking in the past month. These declines in drinking actually began before the downturns seen with illicit drugs. However, there is less decline in the proportion of kids who report being drunk in the past month. This suggests that there is a continuing contingent of regular excessive drinkers. It is sometimes suggested that declines in illicit drug use are offset by increases in alcohol use. That seems not to be the case.

What gets lost when statistics are presented this way is that heavy drinking is concentrated in a *very* small segment of all adolescents. This small group consumes the overwhelming majority of all alcohol. Binge drinking, defined as those who report drinking 5 or more drinks per occasion, is reported by 3% of those 12–14 years old and 18% of those 15–17. Accordingly, it has been estimated among all those 12–14, about 3% consume 80% of the alcohol. For those 15–17, only 12% of the adolescents in that age group consume almost 89% of the alcohol.

This survey also asks questions about kids' notion of the risks that accompany the use of various drugs, their sense of how easy it is to get alcohol or other drugs, as well as their level of disapproval of alcohol/drug use. Consistently the level of use of any drug is related to the individual's perceptions of riskiness and the level of personal disapproval. As perceptions of risk go down, use goes up; similarly, as the level of disapproval goes down, use increases.

Despite widespread alcohol use, adolescents tend to be uninformed about the effects of alcohol as a drug. Particularly in middle adolescence, short on facts, they tend more than adults to rely on myths. For example,

Table 11.1 Alcohol and Other Drug Use by Eighth, Tenth, and Twelfth Graders, 2003

	Lifetime Use (%)			Use in Past 30 Days (%)		
Substance	**8th Grade**	**10th Grade**	**12th Grade**	**8th Grade**	**10th Grade**	**12th Grade**
Alcohol	47.0%	66.9%	78.4%	19.7%	35.4%	47.5%
Cigarettes	31.4	47.4	57.2	10.2	16.7	24.4
Smokeless tobacco	11.2	16.9	18.3	4.1	5.3	6.7
Any illicit drug use	22.8	41.4	51.1	9.7	19.5	24.1
Any illicit drug other than marijuana	13.6	19.7	27.7	4.7	6.9	10.4
Marijuana	17.5	36.4	46.1	7.5	17.0	21.5
Inhalants	15.8	12.7	11.2	4.1	2.2	1.5
Hallucinogens	4.0	6.9	10.6	1.2	1.5	1.8
Ecstasy	3.2	5.4	8.3	0.7	1.2	1.5
Cocaine	3.6	5.1	7.7	0.9	1.3	2.1
Heroin	1.6	1.5	1.5	0.4	0.3	0.4
w/needle	1.0	0.9	0.7	0.3	0.2	0.3
no needle	1.1	1.0	1.8	0.3	0.3	0.4
Amphetamines	8.4	13.1	14.4	2.7	4.3	5.0
Methamphetamine	3.9	5.2	6.2	1.2	1.4	1.7
Tranquilizers	4.4	7.8	10.2	1.4	2.4	2.8
Steroids	2.5	3.0	3.5	0.7	0.8	1.3

From: *Monitoring the Future.* 2003 data. Johnston LD, O'Malley PM, Bachman JG, Schulenberg JE. *Monitoring the Future Volume I. Secondary School Students.* Bethesda, MD: NIDA, 2004.

beer, the overwhelmingly favorite beverage, is thought to be less intoxicating than distilled spirits. One study some years ago showed that of the adolescents surveyed, 42% believed 5 to 7 cans of beer can be drunk in two hours without risk of intoxication, or believed that cold showers can sober someone up, or that driving would be not be "much worse" under the influence. A part of adolescents' thinking is the notion that they are invulnerable, that nothing can or will hurt them. As a result, adolescents do not consider their being in an accident a real possibility, much less one that might result in serious injury or death.

Similarly, this thinking is evident in their attitudes toward nicotine. Teenagers seem to have bought the notion that "light" cigarettes pose fewer health hazards and are less likely to prompt addiction than regular cigarettes. Adolescents chalk up adult smoking to addiction. They attribute smoking by adolescents as efforts to "be in" or to "make a statement." Certainly this is true, but the role of dependence to explain nicotine use among their age peers is largely ignored.

Not unexpectedly, adolescents view alcohol or other drug use quite differently than do their parents. If asked about motives for adolescents' drug use, parents almost always cite things with negative connotations, such as boredom, rebellion, loneliness, or social pressure. However, when kids are questioned, the reasons they put forward tend to be positive—for fun, curiosity, good feelings and relaxation. One of the primary ways in which media's portrayal of smoking has an impact is its depiction of smoking as the norm and an activity of attractive people, rather than as unhealthy, frowned upon by others, and deviant. Far before adolescence, children are aware of different drugs and the varying ways in which they are used. As early as the first grade, children have fairly well-formed notions of whether they will try different drugs, be it alcohol, tobacco, marijuana, or inhalants, when they get older. Sure enough, follow-up of these kids shows that those who voiced an intention to try drugs indeed did so. Such intentions may be one of the early warning signs of subsequent use as teens.

Adolescents use alcohol in many different ways, some of which are a normal part of the whole process. The "try it on" thread runs throughout adolescence. Alcohol is just one of the things to be tried. With drinking being a large part of adult society, it is natural that the adolescent struggling toward adulthood will try it. Drinking is also attractive for either rebellious or risk-taking behavior. In addition, given its pharmacological properties, alcohol can also serve to anesthetize the pain of adolescents who are isolated or who are subjected to abuse by family or peers. Whatever the supposed reasons for use, problems can follow in the wake.

Associated Problems

Not unexpectedly, there are also problems accompanying adolescent drinking and drug use. To cite just a few of the statistics from the ever-growing pile:

- Twenty-eight percent of high school seniors report having had 5 or more drinks in a row in the past two weeks.
- One of 3 high school seniors report having been drunk in the past month.
- Adolescents who began drinking before age 15 are 5 times as likely to develop alcohol dependence than those who begin drinking at age 21.
- In a large study of adolescents age 14 or 15 seen in an emergency room for life-threatening injuries, 71% tested positive for alcohol or drugs.

- A statewide study of all emergency room visits by those ages 12–25, found 32% were positive for alcohol. In examining subgroups, for those ages 12–17 years 12% were positive; for ages 18–20 the rate was 20%; for ages 21–25 the rate was 40%.
- In the United States, 73.6% of all deaths among youth and young adults ages 10–24 years result from just four causes—motor vehicle crashes, other unintentional injuries, homicide, and suicide. All of these are alcohol-related.
- The use of alcohol and other drugs in early adolescence increases the risk of dropping out of school, becoming pregnant or impregnating someone, becoming a teenage parent, and living independently from parents or guardians prematurely.

One way to understand the high incidence of problems with substance abuse in adolescence is in terms of the adolescent developmental tasks cited earlier. The first task described was the acceptance of one's biological role. For women, the onset of their menstrual cycle provides clear biological evidence of their transition into adulthood. For males, the transition may be more difficult. But for both in contemporary America the question of how to know one is an adult is often difficult. For many adolescents, drinking serves as a rite of passage. Not only is it an adult activity, but it is also a way to be part of the crowd. Drinking can provide entry to a group of peers. Even as an adult, one is often encouraged to drink and given messages that not to drink is to be antisocial. For adolescents, with their intolerance of differences and their increased vulnerability to following along with peers' behavior, not drinking at a party where others are drinking may be even harder than for adults.

As some heads cannot carry much wine, so it would seem that I cannot bear so much society as you can. I have an immense appetite for solitude.
HENRY DAVID THOREAU
Letter to Daniel Ricketson, 1857

The second developmental task is the struggle to become comfortable with one's sexuality. This can be threatening to many adolescents. Alcohol can be used to avoid intimacy or to seek intimacy without responsibility. It can also help them avoid dealing with concerns or confusion related to sexual orientation. "I sure missed last night—I was really plastered!" can be said by either boys or girls to disavow what happened the night before. The same is true in the sexual realm, as a means of experimenting without taking responsibility. In our society, being drunk has long provided a "way out." Often people are not held accountable for actions that occur when they are drunk. Thus, getting drunk can often help adolescents express these increasingly powerful impulses, without really taking direct responsibility for their behavior. This can include not taking proper precautions, as the rising number of AIDS cases among this group and unwanted teenage pregnancies can testify.

The third important task mentioned is the choice of an occupational and social identity. Part of the task of gaining an independent identity involves experimentation in all realms. Adolescents may use alcohol for help in experimenting with various roles and identities. Closely connected to this experimentation is risk taking, some of which involves

Alcohol postpones anxiety, then multiplies it.
MASON COOLEY, 1991

physical danger. Adolescents are said to have a "sense of invulnerability." Unfortunately, alcohol can further increase this sense of invulnerability and lead to risk taking with dangerous consequences.

Part of the task of attaining independence is learning to set limits for themselves, to develop self-control. For some adolescents, this is more difficult than for others. It is particularly difficult about issues like drinking where societal messages and alcohol advertising suggest that "having more than one" is appropriate adult behavior. In the process of learning self-control, adolescents react negatively to adults setting limits. If parents are too aggressive in forbidding alcohol use, it may backfire. Further confusing matters is the fact that adolescent development is characterized by changes in patterns of thinking. Before the ages of 12 to 13 years, adolescents generally adhere to concrete rules for behavior. From ages 13 to 15 years, adolescents are likely to question the justification of set rules. They feel that conventions are arbitrary, so rules supporting them are invalid. By the age of 16, most of them begin to realize that some rules are necessary.

As these adolescent developmental tasks are accomplished, the number of problem drinkers declines. Also, problems associated with drinking decline. But for a significant proportion of adolescent drinkers, these problems will persist and grow worse. For far too many, the problems attendant to drinking may end in death or disability.

Risk Factors

When thinking of risk factors for substance use and abuse, it is easy to feel lost under a pile of data. One way to think of these is in terms of concentric circles. At the center are the risk factors that reside in the individual. Surrounding these individual-based factors are external factors that can be just as influential.

In terms of the *individual* the most potent risk factor is genetic endowment. This can present a risk as a predisposition to alcohol and other substance use problems. Another risk factor is one's temperament: the tendency for risk taking, or novelty seeking, or being less socially inhibited. (See Chapter 4.) Age at first use has been said to increase the risk for problems. However, it now appears that age of initiating regular use and the age at which heavier use appears may be more significant landmarks than first use. Appearing older than peers increases risk. Other things that increase vulnerability are rebelliousness, nonconformity, resistance to authority, alienation from one's culture, feelings of failure, hopelessness, a failure to form close relationships, along with inadequate tools for coping, or low self-esteem.

The NIAAA has initiated a series of rigorous studies of the natural history of alcohol use disorders; these studies are providing more insight into alcohol use disorders. Among the factors that stand out is the presence of childhood mental disorders, including conduct disorder, attention-deficit hyperactivity disorder, and major depressive disorders. A common denominator of these disorders might be a more general trait indicating psychological dysregulation, which has a significant genetic component. Also now we recognize that the adolescent brain is still maturing during adolescence, and that the rate of maturation may be a factor in placing some at risk, as well as being a process disrupted by alcohol use.

Beyond the factors residing in the individual, there are risk factors that are associated with characteristics of the *family*. There is increased risk of substance use problems in those who grow up in families with less cohesiveness, where there is less of a feeling of "family-ness." Also, parenting styles can increase risk—an absence of supervision, over-permissiveness, an absence of clear disapproval of teen substance use. In addition, access to alcohol or drugs in the home increases risk. A history of childhood neglect, or physical or sexual abuse, is also a risk factor. In terms of the family's alcohol use, while parents' drinking exerts an influence, this influence is modest compared to that of siblings.

Peers can be another source of risk. Risk increases if peer groups include those who use and are experimenting with alcohol and/or other drugs, or provide access to them. Typically teens' use of alcohol and other drugs mirrors that of their friends. Of course this raises the perennial chicken and egg problem. However, there is the sense that teens who are susceptible to alcohol and drug use find one another, as opposed to recruiting their "innocent" peers. The teen years are marked by belonging to cliques: the jocks, the nerds, the cheerleaders, the preppies, the arty types. And then there is the inevitable group, known as the "druggies." This is the group where those who don't fit elsewhere may find a home.

I pray thee let me and my fellow have
A haire of the dog that bit us last night.
JOHN HEYWOOD, C. 1500

School experiences aside from friends are associated with risk factors. Those who drop out of school are at greater risk. Interestingly, attending a private school does not reduce the risk of alcohol or other drug use. But the levels of use are highest among kids who attend alternative high schools. Having a job can be a risk factor. Those who work at an outside job are more likely to use substances, and the risk increases with the number of hours worked. To what extent this is an issue of money or of increased opportunities due to associations with older persons is unknown.

Further removed from the individual level are the factors that reside in the *community*. Unsafe, chaotic communities, without social services or recreational opportunities, but possibly a drug trade, can spawn substance abuse, as well as being associated with higher levels of violence. Communities differ too along other dimensions, such as access to alcohol. Then there is the larger social scene which touches everyone.

Protective Factors

There are also factors that reside within the individual, the family, and the community that are protective factors, characteristics that are associated with lower risks of alcohol and other drug problems. Protective factors include strong ties to family and community; involvement in church/religious groups; style of parenting that involves setting limits, supervision, and explicit expectancies around substance use; certain personality characteristics such as a sense of optimism, self-esteem, being a non–risk taker; living in a stable community without drug trade, no street violence. Thus, many are the mirror image of risk factors.

Signs of a Possible Problem

Often the temptation is to dismiss adolescent alcohol or other drug problems, considering them as just a stage, a normal feature of adolescence. On the other hand, it is possible to presume that any use of substances will destine the adolescent to dependence. This too is not the case. The following signs may signal a substance use problem. However, they are not exclusively linked to substance use. Thus, if an evaluation rules out substance use, further exploration is required to address what is going on.

School activities
- Unexplained drop in grades
- Unexplained drop in school performance
- Irregular school attendance

Health indicators
- Accidents
- Frequent "flu" episodes, chronic cough, chest pains, "allergy symptoms"
- Feelings of loneliness or depression
- Inability to fight off common infections, fatigue, loss of energy
- Short-term memory impairment
- More than "the normal" adolescent mood changes, irritability, anger

Family relationships
- Less interest in school or family social activities, sports, and hobbies
- Not bringing friends home
- Failing to return home after school
- Unaccounted-for personal time
- Failing to provide specific answers to questions about activities
- Unexplained disappearance of possessions in the home
- Verbal (or physical) mistreatment of younger siblings

Relationships with friends
- Old friends dropped
- New group of friends
- Attendance at parties where parents or adults are not present
- Strange phone calls

Thou wine are the friend of the friendless, though a foe to all.
HERMAN MELVILLE
Mardi, 1885

Personal issues
- Increased money or poor justification of how money was spent
- Personal priorities changed
- "Druggie" clothing and jewelry

- "Drug" memorabilia
- Preference for isolation, solitude

Wine does not intoxicate people—they do it to themselves.
Chinese proverb

Indicators of a significant problem would include any covering up or lying about drug and alcohol use or activities, losing time from school because of alcohol or drug use, being hospitalized or arrested because of drinking or drug-related behavior or truancy, as well as the alcohol or drug use itself. Alcohol or drug use at school generally indicates heavy use. Be alert to these signs and symptoms in children of alcoholics, who have a genetic predisposition and a parent for whom alcohol is a loaded issue.

Natural History

One way to think about the emergence of alcohol use disorders is as a series of stages. One such perspective is sketched out in Figure 11.1. There are 6 stages: Abstinence, Experimentation, Regular Use, Problem Use, Abuse, and Dependence.

This model is very similar to the stages and progression that was sketched out by Vernon Johnson and discussed in detail in Chapter 7. There is one significant difference: Johnson had 4 stages, learning the mood swing —> seeking the mood swing —> harmful use —> drinking to feel normal. The transition between stages 2 and 3 was defined by Johnson as an "invisible line." What signaled that this line had been crossed was the continued use of alcohol despite negative consequences. Johnson's formulation was derived from reports of adults. It is not unreasonable that for the 38-year-old who has been drinking for over 2 decades, the events taking place at that point of transition have long faded from memory. However if one could move back in time, it might be a different story.

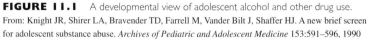

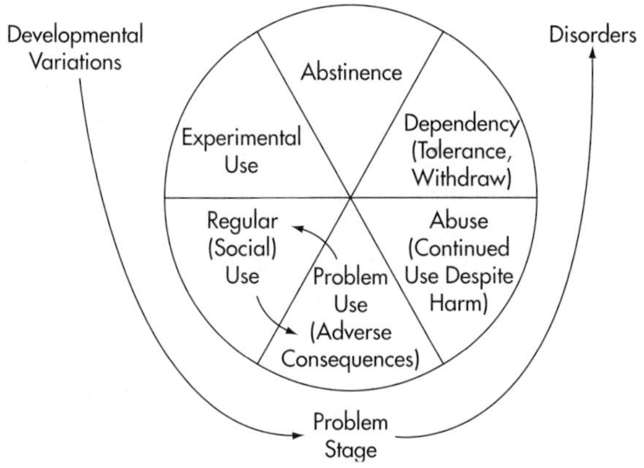

FIGURE 11.1 A developmental view of adolescent alcohol and other drug use.
From: Knight JR, Shirer LA, Bravender TD, Farrell M, Vander Bilt J, Shaffer HJ. A new brief screen for adolescent substance abuse. *Archives of Pediatric and Adolescent Medicine* 153:591–596, 1990

Table 11.2 Natural History of Substance Use Problems: Signs and Symptoms of Adolescent Substance Use

Stage	Pattern of Use	School	Peers	Family	Self
Experimentation	Occasional	← Few effects →			
Regular use (Seeking the mood swing)	Weekends Occasional weekdays	Grades may become erratic	Hanging around drug-using crowd	Some increase in family conflict Some isolation, secrecy	Changes in dress or choice of music, increased mood swings
Problem use (Negative consequences)	Weekends Occasional weekdays	Grades may become erratic	Hanging around drug-using crowd	Some increase in family conflict Some isolation, secrecy	Changes in dress or choice of music, increased mood swings
Abuse (Preoccupation with use)	Occasional weekdays, e.g., before or after school	Decreased school performance	Avoids straight friends	Verbal and physical fights	Depression, stealing, fabrication, and misperception of events
Dependence (Use to feel normal or as a requisite for functioning)	Daily, instead of usual activities	May drop out or be expelled	Alienation from original friends, antisocial behavior, sexual acting out	Increased shame and conflict	Guilt, remorse, depression, anger, paranoia, physical deterioration

Modified from Kinney J. *Alcohol use and its medical consequences: Alcohol use, abuse and dependence.* Timonium, MD: Milner Fenwick, 1989.

Imagine taking a microscope to examine the space between Johnson's second and third stages, the point of the invisible line. What one would see is neither "invisible" nor a "line." Rather one finds terrain that in essence is the equivalent of the stage "Problem Use" as found in Figure 11.1. This is the stage in which things are fluid. There is the potential for the individual to recognize problems, identifying behaviors and situations which are related to problematic use, and make significant changes that reduce further risk. Alternatively, in the absence of change, there is significant probability that it will proceed into harmful use/abuse and from there to dependence. The characteristics of each of these stages are summarized in Table 11.2.

Research Insights

The above is a useful paradigm that has emerged from those working with adolescents, drawing too upon what is known about adults. Major research is only now being conducted on adolescent alcohol use disorders. Inevitably down the line this will entail our rethinking how we view alcohol use disorders in adolescents. Some of the highlights:

- In this research, the terminology being used is the broad category of "alcohol use disorders," which encompasses the formal classifications found in the American Psychiatric Association's *Diagnostic and Statistical Manual* (*DSM*) under "alcohol abuse" and "alcohol dependence."
- There is considerable variability in adolescent substance use disorders, as well as treatment outcomes. A portion of adolescents with a diagnosis of abuse seemingly use alcohol in a nonproblematic fashion in later life.
- The diagnostic criteria used with adults are not a perfect fit when it comes to teens. (See page 366.)
- Of concern is the discovery that in adolescents there are physical changes in the brain, along with impairments in neurological functioning that can accompany alcohol use disorders. Impairment in attention, in some kinds of memory and language, and in problem-solving skills have been identified, most typically among more serious cases of dependence. While modest, these impairments are real and persist for several years following treatment. Follow-up is only now being conducted, so the degree of permanence of these impairments is not fully known.

  Often unappreciated is the fact that while teens may be sexually mature and look adult, in fact the adolescent brain continues to develop during throughout the teenage years. Alcohol involvement appears to interfere with the maturation of the nervous system; the area affected is the hippocampus, a portion of the brain involved with aspects of memory and emotion. Imaging studies have shown a reduction of the volume of the hippocampus among some teens who have been drinking heavily.
- There are those who speak of marijuana or tobacco as gateway drugs. This is prompted by the notion that the use of some common substances increases the risk of using other illicit drugs. An alternative view is termed the common risk model. In this view—which research seems to support—general factors increase the likelihood of using alcohol or drugs. However, the particular substance used is often a matter of circumstances.

O thou invisible spirit of wine, if thou hast no name to be known by, let us call thee devil.
WILLIAM SHAKESPEARE
Othello

Working with Adolescents

Conundrums and Challenges

Adolescent substance abuse and dependence clearly exists and requires treatment. However, the more difficult tasks are tied to earlier stages of adolescent substance use, specifically: experimentation, the emergence of a regular pattern of use, and the occurrence of problems associated with use. There is a major conundrum. As a society there is deemed to be no socially or legally acceptable use prior to age 21. But the reality is that a third of tenth graders and nearly half of high school seniors can be described as regular drinkers, having had a drink in the past month. If adults' imploring—be it parents, teachers, coaches, clergy, government officials, or substance abuse counselors—"you really shouldn't" was going to have had an impact, presumably we should have seen it by now! With such a substantial percentage of adolescents being regular drinkers, it is disingenuous to try to respond to those who drink as if they were particularly deviant or troubled.

Another reality needs to be acknowledged. The opinion of a parent, or a teacher, or a school nurse simply doesn't carry much weight, especially after the fact. To drink or not to drink is ultimately going to be the decision of the adolescent. The best others can do is to provide information that may make this as informed a decision as possible. Collectively, as adults, we can have more influence in delaying the onset of use and through the steps we take to lessen high-risk drinking when teens choose to drink. However, the latter isn't possible if there is a societal atmosphere of denial and collusion not to acknowledge what is going on. For clinicians who are going to work with adolescents, it is imperative that they be able to respond to adolescent alcohol/drug use as a given, and not presume the task is convincing adolescent clients that drinking (drug use) is wrong. If a clinician is unable to lay aside these judgments, then their ability to work with adolescents will be exceedingly limited.

The clinical field has made some initial moves to respond in new ways, in exploration of harm reduction perspective. Since, in many respects there is such denial that adolescent alcohol/drug use occurs, we continue to have more questions than answers. For example, in respect to adolescent alcohol use, following experimentation, what does a "regular" pattern look like? "Regular" can vary from daily, to only Saturday nights, or only to some Saturday nights, at most once a month. Are there "regular" patterns that are likely to be more problematic than others? A related issue is whether there is an evolution of the "regular" pattern. Is use becoming more frequent and involving greater consumption? Is it more like viewing a static picture or viewing a kaleidoscope? What kinds of activities accompany drinking? Is it sitting around at someone's house, talking and listening to music, or is it driving in large groups, searching for a party? Have the adolescents created some safeguards for themselves, even though they may not spell it out for their parents? Such safeguards may involve a decision to sleep over at someone's house, so no one is driving if there is going to be drinking. Or is there a designated driver who drinks nothing? Among girls it may involve an agreement that they arrive and leave together; no spontaneous and potentially ill-advised change of plans is allowed. However, if adolescents and their parents, caregivers, and other adults in their lives continue to pretend alcohol and substance use isn't happening, there is no opportunity to address these issues that can be central in reducing problems and reducing the risk of harm.

Are we taking drunken drivers off the road only to turn them into drunken pedestrians?
LAWRENCE HARRIS
North Carolina State Medical Examiner, commenting on motor vehicle deaths involving pedestrians, 1986

Clinical Approaches

In working with adolescents, there are some general points to consider. It is wise to avoid obvious authority symbols, such as white lab coats, framed diplomas dripping off the walls, and a remote clinical attitude. Adolescents probably already have some difficulty with authority figures, anyway, and they don't need you added to that list. Being somewhat informal in dress and setting can remove one barrier. On the other hand, spiked hair, playing CDs, and sitting on a floor cushion sucking on a "roach" when they arrive won't go down very well either. They want you to know about those things, but not be into them. An attempt to fake out adolescents will fail. They are a hard group to fool, and they place a high premium on honesty. Respect this and honestly be yourself. This means asking for a translation of their vocabulary if you are not familiar with the terms.

Empathy rather than sympathy is the goal. This is true of all therapeutic relationships. Sympathy is feeling like the other person. Empathy is knowing how the person feels but not feeling like he or she does at the moment. For instance, it is simply not helpful to be depressed along with the person.

In general, three types of therapy are done with adolescents. One involves manipulation of the environment. This can include arranging for the father to spend more time with his child, getting the kid who hates Shakespeare into a different school program, or organizing a temporary placement for the child whose parents are nonsupportive at the time. These can be very valuable interventions.

Standard insight therapy—psychologically or psychiatrically oriented therapy—is not often used. Not many adolescents are ready for, or even could benefit from, this kind of therapy. The ones who can benefit from it tend to be bright, advantaged young people who seem more capable and older than their peers or than their chronological age would suggest.

The most commonly productive therapy is what could be termed a relational approach. This requires time for you and the adolescent to become well acquainted and for the adolescent to feel comfortable with you. You are a neutral person, available to the adolescent in a very different way than are parents or peers. For many adolescents AA, particularly a young persons' group, can be a helpful way to be involved in a relational therapy, and also to have successful adult role models for sobriety.

Confidentiality

The issue of confidentiality always comes up. It can be a mistake to guarantee that "nothing you say will ever leave this room." The therapist has a responsibility to others as well as the adolescent client. Given blanket protection, what happens when the kid announces he plans to rob the local deli or another says she plans to drive the family car off the road at the first opportunity? A different approach was suggested by the late Hugh MacNamee, M.D. His practice was to tell whomever he saw that though most of what they said would be held in confidence, if they told him anything that scared him about what they might do, that would be harmful to themselves or others, he was going to blow the whistle. He made it clear he would not do so without telling them; nonetheless, he would do it. In his experience, adolescents accept this, maybe even with relief. It may help to know that someone else is going to exert some control, especially if adolescents are none too sure about their own inner controls at the moment.

In a similar vein, Dr. MacNamee suggested keeping the adolescent posted on any contacts you have with others about him or her. If a parent calls, start off the next session by informing the adolescent, "Hey, your Dad called me, and he wanted . . ." If a letter needs to be written to a school, probation officer, or someone else, share what you are writing with the adolescent. The chances are fairly good his or her fantasy about what you might say is worse than anything you would actually say, no matter what the problem. Because trust is such an issue with adolescents, it is important that you be willing to say to them what you would say about them.

Although the aforementioned is a good general approach to the issue of confidentiality, you may need to be aware of other complicating factors. This refers to the legal issues of a child's right to care versus parental rights to be informed. There may be circumstances in which an adolescent has a legal right to be seen and treated without parental knowledge or consent. In any case, the ground rules you are following must be clear to the adolescent client.

A Framework for Addressing Adolescent Substance Use/Problems

Dealing with alcohol and other drug use issues in adolescents isn't restricted to those who are in the substance abuse field. Indeed some of the most important tasks occur far before an adolescent would arrive at the doorstep of a substance abuse treatment agency.

The framework that follows, designed as an annotated checklist, is adapted from a protocol for pediatricians.[1] It sets forth the central tasks involved in assessing and responding to substance use, and can serve as a blueprint for clinicians generally.

[1] Adapted from Project Cork. *Interview Guidelines for Pediatricians.* Hanover, NH: Project Cork, 2000. Used with permission.

Confidentiality

- Reassure the patient that your discussion is confidential and that you will not disclose the details of your conversation with parents without the patient's permission, unless a serious health risk exists.

Assess Risk by Discussing

- Family relationships. Relationships with parents/step-parents and siblings.
- School performance. Academic performance, attendance, relationship with teachers, and personal goals.
- Leisure activities. "What are the things that you like to do when you're not in school?"
- Self-esteem. "Describe yourself. What are your strengths?"
- Other health risk behaviors; e.g., smoking, sexual activity, nicotine, diet.

Bring Up the Topic of Drugs and Alcohol

- Introduce the topic in a nonjudgmental way; e.g., "I know that some kids your age use alcohol, or smoke, or use other drugs."
- Use a health context. Introduce the topic of substance use in the context of concern for the patient's health; e.g., "I'd like to know a little bit about you and alcohol and drugs and how you feel about this, because it's important to your health."

Screening for Substance Use Problems (CRAFFT)[2]

1. Have you ever ridden in a ***C***ar driven by someone (including yourself) who was high or had been using alcohol or drugs?
2. Do you ever use alcohol or drugs to ***R***elax, feel better about yourself, or fit in?
3. Do you ever use alcohol or drugs while you are by yourself (***A***lone)?
4. Do you ever ***F***orget things you did while using alcohol or drugs?
5. Do your ***F***amily or ***F***riends ever tell you that you should cut down on your drinking or drug use?
6. Have you ever gotten into ***T***rouble while you were using alcohol or drugs?

Scoring: A score of two or more positive responses identifies those whose alcohol and/or drug use warrants further assessment.

---

[2]The CRAFFT is intended specifically for adolescents. Drawing upon adult screening instruments (see Chapter 9), the CRAFFT covers both alcohol and other drugs, is brief, and draws upon situations that are suited to adolescents.

Next Steps: For Those Who Have Not Used Alcohol or Other Drugs: Prevention/Anticipatory Guidance

- Assess exposure. "Have you ever been in a situation in which you were tempted to try drugs or alcohol?" "Has this happened to your friends?"
- Express concern about health problems and safety related to alcohol and drug use.
- Allow the patient to describe his or her understandings of the problems of alcohol and drug use. Correct misunderstandings.
- Provide factual information about alcohol and drug use. Offer pamphlets.
- Reinforce positive attitudes expressed by the patient regarding avoidance of alcohol and drug use.
- Suggest strategies for avoiding alcohol or drugs, and situations in which the opportunity for use may arise.

Next Steps: For Those Who Do Use Alcohol and Other Drugs: Harm Reduction

When there is a history of occasional use or experimentation, as well as more regular use, it is important to address the notion of harm reduction. This can include some basic facts about a drug's effects such as effects on judgment and motor response/reaction time. Addiction potential is another useful piece of information; the line between "experimentation" and regular and increasing use can be very fine. Tobacco is a good example. Identify situations in which use may invite risk, such as driving or sexual behaviors (patient education). Discuss ways to avoid these high-risk situations (harm reduction).

Note: For some drugs, any use places the teen at risk: e.g., inhalants, opiates, amphetamines, street drugs. (See Chapter 13.)

- "When someone uses alcohol or other drugs, it is important to know what these drugs do . . ."
- "From a medical perspective, drugs can cause problems in different ways. With some you can quickly become 'hooked,' for example with cigarettes. In other cases, the dangers are the result of the drug's immediate effects, the way it changes judgment and behavior. Alcohol is a good example of that."
- "Also, being the non-drinker or one of those who is straight in a situation in which others are using or drinking may result in your being the one who is faced with having to deal with problems that arise from someone else's use." Provide some basic facts on intoxication/high BACs/unknown amounts/dangers of putting someone to bed, or letting them "sleep it off." Identify someone who could be called in an emergency.
- Keep the door open. Identify yourself as someone to whom questions can be addressed.

For Identified Substance Use Problems, Assess Problem Severity

- Drinking frequency. "Do you drink regularly? About how often? Every day? Once or twice a week?"
- Drinking quantity. "How much did you drink the last time you got drunk? How much do you usually drink? Do you ever drink to pass out? How often do you get drunk?" (Risk of acute problems is related to the frequency of intoxication and activities when intoxicated.)
- Drug use frequency. "About how often do you use drugs? Every day? Once or twice a week?" Get specifics.
- "Where do you drink/take drugs? Parties only? With friends in cars? Home? School? By yourself at home or in school?"
- Dependence. "Do your social activities usually involve alcohol/drugs? What would happen if you couldn't have any alcohol/drugs?"
- Social consequences. "What kinds of trouble have you gotten into because of alcohol/drugs? Do your parents suspect that you drink or take drugs?"

For Identified Substance Use Problems, Negotiate Follow-up

- Allow the patient to describe his/her understanding of his/her alcohol and drug use. "How would you describe your alcohol or drug use? Do you think it has become a problem for you or dangerous to your health?"
- State clearly that the patient has a problem with substance use. Provide concrete health-related and psychosocial evidence.
- Stress the importance of involving others to address the problem. This includes working with the patient's parents. "I'd like to have your permission to talk to your folks about this. It is important that we involve them because for us to provide the best treatment for this, we need their support."
- Negotiate for a follow-up appointment, ideally with the parents present.
- Assume responsibility for acting as intermediary between the patient and his or her parents. "At one of our next visits, I can meet with you and your parents and explain this to your parents in a way that they can understand. Then we can all work together to help you."
- Solicit the patient's verbal agreement to involve parents.
- Solicit patient's agreement to come for follow-up.
- Schedule a follow-up appointment.

Further Assessment and Treatment

Once it has been determined that an adolescent needs "to do something" and has agreed to see someone, what options are available? Some schools have in-house substance abuse counselors. Every state has a system of substance abuse services, which includes clinicians and offices throughout the state. In many major medical centers there are often substance abuse services. The agreement to "see someone" should not be considered as an agreement to enter substance abuse treatment. Indeed for some adolescents, the next step may be some kind of counseling to better evaluate the nature of a substance use problem, as well as assist the adolescent to recognize that these are problems that accompany substance use, essential preliminary work enabling the adolescent to be engaged in treatment. The clear exception to this is when the adolescent is in immediate danger to himself or others, or when a substance use problem is so clear-cut that immediate involvement in treatment is required.

For some adolescents, part of the assessment may involve a thorough medical and psychiatric evaluation. Formal treatment options include outpatient, residential, or hospital-based care and can involve individual, group, and family counseling, plus self-help groups such as AA or NA (Narcotics Anonymous).

Diagnostic Criteria: Adult-Adolescent Differences

As there have been concerns about how screening tests designed for adults work with adolescents, similarly questions have been raised about diagnostic criteria, for both abuse and dependence. This is an issue that will certainly get considerable attention in the process of revising and developing the next edition of the APA's *Diagnostic and Statistical Manual.* Consider the criterion "Drinking a larger amount than intended." It is fair to say that many adolescents have no particular intention about how much alcohol they will consume on any particular occasion. They can't even figure out until the last minute what movie they want to see. The scenario is just as likely to be "screw the movie, let's go hang out at the mall, pick up a video and then . . ." and of course that plan is subject to change along the line. So the notion of their having an amount in mind that they will drink on a particular occasion is foreign to their thinking and developmental stage. Similarly, with relatively new drinkers, the criterion referring to tolerance, and the need for a larger amount to achieve the same effects, may not be applicable.

The NIAAA studies being conducted about diagnostic criteria have gotten attention. Researchers have found that compared to adults, adolescents are less likely to have withdrawal symptoms. Another criterion which seems not to be a good fit for adolescents, in addition to the one noted above about setting limits for use, involves tolerance. All newer drinkers are acquiring tolerance, so the ability to drink more without feeling impaired is true as well for a large number of adolescents. This isn't restricted to those with alcohol problems. Another issue is the presence of *diagnostic orphans.* This refers to those who meet some criteria for either abuse or dependence, but not a sufficient number to qualify for a formal diagnosis. This confirms the suspicion that some modification of the criteria is needed to better reflect the presentation of alcohol disorders in adolescents.

Alcohol/Drug Assessment

Once the issue of confidentiality has been cleared up, it is important to take a family history. Ask about alcohol or other drug problems, prescription or nonprescription. Include questions about the grandparents, uncles, aunts, brothers and sisters, cousins, as well as the parents and step-parents. Another important part of the history includes asking adolescents how they spend their time. Ask them to describe a typical day. Ask what they and their friends do on a typical Saturday night. Ask about their peer groups—peers' ages, activities, and drug and alcohol use. Ask how they are seen and described by other groups in their school, and then ask about the adolescent's own use of drugs and alcohol. Ask about parental relationships. Ask about sleep, appetite, depression, and the possibility of physical or sexual abuse. Also be able to discuss issues of sexuality and sexual orientation. It is also important to determine adolescents' risk for HIV infection.

The fact that adolescent alcohol abuse can go on for as long as 6 years without being diagnosed is a tribute to several factors. There is the ability of these adolescents to hide their problems, complemented by their parents' ability to avoid recognizing problems in their children. It is also a testimony to the failure of health-care providers to address substance abuse and other sensitive issues, as well as the ability of school systems to ignore or expel problem children. It is not unusual for parents to be actively protecting, rescuing, and taking care of a substance abusing adolescent without realizing that this supports and prolongs the abuse. For instance, they make good on forged checks. They hire lawyers and pay fines. They go to bat for them at school or blame school authorities for the problems.

When asking adolescents about drug and alcohol use, begin by asking about the first time they were drunk, how much they drink now, how often, if they have ever tried to stop or cut down. Ask about blackouts, legal problems, and school problems. Ask about pot, crack, cocaine, acid, stimulants, or whatever the current "in" drug is. Increasingly, younger adolescents are beginning their experimentation with intoxication by using inhalants which are easily available in any supermarket or drugstore. Finally, don't assume that an adolescent is providing a wholly accurate history about drug and alcohol use. Denial is a central characteristic of adolescent alcohol or drug problems.

Moving the Adolescent into Treatment

Although occasionally adolescents will spontaneously request treatment, more often they come to treatment under duress. In working with them, it is important to make it clear that your task is to help them and that you are not an agent of their parents, the law, or the school system.

In dealing with adolescents, the importance of working with the family cannot be overemphasized. The parents need to deal with their child's substance abuse. And they must consider their own behaviors that may have protected, covered up, excused, or, for that matter, contributed to the problem. When it is clear that there is a significant problem and all efforts to involve the adolescent in treatment have failed, the parents may need to seek legal help. Most states allow parents to request state assistance if they feel they cannot enforce safe limits for their child. Although this is a very drastic and difficult step to take, it can be important when alcohol abusing adolescents are acting in ways that endanger their lives. Probation can also be a way of mandating treatment for adolescents, but again this only works if the parents can stop protecting the adolescent from the consequences of his behavior.

Substance Abuse Treatment Once it has been determined that an adolescent needs treatment and the adolescent has agreed to treatment, it is important to proceed in a careful way. Because medical and psychiatric complications frequently accompany adolescent substance abuse, a thorough medical and psychiatric evaluation should precede or be an early part of any treatment plan. Treatment options include outpatient, residential, and hospital-based care and can involve individual, group, and family counseling, plus self-help groups, such as AA or NA (Narcotics Anonymous). The American Academy of Pediatrics suggests the use of the guidelines developed by the American Society of Addiction Medicine in determining the type of care required (see Chapter 9).

There are very good alcohol/drug treatment programs for adolescents. There are those, on the other hand, that might most kindly be described as nontraditional. This includes the boot camp programs, which submit kids to a military-like environment, with forced marches and endless push-ups; in some cases this type of treatment has resulted in deaths. Here, too, the Academy of Pediatrics has developed criteria for selecting a treatment program. The following are suggested as things to look for.

1. The program views drug and alcohol abuse as a primary disease, rather than as a symptom.
2. The program includes a comprehensive evaluation of the patient and attends itself to or makes referral for any associated medical, emotional, or behavioral problems identified in the assessment.
3. The program adheres to an abstinence philosophy. Any use is abuse. Drug use is a chronic disease, and a drug-free environment is essential. Tobacco ideally should be prohibited, or nicotine cessation should be part of the overall treatment plan for patients who smoke.
4. There is a low ratio of patients to staff. Treatment professionals are knowledgeable about substance abuse and adolescent behavior and development.
5. Professionally led support groups and self-help programs are integral parts of the program.
6. Adolescents are separate from the adult groups if both are treated at the same facility.

7. The entire family is involved in treatment. The program relates to parents and patients with compassion and concern, with the goal of reunification whenever possible.
8. Follow-up and continuing care are integral parts of the program.
9. As progress is made in the program, patients have an opportunity to continue academic and vocational education and are assisted in restructuring family, school, and social life.
10. The program administration discusses costs and financial arrangements for inpatient and outpatient care and facilitates communication with managed care organizations.
11. The program is as close to home as possible to facilitate family involvement, even though separation of the adolescent may initially be indicated.

The questions to ask are "Does the program work?" "Is the program drug free?" "Is there a strong family component?" "Is there a strong therapeutic component?" "Is there a strong educational component?" "Is the adolescent involved in treatment planning?" "Is there a peer component?" "Are there provisions for aftercare?" "What are the costs and risks of treatment, including both financial cost and time cost?" "What beliefs are instilled?" "What are the staff's credentials, including training, experience, licensure, and certification?" "Is there a full range of services, including pediatric, psychiatric, educational, psychological, and alcohol counselors?" "Is there involvement with AA?" "How does the program feel when one visits it?" "Is the program accredited?" "If so, by whom?"

Treatment of Psychiatric Disorders Psychiatric problems are not uncommon among adolescents with alcohol or other drug use problems. Several studies of adolescents in treatment found that over 80% had another psychiatric disorder. This is not to suggest that this holds true for all adolescents with substance use problems. Possibly the presence of other psychiatric disorders causes more disruptions and thus increases the likelihood of these teens' entering treatment. Among female adolescents with alcohol problems, there is a greater incidence of other substance abuse disorders, as well as depression and eating disorders. There is also a higher incidence of post-traumatic stress disorder. For these girls, this often includes a history of childhood abuse. Attention-deficit/hyperactivity disorder (ADHD), more common among males, doubles the risk of alcohol or other drug dependency in adolescents and increases the likelihood of relapse following treatment.

One of the questions sometimes raised is whether a preadolescent's use of stimulant drugs for treatment of ADHD is later associated with substance abuse in adolescence. Multiple studies have found that children treated with stimulants have no heightened risk for experimentation and use, or abuse or dependence, in adolescence or adulthood. The far greater danger is a failure to treat the ADHD adequately. There are virtually no data on the use of drug therapies for alcohol use disorders in adolescents. Disulfiram has been used with adolescents, but with some reluctance. Given adolescents' greater impulsivity, clinicians are concerned about the greater risk of drinking and the associated disulfiram reaction. The only data on the use of newer anti-craving agents, only recently on the market in the United States, come from European studies where these drugs had longer use.

Adolescents and AA For the adolescent with an alcohol/substance abuse problem, how might AA be of use? The first thought might be that the adolescent would never identify with a group of predominantly 35- to 55-year-olds. In many areas of the country, that stereotype of the AA group does not necessarily hold true; there are now in some locales what are called "young people's groups." There the average age is the low to mid-20s. Even if there are no young people's groups in the vicinity, age need not be a barrier to an adolescent's affiliating with AA. On the contrary, several features of AA might attract and intrigue the adolescent. It is a group of adults who will definitely not preach at him or her. Furthermore, given the collective life experiences within AA, the members are not likely to be shocked, outraged, or, for that matter, impressed by any of the adolescent's behaviors. The members will generally treat the adolescent as an adult, presumably capable of making responsible choices although cognizant that to do so isn't easy for anyone. Within AA there is a ready assortment of potential surrogate parents, aunts, uncles, and grandparents. The intergenerational contact, possibly not available elsewhere to the adolescent, can be a plus. Also, AA remains sufficiently "unacceptable" so as not to be automatically written off by an adolescent wary of traditional, staid, "out-of-it" adult groups. Because being an alcoholic or another drug abuser is still a stigmatized condition, the parents may be more uncomfortable than their children about AA attendance for adolescents. The therapist may need to help parents with this. In making a referral, the same guidelines outlined in the section on AA apply. (See Chapter 10.) The adolescent is full of surprises, and a willingness to attend AA may well be one.

Adolescents and AIDS A growing concern is the rapid increase of AIDS among young adults, meaning they had contracted HIV during adolescence. Any discussion of adolescents and AIDS requires thinking about the role of the other A—alcohol. Alcohol is involved in this equation for two reasons. First, there's the well-known disinhibiting effect of alcohol and the impaired judgment that is a part of that. Sexual encounters are more likely when drinking. It is less likely that condoms will be used, increasing the risk of a variety of sexually transmitted diseases including HIV. Sexual encounters are also more likely to be casual, involving partners with little history and no ongoing relationship. With the advent of AIDS, the important message to be conveyed is that there is no longer, if there ever was, such a thing as casual sex. The stakes are high, and the costs are no longer simply psychological wounds.

The second important factor that has considerable significance in thinking about adolescents, alcohol, and AIDS goes beyond simply altered judgment. It appears that one of the effects of alcohol—in anyone, not just in those who are alcohol dependent or who drink heavily—is to interfere temporarily with the immune system. Possibly for a day or two alcohol has seemingly "turned down the volume" on the body's defenses. Thus, the body's usually available means of fighting off infections and viruses are not up to par. This allows infections to gain a foothold, which may otherwise not have happened.

Adolescent treatment, as well as prevention, programs need also to be involved in AIDS education. Some treatment programs, beyond including an educational component, also discuss the issue of HIV testing; several have adopted this as a routine part of their procedures. Beyond the fact that it really does matter if one is or is not HIV-positive, these activities also reinforce the point that HIV/AIDS is a major issue. It isn't something that can't or wouldn't touch an adolescent's life. These activities emphasize that it is the choices that adolescents make or don't make that have an impact on them.

Treatment Outcome The data on treatment outcomes remain limited. Programs treating adolescents for alcohol use disorders typically have abstinence as the treatment goal. However, the information from follow-up suggests this goal is rarely achieved for extended periods. Nonetheless there is generally substantial improvement in functioning. In one larger study at 1-year follow-up, about 20% were abstinent. There was another 30% who used alcohol occasionally, but had no symptoms of either abuse or dependence. Furthermore, among these drinking, but without symptoms, their psychological and social functioning seemed to more closely resemble that of the abstainers than those for whom problematic use continued.

Based on what is known of adults who report the emergence of alcohol problems in adolescence, it would be expected that any alcohol problem that becomes apparent in adolescence would be characterized as a chronic condition, with a steady downhill progressive course. Among a group of adolescents followed through their mid-20s, in fact 55% were found to have an alcohol use disorder. Clearly the presence of a diagnosis in adolescence increased the risk of alcohol problems later. On the other hand, there was a significant portion for whom this wasn't the case.

It may go against the grain for substance abuse clinicians, and fly in the face of conventional wisdom, but quite possibly for some adolescents alcohol abuse (not dependence) is developmentally limited. For some adolescents there may be a maturing out of alcohol abuse. If indeed this is the case, this is not to suggest that treatment isn't required because adolescents will "grow out of it." First, this is clearly not the case for all adolescents. Second, it is just possible treatment is a major factor that facilitates a maturation out of alcohol abuse. If nothing else, entering formal treatment is likely to get an adolescent's attention! It may also provide some useful time out. Buying 1 year of nonheavy, nonproblem drinking during adolescence is no small accomplishment. It may allow for further maturation, derail dysfunctional patterns, instill better coping skills, and remove the adolescent from a heavy-drinking peer group.

In a review of factors related with treatment outcome, several have been identified: the level of severity, the extent of family and interpersonal problems, the presence of other substance use, and presence of co-occurring psychiatric conditions, especially antisocial behavior and major depression.

Prevention

Considerable attention and money are being directed to prevention. The Center for Substance Abuse Prevention (CSAP) has funded research initiatives as well as community projects to implement the approaches that have been shown to be successful. In considering prevention, several different approaches are used. Some are directed at the environment, the larger society. These include things such as efforts to curb underage sales. Other prevention programs are directed at the individual. These can be broad-based, touching all teens, such as public service ads to promote the use of designated drivers, to sponsoring alcohol-free proms or graduation parties. Other programs directed at individuals try to reach adolescents who are at higher risk. These can include special programs for children from families with a substance use problem, and efforts to identify children with behavioral risk factors, such as ADHD or conduct disorders. (See Chapter 14 for further discussions of prevention.)

One important task for anyone working with adolescents is to be aware of the potential problems that virtually every adolescent will encounter with respect to alcohol and other drugs. Even if adolescents are not currently into drugs or alcohol, anticipatory guidance can be very helpful. This means speaking with them about how they can handle the situation when it inevitably does arise. Contacts with adolescents, for whatever reason, can be used. This might mean the school counselor who meets with the adolescent to discuss next year's course offerings. Or it may be the occasion of the mandatory physical examination required before participation in high school athletics.

In many communities, there are also efforts under way through parent groups and groups of adolescents to support the development of healthy peer values and norms about alcohol/drug use. It is almost impossible to speak of adolescent alcohol or other drug use without hearing the phrase "peer pressure." This for many conjures up the image of someone sidling up to a kid and saying, "Want to try some beer?" or "How 'bout a joint?" The most potent form of peer pressure, however, is what adolescents *think* everyone else is doing. Teens are apt to overestimate the numbers of their peers who drink by up to 100%. Friends do have considerable influence; however, parents and adults do as well. The expectations of adults in the community have an impact.

BOX 11.1 Some Thoughts for Parents—Parents Do Make a Difference

Some Basic Facts

- A major national study found that 4 out of 10 parents think they have little influence over their adolescent's decision to use or not use drugs. Not true.
- Approximately 45% of parents indicate that it is likely their teens will use illegal drugs.
- Teens and their parents suffer from "collective ignorance." High school students overestimate the proportion of students who are weekly drinkers by 100%. Unfortunately, drinking patterns change toward what adolescents mistakenly think is the norm. Parents underestimate use.
- Risk factors for adolescent drinking encompass sociocultural factors, such as alcohol availability; parental behavior and drinking patterns; the influence and drinking habits of siblings and peers; personality traits, particularly those related to impulsiveness and risk taking; and positive beliefs about alcohol's effects.
- Young people reared in home environments that have permissive or casual attitudes about alcohol and who are introduced to alcohol at an earlier age may be more vulnerable to alcohol-related problems in adolescence.
- Access via licensed premises is one of the strongest predictors of drinking and alcohol problems. Among 15- to 18-year-olds, the ability to get served is more significant than peer or parental influences.
- The earlier that children begin alcohol use, the greater the likelihood of later problems.
- Taking on adult roles too early—becoming a teenage parent, living independently of parents or family, or dropping out of school—is more common among those who used alcohol or other drugs in early adolescence. These situations further increase the likelihood of substance use problems as young adults.
- Be concerned about teenage smoking, as a health risk and as a "gateway drug." Pack-a-day adolescent smokers are 3 times more likely to drink alcohol, 7 times more likely to use smokeless tobacco, and 10 to 30 times more likely to use illicit drugs than are nonsmokers. Appreciate how addictive nicotine is. Very quickly smoking moves beyond experimentation. For teens who do smoke, promote smoking cessation programs.

Appreciate Your Influence

- Parents are a more potent influence than are peers and siblings.
- Parents' influence operates as a natural harm-reduction mechanism that helps protect teenage drinkers from developing alcohol problems.
- Parents influence their children's drinking through family interactions, by modeling and reinforcing standards, and through the attitudes and skills they impart to guide behavior in new situations. Thus, parental influences endure.
- An important predictor of whether a teenage boy will have an alcohol-related driving offense or accident is whether his parents are neutral (rather than negative) about teenage drinking.
- The quality of family relationships and the amount of time adolescents spend with family are more important influences on adolescents' substance use than is the kind of family in which teenagers are living—whether with both parents, with a parent and step-parent, in a single-parent home, or with nonfamily members.
- Adolescents' perceptions of the parenting style in their homes are linked to adolescent substance use. Teens who view their parents as generally authoritative (know what they are talking about), as not permissive (who have standards and clear expectations), and as less authoritarian (not "Do it because I say so") do better in school and are less likely to abuse substances.
- Adolescent drinking behavior is found to be largely unrelated to the socioeconomic circumstances of the family. A supportive family environment is associated with lowered rates of alcohol use.
- Parents' who use illegal drugs have teens at much higher risk of drug use.
- Parents' health habits influence their children. This ranges from wearing bike helmets, to using seat belts, to having healthy drinking patterns, to being smokers. The younger the child, the more powerful is the parents' model. If you have any concern about your own substance use, act on this. Very few people worry about their alcohol or other drug use needlessly. If you are a smoker, is now the time to quit?

(continued on next page)

BOX 11.1 *continued*

Be Realistic

- Parents who recognize the potential for their adolescent's becoming involved with alcohol are more likely and able to intervene if this occurs. They are also more likely to supervise teen parties given at their home.
- Parents see substance use as motivated by factors with negative connotations, such as boredom, rebellion, loneliness, and social pressure. Their children are more likely to cite factors that are more positive, such as curiosity, fun, and insight/experience.
- Appreciate the complexity of this issue. There is no one thing that leads to or one single thing that prevents substance use.
- At some point every teen is in a situation in which alcohol or other drugs are present. Help your child anticipate how he or she can respond gracefully, to avoid embarrassing themselves or others.

What You Can Do

- Use your influence—with your children, with the parents of your children's friends, and within your community.
- Support policy initiatives to reduce access to alcohol.
- Provide anticipatory guidance.
- Expect others in your child's life—pediatrician, coach, clergy—to discuss substance use.
- Be sure your son or daughter knows how to respond to an alcohol/drug emergency.
- Help make the norms in your community apparent.
- Become informed.
- Talk to other parents.
- Set an example. Let your children and others know where you stand on drug and alcohol use.
- Never forget that what you do or fail to do can be a matter of life or death.

From: *Parents Make a Difference,* Hanover, NH: Project Care, 2002.

In thinking about prevention, there is something that cries out for attention. This is preparing adolescents to deal with alcohol or other drug emergencies. There is opposition in some quarters, on the basis that it may be sending a mixed message. Get real. One doesn't withhold potentially life-saving information because kids might think that implies approval of drinking. The reality is that it is likely to fall to the adolescent who isn't drinking to do what needs to be done in such circumstances. It is important that he or she knows how to respond to possible overdose, such as knowing the dangers of letting a really drunk kid "just sleep it off." Adolescents need to learn that when they are in the presence of drinking, they need to be their brother's—and sister's—keeper. (See chart, page 408, on responding to alcohol emergencies.)

For some adults, there is the temptation at some point to "finally" take a stand regarding adolescent drinking. Unfortunately, this often occurs after a lengthy period of vacillating behavior. Finally, something dramatic is done, which may not be well thought out. For example, several years ago there was a growing awareness and concern about alcohol use in a local high school. There were the usual incidents for the age group—having unchaperoned parties with drinking, parents allowing alcohol to be served in their homes, drinking and driving, taking alcohol to school dances, and going to dances after drinking. That year the soccer team had an outstanding season and made it to the play-offs for the state championship. A parent put a bottle of champagne on the bus. The team subsequently won. In the course of the celebrating, someone remembered the champagne on the bus. The players proceeded to pour it over one another. This led to a public uproar. In the aftermath, the team members refused to tell who got the champagne from the bus. Interestingly, the parent who provided the champagne never confessed, either. As a result, the next year's team was not allowed to participate in any postseason games, regardless of their playing record. Beyond the questions of delaying punishment for such an extended period or penalizing players who may not have even been present, there was a further irony. Not only were the students following a well-established tradition witnessed at the conclusion of every professional championship series, but this incident may have represented the most appropriate, most nondestructive use of alcohol ever displayed in the school. But this was the time to "put the foot down." Although an extreme example, this points out the capacity to undermine one's efforts if action is taken precipitously.

Wine is a good familiar creature, if it be well used.
WILLIAM SHAKESPEARE
Othello

Minority Youth

With the exception of Native Americans, minority youth use less alcohol and other drugs than do whites. Much of what has been said about the presentation and treatment of substance abuse does not capture the problems of many urban minority youth. Regardless of whether these youths are African-American, Hispanic, or Native American, they are far more likely to live in substandard housing, be in families with fewer economic resources, have less access to medical care, attend substandard schools, or be school dropouts. If they live in urban areas, they are more likely than their white peers to live in areas in which drug use is prevalent and accompanied by violence in the community.

COLLEGE STUDENTS

Patterns of Alcohol and Other Drug Use

Alcohol and drug use on the college campus has received considerable attention over the past decade. A national survey of college students and young adults, conducted regularly by the National Institute on Drug Abuse,[2] shows that, with a few significant exceptions, college students'

---

[2]There have been 3 major national surveys that gather information on alcohol and other drug use patterns. One is conducted by the National Institute on Drug Abuse and is called *Monitoring the Future.* The survey is not restricted to college students but also includes young adults not attending college. There is also the Core Survey sparked by the funding of prevention and educational efforts on college campuses by the U.S. Department of Education's Fund for the Improvement of Secondary Education. The intent was to ensure that each individual school would have information about the use and extent of alcohol/drug problems, as well as to provide a national snapshot of the situation among this age group. The third national survey is the College Alcohol Study, which uses a sample of 140 four-year institutions and is funded by the Robert Wood Johnson Foundation. It was first conducted in 1993 and was repeated in 1997 and 1999. The results of these different surveys are generally comparable in terms of defining the nature of alcohol and other drug use. However, each has some unique questions that allow one to look at different aspects of substance use and abuse.

TOBACCO RESEARCH INSTITUTE
Compared with non-college peers, college students are more likely to drink heavily and less likely to smoke, so I think we should market a brandy-laced cigarette.

Table 11.3 Past Month Substance Use for College Students and Non-College Peers, 2003

	College	Non-College
Alcohol, past two weeks	66.2%	58.3%
daily drinker	4.3	5.1
binge drinker	38.5	33.9
Cigarettes	22.5	37.8
Marijuana	19.3	22.1
Amphetamines	3.1	4.0
Tranquilizers	2.8	3.2
Hallucinogens	1.8	1.8
Inhalants	0.4	0.4
Heroin	<0.05	0.1
Other narcotics	2.3	4.8

From: Johnston LD, O'Malley PM, Bachman JG, Schulenberg JE. *Monitoring the Future: National Survey Results on Drug Use, 1975–2003. Volume II College Students and Adults Ages 19–45.* Bethesda, MD: National Institute on Drug Abuse, 2004.

substance use patterns are generally similar to those of their age peers who are not attending college. College students are more likely to be drinkers, and far more likely to be heavy drinkers, though they are less likely to be daily drinkers. Despite the upsurge in smoking by college students, they are, nonetheless, far less likely to be smokers than those who are not attending college. They are less likely to use illicit drugs. The respective patterns of substance use are summarized in Table 11.3.

The higher rates of both college student drinking and heavy drinking may, in part, be attributable to two demographic factors. First, alcohol use increases when young adults move away from their parents and begin living independently. Second, drinking declines after marriage for both men and women. Those who do not go to college are more likely to live at home or be married, both of which are associated with less drinking. In combination, these factors may explain some of these differences in drinking patterns.

According to the most recent Core Survey involving more than 93,000 students, 84.5% of all students used alcohol in the preceding year. How often and how much do these students drink? About 17% drink infrequently, meaning 1–6 times in the past year. Forty-two percent are moderate drinkers, drinking between once a month and once a week. The remaining 24% are frequent drinkers, drinking 3 or more times per week.

How about the amount of alcohol that is consumed? Not surprisingly, there is considerable variation. In the week prior to the Core Survey, 36% of students had not used alcohol; 12% had had only 1 drink; 30% reported from 2 to 10 drinks; and 23% reported 10 or more.

Just as is true of the general population, there is no "average" college drinker. Also, as is true in the general population, a minority of college students drink far more than their statistical share of alcohol. A survey of alcohol use at a New England private college illustrates this. The results of a campus survey of drinking patterns were examined by dividing students into four quartiles by levels of drinking (each quartile represents 25% of the students). The lowest quartile consumed 1.5% of all alcohol, the second quartile consumed 11.5%, and the third quartile consumed 23.0%. The highest drinking quartile consumed 64%, close to two-thirds of all the alcohol. In translating that to a "typical week," 57% of students had had from 0 to 6 drinks. At the other end of the continuum were the 2.3% of the students who reported having had between 40 and 50 drinks. What this means is that, during an average week, less than 3% of students drink as much alcohol as all the alcohol consumed by a group representing 57% of their classmates. The last College Alcohol Survey demonstrated the same pattern nationally: slightly under one quarter (22.7%) of students consume a disproportionate amount, about two-thirds of all alcohol.

If four students split 10 beers one would drink none, one would drink one, one would drink two, one would drink six, and they'd all split the last one.

Gender Differences

Differences present during high school continue into college. Women drink less per occasion and drink less frequently. The proportion of women who drink approximates that of men, but they are less likely to be heavy drinkers or daily drinkers. Women are also less likely to use illicit substances. Their use of tranquilizers, however, is on par with that of male students. In 1993, there was a first—the proportion of women who were daily smokers exceeded that of men. That continues.

Racial and Ethnic Differences

The traditionally African-American schools have significantly lower levels of alcohol and other drug use and a lower rate of problems associated with use. In addition, African-Americans drink less than white students, wherever they are attending school.

Trends

There has been a general overall decline in licit and illicit substance use since 1980, as evidenced by the *Monitoring the Future Survey.* In 2003 the prevalence of current marijuana use at 19% represented a decline of close to 45%. Use of any other illicit drug has dropped by more than 60% in this almost quarter century. The proportion of college students who have had alcohol in the past month has declined by 19%. Binge

Table 11.4 Trends in College Students' Drinking Patterns 1980–2003

	Percent of Students			
Drinking Pattern	**1980**	**1990**	**2000**	**2003**
Current drinker	81.8%	74.5%	67.4%	66.2%
Daily drinker	6.5	3.8	3.6	4.3
Binge drinking	43.9	41.0	39.3	38.5

From: Johnston LD, O'Malley PM, Bachman JG, Schulenberg JE. *Monitoring the Future: National Survey Results on Drug Use, 1975–2003. Volume II College Students and Adults Ages 19–45.* Bethesda, MD: National Institute on Drug Abuse, 2004.

SURVEYOR WHO doesn't understand The question
In our survey of over 47 college campuses, we found that almost 90% of college students abuse rugs. They spill beer on them. They vomit on them. They never vacuum or steam clean them.

drinking too has declined, by 14%, with 39% of students reporting having had 5 or more drinks (4 for women) in the past 2 weeks. Similarly, daily drinking has declined by a third. The trends in drinking patterns are presented in Table 11.4.

Interestingly, students' drinking practices did not change substantially following the changes in the legal drinking age that occurred in the 1980s. When the legal drinking age was raised, there was only a transient impact on college students' drinking. There was a decrease in consumption immediately after such legislation was passed, but with time the numbers of students drinking returned to the previous levels.

A Comment on Binge Drinking

While clearly of concern, there is a question that needs to be considered in terms of binge drinking: What is the duration of "the drinking occasion"? If students are attending a party that goes from 9 p.m. to 2 a.m., the 5 drinks that define a binge represent 1 drink per hour. That is the rate at which alcohol is metabolized; the student party-goer could go home with essentially a zero blood alcohol level. That is a different scenario than the group that heads to a local pub and has 5 beers in an hour and a half.

A thematic issue of *Psychology of Addictive Behaviors* (vol. 15, no. 4) was devoted to binge drinking. The issue examines the utility of binge drinking as a marker for high-risk drinking, the advantages and disadvantages of the use of the concept, and some alternative perspectives and indicators of alcohol problems. Several articles question the use of binge drinking as an indicator for intoxication and provide results of studies that indicate this is not an adequate measure. One study found that among those who were classified as binge drinkers the last time they drank, based on the length of the drinking episode, weight, and gender, the majority (63%) would have had a BAC under 0.10; about half (48%) would have had a BAC under 0.08, and 30% would have had a BAC under 0.06%. Similarly, a study of college students and young adults as they were returning from bar-hopping in Tijuana found that the definition of "binge drinking" was not a good measure of the levels of actual intoxication.

A just published report further supports these views. Breath tests were administered to more than 800 students as they returned to their dorms between 10 p.m. and 3 a.m. Among the students whose self-reports would classify them as heavy drinkers based on consumption during the past two weeks, virtually half had a zero BAC on that evening. For males who said they had 5 drinks (4 for women) on the evening of the breath test, the average for their BACs was under the legal level of intoxication (0.08). Very high BACs, of 0.15 or above, were quite rare, found in only 1.3% of the students tested. The general consensus is that while heavy drinking is indeed a concern, binge drinking is an inadequate measure and means to identify high risk, problem use. Indeed, it serves to exaggerate problems related to college drinking, and as one author has noted tends to demonize students.

Problems Associated with Substance Use

Data on the magnitude and nature of problems related to alcohol and substance use on college campuses were very scant for a long time. The Core Survey and Campus Alcohol Survey significantly remedied this. Colleges individually did not systematically gather such data. If this information was collected, it was generally treated as confidential and rarely published in professional literature. Colleges are concerned about their public image. There was the concern that, if this data were available to the press, the institution might be viewed less favorably by the public, alumni, prospective students, or, more important, their parents, potential donors, and, for public institutions, the state legislature, which controls the purse strings. A range of problems can accompany drinking. Table 11.5 summarizes the percentages of students who report having experienced different consequences throughout the past year.

An important issue related to experiencing an alcohol problem is the extent to which the occurrence of these problems is influenced by the person's own drinking pattern. Results from the Campus Survey, summarized in Table 11.6, show that, the more frequently students report binge drinking, the greater the likelihood of their experiencing negative consequences.

Alcohol use is recognized as contributing to campus violence and harassment. The Campus Alcohol Survey shows that the consumption of alcohol or other drugs is also tied to having been a victim of violence or harassment. This is summarized in Table 11.7.

Academic performance, too, is related to alcohol consumption. One thing that distinguishes the *D* or *F* student from the *A* student is that the poorer student drinks over twice as much per week.

Table 11.5 Collegians' Alcohol Problems in the Previous Year

Problem	% Reporting
Had a hangover	62.6
Got nauseated or vomited	53.2
Done something later regretted	38.2
Missed a class	33.1
Drove a car while under the influence	32.5
Had a memory loss	31.7
Got into an argument or a fight	30.8
Was criticized by someone	30.3
Performed poorly on a test or another project	23.5
Was hurt or injured	14.3
Had trouble with police or other authorities	13.7
Was taken advantage of sexually	11.7
Thought they might have a problem	10.7
Damaged property, pulled fire alarm, etc.	8.2
Tried unsuccessfully to stop using	5.8
Seriously thought about suicide	4.6
Took advantage of another sexually	4.6
Was arrested for DWI	1.5
Seriously tried to commit suicide	1.4

From Presley CA, Leichliter JS, Meilman PW. *Alcohol and Drugs on American College Campuses.* Carbondale, IL: Core Institute, Southern Illinois University, 2001. www.siu.edu/departments/coreinst/public_html/recent.html

Effects of Problems on Others

An individual's drinking has an impact on others. Borrowing a phrase associated with smoking, "secondhand smoke," the negative consequences for others have been termed "secondhand drinking." As is shown in Table 11.8, the campus rate of binge drinking has an impact on the extent of these consequences for others.

Perceived Benefits Associated with Drinking

An important element in the consequences of campus alcohol use is often overlooked by researchers and college administrators. But students

Table 11.6 Rate of Alcohol Problems by Drinking Pattern

	Binge Drinking Pattern		
Problem	**None (%)**	**Infrequently (%)**	**Most Frequently (%)**
Do something you regret	18	22	42
Not use protection when you had sex	4	19	20
Damage property	2	9	20
Hurt or injured	4	11	27
Drove after drinking	19	40	57
Trouble with campus or local police	1	5	13
Five or more alcohol-related problems since the start of school year	4	17	48

From: Wechsler H, Lee JE, Kup M, Lee H. College binge drinking in the 1990s: A continuing problem. *Journal of American College Health* 48(3):202, 2000.

Table 11.7 Harassment or Violence and Alcohol/Drug Consumption, 1999

Type of Incident	% Reporting Incident	% of Who Had Consumed Alcohol or Other Drugs Before Incident
Ethnic or racial harassment	5.4	15.5
Threats of physical violence	9.5	34.2
Actual physical violence	5.1	38.0
Theft involving force or threat of force	1.7	24.3
Forced sexual touching or fondling	5.2	40.4
Unwanted sexual intercourse	3.5	36.2

From: Presley CA, Leichliter JS, Meilman PW. *Alcohol and Drugs on American College Campuses.* Carbondale, IL: Core Institute, Southern Illinois University, 2001. www.siu.edu/departments/coreinst/public_html/recent.html

Table 11.8 Secondary Effects of Campus Drinking

Problem Reported by Nonbinge Drinkers	% of Students Reporting Problems by School's Level of Binge Drinking		
	Low Binge Rate	Medium Binge Rate	High Binge Rate
Being insulted or humiliated	21	30	34
Had serious argument or quarrel	13	18	20
Pushed, hit, or assaulted	7	10	13
Had property destroyed	6	13	15
Had to care for a drunken student	31	57	54
Studying or sleep interrupted	42	64	68
Unwanted sexual advance	15	21	26
Victim of sexual assault or date rape	2	1	2
Experienced at least one of the above	62	82	87

From: Weschsler H, Davenport A, Dowdall G, Moeykens B, Castillo S. Health and behavioral consequences of binge drinking in college: A national survey of students at 140 campuses. *Journal of the American Medical Association* 272(21):1672–1677, 1994.

don't miss it. That is the perceived benefits associated with use. The negative consequences of drinking get all of the attention. If that were all there was to it, if virtually only bad, or bad and neutral, outcomes were associated with drinking, isn't it likely that campus drinking patterns would look quite different? A recent study examined the positive consequences that college students associate with drinking. There are many. Equally important, when students weigh the intensity of negative and positive outcomes, the positive consequences are judged to be greater, and positive outcomes are seen as occurring far more frequently than negative fallout. Just as students can recount a negative episode and re-experience the embarrassment or guilt, so too can students recall the specific pleasures associated with a drinking event. "I had a blast dancing at the bar with friends." "I could really talk to others and express my true feelings." Among the things cited as benefits are more fun, better times with friends, less tension, and easier socializing. To draw upon learning theory, the positive responses associated with alcohol occur more frequently and are encoded in each event, reinforcing the belief that drinking leads to more fun. For the most part, this is equally true for men and women, although men do report both greater positive and negative

Most of the confidence which I appear to feel, especially when influenced by noon wine, is only a pretense.
TENNESSEE WILLIAMS, 1977

consequences and women may be more open than men to moderating drinking after negative consequences.

Students at Risk

There are several groups of students who are at greater risk for acute problems. *Inexperienced drinkers* are among those with the greatest risk. Many student health services find that freshmen are those most likely to be seen for overdoses and acute alcohol poisoning. In the vicinity of 15% to 20% of the typical freshman class didn't drink in high school. Most of them become drinkers during their first year of college. Problems accompany this transition from nondrinker to drinker, as well as the transition from infrequent to regular drinker. Underage drinkers, also the younger drinkers, are more likely to experience negative consequences. They have a 50% greater rate of being injured (15% vs. 10%). In addition, they have significantly higher rates of driving after drinking, doing something they later regret, having unplanned sexual activity, and damaging property.

Fraternity and sorority members are another group at special risk for acute problems. Much of the social life of these organizations can revolve around drinking. Members of Greek organizations consistently are found more likely to be drinkers, as well as heavy drinkers. Drinking games are part of the Greek scene. While thought of as the domain of male students, women also take part. This is one way that incoming students are socialized into a problematic drinking pattern. There has been some exploration of personality traits that are associated with playing drinking games. Being a risk taker, a sensation seeker, as well as being impulsive and less socially inhibited are associated with drinking games. When asked motives for playing drinking games, among those mentioned are fun/celebration and sexual manipulation. Drinking games are strongly related with negative consequences and instances of sexual victimization.

The *level of high school drinking* is possibly the best single predictor of alcohol problems in college. A number of years ago, a study conducted by the Health Service at the University of Pennsylvania found that the best predictor of alcohol problems during college was the frequency of drinking to intoxication reported by incoming students. Incoming freshmen who were the heaviest drinkers in their class and who had had a prior alcohol-related incident were at much higher risk for problems during college. By the end of their sophomore year, these students had more overall visits to the health center, more alcohol-related visits to the health center, and a lower grade point average.

Athletes, according to folk wisdom, drink less than other students. The assumption has been that they have less free time, are more concerned with fitness, and are bound by training rules. This is not the case.

Both the Core Survey and the Campus Alcohol Survey have found that those engaged in intercollegiate athletics are more likely to be drinkers and to be heavier drinkers than nonathletes. Male athletes who are also fraternity members have the highest levels of heavy alcohol use. The NCAA (National Collegiate Athletic Association) regularly surveys alcohol and other drug use among member schools. Its 2001 survey included 732 schools, with responses from 21,200 athletes. Among these athletes, 80% reported using alcohol, followed by marijuana (33%), cigarettes (25%), and smokeless tobacco (23%).

Athletes have a higher rate of negative consequences than the general student body. There are several exceptions. One is driving after drinking. The other is suspecting that they may have a problem. Some do acknowledge that their drinking interferes with athletic performance. Fully 33% say that their drinking has led to a poorer performance in practice or a game. In addition to those, 11% report that that has happened more than once or twice. There are also 12% who acknowledge that their drinking has led to their being late for or missing practice or a game. The rates of negative consequences are summarized in Table 11.9. Just as African-American students drink less than whites, so too for African-American athletes, who drink less and have fewer negative consequences.

Most athletes who drink say they have more than 1 or 2 drinks on a typical drinking occasion. Most notably, 30% report 6–9 drinks, and 13.5% say they usually have 10 or more drinks at a sitting. The alcohol-sports connection isn't limited only to athletes. Campus sports fans too drink more heavily than do students who don't describe themselves as sports fans, and they also have more alcohol-related problems than nonfans.

In addition to alcohol, a concern that is unique to college athletes is the use of performance-enhancing drugs. In case anyone may have missed it, in larger schools, college athletics is big business. There are a fair number of schools at which the football coach earns more than does the college's president. College athletic programs, particularly among Division I schools, essentially serve as the minor leagues for professional sports. Beyond whatever pressure there is to win one for the Gipper, or the school, any student who has ever nourished a dream of a post-college professional career has certainly at least thought about the potential benefits of performance-enhancing drugs. While the data are sparse, it appears that a substantial number of college athletes have more than thought about using performance-enhancing agents. A survey of 5 college ice hockey teams found that over half of the members had used metabolic stimulants at some point in their careers. A quarter were current users. Close to 100% recognized use of those stimulants was banned by the NCAA. Furthermore, virtually all were aware that some of these substances were linked to serious side effects, such as those associated with ephedrine use, such as insomnia, hypertension, even sudden death. Nonetheless, a third of those polled indicated they would use a banned

Table 11.9 Alcohol-Related Problems Among Athletes and the General Student Body

Problem	% of All Students	% of Athletes
Had a hangover	62.6	66.5
Got nauseated or vomited	53.2	53.6
Did something later regretted	38.2	45.0
Missed a class	33.1	44.5
Drove a car while under the influence	32.5	30.8
Had a memory loss	31.7	30.5
Got into an argument or a fight	30.8	36.3
Was criticized by someone	30.3	35.1
Performed poorly on a test or another project	23.5	34.5
Was hurt or injured	14.3	21.1
Had trouble with police or other authorities	13.7	18.5
Was taken advantage of sexually	11.7	12.0
Thought they might have a problem	10.7	8.2
Damaged property, pulled fire alarm, etc.	8.2	10.5
Tried unsuccessfully to stop using	5.8	6.2
Seriously thought about suicide	4.6	4.7
Took advantage of another sexually	4.6	6.2
Was arrested for DWI	1.5	2.8
Seriously tried to commit suicide	1.4	2.0

From: Presley CA, Leichliter JS, Meilman PW. *Alcohol and Drugs on American College Campuses.* Carbondale, IL: Core Institute, Southern Illinois University, 2001. www.siu.edu/departments/coreinst/public_html/recent.html

National Collegiate Athletic Association. *Study of Substance Abuse Habits of College-Student Athletes.* Indianapolis, IN: NCAA, June 2001. www2.ncaa.org/media_and_events/ncaa_publications/research/index.html substance

substance if it would help them get into the National Hockey League. Whatever the risks, the possible rewards loomed larger.

A poll of coaches and other staff associated with athletic programs provides a similarly disturbing picture of college athlete drug use. Thirty percent of schools do not have a total ban on alcohol use during recruitment of student players, most of whom are presumably underage. At 81%

of colleges the drug/alcohol education provided via athletic departments to student athletes consists of 1 or fewer sessions per semester. Less than half of the schools have a drug-testing program. Of schools with drug testing, one-third test for anabolic steroids, although 98% test for marijuana. In the event of a first-time positive drug test, 94% inform the director of athletics; 91% inform the student/athlete; 88% inform the coach; 79% inform the trainer, 52% inform a school counselor; 45% the team doctor, and 44% inform the parents. By a third positive test, the odds of the athlete being informed go up to 98%; the chances of a school counselor and the team doctor being informed go up to 56% and 55%, and chances of a parent being told are doubled, reaching almost two-thirds. In terms of actions taken, for a first positive test 44% of the schools will suspend a student from the team. This rises to 71% for a second positive test, and 72% for a third positive test. As for referral for treatment, 85% of the Division I schools have steps in place to make a referral for athletes diagnosed with abuse or dependence. For Division III schools the figure is less than two-thirds.

Natural History of Collegians' Alcohol Use

Researchers at the University of Washington have done considerable work in studying the effects of brief interventions, including the use of brief interventions among college students. To conduct this research, there was the need to define the natural history of alcohol use and alcohol problems during the college years.

In any study of the effectiveness of a treatment or prevention activity, there are several important factors to consider. One is the need for an appropriate comparison, or control, group. This is because any treatment ought to lead to a better outcome than if nothing had been done—hence the question "What is the natural history for the condition?" Many surveys have found that, during college, the rate of drinking and the associated problems do decline. If that is so, does an intervention produce better outcomes than would have occurred anyway? If not, is there a difference in the rate at which alcohol problems resolve? Can the "natural" rate of improvement be sped up? If so, that is a justification for the intervention. A related question is "How long should the follow-up period be to determine if changes endure?" This is a question especially important when evaluating the effects of prevention programs. It is not uncommon to find that students who have received a prevention program differ from a comparison group immediately after the program, or at a month or even after several. But by a year, these differences may have evaporated. The same question arises in respect to treatment effectiveness. Has enough time passed so that one can be confident that any improvement is not transitory? To put it differently, has enough time passed so that, if things were going to fall apart, that would have happened?

University of Washington researchers traced drinking patterns over the course of 4 years of college, tracking drinking frequency, quantity consumed, and negative consequences. The typical incoming student drank more often than he or she did in high school. However, after the first year, he or she drinks less often. Then as an upperclassman and with reaching that magic twenty-first birthday, drinking frequency increases. But what about the quantity consumed? This may come as a surprise: there is a modest increase during the first 2 years. However, when students are upperclassmen, the total amount of alcohol consumed declines, despite the fact that there are more drinking occasions. In effect, they drink more often but less on each drinking occasion.

This is the way I look when I'm sober. That's enough to make a person drink, wouldn't you say?

Kristine, after not having a drink for two days, from the movie *Days of Wine and Roses,* 1962

You'd be surprised how much fun you can have sober. When you get the hang of it.

Joe, from the movie *Days of Wine and Roses,* 1962

While the previous paragraph described the picture for students as a whole, there was a subgroup who was clearly "nonaverage." They entered college with a history of problematic alcohol use. The study followed this at-risk group, too. (For the students to qualify as "at risk," there had to be one incident of binge drinking in the past month and a history of several negative consequences on at least 3 occasions in the preceding 3 years.) What was immediately evident was that at-risk students entered college, drinking more often and larger amounts than the average student. Over their 4 years of college, their frequency of drinking remained relatively constant. At graduation they were drinking about as often as they had in high school, 4 years before. However, as a group, throughout the college years, there was a steady decline in the quantity they drank. These at-risk students were drinking significantly less at graduation than they did as entering freshmen. With the decline in quantity, there was a corresponding decrease in the number of alcohol-associated negative consequences. During college, the level of negative consequences was never as high as it had been in high school.

Clearly, the drinking of high-risk students changes during college, with a decline in the how often they drink, how much, and how many problems that result. Nonetheless, when their pattern is compared with that of students generally, one thing still stands out. Whether it's frequency, quantity, or the negative consequence—the high-risk group consistently has higher levels. Its lowest level on each of these measures is still higher than the highest for the general student body. So while levels of risk decline, they consistently exceed the highest risks for the average collegian.

The Exceptions

That is the global picture for the general college population as well as at-risk students. Within both groups, there are those who follow a different path. For some, college is where alcohol problems first emerge. There is a significant minority—23%—who leave college with more than a diploma. They have also developed an alcohol problem. On the other hand, the same is true of the at-risk drinkers. Not all of them turn in the six-pack for a briefcase, send out a résumé, buy a suit, and live happily ever after. Half leave with drinking problems at the level they were when they entered as freshmen. For 40% of these, the situation is essentially the same. But there are 10% whose problem has become worse.

What factors are at work to help make sense of these patterns? Several perspectives are useful.

Maturation

Clearly there is a *maturational process* at work. Leaving home and going off to college for many is a significant developmental milestone. This is a time when parental bonds soften, including the rules that accompany living with parents. This is a period of increased independence. Alcohol is part of the picture. There are also *expectancies* operating—the belief that alcohol is a part of relaxing, reducing stress, and being more comfortable socially, as well as the sense that drinking is part of college life, independence, and adulthood. College students typically have positive expectancies for drinking. They may, too, erroneously believe that the degree of enjoyment associated with alcohol is related to the amount consumed, so "If some is good, more is better."

Learning

Wine should be taken in small doses; knowledge in large ones.
Chinese proverb

The University of Washington researchers suggest, too, that *learning* is also taking place, especially for the rank-and-file relatively inexperienced and newer drinkers. In essence, they discover the fallacy in the perspective that more is better. As the researchers put it, they discover there is "a point of diminishing returns." There exists a point at which more alcohol does not bring more enjoyment but has the opposite effect. As one upperclassman put it, "It's no longer fun to get smashed the way we used to." This is equally true for the at-risk students as well as students generally. Over the course of their 4 college years, they drink less and with fewer negative consequences. While entering college is a developmental milestone, so is graduation. The college years are essentially a period of transition.

Social Norms

It has long been recognized that among adolescents generally, one of the best predictors of a particular teen's drinking is the drinking pattern of his or her friends. What people think "everyone" is doing, has an impact. Many adolescents too have been found to have inaccurate perception of the drinking patterns in their schools or town. Typically they overestimate the rates of heavy drinking. It is hypothesized that this either frees or pressures adolescents to alter their drinking to approximate what they think is the norm.

Always do sober what you said you'd do when you were drunk. That will teach you to keep your mouth shut!
CHARLES SCRIBNER, JR.
from his obituary, *New York Times,* 1995

In the late 1980s and early 1990s, the same kind of misperception of the actual norms was found to be true on the college campus. Accordingly, a campus prevention approach was designed that goes by the term "social marketing," essentially an effort to educate students as to the actual drinking patterns. Commonly these are media campaigns that use articles and ads in the campus newspaper, or posters, or other such efforts. One of the first such programs, launched in the late 1980s at a midwestern medium-size university, found that the campus binge drinking rate fell markedly, with the rate of binge drinking dropping from 45% to 28% over a 6-year period. Similarly, a large southwestern public university found its campus's binge drinking rate declining from 43% to 31% over 3 years. These kinds of results prompted others to adopt a social marketing approach.

An evaluation of the southwestern university program just mentioned also found that along with the decline in binge drinking, there was a change in student attitudes, especially in how students characterized their own and others' alcohol and drinking behavior. Over the course of the study, there were changes in the number of students who agreed with the following statements:

Belief	% Agreeing	% Decline in Agreement
• "Most college students have 5 or more drinks when they party."	40	30
• "Most UA students drink heavily during Spring Break."	78	8
• "Alcohol-free events are not as much fun as an event with alcohol."	27	27
• "I would rather go to a party that served alcohol than one that did not."	48	17
• "Most college students are not interested in alcohol-free events."	41	20
• "Drinking alcohol increases sexual opportunity."	52	15

Notice which statement generates the highest rate of agreement and was least changed over time: "Most UA students drink heavily during Spring Break." Notice, too, how "Spring Break" is capitalized. This suggests it isn't just a time period; it is an event. Does it spark fantasies that rank right up there with the perfect New Year's Eve? Spring break is a time when students are dispersed, off campus, with no student able to know what is truly transpiring with others. If asked to assess drinking during "Spring Break," what do you base your estimate on? Likely, your imagination or *People* magazine is your major source of information. Does anyone factor in those who don't do anything special, who hang out at home, sleep in, maybe catch up on some reading, and get bored? But then, that's "spring break" not "Spring Break!"

Understandably, social marketing has been getting a lot of attention. However, there are some caveats. For social marketing efforts to have the desired impact—whatever the setting or behavioral changes desired—certain conditions need to be met. First, it's necessary that a significant number of individuals, in this case students, have a misperception. Furthermore, in this case, the incorrect estimates need to be errors in the direction of overestimates. Secondly, the misperception must involve behavior that people can't, individually, know with full certainty. Thirdly,

Good wine needs no bush,
And perhaps products that people really want need no hard-sell or soft-sell TV push.
Why not?
Look at pot.

OGDEN NASH
"Most Doctors Recommend or Yours for Fast Fast Fast Relief," 1972

the individuals being targeted with a message, must care about the group whose values, behaviors, and so forth are being held up as a standard, or norm. Whether one sees oneself as in or out of step with "the group" has to matter at some level for this to motivate behavioral change.

So what are the implications for campus programs? Some studies have shown that some groups on campus, such as those in Greek organizations, are less susceptible to broad social marketing campaigns. This shouldn't be surprising. The group that matters most to them is their own fraternity or sorority, so they may care little what the general campus is doing. In addition, they *do* know what the drinking norms are in their group. So there is no discrepancy that can be exploited.

Some relatively recent research published suggests another potential limitation to social marketing. The most recent Campus Alcohol Study (1999) indicated that unlike a decade earlier, most students *are* accurately estimating the level of binge drinking on their campus. The discrepancy seen earlier has eroded. The majority of students at 60% of schools rated the level within 10% of the actual rate. For 31% there was an underestimate; for only 8% was there an overestimate. Thus only 8% of schools are seemingly good candidates for social marketing. Those with accurate perceptions don't need it. And for the roughly one-third who underestimate the level, there is the danger of inviting students to increase their drinking to match the true norm!

It is tempting to think of social marketing as a magic bullet. There is something else to consider. The number of students who report binge drinking is different from the number of binge drinking events. Possibly the total number of binge drinking episodes that has as much impact on the atmosphere of a campus, as does the number of students involved. Consider the following scenario. One student who is a binge drinker does so 1 out every 10 drinking occasions. Another student who is a binge drinker drinks that way virtually 100% of the time. If the infrequent binge drinker is the person who changes, the impact on the total number of binge drinking episodes is far less than if it's the person who binges every time who changes his drinking pattern.

Another recently identified caveat is that there are in fact different types of norms; this has rarely been noted in discussions of campus social norms and social marketing. Typically when discussing social norms what is meant is *descriptive norms,* that is, the perception of drinking behaviors which describe the drinking patterns on campus. Social norms also can be viewed from the reference point of the "thou shalts" and "thou shalt nots," *injunctive norms,* which are always present. This aspect of social norms has been little discussed. How would students describe the dominant rules regarding drinking? A number of years ago, an effort at Rutgers University drew upon the concept of injunctive norms in efforts conducted within the dormitories. One component of a larger campuswide effort was the requirement for dormitory groups to articulate the expectations they wished to establish and adopt for their own and others' behavior related to drinking.

Campus Policy

In considering campus drinking practices, the question arises as to whether there are campus factors that are protective, associated with lower levels of heavy drinking. The Campus Survey compared schools that had an alcohol ban for all students versus schools without such a ban. First, there wasn't a difference between the schools in terms of the students they attracted; both kinds of schools have the same proportion of heavy high school drinkers. But at the schools with an alcohol ban there was a substantially lower rate of heavy drinking, 30% lower. Of interest is that collegians who had been heavy drinkers in high school were not more likely to be heavy drinkers in college. So for them, the college atmosphere was a moderating influence. But among the heavy drinking college students, the rate of alcohol problems was the same, regardless of the institution's alcohol policy.

Social Capital

Another factor has been identified as associated with lower levels of college binge drinking. Schools were rated by the average time per month that their students spend doing volunteer work, which was referred to as "social capital." Of note is that schools with a higher than average level of volunteer student effort also had a 25% lower level of binge drinking, even though the schools were similar in most other respects. It is interesting to speculate how this phenomenon might be explained. One possibility is that engaging students in the community beyond the campus's ivy-covered walls facilitates the students' maturation process. This is turn may affect the campus climate.

Community Characteristics

Beyond the immediate campus environment, the larger community in which the college is located also influences drinking behaviors. Interestingly, there are marked differences from school to school in rates of student drinking and driving. This isn't a random event. Schools with the lower rates of drinking and driving are generally located in states and communities with more restrictions and greater enforcement of underage drinking. Another difference between colleges is the number of bars and drinking establishments that fringe the campus. The sheer density of drinking establishments surrounding the campus correlates with students' levels of heavy drinking.

Access to Alcohol

Think of "access" in the broadest sense, legal access, to physical access, and also economic access, meaning cost. Many colleges and universities find that their closest neighbors include a disproportionate number of alcohol outlets: package stores, bars, taverns, and cafés. The sheer number is not the only problem. They are doing their own version of social marketing, promoting their wares in an aggressive fashion. There are the Happy Hours, 2 for 1 specials, the pitchers of beer, and half-price drinks

If you are poor, avoid wine as a costly luxury;
if you are rich, shun it as a fatal indulgence.
Stick to plain water
HERMAN MELVILLE
Mardi, 1855

for women between the hours of 5 and 7. Is there a holiday that does not warrant some special attention: St. Patrick's Day, Columbus Day, Ground Hog's Day, Election Night? These places can afford to undercut each other in terms of price, because they make up for it in volume.

Of course, licensed establishments are not the only or even the primary source of alcohol for most students. Older students are a major supplier, followed by parties. Students report that alcohol is a bargain. In a follow-up to the College Survey, students from 10 large universities provided the cost of different kinds of activities. It appears that alcohol is the cheapest form of entertainment:

Social Activity	Average Price
Beer from a keg	$ 0.25
Beer from a can	$ 0.37
Drink special at bar/club	$ 0.75
Admission, all-you-can-drink party	$ 1.50
Cup of coffee (off-campus)	$ 1.09
Movie ticket	$ 5.86
Concert	$27.33

Impetus to Institutional Action

The earliest pressure to address alcohol and substance use problems—back in the 1970s—came from recovering alumni. Many campus alumni magazines have periodically printed first-person accounts by recovering alumni. Typically these individuals do not blame their alma maters for causing their alcohol dependence, but they claim that the campus environment provided fertile ground for its later emergence. Another factor in the 1970s that gave rise to campus initiatives was the availability of federal monies for pilot demonstration educational programs specially targeted at college students.

Certainly the attention paid to alcohol problems on college campuses is a manifestation of society's generally increasing awareness of alcohol and substance use problems. However, some factors have been unique to the campus community.

Institutional Liability

The rise in the legal drinking age highlighted the issue of institutional liability. Although the number of cases that have been litigated has been small, they have received attention. Under its "duty to care," a college is responsible for the well-being of its students. Although the institution's obligation to supervise student conduct may be limited, it cannot claim a total absence of responsibility. The institution can be deemed involved based on its sponsorship and regulation of student organizations. Another domain in which there is potential liability is in the institution's role as proprietor, with the duty to maintain safe premises. This includes handling rowdiness at football games or parties and protecting others from a student who is known to be abusive.

NCAA Policies

Colleges must also contend with the issues of organized sports, such as the National Collegiate Athletic Association (NCAA) mandatory drug testing to establish a student's or team's eligibility. The NCAA mandatory drug testing is, in theory, only one component of a larger substance use educational and prevention effort. However, testing has received the most attention and institutional resources. In addition, federal initiatives to establish drug-free campuses have provided further impetus for institutional action. The drug-free campus legislation has made distribution of federal funds contingent on colleges' establishing programs to promote nonuse among students and employees. These mandated programs are to include clearly established disciplinary actions for those who are found to be in violation of the campus policy.

Impediments to Campus Programs

Although campus efforts to address student alcohol and substance use now seem to have been around forever, that isn't the case. For example, the American College Health Association (ACHA), which has a reputation for its progressive stance toward health-care issues, incorporated alcohol services into its standards for member institutions only in 1987. Although they are far from disinterested, many campus administrators have little sophistication with respect to alcohol and substance use problems. As elsewhere, personal biases and impressions here substitute for information and data.

Also, a number of myths continue to hold sway. One is the view that heavy drinking is "just a stage"—with a diploma, a little more maturity, and some adult responsibilities, this developmental period, marked by excessive alcohol consumption, will pass. While this is true, there are exceptions. Plus, given the dangerous situations that can occur, a student may not survive to outgrow the problem. Given the strong reliance on alcohol and other drug education as the basis of programs, there are those who apparently think problems represent an educational deficit, with students merely uninformed about alcohol or other drugs. This ignores the fact that students arrive on campuses having already been targets of educational programs throughout grade school, middle school, and high school. This position also overlooks the fact that changes in knowledge do not necessarily lead to changes in behavior. (While education is a common element, programs that are built primarily or solely around education have little impact.)

There are those, too, who see substance use problems as a case of bad manners, which is essentially a moral issue. Those with alcohol problems are regarded as having poor attitudes and questionable values. The goal, therefore, is to have students "shape up." Discussion of "responsible" drinking can reinforce this orientation. The obvious counterpoint to responsible drinking is irresponsible drinking. Many students may be at substantial risk but do not view themselves, or are considered by peers as being, irresponsible. Students, too, can mistakenly be viewed as non-drinkers who are thrust into a drinking culture. On the contrary, the majority of students enter college with an established drinking pattern. Many qualify as at-risk problematic drinkers.

Campus Initiatives

Alcohol and Drug Policy

An important component of an institution's effort is formulating an alcohol/drug policy. A policy should not read like a penal code. It should set forth a clear, direct statement of the institution's stance toward alcohol and other drug use and the steps and means it intends to use in addressing these. Consider, as a parallel, institutional statements on academic honesty. In such statements, the institution's stance is clear. The standards set for members' behavior are unambiguous. There is not, however, an effort to establish comprehensive policing efforts to ensure compliance. However, if violations of the honor code come to the administration's attention, they will be treated without hesitation as serious breeches of the ethos underpinning the community's intellectual life.

A question that commonly comes to light when alcohol policies are discussed is "Can we enforce the policy?" One response is opting to go no further than creating "all the policy we think we can enforce," which often is little. There has been the perception that more limited statements would reduce liability, which is not the case. No institution can protect itself from suit in our litigious society. The institution is often the deep pocket. The best protection for the institution if litigation occurs is a comprehensive student education and treatment referral program.

A comprehensive program needs to involve all sectors of the campus community. This does not mean that everyone need be a "true believer" in the same fashion. For some, public relations may be a major concern; for others, the impetus for involvement may be institutional liability; and for others it may be the record on the playing field or not jeopardizing the school's status with the NCAA by coming up with positive urine screens. For others, the quality of life is a major motivation; for others, the academic life. For some, it is a health concern, and for others it may be personal identification with the issues of children of alcoholics or alcohol dependence. A model program can encompass all of these motives, not deeming some as more legitimate and noble than others. Ultimately, campuswide involvement occurs when alcohol issues are recognized as intruding on each of us.

In defining the need for change, one segment of the community often overlooked when formulating policy is the students. The administration formulates policy, makes the basic decisions, and then puts it to the students for some review and comment, which is often unfavorable. Those charged with planning then become bogged down in attempting to determine how to engineer students' acceptance. Students' negative responses may speak as much to their exclusion from the process as to their resistance to the program efforts proposed. Recent surveys have found that the majority of students do support a variety of policy initiatives.

They are not long, the weeping and the laughter,
Love and desire and hate;
I think they have no portion in us after
We pass the gate.
They are not long, the days of wine and roses:
Out of a misty dream
Our path emerges for a while, then closes
Within a dream.

ERNEST C. DOWSON

"Vitae Summa Brevis," 1896

Campuses are touched by the larger culture. One area where this is most strongly evident is campus athletics, particularly in Division I schools. In 1999, an invitational symposium on intercollegiate athletics was convened to consider steps to mitigate campus alcohol and other drug problems. Representatives were drawn from campuses ranging in size from Division I to Division III. This meeting was prompted by several factors. One was the recognition that college athletes are more prone than students in general to alcohol and other drug use and associated negative consequences. But also, college athletics can contribute to a range of problems on campus and surrounding communities. There is the impact of the pro-drinking advertising that accompanies sports sponsorships. Other problems result from widespread drinking both before and during home game weekends. This is particularly true at larger institutions, with their long-standing traditions of pregame parties, tailgating, and postgame affairs.

The symposium participants agreed on the importance of reaffirming the educational mission as the top priority of colleges and universities. The school is, foremost, a place for students to learn and to develop ethical values, not an entertainment venue or a business enterprise. The gathering adopted the following recommendations, which don't hold just for athletes but can be seen as the basis of general campus policy:

- The NCAA should reassess its policies for accepting alcohol advertising and sponsorship, because alcohol advertising of college sports sends a mixed message to underage students on campus and in the community. College and university presidents should consider following the lead of the University of North Carolina at Chapel Hill, the University of Minnesota, and the University of Kentucky and similarly divest their sports programs of alcohol advertising.
- Schools should enforce consistent alcohol control measures for public events, such as pregame tailgating and in-stadium alcohol availability, to avoid double standards. Schools should further ensure that such pregame events do not compete for student attention with scheduled classes. Control measures should focus on high-risk drinking and related behaviors, as well as on marketing practices that encourage high-risk consumption.
- Schools should work with their surrounding communities in collaborative prevention activities.
- Schools should examine their sports recruiting practices and the attendant underage drinking by high school visitors during recruit

weekends. They should encourage frank communication with recruits (and their parents) about the dangers of hazing, high-risk drinking, and campus policies prior to athletes' arrival on campus.

- Schools should reduce risks posed by postgame celebration and consolation occasions by encouraging coaches and team leaders to host such social gatherings in ways that do not involve alcohol and other drugs.
- Schools should examine the pros and cons of accepting support from the alcohol industry in whatever form, including so-called responsible drinking campaigns.
- Schools should be alert to the health status of their student athletes. For some students, treatment may be indicated.

Environmental Initiatives

Efforts to address alcohol and other drug problems are increasingly looking at broader issues that can contribute to substance use problems.

Assessment of Social Fabric of the Campus This includes considering the nature of social life and particularly the extent to which this is tied to Greek organizations and heavy drinking. Are there any or many alternatives to Greek organizations, or is the campus dependent on fraternities and sororities to provide social opportunities? Tied to this discussion is concern about the campus's ability to foster a community that consists of culturally and ethnically diverse groups.

Alcohol-Free Residence Halls More and more colleges are providing students the choice of residences that are alcohol free. Rates of drinking and negative consequences are lower among students in these dorms. Also, many campuses find there are more students interested in alcohol-free dorms than there are rooms available. The presence of alcohol-free dorms also makes a statement to the general community. It supports nondrinking in a visible fashion and makes it a legitimate, official choice.

Athletics and Alumni Events The NCAA guidelines contain initiatives that a number of campuses have instituted. There have been efforts to put an end to tailgate parties before football games, to restrict the service of alcohol at college events of any kind, to establish and enforce restrictions against drinking in public areas of campus, and others.

Reduction of Alcohol Promotions The beverage industry spends a significant amount of money promoting alcohol on campus. Promotional efforts directed at campuses have ranged from providing kegs of beer as prizes for campus events, such as blood drives, to distributing beer mugs or baseball caps with logos. Some students are compensated for being campus promotional representatives, distributing advertising paraphernalia, such as caps, posters, and napkins with the brewer's logo. Beer companies are major advertisers in campus newspapers and other campus publications. Thus, these have led to the adoption of marketing guidelines for promoting alcoholic beverages or limiting alcohol beverage promotions.

Outreach to the Local Community Many campuses are working with local town and city governments to address alcohol-related problems, including the density of drinking establishments near campus, the enforcement of open container laws, the reduction of underage sales by package stores and the serving of underage drinkers in bars, and efforts to keep high school students out of the fraternities. Towns that may have historically looked the other way when it came to alcohol issues are being asked to stop doing so.

Applications of Research Findings An area gaining greater attention in the general substance abuse literature is the role of contingency management, offering frank rewards for desired behaviors. One research group applied this to a fraternity party setting, with people having the opportunity to win a cash prize if they had a BAC below 0.05. Over a series of parties, twice as many were intoxicated at the parties at which there was no prize option than were present when the lottery was held. Never underestimate the attraction of winning the lottery!

Intervention and Treatment

Given the natural history of alcohol use, colleges are confronted by several clear problems. Occasions of intoxication are common. Along with them is the risk of negative consequences, ranging from incidents of violence, to unwanted sexual encounters, to injuries. Such episodes are likely to bring a student to official attention. In addition to efforts that will reduce the campus-wide level of high-risk drinking, there are also interventions that must be directed at particular individuals.

Alcohol Emergencies

There may not be much to recommend education as *the* major means of dealing with college alcohol issues. However, there is one piece of information that is essential for any member of the campus community—how to recognize and respond to an alcohol emergency. This information is the alcohol-use equivalent of knowing CPR. Many schools make concerted efforts to inform students about what to do and what not to do in the case of an alcohol overdose. This information is posted alongside guidelines on how to contact emergency services, such as campus police or the fire department. Box 11.1 is the information that Haverford College (Pennsylvania) provides. It is found in the student handbook, and the emergency guide is posted prominently around campus, virtually as visible as fire extinguishers.

Brief Interventions

College students represent a segment of the population crying out for brief interventions. The number at risk is substantial, and the potential for making changes is significant. Every campus alcohol program needs

BOX 11.1 Alcohol First Aid

Severe intoxication and/or alcohol poisoning can be dangerous. Here are some basic guidelines to help you size up the scene and decide how to deal with a drunken friend.

Do

1. Assist the person to be comfortable. Make sure the person is in a safe place.
2. Use a calm, strong voice; be firm.
3. Assess if the person is in a life-threatening situation, and get help if you need it.
4. Lay the person down on their side with knees up so they won't choke if they vomit.
5. Check breathing every 10 minutes.
6. Do not leave the person alone.
7. Be sure the person doesn't swallow or breathe in vomitus.

Don't

1. Give the person cold showers.
2. Don't try to walk the person around.
3. Don't provoke a fight by arguing or laughing at someone who is drunk.
4. Don't try to counsel the person. Confront the behavior later, when he or she is sober.
5. Don't give anything to eat or drink. Coffee and food won't help, and the person may choke.
6. Don't permit the person to drive.
7. Don't give any drugs; they will not sober someone up; in combination with alcohol, they may be lethal.
8. Don't induce vomiting.

Emergency Guide Call Safety and Security if

- The person cannot be aroused by shaking or shouting.
- The person's breathing is shallow, irregular, or slowed to fewer than 6–7 breaths per minute.
- The person drank alcohol in combination with any other drugs.
- The person sustained a blow to the head or any injury that caused bleeding.
- The person drank a large quantity within a short period and then collapsed.

If You Are Not Sure What to Do, but Think That the Person Needs Help, Call for Medical Advice.

to determine the threshold of concern with respect to individuals. Phrased another way, what is the institution prepared to overlook? The threshold for concern should be low. It is suggested that the best stance is to err on the conservative side. Whether an alcohol incident represents an isolated event or a chronic problem will never be outwardly and immediately apparent. Thus for those who come to attention, some intervention is warranted.

Research Model One model for a brief intervention was part of the University of Washington study which tracked the natural history of drinking. Some of the incoming high-risk students were randomly assigned to a preventive intervention. They were contacted during the winter term to schedule an individualized feedback session in 2 weeks. These students were asked to self-monitor their drinking during the period prior to the appointment. During the visit, drawing upon the 2-week diary and the earlier survey, in the discussion, the student received information about his or her drinking, compared with others. Also covered was the student's sense of the risks and benefits of drinking, highlighting any discrepancies between current behavior and aspirations, goals, and plans. Efforts were also spent countering any myths about alcohol and its effects. At the conclusion, the student got a 1-page handout of tips on reducing drinking risks.

This approach was based on a harm reduction model. There was no discussion of legal issues and being underage and no efforts to persuade the student to stop alcohol use. A manual was used to guide and structure the session. The following year, the sophomore year in college, there was a follow-up contact. This was individualized, again summarizing the person's drinking in relation to others. (For those at highest risk, in addition there was a phone call, expressing concern about the students' level of risk. They were also offered the possibility of further follow-up contacts to see how things were going. A small minority took advantage of this.) This preventive intervention had a clear impact when these students were compared with their at-risk classmates who did not receive it. The changes set in motion persisted over the remaining 3½ years of college. This intervention can be thought of as having facilitated and sped up the "maturing out" process.

Application to Health Care Center The challenge is always how to transfer to the everyday world procedures created in the research arena. At the University of Washington, the task devising a brief intervention that could be conducted was in the health center. This meant that the original research procedures had to be streamlined dramatically and boiled down to activities that the health center clinician can do in 3 to 5 minutes.

Here is what was devised. Students going to the health center are invited to arrive 15 minutes early to take a computerized interactive assessment covering a number of health issues. If a student's responses suggest he or she is at risk for alcohol problems, the computer automatically generates additional questions. The questions and available feedback anticipate common responses. At-risk students typically express disbelief to find they are in the upper levels of consumption: "Ninety-eighth percentile?" "No way." "*Everyone* I know drinks as much or more." To counter this, a number of questions ask for estimates of the "average" college student. Students can request feedback based on the assessment and elect to make a copy available to the practitioner the student is scheduled to see. (To ensure privacy, and to deal with issues such as informed consent, the student does not provide any identifying information in the computer session.)

During the medical appointment, the doctor or nurse reviews the feedback sheet with the patient. These feedback sheets were carefully designed to get the student's attention, as well as to make it easy for the doctor or nurse to zero in on the key information. The practitioners are trained to ask themselves the following questions:

- "What is the pattern of use?"
- "What most concerns me about the student's risks?"
- "What would make it worth the student's while to moderate his or her alcohol use?"
- "What will get in the way of the student's using the information?"
- "Where will I have my biggest impact, such as teaching one skill, or emphasizing the decision is the student's?"
- "Is the student at imminent risk, or is there significant motivation to change that follow-up or referral if warranted?"

After considering these questions, the clinician has 4 basic tasks. To help staff remember what these are, the acronym REAP has been coined. **Re**view the students' current drinking habits and risks. **E**ncourage students to reduce risks by moderating consumption. **A**dvise students on specific strategies to reduce risky drinking. **P**rovide materials, follow-up, or referral if needed. The materials include a computer-generated personalized tip sheet, as well as a moderation management handout. A month later, there is a follow-up contact.

Assessment and Treatment of Substance Use Problems

The brief intervention is a preventive activity. Inevitably there will be contacts where a more serious problem is evident. There are also situations that bring someone to the health service in which alcohol is clearly implicated—accidents, injuries, alcohol poisonings, and requests for the morning-after pill. Or a student may come to the attention of college administration as the result of an alcohol-related event—a fight which involved the police, dorm damage, or arrest for a DWI. Whatever the route, an assessment is required. Whether this is something that can be undertaken by a substance abuse clinician who is part of the health service or counseling service, or whether this is something that is automatically referred out will vary by campus.

If treatment is warranted, the question becomes whether this is something that the health center service staff is capable of providing or whether a referral should be made to a community agency or clinician. There is also the student's openness to treatment. The institution does have some significant leverage as the student considers whether or not to

FOCUS ON DRUGS

Adolescent Smoking Cessation

Too often discussion of adolescents and nicotine are addressed only within the context of prevention. However, as the *Monitoring the Future* study shows, for a significant portion of adolescents, it's past the point of prevention. In 2002 a quarter of high school seniors were current smokers as were 11% of eighth graders.

Importantly a significant majority (85%) of adolescent smokers think about quitting and over 90% have made an effort to quit during the past year. Success in quitting is tied to a number of things. As might be expected, the level of dependence, marked by the number of cigarettes smoked per day, predicts success or failure to quit. Other factors teens mention as helping with cessation are having nonsmoking friends, and the nature of their schools' rules and the level of enforcement which in combination make smoking more difficult. When asked "Why do you want to quit?" the top reason offered by girls is health (65%) and among boys its athletic performance (51%). Also mentioned are cost, social influences, setting an example for others, general appearance, plus no perceived positive reinforcement for smoking.

It is unclear the extent to which adolescents are aware of the kinds of programs or approaches available to assist with smoking cessation. Or as one study found, they may tend not to think of themselves as such hardcore smokers that they need external assistance. The same modalities used with adults are being used with teens—nicotine replacement, medications, brief interventions, motivational enhancement.

Currently only a handful of smoking cessation programs are specifically tailored to adolescents. One of these is a program designed by the American Lung Association, called Not-on-Tobacco (N-O-T). It is among the more intensive initiatives, and is offered over a 10-week period. When compared to a brief intervention, Not-on-Tobacco has far better outcomes especially among those with higher levels of nicotine dependence. In fact the evidence to date suggests that brief treatments are only effective with the low-dependence smokers. Another approach being explored is promoting smoking cessation in teen worksites. It has been initiated in a large supermarket chain; each store typically has over 40 teen employees. Dubbed SMART, it involves diverse components ranging from mailings, health education promotions, contests, games, and peer-led groups. The interactive components are organized at the work site, out of the employee break room.

Beyond the workplace, the other obvious site to offer smoking cessation programs is in schools. Evidence to date from a statewide effort in Illinois shows that these can succeed. Obviously, the first step is getting students to attend! An important factor which predicts attendance is offering smoking cessation programs during the school day, rather than as an evening or after-school extracurricular activity. Other factors which predict participation are prior unsuccessful efforts to quit smoking, and higher levels of dependence, which seemed to translate into greater motivation Some characteristics of the school also influence student participation, such as the percentage of low-income students, which reduced participation, and levels of support for not smoking, as well as the degree of disapproval of smoking.

While research is limited, the findings suggest some factors that deserve further exploration and may enhance the effectiveness of adolescent smoking cessation initiatives. One is the need to be alert to possible depression provoked by smoking cessation. Another is that for a large group of adolescent girls, concerns about weight are closely tied to smoking. For these young women smoking might be viewed as a means of weight control. Adolescent women who are daily smokers are four times as likely to fast, use diet pills, and purge as a way to control weight. Adolescents also may prove to be a unique asset to one another. Nonsmoking teens may be an untapped resource in promoting other teens' cessation efforts. Of those surveyed, fully 90% of the adolescents reported knowing someone whose smoking was a concern to them, most commonly a parent or friend. In addition, they indicated a strong willingness to provide support to help that person quit.

seek treatment. There will be times when the institution has good reason to insist that continuation in school is dependent on entry into treatment and compliance with treatment recommendations. There are times that a medical leave may be advisable. If so, when the student returns, attention needs to be made to follow-up, continuing supportive efforts, relapse prevention, and involvement in self-help.

Antismoking Efforts

While alcohol use is a major concern, attention is also being directed to other drug use on campus. Tobacco is a particular concern. There are efforts to prevent the initiation of smoking and other tobacco use as well as offering smoking cessation programs for current smokers. Just as first-year students are at greatest risk of alcohol problems, they too are at greater risk for becoming smokers. Over half of college seniors who smoke began smoking when in college. Two factors recognized to be associated with smoking—depression and dieting concerns—may be most pronounced among incoming students. Also of concern is that smoking cessation during the college years is rare. In the vicinity of 85% of daily smokers and almost half of occasional smokers continued to smoke.

The American College Health Association, along with other national health organizations, has been concerned about the rise in tobacco use among college students and has recommended colleges enact a variety of measures. These include establishing smoking bans in and around all campus buildings—including student housing—and prohibiting the sale, advertisement, and promotion of tobacco products on campus. Public institutions were interviewed to assess the degree to which such measures have been adopted. Over half have smoking bans in all campus buildings and residences—which students also strongly support—68% have no tobacco sales on campus, and 32% of the schools' newspapers do not accept tobacco advertising.

Closing Thoughts

In conclusion, consider how campus efforts might be evaluated. A variety of parameters can be used to measure program impact, such as levels of dorm damage, the number of emergency visits to the local hospital emergency department, the number of cases involving alcohol or other drug use that come before the campus judiciary system, and how each of these is handled. However, there is another dimension. It does not easily lend itself to measurement but is also important. This is captured by the following vignette.

At the prodding of concerned friends, a fraternity member was seen by a substance use counselor and eventually entered treatment. This set off a wave of referrals from the student's fraternity, one of which turned out to be the current president. This student was treated as an outpatient on campus and became active in AA as part of continuing treatment. Following that year's fraternity rush, the first house meeting with the new pledge class was held. Of those present, each in turn introduced himself. In a parody of introductions at AA meetings, one of the first pledges to introduce himself, after giving his name, added "and I'm an alcoholic." This was met with tittering and laughter. Each subsequent pledge introduced himself in a similar fashion, concluding with "and I'm an alcoholic." Finally it was the president's turn. He looked around at each person and introduced himself in a quiet but forthright way: "I'm Joe, and I really am an alcoholic." There was dead silence.

Ultimately the goal is for change to permeate the community, so that everyday encounters between persons, of the sort that go unnoticed by others, will embody increased awareness and an appreciation of the problems that can accompany alcohol and other drug use. Such moments as the one in the fraternity house represent the outcome of many years' work and are among the most eloquent testimonies to a campus's efforts.

THE ELDERLY

On one of the earliest television talk shows, Art Linkletter, the host, was interviewing children. The topics were a bit different then than they are today. The children came up with the following answers to a question he posed: "You can't play with toys anymore. The government pays for everything. You don't go to work. You wrinkle and shrink." The question was "What does it mean to grow old?" These responses contain many of the stereotypes our society attributes to the elderly. They also show that this negative picture develops from a very early age. There is a stigma about growing old. The notion is that for the elderly there is no play or fun, no money, no usefulness, and no attractiveness.

In considering the elderly, it is important to recognize that we really are talking about ourselves. It is inevitable: we will all age; we will all become elderly. A participant at a geriatric conference reported being asked by a friend, "What can I do to keep from getting older?" The response the person received was simple: "Die now!" There is no other way to avoid aging. So, for those not yet elderly, in thinking about the older person, imagine yourself years in the future, because many of the circumstances will probably be the same.

In the year 2000, there were more than 35 million Americans age 65 and older. This is the group arbitrarily defined as the elderly, or aged. The elderly are the fastest growing segment of the population. Since 1950 the elderly portion of the population has virtually tripled, while the rest of the population did not quite double. In 1970, the average age of the population was 28 years. In the year 2000, it climbed to 36.6 years. Increased longevity has contributed to this change, as has a declining birthrate among younger persons. The post–World War II baby boom generation is now in its late 40s and 50s, further contributing to the increase in the average age of the population. The elderly constitute 12.3% of the total population. In fact, there are as many people age 65 and over as there are under age 10.

Stresses of Aging

Despite the inevitability of aging and physical problems arising as the years pass, there is an important thing to keep in mind. It has been said many times and in many ways that you are as young as you want to be. This is possible, however, only if a person has some strengths going for him or her. The best predictor of the future—specifically, how someone will handle growing old—is how the individual has handled the previous years. Individuals who have demonstrated flexibility as they have gone through life will adapt best to the inevitable stresses that come with getting older. These are the people who will be able to feel young, regardless of the number of birthdays they have celebrated.

Dishonor not the old: we shall all be numbered among them.
Apocrypha Bensira 8:6

Interestingly, as people get older, they become less similar to one another and more individual. One person commented that, as people grow older, they become "more like themselves." The only thing that remains alike for the members of this group is the problems they face. There is a reason for this. In going through life, people rely most heavily on the coping styles that seem to have served them well previously. With years and years of living, gradually individuals narrow down their responses.

What looks, at first glance, like an egocentricity or eccentricity of old age is more likely a lifelong behavior that has become one of the person's exclusive methods for dealing with stress. An example illustrating this point arose in the case of an elderly surgical patient for whom psychiatric consultation was requested. This man had a constant smile. In response to any question or statement by the nurse or doctor, he smiled, which was often felt to be wholly inappropriate. The treatment staff requested help in comprehending the patient's behavior. In the process of the psychiatric consultation, it became quite understandable. Friends, neighbors, and family of the man consistently described him as "good ole Joe, who always had a friendly word and a smile for everyone, the nicest man you'd ever want to meet." Now, under the most fearful of situations, with many cognitive processes depleted, he was instinctively using his faithful, basic coping style. Very similarly, the person who goes through life with a pessimistic streak may become angry and sad in old age. People who have been fearful under stress may be timid and withdrawn in old age. On the other hand, people who have been very organized and always reliant on a definite schedule may try to handle everything by making lists in old age. What is true in each case is that the person settles into a style that was successful in earlier life.

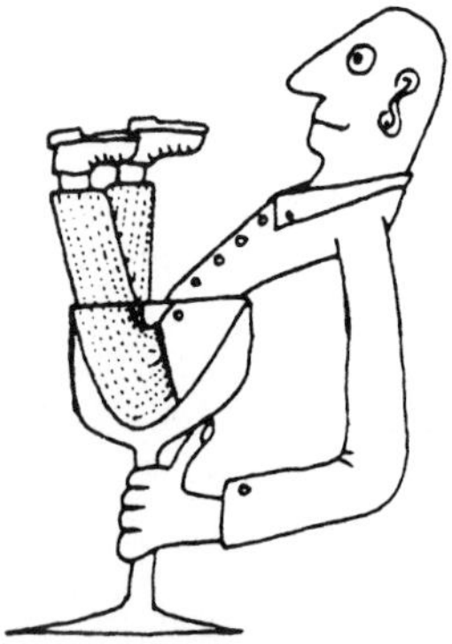

In dealing with elderly people it is important to keep in mind that the particular stresses that are common to this group differ somewhat from those of younger people. Stresses may arise from social factors, psychological factors, or biological problems. Iatrogenic stresses (harm caused by efforts to heal) can also occur as the helping professions serve (or inadequately serve) elderly people.

Social Stresses

Social stresses can be summarized under the phenomenon of the national addiction to youth. Television commercials highlight all types of products that can be used to disguise the process of aging. There is everything from hair colorings to dish detergents, which if used will make a mother's hands indistinguishable from her daughter's. Look around you. Who is being hired and who is being retired? Aging is equated with obsolescence and worthlessness. People who have been vital, contributing members of an organization suddenly find themselves with the title "honorary." It is often not an honor at all. It means these people have become figureheads; they have been replaced. The real work has been taken over by someone else—someone younger.

Social policy has also neglected the needs of older people. A decade ago the National Institute of Mental Health spent a mere 1.1% of its budget for research on problems of the elderly. Only 1% of its budget for services went to provide for the care of elderly people. This figure is now changing, but it suggests an underlying attitude of disinterest in older people's needs.

The process of receiving medical care and paying medical bills can in itself be a stressor for older people. Elderly people have twice as many visits to a physician, their average hospital stay is 3½ times longer than for persons under age 65, and the hospital stay costs 5 times more than for the under-65 age group. Insurance coverage (including Medicare) is often inadequate, especially for preventive services. The chronic illnesses older people suffer often require much time and few high-tech interventions; the American insurance system reimburses especially poorly for this type of care.

Time is the rider that breaks youth.
GEORGE HERBERT
Jacula Prudentum, 1651

The real issue is one of attitude. If one examines the dynamics behind this attitude, then one can see why there has been disinterest and avoidance. Generally the medical profession and other helping people, including family and friends, are overwhelmed by the multiplicity, chronicity, and confusing nature of the disorders of aging. Caregivers often feel helpless in dealing with the elderly and harbor self-doubts about whether they can contribute in a satisfactory manner that is also personally gratifying. To put it another way, most of us like to see results, to see things happen, to believe there is a "before" and an "after" picture, in which the difference is clear. Also, it is important to feel that the part we have played, however big or small, has made a difference.

Helpers like it when someone puts out her hand and says, "Thank you." The elderly often say, "Don't bug me. I don't want help." If you consider who it is that voluntarily goes into most clinical agencies, it is not the elderly. Those elderly who do go have usually been coerced.

Helpers do not like complainers. What do the elderly say? "This hurts; that hurts. You're not nice enough. You don't come soon enough. My old doctor was much better. Do this; do that." Helpers like patients who receive maximum cures in the minimum amount of time. This certainly is not the elderly. There are more visits, for more problems, requiring more time. Helpers like patients who get well. How many of the elderly are cured? How can you take away their diabetes, their arthritis, the pain from the memory of a lost spouse? Helpers like patients who take their advice. With the elderly, helpers suggest A but they'll often do B.

These interactional dynamics are understandable but only aggravate the problem. They may rub the helper's instincts the wrong way. The result is that many potential caregivers decide they do not like working with the elderly, and it shows. Very few clinicians volunteer to take on elderly clients. If an elderly client goes to a helping agency, the chances are good that the person who sees the client will soon decide to transfer the case to someone more "appropriate" or will refer the client to another agency.

Another factor that gets in the way of their receiving adequate care from helping people is that the elderly may resent the helper's youth, just as the helper fears the client's elderliness. Also, the elderly generally dislike the dependent status that goes along with being a client or patient. It is the opposite of what they want, which is to be independent and secure and to feel a sense of worth. Being in treatment implies that something is wrong with them. It also means that someone else is partially in charge and telling them how to run their lives.

Psychological Stresses

The greatest psychological stress the elderly must face is loss. In the geriatric population, losses are steady, they are predictable, and they often occur in bunches. And even if they do not, they are still numerous. What are the specific losses?

There is the loss that comes from the illnesses and deaths of family and friends. The older you get, statistically the more likely that those about you will begin to falter. So there are the obvious losses of support and companionship. Not necessarily as obvious is that the deaths of others also lead to questioning about loss of self, anticipation of one's own death. This may sometimes be the source of anxiety attacks among the elderly.

There is the loss that comes from the geographical separations of family. This begins earlier in life, as children go to school and later leave home for college or the armed services and then eventually marry. For the elderly, this may be especially difficult, because 50% of all grandparents do not have grandchildren living close by. As new generations are being born, they are not accessible to the older generation, whose lives are coming to a close.

There is the loss of money through earned income. Whether income is supplemented through pensions, social security, or savings, the elderly usually do not have as much money as they did earlier in their lives. Dollars do not only represent buying power; they also have symbolic values. Money represents power, stature, value, and independence. Lack of money has obvious implications in vital areas of self-esteem.

Tears, idle tears, I know not what they mean,
Tears from the depth of some divine despair
Rise in the heart, and gather to the eyes,
In looking on the happy autumn days
And thinking of the days that are no more.
ALFRED, LORD TENNYSON
"Tears Idle Tears," 1847.

There are the losses that accompany retirement: loss of status, gratification, and often most important, identity. With retirement, you lose who you have been. This refers not only to retirement from a job but also to retirement from anything—from being a mother, from being a grandmother, or from just being a person who is capable of walking around the block. Often accompanying retirement is a loss of privacy. For married couples, retirement may mean more togetherness than they have had for years. Both spouses will have to change routines and habits and be forced to accommodate the presence of the other. The expectations may also be tremendous. Retirement, in most people's fantasies, is thought to usher in the "golden years" and provide the opportunity to do the things that have been put off. This may well be a letdown.

There is also the loss of body functions and skills, which may include a loss of attractiveness. Older people may develop body odors. They lose their teeth. They are more prone to infection. For women, the skin may become dry, including the skin of the vagina, which can lead to vaginal discharges and dyspareunia (painful intercourse). For men, there is general loss of muscle tone. Everything begins to stick out where it shouldn't. As physical problems arise, this may lead to loss of skills. A carpenter who has arthritis or the tremors of Parkinson's disease will be unable to do the things that were formerly possible and rewarding.

The elderly may try to handle stress in a number of ways. One is the widely used defense of denial. In response to an observation that a client's hand is more swollen, he may well say, "Oh, no, it's no different than it's always been." If a close friend is in the hospital and very seriously ill, she may dismiss the seriousness and claim it is just another of her spells—she'll be out, perky as ever, in a day or two.

Another common way of handling loss is by somatization. This means bringing the emotional content out in the open, but "saying" it in terms of its being the body that hurts. This is why so many of the elderly are labeled hypochrondriacal. When he says his knee hurts and he really cannot get up that day, what he also may be saying is that he hurts inside, emotionally. Because he may not get attention for emotional pains, having something wrong physically or "mechanically" is socially more acceptable.

Another way of handling loss is restricting affect. Instead of saying it does not exist, as with denial, there is a withdrawing. The person becomes less involved, so she does not hear about the bad things happening. By being less a part of the world, she is less vulnerable.

Unfortunately, all these defenses boomerang and work against the elderly. Love, affection, and concern are expressed through words, behavior, and many nonverbal cues—a smile, a nod, a touch. After so many

There's a shadow hanging over me,
Oh yesterday came suddenly.
JOHN LENNON AND PAUL MCCARTNEY
"Yesterday", 1965.

Do not go gentle into that good night,
Old age should burn and rave
at close of day;
Rage, rage against the dying of the light.
DYLAN THOMAS
"Do Not Go Gentle into That Good Night," 1952

years of living, the elderly certainly know the signs of affection and caring as well as those of distancing and detachment. By withdrawing when they are fearful, they may see others reciprocally withdrawing; the elderly may then be left without any source of affection, interest, or caring. This, in turn, they read as dislike, and they may feel their initial withdrawal was justified. Therefore, one of the prime treatment techniques with the elderly is to reach out to them, literally. Smile, touch them, sit close to them. Attempt to reach through the barrier they may have erected with their protective psychological defenses.

The elderly frequently are hurt by what helping people instinctively say when reaching out to the aged. Statements such as "You're lucky to be alive," "Quit worrying about things," "Grow old gracefully" are often misinterpreted by the elderly as someone telling them to ignore their losses, or they may interpret this as being told that the person does not want to get close to them. The elderly's response is that they do not want to grow old gracefully; they do not want to be "easy to manage"; they want to go out with a bang and leave a mark—they want to be individuals to the last day.

How about sex and the elderly? The most prevalent myth is that the elderly have no interest in sex. Physiologically, aging itself need not greatly affect sexual functioning. With advancing years, it takes a little longer to achieve an erection and a little more time to the point of ejaculation, orgasm is a little less intense, and a little more time is required before orgasms can be reexperienced. However, if the elderly are physically healthy, there is no reason they should not be sexually active. The biggest factors influencing sexual activity in the elderly are the availability of a partner and social pressures. Among the elderly, when a partner dies, the survivor may not be encouraged to date or remarry. What is considered virility at age 25 is seen as lechery after age 65. Even when both partners are alive, if they are living in an institution or in the home of their adult children, sexual activity may be frowned on or "not allowed."

I can still have sex anytime I want to. I just don't want to very often.

Another loss is that of sensation. With aging, the senses become less acute. What this means is that the elderly are then deprived of accurate cues from their environment. This may be a big factor in the development of suspiciousness in older persons. Any paranoid elderly person should have his or her hearing and vision evaluated. The most powerful loss, the loss no elderly person is prepared to understand or accept, is the loss of thinking ability. This loss may occur imperceptibly over time. It comes from the loss of cortical brain function. Suddenly a person who has been an accountant or a schoolteacher, for example, is adding 2+2, and it doesn't equal 4 every time. This is embarrassing and scary. Although the person may be able to stand losing other things, to lose one's mind is the ultimate indignity.

The result of all or any of these losses is that self-respect, integrity, dignity, and self-esteem are threatened. The implication can be that usefulness is questioned and life is ebbing away. The feeling may be that "my work is over."

Biological Stresses

Of the elderly, only 5% are institutionalized in nursing homes, convalescent centers, or similar facilities. However, about half of the elderly have some serious physical disability, such as heart disease, diabetes, lung disease, or arthritis. About 25% also have a significant functional psychological problem, with depression being the most prevalent. Understandably, as life expectancy increases and we live longer, there is more vulnerability to the natural course of disease.

Depressive illness is very prevalent among the elderly. There may be a physiological basis for this. The levels of neurochemicals (serotonin, monoamine oxidase, and norepinephrine) thought to be associated with depression change in the brain as people get older. These depressions, then, are not necessarily tied solely to situational events. However, because so many things are likely to be going on in the surrounding environment for the elderly, it is too easy to forget the potential benefits of judiciously prescribed antidepressants. Malnourishment, for instance, is all too common in the elderly. Nutritional deficiency can cause several syndromes that may look like depressions. Many physical ailments, such as thyroid dysfunctions, and illnesses caused by the disease processes themselves, manifest as depression.

May you live all the days of your life.
JONATHAN SWIFT.
Polite Conversation, 1738

Depression in the elderly may not be the same as depression in younger persons, with tearfulness, inability to sleep, or loss of appetite. Some of the tips for recognizing depression in the elderly are an increased sensitivity to pain, a refusal to get out of bed when physical problems don't require bed rest, poor concentration, a marked narrowing of coping style, and an upsurge of physical complaints. Often, the poor concentration leads to absent-mindedness and inattentiveness, which are misdiagnosed as defective memory and ultimately as "senility," while the depression goes unrecognized and untreated. "Senility" is really a useless clinical term. The proper term is "dementia," which means irreversible cognitive impairment. However, all cognitive impairment should be considered reversible (delirium) until proven otherwise. It should also be remembered that alcohol abuse, as well as sometimes creating problems itself, can, in patients with dementia, make the confusion worse. The elderly deserve an aggressive search for potentially treatable, reversible causes of organic brain syndromes by qualified medical personnel.

First I lost my hair. Then I lost my wife. My children have all moved away. My best friends have died, my vision is going, my hearing is going, and now you want me to give up alcohol. It's all I've got left.

Suicide among the elderly is a very big problem. Of those who commit suicide, 25% are over age 65. The rate of suicide for those over 65 is 5 times that of the general population. After age 75, the rate is 8 times higher. In working with the elderly, a suicide evaluation should not be neglected, because so many depressions are masked.

A variety of changes associated with aging make the elderly more vulnerable to the acute effects of alcohol. Body water content declines and the body fat content increases with age. Between the ages of 20 and 70, there is a 10% decrease in lean body mass. With a given amount of alcohol, these combined reductions lead to a higher blood alcohol level among the elderly. Furthermore, with aging there is diminished blood flow through the liver. This means that while the rate of metabolism is unaltered the alcohol is cleared more slowly. For any given amount, the peak blood alcohol level will be 20% higher for a 60-year-old than for a 20-year-old. At age 90, the peak blood alcohol level is 50% higher. Those elderly persons who may have some existing impairment in cognitive functioning have even greater sensitivity to alcohol. In addition to the increased acute effects of alcohol, a variety of other physical changes make the elderly more vulnerable to the medical consequences of use. By age 75, there is a 50% reduction in lung capacity, the kidneys work at only 45% of their earlier capacity, and heart function is reduced by 35%.

Iatrogenic Stresses

"Iatrogenic" refers to harm caused by efforts to heal. Some of the stresses on the elderly are, in fact, the product of the health-care system and the insensitivities to the psychological and basic physiological changes in the elderly. All too often, medication is overprescribed in an attempt to keep behavior controlled rather than diagnosed. Too few clinicians take into account the dramatically altered way the elderly metabolize medications, which means that fewer medicines in combination and lowered doses of drugs are frequently required. There is also a tendency by everyone concerned to ignore the fact that alcohol, too, is a toxic drug. The combination of alcohol with other medications in light of the altered metabolism for both can create serious problems. Rarely is there any thought of whether the elderly patient can afford the medicine prescribed. Also, the elderly person's ability to comply with directions for taking medications is overestimated.

A poignant example of problems with medications is the case of an elderly woman who was discharged from the hospital with a number of medications. She had been admitted with severe congestive heart failure but had responded well to drug therapy for her hypertension and fluid retention. Within 2 weeks of her return home, her condition began to deteriorate, which was a source of dismay and consternation to her physicians. She was thought surely to be purposefully causing her ailments, and a psychiatrist, who was asked to consult on the case, decided to make a home visit. The woman knew which medications to take, when, and for what conditions. However, there was one problem. As she handed the bottle of capsules to the psychiatrist, with her crippled arthritic fingers, the "diagnosis" became obvious: the child-proof cap. She had been unable to open the bottles and therefore unable to take the medicine. This is a vivid reminder of the need to consider all the available information in assessing the problems of the elderly.

Patterns of Alcohol and Other Drug Use

Substance use patterns of the elderly differ from other groups in the population.

Alcohol

The elderly have a lower rate of alcohol use than other age groups. In part due to the historical era in which they grew up, the proportion of lifetime abstainers is higher among the elderly than in the general population. Nonetheless, surveys show that over half of older adults do use some alcohol. Among the elderly, typically, those who drank when younger are unlikely to stop entirely, unless health problems intervene. However, their drinking is far less frequent. So only half of those who had alcohol during the past year had a drink in the past month, thereby qualifying as current drinkers. Of these current drinkers, 15% had at least 1 occasion of 5 or more drinks, and 5% had multiple occasions.

This is your wine and cheese crowd, and nothing ever goes wrong at such events.

New York City policeman commenting on picnickers attending a summer philharmonic concert in Central Park, *New York Times,* 1984

As is true of other age groups, the prevalence of drinking varies considerably by geographic region. Similarly, men are more likely than women to be drinkers.

Drinking among older people is important even when it does not qualify as alcohol abuse. This is because what is considered "social drinking" can cause or aggravate a range of health problems. Little is known about the relationship of alcohol use to life stresses and changes, although there has been speculation. The advent of retirement communities has provided an interesting opportunity to examine some aspects of these questions. It appears that in these settings—which offer their residents a variety of leisure activities, such as golf, swimming, craft classes, and discussion groups—social isolation is not tied to higher levels of alcohol use. On the contrary, the heaviest drinkers (defined as drinking at least 2 drinks per day), who constituted 20% of those studied, were also those who were socially more active. Since entering the community, one-third of the individuals noted a change in drinking patterns, with three-fourths of those people reducing their alcohol use. The other one-fourth (8% of the total group) said their drinking had increased. One of the questions raised is whether social activity in retirement communities is tied to alcohol use and facilitates, or even promotes, heavier drinking by some individuals.

Nicotine

About two-thirds of the elderly used tobacco at some point. Ten percent currently smoke.

Over-the-Counter Preparations

For many people, use of over-the-counter medications is the first response to an illness or a medical problem. These self-prescribed preparations are used more extensively than are prescription medications. The typical American household is estimated to have an average of 17 different over-the-counter products on hand. In response to the question of how they handle everyday health problems, 35% of elderly people report they do not treat the problem, 35% report using an over-the-counter medication, 15% use prescription medications available in the home, 11% use some other home remedy, and 13% contact their doctor or dentist. If elderly people take any action in response to a health-care problem, the odds are good that they will use an over-the-counter preparation.

When chronic illness accompanies aging, there is an understandable tendency to find preparations to ease discomfort. Elderly people are more likely than any other segment of the population to use these preparations. They take 7 times more over-the-counter drugs than do members of any other age group. One study of healthy elderly people identified 54% as regularly using over-the-counter drugs. Fifty percent of that group reported that they typically used analgesics, laxatives, or antacids 4 to 6 times per week. Of those who use over-the-counter drugs daily, 80% are believed to simultaneously be using prescribed drugs, alcohol, or both. Some may often use 6 or more preparations.

The number of over-the-counter preparations is growing. Potent medications that previously required a doctor's prescription, such as ibuprofen and naproxen, are now available without one. In addition, health-care professionals do not rank very high as a major source of information about over-the-counter preparations. Among elderly people, advertising has been identified as the primary source of information by a quarter of those surveyed. Friends, relatives, and neighbors constitute the next largest group, acting as the source of information for 20% of those surveyed. The label on the product itself was noted by 13% as the source of information. Pharmacists were consulted as the source of information for 20%, and physicians were consulted by only 14%.

Prescription Drugs

The elderly take a disproportionate percentage of all prescription medication. Upward of 60% of elderly people have some medications that are prescribed; in many studies, more than 80% do. Some of the drugs most commonly prescribed are also those with a high potential for adverse drug reactions.

Adverse Drug Reactions Adverse drug reactions are more common among elderly people. One major reason for this is that they use more drugs than do younger people. Because of multiple chronic illnesses, they may be under the care of more than one physician, none of whom may be fully informed about the complete range of medications the patient is taking. As drug regimens become more complex, there is a greater probability of error by the patient as well as greater potential for interactions between drugs. Concurrent use of drugs, even 10 or more hours apart, can significantly affect absorption, distribution, metabolism, and toxicity. The more drugs being used, including alcohol, the greater the potential for adverse interactions. A study of hospitalized patients found that all patients taking more than 8 drugs had at least 1 interacting pair of drugs in that mix. A study of 75-year-olds living at home found that there was an average of 5.6 drugs being taken. The primary-care physicians were unaware of 25% of these. Even before factoring in any alcohol use, there was a significant risk of drug interactions for 15% of the patients.

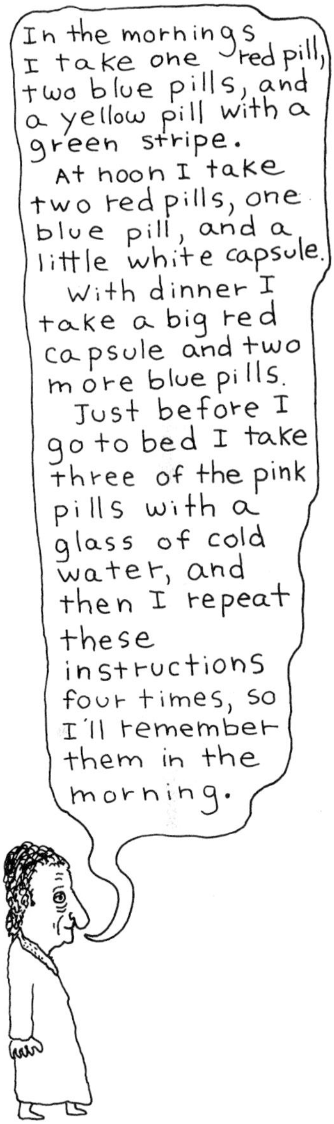

Alcohol-Drug Interactions The unique physiological changes that accompany aging and affect drug distribution and metabolism contribute as well to the increased risk of drug-alcohol interactions. The risk of an adverse drug reaction in those 50 to 59 years old may be as much as a third greater than for those in their 40s. Above age 60 there appears to be a further twofold to threefold increase. Diagnosis of adverse drug reactions may be hampered because of their resemblance to illnesses common in old age, such as gait disturbances and cognitive impairment.

Many commonly prescribed drugs can interact with alcohol. Such interactions can occur by several mechanisms. Some of the effects are due to changes in liver metabolism that occur with age. Remember that normal changes in liver function are compounded by the presence of alcohol. For this reason, medications as common as aspirin and acetaminophen, from oral anticoagulants, to the oral medications used with diabetes, to antihistamines, to pain medications can present problems in the presence of alcohol. There are other interactions that occur for other reasons besides changed liver function. For example, anti-ulcer drugs, such as cimetidine, inhibit alcohol metabolism in the stomach, resulting in greater absorption of alcohol and higher blood alcohol levels per drink. Since elderly people already obtain higher blood alcohol levels per drink due to age-related changes in drug distribution, this effect is of special importance. Alcohol used at the same time as some nonsteroidal anti-inflammatory drugs may substantially increase the risk of the gastrointestinal inflammation and bleeding these drugs can cause. Then there is increased sedation, delirium, and psychomotor impairment, which can occur when alcohol is used with benzodiazepines and other drugs that affect the central nervous system.

Illicit Drug Use

Illicit drug use has long been considered rare among elderly people. This is attributable to several factors. One is that rates of alcohol and drug use decline as people age. Second, those with substance use problems have increased mortality and simply die earlier. Third, the current elderly and those preceding them grew up in an era in which illicit drug use was relatively rare. However, all of this is about to change. The first of the baby boomers, those born after World War II who were the hippies and flower children in the 1960s, are now beginning to celebrate their 60th birthdays. Though the rates of current illicit drug use are not at the levels they would have reported two or three decades ago, illicit drug use is not wholly ancient history.

Table 11.10 Illicit Drug Use by Age Group, 2003

Age Group	Lifetime	Past Year	Past Month
40–44	65.3%	14.0%	8.1%
45–49	62.3	12.6	6.8
50–54	52.0	7.4	3.9
55–59	38.3	4.4	2.0
60–64	23.8	2.9	1.1
65+	9.9	0.7	0.6

From: NIDA. *Results for the 2003 National Survey on Drug Use and Health: National Findings.* Rockville, MD: 2004.

Note: In 2003 baby boomers born between the years 1946 and 1964 would have been between the ages of 39 and 57.

As is evident from examining Table 11.10, the rate of lifetime illicit drug use is growing. For those in their 40s and 50s the rate of lifetime illicit drug use is 5 to 6 times greater than that of the current over-65-year-old group. This is going to have implications for the treatment community. Already there are signs of this. Among methadone maintenance programs, for example, one-third of the patients are over age 40, and one-fourth are between 40 and 49. Looking down the line, it has been estimated that by the year 2020, the treatment capacity to serve the elderly with alcohol and other drug problems will need to be quadrupled.

Alcohol Use and Health Status

Let me die in a tavern; let the wine be placed near my dying mouth, so that when the choirs of angels come, they may say, "God be merciful to this drinker!"
THE ARCHPOET
Confessio, 12th century

No body system is immune to the effects of alcohol. (See Chapter 6.) Among elderly people, a smaller amount of alcohol can create more medical problems. Hypertension, which is common among the elderly, is more common among those who drink. For those over 50, two to three drinks per day is associated with an increase in blood pressure. For those having 3 drinks per day, about one-half (52%) have hypertension, compared with only a third (35%) who are nondrinkers. That is a 50% higher rate. Drinking is also associated with injuries, particularly falls. Those who drink 1,000 grams of alcohol per month have risks of falls that are 8 times that of abstainers. A large study of residents of a retirement community found that those who drank 3 drinks per day were 3.5 times more likely to commit suicide than abstainers. Heavy drinking is also associated with decreases in bone density, which in turn contributes to the risk of injury from falls. Drinking is associated with dementia and confusion among the elderly. Also, while alcohol-related confusion improves with abstinence, this happens more slowly and is less complete than with younger people. In terms of death rates, overall mortality for women increases at levels above 2 drinks per day, and for men at 4 drinks per day.

In light of all this, the current NIAAA recommendation is that both elderly men and women limit daily alcohol consumption to 1 drink per day.

Alcohol Problems

Not only do the patterns of substance use, including alcohol, vary among elderly people, but the associated problems and presentations do as well. Between 2% and 4% of elderly people meet the criteria for alcohol abuse or alcoholism. Approximately 10% have problems related to drinking, even if not severe enough to meet the criteria. In general, men have a much higher likelihood of being problem drinkers than do women, the prevalence decreases with increasing age, and there is considerable geographic variation in the prevalence of alcoholism. In medical settings, the prevalence is higher, and it appears to increase with increasing level of care. In primary-care settings, 10% to 15% of elderly patients are alcohol abusers or dependents, while up to 25% of hospitalized elderly people are. Recognizing alcohol problems among elderly people in medical settings can be very challenging. In the past, physicians recognized and intervened with only a small proportion of these patients. Nonetheless, studies of treatment populations consistently find that about 10% of patients entering alcohol treatment programs are age 65 and older.

Natural History of Alcohol Problems in Later Life

A unique study involving a 10-year follow-up of problem drinkers sheds light on the course of alcohol problems as people approach old age. Problem drinkers were enrolled in the study when they were between the ages of 50 and 65. They were followed up at year 4, and then at 10 years. At that time there were a number of comparisons made between those whose problem had resolved, versus those for whom it continued, versus a comparison group without a history of alcohol problems. Several interesting things stood out. Those whose drinking problem resolved were more likely to have friends who were less approving of drinking. Those whose problems resolved had fewer signs of dependence, had fewer episodes, and they were less likely to say they drank to forget or to get high. In addition, their problems tended to appear later in life.

In comparing the resolved problem drinkers with "normal" controls at 10 years, in many areas they were quite similar. But of the resolved problem group, for the 75% who continued to drink, the level of drinking was higher than it was for those who had never had an alcohol problem. Those who had had a problem used more psychoactive substances and had more depressive episodes. In addition, they were more likely to report "motivated" drinking, for the purpose of getting high and forgetting problems. Only 11% of the entire group reported having had alcohol treatment. It was equally common among the resolved and the continuing problem groups, so here treatment did not promote higher rates of improvement. While clearly improved, on a variety of measures the resolved problem group was still not functioning on par with the general population. This is of interest because treated alcoholics at 10-year follow-up are essentially indistinguishable from the general population.

What factors were associated with the resolution of problems? Several things are of interest. At the point of a 4-year follow-up, those whose problem later improved reported more acute medical problems. Possibly these had served as a wake-up call and prompted a reduction in alcohol use. Also, those whose alcohol problem diminished were more likely to give up other substance use, especially nicotine. For the group as a whole, those whose problem resolved were more likely to be abstinent. Another change that they made was in the type of coping patterns they used. They became more likely to use what are called "approach" coping strategies when confronting problems or stress. Rather than employing a "going-it-alone" style, they began to reach out to others.

Types of Alcohol Dependence

Alcohol problems can make their appearance at any point in life. A majority of the elderly with alcohol dependence have a long-standing problem that began much earlier in life. For whatever reasons, probably one being good genes, they have been relatively resistant to alcohol-related medical problems through middle age. They often begin to experience deterioration of physical and cognitive functioning when they reach their 60s and 70s. Then there are those for whom alcohol dependence only develops in old age. These 2 differing patterns of alcohol dependence are commonly termed as either "early-onset" or "late-onset." Researchers have adopted different age cutoff points to distinguish these varieties, cutoff points that fall anywhere between ages 40 and 60. Despite the differences in distinguishing between the two varieties, there is general agreement that, of elderly people with alcohol dependence, approximately 50% began drinking heavily before age 40 and approximately two-thirds before age 60. Thus, the ratio of early-onset to late-onset alcoholism is around 2:1. Some differences between those with early- and late-onset alcohol dependence are summarized in Table 11.11.

Wine and cheese are ageless companions, like aspirin and aches, or June and moon, or good people and noble virtues.
M.F.K. FISHER
Wine and Cheese, 1981

Many factors may contribute to the development of late-onset alcohol dependence. Problems from alcohol use sometimes emerge in later life with minimal changes in alcohol consumption. Because of the normal aging process, what had previously been a benign heavy social drinking pattern for some individuals becomes problematic. Some elderly people, however, seem to develop drinking problems as a maladaptive response to social stresses, such as retirement, loss of a spouse, grief, economic hardships, social isolation, and changes in living situations. At any age, alcohol may be used to cope with major life stresses. For some of the elderly, the stresses of aging may have been too great or may have come too fast. They turned to alcohol as a coping mechanism. However, the view that changing life circumstances and social isolation provokes alcohol problems in elderly people is largely speculative.

Table 11.11 Characteristics of Early- and Late-Onset Alcohol Dependence

Characteristics	Early-Onset (%)	Late-Onset (%)
Separated or divorced	22	55
Widowed	33	9
Time spent in jail	78	55
Symptoms of organic brain disease	11	36
Serious health problem	44	91
Family history of alcoholism	86	40

From: Bienfeld D. Alcoholism in the elderly. *American Family Physician* 36(2):163–169, 1987.

An awareness of differences between early- and late-onset alcoholism is important both for screening and for treatment. For those with early-onset alcoholism, the odds are greater that some of the usual social indicators of alcoholism can be elicited when reviewing the person's medical and social history. There is also a greater probability of prior alcohol treatment among early-onset alcoholics. One treatment program found that slightly over one-third of early-onset patients had had prior treatment. Even among those with late-onset alcohol dependence, however, 17% had had some prior treatment. In treatment programs, emphasis on developing alternative coping strategies is of particular importance for late-onset alcoholics.

Presentations

Alcohol problems among elderly people often have nonspecific presentations. The negative consequences of alcohol use that immediately come to mind as signaling a problem, such as job difficulties or family or legal problems, are less common. Elderly people who are alcohol dependent are more likely to present with medical complications from the drinking. The range and frequency of medical problems common in elderly with alcohol dependence are presented in Table 11.12. Among elderly people, some of the presentations are often mistaken for other age-related illnesses or medical conditions, such as malnutrition, falls, other accidents, depression, confusion, less attention to self-care, and unexpected reactions to prescribed medications.

Screening

The importance of taking an alcohol and other drug use history does not decline with the patient's increasing age. The commonly used MAST

Table 11.12 Current and Past Medical Diagnoses in Elderly Patients with Alcohol Dependence

Diagnosis	Current Diagnosis (Number)	Past Diagnosis (Number)	Total Number	%
Alcoholic liver disease	37	2	39	18
Hypertension	71	2	73	33
Chronic obstructive pulmonary disease	65	1	66	31
Coronary artery disease	36	5	41	19
Arteriosclerosis	9	2	11	5
Neurological disorders				
Organic brain disease	52	2	54	25
Cerebral vascular disease	12	2	14	7
Cerebral degeneration	13	0	13	6
Diabetes	17	1	18	8
Peptic ulcer disease	4	29	33	15
Alcoholic gastritis	6	3	7	3
Prostate hypertrophy (men)	16	19	35	23
Psoriasis	8	3	11	5
Degenerative joint disease	38	6	44	20

Adapted from Hurt RD. Alcoholism in elderly persons: Medical aspects and prognosis of 216 inpatients. *Mayo Clinic Proceedings* 63:756, 1988.

(Michigan Alcoholism Screening Test) has been adapted for the elderly populations (see Table 11.13).

One goal of history taking is to identify alcohol or other drug dependence. An additional goal of history taking that assumes greater importance with increasing age is to identify medically hazardous alcohol use, including potential alcohol-drug interactions. Asking about quantity and frequency of use is therefore as important as asking about adverse consequences of drinking. Several techniques have been shown to help enhance the accuracy of self-reported quantity and frequency of drinking. Asking about each type of alcoholic beverage separately will increase the accuracy of reporting. The "time line follow-back" procedure uses a calendar and visual aids to enhance reporting of alcohol consumption. This procedure asks about drinking on each specific day of the week for as far back as the interviewer deems important. Heavy drinking

Table 11.13 Michigan Alcoholism Screening Test Geriatric Version (MAST-G)

1. After drinking have you ever noticed an increase in your heart rate or beating in your chest?	___Yes	___ No
*2. When talking to others, do you ever underestimate how much you actually drink?	___Yes	___ No
3. Does alcohol make you sleepy so that you often fall asleep in your chair?	___Yes	___ No
*4. After a few drinks, have you sometimes not eaten or been able to skip a meal because you didn't feel hungry?	___Yes	___ No
*5. Does having a few drinks help you decrease your shakiness or tremors?	___Yes	___ No
*6. Does alcohol sometimes make it hard for you to remember parts of the day or night?	___Yes	___ No
7. Do you have rules for yourself that you won't drink before a certain time of the day?	___Yes	___ No
8. Have you lost interest in hobbies or activities you used to enjoy?	___Yes	___ No
9. When you wake up in the morning, do you ever have trouble remembering part of the night before?	___Yes	___ No
10. Does having a drink help you sleep?	___Yes	___ No
11. Do you hide your alcohol bottles from family members?	___Yes	___ No
12. After a social gathering, have you ever felt embarrassed because you drank too much?	___Yes	___ No
13. Have you ever been concerned that drinking might be harmful to your health?	___Yes	___ No
14. Do you end an evening with a night cap?	___Yes	___ No
15. Did you find your drinking increased after someone close to you died?	___Yes	___ No
16. In general, would you prefer to have a few drinks at home rather than go out to social events?	___Yes	___ No
17. Are you drinking more now than in the past?	___Yes	___ No
*18. Do you usually take a drink to relax or calm your nerves?	___Yes	___ No
*19. Do you drink to take your mind off your problems?	___Yes	___ No
*20. Have you ever increased your drinking after experiencing a loss in your life?	___Yes	___ No
21. Do you sometimes drive when you have had too much to drink?	___Yes	___ No
*22. Has a doctor or nurse ever said they were worried or concerned about your drinking?	___Yes	___ No
*23. Have you ever made rules to manage your drinking?	___Yes	___ No
*24. When you feel lonely, does having a drink help?	___Yes	___ No

Note: Questions marked by an asterisk represent the Short MAST—Geriatric Version.

Scoring: Each positive response is a score of 1 point. Five or more positive reponses are seen as possibly indicative of an alcohol problem, for full MAST-G.

From: Blow FC. *Substance Abuse among Older Adults. Treatment Improvement Protocol (TIP) Series 26.* Rockville, MD: Center for Substance Abuse Treatment, 1998. (418 refs.)

determined by this method has been shown to be a good indicator of problem drinking.

Obstacles to Identification and Intervention

Many of the screening instruments in common use are based on the behavior of younger people and men and do not transfer well to older people. Since many older people are retired, for instance, they do not have

problems at work. Since many live alone, they are less likely to have alcohol-induced marital problems. Hence the MAST Geriatric version.

It is particularly challenging to identify problem drinking in people with cognitive impairment. Family, friends, and neighbors are important sources of information about those who are unable to give a good history themselves.

Other factors also contribute to poor recognition of alcohol problems in older people. Classic signs of alcohol dependence may be obscure. Tolerance, manifested by requiring more alcohol to achieve the same effect, is one classic component of alcohol dependence. Older people, who obtain higher blood alcohol levels per drink, may honestly report requiring less alcohol intake to get the same effect as before. Withdrawal, though its signs and symptoms are little different in older people, may not be recognized until late in the course. Many other possible causes of tachycardia, hypertension, delirium, and so on that signal withdrawal will be thought of first in elderly people. Social decline is often marked by nonspecific features, such as dropping the bridge club, which differs from the presentation in younger people.

As happens in other segments of the population, elderly people are likely to be protected by family, friends, and caregivers. These people may fail to see the problem, ignore what they suspect, or justify not intervening in an alcohol problem, because no one wants to take away someone's "last pleasure." Thinking "What do they have to live for, anyway? They have been drinking all these years, they'll never stop now, and I don't want to be the one who asks them to give up the bottle" is also common. There are times that the elderly person is dependent on some outside assistance to continue drinking. For example, a neighbor or housekeeper may ensure access to alcohol by purchasing it for the homebound person. In situations where family members or friends support problem drinking or are reluctant to intervene, it is important to point out that problem drinking is not pleasurable drinking. Such complications of heavy drinking as cognitive impairment, gait disturbances, and other physical dependencies are greatly feared by most older people. These impairments often lead to nursing home placement, which most elderly people wish to avoid at almost any cost.

Detoxification and Treatment

Detoxification protocols need to be adjusted for elderly people. Generally, because of autonomic and cardiovascular instability, detoxification is better managed in a hospital than on an outpatient basis. Although the general strategy is similar for managing withdrawal in younger patients, there are several caveats. Withdrawal is likely to take longer in elderly people, especially those with cognitive impairment. The use of benzodiazepines, as a preventive measure, in the absence of withdrawal symptoms is unwise, because it might provoke delirium. It is generally recommended that their use be delayed and prescribed only in response to specific signs and symptoms of withdrawal. Drugs with a short half-life are preferable to longer-acting agents. The usual dosage can be reduced by one-half to two-thirds. In a person also dependent on benzodiazepines, withdrawal may take considerably longer than alcohol withdrawal alone.

The use of Antabuse® (disulfiram) has been suggested by some as potentially useful. Careful consideration needs to be given to the risks and potential benefits. Among elderly people, the risks may be considerable. Physically, they are more frail. Their metabolic ability to handle disulfiram is a factor. They may be less able to comply with the restrictions because of cognitive impairments. Their greater use of over-the-counter preparations increases the probability of inadvertent drug reactions. A disulfiram reaction that might be uncomfortable for someone younger may represent a medical crisis and have a lethal outcome for someone elderly. Of note, the newer anti-craving agents, naltrexone and acamprosate, are not only well tolerated, but also reduce the risk of relapse.

Elderly people need the same type of rehabilitation services as younger persons—education, counseling, and involvement in self-help groups. Treatment programs typically incorporate elderly people in their general programs. The prognosis is as good for elderly people as it is for younger persons. The elderly are as likely as younger persons to affiliate with AA and participate in aftercare. Also of note, the elderly too are as likely as younger persons to respond to brief interventions. In addition to the treatment program's standard regimen, elderly people also require a thorough medical evaluation and potentially more extensive social service involvement at discharge and to facilitate aftercare.

The earliest research on treatment outcomes from the early 1980s indicated that elderly alcoholics had outcomes comparable to those of younger patients. This was interpreted as refuting the need for specially focused programs for older persons. For most clinicians, the issue of specialized versus standard programs is likely to be nothing more than an academic interest, because so few programs have been developed for elderly people. However, more recent studies have demonstrated that programs tailored to elderly people enhance outcomes by reducing treatment dropout, by increasing rates of aftercare, and by dealing with relapses if they occur so that the person is not lost to treatment.

Many of the benefits of programs designed for elderly people can be achieved within the standard programs, with some inventiveness. Referring agencies and health-care providers need to be sensitive to the accommodations that can easily be made to serve elderly people better. Matching patients with clinicians who are knowledgeable about and comfortable in treating elderly people within standard programs and who are able to work at a slower, gentler pace can be beneficial. Furthermore, abrasive confrontation, which is used in some programs, is not likely to be effective with elderly persons. Programs that emphasize that style of group work may be poor choices for a referral.

Groups are important to elderly people in many ways. They reduce the sense of isolation, can enhance communication skills, provide a forum for problem solving, and address denial. Small group sessions or individual therapy within a general treatment program can help develop the special skills the older person may need for coping with losses, enjoying leisure time, and developing new relationships after the loss of old ones. A particular element found to be important for elderly people is referred to as life review. Groups need to allow for the elderly person's reminiscence and processing of the past. This is important for all elderly persons to see their lives as a whole. For those in treatment for alcohol problems, incorporating this process in a way that does not diminish self-esteem or devalue the elderly person's life is important. This is not only important in formal alcohol treatment but in contacts with health-care and social service professionals as well.

Treatment of the cognitively impaired alcoholic is especially difficult. Often a prolonged period of enforced abstinence from alcohol will be needed in order to determine if the person will recover sufficient cognitive function to pursue and participate in treatment. If not, a permanently supervised living situation, such as a nursing home or group home where alcohol is not available, will probably be needed.

Prevention

Your middle-age patient of today is another clinician's elderly patient several years hence. Today's adolescent is establishing a framework for making independent decisions about self-care and health-care practices. These will have a bearing on lifelong health habits. What kind of questions should any individual consider before he or she decides to take medication? What specific questions are important for the particular patient? Patients rarely consult their doctors before making such decisions. In fact, no doctor would want to be contacted on that basis. A resource available to everyone is the pharmacist. Though almost always available, the pharmacist is an underutilized resource. One of his or her jobs is public education and information. Patients need instruction about the kind of questions to ask: Are there any contraindications when using this product? Is there a need for concern about interactions with this prescription medication? Are there any side effects?

Working with Elderly People

Remember that elderly people are survivors. Those who are old now have lived through hard times. Getting through the Great Depression and a world war required strength. Those who survived have a wealth of experience to bring to coping with the stresses of aging. Make it clear that you respect their strengths and experience and that you have high expectations for their ability to overcome their problems.

Because many elderly persons are reluctant to seek or receive help, a family member is often the person to make the initial contact. The family's views of the situation, their ideas and fears, need to be discussed. Whatever the problem, the chances are good that something can be done to improve the picture and improve functional status. It often comes as a surprise to families that there is hope for recovery. Professionals can help the family, too, as they cope with a difficult situation, such as by arranging for Meals-on-Wheels or making simple suggestions about how to make routines easier.

In conversation with elderly people, do not stick with neutral topics, such as the weather, all of the time. Discuss topics of common interest to you both, such as gardening or baseball, as well as some controversial topic, something appealing. You can enhance self-esteem by letting the person know that not only do you want their opinions but you also want them to listen to yours.

Multiple resources may be needed to assist elderly people. Many older adults with alcohol problems need to become reinvolved in the world. Meaningful contacts can come from a variety of people, not just from professional helpers. The janitor in the client's apartment building, a neighbor, or a crossing guard at the street corner may all be potential allies. If the person was once active in a church group, a civic organization, or another community group but has lost contact, recommend that he or she get in touch with the organization. There is often a member who will visit or be able to assist in other ways. Many communities have senior citizen centers that offer social programs, Meals-on-Wheels, counseling on Social Security and Medicare, and transportation.

When cognitive impairment is a factor, providing cues to orient the person may be helpful. Mention dates, day of the week, and current events. Do not, however, expect a cognitively impaired person to retain such information or to learn new skills. Since remote memory is usually preserved longer than recent memory, discussing past events and interests may be socially rewarding.

If you give specific information to the client, write it down legibly. This makes it much easier for the client to comply. If family members are present, tell them the directions, too. In thinking about compliance and what can be done to assist the elderly in participating in treatment, take some time to think about how your agency functions. What does it mean for an elderly person coming to see you? Are there long waits at several offices on several floors? Does it require navigating difficult stairs, elevators, and hallways in the process? Are there times of the day that make use of public transportation easier? Consider such factors, and make adjustments to make it much easier for your elderly clients. In specific terms, make every effort to do things in as uncomplicated, convenient, nonembarrassing, and economical a fashion as possible.

I think I don't regret a single "excess" of my responsive youth—only in my chilled age, certain occasions and possibilities I didn't embrace.

HENRY JAMES

Letter to Hugh Walpole, 1913

Separate sympathy from empathy. Sympathy is feeling sorry in company with someone. The elderly don't want that; it makes them feel

like children. Empathy means you understand or want to understand. This is what they would like.

Be aware that you may be thought of and responded to as any number of important people in your client's long life. Also, you may alternately represent a grandchild, a child, a parent, a peer, and an authority figure to them at various points in treatment, even within the same interview, and at the same time.

Have integrity with the elderly. Do not try to mislead or lie to them. They are too experienced with all the con games in life. If they ask you questions, give them straight answers. This, however, does not mean being brutal in the name of honesty. For example, in speaking with a client, you might say, "Many other people I talk with have concerns about death; do you?" If the client responds, "No, I haven't thought much about it," you don't blurt out, "Well, you'd better think about it, since you have only 6 months to live." That is not integrity.

In working with the elderly, set specific goals. Make sure that the initial ones are easily attainable. This means they can have some surefire positive experiences. With that under their belts, they are more likely to take some risks and attempt other things.

Make home visits. These can be the key to working with this group. It may be the only thing that will break down their resistance and help them enter treatment. Very few will seek help on their own initiative. So, if someone is not willing to come to your office, give him or her a call. Ask if you can make an appointment to see him or her at home. If the response you get is "I don't want you to come," don't quit. Your next line is "Well, if I'm ever in the area, I'd like to stop by." After your visit, you may well find his or her resistance has disappeared. The home visit can be vital in making an adequate assessment. Seeing the person in his or her own home, where security is at its peak, provides a much better picture of how the person is getting along, as well as the pluses and minuses of the environment. It also allows the client to be spontaneous in emotions and behavior. If you regularly make home visits, beware of making the person "stay in trouble" to see you. Don't just visit in a crisis. Instead, stop in to hear about successes. Your visits may be a high point for the person, who may not like to think of losing this contact. Make a visit the day after the client's first day on a new volunteer job, for example.

Beware of those who arrange trivial activities for older people to occupy their time. Craft classes, for instance, ought to teach usable skills, not just keep people busy. Many elderly people also have something they can teach others. For example, the carpenter who is no longer steady enough to use tools will be able to provide consultation to people who want to remodel their homes. Elderly people have a richness of life experiences and much to contribute.

It is always important that the substance abuse clinician work closely with the client's physician and health-care providers. There are few situations when it is more important that everyone is singing from the same page.

WOMEN

Alcoholism, heavy drinking, problem drinking, and other drug use were long assumed to be problems of men. Accordingly, for a long time research on substance abuse problems among women was very limited. With respect to alcohol, a literature review indicates that only 28 English-language studies of women with alcoholism were published between 1928 and 1970. Another assumption has been that, when present, alcoholism is alcoholism and drug dependence is drug dependence, regardless of gender.

Despite the growing attention to women's problems, the available data are not easily synthesized. One problem results from the fact that researchers frequently study women who enter treatment. This limits what can be said about the extent, nature, and magnitude of problems among women in general. Further complicating the situation is the fact that those being studied seemingly represent all of the possible combinations of alcohol and other substance use. Subjects of research studies range from alcohol-dependent women, to women with drug dependence, to women with alcohol dependence who use/abuse/are dependent on other substances, to female substance users who drink/drink heavily/are alcohol dependent. The extent to which these populations are distinctive or overlapping is unknown, so generalizations from any of these individual studies is difficult. In addition, some research to date has used relatively small samples and has focused on narrow topics, such as the use of day care by urban women in substance abuse treatment. While such details are very important, a multitude of detail doesn't necessarily make seeing the big picture easier. Although facts proliferate and there is more information, there is not always greater understanding.

Gender Differences

Women represent a growing percentage of drinkers, including those with alcohol problems and those with alcohol dependence. For younger women in the general population, the proportion of drinkers is beginning to equal that of men. The differences between male and female drinking rates are due in part to the large number of abstainers among older women. These older women, born on the heels of Prohibition, are of an era in which women's drinking was less socially acceptable and far less prevalent. The behavior of their granddaughters is quite different.

Table 11.14 summarizes the substance use patterns of women with respect to patterns of men. Table 11.15 provides information on the use

Table 11.14 Substance Use in the Past Year by Gender, 2000

Substance	% of Men	% of Women
Alcohol	68.3	60.0
Nicotine	33.1	27.4
Any illicit drug use	13.8	9.3
Marijuana	10.8	6.5
Cocaine	2.3	1.2
Crack	0.6	0.3
Inhalants	1.3	0.6
Hallucinogens	2.0	1.3
Prescription (nonmedical use)	3.2	2.1

From: Substance Abuse and Mental Health Services Administration. *National Household Survey on Drug Abuse: Main Findings 2000.* Rockville, MD: Substance Abuse and Mental Health Services Administration, 2000.

Table 11.15 Women's Substance Use in the Past Year by Age Groups, 2000

	Age Groups (%)				
Substance	**All Women**	**12–17**	**18–25**	**26–34**	**> 34**
Alcohol	60.0	32.7	68.9	71.5	59.7
Nicotine	29.3	21.8	35.0	33.3	24.9
Marijuana	6.5	13.7	20.0	6.5	2.7
Cocaine	1.2	2.0	3.4	1.9	0.5
Crack	0.3	0.6	0.5	0.7	0.2
Hallucinogens	1.3	3.6	5.6	1.0	0.2
Inhalants	0.6	3.0	1.8	0.4	—
Prescription (nonmedical use)	2.1	4.0	4.4	2.6	1.3
Heroin	0.8	0.3	0.7	0.9	0.9

From: Substance Abuse and Mental Health Services Administration. *National Household Survey on Drug Abuse: Main Findings 2000.* Rockville, MD: Substance Abuse and Mental Health Services Administration, 2000.

patterns of women in different age groups. This information is drawn from the *National Household Survey,* conducted regularly on behalf of the National Institute on Drug Abuse.

Differences Among Women

Racial and Ethnic Considerations

Race and ethnicity would be anticipated to be an important basis for differences among women. While data remain limited, there are differences with respect to patterns of use. White women are more likely than either Hispanic or African-American women to be drinkers and to be smokers. African-American women are more likely to have used illicit drugs in the past year, primarily attributable to higher levels of marijuana use. Where there seem to be racial/ethnic differences, most noticeable in the category of illicit drug use, the differences disappear when age, education, and household income are taken into account. Table 11.16 summarizes substance use for women from 3 ethnic groups.

Table 11.16 Women's Substance Use in the Past Year by Race/Ethnicity, 1996

Substance	All (%) Women	White	African-American	Hispanic
Alcohol	58.6	64.3	52.9	48.8
Nicotine	27.0	32.0	28.1	21.4
Any illicit drug	8.0	7.8	10.5	7.0
Marijuana	6.0	5.9	7.7	5.2
Cocaine	1.3	1.2	1.5	2.1
Crack	0.5	0.5	0.4	1.4
Inhalants	0.7	0.9	0.2	0.4
Prescription*	2.5	2.6	2.4	2.0
Stimulants	0.7	0.7	0.4	0.8
Sedatives	0.2	0.3	0.3	0.1
Tranquilizers	1.0	1.1	0.5	0.4

*Nonmedical use

From: NIDA: *National Household Survey on Drug Abuse: Population Estimates 1996,* Rockville, MD: NIDA, 1997

Sexual Orientation

With the limited attention to substance use problems of women generally, it is not surprising that there has been very little discussion directed to lesbian and bisexual women. Beyond sexism, lesbian addiction goes unaddressed because of homophobia and the attendant societal stigma. Research is exceedingly limited, although work is being done. In larger cities there are treatment programs being conducted specifically for lesbian and bisexual women.

It has been suggested that lesbians and bisexual women are at greater risk for substance use problems than are heterosexual women. Some early estimates were that from 25% to 35% of lesbians have a serious substance use problem. This elevated level of substance use disorders was attributed in part to the "fact" that much of lesbian social life supposedly revolves around bars. More recent studies do not support this. Better designed research has found no significant differences between lesbian/bisexual women and heterosexual women, either in terms of drinking patterns or rates of alcohol problems. The one striking difference that has been found between lesbian/bisexual women and heterosexual women is in the proportion of lesbian women who are smokers. Lesbian/bisexual women also have higher rates of marijuana use.

A subgroup of lesbians that may be particularly vulnerable to substance use problems are adolescents. A common theme in any study or report of lesbian, gay male, and bisexual youth is the chronic stress created by the verbal and physical abuse they receive from peers and adults. This can lead to a number of problematic outcomes, ranging from difficulties at school, to running away or being ejected from home, to encounters with the law, to prostitution, to substance abuse and suicide attempts.

Even though the rate of problems may not be elevated to the degree that had been presumed, there are unique treatment issues. Lesbian/bisexual women entering treatment will confront special issues, such as when and how to reveal their sexual orientation and deal with the associated prejudices. There is a small but rich literature with respect to treatment, the issues to be confronted, the perceptions of treatment, and the treatment process, both in formal treatment and in the use of self-help groups.

The toll of AIDS in the gay community is well known. Lesbian women are also at elevated risk for HIV/AIDS if sexually active with a partner who is an intravenous drug user. Data suggest that a very high percentage of all HIV/AIDS cases (possibly upward of 90%) reported among women who had only had a female partner involved intravenous use by the partner.

Age-Related Differences

Despite the fact that age has not received particular attention, it is repeatedly cited as the factor related to the differences that are identified among women. For example, among alcohol-dependent women, younger women have been recognized as being at greater risk for other drug use. They have also been recognized as being at substantially higher risk for attempted or completed suicide attempts. One study of the effects of age demonstrated considerable differences between women born before versus those born after 1954.[4] That year was chosen as the point for distinguishing age groups to divide the sample into those who had reached adulthood before or after the early 1970s, a period in which there were dramatic cultural changes. The question being examined was "Have shifts in cultural norms and behavior with respect to substance use, as well as women's roles, influenced the natural history of those who enter treatment?" This seemed to be the case. The following is a list of the age-related differences identified among these women. Despite being a decade old, these findings dramatically point out the impact of cultural eras and social change.

- *Substance use patterns.* Younger women (those then under age 35) were more likely than older women to be using marijuana, cocaine, stimulants, opiates, and hallucinogens on a weekly basis. One-third of younger women reported weekly use of marijuana, and one-third reported weekly use of cocaine. While 16% of younger women reported daily drinking, this was 2.5 times more common in older women, with 40% reportedly being daily drinkers.
- *Onset of use.* Over one-half of younger women (56%) had started drinking before age 16, whereas only 14% of older women had begun drinking by that age. If age 18 is the point of adulthood, 83% of younger women, compared with less than one-half of older women (46%), had spent their entire adult lives as drinkers. The differences based on age for drug use during adulthood are even more extreme. For older women, 14% had been using drugs since age 18, but 74% of younger women had been using drugs all their adult lives.
- *Settings for use.* Women's drinking has frequently been characterized as solitary, private, and hidden. This is less true of younger women, with slightly over one-half reporting their drinking or drug use to always or usually takes place with others. Only 20% of older women reported that their use occurred primarily in the company of others. Thus, the pattern of solitary, private use is true of older women.
- *Correlates of use.* Younger women were more likely to have used alcohol or other drugs during pregnancy. They were also more likely to have had incidents of consuming the equivalent of a fifth of liquor per day and more likely than older women to have hit someone or been violent toward others. Younger women had a 2.5 times higher

[4]The then 35-year-olds are now 50.

incidence of eating disorders, with 25% having either anorexia or bulimia or alternating periods of starving and binging and purging. Rates of depression were similar across age groups. In comparison with older women, the younger group had considerably more work-related problems—for example, relationships with supervisors and coworkers, in the quality of work performance, in time off the job, and in injuries on the job. Younger women were also more likely to have been the driver in a motor vehicle accident, to have been arrested, or to have been jailed overnight. In the year before treatment, younger women had more hospitalizations for psychiatric care, received more emergency room medical treatment, and had hospitalization and outpatient medical care similar to that of older women.

- *Violence and abuse.* Younger women also had a history of greater physical abuse as children (36%). As adults, the prevalence of abuse escalated, with 48% of younger women reporting physical abuse and 32% reporting rape or coerced sexual intercourse. This is in contrast to older women, of whom 23% reported a history of physical abuse before age 18, rising to 35% after age 18. For younger women, relationships with boyfriends and spouses were marked by domestic violence and abuse. Among married women, younger women were 2.5 times more likely than were older women to have a spouse with an alcohol or a substance abuse problem.
- *History.* Younger women demonstrated a wider range of problems and more incidents of social difficulties before age 15. These included truancy (30%), suspensions or expulsions from school (23%), arrests (14%), running away from home more than once (28%), vandalism (19%), shoplifting and stealing (53%), and initiation of physical fights (27%). Younger women reported being more sexually active in early adolescence, with 20% having had sexual intercourse with more than one person before their fifteenth birthday.
- *The widowed.* Although elderly widows have not been identified as a subgroup at special risk, the question of the relationship among grief, bereavement, and the subsequent use of alcohol was examined among women admitted for substance abuse treatment. Tranquilizer use has been recognized as greater among widows, even in the absence of a therapeutic effect. Three-fourths of widows had a history of heavy alcohol use before the deaths of their husbands. There was a significant subgroup who did appear to be at increased risk for the development of an alcohol problem after the death of their husbands. These were women who had no family history of alcohol problems but whose deceased husbands had been alcohol dependent and had been untreated. Alcohol problems emerged in these women as a response to pathological grief, which was the legacy of the alcoholic marriage.

Natural History of Alcohol and Other Drug Problems in Women

In what other ways do the alcohol and other drug problems of women differ from those of men? The major differences that have been described are noted in the following list.

- *Specific triggers.* More alcohol-dependent women than men can point to a specific trigger for the onset of heavy drinking. This might be a divorce, an illness, the death of a spouse, children leaving home, or some other stressful event. If a woman seeks help at such a point, both a careful alcohol use history and education about the potential risks of alcohol use are warranted. The danger of relying on alcohol or other drugs is that the crisis can take on a long-term life of its own. The challenge to those dealing with a woman in the face of life changes and crises is in providing empathy rather than sympathy. Either overtly or covertly, the danger is often to imply that, if that had happened to us, we would probably have responded in the same fashion. The current dangerous misuse of alcohol and other drugs can become lost in the forest of other problems. A history of abortion is also associated with an increased risk of substance use problems.
- *A telescoped course.* Women's alcohol dependence is often described as "telescoped." This means the disease appears later and progresses more rapidly. The period of time between the onset of heavy drinking and entry into treatment is shorter among women, too. The same is apparently true of other drug use, with a shorter time from first use to dependence.
- *Medical complications.* Female alcoholics are more susceptible to medical complications than are male alcoholics. For men, the presence of medical complications is tied to long-term, regular, heavy use. The several six-packs a day over time will take their toll. For women, the situation may be different. Medical complications among women may be less a product of the amount usually consumed but tied to the frequency of heavy drinking occasions. Thus, very heavy drinking once or twice a week may wreak more havoc than if the same amount of alcohol were spread out over time. Women have particular susceptibility to liver disease. This may well be tied to the differences in the way men and women metabolize alcohol (see Chapter 3). Women with alcohol dependence have consumed significantly less alcohol during their drinking career than have men, perhaps 45% less, yet they still experience difficulties of a similar magnitude. There are some physical measures that confirm women's greater vulnerability to alcohol. This greater vulnerability to alcohol's effects has been found in measurements of changes in the brain associated with heavy drinking; women have a greater reduction in gray and white matter.

- *Entry into treatment.* Women with alcohol dependence tend to enter treatment earlier than men. The time between the onset of heavy drinking and a referral for treatment is likely to be shorter. This is believed to be due to higher rates of medical complications. Women, too, tend to exhaust the social supports and resources needed to continue alcohol use. Also, women have a greater number of alcohol-induced problems than do men, even when the length of drinking, the presence of psychiatric problems, and work status are taken into account. Men, however, outnumber women entering treatment by almost 4 to 1. In terms of what prompts treatment and the perceptions of problems when entering care, women have been found to differ from men in several ways. Generally women report more depression, anxiety, powerlessness, hopelessness, and guilt than men report. This is not the result of their having more psychiatric illness but is part of the female symptom pattern of alcohol dependence. While reporting less support for entry into treatment, women, more than men, credit pressure from others as a major factor in their seeking treatment, whether from children, other relatives, coworkers, or their physicians.
- *Violence and abuse.* Women entering treatment often have experienced recent episodes of violence.
- *Family Issues.* If the woman is unmarried or a divorced single parent, there are not only additional emotional demands but also economic burdens. In the aftermath of divorce, almost three-quarters of women and their children are economically less well off, if not downright poverty stricken. Entry into treatment may stretch an already difficult financial situation. A concern unique to women is fear of losing custody of children. This is especially an issue for women who are involved with illicit drug use. In a marriage in which one spouse is alcoholic, when it is the woman, there is a significantly greater likelihood of divorce. If the wife has alcoholism, there is a 9-times-greater chance of divorce than is found for male alcoholics. An important consequence is that the family and emotional support systems that are an asset in recovery are less likely to be present. Interestingly, whatever the woman's marital situation, it has been found that women entering treatment do not receive the solid support for that decision that men generally receive from family and friends. Women with alcohol and/or other drug problems are more likely than are men to have a drug-dependent partner.

Give me something that's mysterious

- *Other drug use.* Women have higher rates of use of drugs other than alcohol and of other drugs in combination with alcohol than do men. They are prescribed mood-altering drugs much more frequently than men. In contrast to men, women are at greater risk for non-medical use of prescription drugs, particularly benzodiazepines and narcotic analgesics. A sample of women alcoholics found that 70% had a history of having been prescribed psychoactive drugs, a rate 1.5 times greater than for alcoholic men. Of the women prescribed psychoactive drugs, one-half could recall at least one occasion of having used alcohol in combination with the medication; also, one-half had been prescribed more than one category of drug. This suggests the need for obtaining a very careful drug use history, with a wary eye for multiple drug use and abuse.

- *Workplace and vocational spheres.* In the workplace and vocational arenas, differences between men and women are evident. With respect to employment and vocational status, women with substance use problems—just like women in the general population—have fewer vocational skills and training and are less likely to be employed, to hold high-status jobs, to be self-supporting, and, if drugs are involved, to be financing their own drug use. In these circumstances, women may support their drug addiction with petty larceny, shoplifting, and prostitution. They also have fewer vocational skills and training. Women are more likely than men to lose their jobs. Women with alcohol or other drug problems are more likely to be dependent on a family member or on public welfare for survival than are men.
- *Perceptions.* Women with dependence are reported to have lower expectations for their lives than men and to express more concern with survival and minimizing discomfort. More commonly women do not see either alcohol or other drug use as their primary problem. Thus, they are inclined to express concern about the ability of a substance abuse program to assist them. This also means that it is particularly important for treatment personnel to help them make the connection between their life problems and alcohol or other drug use.
- *Personality.* Little is known about the personality factors that may predate the emergence of alcohol dependence in women. A follow-up in later life of a sample of women college students found that the factors predictive of alcohol dependence in later life were considerably different from those among men. The best predictor for alcohol dependence in women might be termed "purposeful drinking"—that is, drinking to relieve shyness, to get high, to be happy, and to get along better. Research also indicates that women who are heavy social drinkers have the expectation that drinking will relieve worries, nervousness, and tension.
- *HIV/AIDS.* A problem of growing concern is the rise of HIV infection and AIDS among women, primarily related to their own intravenous drug use or to their having a sexual partner with AIDS. It appears that young women with alcohol and multiple substance use problems are a population at particular risk. While a 3:1 ratio of male-to-female intravenous drug users has been frequently cited, among younger women this disparity is disappearing. Women appear to have a faster transition from drug use initiation to dependence; tend to be introduced to drug use by partners; have drug-using partners, which promotes access to drugs; are more likely to engage in needle sharing; and, with the potential for prostitution, are likely to

From birth to age eighteen, a girl needs good parents. From eighteen to thirty-five, she needs good looks. From thirty-five to fifty-five she needs a good personality. From fifty-five on, she needs good cash.
SOPHIE TUCKER, 1953 (AT AGE 69)

have greater ease in maintaining a steady supply of drugs. All of these factors contribute to an increased risk of HIV/AIDS infection. Beyond the risk to these women, the other issue of concern is perinatal transmission in pregnancy. A public health priority is intervention to reduce the spread of HIV/AIDS in this population.

- *Family relationships.* There are gender-based differences that are evident in women's relationships to family and spouse or partner. Women who come from families where drugs were commonly used as a primary coping strategy are themselves more likely to become addicted. Women with substance use problems have often experienced greater familial disruption than have men with such problems. In contrast to men, both alcohol- and opiate-involved women come from drug abusing and disorganized families. Female heroin addicts are more likely than are male heroin addicts to have first been introduced to heroin by family members or others close to them. The development of dependence is linked to the family's approval of use or the absence of clear disapproval of use, in combination with easy access to the drug.
- *Emergency room care.* With respect to the drinking population, women are overly represented in emergency room visits, as indicated by data drawn from the Drug Abuse Warning Network (DAWN). It is speculated that this is due to women's greater vulnerability to overdoses at lower levels of consumption and their greater likelihood to use alcohol in combination with other drugs. With many overdoses reported as accidental, one important intervention is education about the effects of alcohol and other drugs, alone and in combination. Among women admitted to a large regional trauma center, a routine screening involving lab tests, the MAST screening test, and one-third were determined to have an alcohol problem.
- *Suicide.* Alcohol problems in women greatly increase the risk for suicide. One study determined that alcoholic women have a history of suicide attempts 5 times greater than that of nonalcoholic women, with 40% of the alcoholic women in the study reporting a suicide attempt. Furthermore, close to 50% who make one attempt will make a future suicide attempt. Youth and alcohol/drug use and abuse in women are a high-risk combination.
- *Pregnancy.* Women ages 18–44 are considered to be of child-bearing age. Within this group, 6.4% of nonpregnant and 2.8% of pregnant woman report using illicit drugs. During pregnancy there is a reduction in illicit drug use, with the rate of abstaining increasing from 28% in the first trimester to 93% by the third trimester. Marijuana represents three-quarters of the illicit drug use. However, following delivery, there was a significant resumption of use, and only one-third continued to refrain from illicit drug use. Among those using illicit drugs, half of the pregnant and two-thirds of nonpregnant women also used alcohol and tobacco.

Assessment

Of the screening tools described in Chapter 9, the TWEAK is the one developed specifically for women. While it may be obvious, in assessing drinking patterns and quantity, the result is dependent on the size of the glass. A study of women who were attending a public prenatal clinic, provides a dramatic reminder of this. When women were shown glasses of different sizes and asked to select the one(s) that applied to them, the quantity of alcohol they regularly consumed skyrocketed. For beer, the amount consumed had to be increased by a third. For spirits, the actual amount consumed was 300 times higher. Overall in this group of high-risk women, the "4 drinks" became 10 drinks.

Treatment Approaches

There are several treatment approaches that are unique to women. *Residential treatment* programs created for women and their children described further below are becoming more common in many communities. Evaluation studies suggest that such settings increase retention in treatment. Also of significance is their impact on the overall family unit. There is improvement, not only in the women but also in the children. At 6- and 12-month follow-ups, children had fewer emotional and behavioral problems. *Brief intervention,* particularly with women who are pregnant or of child-bearing age, is a promising approach. As with other populations, the use of brief treatments reduces the quantity of alcohol consumed as well as reducing episodes of heavy drinking. In one study's follow-up 4 years later, the greatest reduction was among women who became pregnant following the brief intervention. Given the social costs as well as the consequences for the woman and her child, such brief intervention is important.

With the interest in substance use among pregnant women, there has been some exploration of what is involved in getting people off of the most common drugs used in combination: alcohol, nicotine, and caffeine. Typically these cluster together. Find a smoker and the odds are you also have a drinker. Those who use multiple substances were less likely to quit one than are those who use only one substance. In one case study being a nonsmoker predicted quitting alcohol. And being neither a smoker nor a drinker predicted quitting caffeine. However, if those who were into all three did manage to quit one, then they were more likely, rather than less likely, to proceed and cease other legal substance use. So for them it was seemingly an all or none. One of the challenges is to figure out the best treatment strategies in approaching multiple legal drug use cessation. At this point, we don't know—is it all at a time, in sequence, or if in sequence then how the sequence should be staged. Is there a danger in staging, with having cessation too close or too far apart?

Treatment Themes

Beyond the items already touched on that can influence the course of the disease process and when and how women are identified and diagnosed, there are also issues relevant to the treatment process itself.

Mothering and female sexuality are aspects of self-esteem unique to women. If a woman has children, some of the questions she may well be asking herself include the following: "Am I a good mother? Can I be a good mother? Have I hurt my children? Can I ever cope with my children if I don't drink or use drugs?" These may not be explicit in the therapy sessions, but they do cross her mind. They begin to be answered, positively, one hopes, as she gains sober and straight time. Family meetings may also be one way she gains answers to these questions. However, in some cases where there has been child abuse or a child is having difficulties, a referral to a children's agency, a family-service agency, or a mental health clinic may be important in dealing with these situations. One of the things any mother will need to learn if she is to regain her self-esteem as a mother is a sense of what the "normal" difficulties are in raising children.

In terms of sexuality, there may be a number of potential questions. If she has had a divorce or an affair, a woman may well be wondering about her worth and attractiveness as a woman. Even if the marriage is intact, there may be sexual problems. On one hand, the sexual relationship may have almost disappeared as the drinking progressed. On the other, it may have been years since she has had sexual intercourse without the benefit of a glass of wine or a couple of beers. Again, time in sobriety may well be the major therapeutic element. But couples therapy and/or sexual counseling may be needed if marital problems are not resolved. In cases where the sexual problems preceded the active drinking, professional help is certainly recommended. Sobering up is not likely to take away the existing problem in some miraculous fashion. To let it fester is to invite even more problems.

What about single women and women caught in an unsatisfactory marriage? Some find themselves "suddenly" involved in an affair or an extramarital relationship. With a little bit of sobriety, they are very ripe to fall in love. This may have several roots. The woman may be questioning her femininity, and the attentions of a man may provide some affirmation of her status as a woman. Also possible is the fact that with sobriety comes a sense of being alive again. There is the reawakening of a host of feelings that have long been dormant, including sexual feelings. In this sense it may be like the bloom and intensity of adolescence. A romantic involvement may follow very naturally. Unfortunately, it can lead to disaster, if followed with abandon. This can be equally true for men.

A word of caution to male therapists working with women is warranted. If you are the first person in many years to accept her and if you have been making attempts to raise her self-esteem, she may mistake her gratitude for a personal emotional attachment to you. Your recognition of this "error" is imperative. If you provide contacts for her with other women in recovery, she may be better able to recognize this pitfall as well.

For women in treatment, children are another concern. If a woman has young children, long-term residential treatment may be very difficult to arrange. Many women have no husband in the home, and extended family members do not always live down the street, as was once the case. However, for that very reason, it may be all the more important for the woman to begin her recovery in a residential center, where intense therapy may take place without the distractions of daily family life. Models of treatment to overcome this problem are being tried in many areas throughout the country. But in too many places the usual facilities are still the only ones available. You will need to stretch your creativity to the limit to deal with this problem. Potentially, friends, extended family—even if they are called in from a distance—or a live-in sitter can be used. When inpatient treatment is warranted, there may be no way to allow a client the optimum advantage of an extended residential treatment. If this is the case, intensive day treatment is a possible option. Even if inpatient care can be arranged, you may be faced with a woman's intense guilt over, and resistance to, leaving her children. There are no easy formulas, and the therapist is left to work out the best solution possible in each case.

The latest figures from the General Services Board of AA indicate that women are well represented in AA. It appears that whatever the differences between men and women, AA manages to achieve similar rates of success with both. It is as important to make a referral to AA or NA for your female clients as for male clients. A few trips to local meetings should assure her that it is no longer the male stronghold it once was. In many communities, one will also find women-only groups. A common criticism of Alcoholics Anonymous and the related 12-step programs is that they foster continuing female dependence. This, however, is not a universally accepted view. As one feminist author commented, "Those I see going into 12-step programs are basically trying to stay alive. They are not the people that one would see at political meetings. Without recovery they would probably be dead, and dead women don't have any politics."

There has been little systematic research on whether there are differences in treatment outcomes by gender. Both males and females with similar demographic characteristics, in comparable stages of their illness, are presumed to do equally well in similar treatment settings. A few recent studies do suggest that women may have more satisfactory outcomes a year posttreatment than do men. However, women's rates of entrance, retention, and completion of treatment are found to be significantly lower than rates for men.

Access to treatment may be a dimension on which men and women differ. For women there are the issues of child care and affordability of treatment, because women have greater chances of losing their jobs and having lower wages and benefits, and they may be the family's sole source of support. Women may need more ancillary supports and services because of their status as single mothers or as victims of domestic violence or the absence of supportive people in their environment. Training in and skillful application of the information on women's issues generally can minimize women's distrust of social service system providers. Attitudes toward addicted women are often negative, and chemically dependent women are often subjected to sexual harassment. Pregnancy and childbirth are points where intervention is often effective with alcohol- and other drug-involved women.

Valley View Recovery Center for Women and Children
I trained to be an alcohol counselor. No one ever taught me to change diapers.

In light of the impediments to women's entering and remaining in treatment, programs designed specifically for women have begun to emerge. The Center for Substance Abuse Treatment (CSAT) funded demonstration projects in the mid-1990s known as Residential Women and Children (RWC) and Pregnant and Postpartum Women programs. These programs were unique in several respects. They were residential programs designed to involve stays of 6 or 12 months, they included not only women but also young children, and they provided a comprehensive range of services for clients and their children. In addition to the usual substance abuse treatment there were prenatal care, pediatric and medical services, mental health treatment, vocational training, parent classes, legal services, nursery and preschool for children, transportation, and assistance with securing transitional housing. The earliest evaluations of these programs have only recently been published. The outcomes have been very positive. One such report describes the outcomes for women with serious drug problems. Alcohol was the common ingredient, but crack cocaine, powder cocaine, heroin, methamphetamines, over-the-counter drugs, and marijuana also were used. These were women with multiple problems: unemployed (92%), few skills, little education (over half without a high school education); pregnant at admission (25%); separated/divorced/never married (82%); 3 or more children (54%); medical problems (60%); criminal justice system involvement at admission (50%); and had children removed from the home by child protection services (47%). The mean age was 30 years old, and the mean years of substance use was over 15. At one-year follow-up, 70% of those who had stayed six or more months had maintained complete abstinence. In addition, health status was significantly improved, two-thirds were employed or in vocational training programs. Arrest rates or involvement in illegal activities was about 2%. Over 80% lived with at least one child. Only 5% lived with a drug-involved spouse or partner compared to 44% prior to treatment.

Residential care for women and their children, ideally, is family-centered care for both. As part of the evaluation of women's residential programs there has been some exploration as well on their impacts on the children. Many of these children are at risk for future problems. There may be biological risks (such as prenatal exposure to AOD). In addition they confront an array of environmental risks including low income, low maternal education, maternal mental illness, instability in caregivers, residential instability, child abuse and neglect, little father involvement, and experiences in foster care. Their presence in the residential setting shouldn't be seen merely as a nice touch for the mothers' benefit, but the opportunity to provide services to these children as well. In one description of such a family-based setting, it was noted that serving these children on site is more effective than trying to use community-based services. Beyond providing for better integration of services, just imagine the logistics. Ask any soccer mom what would be entailed in arranging for doctor's appointments, speech therapy, remedial reading, play groups, and school activities for potentially 15 to 20 children. In such a residential family-centered setting, women are not just getting parenting classes. There is active support for parenting, in a variety of ways from mother-child activities, to support and modeling. After the period of residential care, services to children ought to be included in aftercare planning, with home visits, case management, and supportive services for children in their school or nursery school settings.

In looking at factors which seemed to be related to relapse, living with a drug-involved partner seemed by far to be the single greatest risk factor. This has also been found true in other studies. For one, those with drug-using partners are likely to leave treatment earlier. Drug-using partners not only come with their drugs; they come with an accompanying set of problems, being more likely to be unemployed, have less education, have legal problems, and more health problems. They are seen as less supportive, and in fact are more likely to undermine treatment by providing money for drugs.

Treatment Issues for Pregnant Women

Pregnancy and childbirth are points when the potential for intervention is often greatest. Medical treatment for pregnant alcohol and drug dependent women must include perinatal services, pharmacotherapy, health education, and referral. Perinatal services should encompass evaluation and treatment by a perinatologist and a perinatal nurse clinician. HIV counseling and testing and nutritional counseling are important. The mother should deliver in a hospital where emergency services are readily available in case of complications. Many infants are low birth weight and need intensive care. For women who are drinking heavily, even if abstinence cannot be achieved, a reduction in drinking reduces the risks of fetal alcohol syndrome and fetal alcohol effects.

See Chapter 13 for more discussion of other drug use and pregnancy. However, there is a disturbing social development that needs to be mentioned: the emergence of court actions filed against pregnant women who are dependent on drugs, particularly cocaine, and alcohol to a lesser degree. Women have been charged with child abuse on the basis of administering cocaine to the fetus through the umbilical cord. Unfortunately, judges, legislators, and prosecutors, like the public in general, have obtained most of their information about drug- and alcohol-dependent pregnant and parenting women from the popular press. The coverage of the so-called crack epidemic and crack babies has been inaccurate and alarmist. Careful research and measured responses have not been widely covered, and thus there exists the prevailing assumption that children exposed prenatally to crack are inevitably and irremediably damaged.

The reactions to the problems of drug- and/or alcohol-dependent pregnant women have thus been largely punitive. Hundreds of women have been prosecuted on unproven theories of fetal abuse and drug delivery through the umbilical cord. These prosecutions continue, despite the fact that no appellate court in the country has upheld one. Thousands of women have also been reported under civil child neglect laws and have been investigated for being neglectful or abusive parents based solely on a positive urine toxicology specimen at the birth of the child. African-American women have been arrested and reported disproportionately to authorities, despite evidence that white and African-American women in similar situations use illegal substances at approximately the same rate. Judges often assume, incorrectly, that drug-dependent pregnant women have access to appropriate drug treatment, to contraceptive and abortion services, and to prenatal care. Moreover, they do not view addiction as a disease or understand that relapse may be part of recovery. The public policy statements of leading medical and public health organizations opposing punitive responses has helped. The continued prosecution of pregnant women, cutbacks in services for pregnant and parenting drug users, and the continued belief among many leaders that children's physical and emotional health problems can be blamed exclusively on cocaine or other drugs suggest the need for extensive judicial and public education and organized opposition to punitive approaches to this health problem.

THE WORKPLACE

Some Basic Statistics

In 1994, the *National Household Survey* for the first time included questions about alcohol and other drug use in relation to work. Those surveyed were asked about work-related issues, such as missed work, whether they had been fired, workplace accidents, their occupation, size of the workplace, whether they had ever been provided with information about the alcohol and other drug polices at work, the existence of an EAP (employee assistance program), the use of drug testing, and their attitudes toward testing. The most recent data available are from the 2000 survey. In the population ages 18 to 49, of full-time workers, 8.1% reported heavy alcohol use and close to the same proportion, 7.4%, reported either alcohol abuse or dependence. In terms of illicit drug use, 8.3% were current users of an illicit substance, and about a third of those reported drug abuse or dependence during the past year.

Patterns of heavy alcohol as well as illicit drug use vary among segments of the workforce. For one, the rates of heavy drinking and illicit drug use are higher among part-time workers (9%) and the unemployed (16%). Within the full-time workforce there also are significant differences related to gender and age. Compared to women, men have twice the rate of heavy drinking and one and a half times the rate of alcohol abuse or dependence. Similarly with illicit drugs, men are twice as likely to be current users or to have reported symptoms indicating a diagnosis of abuse or dependence in the past year. Age differences are reflected in the fact that heavy drinking is twice as common among those 25 and younger compared to those 35 to 50, with respective rates of 13.5% versus 6%. The differences between age groups is even more striking for illicit drug use. Younger workers are about 3 times more likely to have used illicit drugs in the past month than the older workers. And they are more than 5 times as likely to report either abuse or dependence. Interestingly, for all age groups, the differences between any illicit drug use or heavy drinking in the past month are modest. In fact more younger workers report past-month drug use (14.9%) than report heavy drinking (13.5%). Those who used illicit drugs or are heavy drinkers were more likely to have worked for 3 or more employers during the past year. They were also more likely to have voluntarily left a job. In addition, they also report more absenteeism.

Between 1994 and 2000 there was over a 50% increase in those who reported employment-related drug testing. Fifty-two percent of full-time workers reported drug testing at hiring, 30% reported random drug testing, and 42% reported testing upon reasonable suspicion, such as after accidents. Among large employers, as of 2003, it was estimated that in the vicinity of 80% have some kind of drug testing program.

Over the years, studies have consistently found that substance use has a statistically significant effect on labor supply, absenteeism, and retention, and it influences a variety of performance measures. As business and industry began to recognize the costs to them of employees with alcohol problems, programs emerged to identify problems and initiate treatment. The earliest work-based programs emerging in the 1970s focused on alcohol and were sometimes called occupational alcohol programs. That term has been replaced by employee assistance programs (EAPs). Attention is no longer primarily or narrowly directed to alcohol or even substance use, but includes the array of issues that might influence job performance, whether family problems, financial problems, or mental health concerns. These programs are sometimes called enhanced EAPs. An examination of the effect of moving to an enhanced EAP model showed that the average number of women and minority cases per worksite increased by 58%, white male cases by 45%, and total EAP cases by 53%. This change in program orientation was also accompanied by efforts to draft brochures and the like to reach out to women and minorities.

EAP programs are more common in work sites with 50 or more full-time employees as well as those with unions. More large companies have begun to self-insure rather than purchase market group health insurance. The self-insured firms are more likely to have an EAP, suggesting that is a service desired by the workforce. The median cost per employee for internal and external programs in 2000 was $21.83 and $18.09, respectively. EAP programs, too, are increasingly interested not just in addressing problems but in preventing them. So now there are employee wellness programs. These can include stress reduction courses, programs on nutrition, or exercise programs, and in many places fitness centers are on site. Alcohol risk reductions are included in these other general wellness risk programs. There are also some preliminary explorations of the use of web-based educational and screening efforts.

Historically drinking has been interwoven with work. There has long been the office party, the company picnic, the wine and cheese reception, the martini lunches, the "drink date" to review business, the bar car on the commuter train, the old standby gift of a bottle for a business associate, the round of drinks to celebrate the closing of a business deal, and the construction crew's stopping off for beers after work. Over the past several years the meshing of drinking and business has come under fire. First, the IRS decreed that the martini lunch is not a legitimate business expense. Then the growing interest in physical fitness took its toll. Concern about liability when alcohol is a part of company-sponsored parties came into play. Alcohol use at company parties has recently received more attention, although court cases addressing this go back to the mid-1970s. Nonetheless, for too long drinking in many work situations was not only accepted but expected. Whenever alcohol use is tolerated, the potential for alcohol problems among susceptible individuals rises, more so if drinking is subtly encouraged.

Portrait of a man who stops in a bar for 3 drinks on his way home from work every night.

With the passage of the drug-free workplace legislation in the 1980s, drug use also became a workplace concern. It was at this point that drug testing became common. The assumption was that testing would serve as a deterrent and preventive measure. However, there is little support for this view, as noted in the mid-1990s in a major report of the National Academy of Sciences. Even if, for the sake of argument, one granted that they served as a deterrent, questions remained. For example, how many cases would need to be prevented to justify testing everyone at a cost of $40–$50 per test. In addition, drug testing typically indicates past use; does all such use have implications for workplace performance?

Some of these questions are now being answered. A recent study conducted in a major manufacturing company provides some interesting insights. The study was intended to answer the question "What drug testing policy would be associated with the lowest level of medical care costs?" In the company examined, there was random drug testing, at variable intervals and involving variable percentages of the workforce. A positive drug test was grounds for firing. What was found was that random testing of under half of employees (42%) would reduce medical costs to the lowest level possible. Presumably, for that organization, a 42% testing rate was high enough to lead employees to think that there was a reasonable chance of being tested. Since one didn't have to test a higher proportion of employees to achieve the deterrent effect, the costs of any additional tests might be seen as wasted. A further question was examined, the relationship of the rate of testing and injuries. Indeed, it was determined that by doubling the rate of testing, it would be possible to cut the rate of accidents in half. However, there was a kicker. The rate of injuries was already very, very low, under 1% per month. Cutting that percentage further was seen as having only a marginal benefit and would require testing hundreds more employees.

The following year, in 2004 further clarification was provided. Using information from 2 years of the NIDA *National Household Survey,* the question was examined whether in fact drug testing—whether pre-employment, random testing, or suspicion-based testing—has an impact on the likelihood and frequency of employee drug use. Indeed it does. The employees of firms that have drug testing programs have both lower levels of drug use and fewer chronic drug users. However, this raises the question of whether the drug testing itself deters use, or whether those who use drugs are drawn to work settings without such testing programs.

Clearly the focus of the Drug-Free Workplace Legislation was on drugs as opposed to alcohol. At the same time, these initiatives have conveyed the message that alcohol no longer enjoys a status of being "okay," while all other drugs are "bad." Substance use of whatever variety can and does interfere with performance and productivity and is therefore a legitimate business concern.

In a similar vein, for a long period, smoking at work was an accepted practice. This is no longer the case, and many worksites, in addition to banning smoking in the workplace, have offered smoking cessation programs to help employees quit. No longer being able to smoke at work has certainly raised the quit rate. There is also the phenomenon of "exiled" smoking—people taking smoking breaks—and questions are now being raised about the impact of this practice. One is "What is the impact on performance of smokers' experiencing withdrawal?" and another is "What is the impact on nonsmokers' morale as they witness coworkers' taking authorized and unauthorized cigarette breaks?"

A partial response to the first of these questions is provided by examining the effects of withdrawal on pilots who are regular smokers. Using flight simulators, the pilots were examined after 12 hours of abstinence. In brief, all tests showed declines in cognitive functions and higher levels of reported nervousness, tension-anxiety, fatigue, difficulty concentrating, less alertness, disorders of fine motor adjustments, prolonged reaction times, anger and irritability, drowsiness, and impaired judgment. Physiological measures showed changes in blood pressure and heart rate.

Some companies have extended the ban on indoor smoking to include the entire workplace property, a tactic known as a "smoke-free grounds." This makes the option of just stepping outside for a smoke no longer possible. After the extended ban, the quit rate during one company's smoking cessation program was 52%. That rate far exceeds the outcomes for virtually all smoking cessation programs, for which very good outcomes are around 20%.

Smoking in the workplace has received attention in another context. This is related to efforts to protect workers from the effects of secondhand smoke. This played a part in the lobbying that led to the ban of smoking on airplanes, which exposed flight attendants to passive smoke. More recently, the same issue has arisen in the context of bars. A growing number of municipalities have enacted smoking bans in bars as well as restaurants. Research has confirmed what was long suspected: The bulk of ventilation systems installed in restaurants and bars are largely ineffective. As a result, in many restaurants there is no such thing as a nonsmoking area. Whenever there is a single ventilating system, the air from smoking and nonsmoking areas is collected by that single system and redistributed.

Another group of workers for whom there is concern in respect to nicotine is farm workers. This is because tobacco leaves can effectively act as giant nicotine patches and cause nicotine poisoning. This condition is called *green tobacco sickness.* Symptoms include weakness, headache, nausea, vomiting, dizziness, stomach cramps, breathing difficulty, abnormal temperature, diarrhea, chills, along with fluctuations in blood pressure or heart rate, and increased perspiration and salivation. Treatment includes changing clothing to reduce exposure from any nicotine on garments, showering, rest, and cessation of work and possible medication to handle the nausea and vomiting. Many of those who harvest tobacco are low-wage workers, often migrant workers, with limited access to health care, and often victims of exploitation. Protective clothing can potentially reduce the risk, but enforcement of regulations where these do exist is limited.

High-Risk Factors

Although a job cannot be said to cause alcohol/drug dependence or abuse, it can contribute to its development. Some of the factors that Trice and Roman, authorities in the area of workplace alcohol issues, have identified as job-based risk factors include the following:

- Absence of clear goals (and absence of supervision)
- Freedom to set work hours (isolation and low visibility)

- Low structural visibility (such as salespeople away from the business place)
- Overinvestment in one's job
- Occupational obsolescence (especially common in scientific and technical fields)
- New work status
- "Required" on-the-job drinking (such as salespeople's drinking with clients)
- Reduction of social controls (occurs on college campuses and other less structured settings)
- Severe role stress
- Competitive pressure
- Presence of illegal drug users

More recently researchers have recognized that working with alcohol itself, such as in the hospitality industry, can be a risk factor. Another form of work-related drug problem comes not from the individual's use but others' use. The smoking ban in restaurants and bars may be appreciated by the patrons. The real beneficiaries are bartenders and the waitstaff, who never had the option of leaving and were trapped in a smoky haze for their 8-hour shifts.

The Workplace Response

If bringing up the drinking practices and potential problems of a family member or close friend makes someone squirm, the idea of saying something to a coworker is virtually unthinkable. Almost everyone accepts a separation between work and home or professional and private life. So until the alcohol problem flows into the work world, the worker's use of alcohol is often considered no one else's business. That does not mean that no one sees a problem developing. The suspicion is that someone with even a little savvy can often spot potentially dangerous drinking practices. The office scuttlebutt or the work crew's bull sessions plus simple observation make it common knowledge who really put it away this weekend, the person who just got picked up for a DWI, or who you can always count on to join in whenever anyone wants to stop for a drink after work.

There are two things that will be believed of any man whosoever, and one of them is that he has taken to drink.
BOOTH TARKINGTON

Even if an employee does show some problems on the job, whether directly or indirectly related to alcohol use, coworkers may try to help out by doing extra work or at least by not blowing the whistle. Because employee assistance programs, if they are available, are based on identifying work deterioration, any attempt by coworkers to help cover up job problems makes spotting the problem all the more difficult. If a company does not have a program to help those employees with alcohol/drug problems, odds for a cover-up by coworkers are even greater. Another important party in this concealment strategy is predictably the spouse, who usually doesn't want to do anything to threaten the paycheck.

Portrait of a man
who thinks he's clever
when he's drunk

Historically if an alcohol problem officially came to light, the employee usually got fired; this may still happen in many companies. In such instances the enterprise may lose a formerly valuable and well-trained worker—statistically, a costly "solution." The current thinking is that it is cheaper for a company to identify problems earlier and to use the job as leverage to get the employee into treatment and back to work.

Workplace Interventions

Facts and experience suggest that the occupational environment is one of the most efficient and economical means of providing an opportunity for early identification and treatment of alcoholism and alcohol- and other drug-related problems. Early intervention increases the chances for recovery for the following reasons:

- Physical health has not deteriorated significantly.
- Financial resources are not as depleted as would be later on.
- Emotional supports still exist in the family and community.
- Threat of job loss can be used as leverage.

The following are among the more common signs and symptoms that point to a troubled employee and thereby help identify the problem drinker or substance abuser:

- Chronic absenteeism
- Erratic behavior
- Physical signs, alcohol-induced medical problems
- Spasmodic work pace
- Lower quantity and quality of work
- Partial absences
- Avoidance of supervisors and coworkers
- On-the-job drinking or drug use
- On-the-job accidents and lost time from off-the-job accidents

Training supervisors and others to recognize these signs and symptoms is important, so that early detection can occur. Training is also critical in helping employers document, not diagnose. Where there have been broad educational efforts through information sessions, posters, pamphlets, and so forth, there has been an increase in peer or self-referrals. Such referrals may make up the bulk of referrals to a program. The culture of the workplace has a significant impact on the use and acceptance of EAPs. While supervisory personnel are a major factor, equally important are the attitudes of close coworkers. The workplace medical clinic is also well positioned to promote screening and to conduct brief, office-based interventions. One recent Swedish study found that, when employees were offered an alcohol screening as part of a routine occupational health visit, 98% took advantage of the opportunity. Of those screened, 21% were found to have excessive alcohol consumption and were contacted to arrange a follow-up visit. Of those contacted by telephone, 80% went in for a follow-up visit, compared with only 17% who were sent a letter. Of equal interest is that this program also prompted persons who had not been initially screened as positive for a possible alcohol problem to call for an appointment.

Implications for Treatment

It is important that substance abuse professionals be knowledgeable about workplace programs. They can thereby better coordinate treatment efforts for the employed client.

Does the individual's employer have an EAP? If so, who is the EAP clinician? What services are offered? For any client, it is important that you be aware of any work-related problems. If so, what is the current job status? Has a disciplinary procedure been instituted, or has the employee been informally warned and referred for treatment? In addition, to avoid future conflict, learn about any union involvement. Such information can help in formulating realistic treatment plans.

It is important to be sensitive to the policies and politics of the employed client's work setting. Without this knowledge and awareness, there is the danger of violating confidentiality or conversely of not taking full advantage of the opportunity to cooperate with the employer on the client's behalf. If there is a company policy, learn about it, so that you can plan realistically and avoid treatment-work conflicts. The nature of the client's work and the potential impact of any prescribed medication must be considered. A follow-up plan must consider the working person's hours and geographical location. The flexibility and accessibility of the treatment facility can be key factors in successful rehabilitation. Evening office hours and early-morning and weekend appointments may have to be arranged, so that treatment will not interfere with the job. On the other hand, if there is an EAP with clinical personnel, this may be the most appropriate site for follow-up and continuing care, after the initial intensive treatment.

You may also find that some individuals will have to be treated as outpatients even when inpatient services are more appropriate. The employee may not be able to take the time off or may not have adequate insurance coverage. Insurance plans are far less likely to cover inpatient treatment; if they do, the stay will be very limited. The rationale is that outpatient care is less expensive and that little or no evidence indicates that inpatient care provides better treatment outcomes. These assumptions are based on data derived from group statistics. Both ends of the spectrum are lost to the statistical average. All clients are not alike, and blanket assumptions regarding treatment can be hazardous to a client's health.

Many larger companies are also becoming involved in managed health-care plans. This means that there are designated providers, as in an HMO (health maintenance organization), which provide either the

medical care that is needed or the required prior approval for a treatment referral, if the insurance is to cover the costs. The rationale for such arrangements is that unnecessary services will be eliminated and health-care dollars will be used more wisely. While laudable in concept, in practice this arrangement has caused concern. With respect to alcohol and substance abuse services several problems have been identified. Some managed health-care systems have developed contracts with specific treatment agencies to provide all necessary services. Payment is often based on a per capita formula, with a set reimbursement paid for a diagnostic category, rather than reimbursements being made on the basis of actual costs incurred. Thus, there is a clear incentive to limit services—for example, to favor outpatient care over inpatient treatment or to have outpatient treatment consist of a specified number of visits. This may work for the "average" client. However, the average person in treatment is, by analogy, like the statistically average drinker we described in Chapter 2—virtually nonexistent. The provision of individualized treatment needed to ensure optimal care is sacrificed for indiscriminately delivering the statistically predetermined norm.

Workplace programs have made significant progress in demonstrating that the "human approach" is good business. Yet there is still a great deal to be done, and it can be better accomplished with cooperation among those involved in the occupational program field and substance abuse clinicians.

OTHER SPECIAL POPULATIONS

An "average client" is virtually nonexistent. All kinds of factors have an impact, particularly cultural factors, including race and ethnicity, in combination with age and gender. These have an important impact in several ways. These factors, for example, determine what kinds of behavior are viewed as evidence of a problem, to whom people turn for help and under what circumstances, and a client's comfort in using professional care. In light of this, the substance abuse field as well as many others is beginning to discuss issues of cultural diversity and acknowledge the unique constellation of characteristics found in segments of the population. Population sub-groups are commonly termed "special populations." Being informed about cultural issues of importance to members of a segment of the population is often termed "cultural sensitivity."

In this chapter, neither racial nor ethnic groups are discussed specifically. The U.S. census provides the following groups for people to designate their race: (1) White, (2) Black or African-American, (3) American Indian and Alaska Native, (4) Asian, (5) Native Hawaiian and Other Pacific Islander, (6) Some other race. In the 2000 census for the first time, people were able to select more than one race to describe themselves, and about 10% did so. Hispanic or Latino status is not considered a race—Latinos can be either white, black, or both. Hispanic/Latino designates a cultural orientation and encompasses those who whose heritage is tied to Spanish-speaking areas in the Americas—Mexico, the Caribbean, Central and South America. These groups are probably those who first come to mind if one mentions race/ethnicity. However, there are countless other identifiable cultural groups, each with its distinctive characteristics that are relevant for the clinician, be it the Portuguese New England fisherman; or the Amish who live in Pennsylvania, Ohio, and Indiana; or the Tibetan neighborhood in a small midwestern city. Even within a particular group there can be considerable diversity. This can be based on geographical location, whether a client is a recent immigrant or native born, and of what generation in the family's constellation.

A client's cultural heritage and orientation is important in the clinical arena. In working with the member of any special population group, one of the client's relationships is to his or her traditional culture as well as to the larger, dominant culture. This is sometimes referred to as cultural orientation, meaning the sets of rules an individual instinctively follows. The basic question is to what extent the client identifies with a traditional ethnic group and to what extent he or she thinks and is comfortable in functioning not as a member of a particular ethnic group but as part of the American mainstream. Some of the terms used to describe these different orientations is "assimilated" (as opposed to "nonassimilated") and "bicultural." In brief, those individuals who are not assimilated think of themselves in terms of the values and rules of behavior of their group of origin. Those who are assimilated may or may not be familiar with the traditional ways; however, they are most comfortable functioning in the usual style of the dominant American culture. Those described as bicultural are able to function by the rules either of their native culture or the majority American culture.

In working with clients who are members of ethnic groups, a sense of their cultural orientation is important. Table 11.17 indicates the different areas that might be considered.

In working with clients who are members of any cultural group other than your own, it is important to become familiar with the values, practices, and ways of seeing the world that are part of that group. Often a useful place to start is by considering the nature of your biases and the source of any preconceived notions.

Suggesting that a referral be made to a counselor or clinician who is from the same cultural group as the client may be good advice, but it isn't always possible to do. At the very least it is important to know about the client's culture's history and traditions. In terms of alcohol problems, how are drinking problems defined? What are the behaviors that within the community would signal an alcohol problem? To whom do people tend to turn for help in time of trouble? Are there any biases against

Table 11.17 Assessing Cultural Orientation

	Traditional Culture or Culture of Origin	Majority Culture
Social	• close friends from same ethnic background • leisure activities within ethnic community	• close friends not restricted to ethnic group • leisure not primarily within ethnic community
Language	• fluent in native language • uses primarily native language	• not fluent in native language
Spiritual/traditions	• familiar with and participates in ethnic ceremonies and celebrations	• unfamiliar with or does not participate in native festivities
Family	• defined by customs of the ethnic culture	• considers family the nuclear family unit, i.e. spouse, or parents and children

seeking professional care or getting help from an "outsider"? Are there any customs that would make getting help more difficult? Be alert to any barriers caused by language. Do not be surprised to be watched closely for signs of prejudice or disinterest. As necessary, certainly acknowledge the limits and differences of your own experience and background. Wise advice that holds here as elsewhere is that the patient is the best instructor, but it requires that you open yourself to learning.

RESOURCES AND FURTHER READING

Adolescents

Addiction 99(Supplement 2):entire issue, 2004. This entire issue is devoted to adolescent substance abuse treatment with a review of research on epidemiology, treatment approaches, and treatment outcome.

Alcohol Health and Research World 22(2):entire issue, 1998.

Alexander DE, Gwyther RE. Alcoholism in adolescents and their families: Family-focused assessment and management. *Pediatric Clinics of North America* 42(1): 217–234, 1995. (102 refs.)

Allen M, Donohue WA, Griffin A, Ryan D, Turner MMM. Comparing the influence of parents and peers on the choice to use drugs: A meta-analytic summary of the literature (review). *Criminal Justice and Behavior* 30(2): 163–186, 2003. (122 refs.)

American Academy of Pediatrics, Substance Abuse Committee. Indication for management and referral of patients involved in substance abuse. *Pediatrics* 106(1): 143–146, 2000. (18 refs)

Andrews JA, Tildesley E, Hops H, Duncan SC, Severson HH. Elementary school age children's future intentions and use of substances. *Journal of Clinical Child and Adolescent Psychology* 32(4):556–567, 2004. (44 refs)

Aung AT, Hichman NJ, Moolchan ET. Health and performance related reasons for wanting to quit: Gender differences among teen smokers. *Substance Use & Misuse* 38(8): 1095–1107, 2003. (28 refs.)

Bachman JG, Safron DJ, Sy SR, Schulenberg JE. Wishing to work: New perspectives on how adolescents' part-time work intensity is linked to educational disengagement, substance use, and other problem behaviours. *International Journal of Behavioral Development* 27(4): 301–315, 2003. (77 refs)

Balch GI, Tworek C, Barker DC, Sasso B, Mermelstein RJ, Giovino GA. Opportunities for youth smoking cessation: Findings from a national focus group study. *Nicotine & Tobacco Research* 6(1):9018, 2004. (33 refs.)

Barkley RA, Fischer M, Smallish L, Fletcher K. Does the treatment of attention-deficit/hyperactivity disorder with stimulants contribute to drug use/abuse? A 13-year prospective study. *Pediatrics* 111(1):97–109, 2003. (74 refs.)

Camenga DR, Klein JD. Adolescent smoking cessation. (review). Current Opinion in Pediatrics 16(4):368–372, 2004. (38 refs.)

Deas D, Thomas SE. An overview of controlled studies of adolescent substance abuse treatment. *American Journal on Addictions* 10(2):178–189, 2001. (50 refs.)

Delnevo CD, Hrywna M, Abatemarco DJ, Lewis MJ. Relationships between cigarette smoking and weight control in young women. *Family & Community Health* 28(2):140–146, 2003. (23 refs.)

Hanson K, Allen S, Jensen S, Hatsukami D. Treatment of adolescent smokers with the nicotine patch. *Nicotine & Tobacco Research* 5(4):515–526, 2003. (36 refs.)

Hogan MJ. Diagnosis and treatment of teen drug use (review). *Medical Clinics of North America* 84(4):927–966, 2000. (126 refs.)

Hopfer CJ, Crowley TJ, Hewitt JK. Review of twin and adoption studies of adolescent substance use (review). *Journal of the American Academy of Child and Adolescent Psychiatry* 42(6):710–719, 2003. (35 refs.)

Hunt MK, Fagan P, Lederman R, Stoddard A, Frazier L, Girod K, et al. Feasibility of implementing intervention methods in an adolescent worksite tobacco control study. *Tobacco Control* 12(Supplement 4):40–45, 2003. (39 refs.)

Killen JD, Robinson TN, Ammerman S, Hayward C, Rogers J, Samuels D, et al. Major depression among adolescent smokers undergoing treatment for nicotine dependence. *Addictive Behaviors* 29(8):1517–1526, 2004. (30 refs.)

Knight JR. The role of the primary care provider in preventing and treating alcohol problems in adolescents. *Ambulatory Pediatrics* 1(3):150–161, 2001. (116 refs.)

Kropp RY, Halpern-Felsher BL. Adolescents' beliefs about the risks involved in smoking "light" cigarettes. *Pediatrics* 114(4):445–451, 2004. (33 refs.)

Madan A, Beech D, Flint L. Drugs, guns, and kids: The association between substance use and injury caused by interpersonal violence. *Journal of Pediatric Surgery* 36(3):440–442, 2001. (13 refs.)

Moolchan ET, Ernst M, Henningfield JE. A review of tobacco smoking in adolescents: Treatment implications (review). *Journal of the American Academy of Child and Adolescent Psychiatry* 39(6):682–693, 2000. (99 refs.)

Patten CA. A critical evaluation of nicotine replacement therapy for teenage smokers (review). *Journal of Child and Adolescent Substance Abuse* 9(4):51–75, 2000. (100 refs.)

Patten CA, Lopez K, Thomas JL, Offord KP, Decker PA, Pingree S, et al. Reported willingness among adolescent nonsmokers to help parents, peers, and others to stop smoking. *Preventive Medicine* 39(6):1099–1106, 2004. (46 refs.)

Pbert L, Moolchan ET, Muramoto M, Winickoff JP, Curry S, Lando H, et al. The state of office-based interventions for youth tobacco use (review). *Pediatrics* 111(6):E650–E660, 2003. (127 refs.)

Porter RS. Alcohol and injury in adolescents. *Pediatric Emergency Care* 16(5):316–320, 2000. (15 refs.)

Rigotti NA, Regan S, Moran SE, Wechsler H. Students' opinion of tobacco control policies recommended for US colleges: A national survey. *Tobacco Control* 12(3):251–256, 2003. (21 refs.)

Rome ES. It's a rave new world: Rave culture and illicit drug use in the young (review). *Cleveland Clinic Journal of Medicine* 68(6):541–550, 2001. (14 refs.)

Rotunda RJ, Scherer DG, Imm PS. Family systems and alcohol misuse: Research on the effects of alcoholism on family functioning and effective family interventions (review). *Professional Psychology: Research and Practice* 26(1):95–104, 1995. (106 refs.)

Turner LR, Mermelstein R, Berbaum ML, Veldhuis CB. School-based smoking cessation programs for adolescents: What predicts attendance? *Nicotine & Tobacco Research* 6(3):559–588, 2004. (34 refs.)

Vakalahi HF. Adolescent substance use and family-based risk and protective factors: A literature review (review). *Journal of Drug Education* 31(1):29–46, 2001. (117 refs.)

Wakefield M, Flay B, Nichter M, Giovino G. Role of the media in influencing trajectories of youth smoking (review). *Addiction* 98:79–103, 2003. (204 refs.)

Wilens TE, Faraone SV, Biederman J, Gunawardene S. Does stimulant therapy of attention-deficit/hyperactivity disorder beget later substance abuse? A meta-analytic review of the literature (review). *Pediatrics* 111(1):179–185, 2003. (56 refs.)

College Students

Baer JS, Kivlahan DR, Marlatt GA. High-risk drinking across the transition from high school to college. *Alcoholism: Clinical and Experimental Research* 19(1):54–61, 1995. (27 refs.)

Beirness DJ, Foss RD, Vogel-Sprott M. Drinking on campus: Self-reports and breath tests. *Journal of Studies on Alcohol* 65(5):600–604, 2004. (16 refs.)

Bents RT, Tokish JM, Goldberg L. Ephedrine, pseudoephedrine, and amphetamine prevalence in college hockey players: Most report performance-enhancing use. *Physician and Sportsmedicine* 32(9):30–34, 2004. (20 refs.)

Borsari B, Carey KB. Effects of a brief motivational intervention with college student drinkers. *Journal of Consulting and Clinical Psychology* 68(4):728–733, 2000. (24 refs.)

Carter CA, Kahnweiler WM. The efficacy of the social norms approach to substance abuse prevention applied to fraternity men. *Journal of American College Health* 49(2):66–71, 2000.

Dimeff LA, McNeely M. Computer-enhanced primary care practitioner advice for high-risk college drinkers in a student primary health-care setting. *Cognitive and Behavioral Practice* 7(1):82–100, 2000. (87 refs.)

Engs RC, Hanson DJ. University students' drinking patterns and problems: Examining the effects of raising the purchase age. *Public Health Report* 133(6):647–673, 1988. (61 refs.)

Fournier AK, Ehrhart IJ, Glindemann KE, Geller ES. Intervening to decrease alcohol abuse at university parties: Differential reinforcement of intoxication level. *Behavior Modification* 28(2):167–181, 2004. (34 refs.)

Halperin AC, Rigotti NA. US public universities' compliance with recommended tobacco-control policies. *Journal of American College Health* 51(5):181–188, 2003. (26 refs.)

Ham LS, Hope DA. College students and problematic drinking: A review of the literature. *Clinical Psychology Review* 23(5):719–759, 2003. (152 refs.)

Johnston LD, O'Malley PM, Bachman JG. Monitoring the Future. *National Survey Results on Drug Use, 1975–2003. Volume II: College Students and Young Adults*. Rockville, MD: National Institute on Drug Abuse, 2004.

Leichliter JS, Meilman PW, Presley CA, Cashin JR. Alcohol use and related consequences among students with varying levels of involvement in college athletics. *Journal of American College Health* 46(6):257–262, 1998. (27 refs.)

National Collegiate Athletic Association (NCAA). *Study of Substance Abuse Habits of College-Student Athletes.* Indianapolis, IN: NCAA, 2001. http://ncaa.org/library/research/substance_use_habits/2001/substance_use_habits.pdf

Nelson TF, Wechsler H. Alcohol and college athletes. *Medicine and Science in Sports and Exercise* 33(1):43–47, 2001. (14 refs.)

Park CL. Positive and negative consequences of alcohol consumption in college students. *Addictive Behaviors* 29(3):311–321, 2004. (20 refs.)

Perkins HW, ed. *Social Norms Approach to Preventing School and College Age Substance Abuse: A Handbook for Educators, Counselors, and Clinicians.* San Francisco: Jossey-Bass, 2003.

Rimal RN, Real K. Understanding the influence of perceived norms on behaviors. *Communication Theory* 13(2):184–203, 2003. (62 refs.)

Walker ET. Missing the target: How performance-enhancing drugs go unnoticed and endanger the lives of athletes. *Villanova Sports and Entertainment Law Journal* 20(1):181–209, 2003. (180 legal refs.)

Walters ST. In praise of feedback: An effective intervention for college students who are heavy drinkers. *Journal of American College Health* 48(5):235–238, 2000. (16 refs.)

Wechsler H, Kuo MC, Lee H, Dowdall GM. Environmental correlates of underage alcohol use and related problems of college students. *American Journal of Preventive Medicine* 19(1):24–29, 2000. (32 refs.)

Wechsler H, Lee JE, Gledhill-Hoyt J, Nelson TF. Alcohol use and problems at colleges banning alcohol: Results of a national survey. *Journal of Studies on Alcohol* 62(2):133–141, 2001. (21 refs.)

Wechsler H, Lee JE, Nelson TF, Lee H. Drinking levels, alcohol problems and secondhand effects in substance-free college residences: Results of a national study. *Journal of Studies on Alcohol* 62(1):23–31, 2001. (28 refs.)

Wechsler H, Lee JE, Nelson TF, Lee H. Drinking and driving among college students: The influence of alcohol-control policies. *American Journal of Preventive Medicine* 25(3):212–218, 2003. (31 refs.)

Weitzman ER, Folkman A, Folkman KL, Wechsler H. The relationship of alcohol outlet density to heavy and frequent drinking and drinking-related problems among college students at eight universities. *Health & Place* 9: 1–6, 2003. (14 refs.)

Weitzman ER, Kawachi I. Giving means receiving: The protective effect of social capital on binge drinking on college campuses. *American Journal of Public Health* 90(12):1936–1939, 2000. (27 refs.)

Wetter DW, Kenford SL, Welsch SK, Smith SS, Fouladi RT, Fiore MC, Baker TB. Prevalence and predictors of transitions in smoking behavior among college students. *Health Psychology* 23(2):168–177, 2004. (46 refs.)

The Elderly

Adams WL. Alcohol and the health of aging men. *Medical Clinics of North America* 83(5):1195–1210, 1999. (107 refs.)

Appel DW, Aldrich TK. Smoking cessation in the elderly. *Clinics in Geriatric Medicine* 19(1):77+, 2003 (96 refs.)

Atkinson RM. Late onset problem drinking in older adults (review). *International Journal of Geriatric Psychiatry* 9(4):321–326, 1994. (28 refs.)

Barrick C, Connors GJ. Relapse prevention and maintaining abstinence in older adults with alcohol-use disorders. *Drugs & Aging* 19(8):583–594, 2002. (71 refs.)

Brower KJ, Mudd S, Blow FC, Young JP, Hill EM. Severity and treatment of alcohol withdrawal in elderly versus younger patients. *Alcoholism: Clinical and Experimental Research* 18(1):196–201, 1994. (12 refs.)

Conigliaro J, Kraemer K, McNeil M. Screening and identification of older adults with alcohol problems in primary care. *Journal of Geriatric Psychiatry and Neurology* 13(3):106–114, 2000.

Fingerhood M. Substance abuse in older people (review). *Journal of the American Geriatrics Society* 48(8):985–995, 2000. (125 refs.)

Flaherty JH. Commonly prescribed and over-the-counter medications: Causes of confusion (review). *Clinics in Geriatric Medicine* 14(1):101–121, 1998. (281 refs.)

Gfroerer J, Penne M, Pemberton M, Folsom R. Substance abuse treatment need among older adults in 2020: The impact of the baby boom generation. *Journal of Substance Abuse Treatment* 69(2):127–135, 2003. (36 refs.)

Jennison KM. The impact of stressful life events and social support on drinking among older adults: A general population survey. *International Journal of Aging and Human Development* 35(2):99–123, 1992. (85 refs.)

Lemke S, Moose RH. Outcome at 1 and 5 years for older patients with alcohol use disorders. *Journal of Substance Abuse Treatment* 24(1):43–50, 2003. (24 refs.)

Oslin D, Liberto JG, O'Brien J, Krois S, Norbeck J. Naltrexone as an adjunctive treatment for older patients with alcohol dependence. *American Journal of Geriatric Psychiatry* 5(4):324–332, 1997. (11 refs.)

Whelan G. Alcohol: A much neglected risk factor in elderly mental disorders. *Current Opinion in Psychiatry* 16(6):609–614, 2003. (30 refs.)

Women

Ashley OS, Marsden ME, Brady TM. Effectiveness of substance abuse treatment programming for women: A review. *American Journal of Drug and Alcohol Abuse* 29(1):19–53, 2003. (102 refs.)

Blume S, Frausto T, Guschwan M, Silverman S, Trautman R, Virzi O, et al. Position statement on the care of pregnant and newly delivered women addicts. *American Journal of Psychiatry* 158(7):1180, 2001. (0 refs.)

Champion HLO, Foley KL, DuRant RH, Hensberry R, Altman D, Wolfson M. Adolescent sexual victimization, use of alcohol and other substances, and other health risk behaviors. *Journal of Adolescent Health* 35(4):321–328, 2004. (55 refs.)

Ebrahim SH, Gfroerer J. Pregnancy-related substance use in the United States during 1996–1998. *Obstetrics and Gynecology* 101(2):374–379, 2003. (24 refs.)

Haas AL, Peters RH. Development of substance abuse problems among drug-involved offenders: Evidence for the telescoping effect. *Journal of Substance Abuse* 12(3):241–253, 2000. (35 refs.)

Hall JM. Lesbians and alcohol: Patterns and paradoxes in medical notions and lesbians' beliefs (review). *Journal of Psychoactive Drugs* 25(2):109–119, 1993. (109 refs.)

Hommer DW, Momenan R, Kaiser E, Rawlings RR. Evidence for a gender-related effect of alcoholism on brain volumes. *American Journal of Psychiatry* 158(2):198–204, 2001. (29 refs.)

Kaskutas LA, Graves K. Pre-pregnancy drinking: How drink size affects risk assessment. *Addiction* 96(8):1199–1209, 2001. (26 refs.)

Killeen T, Brady KT. Parental stress and child behavioral outcomes following substance abuse residential treatment: Follow-up at 6 and 12 months. *Journal of Substance Abuse Treatment* 19(1):23–29, 2000. (23 refs.)

Manwell LB, Fleming MF, Mundt MP, Stauffacher EA, Barry KL. Treatment of problem alcohol use in women of childbearing age: Results of a brief intervention trial. *Alcoholism: Clinical and Experimental Research* 24(10):1517–1524, 2000. (38 refs.)

Pirie PL, Lando H, Curry SJ, McBride CM, Grothaus LC. Tobacco, alcohol, and caffeine use and cessation in early pregnancy. American Journal of Preventive Medicine 18(1):54–61, 2000. (32 refs.)

Porowski AW, Burgdorg K, Herrell JM. Effectiveness and sustainability of residential substance abuse treatment programs for pregnant and parenting women. *Evaluation and Program Planning* 27(2):191–198, 2004. (16 refs.)

Reardon DC, Ney PG. Abortion and subsequent substance abuse. *American Journal of Drug and Alcohol Abuse* 26(1):61–75, 2000. (23 refs.)

Redgrave GW, Swartz KL, Romanoski AJ. Alcohol misuse by women (review). *International Review of Psychiatry* 15(3):256–268, 2003. (146 refs.)

Saules KK, Pomerleau CS, Snedecor SM, Mehringer AM, Shadle MB, Kurth C, et al. Relationship of onset of cigarette smoking during college to alcohol use, dieting concerns, and depressed mood: Results from the Young Women's Health Survey. *Addictive Behaviors* 29(5):893–899, 2004. (15 refs.)

Simoni-Wastila L, Ritter G, Strickler G. Gender and other factors associated with the nonmedical use of abusable prescription drugs. *Substance Use & Misuse* 39(1):1–23, 2004. (47 refs.)

Stein MD, Cyr MG. Women and substance abuse (review). *Medical Clinics of North America* 81(4):979–1007, 1997. (125 refs.)

The Workplace

Akbar-Khanzadeh F. Exposure to environmental tobacco smoke in restaurants without separate ventilation systems for smoking and nonsmoking dining areas. *Archives of Environmental Health* 58(2):97–103, 2003. (26 refs.)

Arcury TA, Quandt SA, Preisser JS, Bernert JT, Norton D, Wang J. High levels of transdermal nicotine exposure produce green tobacco sickness in Latino farmworkers. *Nicotine & Tobacco Research* 5(3):315–321, 2003. (27 refs.)

Cranford M. Drug testing and the right to privacy: Arguing the ethics of workplace drug testing. *Journal of Business Ethics* 17(16):1805–1815, 1998.

Emener WG, Hutchison WS Jr., eds. *Employee Assistance Programs: Wellness/Enhancement Programming* Springfield IL: Charles C. Thomas Publisher, Ltd, 2003.

French MT, Roebuck MC, Alexandre PK. To test or not to test. Do workplace drug testing programs discourage drug use? *Science Research*. 33: 45–65, 2003

Giannakoulas G, Katramados A, Melas N, Diamantopoulos I, Chimonas E. Acute effects of nicotine withdrawal syndrome in pilots during flight. *Aviation, Space, and Environmental Medicine* 74(3):247–251, 2003. (74 refs.)

Hartwell TD, Steele PD, Rodman NF. Workplace alcohol-testing programs: Prevalence and trends. *Monthly Labor Review* 121(6):27–34, 1998. (27 refs.)

Karuntzos GT, Dunlap LJ, Zarkin GA, French MT. Designing an employee assistance program (EAP) intervention for women and minorities: Lessons from the Rockford EAP Study. *Employee Assistance Quarterly* 14(1):49–67, 1998. (37 refs.)

Kramer RM. The role of the EAP in the identification and treatment of substance abuse. *Clinics in Laboratory Medicine* 18(4):747–759, 1998.

Osinubi OYO, Sinha S, Rovner E, Perez-Lugo M, Jain NJ, Demissie K, Goldman M. Efficacy of tobacco dependence treatment in the context of a "smoke-free grounds" worksite policy: A case study. *American Journal of Industrial Medicine* 46(2):180–187, 2004. (19 refs.)

Ozminkowski RJ, Mark TL, Goetzel RZ, Blank D, Walsh JM, Cangianelli L. Relationships between urinalysis testing for substance use, medical expenditures, and the occurrence of injuries at a large manufacturing firm. *American Journal of Drug and Alcohol Abuse* 29(1):151–167, 2003. (25 refs.)

Repace J. Flying the smoky skies: Secondhand smoke exposure of flight attendants. *Tobacco Control* 13(Supplement 1):8–19, 2004. (56 refs.)

Siegel M, Skeer M. Exposure to secondhand smoke and excess lung cancer mortality risk among workers in the "5 B's": Bars, bowling alleys, billiard halls, betting establishments, and bingo parlours. *Tobacco Control* 12(3):333–338, 2004. (42 refs.)

Substance Abuse and Mental Health Services Administration Office of Applied Studies, Zhang Z, Huang LX, Brittingham AM. *Worker Drug Use and Workplace Policies and Programs: Results from the 1994 and 1997 NHSDA*. Rockville, MD: Substance Abuse and Mental Health Services Administration, 1999.

White T. Drug testing at work: Issues and perspectives. *Substance Use & Misuse* 38(11/13):1891–1902, 2003.

Zarkin GA, Bray JW, Karuntzos GT, Demiralp B. The effect of an enhanced employee assistance program (EAP) intervention on EAP utilization. *Journal of Studies on Alcohol* 62(3):351–358, 2001. (24 refs.)

CHAPTER 12

Other Psychiatric Considerations

Substance use disorders are in themselves psychiatric conditions. In this chapter, the focus is on broader psychiatric issues of importance for the substance abuse clinician. These topics include suicide evaluation and prevention, the elements of the mental status examination, the major categories of co-occurring psychiatric illness, and the medications used in their treatment. The classifications for mental illness are important on several counts. One is that some clients will have a separate, coexisting psychiatric illness in addition to their alcohol or drug abuse or dependence. Another is that many colleagues are from the mental health field. It is important to be comfortable with the terminology they use and issues with which they deal. Finally, alcohol or other substance use problems will often mimic psychiatric conditions. Being informed about these conditions is vital when the task is determining if the behavior being observed or reported is a symptom of a substance use problem or another psychiatric illness.

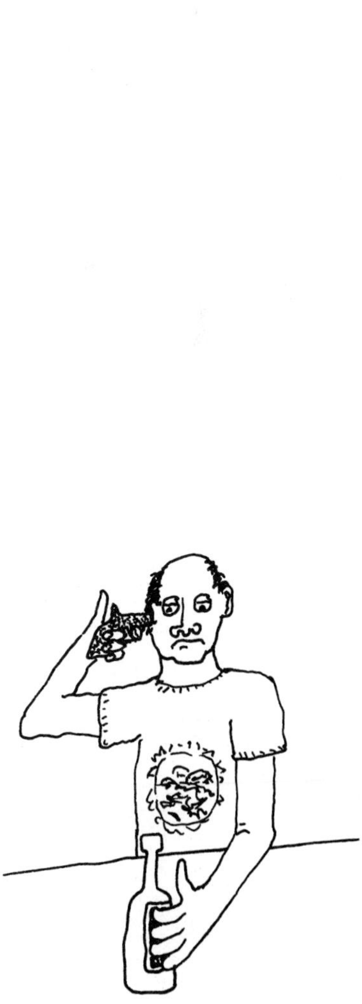

SUICIDE EVALUATION AND PREVENTION

Substance use—alcohol use, in particular—and suicide go together. Recall from Chapter 1 that, in a substantial number of suicide attempts, the individual has been drinking and that approximately 40% of all completed suicides are alcohol-related. The suicide rate for alcoholics is 55 times that of the general population. Before we are overwhelmed by these statistics, we should consider why suicide and alcohol are connected and what we can do about this.

For practical purposes, there are several groups to be considered when examining suicide. First are the *completers,* those who take their lives and intended to. Classically these are lonely white men over 50 years of age or lonely teenagers. They use violent means, such as a gun or hanging. Their methods are calculated and secretive. Second are those who succeed but did not intend to. These are the *attempters.* Classically they are white women, ages 20 to 40, often with interpersonal conflicts, whose method is pills. The suicide attempt is often an impulsive response. Attempters die by mistake or as a result of miscalculation. For example, they lose track of dosage, or something goes wrong with their plans for rescue. The attempter's intent is not so much to die as to elicit a response from others. Emergency room psychology, which dismisses these clients with irritation and anger, is inappropriate. Someone who is trying to gain attention by attempting suicide is in reality quite sick and deserves care. Third are the *threateners.* These are individuals who use suicide as a lethal weapon: "If you leave me, I'll kill myself." They are often involved in a pathological relationship. Threateners usually do not follow through, but they are frightened and guilt-ridden. In responding to them the therapist will attempt to challenge the threat and thereby remove the deadlock it has created. Finally, there is another group to be considered in suicide assessment. These people are termed *parasuicidal.* They are people who harm themselves for the release of either tension or emotional pain. Commonly, they have a history of physical or sexual abuse or severe neglect as children. Though they may intentionally seriously injure themselves, they usually do not have suicide in mind when they do so. They differ from attempters in that, unlike attempters, the impetus is not to get the attention of others but to relieve internal emotional pain. However, there are always errors and deaths occur.

Statistics and High-Risk Factors

The statistic to keep in mind is that suicide is the second-leading recorded cause of death in people under 18 or over 65 years of age. Sixty percent give some prior indication of their intent, thereby making suicide preventable. Typical indications include hypothetical statements such as "I have a friend who has been feeling down . . ." or "What would you think if someone said . . ."; or stockpiling drugs or giving away their possessions. New behaviors can be important cues. People doing things they have never done before may indicate they have suddenly decided to commit suicide and are now at peace—for example, they might suddenly be playing cards, dancing, or taking out the garbage when they have never made a practice of this before.

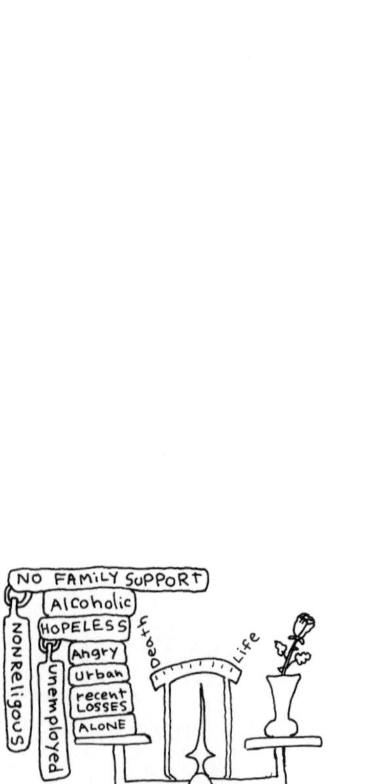

Certain high-risk factors should be identified. These include experiencing the recent loss of a loved one; being single, widowed, and/or childless; living in an urban area; and being unemployed, nonreligious, or "oppressed." High-risk emotional factors include anger plus hopelessness, broken or pathological family/friend communications, and isolation in a marriage or another ongoing relationship. Verbal high-risk cues take the form of both direct statements (such as "I'm going to kill myself") and indirect indications (such as "I won't be around to give you any more trouble"). People entering and leaving a depression are especially vulnerable, as are those with chronic illnesses, such as arthritis, high blood pressure, ulcers, and malignancies.

Recall that 65% of all suicide attempts are related to alcohol. Several reasons explain this correlation. First, the chemical nature of alcohol tends to release certain brain areas from control. The guarding mechanisms are let down. Hidden thoughts and impulses are released. (You may have witnessed incidents such as an intoxicated employee calling the boss a creep.) Second, because of the chemical action of alcohol, a state is created wherein the integrative capacity of the brain is diminished. This is a condition in which aspects of memory and concentration are lost. Third, when alcohol is used as a medicine, it is, unfortunately, a good one to initially produce a mood of relaxation and pseudostability. In this state, people may think things are just the way they should be. They feel cool, calm, and collected, so that suicide at this point may seem relevant and a good idea: "I'll just jump. It's the rational solution." Also, alcohol acts as a true depressant, with obvious potential consequences. Finally, alcohol may also bring out psychological vulnerabilities. It may place people on the edge of reality, lead to loose associations, bring out psychosis, disinhibit normal fears, and produce voices, saying, "The world is better off without you." In all these cases, alcohol acts as a catalyst, both physically and psychologically.

The most fertile ground for suicide is in cases of clinical depression. Most people who simply have the blues are not suicidal. They might think, "Gee, I wish I were dead; things are going so badly," or "I don't know how I'll make it. I might just drive off the road if things don't get better." Things usually do get better, however. On the other hand, clinical depression is characterized by a consistently low mood over a period of weeks, plus weight changes, sleep problems, and other physical symptoms. Pessimism is a symptom of the illness, just as fever is a symptom of the flu. Feelings of how bad things are are part of the depression. Depression, therefore, is bad enough alone, but combined with alcohol, it is a potent mix: "There is no way out." "I'm a bad person—the only way out is to kill myself."

How to Ask about Suicide

The therapist should always ask about suicide with any person who is depressed. The thing to remember is that therapists have never killed anybody by asking, although they have certainly missed helping people they could have helped by not asking. There is no way to instigate a suicidal attempt by commonsense asking. It will come as a relief to your clients if you do ask them. Use your own emotional barometer to find out whether they are depressed or whether they are sad. Check yourself in an interview every so often. Forget about the client for a moment and ask yourself, "How am *I* feeling right now? Am I sad, angry, scared? What am I feeling?" It is probably a pretty good barometer of how the client is feeling. Clients often say they feel great; check your own gut reactions and trust them.

Ask every client about suicide, but let rapport develop first. Do not just have the client come in and immediately ask intimate questions, such as "How's your sex life?" "Been hallucinating lately?" or "Feel like killing yourself?" The client will probably want to kill you. Let rapport develop, and later say, "Now, we've talked about a lot of things these past 20 minutes. Have any of them ever gotten you to the point of feeling you couldn't go on any longer?" Don't leave it there; explain that you are asking about suicide. Always say the word "suicide." Do not just ask clients if they have ever thought of "throwing in the towel" or some other euphemism. They can take you quite literally and might say, "Well, no. I dried myself pretty well this morning." You have to get yourself to say "suicide." Practice. It is not so easy to come right out and say it. The first few times it bombs, something like this: "Gee, we've talked about a lot of things. Have any of them ever gotten you to the point of thinking about committing s-s-ah-s-th-?" It's almost the kind of thing you need to practice in front of a mirror: "Su-i-cide. Suicide."

Clients may say, "Boy, you're kidding!" but it's not a hostile response. If anybody does say yes—and the client probably will tell you if he or she has been thinking about it—obtain as much information as you can. Then go on to say, "Well, when was the last time you thought of it?" and "How about today?" Whenever the client was last thinking of it, find out when that was. What was going on, when the thoughts of suicide surfaced. Ascertain the person's plans for committing suicide as specifically as possible. In cases of most serious intent, the client will probably say, "Well, not only have I been thinking of it today, but I've been cleaning my gun. It's in my car, and my car's outside." In other words, get all the data.

Responding to Suicidal Patients

Try to defuse the situation psychologically and in practical ways. For instance, offer alternatives, such as "On the other hand, what specific reasons do you have for living?" Try to get to a positive reason. Start initiating reasons to live. The more seriously depressed the client, the fewer reasons will come to mind. Remember, that is part of the illness. The client will say, "Nothing," and cry. At that point, try to reiterate things he or she told you earlier about him- or herself that are reasons to live—a child, a spouse, a business. Provide the reason to live: "That child really needs you." If the client doesn't come up with anything, allow him or her 60 seconds to think of something, even one reason, and then support that enthusiastically: "You're right. Tremendous!" Fill in the picture, and lead him or her into ways that can be acted on concretely. If it is a child, for example, ask where the child is now. How can the client as a parent be of help to the child?

Another important thing is to make a referral, whenever possible, to a mental health clinic or mental health specialist. As a counselor, you have a key role in identifying potential suicides. You cannot expect yourself to single-handedly treat and manage the situation. Request a consultation for further evaluation. Possibly the person has a clinical depression and needs medication or the supervision of an inpatient facility. So call and make an appointment before the client leaves the office. In conjunction with the mental health clinic, a decision can be made about how quickly the person should be seen—immediately, later today, or tomorrow. If the client is already being seen by a therapist, contact the therapist. A therapist who is unaware of the situation will want to know and will be able to provide guidance for you, so that you are working together. Don't be afraid you are stepping on anyone's toes. Anybody contemplating suicide cannot have too many people in his or her corner.

Maybe here we can lay to rest any discomfort that arises from the philosophical debates on whether someone has a right to commit suicide. There is considerable discussion about the right to die. Looking at it from the practical side of the issue, anyone who thinks he or she has that right would just go ahead and do it. The person wouldn't be in your office. Anyone who "happens" into a counselor's office, or phones, and acknowledges suicidal thoughts, directly or indirectly, is not there by chance. These individuals are seeking help in settling the internal debate over life versus death. You, as do other helping people, must come down clearly on the side of living. When depressed, a client cannot rationally make this decision. Once the depression clears, most clients are very pleased that you prevented their action on suicide plans.

If a client has a weapon, ask that it be checked at the reception desk or elsewhere on the premises. If it is at home, ask that someone else take possession of it and notify you when that is done. Even if a client's mood improves during the interview—and it usually improves during the interview—never let a client who is suicidal leave your office without your double-checking the person's plans for the rest of the day. Be specific. Call home to make sure someone will be there, if that is the expectation. Give the client chores and support. Have somebody there to watch the client around the clock and to give the attention he or she needs. Set up another appointment to see the person within 48 hours. Have the client call you to check in later that day, or you make the call. Be specific. Say, "I'd like to call you between 4 and 5," or at least "this afternoon." It is better not to give an exact time because that is often hard to meet. This kind of paternalism is needed at this time. The weaning of dependence and fostering of independence come later. Give reinforcements: "What do you like to do? What do you have to do? Do it and let me know how it goes."

In talking with a client, the only times that you may foresee something going wrong are in the following situations. If the client's theme is rejection and loss, for example, be careful you don't reject the person or put him or her off. Take care to avoid supporting negative feelings. If you agree with the client about how bad things are—for example, the client says, "I am a worthless person. I beat my child"—you may easily get into your own negative feelings about this. You might communicate, "Well, you're right; that was a horrible thing to do." Don't support their punitive guilt response. Similarly expressions of empathy can be misplaced. Clients may say how bad they feel. You are tempted to say, "I understand how bad you feel. I often feel that way myself." You're trying to sympathize and share the misery, but clients interpret this as permission to feel the way they do. You're getting away from the reasons the client has to live and are underscoring the pessimism. It's better to reinforce the reasons to live.

Get histories of previous suicide attempts. Anyone who has tried it once has a poor track record. A family history of suicide, other losses in childhood from divorce or illnesses or a history of childhood sexual abuse also increase the risk. For someone who has either attempted suicide or is thinking about it, reduce the person's isolation from family and friends. Hospitalization under close supervision may be needed if supports are lacking. Take away guns, ropes, pills, and so on. Have the client give you the weapon personally. Shake hands with the client as he or she leaves the office, and give something of yourself for the person to take with them, such as a piece of paper with your name and phone number. Try to make sure the client does not have what would constitute a lethal dosage of medication. Any supply of tricyclic antidepressants greater than 1,000 mg or a 5-day supply of meprobamate (Miltown) (8,000 mg) can be lethal.

Consider a special situation. If you happen to get involved in an emergency in which someone is about to shoot him- or herself, jump from a window ledge, or do something else rash, try to be calm. Keep your voice down. Do not ask philosophical questions, but ask practical questions: "What's your name?" "Where are you from?" Try to have a nonthreatening conversation. This is a grueling situation and can last for hours. Wear the person down. Do not ever be a hero. Do not rush a person with a gun. Stay alive to help the people who can be helped.

Trust your gut reactions. Don't feel that if you are unsuccessful, it is your fault. Don't ever forget that your job with suicidal clients is not to be God. Being God's helper is enough.

MENTAL STATUS EXAMINATION

The mental status examination is one of the tools used by mental health professionals. Its purposes are to guide observation and to assist the interviewer in gathering essential data about mental functioning. It consists of standard items, which are routinely covered, ensuring that nothing important is overlooked. The format also helps mental health workers record their findings in a fashion that is easily understood by their colleagues.

Three aspects of mental functioning are always included on a mental status examination: mood and affect, thought processes, and cognitive functioning. "Mood and affect" refers to the dominant feeling state. Mood and affect are deduced from the client's general appearance; feelings the client reports; and posture, body movements, and attitude toward the interviewer. "Thought processes" zero in on how the client presents his or her ideas. Are the thoughts ordered and organized, or does the client jump all over the place? Are the sentences logical? Is the content sensible, or does it include delusions and bizarre ideas? Finally, "cognitive functioning" refers to intellectual functioning, memory, ability to concentrate, comprehension, and ability to abstract. This portion of the mental status examination involves asking specific questions about current events, definitions of words, or meanings of proverbs. The interviewer considers the individual's education, lifestyle, and occupation in making a judgment about the responses.

Becoming skilled in doing a simple mental status examination can help you spot clients with particular problems. It can also greatly facilitate your communication with mental health workers. Just telling a psychiatrist or psychiatric social worker that the person you are referring is "crazier than a bedbug" isn't very useful.

MAJOR CATEGORIES OF CO-OCCURRING PSYCHIATRIC ILLNESS

Understanding the relationship between alcohol or other drug use and mood, thoughts, or behavior is one of the most challenging and essential components of anyone's work in the substance abuse field. An effort to determine the relative contributions of addictive and nonaddictive psychiatric disorders to abnormal mental states is essential for several reasons. First, the prevalence of co-occurring psychiatric disorders is so great in persons with alcohol use disorders that having a co-occurring psychiatric condition is an expectation, not an exception, in treatment settings. Second, studies have shown that the risk of having a problem with alcohol use increases 10 times if a person has schizophrenia or 15 times if a person has an antisocial personality disorder. Third, alcohol dependence and withdrawal can produce symptoms that resemble many other psychiatric disorders. For this reason, psychiatry, perhaps more than any other medical discipline, must respect alcohol dependence as "the great mimicker." Fourth, the co-occurrence of a psychiatric condition with alcohol dependence significantly worsens the clinical course and outcomes for individuals with both disorders. Because of this, it is imperative that all mental health workers screen and assess alcohol use disorders for all people seeking mental health treatment and that all addiction staff screen and assess for co-occurring psychiatric disorders. Furthermore, if alcohol or drug use co-occurs with another psychiatric disorder, both disorders should be treated concurrently and aggressively. This treatment should be based on an integrated treatment plan.

In this text, we have placed considerable emphasis on the fact that psychological problems are not the cause of alcohol dependence per se. However, in trying to get that message across, it is important not to lose sight of the fact that an individual may have both alcohol dependence and another psychiatric condition. Whether dependence grows in the soil of some other psychiatric condition (sometimes termed "secondary" or "reactive alcoholism") or whether it co-occurs with another psychiatric problem, when present, it develops a momentum of its own. The client's ability to establish and maintain sobriety may be dependent on actively treating other psychiatric conditions as well. The clinician confronted by clients with co-occurring addictive and mental disorders faces both diagnostic and treatment challenges, and all too frequently the client faces administrative and systemic barriers.

The next sections cover the major classes of psychiatric illness as they relate to alcohol use disorders.

Mood Disorders

Mood and emotion are what you feel and how you show it. Mood disorders are feelings that go beyond the normal experiences of sadness or elation. About 9% of Americans suffer some form of mood disorder every year. There are two extremes—people who are manic and those who are depressed. In addition people can fluctuate between these extremes, a condition termed bipolar disorder. Lesser degrees of depression over longer periods of time are called dysthymia, and a lesser degree of mania is termed hypomania (see Table 12.1). People in a *manic episode* show characteristic behavior. Often they have grand schemes, which to others seem outlandish. Their conversation is very quick and pressured. Often they jump from topic to topic. They may watch two television shows at the same time while they look through magazines. If there were a conversation about the state of the union, a person when manic might say, "And, yes, Texas is a very pretty state. President Bush was the governor of the state, and the governor of my car is out of kilter. The left tire is flat, out of air like a balloon Suzy got a balloon at the circus where she stained her best dress with cotton candy. . . ." Although there is a logical connection among these thoughts, there is an inability to concentrate on any single thought. This pattern of thinking is termed "loose associations." One thought is immediately crowded out by the next. Someone who is manic may also be aggressive and irritable or, alternatively, may feel themselves very attractive, sexually irresistible, or capable of superhuman performance. People when manic are perpetually in high gear,

Table 12.1 Mood Disorders

Mood Disorder	Clinical Features	Prevalence among Persons with Alcohol Use Disorders Seeking Treatment
Major depression	Depressed mood, diminished activity, weight loss, insomnia, fatigue, poor concentration, worthlessness, suicide ideation	14%
Dysthymia	Low mood for most days for at least 2 years, similar symptoms to depression but not as intense	11
Mania	Elevated mood for more than a week, grandiosity, decreased need for sleep, excessive involvement in high-risk activities, excessive drinking	13
Hypomania	Elevated mood for at least 4 days, symptoms similar to mania but less intense	3

have difficulty sleeping, and may have trouble concentrating. Simply being in their company might make you feel exhausted. Auditory and visual hallucinations complicate the more extreme forms of mania.

Depression, which is the other side of the mood coin and is far more common, has all the opposite characteristics. Rather than being hyped up, people with depression grind to a halt. They find very little pleasure in most activities and often feel hopeless. Movements, speech, and thinking may be slowed down. Biological changes can accompany depression and are called vegetative symptoms. These include disturbances of normal sleep patterns, slowed motor activity, changes in appetite, and weight loss or gain. In extremes, the person with depression stops eating, is unable to rest, experiences a complete depletion of energy, and expends available motor energy in repeated, purposeless motions, such as hand-wringing and pacing. Such depression is associated with a sense of self-reproach, irrational guilt, worthlessness, hopelessness, and loss of interest in life. In full force, these phenomena may culminate in suicidal thoughts, plans, or actions. In psychological autopsies after a completed suicide, depression is found in up to 70% of the deaths. Severe depression is a life-threatening disorder.

Most depression and mania are believed to have a biological basis. They are also episodic disorders. Between episodes, the mood states typically return to a normal state. This is not to imply that one simply sits back and waits for the manic or depressive episode to pass. With individuals who are significantly depressed, suicide is an ever present possibility. Individuals with mania incur phenomenal life problems, which may wreak havoc for themselves as well as for their families. These conditions are highly treatable with medications (see the following section "Psychotropic Medications"). Talking therapies, particularly cognitive behavioral therapies, may be helpful in less severe conditions but are of little use when someone's perception of reality and thought processes are seriously altered.

Alcohol use and alcohol dependence are intertwined with mood disorders in several ways. The most important one is that of persons with alcohol use disorders seeking treatment, up to 40% will have a mood disorder and the vast majority of these conditions are not alcohol induced and require treatment. Alcohol can produce a toxic depression that embraces the full range of depression's symptoms, including anorexia, insomnia, physical complaints, suicidal thoughts, and despair. Experimental studies have demonstrated that heavy drinking can induce depressive symptoms. This is true of those with alcohol dependence and those without dependence. A temporary depression is frequently described as a feature of dependence that can remit with abstinence. Women are more likely than are men to present with symptoms of depression. Beyond the acute effects of the drug alcohol, chronic alcohol abusers often confront deteriorating social relations, loss of employment, homelessness, associated trauma, and loss of health, which are factors also associated with depressed states.

As mentioned in the section on suicide, any alcohol use by someone with depression is contraindicated. This is an additional concern for alcoholics. It is estimated that 4% to 15% of alcoholics commit suicide. And, of people who commit suicide, 40% have a history of an alcohol use disorder. Although suicidal behavior in general increases with alcohol consumption, active alcoholics attempt suicide far more often than do nonalcoholics when drinking. Several factors contribute to this. Alcohol dependence may be an indicator of a suicide-prone individual; the condition itself can be considered a form of slow suicide. The loss of cognitive function resulting from alcohol abuse creates an increasing gap between personal expectations and actual performance, resulting in despair. The multiple losses that alcoholics confront can compound a sense of hopelessness. In assessing an alcoholic's suicide potential, further risk factors to consider are the loss of a close interpersonal relationship within the previous 6 weeks, unemployment, serious medical illness, living alone, and suicide communications. The alcoholic with suicidal thoughts, whether inebriated or not, needs to be taken seriously. As an important aside, a reactive depression may also be seen in the family members of a substance abuser. Alcohol dependence is a family illness, and 1 out of 3 American families has direct contact with someone who has a serious alcohol problem. Family members may develop depression as their defenses are overwhelmed by the constant stress of dealing with emotional and physical abuse, economic instability, and their perceived impotence to change their loved one's behavior. Obviously, for most, a referral to Al-Anon is far more appropriate than a prescription for antidepressant medications.

Because some symptoms of depression are the result of alcohol dependence—representing substance-induced depression—the symptoms of depression seen in alcohol-dependent individuals do not always require separate treatment. In these instances, it is likely that the depression will not lift with abstinence and alcohol treatment. At the point of entry into treatment, it may be difficult to get the information needed to distinguish initially between an independent, primary depression and depression that results from alcohol dependence. The client may have difficulty providing an accurate chronology of events due to cognitive deficits that are a part of both alcohol dependence and depression. The most reliable information is often provided by family and friends.

The cause of depression for a person abusing alcohol may become apparent only over time. If the depressive symptoms lift with abstinence, then one can be confident that the mood disturbance was secondary to the alcohol abuse. Recent research suggests most depression in persons with alcohol use disorders is independent of the alcohol use. If there are persistent, intense depressed symptoms after several weeks of abstinence, then the clinician should consider the possibility of a co-occurring mood disorder, and concurrent treatment for depression may be indicated. An extended period of sobriety before making the diagnosis of depression, though preferable, may not always be possible. On occasion, the clinician may be so impressed with the severity of depressive symptoms that waiting for several months cannot be justified. This is critical, because without effective integrated treatment these clients are likely to see themselves as treatment failures. For them, things have not gotten better with sobriety. Also, they may be urged by AA friends or treatment personnel simply to "work the program harder." In fact, they have been giving it their all. All treatment programs for persons abusing alcohol must include education about depression—including information on its biological basis and how medications can be useful. Discomfort may surface around the use of medications, especially because many treatment programs caution clients about the dangers of psychoactive drug use. Clients need to be reassured that the medications prescribed for depression have no addiction potential and are not associated with abuse. It is also important to keep in mind that several medical conditions, such as thyroid disease, can cause mood disorders as well.

Another association between mood disorders and alcohol use is that drinking can escalate during the period of mood disturbance. Research indicates that 20% to 60% of clients with bipolar disorder report excessive use of alcohol during the manic phase of their illness. It is unclear whether this is an effort to self-medicate their disturbing manic symptoms or whether it is a result of the poor judgment that is part of this phase of the illness. Regardless of why alcohol use increases, the consequences of the disinhibiting effects of alcohol, on top of the impaired judgment generally present, are often disastrous. The focus of therapy for bipolar clients with alcohol abuse is two-pronged. The primary disorder may require medication (lithium, other mood stabilizers, and/or antipsychotic agents) while simultaneous counseling and education are necessary to address alcohol use issues. In individuals with primary depression, 20% to

30% report increased alcohol intake during their mood disturbance. Persons with mood disorders are at higher risk of developing a co-occurring alcohol use disorder and should be warned of this possibility as a preventive measure.

Disorders Involving Psychosis

Psychosis is a disturbance of perception and thought process that is frequently associated with disturbances in function. While psychotic symptoms may be associated with a variety of psychiatric disorders, including substance-related disorders, it is often prominent in schizophrenic disorders. Schizophrenia and other psychotic disorders are a group of chronic, fluctuating disturbances that are among the most incapacitating of the mental disorders. They exact an enormous cost in human suffering and public and private resources. These disorders have a biochemical basis but are subject to environmental influences.

Schizophrenia occurs in about 1% of the general population. Schizophrenia is heterogeneous in its presentation. Those with schizophrenia may have "positive" or "negative" symptoms. Positive symptoms include hallucinations (sensory perceptions with no corresponding stimulus), delusions (fixed, false beliefs), and incoherence of thought with resultant disorganized speech. Negative symptoms include shyness or withdrawal from social contacts, difficulty communicating, and a restricted emotional range, making them appear dull and listless. Attention and cognitive disturbances are frequently present. Attempts to communicate are very difficult because the person with schizophrenia may perceive reality very differently than do people without schizophrenia. The individual with schizophrenia often misinterprets environmental stimuli. This altered perception can be very subtle or very marked. Clients with schizophrenia may make unwarranted connections between events. For example, a client may hear a car backfire, see the landlord in the hallway, and develop a concern that the landlord is "out to get me." If the client then hears imaginary voices saying, "He'll shoot first, ask questions later," the person's sense of paranoia becomes even greater. The treatment of schizophrenic disorders, as well as other psychotic disorders, includes medications (see following section) as well as ongoing supportive counseling and other rehabilitative efforts.

Some conditions associated with alcohol abuse closely resemble psychotic disorders. One study found a history of psychotic symptoms in over 40% of alcoholics who sought treatment. One such condition that may be misdiagnosed and thus lead to the inappropriate use of antipsychotic medication is that of *alcoholic hallucinosis.* Although seen in less than 3% of chronic alcoholics, it is so easily confused with schizophrenia that it should be considered in all cases of acute psychosis. It is often part of withdrawal states, but it can also occur in an actively drinking individual. The symptoms include auditory, tactile, or visual hallucinations, and the person typically develops persecutory delusions related to these hallucinations. Several features help distinguish alcohol hallucinosis from schizophrenia. The client has a history of heavy alcohol use. The majority of alcoholics with this condition will have their first episode after the age of 40, while schizophrenia typically appears earlier in life. The client usually has no family history of schizophrenia, but there may be a family history of alcohol dependence. Unlike schizophrenia, there is little evidence of a formal thought disorder—for example, loose associations and disorganization of thinking. The content of the hallucinations is fairly simple, unlike the less understandable or bizarre hallucinations of schizophrenia. In alcohol hallucinosis, the resolution of these symptoms is usually quick, occurring over the course of 1 to 6 days. Management should include hospitalization, close observation, some minor tranquilizers, and the limited use of antipsychotic medications. *Wernicke-Korsakoff syndrome* (see Chapter 6) also includes psychotic symptoms. This is an irreversible organic brain syndrome resulting from chronic alcohol abuse; it is characterized by prominent memory impairment and striking personality changes.

FORMAL THOUGHT DISORDER

Aside from the psychotic symptoms that may result from alcohol use, estimates of the prevalence of alcohol use disorder's co-occurring with schizophrenia range from 14% to 50%. These may be seen with levels of alcohol consumption that would typically not be thought of as problematic in the general population. The combination of schizophrenia and alcohol abuse often results in a rocky clinical course and a poor prognosis. Without specialized services, these individuals may have difficulty complying with any treatment plan. They frequently do not take medications as prescribed and may be unwilling or unable to follow recommendations for abstinence from alcohol. Efforts to end drinking in this population must be based on an assessment of what alcohol provides for the individual. If drinking is used to reduce anxiety around hallucinations, then increasing antipsychotic medication may be appropriate. If drinking is used to reduce uncomfortable side effects from antipsychotic medication, then a reduction in or substitution of medications may be necessary. If drinking represents an effort to achieve peer acceptance, then nonalcohol-centered social alternatives should be developed. For these clients, the need for compliance with prescribed medication cannot be overemphasized. Abstinence for some persons with schizophrenia may be indicated because even moderate drinking may, for them, be disruptive, suggesting a vulnerability to the effects of alcohol.

When schizophrenia is accompanied by alcohol abuse, the standard alcohol or drug regimen may be seen by patients as threatening. Poor treatment outcomes in traditional alcohol treatment settings have been associated with the severity of psychiatric symptoms. Persons with schizophrenia tend to do poorly in group settings with lots of confrontation. But the same patients can be treated quite effectively in less threatening groups. In recent years attention has turned to matching treatment interventions and to the motivational state of the patient. Engagement, persuasion, active treatment, and relapse prevention phases have been outlined to guide treatment planning and treatment goals. Incorporating motivational interviewing techniques can accelerate movement through the phases of recovery. If AA is to be used as part of the treatment plan, then these persons must be thoroughly prepared for AA experiences after they have accepted the need for abstinence. The host group should be assessed in advance for receptiveness to the psychiatrically impaired. Specialized dual recovery self-help groups for this are ideal and are increasingly available in many regions. Recent reviews of integrated treatment for schizophrenia and alcohol use disorders have shown promising results in achieving stable recovery and improved functioning.

Anxiety Disorders

Anxiety disorders are relatively common and involve incapacitating nervousness, tension, apprehension, and fear. These symptoms may appear episodically and without warning as in panic attacks. The anxiety may be a fear of particular places or situations (*agoraphobia*), or the anxiety may be a symptom of fearing a specific object, such as spiders (a simple *phobia*). For others it may take the form of unrelenting, recurrent ideas (*obsessions*), or the need to perform repetitive rituals (*compulsions*). The anxious person may experience physical symptoms, including diaphoresis (sweating), tremor, nausea, diarrhea, pallor, rapid pulse, shortness of breath, headache, or fatigue. These "panic attacks" can be very frightening. In contrast to other mental disorders, which may also be associated with a significant amount of anxiety, the anxiety disorders do not involve major disturbances in mood, thought, or judgment. Care must be taken to rule out other medical problems or medications as the cause of anxiety symptoms.

The relationship of anxiety disorders to alcohol problems remains controversial. As with mood disorders, the anxiety experienced may be independent of or secondary to alcohol dependence. Most clinicians know of clients who drink to control symptoms of panic or phobic disorders. This self-medication may then take on a life of its own, leading to alcohol abuse or dependence. There is a high prevalence of anxiety disorders among those in alcohol treatment. Several studies have reported the rate of associated anxiety disorders to be in a range between 22% and 44%, with specific phobias must common, followed by generalized anxiety disorder infrequency. Investigators concede that the sequence of anxiety and drinking is highly variable among individuals.

Understanding the relationship of anxiety symptoms to the drinking behavior is essential. Abstinence alone may "cure" the anxious symptoms if they are the consequences of drinking. On the other hand, severe anxiety may increase the dually diagnosed client's vulnerability to relapse. Treatment decisions must be based on a careful history of symptoms and observation of the individual following detoxification. If a co-occurring anxiety disorder is felt to be present, an integrated treatment plan might include the use of psychotherapy, behavioral therapy, and/or medications. Participation in safe, supportive 12-step programs may also reduce the symptoms of anxiety disorders. Antidepressants, such as desimipramine or sertraline (Zoloft®), may be effective with certain anxiety disorders and have very little abuse potential. Benzodiazepines are often effective for the symptoms of anxiety, but because of their high abuse potential, they should be lower on the list of medication alternatives. Buspirone (BuSpar®), without euphoric properties, but with a good safety profile and with few drug interactions, can be useful in treating an anxiety disorder in individuals with alcohol dependence. Cautious prescribing practices and a regular monitoring of clinical progress will minimize the risk of drug abuse and maximize the chances of successful recovery.

Personality Disorders

Everyone has a unique set of personality traits, which he or she exhibits in a range of social situations. When these traits are so rigid and maladaptive that they repeatedly interfere with a person's social or occupational functioning, they constitute a personality disorder. People with these disorders have the capacity "to get under everyone's skin." There are 10 types of personality disorders described in *DSM-IV TR,* but the 3 most commonly associated with alcohol problems are the antisocial, obsessive-compulsive, and borderline types.

A person with an *antisocial personality disorder* is frequently in trouble, getting into fights, conning others for personal profit, committing crimes, and having problems with authority. Antisocial personality disorder appears to be inherited independent of the predisposition to develop alcohol dependence, and studies have found rates as high as 20% in people with the disorder. Although these two disorders are not genetically linked, those with antisocial personality disorder are at high risk for developing alcohol dependence. In addition, chronic alcohol consumption can lead to personality changes that closely resemble the antisocial personality. However, these behaviors may disappear following abstinence. Studies have found that from 10% to 20% of men and about 5% to 10% of women in alcohol treatment facilities meet the criteria for antisocial personality disorder. Women with alcohol use disorders are 6 times more likely to have antisocial personality disorder than women without alcohol problems. For this group the prognosis is poor. Their social problems do not disappear with abstinence. They are generally resistant to any type of intervention, lack remorse for their behavior, and frequently alienate caregivers and peer support groups.

People with *obsessive-compulsive personality disorder* are preoccupied with perfectionism and control at the expense of flexibility and efficiency. They may repeatedly check to see if doors are locked or ovens are off, sometimes missing important appointments. They may scrub a wall so often that the paint is worn off in their effort to eliminate germs. Things must be perfect and their effort to achieve this state may prevent them from finishing the task. They may hoard objects and sometimes get crowded out of their own living space by magazines, books, and "collectibles." Alcohol may initially give them a break from their ritualistic behavior, but can quickly become a disorder in itself.

Those with a *borderline personality disorder* may act impulsively, with multiple suicide attempts; may exhibit inappropriate emotions, such as intense anger or ingenuine affection; may have feelings of emptiness or boredom; and may have frequent mood swings. They also frequently use alcohol in chaotic and unpredictable patterns, and 13% to 28% of alcoholics seeking treatment have been given this diagnosis. It is again important to attempt to separate out the sequence of behavioral problems and alcohol abuse in developing appropriate treatment plans. People with borderline personality disorder also evoke strong negative feelings from their caregivers. All suicidal behavior, from threats to attempts, must be taken seriously. Treatment objectives include the creation of a safe and secure relationship and environment.

Attention-Deficit/Hyperactivity Disorder

Some children are unable to remain attentive in situations where it is socially necessary to do so. This is often first recognized in the challenging environment of elementary school, but it can also be apparent in the home. In the past these conditions were termed hyperactivity or minimal brain dysfunction; they are now known as attention-deficit/hyperactivity disorder (ADHD). ADHD occurs in 3% to 5% of school-aged children, and boys are 4 times more likely than girls to have the illness. Follow-up studies of children with ADHD have noted an increased risk of alcohol dependence in adulthood. The examination of alcoholics' childhoods also shows a higher incidence of ADHD. One hypothesis is that a subgroup of alcohol abusers begin to drink to stabilize areas of the brain that are "irritable" due to damage earlier in life. For them, alcohol can be considered self-medication. Alcohol may improve performance on cognitive tasks, allow better concentration, and offer a subjective sense of stability. Such a response to alcohol would be highly reinforcing and thereby would increase the risk of addiction.

With adults, it is very difficult to sort out the cognitive impairment caused by alcohol from a preexisting, underlying deficit. As is true with anxiety disorders, here too prolonged abstinence is desirable prior to making a diagnosis. On the other hand, these clients may be unable to achieve and maintain sobriety.

When confronted with an individual who has been through treatment several times and has never been able to establish sobriety, take a careful childhood history. If there is evidence of difficulties in school or other problems suggesting ADHD, further evaluation and treatment with medication may be warranted. The medication prescribed in such cases may belong to the stimulant class; however, for such clients it has a paradoxical "calming" effect. In addition, the association of ADHD and alcohol abuse suggests that parents of children diagnosed as having ADHD be alerted to the steps they can take to reduce the risk of future alcohol problems. Recent studies do not support the conclusion that the use of medication in childhood correlates with eventual substance abuse.

Psychiatric Disorders Due to a General Medical Condition

A psychiatric disorder is diagnosed as due to a medical condition when the symptoms, based on evidence from the history, physical examination, or laboratory findings, are judged to be the direct physiological consequence of a medical condition. The causes can vary. For example, mental disorders can result from trauma to the central nervous system, from a brain tumor, from a stroke, or from a variety of infections. These impairments in brain function limit the person's ability to think and respond meaningfully to the environment. Usually there are significant changes in cognitive function. Problems with memory, an inability to concentrate, or a loss of intellectual capacity are common.

These disorders can represent permanent impairment, or they can be completely reversible. Which of these outcomes occurs depends primarily on whether there has been only temporary interference with the brain's function, such as through the ingestion of drugs or an active infection of the brain, or whether there has been permanent damage to brain tissue. Reversible disorders due to a medical condition are referred to as *delirium.* Typically the onset of delirium is rapid, and if the cause is identified and treated, the person may return to his or her usual self within days. Another component of delirium can be visual hallucinations, especially at night, which can be particularly terrifying. *Dementia* generally refers to irreversible changes in cognition due to medical conditions. Usually these changes have a more gradual onset, with a gradual deterioration of function over the course of years. In addition to the limitations these disorders create for an individual, an equally significant factor may be how the individual perceives them. If the symptoms appear slowly, the individual may be able to compensate—that is, for the most part, appear normal—especially if in a familiar environment with no new problems to solve. On the other hand, if the symptoms appear rapidly, the person may understandably be extremely upset. As the individual experiences a reduction in thinking capacity, anxiety often results and is very apparent.

The treatment of mental disorders due to a medical condition attempts, when possible, to correct the underlying cause. If the medical

condition is a tumor, surgery may be indicated; if it is encephalitis, antibiotics are necessary; if it is drug-induced, withdrawal of the toxic agent is necessary. If permanent impairment is associated with organic mental disorders, rehabilitation measures will be initiated to assist the person in coping with limitations.

Severe cognitive deficits in a chronic alcoholic may lead to the diagnosis of alcoholic dementia. This type of dementia develops insidiously and typically occurs during the drinker's fifth or sixth decade. The symptoms include a deteriorating memory and often dramatic personality changes. Mood swings are common; moods can swing from anger to euphoria. This condition is related to the widespread brain damage and actual shrinkage of brain tissue, which is apparent if the person has a computerized axial tomography (CAT) scan of the brain. With abstinence, there may be some recovery over the first 6 weeks. These improvements will be marked and be evident on a CAT scan. Abstinence, unfortunately, is difficult to achieve. The impairment in thinking doesn't allow the standard counseling and educational approaches to take hold. Generally some degree of dementia persists after abstinence.

The elderly are particularly susceptible to mental disturbances caused by alcohol. Metabolism slows with age, leading to higher blood levels of alcohol than is present with the same level of consumption earlier in life. Their increased use of prescribed medication also increases the likelihood of a medication/alcohol interaction, often leading to episodes of confusion. In a study of elderly patients seen in one emergency room, confusion was virtually three times more common for those with an alcohol problem. Older people apparently have a heightened sensitivity to all psychoactive compounds, leading to greater cognitive changes while drinking. As demographic changes in the United States result in a higher percentage of older Americans, practitioners will be increasingly challenged to identify alcohol-related cognitive deficits and not simply chalk them up to aging. An alcohol-related diagnosis is often missed in this population because the elderly tend to be protected by their friends and family. They may not meet strict *DSM-IV* criteria for alcohol abuse or alcohol dependence, but they still may be drinking pathologically.

Other Drug Dependence and Alcohol Abuse

Alcohol abuse among those who are primarily abusing other licit and illicit substances is frequently overlooked. In one study, 70% to 77% of clients entering treatment for benzodiazepine (an anti-anxiety agent) abuse also met the criteria for alcohol abuse; of opioid addicted persons in treatment, 20% to 35% were found to have alcohol-related problems. The danger in such instances is that an alcohol problem is treated lightly, no alcohol assessment is done, nor alcohol treatment provided. The cocaine abuser who routinely uses alcohol to offset the stimulant's effects may not be aware of a developing alcohol dependence. The alternative is equally true. It is also necessary to look for other drug dependencies in those with identified alcohol problems. The rate of other drug abuse or dependence in treatment samples of alcoholics ranges from 12% to 43%.

Other Addictive Behaviors

The concept of addiction is also being applied to behaviors that do not involve alcohol or other drug abuse—most notably, eating disorders and pathological gambling. Some people refuse food intake because they believe they are too fat, although the scales say differently (*anorexia nervosa*). Others stuff themselves and purge by vomiting or abusing laxatives over and over (*bulimia*). Each of these behaviors has an addictive quality: anorexia nervosa is an addiction to food avoidance, while bulimia is an addiction to food binges. Anorexia and bulimia occur primarily in females. Social influences, such as how one should look, are important contributors to the development of these disorders. Case reports of associations between eating disorders and alcohol abuse are increasing as recognition of each illness improves. A striking phenomenon is the frequency of referral for alcohol treatment of individuals who had eating disorders in earlier years. Among those with anorexia, there appears to be a higher incidence of a family history of alcohol problems which also increases the risk of developing this dependency. Although prospective studies are needed, the potential risk of alcohol problems among those with eating disorders should be recognized.

Gambling is another example of an impulse-control disorder that can disrupt personal, family, and vocational goals. Those with a gambling addiction speak of the arousal they seek in much the same way alcoholics describe drinking. They are preoccupied with planning the next gambling venture, they continue to gamble despite efforts to cut back, and they may become restless or irritable when attempting to stop. When not gambling they may be workaholics or binge workers who require a deadline to motivate action. While the treatments for eating disorders and gambling are complex, the use of Overeaters Anonymous and Gamblers Anonymous groups in America speaks to the growing recognition of these addictive behaviors.

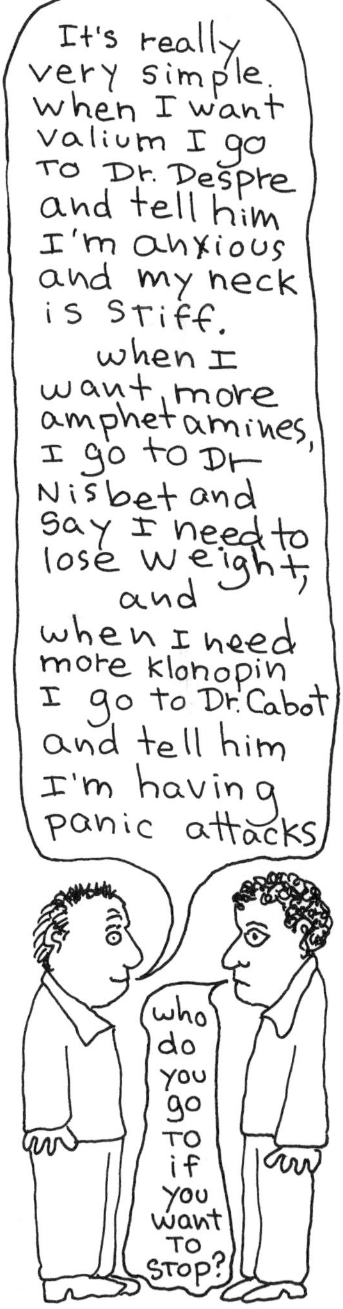

Clinical Considerations

Because of the high prevalence of co-occurring psychiatric conditions, all clients should be screened for co-occurring disorders. Screening is the determination of the likelihood that a person has a co-occurring mental disorder and establishes whether the person has a need for an in-depth assessment. The screening should be brief and occur soon after the client presents for services. The Mental Health Screening Form III is a practical tool that covers most of the disorders discussed in this chapter (available

without charge at www.asapnys.org/Resources/mhscreen.pdf. When screens are positive for a possible co-occurring psychiatric condition, substance abuse treatment personnel should either conduct a thorough assessment or consider consultation from a psychiatrist or mental health worker. When a co-occurring condition is diagnosed, it and the alcohol disorder are considered primary. Treating both conditions simultaneously is necessary and requires an integrated treatment plan. The treatment of psychiatric illness must be coordinated carefully with rehabilitation efforts. Under any circumstances, extra support and education are essential. Effective programs need to recognize that recovery tends to occur over months or years and that long-term, community-based strategies are required. The client needs to appreciate that he or she is being treated for two very different conditions. For long-term success, control of both is equally important. Efforts to help the client integrate information from both treatment perspectives require thoughtful treatment planning and follow-up.

Homelessness, Alcohol Use, and Chronic Mental Illness

Although homelessness is not an illness, it represents a point at which chronic mental illness intersects with alcohol problems. Alcohol dependence is one pathway toward homelessness. On the other hand, homelessness can be a condition that precedes increased alcohol abuse. Either way, alcohol-related problems within the homeless population are enormous. On any given night, more than 700,000 people in this country are without adequate shelter, and about two-fifths of them are affected by alcohol abuse. Certainly the "skid row bum," whose repeated detox and jail stints leave lasting impressions on health-care providers, remains inextricably linked with homelessness in the popular consciousness. Historically the "chronic public inebriate" frequently ended up on the streets. Increasingly these individuals are being swept into the criminal justice system through cycles of arrest, release without adequate treatment and support, and rearrest. Homeless persons with alcohol dependence have unique service and housing needs, requiring creative responses.

The homeless alcohol abuser has been shown to be multiply disadvantaged, with higher rates of physical, mental, and social problems than the nonalcohol abusing homeless person. Most homeless alcohol abusers are male, white, and elderly. Many have troubled marital and family histories and poor employment records, and many are transient and socially isolated. They are frequently incarcerated for petty crimes and often are victims of violent attacks. The majority of alcohol abusing homeless persons have an additional psychiatric diagnosis. Homeless alcohol abusers are at high risk for neurological impairment, heart disease and hypertension, chronic lung disease, liver disease, and trauma. These clinical features complicate engagement, intervention, and recovery.

Successful treatment of alcohol dependence depends on social and physical environments where sobriety is positively supported. These are hardly the conditions encountered in a street existence. Therefore, the service needs of the homeless go beyond the provision of substance abuse treatment. Providing only detoxification and short-term inpatient care will reinforce the revolving door scenario that too often typifies homeless persons with alcohol problems. Assistance and support for finding appropriate, affordable, and alcohol-free housing are the backbone of treatment for this special population. To accomplish even this basic goal, bridging the person's disaffiliation, distrust, and disenchantment is necessary. Overcoming these adverse motivational forces requires a great deal of clinical skill. It also requires a great deal of patience, since homeless persons with alcohol problems are among the most severely and chronically ill clients that a counselor is likely to encounter. The needs of the homeless alcohol abuser go beyond the capacity of any single provider. Clinicians need to continue to form coalitions with advocates, politicians, and community resources to develop adequate service systems for this disadvantaged population.

PSYCHOTROPIC MEDICATIONS

Neither alcohol nor other drug problems exist in a vacuum. Those with substance abuse problems can also have a variety of other problems—some physical, some psychiatric. These patients may be receiving treatment or treating themselves. The treatment may involve prescription or over-the-counter medications. The more one knows about medications in general, the more helpful one can be to a client. The group of medications of particular interest in relation to alcohol or other drug use are those with psychotropic effects. Any drug that influences behavior or mood falls into this category. Because of the abuse potential of some of them and their ability to mimic intoxicated states, these medications are of the greatest concern to the substance abuse clinician. At the same time, they may be the most widely misunderstood.

Good medicine is bitter, but it cures illness.
CONFUCIUS

Those with substance or abuse dependence, and particularly alcohol-dependent people, tend to seek instant relief from the slightest mental or physical discomfort. The active alcoholic may welcome any chemical relief and is at risk for using some medications in an abusive manner. The recovering person, on the other hand, may be so leery of any medication that he or she may refuse to use those medications that are very much needed. Thus, some familiarity with the types of psychotropic medications and their appropriate use is important. They are not alike, either in terms of their actions or in their potential for abuse.

Taking a good medication history is imperative in dealing with clients. The following are some of the questions a clinician should have in mind: "What medications do you currently take? Is it prescribed, when was it prescribed, and by whom was it prescribed? Are you following the prescription? Do you take more or less or use a different schedule? Is the drug having the desired effects? What, if any, side effects exist? Do you have any medication allergies? What is your philosophy about medications? Have you ever abused medication in the past?" These questions can help identify any abuse of current medications and can prevent future abuse in vulnerable, recovering individuals.

Tremendous confusion may arise from a communication gap between the patient and the prescribing physician. The physician prescribes a medication intended to have a specific effect on a particular patient. The patient is sometimes unclear about (and usually doesn't question) the need for medication. There may be limited access to the physician for follow-up calls. Only feedback from the patient enables the doctor to make adjustments, if necessary. The regimen for taking a drug is important, also. Often, as the patient begins to feel better, he or she stops or cuts the dose of a prescribed drug. This sometimes occurs because patients assume that, once the symptoms are gone they no longer need the medication, rather than realizing that it is the medicine that is keeping the symptoms under control. Clients should be encouraged to consult with the physician before altering the way medications are taken. Because treatment requires good communication, you should help the client ask questions about the treatment and the drugs involved. Also be sensitive to the problems that the cost of medications can present for some clients. Those without insurance can find the cost prohibitive. This may mean that they skimp on taking medicines as prescribed to make their supply last longer. Or they may put off having a prescription refilled on schedule, because their budget simply can't be stretched that far, at that time.

The desire to take medicine is perhaps the greatest feature which distinguishes man from animals.
SIR WILLIAM OSLER, 1925

Every drug has multiple, simultaneous actions. Only a few of these are sought when a particular drug is prescribed. The intended effects are the drug's therapeutic effects; all the other effects are considered the drug's side effects in that particular instance. In selecting a medication for a patient, a doctor seeks a drug with the maximum therapeutic impact and the fewest side effects. Ideally the prescription of a particular drug should be a collaborative effort. Enough information must be exchanged to enable the patient to give valid consent to the doctor for the prescription. The following is a discussion of the four major categories of psychotropic medication: neuroleptics, the antipsychotic medications, antidepressant medications, mood stabilizers, and anti-anxiety agents. Each has different actions and is prescribed for different reasons.

Antipsychotic Medications

The antipsychotic medications, sometimes referred to as neuroleptics, are drugs which relieve psychotic symptoms. In addition to the antipsychotic effect, they also have a tranquilizing and a sedative effect, calming behavior and inducing drowsiness. Antipsychotic medications have allowed many patients to live in the community rather than institutions.

There are two general categories of antipsychotics, with different side effects. Those most commonly used are termed the atypical antipsychotics (in comparison to the older typical or traditional group). The atypicals are also used in the acute phase of mania for mood stabilization. Side effects vary from medication to medication, as is true of the typical or traditional medications. Serious but reversible side effects in some of the most widely used medications in the atypical category include weight gain, increase in serum lipids, and onset of Type II (late-onset) diabetes. The potential for irreversible neurological side effects with the use of the typical or traditional antipsychotics further mandates their judicious use.

The medications in this group have various side effects, making them either more or less sedating. The medication prescribed is selected on the basis of the patient's constellation of symptoms. Thus, a drug with greater sedative effects might be selected for a person exhibiting manic, or agitated, behavior. Some antipsychotic drugs are currently available in a long-acting injectable form called decanoate. These shots can be useful in ensuring medication compliance in clients with a history of poor compliance. The antipsychotic, neuroleptic, medications most frequently encountered are listed in Table 12.2.

As with most medications, antipsychotic drugs interact with alcohol. A common effect of combining alcohol with sedating medications is potentiation: the two agents act in concert to exaggerate the sedative effects, which can cause problems. Alcohol can also increase the levels of neurotransmitters that the neuroleptic drugs are attempting to block, leading to reduced effectiveness.

Antipsychotic drugs are much less likely to be abused than other psychocative agents. They are not chemically similar to alcohol and are therefore not subject to cross-tolerance or addiction. The sensations they produce are generally not experienced as pleasurable and are therefore infrequently sought out. For these reasons, an antipsychotic agent may be prescribed, not to relieve psychotic symptoms but for its sedative or tranquilizing properties. Several of the side effects, involving involuntary movements, caused by the antipsychotic drugs are unpleasant. Medications can be used to reduce these unpleasant side effects, including benztropine (Cogentin®) and trihexiphenidyl (Artane®) and medications from the benzodiazepine group of anti-anxiety medications. The latter (anti-anxiety agents) can induce pleasurable mental changes and may be abused by clients.

Antidepressant Medications

The antidepressants, another major class of psychotropic medications, are used to treat the biological component of depression. They must be taken at a high enough dose to achieve a therapeutic level. A period of regular use (often 2 to 4 weeks) is also necessary before these medications have their full effect. Therefore, an initial complaint of patients is

Table 12.2 Antipsychotic Medications

Drugs in Category	Daily Dose Range	Potential Overdose Danger
Antipsychotic Medications (Atypicals)		
Action: believed to bind at some dopamine and serotonin receptors for major portion of effects to either enhance, block, or modulate neurotransmitters' effects		
Olanzepine (Zyprexa®)	2.5–10 mg	Low
Potential side effects: sleepiness, postural hypotension (drop in blood pressure when rising from a chair or bed), constipation, significant weight gain, hyperlipidemia (increase in blood cholesterol or triglyceride levels), development of Type II diabetes, dizziness, muscle rigidity and weakness, possible liver enzyme elevations		
Risperidone (Risperdal®)	0.5–6 mg	Low
Potential side effects: sleepiness, dizziness, heart palpitations, weight gain, sexual function complaints increased fatigue, dose-related, extra-pyramidal effects (involuntary movements, tics, tremors)		
Quetiapine (Seroquel®)	50–750 mg	Low
Potential side effects: sleepiness, postural hypotension, dizziness, constipation, dry mouth, weight gain		
Ziprasidone (Geodon®)	40–160 mg	Low in early trials
Potential side effects: possible cardiac arrhythmias, drowsiness, nausea, constipation, diarrhea, dizziness, restlessness, abnormal muscle movements, rash, cough, runny nose		
Aripiprazale (Abilify®)	100–900 mg	Low
Potential side effects: constipation, akathisia (a mix of agitation and physical restlessness), difficulty sleeping, insomnia, lightheadedness		
Cloazpine (Clozaril®)	100–900 mg	High
Potential side effects: drowsiness, sedation, dizziness, headache, tremor, excessive salivation and sweating, hyperlipidia, development of Type II diabetes, dry mouth, rapid heart rate, hypotension, fainting, weight gain, seizures Due to multiple and potentially dangerous side effects generally used when other antipsychotic agents have been ineffective.		
Typical Antipsychotic Medications (Traditional)		
Action: precise mechanism unknown; thought to act as dopamine 2 antagonist		
Chlorpromazine (Thorazine®)	50–500 mg	Moderate
Haloperidol (Haldol®)	1–15 mg	Moderate
Fluphenazine (Prolixin®)	25–100 mg IM q 1–4 week 5–60 mg/day p.o.	Moderate
Thiothixine (Navane®)	5–60 mg	Moderate
Perphenazine (Trilafon®)	4–24 mg	Moderate
Molindone (Moban®)	50–225 mg	Moderate
Potential side effects: sedation, dry mouth, Parkinsonian symptoms, involuntary facial movements (dyskinesia), constipation, difficulty with urination, blurred vision, muscle rigidity and weakness, weight gain (except for molindone) Note: This applies to all		

that the medicine isn't helping. Side effects vary according to the category of antidepressant. These are most pronounced when the person first begins taking the drug. The physician may choose to have the patient take the medication at a particular time of the day to minimize side effects. There are several types of antidepressants, grouped according to their chemical properties and how they act.

The SSRIs—the acronym for **s**elective **s**erotonin **r**euptake **i**nhibitors—are currently the most commonly prescribed and most widely used antidepressant medications. In general, they have fewer side effects than the other categories of antidepressant medications. The most commonly encountered side effects include gastrointestinal symptoms, headache, insomnia, and agitation. The tricyclics are the oldest category of commonly used antidepressants. Common side effects include dry mouth and constipation. A third category, known as **m**ono**a**mine **o**xidase **i**nhibitors (MAOIs), requires additional dietary restrictions, to avoid bad side effects. Beyond the dietary restrictions, drugs in this category have numerous other side effects as well.

Venlafaxine and Duloxetine, SNRIs (serotonin-**n**orepinephrine **r**euptake **i**nhibitors), have actions similar to those of both the SSRIs and the tricyclics without the unpleasant side effects or significant threat of overdose of the tricyclics. While mitazepine too directly affects both serotonin and norepinephrine, it is not a reuptake inhibitor. Bupropion is another commonly prescribed antidepressant. It is presently the only medication in its category and is chemically unrelated to the other antidepressants. It is *exactly* the same medication marketed as Zyban® for smoking cessation. Although in the antidepressant category, trazadone is used more often for its side effect of sedation than for its antidepressant effect.

The most common antidepressants are listed in Table 12.3. There is no clear evidence that antidepressant medications invite abuse or create dependence. However, overdoses of some of these medications, such as the tricyclics, can be lethal. Again, in combination with alcohol, problems can arise because of the additive effects.

Mood Stabilizers

Mood stabilizers are used to treat bipolar (manic-depressive) disorder (see Table 12.4). A few comments on lithium carbonate are worth mention. It can be helpful in either depression or mania and is a common medication used in controlling bipolar disorder. The dose is geared to body weight, and the level is monitored periodically through blood samples. Because lithium produces no pleasant effects, it is unlikely to be abused. The opposite behavior, taking too little, is the more common problem. Feeling greatly improved, those on lithium may decide it's no longer necessary. However, maintaining stability usually depends on continuing to take the medication.

Table 12.3 Antidepressant Medications

Drugs in Category	Daily Dose Range	Potential Overdose Danger
SSRIs (Selective Serotonin Reuptake Inhibitors)		
Action: believed to increase the neurotransmitter serotonin by preventing the usual reuptake of serotonin by the presynaptic (sending) nerve cell, making more serotonin available for transmission to the postsynaptic (receiving) nerve cell		
Fluoxetine (Prozac®)	10–80 mg	Low
Paroxetine (Paxil®)	10–80 mg	Low
Sertraline (Zoloft®)	25–200 mg	Low
Citralopram (Celexa®)	20–40 mg	Low
Escitralopram (Hexapro®)	10–20 mg	Low
Potential side effects: sexual dysfunction, decreased libido, nausea, headache, nervousness, insomnia, drowsiness, diarrhea, weight gain or loss		
Tricyclics		
Action: believed to involve potentiation of norepinephrine and possibly serotonin activity by blocking reuptake by the presynaptic (sending) nerve cell, making more serotonin available for transmission to the postsynaptic (receiving) nerve cell		
Imipramine (Tofranil®)	30–200 mg	High
Desipramine (Norpramin®)	25–200 mg	High
Amitriptyline (Elavil®)	10–200 mg	High
Nortriptyline (Pamelor®)	30–150 mg	High
Doxepin (Sinequan®)	25–300 mg	High
Protriptyline (Vivactil®)	15–60 mg	High
Potential side effects: dry mouth, increased hearth rate, EKG changes, urinary hesitation, constipation, blurred vision, sedation, weight gain		
Monoamine-Oxidase Inhibitors (MAOIs)		
Action: believed to act by inhibiting the enzyme monamine oxidase, responsible for the breakdown of monoamines (norepinephrine, epinephrine, and serotonin); inhibition results in increased levels of these neurotransmitters. Note: Because of the possible interactions of MAOIs with foods containing tyramine (for example, cheeses, red wines, processed meat such as pepperoni) and with multiple medications that results in marked blood pressure elevation, use of the MAOIs requires that the patient be very diligent about diet and the use of other medication; thus, MAOIs are infrequently prescribed.		

(continued)

Table 12.3 continued

Monoamine-Oxidase Inhibitors (MAOIs)

Drugs in Category	Daily Dose Range	Potential Overdose Danger
Tranylcypromine (Parnate®)	30–60 mg	High
Phenylzine (Nardil®)	15–90 mg	High

Potential side effects: overstimulation, anxiety, agitation, mania, restlessness, insomnia, drowsiness, dizziness, gastrointestinal symptoms, headaches, rapid heartbeat. Hypertensive crisis when food containing tyramine is eaten or medications with sympathomimetic effects, such as cold preparations taken

SNRIs (Serotonin/Norepinephrine Reuptake Inhibitors)

Action: believed to potentiate the action of serotonin, norepinephrine, and possibly dopamine by inhibition of the reuptake mechanism

Venlafaxine (Effexor®)	75–300 mg	Low
Duloxetine (Cymbalta®)	40–60 mg	Low

Potential side effects: elevated blood pressure, headache, sweating, nausea, insomnia, dizziness, anorexia, anxiety, sleepiness, difficulty with orgasm

Other

Bupropion (Wellbutrin®) (marketed as Zyban® for smoking cessation)	100–450 mg	Low

Action: unknown; believed to be due to action on dopamine and noradrenergic systems

Potential side effects: agitation, dry mouth, sweating, gastrointestinal upset, insomnia, seizures, dizziness

Nefazadone (Serzone®)	100–600 mg	Low
Trazadone (Desyrel®)	50–600 mg	Low

Action: unknown; possible inhibition of reuptake of serotonin and norepinephrine

Potential side effects: both medications—dry mouth, nausea, constipation, sleepiness, dizziness, lightheadedness, vision problems, confusion; trazadone—hypotension, priapism (rare) (persistent erection in the absence of stimulus)

Mirtazepine (Remeron®)	15–45 mg	Low, but few reports*

Action: unknown; antidepressant activity may be related to a direct enhancement of noradrenergic neurotransmitters and thereby a subsequent increase in serotonin

Potential side effects: sleepiness, dizziness, increased appetite and weight gain, increased triglyceride and cholesterol levels

*Rarely used due to possible liver damage.

Table 12.4 Mood Stabilizers

Drugs in Category	Daily Dose Range	Potential Overdose Danger
Lithium		
Action: unknown; alters sodium transport and causes a shift toward intraneuronal metabolism of catecholamines, but specified biochemical mechanism of action in mania is not known		
Lithium carbonate (Lithobid®, Eskalith®, Lithonate®)	600–1800 mg	High
Potential side effects: hand tremor, nausea, weight gain, increased output of urine and increased fluid intake, fatigue, lethargy, hypothyroidism		
Anticonvulsants		
Action: anticonvulsant; mechanism of action/effectiveness in mania is unknown. A number of medications formerly used to control seizures (anticonvulsants) are now used as mood stabilizers.		
Divalproex (Depakote®)	500–1500 mg	High
Valproic acid (Depakene®)	15–60 mg per 2.2 pounds body weight	High
Potential side effects: gastrointestinal symptoms, asthenia, weight gain, sleepiness, dizziness, tremor, possible liver problems		
Carbamazepine (Tegretol®)	400–1200 mg	High
Potential side effects: dizziness, drowsiness, unsteadiness, nausea, vomiting, skin rashes; rare but serious effects on bone marrow and white blood count		
Lamotrigine (Lamictal®)	100–400 mg (adults)	Moderate to high
Potential side effects: headache, nausea, vomiting, dizziness, diplopia (double vision), blurred vision, unsteadiness, runny nose, skin rash; life-threatening skin disorders have been reported in 0.3% of adults taking Lamictal® (they are more common in children taking lamotrigine for epilepsy)		
Topirimate (Topamax®)	50–400 mg	Undetermined
Potential side effects: somnolence, dizziness, vision problems, unsteadiness, speech problems, psychomotor slowing, "pins and needles," nervousness, nausea, memory problems, tremor, confusion, fatigue		

Note: Not helpful in acute mania.

In addition to lithium, carbamazepine (Tegretol®) and valproic acid are used with patients who cannot take lithium because of side effects, or they are taken in addition to lithium. The use of alcohol with either of these is contraindicated because of additive effects and because there is the possibility that either of them, on its own, can cause liver damage. This would be made worse by alcohol use.

Table 12.5 Anti-Anxiety Agents

Drugs in Category	Daily Dose Range	Potential Overdose Danger
Benzodiazepines		
Action: depression of activity at all excitable tissues; in general, acts at receptors on neurons that are linked with or potentiate the GABA (gamma-amino-butyric acid) system, which inhibits neuronal activity; chloride ion flow into neurons is facilitated by the GABA system, resulting in sedation		
Alprazolam (Xanax®)	0.25–6 mg	Low
Chlordiazepoxide (Librium®)	5–100 mg	Low
Clonazepam (Klonopin®)	0.5–4 mg	Low
Diazepam (Valium®)	2–40 mg	Low
Oxazepam (Serax®)	10–45 mg	Low
Potential side effects: similar to alcohol; impaired cognitive function, impaired psychomotive performance, sedation; development of tolerance		
Non-benzodiazepines		
Action: unknown; has an affinity for dopamine 2 receptors; may act on other neurotransmitter systems; has no known dependency potential		
Buspirone (BuSpar®)	15–60 mg	Low
Potential side effects: minimal		

Note: The table is restricted to the most commonly prescribed medications.

I'll trade you two Valiums and a Xanax for an ativan.

Anti-Anxiety Agents

The final group of psychotropic medications are the anti-anxiety agents, also called anxiolytic agents. The major action of these drugs is to promote tranquilization and sedation. Quite properly, alcohol can be included in any list of drugs in this class. The anti-anxiety agents have sometimes been called the minor tranquilizers. They have no antipsychotic or significant antidepressant properties and are very effective in the treatment of anxiety disorders. Short-acting forms are frequently prescribed as sleeping aids. However, their high potential for abuse and dependence makes them less likely to be the first medication prescribed for anxiety, especially in persons who have any history of abuse of alcohol or other drugs. There are two different types of anti-anxiety drugs, the benzodiazepines and newer agents, called the "nonbenzodiazepines." The most common anti-anxiety agents are listed in Table 12.5.

The medications in this class, along with barbiturates (now rarely prescribed), are those most likely to be troublesome for those with alcohol dependence. The potential for abuse of the anti-anxiety agents has become more broadly recognized. Valium®, Xanax®, and Ativan® (benzodiazepines) are the anti-anxiety agents that have been most widely associated with abuse and dependence. In the past, Quaalude® and Placidyl®—which are no longer available for prescription in this country—as well as Miltown® and some barbiturates—led to abuse and dependence problems. Newer anti-anxiety medications, such as buspirone (BuSpar®) and hydroxyzine (Atarax®, Vistaril®), have demonstrated far less abuse potential.

Beyond problems of possible abuse, there are other dangers with the benzodiazepine anti-anxiety agents and alcohol. Taken in combination, they potentiate one another. Medical ethicists and legal scholars all are familiar with the case of a 21-year-old woman named Karen Ann Quinlin, whose family was the first to have fought in court to have a family member removed from a respirator, to be allowed to die. In 1985, she had been in a coma for almost a decade. Many people are unaware that the cause of her irreversible coma was attributed to the combination of alcohol and Valium®.

Every form of addiction is bad, no matter whether the narcotic be alcohol or morphine or idealism.
CARL JUNG

Because of their similar pharmacology, alcohol and the benzodiazepine anti-anxiety agents are virtually interchangeable. This phenomenon is the basis of cross-addiction and is the rationale for their use in alcohol detoxification. It is their very interchangeability with alcohol that makes them very poor anti-anxiety drugs for those with an alcohol problem, except for detoxification purposes.

Eat not to fullness; drink not to elevation.
BENJAMIN FRANKLIN

On the whole, Americans are very casual about medications. Too often, prescriptions are not taken as directed, are saved up for the next illness, or are shared with family and friends. Over-the-counter preparations are treated as candy. The fact that a prescription is not required does not render it harmless. Some possible ingredients in over-the-counter drugs are antihistamines, stimulants, and of course alcohol. These can cause difficulty if taken in combination with alcohol or may themselves be abused.

RESOURCES AND FURTHER READING

Berglund M, Ojehagen A. The influence of alcohol drinking and alcohol use disorders on psychiatric disorders and suicidal behavior. *Alcoholism: Clinical and Experimental Research* 22(7 Supplement):333S–345S, 1998. (112 refs.)

Buckley PF. Substance abuse in schizophrenia: A review. *Journal of Clinical Psychiatry* 59(Supplement):26–30, 1998. (60 refs.)

Byrne P, Jones S, Williams R. The association between cannabis and alcohol use and the development of mental disorder. *Current Opinion in Psychiatry* 17(4):255–261, 2004. (53 refs.)

Crawford V, Crome IB, Clancy C. Co-existing problems of mental health and substance misuse (dual diagnosis): A literature review. *Drugs: Education, Prevention and Policy* 10(Supplement):S1–S74, 2003. (138 refs.)

Drake RE, Essock SM, Shaner A, Carey KB, Minkoff K, Kola L, Lynde D, Osher FC, Clark RE, Rickards L. Implementing dual diagnosis services for clients with severe mental illness. *Psychiatric Services* 52(4):469–476, 2001. (87 refs.)

Drake RE, Mueser KT, Brunette MF, McHugo GJ. A review of treatments for people with severe mental illnesses and co-occurring substance use disorders (review). *Psychiatric Rehabilitation Journal* 27(4):360–374, 2004. (93 refs.)

D'Souza DC, Perry E, MacDougall L, Ammerman Y, Cooper T, Wu YT, et al. The psychotomimetic effects of intravenous delta-9-tetrahydrocannabinol in healthy individuals: Implications for psychosis (review). *Neuropsychopharmacology* 29(8):1558–1572, 2004. (148 refs.)

Johnson J. Cost-effectiveness of mental health services for persons with a dual diagnosis: A literature review and the CCMHCP. *Journal of Substance Abuse Treatment* 18(2):119–127, 2000. (95 refs.)

Kushner MG, Abrams K, Borchardt C. The relationship between anxiety disorders and alcohol use disorders: A review of major perspectives and findings (review). *Clinical Psychology Review* 20(2):149–171, 2000. (120 refs.)

McEvoy JP, Allen TB. Substance abuse (including nicotine) in schizophrenic patients. *Current Opinion in Psychiatry* 16(2):199–205, 2003. (16 refs.)

Mueser KT, Drake RE, Wallach MA. Dual diagnosis: A review of etiological theories (review). *Addictive Behaviors* 23(6):717–734, 1998. (146 refs.)

Mueser KT, Torrey WC, Lynde D, Singer P, Drake RE. Implementing evidence-based practices for people with severe mental illness (review). *Behavior Modification* 27(3):387–411, 2003. (114 refs.)

Negrete JC. Clinical aspects of substance abuse in persons with schizophrenia (review). *Canadian Journal of Psychiatry* 48(1):14–21, 2003. (58 refs.)

Nunes EV, Levin FR. Treatment of depression in patients with alcohol or other drug dependence: A meta-analysis (review). *Journal of the American Medical Association* 291(15):1887–1896, 2004. (83 refs.)

Rosenberg SD, Drake RE, Wolford GL, Mueser KT, Oxman TE, Vidaver RM, et al. Dartmouth Assessment of Lifestyle Instrument (DALI): A substance use disorder screen for people with severe mental illness. *American Journal of Psychiatry* 155(2):232–238, 1998. (48 refs.) Note: This instrument is presented in Chapter 9.

Sacks S. Co-occurring mental and substance use disorders: Promising approaches and research issues (review). *Substance Use & Misuse* 35(12/14):2061–2093, 2000. (138 refs.)

Sacks S, Ries RK. *Substance Abuse Treatment for Persons with Co-Occurring Disorder. A Treatment Improvement Protocol, No. 42.* Rockville, MD: Center for Substance Abuse Treatment, 2005.

Stahl SM. *Essential Psychopharmacology: Neuroscientific Basis and Practical Applications, Second Edition.* Cambridge, UK: Cambridge University Press, 2000. Note: Covers the actions and uses of all psychotropic medications, with excellent cartoon illustrations of actions of medications.

Verheul R. Co-morbidity of personality disorders in individuals with substance use disorders. *European Psychiatry* 16(5):274–282, 2001. (62 refs.)

Wilens TE, Faraone SV, Biederman J, Gunawardene S. Does stimulant therapy of attention-deficit/hyperactivity disorder beget later substance abuse? A meta-analytic review of the literature (review). *Pediatrics* 111(1):179–185, 2003. (56 refs.)

Williams JM, Ziedonis D. Addressing tobacco among individuals with a mental illness or an addiction (review). *Addictive Behaviors* 29(6):1067–1083, 2004. (109 refs.)

CHAPTER 13

Drugs of Abuse Other Than Alcohol

The focus of this book has been on alcohol. Alcohol and our other socially legal drug, nicotine, along with caffeine, are the most widely used psychoactive agents. An understanding of alcohol—its actions, the process of abuse, and dependence—provides a solid backdrop for considering any substance use. For those who use alcohol it is not uncommon that other drug use is also a part of the picture. When trying to deal with multiple drugs it is possible to feel overwhelmed by facts, in terms of acute effects, actions, side effects, withdrawal effects—lists, lists, lists. To help deal with that overload, this chapter endeavors to provide a tool box of basic concepts, which can help make sense of the phenomena that underlie drug use and help make drug effects intelligible. Following a discussion of the overall patterns of use and associated social problems, the chapter considers basic pharmacological concepts, followed by an overview of the major classes of drugs of abuse. Somewhat more attention is directed to nicotine and marijuana than other drugs, due to their wider use.

DRUG USE PATTERNS

The National Institute on Drug Abuse (NIDA) conducts 2 regular surveys of substance use—the *National Household Survey,* which samples the total population, and *Monitoring the Future,* a survey of high school students and young adults. In general there was an overall decline in illicit substance use during the 1980s. There was overall an almost 50% decline between 1979 and 1992. There was then a brief rise in use, but in 1995 use again began to fall. The other notable trend is that there was a drop in the age of first use over the past decade.

Table 13.1 Drug Use in 2003 by Those Age 12 and Older

Substance	Past Year	Past Month
Alcohol	65.0%	50.1%
Nicotine	35.1	29.8
Any illicit drug	14.7	8.2
Marijuana and hashish	10.6	6.2
Cocaine	2.5	1.0
Crack	0.6	0.3
Heroin	0.1	0.1
Hallucinogens	1.7	0.4
LSD	0.2	0.1
PCP	0.1	0.0
Ecstasy	0.9	0.2
Inhalants	0.9	0.2
Nonmedical use of any psychotherapeutics	6.3	2.7
Pain relievers	4.9	2.0
Oxycodone	1.2	0.8
Tranquilizers	2.1	0.8
Stimulants	1.2	0.5
Methamphetamine	0.6	0.3
Sedatives	0.3	0.1
Any illicit drug other than marijuana	8.5	3.7

From: Office of Applied Studies. *Results from the 2003 National Household Survey on Drug Use and Health. National Findings.* Rockville, MD: National Institute on Drug Abuse, 2004.

Table 13.1 outlines the percentages of those 12 and older in 2003 who reported alcohol, nicotine, and other drug use in the past year and the past month. Clearly alcohol and nicotine are the drugs of choice in the United States. While other drug use and its associated problems should in no way be discounted, the fact remains that alcohol and nicotine are far and away the American favorites. Sometimes this fact gets lost in discussions of "the war on drugs."

Age

Overall, about half of current illicit drug users are under age 26. While the rates of use of most drugs in 2003 are higher among youth and young

Table 13.2 Past Month Illicit Drug Use by Age Group, 2003

Drug	12–17	18–25	26 and Older
Any illicit drug use	11.2 %	20.3%	5.6%
Marijuana	7.9	17.0	4.0
Cocaine	0.6	2.2	0.8
Heroin	0.1	0.1	0.3
Hallucinogens	1.0	1.7	0.1
Nonmedical use of psychotherapeutics	4.0	6.0	1.9
Pain relievers	3.2	4.7	1.3
Tranquilizers	0.9	1.7	0.6
Methamphetamine	0.3	0.6	0.2
Sedatives	0.2	0.2	0.1

From: Office of Applied Studies. *Results from the 2003 National Household Survey on Drug Use and Health. National Findings.* Rockville, MD: National Institute on Drug Abuse, 2004.

adults than among older adults, the age distribution of users varies considerably for different drugs. There are some drugs that clearly are used primarily by the young. The percentages of different age groups who have used an illicit drug in the past month are presented in Table 13.2.

In terms of current use, compared to those over age 25, the rate for those ages 12 through 17 is almost twice as high, and the rate for those ages 18 through 25 is over three and a half times higher. While the rates of drug use are typically higher among youth and young adults, there is one notable exception, heroin.

Gender

In 2003, men continued to have a higher rate of current illicit drug use than women (10% vs. 6.5%). However, the differences are narrowing. For the youngest groups, under age 18, the rates of current illicit drug use are essentially the same, at 11.4% of boys and 11.1% of girls. So the gender gap has essentially disappeared in younger generations.

Education

Rates of illicit drug use are correlated with education levels. College graduates are more likely than those who have not completed high school to have used illicit drugs at some point. However, college graduates are less likely to be current users. Thus, while college graduates have higher levels of past use, whether social or experimental use, this use drops off in adulthood. For late adolescents and young adults, whether in or out of college, the rates of current illicit drug use are similar.

Employment

Employment status is correlated with drug use patterns. In 2003, it is estimated that, among the unemployed, the rate of current illicit drug use was 13.5%. This is over twice the rate for those who are employed full-time (6.3%) and higher than for those who are working part-time (6.4%).

Geographic Region

There are regional differences in drug use patterns. While the 2003 data have not been published, in 2000, illicit drug use was highest in the western United States (8%) followed by the Northeast (5.7%), Midwest (5.7%), and South (5.5%). Rates also vary by the type of community. Typically, as reported in 2000, they are highest in metropolitan areas (6.5%) and lowest in entirely rural communities (3.9%). If only younger people are considered, the differences between types of community are less marked.

SOCIAL COSTS

In 2000, the social costs associated with drug abuse were estimated to be $160.7 billion. This figure includes health-care costs, loss in productivity, expenditures for the criminal justice system, federal efforts to reduce supply, local policing, as well as treatment and prevention. A significant portion of the cost of drug abuse is attributable to costs within the criminal justice system. Another significant federal drug-related expenditure of $5,500 million is directed to supply reduction, primarily through policing and military efforts. By way of contrast, $826 million was spent on prevention, and $28 million on treatment in federal prisons.

Within the federal and state prison populations there are striking differences between the proportions of crimes attributable to drinking versus drug use. In general, alcohol is associated with crimes against people. Compared with other drug use, alcohol is twice as likely to play a role in homicides, 6 times as likely to be implicated in assaults, and 10 times as likely to be a factor in sexual assault. On the other hand, other drug use is associated with crimes against property. A drug other than alcohol is 8 times more common than alcohol in robberies, 10 times more common in burglaries, and 10 times more common in larceny/theft, except for auto theft, where the rate is only 2 times as high.

From the perspective of crime victims, what proportion of different crimes are attributable to drug abuse? About 30% of crimes involving property are attributed to drug abuse (larceny 30%, burglary 30%, robbery 27%). In terms of crimes against people, 16% of homicides are attributed to drug abuse, 5% of assaults, and 2.4% of rapes. In 2001, there were more arrests for violation of drug laws than for DWI. Fifteen percent of all arrests are drug related.

Of the total expenditures on corrections and prisons, a significant portion is attributed to illicit drugs, about $40 billion. Over a third of state and federal prisoners are incarcerated for drug-related crimes, primarily infractions of drug laws. A large portion of the drug cases handled by the criminal justice system is simply the result of the drug's illicit status, rather than being associated with other offenses attributable to drug use. Of the estimated 648,500 persons in prison or jail due to drug abuse, 70% of these violated drug laws. This is in comparison to 8% of drug-related incarcerations attributed to robbery or 3% involving homicide.

Ninety percent of all arrests for marijuana are for simple possession. They are not for dealing, for growing, or for committing crimes related to marijuana use. In addition, the penalties fall fairly evenly; there is little distinction in sentencing based on the individual's role in the drug trade system. Users and small-time dealers have sentences equivalent to those much higher up in the pyramid. And, as one author wryly noted, the people at the bottom have no room to plea-bargain or secure lighter sentences if they turn informer. Some of the laws passed that contributed to the rapid rise in the prison population have been the product of emotion, not reason. The most obvious is the distinction that is now made between cocaine as a powder and cocaine in the form of crack. The differences in penalties for use of equivalent amounts is striking. For a quantity of cocaine that as powder would be handled as a misdemeanor, the same amount in the form of crack leads to a felony charge and a 5-year mandatory prison term.

PUBLIC PERCEPTIONS AND PUBLIC POLICIES

Everybody who does not live in a prostitute's bed and on a diet of cocaine snow is called an ascetic nowadays.
George Bernard Shaw

Several factors influence the way in which we view and respond to substance use. The single major factor is legal status. Perceptions of a drug's danger are tied more to its legal status than to its pharmacological properties. There are any number of ways in which we see the problems of alcohol use as belonging to a "them," who are different from "us." The same is true of other drugs, but even more so. Substance use problems are often seen, erroneously, as existing primarily in urban inner cities, among minority groups, or within recent immigrant groups. There is a long historical precedent for this.

A drug's illicit status also has a major impact on how federal money is spent. A large proportion of the money spent on the war on drugs—and the use of this military metaphor should not be lost—is not for treatment or prevention. It is going to policing efforts, be it the Border Patrol, the Coast Guard, or narcotics divisions in police departments. A United Nations report estimates that 80% of the U.S. federal drug budget is spent on supply reduction. (Efforts are divided into supply reduction and demand reduction. Supply reduction consists generally of criminal justice initiatives, and demand reduction involves both prevention and treatment, so the desire and market for drugs are reduced.) This marks a dramatic increase from the early 1980s, when the expenditures for both were essentially equal. Accordingly, the criminal justice system has seen a dramatic rise in the prison population, the bulk of which is attributed to drug-related offenses. In part this has been the result of the introduction of mandatory sentences for drug-related offenses. There is concern that members of minority groups are those most likely to find themselves in prison, despite the fact that there are not correspondingly higher rates of use among this population. This raises serious questions about disparities in policing practices and judicial responses that are based on race.

The cloud of illegality plays a role in the perceptions of what constitutes appropriate treatment. Witness the discussion of methadone maintenance in the treatment of heroin addiction or needle exchange programs as a means of addressing the epidemic of HIV/AIDS, which is tied to the practice of sharing needles. Another topic that is guaranteed to evoke strong responses is discussion of the possible legalization of marijuana use, its prescription for medical use, or the suggestion that we decriminalize possession of small amounts for personal use. In the public health field, harm reduction is a very respectable approach. It is predicated on the recognition that, while preventing all use may be the long-range goal, in the interim there are steps that can be taken to reduce the negative consequences associated with use. Designated drivers are a good example of such a response to driving while intoxicated. Harm reduction, unfortunately, is seen as problematic when illegal drugs are involved. There is the fear among many that harm reduction efforts will inevitably be perceived as condoning use. One of the challenges is to create a public health response that can replace fear tactics with facts and that can see people as needing treatment and intervention, rather than primarily criminal sanctions. Our current criminal justice response is flawed by the failure to distinguish between large international cartels engaged in a major economic enterprise and casual users or small-time dealers, many of whom are only trying to support their own habits—in some cases, because treatment is not available.

Early Control Efforts

The efforts to control alcohol use are discussed in Chapter 1. There are some interesting differences between alcohol use and other drug use. From a cultural perspective, a number of drugs of abuse were originally viewed as therapeutic agents and were part of medical practice. For the

[Members of the commission] simply state that smoking marijuana in the privacy of your home should be perfectly legal—as long as no one gave it to you [or] sold it to you and you didn't grow it yourself.
W. WALTER MENNINGER
On Report by President's Commission on Marijuana and Drug Abuse, 1972

most part, the narcotics—such as morphine—and cocaine were recognized as problematic before the turn of the twentieth century. This recognition in part was prompted by the involvement of physicians in providing these drugs to patients and then being faced by the emergence of addiction. The "typical" narcotic addict at the end of the 1800s was a white female who had been prescribed narcotics for the treatment of a wide variety of "female problems." Beyond physician prescription was the host of patent medicines available, many of which contained narcotics.

Of note historically, drugs that were originally believed to be medically useful and nonproblematic turned out otherwise. For example, cocaine was initially touted as being very useful in weaning people from the opiates; thus, it was seen as a good means of treating opiate addicts. Rather quickly it became apparent that it, too, creates dependence and that one was simply substituting one addictive drug for another. Then there was the introduction of heroin by the Bayer Laboratory in 1898. The same pharmaceutical research team that synthesized heroin produced aspirin in the same month. Heroin was marketed as a cough suppressant and was believed—erroneously—to be superior to other available products. It was thought not merely to suppress coughs but also to improve lung function. Had this mistake not been made, in all probability heroin would never have been manufactured. Within a decade it was recognized that heroin does not promote lung function. However, by then it had taken on a life of its own.

The perceived indiscriminate use of such drugs by medical practitioners, popularly called "dope doctors," as well as their ready availability in over-the-counter preparations, sparked the passage of two key pieces of legislation in the United States. One was the legislation that created the Food and Drug Administration in 1906. It contained what were the earliest federal provisions affecting narcotics. Any over-the-counter preparations containing opiates, cannabis (marijuana), cocaine, or chloral hydrate needed to have a label identifying these and the relative percentage(s). The other key legislation was the Harrison Act, passed in 1914, which classified certain drugs as "controlled substances." This meant that they could no longer be sold over-the-counter but could be dispensed only by physicians and used only for medical purposes. In the earliest days of the Harrison Act, providing these drugs to addicted people was considered a legitimate purpose. However, this understanding of proper use was rather quickly eliminated. Along with that there was the closing of the small number of clinics that had been established to provide drugs to existing addicts.

Sources of Illicit Drugs

The sources of illicit drugs vary with the particular drug. However, each type of drug tends to have its own distinctive and characteristic pattern of manufacture or processing and distribution. In the cases of heroin and cocaine there are large organizations involved, which in effect are counterparts to legal international pharmaceutical companies. Cocaine production, based on processing of coca leaves, which are grown in the countries of the Andes—Bolivia, Peru, and Colombia—in South America, is centered in Colombia. Heroin production is based on the cultivation of opium poppies, which now are being grown predominantly in Afghanistan. In both cases there are large organizations—the drug cartels centered in Colombia and Mafia-like organization(s) for opium.

Prescription drugs become available either through diversion of legally prescribed medications to illegal markets, or via importing from countries where these drugs are legal. For example, the sources of OxyContin on the street are through sales of legitimate prescriptions, prescription forgeries, and burglary of pharmacies. A pill that costs approximately $4 by prescription may sell for from $20 to $40 on the street. A study of persons declaring possession of prescription drugs on entry into the United States from Mexico found the most common drugs being brought in are those used by adolescents and young adults—benzodiazepines, including Rohypnol®, known as one of the date-rape drugs. Synthetic drugs not prescription medications, particularly the stimulants, are manufactured in small laboratories scattered about the United States, particularly in rural areas. Then there is marijuana. There are backyard growers, but increasingly marijuana is becoming a professionally cultivated crop. In northern California cannabis has been described as *the* major cash crop.

Drug Diversion

The potential for the diversion of drugs and their use for unintended purposes is a concern with medications having psychoactive properties. However, steps can be taken in the manufacturing process to help reduce the abuse potential. The failure to have taken this into account is what caused a delay in the FDA's final approval of buprenorphine as an alternative to methadone in the treatment of heroin dependence. Now another drug, naloxone, is added to buprenorphine as it is manufactured. Naloxone is an opiate antagonist, meaning it blocks the ability of opiates to have an effect. When injected, it goes quickly to the opiate receptors, where it displaces any opiates already there. When taken orally or under the tongue, as buprenorphine (Suboxone), it has essentially no effect. Buprenorphine alone has some abuse potential, especially when crushed and injected. If the combination drug is crushed and injected, however, and if the person is already on an opiate, the Naloxone causes the person to go into immediate and very uncomfortable withdrawal. With this mixed formulation, the potential for abuse is significantly reduced. Such a formulation is not a new idea, and the pharmaceutical company that produces OxyContin® has been criticized for not having anticipated the potential for abuse and done this as well.

Pharmaceutical companies certainly cannot be held responsible for the abuse of their products. But it is not unreasonable to expect they will take reasonable steps within their means to reduce the potential for abuse.

Cocaine Lil and Morphine Sue

Did you ever hear about Cocaine Lil?
She lived in Cocaine town on Cocaine hill,
She had a cocaine dog and a cocaine cat,
They fought all night with a cocaine rat.
She had cocaine hair on her cocaine head.
She had a cocaine dress that was poppy red:
She wore a snowbird hat and sleigh-riding clothes,
On her coat she wore a crimson, cocaine rose.

Big gold chariots on the Milky Way,
Snakes and elephants silver and gray.
Oh the cocaine blues they make me sad,
Oh the cocaine blues make me feel bad.

Lil went to a snow party one cold night,
And the way she sniffed was sure a fright.
There was Hophead Mag with Dopey Slim,
Kankakee Liz and Yen Shee Jim.

There was Morphine Sue and the Poppy Face Kid,
Climbed up snow ladders and down they skid;
There was the Stepladder Kit, a good sixfeet,
And the Sleigh-riding Sister who were hard to beat.

Along in the morning about half past three
They were all lit up like a Christmas tree;
Lil got home and started for bed,
Took another sniff and it knocked her dead.
They laid her out in her cocaine clothes:
She wore a snowbird hat with a crimson rose;
On her headstone you'll find this refrain:
She died as she lived, sniffing cocaine.

ANONYMOUS

Included in *Oxford Book of Light Verse*, W.H. Auden, Ed., 1938

No, I was never the victim of a date-rape drug, but I was once the victim of an apricot brandy hicky.

It was for this reason that the manufacturer of Rohypnol®, Hoffman-LaRoche, made changes in the manufacturing process after reports began to circulate about the association of Rohypnol with date rape. (Rohypnol is not approved for use in the United States, but is marketed in Europe and Latin America.) Rohypnol, a benzodiazepine, is odorless, colorless, and tasteless. According to media accounts it has been surreptitiously slipped into women's drinks, and the women do not realize they are consuming a drug. In combination with alcohol, there are additive effects, so intoxication occurs more quickly than with alcohol alone, which is all the woman thinks she is ingesting. In response to these reports, Hoffman-LaRoche added another ingredient to Rohypnol. This does not affect its psychoactive properties, but it does turn any liquid a milky white. So this provides a warning that something is amiss. In addition Hoffman-LaRoche took other steps. It made considerable efforts to assist date rape victims by providing free, comprehensive testing for Rohypnol to EDs, law enforcement agencies, and sexual assault crisis clinics. (The pharmacological properties of Rohypnol [flunitrazepam] are discussed later in this chapter within the section "Sedative-Hypnotics.")

This raises another issue worth noting. Things are not always as they seem. This is especially true of self-reports and the use of street drugs. There is no question about the abuse of flunitrazepam (Rohypnol). There *is* reason to question whether the level of rapes supposedly associated with its use are as extensive as have been reported. One medical center emergency department examined the results of laboratory tests of more than 1,000 consecutive tests that were performed in cases suspected to involve flunitrazepam. The tests involved urine samples. Of the 1,077 tests performed, flunitrazepam was present in only 6 of the tests! Of all the cases, 41% of all assays were negative for all drugs tested. The remaining 59% had one or more detectable drugs, including alcohol. The breakdown was alcohol (36%), marijuana (18%), all other benzodiazepines (6%), and GHB (4%). Another study similarly raises questions about the reliability of reports of flunitrazepam use. Interviews were conducted with women who identified themselves as using flunitrazepam. However, when asked to describe the appearance of the "Rohypnol" they had taken, the descriptions being provided were not for Rohypnol but were consistent with the appearance of other benzodiazepines. Here, too, there was a wide range of other drug use reported. The substance abuse field seems to have its own versions of Internet urban myths.

BASIC PHARMACOLOGICAL CONCEPTS

How to Think about Drug Use

In reviewing textbooks about drugs of abuse, organized in the format of one chapter per drug, it is all too easy to feel you are drowning in facts and a little short on understanding. If this has been your experience, a different starting point is suggested. Forget about the different drugs. Instead, begin by considering several basic, essential principles that are pertinent to understanding *any* drug. These include how drugs are taken into the body; how rapidly they are delivered to the brain; how they are metabolized and the kinds of by-products that may be produced in this process; how rapidly they are removed; abuse potential; and how they affect the brain to produce their effects including sites of action. The following sections discuss these key elements. With this information as background, the next task is to think in terms of different classes of drugs. All drugs in a particular class, by definition, share many features. To know to which class a drug belongs is to have considerable information.

Route of Administration

Route of administration is the term used for how a substance in taken into the body. To very briefly recap the points made in Chapter 3, drugs are administered by different means. They can be taken by mouth, inhaled, or absorbed through the skin; they can be injected into the bloodstream, just under the skin, or into a muscle. The route of administration has an impact on how a drug's effects are experienced. The route of administration influences how quickly the drug reaches the brain, as well as how much of the drug is lost in the process. Recall that when smoking, the drug enters the blood stream quickly but a portion of the drug literally goes up in smoke. Similarly a portion of alcohol is metabolized in the stomach and thus a portion of the amount ingested never enters the bloodstream. On the other hand, a drug that is injected intravenously will be rapidly and totally available.

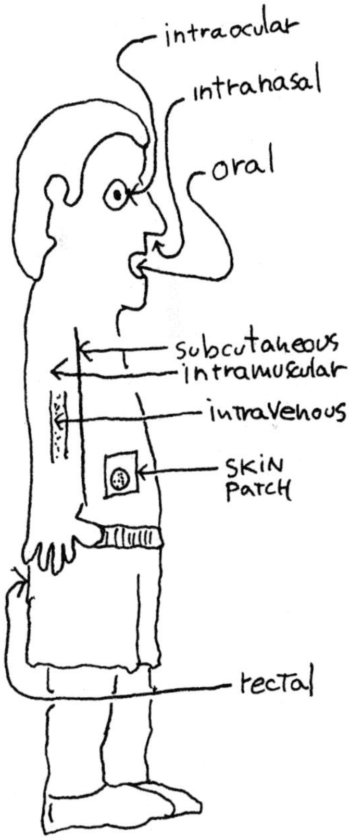

The route of administration also has significance in terms of the kinds of problems that can result from use. These can potentially be greater than the drug's direct effects. As one physician commented to a smoker, "I really don't object to your drug of choice, but how you deliver it!" Many of the long-term health problems are tied to the *smoking,* not to the nicotine. It is the addictive properties of the nicotine that prompt the continuation of the dangerous practice of smoking. Indeed, were all smokers to replace their cigarettes for equivalent daily doses of nicotine delivered via nicotine patches, with the nicotine absorbed through the skin, the rates of respiratory problems, chronic lung disease, bronchitis, emphysema, and lung cancer would decline dramatically. In the same vein, many of the long-term problems associated with smoking marijuana do not come from the THC, in its 61 varieties. They come from the more than 350 other compounds in the smoke and the superexposure to these that is associated with holding the marijuana smoke in the lungs. Due to this smoking style, one joint is equivalent to far more than one cigarette.

Wacky Dust

They call it wacky dust
It's from a hot cornet,
It gives your feet a feeling so breezy
And oh, it's so easy to get.
They call it wacky dust
It brings the dancin' jazz
And when it starts
And only a sap will refuse to
be appled or jazzed.
So I don't know just why it get you so high,
Puttin' a buzz in your heart.
You'll do a marathon, you'll want to go on,
Kickin' the ceiling apart.
They call it wacky dust.
It's something you can trust.
And in the end, the rhythm will stop
When it does then you'll drop,
From happy, wacky dust.

Recorded by Chick Webb and His Orchestra, 1938, with Ella Fitzgerald

Site of Action

The motivation for taking substances is to alter mood states and/or alter perceptions. This is accomplished by the effects of the drug on various areas of the brain as well as which neurotransmitter systems are affected by a drug. Drugs typically have various effects on specific neurotransmitter system(s). These include action on the levels of the neurotransmitters themselves, the chemical messengers, as well as the receptor sites, where the neurotransmitters have their effects. While a simplification, there are certain kinds of predictable possible ways that abused substances can affect the neurotransmitter system. The drugs may prevent a neurotransmitter from breaking down, leading to a build-up of the neurotransmitter. It can prevent amounts of a neurotransmitter secreted into the space between nerve cells from being taken back up by the sending cell (which would normally occur), resulting in more of the neurotransmitter's being available to the receiving cell. Taking a drug may lower the production of a particular neurotransmitter, thus leading to a lower than normal level of that neurotransmitter. Or the drug may block the site where the neurotransmitter acts and thus prevents it from having its usual effects. In such cases, while there is the usual amount present, it can't have an effect. The exact result of this build-up or shortage depends on the effects of that neurotransmitter. Finally, in some cases, drugs not only can affect the chemical signaling system overseen by neurotransmitters but can also have a generalized effect on the nerve cell, acting as a toxin, or making them simply more sluggish.

A discussion of all the neurotransmitter systems and the receptor sites that play a role in substance use and abuse is beyond the scope of this book. The following neurotransmitters are likely those most commonly discussed: GABA (inhibitory, slows communication); norepinephrine (activating, enhances communication); dopamine (associated with feelings of pleasure); serotonin (associated with anxiety, depression, aggressiveness); and glutamate (the major excitatory neurotransmitter).

Another factor that is significant is the site in the brain where the various neurotransmitters are located. Consider marijuana. One of its effects is the alteration of perception. Accordingly it may contribute to accidents that can cause deaths. But there are no known deaths due to its toxic effects. There is no blood marijuana concentration that is lethal. Essentially this is because the brain stem, which controls basic body functions, such as heart function or respiration, does not contain any of the neurotransmitters that are affected by marijuana in any significant way.

Marijuana is . . . self-punishing. It makes you acutely sensitive, and in this world, what worse punishment could there be?
P. J. O'ROURKE
Rolling Stone, 1989

Solubility in Fat and/or Water

Drugs differ in whether they are soluble in water or fat or both water and fat. Recall how the differences between men and women in the body's relative proportions of water and fat influence their blood alcohol concentrations. All else being equal, being of the same weight, with equivalent doses of alcohol, women with proportionately more body fat and less tissue water have a higher blood alcohol level. Whether a drug is fat or water soluble determines how it is distributed in the body and where and how long it is stored. One way in which this is of practical significance is its implications for drug testing. Drugs that are fat soluble leave long-lasting traces in tissues in a way that alcohol does not. Thus, detectable amounts of a drug may be present in blood samples due to their slow release from fat stores, long after the last intake of the drug. One can also test hair samples and fingernails to identify use of a drug. For alcohol, once the blood alcohol drops to zero, there is no similar continuing evidence of recent use, as there is with other drugs. (The measure of carbohydrate-deficient transferrin is a good though an indirect marker of recent drinking. This liver enzyme, which is responsible for transporting iron, is influenced by alcohol consumption.) The active ingredient in marijuana, on the other hand, is very fat soluble and is released slowly from fat. It may therefore be present in urine drug screens of heavy, regular users for weeks after the last use.

Metabolism

How a drug is metabolized and removed from the body suggests the kinds of problems that may result. As was discussed in Chapters 3 and 6, alcohol is metabolized by enzymes that are produced primarily in the liver and to a lesser degree in the stomach. One of these enzyme systems, Cytochrome P450, also known as MEOS, is involved as well in the metabolism of other drugs. Thus, if different drugs are present, both requiring the same enzymes, they are in competition and the removal of both is slowed.

Another potential problem is the by-products formed during metabolism. Recall the danger of drinking non-beverage alcohol is due to the toxicity of substances formed when they are metabolized. In some instances there are by-products that are formed if two drugs are present simultaneously. Alcohol and cocaine is one example. They form cocaethylene. This is a metabolite that has properties similar to those of cocaine but, in fact, may be more toxic to the heart and liver. This byproduct, acting as a "booster," may make drinking while taking cocaine more attractive but problem-ridden. (See pages 137–138.)

Abuse Potential

Drugs vary in their potential for abuse. As discussed in Chapter 5, the speed of action and the duration of the effects are two significant factors that influence this. For example, with cocaine or nicotine, the risk is considerable. The effects are felt very quickly and also wear off quickly, increasing the likelihood of abuse. With some drugs the user has several

Table 13.3 Percentage of Past-Year Users Who Meet Diagnostic Criteria for Abuse or Dependence

Nicotine*	85.0%	Marijuana	16.6%	Tranquilizers	8.6%
Heroin	57.4	Stimulants	13.7	Hallucinogens	8.2
Cocaine	25.6	Pain relievers	12.2	Inhalants	8.2
Sedatives	19.0	Alcohol	11.5		

From: Office of Applied Studies. *Results from the 2003 National Household Survey on Drug Use and Health. National Findings.* Rockville, MD: National Institute on Drug Abuse, 2004.

*Nicotine data were not included in the NIDA report. This number was drawn from *NIDA Notes* 13(3):1–4, 1998, on levels of dependence.

Cocaine habit-forming? Of course not. I ought to know. I've been using it for years.
TALLULAH BANKHEAD

choices in terms of how he or she takes them. With marijuana, there is the choice of smoking it or adding it to the brownies. With cocaine, there are the options of snorting, smoking, and injecting. As someone's drug career unfolds, it is likely that the individual will adopt more effective routes of administration. In the wake of this, with more rapid delivery comes a more intense experience of the drug effects, a condition inviting further use.

The *National Household Survey on Drug Use and Health 2003* provides information on the percentage of current users of various drugs and the proportion of current users whose survey responses indicate the presence of abuse or dependence. As shown in Table 13.3, the relative rates of abuse or dependence provide a good measure of the likelihood that use turns into problematic use.

Based on the responses to the *National Household Survey,* NIDA estimates in 2003 that 21.6 million persons aged 12 or older were dependent on alcohol and/or an illicit drug. This is equivalent to 9.1% of the total population. The bulk of these represent alcohol abuse or dependence (69%). The remainder are roughly divided between an illicit drug alone (18%) and alcohol abuse dependence in combination with an illicit drug problem (14%).

However, there is a glaring omission in these figures. They fail to include nicotine. What might be a more accurate estimate of the true number? Using the NIDA survey estimate for current nicotine use in general population of 29%, and applying the accepted rate of for dependence, means that at least 20% of the population is nicotine dependent. Even if you grant that everyone already identified as abusing or dependent on a substance also is in trouble with nicotine, that still leaves 11% of population with nicotine dependence unaccounted for. Rather than 21.6 million, a better estimate would be at least 56 million with substance abuse or dependence.

Abuse potential is a pharmacological concept. It is based on the effects of a drug. However, outside of a laboratory setting there are social factors that influence the likelihood of abuse. One is social acceptance of use. Closely linked to social acceptance is the opportunity for use. Even if a drug were ranked up there with the greatest pharmacological abuse potential, it would not be widely abused if there were little access to it. Virtually every adult of legal drinking age has the opportunity to use alcohol. Given the manner in which alcohol is used socially, for many the choice is whether to or not to drink. While it is not uncommon for a host or hostess to wander through a party with a tray of drinks for guests, this is hardly the case with illicit drugs. One does not usually find a tray with lines of cocaine or syringes with heroin being passed along with the cheese and crackers and onion dip. The *Monitoring the Future Survey* of students routinely asks questions about attitudes toward use and also the students' sense of how easy it would be to get a particular drug. Similarly the *Household Survey* asks about availability, and perceptions of whether obtaining a drug would be fairly or very easy to do. Among adults in 2003, 56% report marijuana as easy to obtain. For young adults this figure is 78%. Among adults the perception of easy access for cocaine, hallucinogens, and heroin is reduced, being 31%, 19%, and 19%, respectively.

Problems

Many of the problems resulting from alcohol apply to other drug use. As with alcohol, the *pharmacological effects* of a given drug can lead to acute problems in the absence of dependence. As is true with alcohol, even in the absence of dependence there are other significant potential problems. There are problems of acute use be it overdose or the result of intoxication and problems from long-term use. With alcohol as the point of reference, the tendency is to think that major medical problems occur only after extended heavy use. It may literally be decades of heavy drinking before irreversible liver damage or brain damage occurs. However, this is not universally true with other drugs; there is considerable variability among substances. For example, even after relatively short periods of use, inhalants can have serious medical consequences, with permanent brain damage.

With other drugs, the *presence of contaminants* as well as *by-products of metabolism* are a concern. The potential for irreversible toxic effects was brought home in the late 1980s, in the efforts of illicit labs to produce a designer drug, a version of meperidine (Demerol®). A neurotoxin was present in the drugs manufactured. This by-product, MPTP (methyl-phenyl-tetrahydropyridine), is noted for its ability to induce Parkinsonian symptoms. A number of users of that batch developed drug-induced Parkinson's disease, which is wholly nonreversible. Another concern is related to the *route of administration.* Intravenous use as a means of drug administration has special problems—namely, infection from nonsterile techniques and from the sharing of syringes. Also with injection drug use, there can be problems that simply come from

Table 13.4 Estimated Lethal Doses of Abused Psychoactive Substances

Drug	Route of Administration	Safety Ratio	Usual Lethal Dose
Heroin	intravenous	6	50 mg
Isobutyl nitrite	inhaled	8	1.51 ml vaporized liquid
GHB	oral	8	16 gr
Alcohol	oral	10	330 g
DXM	oral	10	1.5
Methamphetamine	oral	10	>150 mg
Cocaine	nasal	15	1200 mg
MDMA	oral	16	2 g
Methadone	oral	20	100 mg
Codeine	oral	20	800 mg
Mescaline	oral	24	8.4 gr*
Rohypnol	oral	30	30 mg
Ketamine	nasal	38	2.7 g
DMT	oral	50	2 g
Phenobarbital	oral	100	>2 g
Prozac	oral	100	>2 g
Nitrous oxide†	inhaled	>150	>525 l
Psilocybin	oral	1000	6 g
Marijuana	smoked	1000	>15 g
LSD	oral	1000	100 mg*

*Extrapolated from animal studies.

†Never toxic if used with adequate oxygen. Nonmedical doses usually 100% N_2O, and death is due to atoxia.

From: Gable RS. Comparison of acute lethal toxicity of commonly abused psychoactive substances. (review). *Addiction* 99(6):686–696, 2004. (103 refs.)

inexperience and uninformed injection practices. As a drug career takes hold, when the drug can be taken by multiple routes there is the likelihood that people will go from less to more dangerous routes, such as from sniffing or oral routes of administration to intravenous use.

Toxicity and Overdose

Drugs vary considerably in the risks of unintentional death from an overdose. Several measures are used in considering toxicity. One of these is known as the median lethal dose, the shorthand for which is LD_{50}. This term, which originated in toxicology laboratory studies, represents the amount of a drug at which half of the animals to which it is administered die. An LD_{50} doesn't represent the dose at which deaths begin to occur, it is the midpoint; already 49% of deaths have occurred. Another relevant value is the median effective dose, known as ED_{50}. This value indicates the dose that 50% of animals need to take to get the desired effects. In thinking about the relative safety of any drug, an important factor is the size of the window between the dose needed to get the desired effect and the dose at which death occurs. When these values are very close together, there is little margin for error. The relationship of the lethal dose to the effective dose is termed the safety ratio.

A recent review drawing upon the literature on drug effects, overdose, and fatalities, assembled this relevant toxicological information for commonly used substances of abuse. All these reports were carefully screened to eliminate reports and studies in which there were multiple drugs present. This data are summarized in Table 13.4, and apply to a healthy, 70 kg adult, without tolerance to the substance or residue from prior administrations, and in the absence of other drugs.

As is apparent there are substantial differences in the safety ratio of different drugs. The most toxic substances have a lethal dose less than 10 times the effective dose. These substances include GHB, heroin, and isobutyl nitrite. The next most acutely toxic substances, with safety ratios from 10 to 20, include alcohol, cocaine, codeine, dextromethorphan (DXM), ecstasy/MDMA, methadone, and methamphetamine.

Keep in mind that this review was limited to the data available. Also, remember that such numbers represent averages and cannot predict the outcome for a particular individual. And an LD_{50} doesn't represent the dose at which deaths begin to occur; it is the midpoint, and already 49% have died. This is not to be confused for a value denoting the beginning of a danger zone.

CLASSIFICATION SCHEMAS FOR SUBSTANCES OF ABUSE

There are a variety of ways in which drugs of abuse can be classified. The particular system used in a discussion can be more or less helpful, depending on the purpose. Whether a drug is licit or illicit certainly makes a difference in considering the social consequences of use. However, this way of categorizing drugs may or may not provide much insight into the medical problems inherent with use or the risk of abuse and dependence. It certainly doesn't say much about the subjective effects that accompany use and the properties that may make them attractive to some people. For those purposes, other schema may be more useful.

Licit versus Illicit

Commonly, distinctions are made between licit and illicit drugs. On the one hand are alcohol and nicotine, and on the other everything else. Prescription drugs don't quite fit into this format. While not illegal, if used for nonmedical purposes this suggests abuse. The licit/illicit dichotomy certainly has implications for law enforcement and societal problems. This distinction can also have health implications. Illicit drugs, by definition, are manufactured without government control or oversight and thus can be of questionable purity and strength. Heroin may have been cut many times, or barely cut at all, and thus the true dose may be higher or lower than what the user expects. Supposed prescription drugs sold on the street may or may not be what they are alleged to be. Caveat emptor (a Latin phrase meaning "Let the buyer beware").

DEA Schedule

The Controlled Substance Act, which originated as the Harrison Act, is a federal law that identifies some drugs as controlled substances and sets forth rules and regulations about their manufacture, use, and distribution. The Food and Drug Administration (FDA) houses the administration machinery for determining the status of a drug. Controlled substances are limited to those for which there is potential for abuse. If controlled, the drug is placed in 1 of 5 categories, depending on the assessment of its potential for abuse, potential for dependence, and current accepted medical use:

Schedule I. Any drug included here has a high level of abuse/dependence. Also, there is no accepted medical use. Included are heroin, LSD, and marijuana.

Schedule II. These drugs are essentially similar to those in Schedule I. There is evidence of the potential for abuse/dependence. The distinguishing feature in Schedule II is that there is accepted medical use. There are restrictions on manufacture and distribution via production quotas and import and export controls. Prescriptions are nonrefillable. Schedule II drugs include methadone, morphine, amphetamines, and cocaine.

Schedule III. Drugs in this category are considered to be at moderate risk or low risk for physical dependence but at high risk for psychological dependence. There are currently established reasons for medical use. Schedule III drugs include Vicodin and Tylenol #3 and #4.

Schedule IV. Drugs in this category are considered to be at low risk for physical dependence but moderate risk for psychological dependence. There are currently accepted indications for medical use. Drugs in this group include Valium, Ativan, Halcion, and Darvon.

Schedule V. Drugs in this category are considered to be at low risk for both physical dependence and psychological dependence. Again, there are currently accepted indications for medical use. Lomotil is an example.

Controlled Substance Analogs

Controlled substances are essentially identified by their chemical formulas. Those manufacturing drugs in illicit laboratories found a way around the law. They changed the drug slightly, so that the drug's chemical composition was no longer that specified by the law. For that reason these drugs are sometimes called "designer drugs." However, the changes were for the most part inconsequential in terms of the drugs' effects. A Porsche is a Porsche; it doesn't matter if it comes in charcoal gray or bright red. To plug up this loophole, an amendment was added to the Controlled Substance Act as part of the Anti-Drug Abuse Act of 1986. It created a new category—*controlled substance analog.* This is a category used for drugs that are chemically very similar to drugs in Schedule I or Schedule II. They are treated as Schedule I drugs, without any redeeming social value.

Emergency or Temporary Scheduling

To deal with the unexpected, in 1984, as part of the Comprehensive Crime Control Act, an amendment to the Controlled Substance Act was passed to allow immediate action in dealing with drugs that show up on the street and are not covered by the existing schedule. The head of the DEA has the authority to declare a drug as Schedule I on a temporary basis, until research can be conducted to ascertain the drug's properties and the appropriate schedule.

Pharmacological Effects

Another way of classifying drugs is to group them in terms of their primary effects. This is essentially the classification schema used in the APA's *Diagnostic and Statistical Manual.* This is of particular use to those working in the clinical field. This is how those who use illicit drugs tend to think about them. This is seen by some of the slang terms, with the references to a family of drugs, such as talk of "uppers" or "downers." People will consider some drugs as more or less an adequate substitute for one another. If someone likes to take LSD but can't get any, peyote might be an acceptable substitute. But it is far less likely for a sedative to be considered an adequate alternative.

Equally important for the clinician, with a few exceptions, drugs in the same class share important characteristics. They are used for a particular effect, have similar effects on the brain, have similar symptoms of overdose or toxicity, and have similar withdrawal syndromes. These commonalities are also the basis for the treatment of withdrawal.

MAJOR CLASSES OF COMMONLY ABUSED DRUGS

Nicotine

Patterns of Use

Nicotine ranks right up there with alcohol, the other licit drug, as one of the most widely used in the United States. In addition, it ranks up there as a major public health concern. Since the late 1960s, when 40% of the adult population smoked, there has been a steady decline in nicotine use. Presently the proportion of the population who are current smokers is 25%. There is another 4% who use other nicotine products—smokeless tobacco, cigars, pipes—but don't smoke cigarettes. About 20% of smokers also use other nicotine products. For a long time, nicotine use was equated with smoking cigarettes. It is only recently that the *National Household Survey* began to ask questions about different forms of tobacco. In terms of absolute numbers, there are 77.2 million using nicotine in the United States. By way of contrast, the number of persons using any illicit drug other than marijuana is estimated to be 9.8 million. So for every 1 person who is using an illicit drug (other than marijuana), there are about 8 smokers.

Demographics of Use

Overall, men are more likely to use tobacco than are women. However, over the years, because men have quit smoking at a higher rate than women, and because among younger people there is virtually no difference by sex, the *gender gap* is disappearing. When it comes to age, the rate of regular tobacco use rises dramatically from age 12 through 16. The percentage of regular smokers virtually doubles for each year, moving from 1.7% of 12-year-olds being regular users to 22% of 16-year-olds. At that point, the rate of increase drops by half through age 22. Twenty-two-year-olds are the age group with the highest proportion of regular smokers, at about 43.5%. However, while the proportion of smokers begins to decline, the rate of decline is much, much more gradual. You have to look to those in their late 50s before the proportion of smokers is equivalent to that of 16-year-olds. With respect to racial/ethnic differences, Native Americans have the highest rate of regular smokers, at 36%, followed by whites (27%), African-Americans (26%), Hispanics (21%), and Asians (13%). The rates of nicotine use vary considerably among Asian people of different ethnicity. The rate of nicotine use among Korean Americans, who have the highest level of use, is essentially twice the rate among Chinese Americans, who have the lowest rate. There are similarly different rates among Hispanic groups. Among adults, higher levels of education are associated with lower levels of nicotine use. In terms of employment status, the highest rate of nicotine use is among the unemployed, and the lowest rate is among part-time workers. Geography is also a factor; the region with the highest percentage of nicotine users is the South; the West has the lowest rate, although the Northeast is not far behind. The size of the community also plays a role; the highest level of smoking is found in rural areas, and the lowest rates are in metropolitan areas.

Tobacco and opium have broad backs, and will cheerfully carry the load of armies, if you choose to make them pay high for such joy as they give and such harm as they do.

RALPH WALDO EMERSON

Civilization, 1870

Associated Drug Use

Smoking is also strongly associated with other substance use. One of the best predictors of other drug use is smoking status. Many studies have found that those who use tobacco are more likely to use other substances—sedatives, hallucinogens, stimulants, and opiates. According to *National Household Survey* (2000) data, compared with those who don't use nicotine, those who smoke are almost 8 times more likely to use cocaine, 14 times more likely to use crack, 16 times more likely to use heroin, and 7 times more likely to use marijuana. In addition, those who smoke cigarettes are more likely to use other drugs that are smoked, so that, having become used to this route of administration of drugs, these users have a greater likelihood of experimenting with other drugs that are smoked. For example, in that study, among those who entered treatment for smoked cocaine, virtually all (97%) had a history of smoking cigarettes prior to cocaine use. Also of interest, if other substances were smoked, on quitting smoking cocaine, people stopped smoking other drugs, with one exception, nicotine. Half quit smoking marijuana and a third decreased their marijuana use when they ceased cocaine use. But only 5% quit smoking cigarettes.

The general association of nicotine use with other drug use is especially striking among teenagers. Those under age 18 who smoke cigarettes are 9 times more likely to have used an illicit drug in the past month. In terms of specific drugs, teenage smokers are 15 times more likely than their nonsmoking peers to have used marijuana, 38 times more likely than nonsmoking teens to have used cocaine, and 7 times more likely to have used inhalants.

Abuse Potential

Nicotine is a drug with a high potential for abuse/dependence. This is dramatically highlighted by the title of one journal article: "The Nicotine Addiction Trap: A 40-Year Sentence for Four Cigarettes." The authors noted that, as of 1990, the point at which the article was published, "over 90% of teenagers who smoke 3–4 cigarettes are trapped into a career of regular smoking which typically lasts for some 30–40 years. Only 35% of regular smokers succeed in stopping permanently before the age of 60, although the large majority want to stop and try to stop." So if people can manage to smoke 3 to 4 cigarettes and get through the initial effects—which, in fact are not pleasant (dizziness and sometimes nausea)—they will be embarking on a smoking career that statistically is likely to go on for at least 4 decades. The bulk of smokers begin smoking as adolescents. Daily about 1,000 adolescents first use nicotine.

Another perspective on the high rate of dependence among those who use nicotine can be gleaned by looking at the proportion of "past-year" smokers who are also current smokers, which is defined as use in the past month. The percentage of past-year users who are also current users is suggestive of the extent of physical dependence associated with use. How does nicotine compare with illicit drugs? Heroin and crack cocaine have the highest level of past-year users who are also current users—essentially, 100%. Next comes nicotine, 84%. This rate is in the range of about 3 times as high as many illicit drugs.

Pharmacological Action

There are different types of nicotinic receptor sites found throughout the brain. They are present in differing concentrations, and there is considerable complexity in how they function. There is evidence, too, that the number and concentration of sites increase with the use of tobacco. The receptors appear to be located both on cell bodies and at the nerve terminals. These receptors are associated with the release of an array of neurotransmitters: acetylcholine, norepinephrine, serotonin, beta endorphin, glutamate, and dopamine, which is recognized for its rewarding properties. Nicotine also leads to the release of growth hormone, prolactin, and ACTH (adrenocorticotropin hormone) by the pituitary gland. Tolerance to nicotine develops very rapidly. The dizziness, nausea, and possible vomiting that accompany the first cigarette is diminished by the second, and virtually absent after several. Research suggests that within a day of regular smoking there is also tolerance to the subjective effects and increased heart rate. Also, examination of accidental nicotine poisonings has shown that the immediate toxic effects disappear even though high levels of nicotine remain in the blood.

Absorption and Metabolism

When smoked, nicotine is carried by tar droplets, which are inhaled and deposited in the air sacs of the lungs. The nicotine then passes very quickly into the bloodstream, via the small air sacs in the lungs. Very rapidly, in 10 to 19 seconds, it enters the brain. Very little smoked nicotine is absorbed through the mucous membranes in the mouth, though. This is because smoked nicotine is slightly acidic, which prevents absorption. However, chewed tobacco products are slightly alkaline and are absorbed by these membranes. The speed with which nicotine reaches the brain depends on the route of administration, with smoking being the fastest. While the nicotine is delivered quickly to the brain, the level of nicotine in the brain declines rapidly as nicotine is then distributed to tissues in other parts of the body. Between cigarettes, the level declines and provides an opportunity for the brain's nicotine receptors to be recharged.

Given the difference in smoking patterns, it is difficult to estimate the dose of nicotine with any precision. In one study, in a group of regular smokers, the level of nicotine per cigarette averaged 1 mg, but ranged from 0.37 to 1.57 mg. For chewing tobacco, the intake is roughly equivalent to 4½ cigarettes if the wad is kept in the mouth for a half hour. The half-life of nicotine averages 2 hours; however, regular smokers often do not space cigarettes 2 hours apart. Consequently, with the regular administration of nicotine, the level of nicotine persists throughout the day, accumulates, and persists throughout the night. Nicotine is metabolized primarily by the liver and a much smaller amount by the lungs, and excretion by the kidneys accounts for at most 20%. The nicotine is broken down into several compounds. The major metabolic product is cotinine. It remains in the body for a longer period than the nicotine. Its half-life is 16 hours, 8 times that of nicotine. The levels of cotinine are typically 15 times higher than the levels of nicotine. For this reason, it is often used as a marker of nicotine use. It is eventually excreted by the kidneys. It is not fully clear what the effects of cotinine are on the body. However, it does have an impact on some neurotransmitters in the brain and affects a number of enzymes. It may also play a role in withdrawal symptoms.

Half-life: The length of time for half of the drug to be removed from the body.

Assessment

The level of dependence and associated craving needs to be taken into account in undertaking smoking cessation. The Fagerstrom Test for Nicotine Dependence (Table 13.5) is commonly used to assess the degree of dependence on nicotine. Those with higher scores are seen as needing assistance in their efforts to stop smoking. The test is also included on numerous websites devoted to health education and smoking cessation efforts.

Treatment

There is a large body of literature on smoking cessation. Typically smoking cessation programs are offered through hospitals and community health facilities or via individual physicians and health-care providers. There are very few residential treatment programs for smokers. At this point, the rate of treatment success, in terms of establishing abstinence from nicotine, is in the vicinity of 15% to 25%. Commonly people try to quit smoking several times before succeeding. In general, smoking cessation programs include patient education, group support, and counseling. When smoking cessation efforts include nicotine replacement, there is a better chance of quitting smoking. There are several forms of nicotine replacement: nicotine gum, nicotine patch, nasal sprays, and inhalers. The gum and patch are available over-the-counter. Nasal sprays and inhalers require a prescription. In addition, a drug originally used for the treatment of depression, bupropion (Wellbutrin®), has been found to

Table 13.5 Fagerstrom Test for Nicotine Dependence

Instructions: Select the number of the answer that is most applicable, and write it on the line to the left.

_______ 1. How soon after you awake do you smoke your first cigarette?
- 0. After 30 minutes
- 1. Within 30 minutes

_______ 2. Do you find it difficult to refrain from smoking in places where it is forbidden, such as the library, theater, or doctors' office?
- 0. No
- 1. Yes

_______ 3. Which of all the cigarettes you smoke in a day is the most satisfying?
- 0. Any other than the first one in the morning
- 1. The first one in the morning

_______ 4. How many cigarettes a day do you smoke?
- 0. 1–15
- 1. 16–25
- 2. More than 26

_______ 5. Do you smoke more during the morning than during the rest of the day?
- 0. No
- 1. Yes

_______ 6. Do you smoke when you are so ill that you are in bed most of the day?
- 0. No
- 1. Yes

_______ 7. Does the brand you smoke have a low, medium, or high nicotine content?
- 0. Low
- 1. Medium
- 2. High

_______ 8. How often do you inhale the smoke from your cigarette?
- 0. Never
- 1. Sometimes
- 2. Always

Scoring:

0–2	Very Low Addiction
3–4	Low Addiction
5	Medium Addiction
6–7	High Addiction
8–10	Very High Addiction

From: Heatherton TF, Kozlowski LT, Frecker RC, Fagerstrom KO. The Fagerstrom Test for Nicotine Dependence: A revision of the Fagerstrom Tolerance Questionnaire. *British Journal of Addictions* 86:1119–1127, 1991.

help reduce craving among those who are quitting smoking. This drug is known as Zyban® when marketed as a drug to assist smoking cessation efforts and is exactly the same as Wellbutrin. The two should *not* be taken simultaneously. The prognosis for quitting increases significantly when both nicotine replacement and bupropion are used together.

Of note is the substance abuse treatment field's lack of involvement in smoking cessation efforts. This is true despite the fact that there is no other group of health-care providers with such a large proportion of smokers. The resistance to addressing smoking cessation as part of other alcohol or drug use treatment is probably the product of several factors: the relatively high level of smoking among staff, the misperception that addressing nicotine dependence along with other substance use problems leads to poorer outcomes, the idea that multiple dependencies should be handled sequentially, and inadequate training in smoking cessation techniques.

Summary: Nicotine

Examples:	Cigarettes, cigars, pipes, chewing tobacco, snuff
Route of administration:	Smoked, chewed
Length of action:	Approximately 2 hours
Desired effects:	Relaxation, stimulation, social acceptance, image, ward off withdrawal
Other acute effects:	Dizziness and nausea (in the inexperienced), increased heart rate
Action:	Agonist at nicotinic receptors in the central and peripheral nervous system; Modulates both inhibitory and excitatory elements of number of neural pathways; May act on some of the same pathways as opiates and sedative hypnotics
Intoxication/overdose:	Rare; Most of the negative effects are from regular and prolonged use, rather than from intoxication and overdose
Common problems:	Dependence; The common medical problems associated with use are in large measure the result of smoking, not the nicotine per se (these include cough, bronchitis, increased respiratory infections, chronic obstructive pulmonary disease, lung cancer, and oral cancers); Apparent increase in other cancers; Death or injury by fire; Among pregnant women there is a higher incidence of low birth weight babies and an increase in spontaneous abortions
Withdrawal symptoms:	Craving, irritability, anxiety, possible depression

Interaction with alcohol:	Increased likelihood of use of one when the other is used; Combined use greatly increases incidence of oral cancers

Nicotine

Drug	Average Amount Taken	Addiction Risk	DEA Schedule
Nicotine	1 mg/cigarette, 4.5 mg/"wad" chewing tobacco	High	N/A

Opiates

Historical Notes

Opium was recognized over 10,000 years ago as having psychoactive properties. The Assyrians are thought to have used it medicinally. Opium poppies were being cultivated in the area now known as Iraq over 2,400 years ago. Opium was known to the Greeks and, along with alcohol, was one of the mainstays of ancient medicine. The only improvement on either alcohol or opium alone was their combination in a preparation known as laudanum. First manufactured in 1500, it combined wine with opium along with some spices and its use continued throughout the 1800s. The disappearance of laudanum was the result of passage of the Pure Food and Drug Act in 1906.

Not poppy, nor mandragora,
Nor all the drowsy syrups of the world
Shall ever medicine thee to that
sweet sleep
Which thou owed'st yesterday.
SHAKESPEARE
Othello

In terms of what distinguishes "opiates" and "opioids," opiates are naturally occurring or partially synthesized, whereas opioids are synthetic opiates.

As a general rule, any psychoactive agent that is naturally occurring in nature tends to be less potent and generally less problematic than are any derivatives created from it by processing. This is really a rather commonsense notion. Why bother going to the trouble of refining or processing if there isn't any improvement? Accordingly, distillation is required to produce alcoholic beverages above 14%. In terms of opiates, it was only in the early 1800s that opium poppies were refined to create morphine, a substance that was about 10 times more powerful. But something else had to happen before the use of morphine became widespread. The real breakthrough in terms of the administration of opiates didn't occur until 1853 with the invention of the syringe. From then on, there was the potential for delivering morphine intravenously, thereby greatly enhancing its effects. (By the mid-1800s, opium smoking had been introduced into the United States by Chinese laborers. However, it never caught on beyond the Chinese community, in large measure because of prejudice and racism.) The first widespread medical use of morphine was in the Civil War. It was used less than judiciously and without an appreciation of the addictive potential. A number of soldiers who lived through the war were described as having the "soldier's illness" or "army disease." The next landmark in terms of the history of opiates was the synthesis of heroin from morphine in 1898. Accordingly, heroin joined opium and morphine as an ingredient of the various tonics and medications then available. Heroin is noted for its rapid onset of action and short half-life. Both features contribute to its abuse potential. Heroin is about twice as potent as morphine—that represents a potency 20 times greater than that of opium. Appropriately, the name given this synthesized product, heroin, comes from the German word "heroisch," which means large or powerful. Its average half-life is 3 minutes.* Though heroin is metabolized quite rapidly, one of the products of its metabolism is morphine, which, of course, has psychoactive effects and stays in the system much longer. (By way of contrast, the products formed by the metabolism of alcohol do not have any mood-altering properties.)

Thou hast the keys of Paradise, oh just, subtle, and mighty opium!

Confessions of an English Opium Eater, 1822

With the passage of the Pure Food and Drug and the Harrison acts, the legal and widespread supply of opium and its major derivatives, morphine and heroin, disappeared. In 1924, heroin production in the United States was outlawed. In 1942, growing opium poppies was similarly outlawed. It was in 1956 that possession of heroin was essentially made illegal, and all remaining stockpiles were to be surrendered to the U.S. government. In other countries—notably, England—heroin is still legally manufactured. England, as a harm reduction effort, makes heroin available via prescription to those who have long-standing heroin problems and who have not succeeded in drug-free treatment programs or substitution programs such as methadone maintenance. England is not alone in this approach. Other countries, such as Switzerland and The Netherlands, have created similar pilot programs to explore this, and it is being considered in Australia.

Heroin is sometimes reported as having a half-life of around three minutes, other times the half-life is reported as around a half hour. This discrepancy apparently relates to the time required for heroin to be transformed into morphine. There is an intermediate product formed between the heroin and the morphine, 6-monoacetylmorphine (MAM), and the discrepancy is how this intermediary product is handled in the calculations. Either way, the half-life is very short. That is the important part!

Patterns of Use

For many drugs, use in the population varies over time; a particular drug waxes and wanes in popularity. In part this is attributed to supply but also to what might be thought of as "generational memories." In the 1980s, heroin use was primarily associated with those described as "the dinosaurs," those in their 40s and 50s. The *National Household Survey* shows that in 2003, unlike other drugs, the majority of users of opiates is *not* the young. Nonetheless, there was a resurgence of heroin use in the early 1990s. A new generation of users emerged, drawn from those in the 13 to 23 age bracket. This increase in use was attributed to a lowering of price, to greater purity, to the fact that cocaine street sellers in some areas had begun trafficking in heroin as well, and to the fact that there is no generational memory of heroin use and its problems. The new users had no experience of the problems of heroin, as they had, for example, with cocaine and especially crack cocaine. With increasing purity, there is also an increase in other routes of administration besides IV use. Those potentially averse to IV use have not been disinclined to experiment with heroin taken in other ways. It is taken intranasally, as well as smoked (chasing the dragon), which involves not rolling cigarettes but inhaling

FOCUS ON DRUGS

Kabul, Afghanastan

Over the past decade, Afghanistan has emerged as the global source of opium poppy associated with 90% of the world's heroin production. In light of that fact, what is the magnitude of drug problems within the country? In a country ravaged by war, having a largely rural population, there is nothing that resembles definitive countrywide survey data. However, the United Nations' Office on Drug and Crime has been gathering information through a variety of sources—from interviews with hospital officials, police, Afghan citizens living in refugee camps, persons engaged in the few treatment programs available in the capital city of Kabul, and drug users themselves to produce some sense of the magnitude, nature, and trends in drug use. These provide a series of snapshots, if not a definitive picture.

The following are some of the highlights:

- In 1996 the United Nations ranked Afghanistan as among the world's poorest countries, placing it 169 of 174 according to a development index. In the following year it was dropped from the list, due to inadequate data.
- Afghans have an average life expectancy of 45 years. Alongside people from Somalia and Haiti its people are among the world citizens most chronically hungry.
- The country has had a virtually unbroken 24-year history of war and conflict.
- In Islam, the use of any intoxicating drugs (*nasha—I-mawad*) is forbidden (*haram*). During the Taliban period, the Department for the Suppression of Vice and Promotion of Virtue imposed severe punishment for drug users who were caught. As the result of shame and fear, drug users are very reluctant to have their drug use be publicly known.
- The first in a series of UN assessments of drug use in Afghan communities was published in 1999. It then reported an apparently growing level of drug use involving a variety of substances—hashish, opium, heroin, pharmaceuticals, and painkillers.
- The UN has expressed concern about drug use in the multiple vulnerable populations: the unemployed, the war-disabled, ex-combatants, displaced persons, refugees, women, and children.
- Heroin is seen as a growing problem in urban areas, particularly Kabul. Afghanistan is the world's leading producer of opium. With increasing policing and security on Afghanistan's borders, there is speculation some traffickers will take the "low-risk" option of selling within the country, even though this yields lower profits.
- Loss is something that touches virtually everyone. There is loss of family, home, jobs, personal security, and—in the case of refugees—even country. More than 2 million Afghans have been killed in the fighting.
- Among the estimated 2.5 million residents of Kabul, 58% of the households are comprised of refugees and returnees.
- An earlier assessment of a refugee camp in Pakistan found that 10% of adults had a drug problem. Given the number of refugees returning to Kabul, that suggests the influx of approximately 40,000 drug users into the city.
- *Estimated number of drug users in Kabul.* Based on interviews with both key informants and drug users, the following very crude estimates of drug use were generated representing the minimum number of users of various substances:

Heroin	7,007
Opium	10,774
Hashish	23,995
Pharmaceuticals	14,298
Alcohol	6,568
Total	*52,642*

- *Treatment.* Compared to those estimated to have a problem with drug use, the statistics suggest that treatment and health interventions are minuscule. In 2003, a total of 452 people were admitted to a Kabul drug treatment program. Of these, 75% were using heroin, and 20% opium. A different program opened in 2003; in its first month it had contact with over 300 people. Of these, two-thirds were women dependent on opium, and 6% were children between the ages of 2 months and 14 years also opium dependent.
- *Demographics.* Among the drug users interviewed for the study, there was considerable diversity in age, occupation, income, and prior residence, suggesting the drug users are a very diverse group.
- *Heroin and opium.* Among drug users interviewed, one-third reported using heroin. Twice that amount

reported using opium. Over half began using heroin when in a refugee camp in either Pakistan or Iran. Only a third had begun using in Kabul. Forty percent had been using for over three years, and another 21% had been using more than 7 years. Injection as a route of administration is becoming more common. An advantage of injecting is not its effects but that it is more private and less socially obvious. Injecting reduces the risk of being apprehended by police who might trace the smoke or smell of burning heroin produced by smoking. For opium a third report smoking, usually by adding it to a cigarette. The others report eating it. The reasons for opium use were varied, encompassing medicinal purposes, to alleviate tiredness, or help with work.

- *Hashish.* About half of the drug users reported use of hashish. A third of these had been using for more than 10 years. Almost all began using in Afghanistan. Reasons for use were varied, from "for enjoyment" to soldiers reporting use "to be free from fear during the war." The cost is considerably less than that of heroin and opium, with people estimating they spent between 20¢ (U.S.) to 80¢ (U.S.) per day.
- *Alcohol.* In Kabul alcohol is more available than in other areas of the country. It is sometimes found at weddings or as part of social events, such as picnics. Nonetheless, only a fifth of the drug users reported ever having used alcohol. Of the minority who had ever used alcohol, 10% reported being habituated, reporting "four glasses or a plastic bag every day," or "five times a day, thirty-five times a week."

United Nations Office on Drugs and Crime, Country Office for Afghanistan, McDonald D. *Afghanistan: Community Drug Profile No. 5. An Assessment of Problem Drug Use in Kabul City.* Vienna, Austria: United Nations Office on Drugs and Crime, July 2003. www.unodc.org/afg/en/reports_surveys.html

the smoke from heroin that is burnt, for example, when placed on a piece of tinfoil. The increased use of heroin was not restricted to urban areas but spread to the suburbs and rural areas as well. The upsurge of heroin use peaked in 1996 and remained relatively stable through 1999, when there was a decrease among the youngest users, according to the *Monitoring the Future* survey.

The Basic Principles of Dealing Heroin

1. Never give anything away for nothing.
2. Never give more than you have to give (always catch the buyer hungry and always make him wait).
3. Always take everything back if you possibly can.

WILLIAM BURROUGHS

The Naked Lunch, Introduction 1959

Detoxification

If a person has been taking opiates on a daily basis for 2 to 3 weeks, some significant withdrawal symptoms are likely to occur. In general, the shorter the duration of the effects of a drug, the more intense the withdrawal will be, but the duration of the withdrawal symptoms will be shorter. Conversely, the longer-acting drugs have less severe withdrawal symptoms, but those symptoms persist over a longer period. In the past, the most common method of detoxification from opiates was to use methadone as a substitute and then gradually tapering the methadone. Recently buprenorphine has become available for use as a detoxification medication with positive results and without many of the restrictions associated with methadone detoxification.

Other detoxification regimens have been introduced. The most controversial of these is known as *ultra-rapid detoxification,* accomplished under sedation. It involves administration of naltrexone, a blocking agent which, by binding with the opiate receptor sites, makes it impossible for the opiates to do so, thus causing withdrawal. This procedure has been criticized on several counts. It has been associated with several deaths and thus is a riskier procedure than other withdrawal regimens, and it introduces risks that are not present with other regimens. (Compared with alcohol withdrawal, opiate withdrawal involves less medical risk. While uncomfortable, it is not associated with mortality and complications.) Also, ultra-rapid detoxification is not covered by insurance and, costing up to $7,500, is seen as exploitative of patients.

In contrast to ultra-rapid detox there is also a procedure known as *rapid detoxification.* It does not require sedation or anesthesia, also uses naltrexone, but in combination with another medication, clonidine, as a pre- and postnaltrexone treatment, along with benzodiazepines and other medications as needed for nausea and vomiting and takes 2 to 3 days. So this is not a simple procedure and while conducted on an outpatient basis it requires careful medical monitoring over a several-hour period. As with alcohol, detoxification per se is not treatment for the dependence syndrome. It simply sets the stage for treatment of dependence.

Summary: Opioids

Category includes:	Heroin, morphine, meperidine, oxycodone, opium, codeine, hydrocodone, fentanyl, methadone.
Route of administration:	Heroin: Intravenous, snorted, "skin-popped," or smoked. Medications: Oral, intravenous or skin patch (fentanyl). Medications that are intended to be taken by mouth such as oxycodone, may be crushed and injected or snorted
Length of action:	Varies by compound. Heroin: 3–4 hours; Morphine: 3–4 hours; Methadone: 12 hours to days
Desired effects:	The "rush" or "high," a feeling of intense pleasure, often described as almost "orgasmic." A state of decreased mental and physical awareness and of decreased physical and emotional pain.
Other acute effects:	Dependence; Sedation; Decreased judgment; Decreased ability to operate vehicles or machinery. Respiratory depression secondary to accidental overdose.
Action:	Appear to bind to opiate receptors in specific areas in the central nervous system where they appear to mimic or block normally occurring opiate-like substances causing an altered mood state which is considered desirable and much sought after by repeated administration.
Intoxication/overdose:	*Vital signs:* respiration decreased, blood pressure decreased, temperature decreased.

	Physical exam: Pupils constricted; Reflexes absent or diminished; Pulmonary edema; Possible convulsions with pain Demerol® and Darvon® (pain medications). *Mental status:* Variable; Possible normal mood; Euphoria; Sedation, possible stupor.
Common problems:	Rapidly acquired tolerance, physical dependence. Respiratory depression secondary to accidental overdose. Cellulitis at site of injection. Sepsis (systemic infections). Endocarditis. Increased likelihood of exposure to HIV infection and hepatitis by sharing of needles. Risk to sexual partners of IV opiate users with HIV. Legal problems related to acquiring opiates illegally.
Withdrawal symptoms:	Drug craving; Dysphoria and anxiety; Yawning; Sleep difficulties; Perspiration; Fever; Chills; Gooseflesh; Abdominal cramps; Nausea; Diarrhea; Muscle cramps; Bone pain; Tears.
Interaction with alcohol:	Each potentiates the effects of the other in overdose situations. Possible decreased efficacy of either when taken by an individual with tolerance to the other (cross-tolerance).
Medical uses:	*Pain* (morphine, meperidine, hydromorphone, methadone, oxycodone, hydocodone); *Cough suppression* (codeine); *Anesthesia* (fentanyl); *Addiction treatment* (methadone, buprenorphine); *Diarrhea* (opium).

Opioids

Drug Generic	**Usual Therapeutic Dose/Day (Adults)**	**Addiction Risk**	**DEA Schedule**
Codeine (multiple products)			
cough	5–15 mg q 4h	High	II
pain	15–60 mg q 4h		
Heroin	No medical uses in U.S.	High	I
Morphine			
(MSIR®)	5–20 mg q 4h	High	II
(MS Contin®)	15–60 mg q 12h	High	II
Opium			
(Paregoric®)	6 mg or 6 ml q 4h	High	II

Opioids (continued)

Drug Generic	Usual Therapeutic Dose/Day (Adults)	Addiction Risk	DEA Schedule
Opioids			
Fentanyl (Duragesic Patch, Atiq, Oralef, Sublimaze)	2–50 micrograms/kg	High	II
Hydrocodone			
Cough (Hycodan)	5–10 mg q 4h	Moderate	II
Pain (Vicodan)	Limit 8/day	Moderate	III
Hydromorphone (Dilaudid)	1–4 mg q 4-6h	High	II
Levorphanol (Levo-Dromoran)	2–3 mg q 6-8h	High	II
Meperidine (Demerol)	55–150 mg q 3-4h	High	II
Methadone			
Maintenance**	5–120 mg/day	High	II
Pain (Dolophine)	2.5–20 mg q 3-4h	High	II
Oxycodone			
(Percodan, Percocet, Tylox)	1 tab q 6h	High	II
(OxyContin)	10–40 mg q 12h	High	II
Propoxyphene (Darvon, Darvocet, Darvon-N)	1 tab q 4h	Low	IV
Partial Opioid Agonists			
Buprenorphine			
Pain (Buprenex®)	0.3–0.6 mg IM or IV	Low	III
Maintenance			
(Suboxone®)	8–16 mg/day		
(Subutrex®)			
Butorphanol			
Pain: IM or IV (Stadol)	1–2 mg q 3–4h	High	IV
Intranasal spray	1–2 mg q 3–4h		
Nalbuphine Pain (Nubain® Subcutaneously)	10 mg IM q 3–4h	Low	IV
Pentazozine			
Pain (Talwin) Subcutaneously	30 mg IM, IV q 3–4h	Moderate	IV
Non-Opioid but with Opioid-like-Effects and Addictive Potential			
Tramadol (Ultram®)	50–10 mg po, q 6h	Low	Not Controlled

**May be higher in tolerant patients

Note. Amounts used significantly in excess of recommended use should be considered abuse. All risk may be higher risk in patients with substance abuse history.

Sedative-Hypnotics (Central Nervous System Depressants)

Sedative-hypnotics constitute the category of drugs to which alcohol belongs. Accordingly many of the drugs in this group have properties similar to those of alcohol. For this reason, some of the most serious interactions with alcohol occur with drugs in this class, both drugs having a depressant effect. For this reason, medications in this class are for detoxification from alcohol. In essence, they are substituted for the alcohol, with the doses then tapering off.

Patterns of Use

In the general population, this is the drug class with the least difference in levels of use based on gender. According to the 2003 *National Household Survey,* in the past year 2.1% of those age 12 and older reported nonprescribed use of the minor tranquilizers, and 0.3% used sedatives. In terms of past-month use, the rates for both were under one percent, 0.8% and 0.1%, respectively. The highest rate of use is among young adults between the ages of 18 and 25, but the rate is still relatively low (1.7%).

Summary: Sedative-Hypnotics

Examples:	Benzodiazepines, barbiturates, meprobamate, chloral hydrate, GHB
Route of administration:	Usually by mouth, rarely intravenous
Length of action:	Varies by substance
Desired effects:	Similar to those of alcohol, reduction of anxiety, possible elation secondary to decrease in alertness and judgment
Other acute effects:	Sedation, impaired judgment, impaired operation of vehicles or machinery, respiratory and cardiac depression with overdose (much less likely with benzodiazepines alone)
Action:	Depression of activity at all excitable tissues; In general, act at receptors of neurons linked with or potentiate the GABA (gamma-aminobutyric acid) system, inhibitory system; Chloride ion flow into neurons is facilitated either by the GABA system (benzodiazepines) or directly (barbiturates), resulting in sedation.
Intoxication/overdose:	*Vital signs:* minimal changes, possibly decreased respirations, more likely with non-benzodiazepines. *Physical exam:* slurred speech, ataxia (unable to walk a straight line), stupor, coma, possible respiratory depression. *Mental status:* slurred speech, confusion, impaired judgment, delirium, coma

Common Abbreviations on Prescriptions

caps = *capsules*
gm = *gram*
gtt. = *drops*
mg. = *milligram*
ml. = *milliliter*
h = *hour*
p.r.n. = *when necessary*
q.d. = *once a day*
b.i.d. = *twice a day*
t.i.d. = *three times a day*
q.i.d. = *four times a day*
q.h. = *every hour*
q.2h = *every 2 hours*
q.3h = *every 3 hours*
q.4h = *every 4 hours*
q._h. = *if to be taken at an hourly interval, hours between doses is inserted*
a.c. = *before meals*
p.c. = *after meals*
ad lib = *use as much as one desires (from "ad libitum")*
p.o. = *by mouth, orally*
i.m. = *injection, intramuscular*
i.v. = *injection, intravenous*
subcutaneous = *under the skin*

Common problems:	Tolerance, physical dependence; Respiratory and cardiac depression with overdose
Withdrawal symptoms:	Similar to alcohol withdrawal. Severity and time of onset vary with half-life of drug; anxiety, elevated vital signs, sweating, tremulousness, altered perceptions, withdrawal seizures possibly leading to death (barbiturates)
Interaction with alcohol:	Potentiation of effects, especially respiratory depression; some degree of cross-tolerance
Medical uses:	Sleep, anxiety disorders, muscle relaxation, alcohol and sedative-hypnotic withdrawal, control of seizures

Sedative-Hypnotics

Drug Generic	Usual Therapeutic Dose/Day (Adults)	Addiction Risk	DEA Schedule
Benzodiazepines			
alprazolam (Xanax®)	0.25–0.60 mg	High	IV
chlordiazepoxide (Librium®)	5–100 mg	Low	IV
clonazepam (Klonopin®)	0.5–4 mg (larger doses for epilepsy)	Low	IV
diazepam (Valium®)	2–40 mg	Moderate/high	IV
flurazepam (Dalmane®)	15–30 mg	Low	IV
lorazepam (Ativan®)	1–6 mg	Moderate/high	IV
oxazepam (Serax®)	10–90 mg	Low	IV
temazepam (Restoril®)	15–30 mg	Low	IV
triazolam (Halcion®)	0.125–0.5 mg	Moderate/high	IV
estazolzm (Prosom®)	0.5–2.0 mg	Low	IV
flunitrazepam (Rohypnol®)*	—	High	—
Barbiturates			
butabarbital (Butisol Sodium®)	15–120 mg	Moderate	III
butalbital (Fiornal®)	1–6 tabs	Moderate	III
pentobarbital (Numbutal®)	100 mg	High	II
phenobarbital	30–400 mg	Low	IV
secobarbital (Seconal®)	100 mg	High	II
Other Compounds			
chloral hydrate	250–500 mg	Low	IV
meprobamate (Miltown®/Equanil®)	200–2400 mg	Moderate/high	IV
carisoprodol (Soma®)	350–1500 mg	Low	Not classified

*Not approved for use in the United States.

Note: Amounts used significantly in excess of recommended use should be considered abuse. All use may be higher risk in patients with substance abuse history.

Gamma-Hydroxybutyrate (GHB): A Special Case

Unlike the drugs just described, GHB in the United States has an exceedingly limited legitimate use. It is marketed as Xylrem and it was only approved in 2002 for treatment of a rare form of narcolepsy. The major source of GHB is not drug diversion but production in illicit clandestine laboratories. It is easily synthesized from readily available chemicals. It is one of the so-called club drugs, and is usually sold in vials or small bottles, and typically consumed by the capful or teaspoonful. It is clear, odorless, tasteless. These as well as its sedating properties contributed to its being cited in cases of sexual assault. On the club scene the attraction of GHB is its relaxant and disinhibiting effect. In the late 1980s GHB was touted for very different effects, to promote body building. The claims for GHB were that it enhanced strength, contributed to muscle development, and enhanced the metabolism of fat. It was promoted by health food stores as a dietary supplement. Adverse reactions led to its being banned from use in nutritional and weight loss supplements in 1991. GHB is problematic because there is a very steep dose-response curve, greater than other sedatives, and doses are far from standardized. It is rapidly absorbed, with peak levels achieved in 20 to 60 minutes, and it lasts no longer than 3 hours. Dependence can occur, and the withdrawal syndrome is similar to that with alcohol.

Stimulants

Stimulant drugs are given that name because of their effect on the central nervous system. In contrast to alcohol and the other sedative-hypnotics, which have a dampening effect on the central nervous system, these drugs increase levels of activity. The group includes both illicit drugs (cocaine and the illicitly manufactured methamphetamines) and prescription medications: methylphenidate (Ritalin®) and amphetamines (Dexedrine®, Adderall®, Desoxyn®). In comparing differences clinically among different stimulants, research shows that, with methamphetamines, there is a more rapid progression from first use to regular use and from first use to entry into treatment. In comparing those who use methamphetamines and those who use cocaine, cocaine use is more episodic, more expensive financially, and likely to be accompanied by heavy drinking. In contrast, methamphetamine use is more likely to be daily, be accompanied by marijuana use, to involve women, and have more medical and psychiatric consequences.

Amphetamines

Amphetamines were widely prescribed in the middle of the twentieth century as a medication for depression and obesity. The number of prescriptions peaked in the United States in the late 1960s, with a total of 31 million. About 4% to 5% of all Americans have used amphetamines at sometime in their lives, 0.5% in the past year. Amphetamines are available

FOCUS ON DRUGS

Club Drugs

"Club drug is a vague term." No question about that. Club drugs do not constitute a pharmacologic class of compounds. The club drugs in the below list fall into multiple drug classes—sedatives/depressants (alcohol, GHB [gamma-hydroxybutyrate], and Rohypnol); stimulants (amphetamines and methamphetamines); opioids (fentanyl); hallucinogens and dissociatives (LSD, ecstasy, ketamine). The common element characterizing the array of substances known as club drugs is the settings in which they are used. Club drugs are those used at nightclubs, music festivals, dance parties, and raves, the rock concerts of this generation. These parties involve all-night dancing, laser light shows, electronic music, and drugs. Attendance can range from several hundred to thousands of people. After originating in England, raves spread internationally. Typically raves are held in private clubs, hence the name "club drugs" for the drugs that are commonly used there.

Among the substances most commonly termed club drugs are ecstasy, ketamine, GHB (gamma-hydroxybutyrate), and Rohypnol. They are seen as enhancing social intimacy, sensory perception, and endurance, allowing users to continue for hours on the dance floor. While Rohypnol is commonly included in discussions of club drugs, the evidence suggests that in fact it is quite uncommon, even though much discussed. (See page 504.)

Generally drugs are purchased at the event, and bought by the capsule or the vial. So typically club drugs are cheap and conveniently distributed as small pills, powders, or liquids. Not unexpectedly, frequently the tablets or vials sold are not what they are purported to be. In the United Kingdom, common additives to GHB include cocaine, amphetamines, and morphine. In the United States common additives are methamphetamine, PCP, and ecstasy.

In addition to the inherent problem of using unknown drugs of unknown strength, the pattern of drug use at raves introduces another problem. The usual practice is to take sequential doses of the same substance or a sequence of different drugs, as the effects of one wear off, a practice known as "bump." This pattern of use invites problems, as the drugs vary in their rates of clearance and metabolism; also, the effects of a particular drug may vary with the dose. And if you really don't know what you consumed . . . plus judgment is impaired . . . who remembers what the supposed sequence was? Plus, alcohol use is the rule, and typically alcohol is the beverage in which these drugs are mixed. Another potential problem arises from the crowded hot conditions common on the club and rave scene. Ecstasy can cause a marked increase in body temperature, which can invite liver, kidney, and cardiovascular problems. Another problem is that ecstasy users can become dehydrated. Or fearing dehydration, folks may drink large volumes of water, inducing "water intoxication," which is potentially life threatening as it causes disturbances in electrolyte balances.

GHB is a sedative that can lead to reduced respiration and coma when used along with alcohol. Many of the club drugs have sedative properties, and particularly when consumed along with alcohol invite the risk of depressed respiration and coma. Over a 6-year period, the number of emergency room visits involving club drugs have increased about tenfold, from several hundred to several thousands. However, in 2002, in combination, GHB and ecstasy—totaling about 7,300 emergency room incidents—represented only a tiny, tiny fraction of the 1 million–plus drug-related emergency room visits.

Club drugs include alcohol, LSD, MDMA (Ecstasy), GHB, GBL, Ketamine (Special-K), Fentanyl, Rohypnol, amphetamines, and methamphetamine.
NIDA, WEBSITE, 2004

Club drug is a vague term that refers to a wide variety of drugs.
LETTER, NIDA DIRECTOR, 2002

as pills, liquids, or powder. Oral or intravenous administration is the most common. A derivative, methamphetamine, is a street drug manufactured in clandestine laboratories, typically located in rural areas. There are sharp regional differences with use of methamphetamines, in part attributed to proximity to points of manufacture. Initially methamphetamine use was centered in California, then the Southwest, due to importation from Mexico. But with the growth of bootleg manufacturing, use has grown proportionally, especially in the plains states.

Cocaine

The use of cocaine peaked in 1985, followed by a marked decline, with the levels of use remaining relatively constant in the 1990s. Cocaine is more common in the young and middle adult age groups, ages 18 to 34, than among younger or older people. Cocaine use, like marijuana use, is more common in men, with the exception of those under age 26, where women's use approaches that of men. Racial differences are far less marked for cocaine use, although rates of use are slightly higher for Hispanic males than for other groups. Cocaine use is higher in metropolitan areas, but distinctions based on geography are not dramatic.

Nobody saves America by sniffing cocaine,
Jiggling yr knees blankeyed in the rain,
When it snows in yr nose you catch cold in yr brain
ALLEN GINSBURG

The change in the route of administration and the emergence of crack cocaine have been a concern. Although any method of cocaine administration is potentially lethal, the dangers increase dramatically with freebasing and smoking rather than snorting (intranasal administration). With freebasing, unlimited quantities can be ingested. While the level of cocaine use has been slowly but continuously declining, paradoxically there has been a marked increase in cocaine-related problems seen in hospitals' emergency rooms. The DAWN (Drug Abuse Warning Network) is a federally supported system to track drug-related incidents by tallying emergency room visits involving drug use and the frequency of a drug's being mentioned in medical examiners' (coroners') cases. Overall there has been a marked rise in drug-involved cases seen in emergency departments, with cocaine-related incidents experiencing the most dramatic rise. Between 1975 and 1985, there was a tenfold increase, from fewer than 1,000 incidents per year to approximately 10,000. By the mid-1990s, there was another tenfold increase to over 120,000 emergency room episodes involving cocaine. Thus, the magnitude of the problems associated with use grew geometrically, even as actual use declined. While initially attributed to the presence of crack cocaine, the numbers have not gone down as the use of crack cocaine has declined.

The shortest way out of Manchester is notoriously a bottle of Gordon's gin; out of any businessman's life there is the mirage of Paris; out of Paris, or mediocrity of talent and imagination, there are all the drugs, from subtle, all-conquering opium to cheating, cozening cocaine.
WILLIAM BOLITHO, 1930

Summary: Stimulants

Examples:	Cocaine, amphetamines, methamphetamines, methylphenidate (Ritalin®)
Route of administration:	Powdered cocaine (cocaine hydrochloride) is snorted intranasally and (rarely) used intravenously or smoked as free base; Cocaine is mostly smoked as "crack"; Amphetamines are taken orally, taken intravenously, or smoked; Methylphenidate is taken orally
Length of action:	Cocaine: smoking produces a high that lasts 20–30 minutes, half-life in plasma is approximately 1 hour, remains in the brain 2–3 days; Methamphetamines: high lasts 8–24 hours, half-life is 6–12 hours; Methylphenidate: half-life is about 2 hours

Desired effects:	Increased alertness, feeling of well-being, euphoria, increased energy, heightened sexuality
Other acute effects:	Anxiety, confusion, irritability, possible medical problems (cardiac, central nervous system, respiratory, etc.) with potential death
Action:	*Cocaine:* similar to amphetamines; Affects dopamine, norepinephrine, and serotonin; Blocks reuptake of dopamine, thereby prolonging dopamine effects; May enhance dopamine transmission in mesolimbic and mesocortical areas of brain; Depletes presynaptic dopamine with prolonged use; May act on opiate system to promote addictive behavior; Toxic sympathomimetic effects, particularly on cardiac, respiratory, and central nervous systems; *Amphetamines and methylphenidate:* direct neuronal release of dopamine and norepinephrine and blockade of catecholamine reuptake produce euphorigenic effects, various pharmacologically toxic sympathomimetic effects
Intoxication/overdose:	*Vital signs:* increased heart rate, elevated blood pressure and temperature, decreased respiration; *Physical exam:* dilated pupils, dry mouth, cardiac arrhythmias, twitching, tremors, convulsions, stroke, coma; *Mental status:* impaired judgment, confusion, disinhibited behavior, paranoid thoughts, hypervigilance, hallucinations, elation and/or depression, suicidal behavior
Common problems:	Dependence, tolerance; Anxiety, confusion, irritability, social withdrawal; Weight loss; Psychosis; Multiple medical problems (cardiac, central nervous system, respiratory, etc.) with potential death; with long-term, chronic use of methamphetamines there is evidence of irreversible damage to central nervous system
Withdrawal symptoms:	Depression (possibly with suicide potential); Excessive need for sleep; Fatigue; Anhedonia (lack of pleasure); Increased appetite; Craving, especially with cocaine; Usually not life-threatening except for suicide potential
Interaction with alcohol:	Alcohol decreases side effects of stimulants (such as anxiety) and withdrawal symptoms, alcohol commonly used along with stimulants

Medical uses:	Cocaine: local (ear/nose/throat) anesthesia; Amphetamines and Methylphenidate: attention deficit hyperactivity disorder (especially in children), narcolepsy, used rarely for depression unresponsive to other treatments

Stimulants

Drug	Usual Therapeutic Dose/Day*	Addiction Risk	DEA Schedule
cocaine	Only medical use is for local anesthesia	High	II
dextro-amphetamine (Dexedrine®)	2.5–60 mg	High	II
methamphetamine (Desoxyn®)	5–25 mg	High	II
dextroamphetamine/ amphetamine salts (Adderall®)	5–40 mg	High	II
methylphenidate (Ritalin®)	10–60 mg	High	II
(Concerta®)	18–54 mg	High	II

*Child's ADHD dose.

Note: Amounts used significantly in excess of recommended use should be considered abuse. All use may be higher risk in patients with substance abuse history.

Hallucinogens and Dissociatives

The hallucinogens and dissociatives include both naturally occurring and synthetic preparations. While they represent different types of compounds, they are commonly combined into one category, because of their shared ability to alter reality and produce hallucination-like effects. Hallucinogenic substances have played a role in human life for thousands of years. It has been recognized through the ages that there were a variety of plants that induced a state of detachment and precipitated visions. These were used largely in social and religious contexts, and never became widely used and abused. These plants contain chemical compounds, such as mescaline and psilocybin that are very similar to serotonin. In 1935 a German pharmaceutical company was exploring the use of ergot, a compound found in rye grass, to develop new pharmaceuticals. Several years later, one of the company's chemists accidentally ingested one of these compounds and reported: "My surroundings . . . transformed themselves in more terrifying ways. Everything in the room spun around, and the familiar objects and pieces of furniture assumed grotesque, threatening forms. They were in continuous motion, animated, as if driven by an inner restlessness. . . . Every exertion of my will, every attempt to put an end to the disintegration of the outer world and the dissolution of my ego, seemed to be wasted effort. A demon had invaded me, had taken possession of my body, mind, and soul."[1] This compound was LSD-25, the number referring to its being the twenty-fifth in a series of compounds that contained Lysergic Acid Diethylamide. LSD is easily manufactured and is the most powerful hallucinogen.

The dissociatives include anesthetics, phencyclidine (PCP), and ketamine. They are anesthetics in that they block pain and induce loss of consciousness, but at subanesthetic thresholds they produce effects similar to those associated with other hallucinogens. "Dissociative" refers to an altered sense of self, of being outside of oneself. There too is a heightened awareness, be it of color or sound. Because of these hallucinogenic properties their use as anesthetics was short-lived. Often patients became agitated, delusional, and irrational as the anesthetic effects wore off following surgery. Due to these problems, in 1965 the clinical trials of PCP as an anesthetic were discontinued. In 1963, ketamine, another dissociative anesthetic, was introduced in the U.S. to replace PCP; but the same problems quickly became evident. Its use in the U.S. is now restricted largely to veterinary practice. Most ketamine available on the streets is diverted from veterinary offices.

Currently, PCP is produced illegally. It is a white powder that dissolves easily in both water and alcohol. It is relatively inexpensive, is active in liquid, vapor, powder and crystalline forms and acts on multiple receptors sites. For these reasons it is one of the most common adulterants found in psychoactive properties, and thus is used to cut more expensive street drugs.

The other drug in this category is MDMA, known as ecstasy. It is a designer drug, an analog of methamphetamine, and has both stimulant and psychedelic properties. Ecstasy was placed on the DEA schedule in 1985 due to the pattern of abuse and because chemically it is closely linked to another drug found to damage serotonin neurons in the brain. Prior to this rescheduling, in addition to its being a recreational drug, it was being investigated as an adjunct to psychotherapy. Women seemingly are more sensitive to the effects of MDMA than are men. The dissociatives, along with the hallucinogens, are associated with the "rave" scene and among the substances known as club drugs.

Patterns of Use

Hallucinogens and the dissociatives are drugs of the young. In 2003, 19- and 20-year-olds were those with the highest rate of use in the past year (7.8%). By age 25, the rate of use drops to 2.8%. Demographic factors be-

[1]NIDA. *Research Report Series: Hallucinogens and Dissociative Drugs.* Rockville, MD: NIDA, November 2001.

yond age that distinguishes users are race/ethnicity and household income. Use is higher among whites and also higher in those with higher household incomes.

Summary: Hallucinogens and Dissociatives

Examples:	*LSD-like drugs:* LSD, mescaline, psilocybin, psilocin, and probably DMA, DOT, and DMT; *MDMA-like drugs:* ecstasy, a club drug; *Dissociative Anesthetics:* ketamine, club drug
Route of administration:	*LSD-like drugs:* ingested or smoked; *MDMA-like drugs:* ingested or smoked; *PCP:* smoked, ingested, or snorted; *Ketamine*: commercially available as a liquid, easily converted to a powder that is snorted; Less frequently, dissolved in water and injected
Length of action:	Varies with the substance, ranges from hours to a few days
Desired effects:	Increased awareness of sensory input; Perceptions of usual environment as novel; Altered body image; Blurring of boundaries between self and environment; Temporary modification of thought processes, claims of special insights, and increased empathy; Hallucinations; Feelings of strength, power, and invulnerability (PCP); Pleasant, floating, dreamlike state (ketamine); Reported sexual stimulation (ketamine)
Other acute effects:	*LSD group:* Panic attacks; Increased blood pressure, palpitations, tremor, nausea, muscle weakness, increased body temperature, ataxia; In some cases, accidental death (if act on drug-induced thought, such as belief one can fly); *MDMA group:* Nausea, jaw and teeth clenching, muscle tension, blurred vision, panic attacks, confusion, depression anxiety, paranoid psychosis, hyperthermia, cardiac arrest; *PCP:* psychotic reactions, bizarre behavior, outbursts of hostility and violence; Feelings of severe anxiety, doom, or impending death; Gross incoordination, nystagmus, hypersalivation; Vomiting; Fever; *Ketamine:* frightening experience of complete sensory detachment described as a "near death" experience, often referred to as the "k-hole"; Paranoia; Boredom; Possible

	coma; *Dextromethorphan:* Hallucinations (tactile, auditory, visual), visual disturbances, paranoia, disorientation, nausea, vomiting, abdominal pain, hyperthermia ("rave-related heatstroke"), cardiac irregularities, high blood pressure
Action:	*LSD-like drugs:* structurally related to serotonin, probably produce many of their behavioral effects by binding to serotonin receptors, such as the 5HT2 receptors; *MDMA-like drugs:* acting at serotonergic, adrenergic, cholinergic, and histaminergic histamine, all neurotransmitter sites, effects seem to be a combination of LSD-like hallucinations and amphetamine-like arousal; PCP: behavioral effects believed to be mediated through an excitatory receptor (NMDA); Ketamine and dextromethorphan: similar to PCP (NDMA receptor antagonist) but shorter-acting
Intoxication/overdose:	
LSD Group	*Vital signs:* elevated blood pressure, increased heart rate, elevated temperature with possible hyperthermia; *Physical exam:* increased reflexes, tremors, weakness, flushing and chills, seizures; *Mental status:* inappropriate mood, elation, hallucinations, bizarre behavior, disorientation, confusion, delusions, impaired judgment
MDMA Group	*Vital signs:* elevated heart rate, high blood pressure progressing to low blood pressure, possible hyperthermia; *Physical exam:* tremor, hypertonicity of muscles (more tense), nausea, decreased appetite, sweating; *Mental status:* elation, inappropriate affect, poor judgment
PCP	*Vital signs:* initially increased respiration but later decreased and possible apnea (stopping breathing), mild to severe blood pressure elevation, possible hyperthermia; *Physical exam:* red eyes, muscle rigidity, increased reflexes, repetitive movements, flushing, salivation, sweating, nausea, vomiting, seizures, possible coma or stroke; *Mental status:* abnormal appearance and behavior, disorientation, inappropriate affect, impaired

	judgment, memory problems, depression, elation, suicidal or homicidal behavior
Ketamine	*Vital signs:* mild to severe blood pressure elevation; *Physical exam:* tachycardia, palpitations, nystagmus, dilated pupils (mydriasis), hypertension, chest pain, slurred speech; *Mental status:* anxiety, slurred speech, hallucinations, confusion, memory loss
Dextromethorphan	May include symptoms of bromide poisoning; *Vital signs:* increased temperature, irregular heartbeat, elevated blood pressure; *Physical exam:* ataxia, nystagmus, dry mouth, dry skin, loss of consciousness; *Mental status:* may vary from somnolence to hyperexcitability, hallucinations, disorientation, paranoia
Common problems:	*LSD group:* flashbacks long after use has terminated, which can lead to depression, panic attacks, or in some cases suicide; Hallucinogenic mood disorder; Psychotic (delusional) disorders with varying courses; Long term visual changes (hallucinogen persistent perceptual disorder) a phenomena of "after-images" or sometimes referred to as "trailing" occurring after use of LSD has stopped, sometimes for years; *MDMA group:* nausea, jaw clenching, teeth clenching, muscle tension, blurred vision; Anxiety, confusion, panic attacks, depression, paranoid psychosis; Hyperthermia; Impaired blood clotting (coagulopathy); Cardiac arrest; Possible degeneration of serotonergic nerve terminals (not clinically confirmed); Memory and cognitive impairment; *PCP:* bizarre behavior; Outbursts of hostility and violence; Feelings of severe anxiety, doom, or impending death; Gross incoordination; Nystagmus; Hypersalivation, vomiting; Fever; Psychotic reactions; *Ketamine:* dependence reported; Hallucinations/flashbacks persisting for months after use; Possible memory impairment; *Dextromethorphan:* possible dependence
Withdrawal symptoms:	*LSD and MDMA* groups: there is no clinical evidence of withdrawal effects when use is terminated; *PCP:* animal studies suggest

	withdrawal symptoms, including poor feeding, weight loss, irritability, buxism, tremors, and preconvulsive activity; *Dextromethorphan:* insomnia, dysphoria, depression; No physical symptoms reported
Interaction with alcohol:	In combination with MDMA or dextromethorphan, possibly increases dehydration (especially when used at raves)
Medical uses:	There is no current accepted medical use of LSD-like and MDMA groups; Cough suppressant (ketamine); Dextromethorphan dosages listed in the following table are the average amounts taken

Hallucinogens and Dissociatives

Drug	Average Amount Taken	Addiction Risk	DEA Schedule
LSD Group			
LSD (acid)	10–400 micrograms	Low	I
Mescaline (mescal button)	100–200 mg	Low	I
Psilocybin	4–10 mg	Low	I
DOM (STP)	3–5 mg	Low	I
DMT	3.3–5 mg	Low	I
MDMA Group			
MDMA (ecstasy)	110–150 mg	Moderate	I
MDA		Low	I
Dissociatives			
PCP	80–500 mg	Low	II
Ketamine	100–200 mg	Low	III
Dextromethorphan	2–10 oz	Moderate	over-the-counter in many "extra strength" cough medications

Cannabinoids

The cannabinoids include marijuana, hashish, and hash oil. While their psychoactive properties have long been known, use rose dramatically during the 1960s, when the percentage of users among young adults went from about 3% in the beginning of that decade to 40% at the end.

Historical Tidbits

Cannabis, the plant from which marijuana is derived, is not native to North America. It was imported from Europe with the earliest colonists as a source of hemp, which was used for cloth and rope. It was long recognized as having psychoactive properties and was used as a medicine during the 1800s. For the most part, abuse wasn't an issue. In the first half of the twentieth century, nonmedical use was restricted to "artists," "bohemians," and other marginal groups. Concerns about use were not sufficient for it to be included in the Harrison Act, passed in the early 1900s. With the passage of the Marijuana Tax Act in 1937, efforts were made to regulate marijuana. The act was supposedly a revenue/tax measure, with individuals who distributed or dispensed or possessed marijuana required to pay a tax of $1, and under particular circumstances register with the government. Failure to pay the $1 tax could lead to substantial fines and prison terms. While not illegal per se, it is evident this was not created as a measure intended primarily to generate government revenues.[2]

I don't respond well to mellow, you know what I mean, I—I have a tendency to . . . if I get too mellow, I—I ripen and then rot.

WOODY ALLEN

In *Annie Hall*, explaining why he is passing on a marijuana party

It was only in 1941 that marijuana was no longer classified as a medication. Interestingly, part of the groundwork for the emergence of marijuana in the 1960s was laid by U.S. government policy during World War II. Foreign sources of hemp were no longer available then, and domestic cultivation became part of the war effort. The goal was to have over 300,000 acres in cultivation by the middle of the war. Most of this was grown in the Midwest, where wild marijuana plants can still be found. With the increasing attention paid to cultivation techniques, marijuana currently often has twice the THC (tetrahydrocannabinol, the psychoactive compound in marijuana) content of the "backyard" varieties of the 1960s.

Betel-nut of India is used as a mild narcotic by about one hundred million people. This is the seed of the Areca Palm, a species of trees found in abundance in India, especially along the southern slopes of the Himalayas. It is also cultivated extensively along the eastern coast and in Ceylon and the adjacent islands. The tree grows to the height of about thirty feet. The nut is about an inch long and a conical shape. It is prepared for chewing by being cut in pieces, sprinkled with quicklime, and wrapped in the leaf of a pepper plant. The quid thus made up is called a buyo, *and it is common custom to prepare for a journey by making a quantity for consumption on the road. The quid loses its virtue after half an hour of mastication; and where indulgence is not limited by poverty, a fresh supply speedily succeeds the exhausted* buyo, *and the process goes on from morning to night, with few and brief intermissions. . . . The habit obtains a very decided hold upon those who use the nut, so that they suffer more from a scanty supply of betel than from short rations of food.*

J.T. CRANE

Arts of Intoxication, 1870

Patterns of Use

Marijuana is by far the most widely used illicit drug. About 7% of the total population over 11 years old used marijuana in 2003. If you ignore those over age 30, the level of use is much higher. The age group with the highest rate of use is those between 18 and 25 years, with over a quarter reporting use in the past year (28.5%). For those over age 25, the rate is 6.9%. Overall, use declined during the 1980s. Between 1979 and 1985, there was a 33% decline in use among those 18 to 25 years old, the age group with the highest level of use. However, in the early to mid-1990s, there was a sharp upturn, which has since leveled off. For marijuana, as for drugs in general, there has been a trend toward first use at an earlier age.

[2]The taxation route as a control policy continues. Effective in January 2005, Tennessee followed the example of other states, and began to assess an excise tax on illicit drugs, including prescription drugs that are obtained illegally. People in possession of illicit drugs have 48 hours to report to a state revenue agent and pay the requisite tax, and this revenue office is barred from providing the identity of those who pay the tax to law enforcement officials.

Marijuana use is more common among men than women, except for those under age 18. With respect to race/ethnicity, Hispanics have the lowest levels of use. Among adolescents 12 to 17, use is significantly higher in metropolitan areas than in nonmetropolitan areas; however, among the 25- to 34-year-old age group there are no such differences, nor are there significant differences between sections of the country. Among current marijuana users and those with heaviest use, there is a significantly higher number who report having tried cocaine than is true of lighter users.

Societal Perspectives

Despite its being an illicit drug, there are those who distinguish marijuana from other illicit drugs. The fact is that, in some social circles, marijuana use is tolerated or accepted, if it is used with discretion. This is a bit like the "don't ask, don't tell" rule regarding gays and lesbians in the military. Many consider marijuana use a private matter and no one else's business if it is not used in situations that invite physical risk or endanger others, such as driving. That societal attitudes are changing is evidenced by the increasing discussion of decriminalization of possession of small amounts for personal use, as well as various referenda to allow the use of marijuana for medical conditions.

The problems that can occur with marijuana use simply are not in the same league as those associated with other drugs, including alcohol. The most significant problem may be cognitive impairments with heavy use that interferes with learning new material, a significant issue, given the young age group of most users. Dependence can occur with marijuana. But a much smaller proportion develop dependence than do those who use many other drugs. Even the problems associated with long-term, heavier use are less dramatic than those that accompany heavy long-term drinking. On the basis of this, there are those who feel strongly that the criminal sanctions that can be brought to bear are disproportionately harsh. Given the levels of social problems that are related to use, there is discussion in some quarters about decriminalizing, if not actually legalizing, use. Those who hold that marijuana should remain an illicit drug cannot point to its drug properties to make the case. While a case certainly can be made, it has to be made on other grounds. Generally these arguments boil down to the position that, as a society, we have enough problems with the drugs that are licit, so why add to our problems?

Clinical Issues

The person who comes to a clinician's attention due to marijuana use may represent a situation containing the same issues as those posed by alcohol abuse. Clearly some problems have resulted from use; otherwise, the individual wouldn't be in a clinician's office. But there may not be dependence. The job of clinicians is not to be police officers. Nonetheless, this is where the legal status begins to cast a shadow over the issue.

By virtue of the fact that someone comes to professional attention, use has clearly become somewhat public. In light of someone's being seen by a clinician, one may question if "moderate" marijuana use is a reasonable clinical goal. Marijuana use can also be problematic in the context of other drug use. Just as marijuana is notorious for causing the munchies, it is also true that, when someone is stoned, the decision to drink or not to drink is hardly an informed, thoughtful one. The client needs to be engaged in the same process of self-examination that is required in the presence of alcohol abuse. Again, follow-up is required to see whether efforts to reduce risk are effective.

There have been efforts to change laws to allow the medical use of marijuana. According to the folk wisdom, there are a number of conditions that can be alleviated by the use of marijuana—these include nausea and lack of appetite that can accompany chemotherapy; chronic pain; HIV- and AIDS-related problems; depression; anxiety; menstrual cramps, migraine, as well as everyday aches, pains, stresses and sleeping difficulties. To date systematic clinical research has not been conducted to assess these beliefs. What many may not know is that there is a medication now available, Dronabinol®, that is THC, the active ingredient of marijuana.

Summary: Cannabinoids

Examples:	Marijuana, hashish, THC
Route of administration:	Smoked, taken by mouth
Length of action:	Smoking: 2–4 hours; ingestion: 5–12 hours
Desired effects:	Sense of relaxation and well-being, euphoria, detachment; modification of level of consciousness, altered perceptions, altered time sense; sexual arousal
Other acute effects:	Slows reaction time and alters perceptions, making it dangerous to operate machinery or drive; Panic; Anxiety; Nausea; Dizziness; Difficulty expressing thoughts; Paranoid thoughts; Depersonalization
Action:	When smoked, absorbed through the lungs; Produces effects through specific binding at cannabinoid receptor sites in the brain that appear to be specific for cannabinoids
Intoxication/overdose:	*Vital signs:* increased respiration rate, increased heart rate, mild increase in temperature; *Physical exam:* red eyes (conjunctival injection), mild dilation of pupils, mild tremor, decreased coordination, decreased strength, less ability to perform complex motor tasks, dry mouth; *Mental status:* feelings of depersonalization, alteration in mood,

	disorganization; anxiety, panic; Memory problems; Paranoid thoughts; Hallucinations
Common problems:	Dependence, panic, anxiety; nausea, dizziness; Difficulty in expressing thoughts, paranoid thoughts, depersonalization, visual distortions, perceptual problems, motor performance may impair driving; Impairment of ability to learn new material; Physical effects with prolonged use include respiratory problems, possible impaired immune function, and possible reproductive problems, including low birth weight infants
Withdrawal symptoms:	Craving, anxiety, irritability, nausea, anorexia, agitation, restlessness, tremor, depression
Interaction with alcohol:	CNS depressant effects; Impairment of driving related skills
Medical uses:	Used to reduce nausea and stimulate appetite in cancer patients, possible treatment of glaucoma

Cannaboids

Drug	Average Amount Taken	Addiction Risk	DEA Schedule
Marijuana	4–40 mg	Moderate	I
Hashish		Moderate	I
Dronabinol® (Marinol®)	2.5–20 mg/day	Low as used medically	III

Inhalants

Inhalants are substances that give off vapors or fumes, which are inhaled for their psychoactive properties. There are 3 kinds of compounds that fall into the category of inhalants. The largest group of inhalants consists of common household products—paints, lighter fluid, paint thinners, other aerosols, felt-tipped pens, correction fluid, cleaning compounds, gasoline, and glue. These are termed the hydrocarbons, based on their chemical composition, and are sometimes referred to as volatile solvents. Another kind, nitrites, take their name from their chemical composition. The butyl nitrites are found in air fresheners and videotape cleaners. Amyl nitrites are known as "poppers" or "snappers," based on the ways they are packaged. They were originally used to treat angina. The third kind of inhalants are the nitrates, which are a form of anesthetics, the most common one being nitrous oxide, known as "laughing gas."

Patterns of Use

Over the past decade, the use of inhalants rose, peaked in 1995, and then declined. Inhalants are most popular among the youngest adolescents. They are easily available and inexpensive. Inhalants can cause permanent brain damage. This is particularly troubling since much inhalant is a group activity, thus exposing a group to this danger. Among eighth graders, inhalants are the second most commonly used drug, even ahead of marijuana. The rate of use drops by half between eighth and twelfth grades. Of high school seniors surveyed in 2003, 3.9% of seniors had used inhalants in the previous year. The rate for tenth graders was 5.4% and the rate for eighth graders, 8.7%.

Inhalant use is highest among Hispanics, followed by whites. African-Americans' use is virtually a third of Hispanics' and half that of whites. In terms of region, use is highest in the West, followed by the North Central region. Use is least common in urban areas and most common outside of cities and suburban areas. Among adolescents, use is virtually twice as high among those who do not expect to attend college. This is one of the few drugs in which use by females exceeds that of males.

Pharmacological Actions

Although the inhalants are a diverse group of compounds, they have several common features. Their molecules are very small, thus allowing them to be absorbed easily by the lungs. Also, their effects are very similar to those of central nervous system depressants. However, their effects seemingly are not due to their impact on neurotransmitters. Being fat soluble, they can be incorporated into cell membranes. This in turn interferes with the cell's level of excitability. The fat-soluble properties of inhalants also account for its distribution into various body organs. This is important because many inhalants and their metabolites are known to be prototypic toxins of the liver, kidneys, and nerve cells. Inhalants' toxicity on the central nervous system was first recognized in the Scandinavian countries; termed "painter's syndrome," it resulted from long exposure to paint fumes.

Summary: Inhalants

Examples:	Paints, other aerosols, organic solvents and cleaning agents, gasoline and other petrochemicals, glue; Vasodilators (amyl and butyl nitrites); Anesthetics (nitrous oxide)
Route of administration:	Inhalation ("huffing")
Length of action:	Varies—several minutes to several hours

Desired effects:	*Volatile solvents:* the "rush"; Euphoria; Behavioral disinhibition; Sensation of floating; Perceptual disturbances, including hallucinations; *Nitrites:* used to postpone or enhance intercourse, especially in gay male population; May cause euphoria; *Nitrous oxide:* euphoria, altered perceptions
Other acute effects:	*Volatile solvents:* cardiac depressants leading to "sudden sniffing death" probably secondary to cardiac arrhythmias, aspiration or respiratory depression, vehicle accidents secondary to intoxication; *Nitrites:* panic reactions, nausea, dizziness, hypotension; *Nitrous oxide:* nausea, vomiting, confusion
Action:	*Volatile solvents:* action is not fully understood and probably varies with the substance inhaled, action on the central nervous system is similar to that of CNS depressants, may act on GABA and glutamate neurotransmitter systems, presumed that inhalants disrupt neural function, intoxication is similar to that of the CNS depressants; *Nitrites:* act by increasing cerebral blood flow, little else known; *Nitrous oxide:* mechanism of action unknown, may involve opiate receptors
Intoxication/overdose:	
Volatile Solvents	*Vital signs:* possible irregular heartbeat; *Physical exam:* ataxia, muscle weakness, dysarthria, nystagmus, diminished reflexes; *Mental status:* euphoria, giddiness, fatigue, confusion, disorientation
Nitrites ("Poppers")	*Vital signs:* decreased blood pressure, increased pulse; *Physical exam:* minimal findings; *Mental status:* minimal changes
Nitrous Oxide	*Vital signs:* increased respiration; *Physical exam:* possible asphyxiation and frostbite of nose, lips, or larynx if inhaled from tank; Loss of motor control; Nausea; Ataxia; Muscle weakness; Dysarthria; Nystagmus; Diminished reflexes; *Mental status:* laughter, giddiness, confusion
Common problems:	*Volatile solvents:* Cardiac depressants leading to "sudden sniffing death" probably secondary to cardiac arrhythmias, aspiration or respiratory depression, atrophy of various areas of brain with attendant behavioral

	symptoms, renal complications, vehicle accidents secondary to intoxication; *Nitrites:* panic reactions, nausea, dizziness, hypotension, negative effects on the hematological and immune systems (anemia, decreased T-cell function); *Nitrous oxide:* paranoid psychosis with confusion (chronic use), depletion of vitamin B-12 with neurological side effects (weakness, peripheral neuropathy), deficits in short-term memory
Withdrawal symptoms:	Psychological dependence symptoms documented (craving, etc.); Physical withdrawal symptoms not well established in humans; Sleep disturbances, nausea, tremor, and irritability reported with volatile solvents; Withdrawal seizures with nitrous oxide in rats
Interaction with alcohol:	Varies by substance, potentiation with volatile solvents
Medical uses:	None, except use of nitrous oxide for anesthesia

Inhalants

Drug	Average Amount Taken	Addiction Risk	DEA Schedule
Volatile solvents (commercial products)	Variable	Moderate	N/A
Nitrites (amyl nitrite, butyl nitrite)	Variable	Unknown	N/A
Nitrous oxide	Variable	Moderate	N/A

Anabolic Androgenic Steroids

Steroids are not used for their psychoactive, mood-altering properties. Drugs in this class are male hormones and are used by athletes to increase muscle development and enhance athletic performance, and are used by people involved with body building. They have been described by some as the male chemical equivalents of breast enhancement in women. While not taken for their mood-altering properties per se, with long-term use there are serious side effects. In addition to the physical problems associated with long-term use, there are also behavioral problems. Anabolic steroid use is thought to cause aggression in some people, hence the term "roid rage."

FOCUS ON DRUGS

Performance-Enhancing Drugs

In 1995, a poll of 198 Olympic-level power athletes was based on the following scenario: you are offered a banned substance with two guarantees. First, you will not be caught, and, second, by taking the substance you will win. Of the athletes asked if they would take the substance, only 3 said they would not. The next scenario proposed: the same undetectable substance will enable you to win every competition entered for the next 5 years but then it would kill you. More than half of those polled reported that they would still use the substance.

Typically substance abuse is thought to involve drugs that act on the brain to alter mood, perceptions, and feeling states. Substance abuse could well be defined more broadly and include substances used to alter not the brain, but the body. This would be the "performance-enhancing drugs." In some instances drugs fall into both camps: the stimulants, the amphetamines, caffeine.

The following overview is of substances currently outside the usual domain of the substance abuse field, but which are getting increased attention. While professional athletes may get the bulk of attention, performance-enhancing drugs are also seen as an issue for those in the college ranks, high school students, and those younger. Although anabolic steroids typically receive the most attention, a number of other substances are also reported to be widely used. The major groups are described below.

Human Growth Hormone (hGH)

This hormone is produced by the pituitary gland. It is known to influence the body's handling of amino acids, one of the body's basic building blocks, promote the synthesis of proteins, as well as support growth-promoting body functions. It is a controlled substance, legally available only by prescription. Persons with an hGH deficiency tend to be short in stature. The presence of excessive amounts leads to the medical condition of giantism.

Studies are quite limited. However, the research to date seems to indicate that while human growth hormone increases muscle size, there is no corresponding increase in performance or strength. Thus, people using hGH only *look* more impressive.

Amphetamines and Stimulants

Amphetamine use is credited with increasing muscle strength, and is valued for providing resistance to fatigue, and, especially among cyclists, valued for improving muscle torque and increasing lung function.

Ephedrine and Ephedra

These are systemwide general stimulants. Among the claims made for them is that they increase alertness, heighten energy levels, and thus add to athletic performance. Outside the locker room realm, they are also touted as appetite suppressants and incorporated in weight loss products. Ephedrine is the major ingredient of many cold remedies and over-the-counter decongestants. There are over 40 species of plants that include these compounds, including the Chinese herb Ma Huang, sometimes referred to as herbal ephedrine. Both the Olympic Committee and NCAA have banned ephedrine, although evidence for its providing a significant performance advantage is limited. In part the ban is related to adverse effects. Among the side effects reported are irritability, rapid heartbeat, sleeplessness, heart palpitations, as well as stroke and heart attack. Herbal weight-loss products containing ephedra were banned in the United States in 2004.

Erythropoietin (EPO) and Blood Doping

Endurance athletes, for example those who run marathons or cyclists, will be aided by anything which increases the blood's capacity to handle oxygen. Hence, all kinds of training regimens, such as living at higher altitudes or sleeping in "altitude tents," have been developed with the goal of enhancing oxygen-carrying capacity. Another technique that has been devised to accomplish this is blood doping, the transfusion of blood, so that there is an increase in hemoglobin, the blood cells that carry oxygen. The drug EPO is a hormone produced in the kidney; it increases hemoglobin, thereby influencing the oxygen-carrying capacity of blood cells.

Studies demonstrate that these efforts do indeed increase the availability of oxygen, as well as increasing endurance. There are, however, some dangers. While the reason is not known, artificially high levels of hemoglobin are associated with stroke, heart attack, and blood clots in the lung. Therefore blood-doping is a banned practice, as is EPO, although there are no easily administered tests to identify it. In face of this, to reduce the use of EPO and doping, the Olympics has set upper limits for hemoglobin values.

Creatine

This is a popular nutritional supplement that has been estimated to represent a $300 million market in the

United States. It came to attention when its use was reported in conjunction with the 1992 Barcelona Olympics, which proved to be a great marketing device.

Creatine is a naturally occurring compound made in the liver, pancreas, and kidneys, and then deposited and stored in muscles. Creatine contributes to the restoraton of muscles after exercise. Accordingly, by increasing creatine content in muscles there is an enhancement of muscles' capacity for restoration. It is viewed as useful in anaerobic events, and is reportedly used widely by college athletes, high school athletes, and persons involved in individual fitness regimens.

In studies involving an array of athletes—swimmers, cyclists, weight lifters—creatine supplementation has been shown to increase performance and endurance. For example, among sprinters, creatine has been shown to improve average sprint times by 1–2%. For races determined by hundredths of a second, this could be significant.

As a nutritional supplement, a product of what is sometimes termed the "neutraceutical industry," creatine is not regulated by the Food and Drug Administration. This means there is no regulation in formulating products, and less pressure/opportunity for safety testing. While there are no apparent problems with short-term use, the effects of long-term use are unknown.

Beta-Hydroxy-Beta-Methylbutyrate (HMB)

This is a nutritional supplement that is marketed as an anti-catabolic. This means it supposedly suppresses the breakdown of protein after a workout and restricts the body to burning carbohydrates and fat to meet its energy requirements. Thus, it is supposed to maintain and increase lean body mass. Indeed, while the basis for its function is unclear, some studies appear to support the claim that HMB supplementation does prevent exercise-induced muscle change. At best, however, the performance studies show modest improvement for persons who haven't been involved in any kind of training or conditioning. For those involved in workout and training regimens, there was no improvement.

Seemingly there are no identified negative side effects. In fact a review of studies showed that it was associated with a lowering of cholesterol, and systolic blood pressure. So it may have cardio-protective benefits even if there are no apparent performance-enhancing properties.

Androstenedione (andro)

This over-the-counter product falls into the category of nutritional supplements. It is marketed as increasing testosterone levels, and a natural alternative to anabolic steroids. Androstenedione is the precursor to testosterone, and is thought to be broken down in testosterone. It has been said that the hype for andro exceeds the scientific study. The evidence to date suggests that no demonstrated improvement accompanies use.

Others

This is far from a complete catalog of drugs associated with athletics and improving performance. In addition are pain medications that enable athletes barely able to walk off the football field to return to the game after half time, or a pitcher in the World Series to continue despite a badly injured ankle requiring some temporary stitches. There are even drugs becoming available to mask the use of banned drugs.

A Point for Reflection

A provocative essay in the *British Journal of Sports Medicine* raises questions worth reflection. Are amateur sports a notion from a bygone era? Are elite athletes as much a product of their genes as evidence of their dedication, hard work, and spirit? If an Olympic athlete has a genetic mutation that naturally provides 40–50% more red blood cells than average, is this an unfair advantage? Does it matter if blood counts are elevated by altitude training, by using a hypoxic machine, by genetic mutation, or by taking EPO, the one avenue deemed unfair? Does allowing everyone to take performance-enhancing drugs level the playing field? In Olympic sports would allowing everyone to use performance-enhancing substances reduce the disparity that now exists because only wealthy nations can afford the expensive technology associated with improving performance? EPO at a cost of about $122 per month would be far less costly than the hyoxic air machine.

What limits should be placed on drug use in sports? Should the emphasis be on health testing, not on drug testing? Is it better to determine a safe level of PCV (packed cell volume, i.e., the proportion of blood comprised of red blood cells) rather than worry how a particular level is achieved, whether through training, natural maturation, or use of drugs? Realistically, can the penalties for being caught ever overshadow the benefits of winning? Is performance enhancement against the spirit of sport or *is* it the spirit of sport?

From: Tokish JM, Kocher MS, Hawkins RJ. Ergonic aids: A review of basic science, performance, side effects, and status in sport. *The American Journal of Sports Medicine* 32:1543–1553, 2004.

Savulescu J, Foddy B, Clayton C. Why we should allow performance enhancing drugs in sport? *British Journal of Sports Medicine* 38: 666–670, 2004.

The use of anabolic steroids is one of the lesser achievements of the Olympic movement. They were supposedly first used by members of the Soviet Union weight-lifting team at the 1954 Olympics. However, it was Yankee ingenuity that made use more widespread. A physician with the U.S. team that year got wind of this use, and on returning home teamed up with a pharmaceutical company to produce what is probably the most widely known anabolic steroid, Dianabol®. The use of performance-enhancing drugs was subsequently outlawed by the International Olympic Committee. At this time there is a very lengthy list of prohibited substances, and drug testing is routine. A number of these substances are included in small amounts in over-the-counter medications and in prescription drugs taken for legitimate medical conditions. So knowing what is or is not okay to use almost seems to require a degree in pharmacology. Ironically, the efforts to identify athletes' use of banned drugs has been the major factor leading to advancements in drug-testing procedures now available in clinical and legal settings.

Patterns of Use

The use of steroids among adolescents appears to have been on the rise since 1991, the first year that NIDA began to include steroids in its national surveys. Nationwide in 2003, 2.5% of eighth graders, 3% of tenth-graders, and 3.5% of twelfth graders had taken anabolic steroids at least once in their lives. This is essentially double the rate of use in 1991. Few data exist on the extent of steroid abuse by adults. Among both adolescents and adults, steroid abuse is higher among males than females. However, steroid abuse is growing among young women. Most of the studies of steroid use have been conducted with particular populations, such as college athletes or adolescents in Nebraska or high school football players in Indiana. Not unexpectedly, users are more likely to be involved in school-sponsored sports programs. Those who use steroids are also more likely to use alcohol, nicotine, and other drugs than are those who do not use steroids. What is of note is the relatively young age of initiation of steroid use. The statewide study of Indiana football players found that half had begun use by the age of 14½, and 15% had begun taking steroids before the age of 10.

Another compound that could be classified as a steroid based on chemical composition is gamma-hydroxybutyrate (GHB). Gamma-hydroxybutyrate, first synthesized in 1960, was initially used as a relaxant to induce anesthesia and also as a short-term anesthetic. However, the properties that make it attractive for substance abuse made it unsatisfactory as an agent to induce anesthesia. It has a number of effects on the central nervous system, primarily as a depressant. In many ways it mimics alcohol. Thus it is classified here as well as by NIDA in its publications as a sedative. As a substance of abuse, GHB has become popular in several very different circles. It is reputed to build muscle mass and therefore has become popular among body builders and competitive athletes. It is also popular at raves and known as a club drug, due to its hallucinogenic and euphoric properties. It is available as a colorless, odorless liquid, powder, or capsules. It may be injected but is usually taken orally. Low doses produce euphoria, but higher doses produce sedation. As a recreational drug, there is one major problem. There is relatively little difference between the dose that induces euphoria and that which causes sedation. So there is a very small margin of error. Because most GBH is produced illegally, there is often considerable variability between the supposed and actual dose. GBH has become known as one of the date rape drugs. Because it is colorless and odorless it can be slipped into someone's drink—alcohol or soda—without notice causing loss of consciousness and amnesia. There is no known antidote for GHB poisoning. In cases of poisoning, overdose treatment involves treating the life threatening symptoms and can entail the use of life supports to maintain respiration, heartbeat, and to keep airways open. Generally, as the drug wears off, people awaken spontaneously.

GHB is now being imported, it also can be made inexpensively and easily in anyone's kitchen. This can introduce further problems because lye is used, and poor laboratory technique can mean that some of the residue of the lye remains. Because GHB is no longer legal, there has been a new development, abuse of the legal and easier to acquire "precursors," substances which when metabolized are converted to GHB, and thus induce the same effects as GHB.

Routes of Administration

Anabolic steroids are taken orally as tablets or are injected into the large muscles. When using steroids, athletes tend to adopt a particular regimen that entails a period of use followed by some time off or the use of different steroids in a predetermined sequence, with time off. Whatever the pattern, it is often called a "cycle." The rationale behind this, for which the medical basis is questionable, is that such a pattern can diminish side effects. The cycle of use is also coordinated with other training activities in the hope of achieving peak performance at the time of competition.

Summary: Anabolic Androgenic Steroids

Examples:	Testosterone compounds,19-nortestosterone derivatives, orally active androgen
Route of administration:	Orally or by injection into large muscles
Desired effects:	Enhancement of appearance or athletic performance with attendant self-confidence and self-esteem
Other acute effects:	Negligible
Action:	Bind to hormone-specific receptor complexes in almost every organ system in the body, also have direct action on neuronal cell membranes mediated by specific receptors

Intoxication/overdose:	Rare; Most of the negative effects are from regular and prolonged use, rather than from intoxication and overdose
Common problems:	Virilizing side effects (vary by gender); In men, increased facial hair, deepening of voice, male pattern of baldness, acne; In women, clitoral enlargement and menstrual irregularities; Feminizing effects in men (such as gynecomastia [breast development]); Reduction in HDL cholesterol; Cholestatic jaundice, hepatitis, liver cancer; Psychiatric side effects (hypomania, mania, depression, panic, and aggressive symptoms all reported)
Withdrawal symptoms:	Depression, fatigue, decreased libido, muscle pain, headache, craving
Interaction with alcohol:	Not well researched
Medical uses:	Replacement of endogenous testosterone, to increase red blood cells and complement factor, treatment of endometriosis and fibrocystic breast disease

Anabolic Androgenic Steroids

Drug	Average Amount Taken	Addiction Risk	DEA Schedule
Testosterone esters (testosterone cypionate)		Moderate	N/A
19-nortestosterone derivatives (nandrolone decanoate, nandrolone phenylpropionate)	Daily doses equivalent of 20–2000 mg testosterone/day	Moderate	N/A
Orally active androgens (danazol, fluoxymesterone, methyltestosterone, oxymesterone, stanzolol)	Daily dose from 4–200 times the usual dose of androgens	Moderate	N/A

Caffeine

Historical Notes

Caffeine, a stimulant drug, is the most widely used psychoactive drug in the world. Its use far exceeds that of alcohol or nicotine. It has been known and used throughout the world for millennia. It is a stimulant drug. However, its effects might be considered fairly subtle. Many who use caffeine regularly are not able to easily distinguish its effects and identify mood or behavioral changes associated with use. For many it is just a beverage. However, if pushed, people might note that caffeine helps get them going in the morning, or helps them stay awake if driving late at night, or may mean they have a hard time falling asleep if they have a cup of coffee after dinner. Because coffee has psychoactive properties, there is some discussion as to whether caffeine should or should not be considered a substance of abuse.

Patterns of Use

Caffeine consumption varies greatly by country. The annual caffeine consumption in both Sweden and Great Britain, for example, is twice the amount used in the United States.

Sources of Caffeine Caffeine isn't only in coffee, tea, soft drinks, and energy drinks. It is also found in chocolate and a number of over-the-counter medications. Table 13.6 lists the caffeine found in a number of common products.

Use in the United States The daily amount caffeine consumed in the United States varies by age. Age groups also vary by their dominant source of caffeine. Soft drinks are the major caffeine source among children and young adults. Coffee is the major source for those in middle age, and it's tea among the elderly. Coffee, tea, and caffeinated soft drinks account for almost 90% of caffeine consumed, the remainder primarily comes from a variety of over-the-counter medications, plus

Table 13.6 Caffeine Content of Common Products

Products	Caffeine Content (mg)
Coffee, decaf	4
Hershey milk chocolate bar	25
Espresso, 1-oz cup	40
Brewed tea, 8-oz cup	50
Coca-Cola, 20-oz bottle	57
Red Bull (energy drink), 8.3 oz can	80
Excedrin pain reliever, 2 tablets	130
Brewed coffee, 12-oz cup	200
Mountain Dew, 64-oz (double big gulp)	294

From: Griffiths RR, Mumford GK. Caffeine: A drug of abuse? *Psychopharamcology. The Fourth Generation of Progress.* American College of Neuropsychopharmacology, 2003. www.acnp.org

Table 13.7 Daily Total Caffeine Consumption in the United States 1996

	Milligrams of	
Age	**Daily Caffeine (Average Users)**	**Caffeine (Heavy Users)***
1–5	14	37
6–9	22	45
10–14	33	74
15–19	66	149
20–24	106	227
25–34	123	258
35–49	170	382
50–64	169	357
>64	136	296
Total	120	

*Heavy users are those in the 90th percentile, meaning 9% consume more and 89% consume less.

From: Knight CA, Knight I, Mitchell DC, Zepp JE. Beverage caffeine intake in the United States, consumers and subpopulations of interest: Estimate from the Share of Intake Panel Survey. *Food and Chemical Toxicology* 43:1923–1930, 2004.

chocolate, and cocoa. The average daily consumption of caffeine (in mg) for different age groups is presented in Table 13.7.

The figures in Table 13.7 are national averages based on the entire U.S. population, including the subgroup which doesn't use caffeine at all. So the average consumption of those who use caffeine is actually higher, and is more in the vicinity of 200 mg per day.

Absorption and Metabolism

Caffeine is rapidly absorbed and distributed throughout the water of the body. The levels of caffeine peak between 30 and 75 minutes after consumption. Caffeine is metabolized by the liver for removal from the body. The half-life of caffeine is about 4–5 hours. Since coffee drinkers are likely to have several cups a day, throughout the day there is commonly a gradually upward rise in the blood concentration of caffeine throughout the day. It's being consumed at a faster rate than it is removed.

Acute Effects

Caffeine acts as a stimulant by inhibiting the GABA receptors in the brain; these natural inhibitors slow communication in the central nervous system. A dose of 100–200 mg, (1 to 2 cups of coffee) is associated with increased alertness, relief of drowsiness, improved thinking and increased endurance. However, caffeine impairs fine motor coordination. With higher doses of 250–700 mg, caffeine can induce anxiety, feeling jittery, insomnia, nervousness, hypertension. Levels above 1,000 mg can cause rapid heart beat, sleeplessness, tinnitus (ringing noise in the ear), and cognitive difficulties. A fatal oral dose of caffeine can occur after consumption in excess of 5,000 mg, the equivalent of 40 strong cups of coffee taken in a very short period.

The body very quickly and rapidly accommodates to the presence of caffeine, meaning that tolerance is established. A person's response to consuming caffeine depends on several factors. For one, there are differences between people's *innate sensitivity* to caffeine. In addition, *tolerance* comes from previous use. The regular coffee drinker might have a cup and a refill and not notice much difference. For those who drink caffeine irregularly, a half of a Mountain Dew may have a far greater impact. Another factor is the *dose,* the amount of caffeine ingested. In contrast to alcohol which we think of in particular quantities such as a can of beer, or a glass of wine, few people have any idea about the amount of caffeine they ingest. For example, someone could easily eat a chocolate bar, and not long afterwards drink a cup of coffee with a half-cup refill, followed by a pain capsule, each of which would be delivering a dose of caffeine.

Various studies have demonstrated that caffeine does improve performance by increasing focus and attention, and heightening the energy level. It also enhances performance in safety-critical situations that involve boring or repetitive tasks. Caffeine makes falling asleep more difficult. Not unexpectedly people in the real world tend to orchestrate their caffeine intake throughout the day to take advantage of the enhancements in performance while avoiding the impediments.

In large measure the impact of caffeine is influenced by the person's regular level of caffeine consumption. Negative effects follow caffeine doses that are higher than usual amounts. Among the most common complaints are feeling anxious or jittery; headaches are also common.

There is something that makes assessing caffeine's effects a bit difficult. Typically tests of a drug's effects are conducted when people have been abstinent and have no drug in their systems. So imagine a regular coffee drinker being tested early in the morning, before the usual mug that is part of the routine of getting going. If that person reports a "positive" response to the caffeine, is this because a "normal" feeling state is being improved? Or is this coffee drinker actually a bit caffeine-deprived and, accordingly, the positive response is the result of treating a mini-withdrawal state?

Chronic Effects

An immediate issue in thinking about caffeine is the extent to which its dependence results from use. Regular caffeine use does produce *tolerance.*

This tolerance is established quite rapidly. One research study demonstrated that within a week's time, an increase in the usual amount of caffeine ceases to interfere with sleep in any way. Other studies have shown that within a couple days of higher caffeine consumption, the initial physiological changes associated with caffeine, such as increased blood pressure, fade.

Compared to other stimulants, particularly amphetamines or cocaine, caffeine ranks as a poor cousin, especially in terms of *drug seeking*. Caffeine does not produce equivalent ratings of "liking" or "euphoria" as do the other stimulants. It does not produce an equivalent change in mood states as occurs with some other stimulant drugs. In terms of ratings, its reinforcing properties were evaluated as similar to nicotine. Use may be promoted as much by what feelings caffeine can curtail (withdrawal) as by the feelings it produces.

Withdrawal is also a mark of dependence. Compared to other psychoactive drugs, the symptoms associated with caffeine cessation are relatively mild. Based on a review of about 50 studies dating back to 1833, the following withdrawal symptoms are reported, in order of descending frequency: (1) headache; (2) drowsiness along with decreased energy; (3) decreased feelings of well-being and contentment, more irritability; (4) being less sociable and talkative; (5) flu-like symptoms, aches, hot or cold spells, nausea; and (6) blurred vision. Along with these, tests typically show impairment in performance. The severity of withdrawal is proportionate to the level of the usual, maintenance dose as well as the length of use. If forced to go without caffeine, approximately half of regular caffeine users experience headaches. A smaller group, about 10%, report more serious effects.

Course of Withdrawal Withdrawal symptoms most typically occur from 12 to 24 hours after the last intake of caffeine. The peak of discomfort occurs between 24 and 48 hours. The duration of symptoms may range from 2 or 3 days or as long as a week until usual levels of energy and alertness return.

Significance of Withdrawal Eighty-two percent of all U.S. adults use caffeine. If even 10% experience levels of more serious withdrawal, from time to time, that represents significant numbers The potential importance of caffeine withdrawal is due more to the sheer size of the population potentially affected than to the nature of the symptoms. At this point there are far more questions than answers to what the impact may be. For example, what problems might caffeine withdrawal pose for a commercial airline pilot? What are the implications in the workplace or in terms of highway safety? What problems might caffeine withdrawal pose for patients after surgery? In response to the later question, some pilot efforts have been made to infuse caffeine intravenously to reduce the likelihood of withdrawal in surgical patients.

Medical Import of Long-Term Use Another significant concern with any substance is the nature of any medical conditions that result from long-term use. It has been noted that while cutting down on caffeine may be recommended for any number of medical conditions ranging from ulcers to cardiovascular disease, to cancers, and anxiety disorders, the actual medical basis for this advice is rather scant. There are no medical conditions that are clearly recognized as caused or aggravated by caffeine.

Caffeine–Other Drug Interactions

As a stimulant, caffeine counters some of the depressant effects of alcohol on alertness and memory. Caffeine also reduces alcohol-induced sleepiness. However, other effects of alcohol are not tempered by caffeine. Caffeine does help with dizziness caused by alcohol, which is sometimes present with alcohol intoxication. The question has been raised whether caffeine increases alcohol tolerance in a more general fashion. There is also an interaction with nicotine, When taken with caffeine, nicotine is perceived to be more pleasurable and reinforcing, and is associated with increased ratings of "liking" in laboratory settings. The liver enzymes that metabolize caffeine also play a role in metabolism of a wide variety of other drugs, from heart medications to those used for treating psychiatric illness. Having a lot of caffeine when taking higher doses of such drugs may mean these enzyme systems are over-loaded, or saturated, and the rate of removal of caffeine and these other drugs will be slowed.

A Substance of Abuse?

Some point out that what is considered abuse in significant part is a social definition. Some note too that for the most part excessive use of caffeine tends to be self-limited. Of course, the same could be said for alcohol, and it is indeed the exceptions that are the concern. On the basis of applying the APA's diagnostic criteria for substance dependence, one study identified about one-third of the general population as caffeine dependent. (See Chapter 4 for diagnostic criteria.) However, within the APA diagnostic criteria, the withdrawal syndrome for caffeine is characterized as not clinically significant. Withdrawal from some other substances can be life threatening; this is not the case with caffeine.

Seemingly a small proportion of people experience severe caffeine withdrawal; they may seek medical attention for anxiety or insomnia resulting from caffeine use. Some refer to this as indicating the existence of *caffeinism.* Others, while not denying some instances of more marked withdrawal, seem to believe that such a term is not quite appropriate. In assessing whether caffeine constitutes a substance of abuse, a relevant question is the extent to which caffeine produces adverse effects for the individual and/or society.

Children's Use of Caffeine

Children are the segment of the population in which caffeine use is most discussed. Concerns too have been raised about the possible impact of caffeine on the course of pregnancy, the impact on the newborn of prenatal caffeine exposure, the impact on children with ADD/ADHD as well as children at large. Children, as well as adults, consume caffeine in their diets. Caffeine is consumed at least weekly by 98% of 5- to 18-year-olds, mostly in carbonated beverages. Seven-year-olds consume an average of 12.3 mg/day, increasing to 24.8 mg/day by age 10. Intake increases with age. In the context of a large study of the relationship of caffeine intake and sleep among 7th, 8th, and 9th graders, the caffeine intake ranged from 0 to 800 mg/day. And yes, caffeine use at higher levels was related to sleep disturbances—less total sleep, increased awakenings, and more daytime sleep.

Of note, children too are variable in their sensitivity to caffeine. For some, caffeine is a super-stimulant. It really revs them up. They too have been found to show signs of dependence and withdrawal. If they consume, say, 4 times their usual dose for a week or two, when stopping children show some signs of being less alert, responding more slowly to different memory and performance tasks. However, there is no evidence of an effect either on the course of pregnancy or on infant development.

A large review study undertaken by staff of the National Institute on Health concluded that the effects of caffeine in children seem to be modest and generally innocuous. As the "generally" implies, this means that there will be some children for whom caffeine may be more of an issue, such as those with particular sensitivity or those with anxiety disorders. Also as tolerance develops quickly and there are some signs of withdrawal, questions are raised about the possible impact of the newer high caffeine-containing energy drinks. There is another question not raised that may warrant thought. If kids are drinking more sodas and soft drinks, these may have a greater danger than the caffeine content. That is the calories. This is especially so in light of what is characterized as an epidemic of childhood obesity.

CLINICAL ISSUES

Assessment

The basic issues that pertain to assessment of alcohol problems are also applicable to other drug use. The DAST screening test is specific to drug use; it is included in Chapter 9. Any client with an alcohol problem needs to be assessed for other drug use. The criteria for diagnosis of abuse and dependence use are in Chapter 4.

Treatment Goals

One of the central questions in dealing with the treatment of other drug problems is the issue of treatment goals. The most troublesome question is "In the absence of dependence, is establishing a moderate level of use an appropriate clinical goal?" Typically trying to help someone achieve moderate use of other drugs is not generally considered an appropriate treatment goal. The potential exception is marijuana. In part this is related to a drug's illicit status. This alone raises the ante considerably. As a culture we do not condone recreational cocaine use or consider "a little" steroid use okay. Neither do we view "chasing the dragon" (smoking heroin) as no big deal. These judgments for the most part are not wholly arbitrary social conventions. In many instances the concern about any use reflects a drug's addiction potential. For example, with cocaine or nicotine, the risk is considerable. Consequently, establishing and maintaining a moderate, low-risk pattern of use is unlikely. Combined with that is the recognition that, with the continuing use of some substances, there is the issue of potential changes in the route of administration, which can introduce further problems. For example, to move from smoking or inhaling heroin to IV use introduces risk of infection associated with injection, as well as increases the risk of dependence.

Also, there are significant health consequences that can accompany long-term use—for example, with steroids. Given the potential health consequences over the short haul—for example, with cocaine or inhalants—any use is considered to be risky. Accordingly, clinical efforts would be directed to helping someone stop using. Most would consider it clinically ill advised, if not downright unethical, to work with someone to achieve a moderate use.

Harm Reduction

While the clinician's goal may be abstinence, that may not be the client's goal. Programs and clinicians can be purists and essentially push away those clients who are not interested in adopting abstinence as the goal of treatment. However, there is an alternative possibility—harm reduction. For the author of this book, the first exposure to harm reduction occurred back in the late 1960s, before harm reduction even had a name. It occurred in a large city, where several free clinics had been set up to serve the "flower people," counterculture, and large youth population. The large foundation funding these clinics requested an evaluation of their effectiveness before continuing funding. The results were far less than the organizers of the free clinics had hoped for. As one staff member plaintively noted, "We're just making drug users smarter." Those served by the clinics were not more likely to curtail or reduce their drug use. However, among those served by the clinics there were fewer overdoses, fewer "bad trips," fewer sexually transmitted diseases, and fewer medical emergencies resulting from street drug use. Thus, while the goal of the clinics may not have been harm reduction, that is what was being accomplished. Creating "smarter," meaning more informed, users yields benefits.

The goal of a harm reduction approach is to reduce the risks and harms for clients that may be associated with use. In the United States this is such a foreign concept that it tends to rub people the wrong way or strike some as unethical. If that is your response, take a deep breath and try to set these biases aside. Consider attending some workshops that explore this approach. Simply dismissing harm reduction without careful thought can short-change clients and limit your own effectiveness. The reality is that clients adopt their own goals for treatment; these cannot be imposed externally. The best that you can do is to help the client thoughtfully consider the options available. In fact, in the course of treatment, the client's goals may change.

Harm reduction includes promoting designated drivers and the promotion of needle exchange. It also includes ensuring that clients are informed about sterile injection practices and injection procedures. (Abscesses that accompany IV use are frequently due to improper injection practices.) For the young adolescent who is using inhalants, harm reduction might be pointing out the lesser danger of marijuana, in effect encouraging the adolescent to consider the use of a less dangerous drug. Harm reduction is at work when programs try to get the word out that there is bad dope being sold on the street. Public health departments regularly do this when there has been a rash of overdoses or medical problems due to contaminants. And, harm reduction is at work at raves, when drug testing is provided to determine if the drugs that people think they are taking are indeed those substances.

Such writing is a sort of mental masturbation—he is always f—gg—g his imagination.—I don't mean that he is indecent but viciously soliciting his own ideas into a state which is neither poetry nor any thing else but a Bedlam vision produced by raw pork and opium.
LORD BYRON
A letter commenting on Keats, 1820

For those who have a bit of problem with the concept, reflect for a moment on those with alcohol dependence who enter the treatment system. In effect, the bulk of these clients have been trying harm reduction on their own and without success. Part of the clinical task is helping people review their alcohol use, to see the different strategies that have been tried to reduce problems and make the drinking work again. If the client is still not convinced, there is a technique that is sometimes used clinically to help people assess the presence of dependence. With the assistance of the therapist, the client embarks on an "experiment," in which the client enters into a contract with the therapist. The client agrees to set a specific number of drinks per day that *he or she* considers reasonable, be it 2, 5, or 10, for a set period—typically, a month. The person agrees to have the established number each day, every day, no more, no less. The "no less" part of the contract is an important aspect. Some people realize that certain situations are bound to mean heavy drinking. If afraid what this may lead to, some people will white knuckle it and, to be safe, drink nothing. Since this experiment is intended to help determine the presence of a problem, the client doesn't get the option of avoiding difficulties by not drinking. Ahead of time, the client also agrees to use the "data" collected during the experiment as evidence of the presence or absence of loss of control. Being unable to stick with the limit he or she sets confirms a need for treatment. A month later, the results of the experiment are evaluated. Was the client able to stick to the amount that had been selected as reasonable? Even if he or she was, how much effort did it take? Was such an expenditure of effort worth it? More often than not, the loss of control and the preoccupation become all too apparent, and individuals then move into formal treatment.

Pharmacological Treatment

Given the increasing knowledge of the changes in the brain that accompany long-term drug use, there is now the possibility for what was previously only a dream—that is, the potential to develop drugs with specific properties that may be helpful in treatment. This is different from the use of medications during withdrawal. The discussion in this chapter does not do justice to the topic but only highlights the main issues. Please see the "Resources and Further Reading" section at the conclusion of this chapter. In brief, there are now 3 major approaches to drug therapies: drug replacement, anticraving drugs, and blocking agents.

Drug Replacement

In some instances drug replacement means substitution of a different drug; in other instances it involves actually prescribing the drug of abuse. The goals of drug replacement are twofold. One is harm reduction. The other is the promotion of an environment in which rehabilitation efforts can get a foothold, in which there is time to engage people in treatment, thereby creating the possibility for long-term, including abstinence-oriented, treatment. Nicotine replacement is a prime example of drug replacement. Whether the nicotine is delivered by patch, an inhaler, or a nasal spray, the delivery route is much safer than smoking. Another example is the use of methadone.

Methadone is a pharmacological substitute for heroin. Many of the risks of heroin are related to the route of administration. With a street drug, neither dealers nor manufacturers abide by FDA standards; thus, there is an ever present risk of contaminants or unintentional overdose. Also, compared with methadone, heroin has a shorter length of action, which requires more frequent administration. On several counts methadone is a far safer alternative to heroin. Furthermore, methadone, while pharmacologically similar to heroin, does not provide the rush that accompanies heroin use, though it does stave off withdrawal. Other drugs have become available as alternatives to methadone. One is buprenorphine. It, too, blocks the effects of other opiates and prevents withdrawal, and it does not produce a subjective high. The other is similar. It is available for office-based dispensing. One of the advantages of buprenorphine over methadone is that it only has to be taken 3 times a week, so daily trips to a clinic are not necessary. For either of these medications, an adequate dose must be given; if patients are being undermedicated, they are far more likely to leave treatment.

Anticraving Drugs

Craving seems to be a more prominent feature of some drugs of dependence than others. Most notable are nicotine, cocaine, heroin, and alcohol. One does not typically associate a similar kind of craving with inhalants, the hallucinogens, or even marijuana. A priority in exploring new medications are those that will reduce craving. To date, the major successes have been around the development of medications to reduce the craving common with alcohol dependence. Wellbutrin, known as Zyban® when marketed as a smoking cessation drug, is an antidepressant medication that reduces the craving associated with nicotine dependence. Research is also suggesting that some patients having particular symptoms, such as anxiety or depression, may respond to psychotropic medications.

Blocking Agents

Naltrexone is an opiate agonist. That means, if present, it binds with the opiate receptors. Therefore, if opiates are taken, they would not be able to have an effect, because the receptors where they have their actions are already "taken." For the person who has withdrawn from all opiates, the use of naltrexone can serve as an insurance policy of sorts. If opiates are taken, there would not be the rush and high that are the motive for use. Disulfiram certainly is a disincentive to drink. If someone uses alcohol while on disulfiram, they will become sick. For this reason disulfiram is sometimes referred to as a blocking agent. It is in terms of dissuading someone from having a drink. But it isn't a blocking agent in the pharmacological sense. The action of disulfiram is due to its slowing the breakdown of a by-product formed when alcohol is metabolized (acetaldehyde); it is this build-up of acetaldehyde that prompts the distress.

Pregnancy and the Use of Drugs Other Than Alcohol

Epidemiology

Substance use during pregnancy is a major concern. Alcohol and some other drugs are teratogens, meaning that they can disrupt fetal development. Alcohol in combination with other drug use is the leading cause of preventable birth defects in the United States. The first national survey of drug use during pregnancy found the following rates of drug use among the 4 million women surveyed: nicotine, 20%; alcohol, 18.8%;

marijuana 2.9%; cocaine, 1.1%, and other illicit drug use, including opiates, less than 1.1%. The total for any illicit drug use among pregnant women was 5.5%.

There are differences in the rate of illicit drug use during pregnancy for different racial/ethnic groups. The most recent estimate of illicit drug use during pregnancy is 11.3% for African-Americans, 4.5% for Hispanics, and 4.4% white women. In terms of absolute numbers, the largest number of pregnant women using drugs is white women, given their being the largest population group. However, differences between racial/ethnic groups are not a product of race/ethnicity per se, or due to cultural differences between groups. The important determinant is socioeconomic. Poverty is associated with drug use. When one takes into account age, level of education, and household income, then these racial/ethnic differences in rates of drug use disappear.

Cocaine-Exposed Infants

Cocaine is highly soluble in both water and fat tissue; therefore, it can easily cross the placenta from mother to fetus. When cocaine is used intravenously or as a free base (crack), passage from mother to fetus is enhanced. The fetus has a limited ability to metabolize cocaine, which may lead to its accumulation in the fetus. A binge pattern of use common with cocaine also contributes to even higher levels of cocaine in the fetus. Transfer of cocaine from mother to infant appears to be greater in the first and third trimesters of pregnancy. One of cocaine's most potent effects is the constriction of blood vessels. Constricted blood vessels in the uterus, placenta, and umbilical cord can retard the transfer of cocaine from mother to fetus. However, this constriction of blood vessels is far from being a protective device for the unborn baby. This constriction also means that there is less passage of everything else, including essential nutrients, and less ability to exchange waste products from the fetus to the mother. It is thought that this decreased blood flow may be as important as the cocaine itself in causing whatever abnormalities occur in fetal development.

There has been considerable media coverage of the detrimental effects of prenatal exposure to cocaine. However, the effects are not as clear-cut as such accounts imply. In any consideration of the effects of cocaine on pregnancy, keep in mind that women who use cocaine throughout pregnancy also have many other risk factors. These include cigarette smoking, alcohol consumption, less education, poor prenatal/medical care, use of other drugs of abuse, younger age, being a single parent, and sexually transmitted diseases. In addition, problems can arise from toxic products that may be mixed with the cocaine.

The following characteristics have consistently been reported as accompanying maternal cocaine use: a greater likelihood of maternal health problems that can have an impact on the neonate (such as infections), impaired fetal growth, smaller infant head circumference, premature birth, and an increased risk of still-births. Cocaine use also appears to be involved with the onset of premature labor. Higher rates of early pregnancy losses and third trimester placental abortions appear to be major complications of maternal cocaine use. However, the highly publicized behavioral problems that were supposedly characteristic of "crack babies" do not seem to be at all universal among children that have been exposed to cocaine prenatally.

Animal studies have helped provide some answers regarding cocaine's effects by using research designs that control for many of the other factors that complicate studies with humans. These studies provide evidence of growth retardation, separation of the placenta, cerebral infarctions (strokes), increased general pre- and postnatal mortality, and limb/digit reductions and eye anomalies. But the risk of such abnormalities seems low in animal models and seems to require high doses. Analysis of all available studies conducted with this population suggests that cocaine is not a major source of human birth defects and that most children are likely to be normal in terms of body structure and later neurological developmental. The problems that are seen may be the result of other factors that are present in the lives of the addicted women, not necessarily attributable to the cocaine per se—again, these factors are poverty, inadequate pre- and postnatal care, inadequate nutrition, other drug use, and other medical problems of the mother.

Opiate-Exposed Infants

The physical problems encountered by the pregnant opiate-dependent woman are enormous. For one, medical complications abound due to the frequent use of dirty needles. Due to the frequent use of needles, the women have abscesses, ulcers, bacterial infections, and hepatitis. Moreover, many opiate-dependent women tend to be extremely sexually active and have a history of sexually transmitted diseases. Sexually transmitted diseases such as gonorrhea, syphilis, herpes, and AIDS are common. Their living conditions are often poor, and many infections are transmitted within these settings. Because these women are poorly nourished, they frequently have vitamin deficiencies, such as vitamin C (associated with nicotine and smoking) and the B vitamins (associated with cocaine use). In addition, iron deficiency anemia and folic acid deficiency anemia occur during pregnancy.

The most common obstetrical complication in opiate-dependent women who have had no prenatal care is preterm birth. These infants have the expected complications seen in infants born prematurely. If the infants are born at full term, they may have pneumonia or meconium aspiration syndrome (respiratory problems from sucking first feces when in the uterus or with the first breath).

The extremely high-risk environment from which the pregnant drug-dependent woman comes predisposes them to a host of neonatal problems. In heroin-dependent women, a significant part of the medical complications seen in their babies is due to low birth weight and prematurity. The incidence of low birth weight may approach 50%. There are a number of conditions known to be associated with low birth weight, regardless of its cause. Medical complications generally reflect (1) the amount of prenatal care that the mother has received; (2) whether she has suffered any particular obstetrical or medical complications, including toxemia of pregnancy, hypertension, or infection; and, most important, (3) multiple drug use, which may produce an unstable intrauterine milieu complicated by withdrawal and overdose. This last situation is extremely hazardous, since it predisposes the neonate to meconium staining and subsequent aspiration pneumonia, which may cause significant problems and increase risk of death.

In both premature and term infants, withdrawal from opiates can occur. Appropriate assessment and rapid treatment are essential to treat withdrawal in these infants, so that they can recover without incident. Narcotic abstinence contributes considerably to problems after birth. However, not all infants born to drug-dependent mothers experience withdrawal. Estimates of the percentage who have some withdrawal symptoms range from 60% to 90%. The neonatal narcotic abstinence syndrome is characterized by signs and symptoms of central nervous system hyperirritability, gastrointestinal problems, respiratory distress, and vague autonomic symptoms, including yawning, sneezing, mottling, and fever. The infants initially develop tremors ("the shakes"), which are mild at first but progress in severity. A high-pitched cry, increased muscle tone, irritability, increased deep tendon reflexes, and an exaggerated Moro reflex—a reflex in newborns, a "startle response"—are all characteristic of opiate withdrawal among newborns.

In infants experiencing withdrawal, the rooting reflex—the impulse to snuggle in and nurse—is increased, and sucking either fists or thumbs is common, yet feedings are difficult and the babies regurgitate frequently. These feeding difficulties occur because of an uncoordinated and ineffectual sucking reflex. Also, the infants may develop loose stools; therefore, they are susceptible to dehydration and electrolyte imbalance. The time of onset of symptoms is variable. Following delivery, the newborn's serum and tissue levels of the drug(s) used by the mother begin to fall. The newborn infant continues to metabolize and excrete the drug. Withdrawal occurs when the level of opiates in the tissues reaches a critically low level. Because of the variation in time of onset and in degree of severity, a spectrum of abstinence patterns may be observed. Withdrawal may be mild and wax and wane; it may be delayed in onset; or there can be a stepwise pattern, with gradual, continuing increases in severity.

More severe withdrawal seems to occur in babies whose mothers have taken large amounts of drugs over a long period. Generally the closer to delivery a mother takes a narcotic, the greater the delay in the onset of withdrawal and the more severe the eventual symptoms in the baby. The maturity of the infant's own systems determine if it is able to metabolize and excrete the drug after delivery. Due to the variable severity of the withdrawal, the duration of symptoms may be anywhere from 6 days to 8 weeks. Drug therapies may be used to accomplish neonatal detoxification. Although the babies may be discharged from the hospital after drug therapy is stopped, their symptoms or irritability may persist for more than 3 to 4 months.

Methadone Use in Pregnancy

Methadone maintenance has proved very helpful in the treatment of pregnant opiate-dependent women. Daily doses range from 10 to 90 milligrams, with an average of 50 milligrams. It is clear that methadone is safe for pregnant women. The major problem encountered is withdrawal symptoms in the baby; other complications resulting from the medication do not occur. If methadone is used appropriately and coupled with comprehensive prenatal care, there is a decline in the complications of pregnancy, childbirth, and infant development.

Medical withdrawal of pregnant opiate-dependent women from methadone generally is not necessary nor recommended. Methadone doses should not be decreased but, rather, continued at a level that provides comfort for the mother and decreases the chances of withdrawal in the mother and fetus. In the third trimester, many women need an increase in methadone dose due to various physiological changes, including weight gain at this time. Early data suggest buprenorphine can also be safely used in pregnancy with satisfactory results.

If a pregnant woman has any specific medical complications, such as hyperthyroidism or diabetes, appropriate medical consultation is essential. Due to the impoverished conditions in which many of the women live, medical, social, and legal problems are common and economic survival tenuous.

Policy and Legal Issues

Being a drug-dependent mother presents many conflicts. One of the basic premises of child rearing and intervention models is that infant behavior is part of a communication system within the caregiving environment. This is a mutually responsive system in which feedback from one partner to the other is used to regulate this system. In early work with drug-exposed infants, this complexity was not appreciated. As a consequence, it was believed that drug exposure per se led to poor developmental outcome. If the mother was considered at all, it was thought that she could only lower the developmental outcome of the child. The Maternal Lifestyles Study, a federally funded multicenter, prospective, longitudinal study, is now attempting to address these issues by studying the effects of prenatal drug exposure on the interplay between the neurobehavioral and regulatory capacities of the child and parenting and environmental factors. There is the belief that here, too, there are often protective factors at work that mitigate against some of the risks imposed by maternal drug use; and interventions that provide needed supports can make a difference.

With respect to social policy, a variety of approaches have been suggested to protect children born to drug-dependent mothers. These include instituting systematic and massive public education and support by community leaders to stress that no drugs be used during pregnancy; giving hospitals the legal power and financial resources to care for babies until they are medically ready for discharge and the home environment is ready to care for them; placing children into foster care if drug-dependent parents cannot care for them; and facilitating the adoption process when parents anticipate little chance for improvement. Special programs for children affected by prenatal drug exposure remain limited. Such programs are needed to address and prevent any developmental disabilities; to provide supportive services to parents or other caregivers, such as foster parents or guardians, who may be caring for the child because of the mother's continued drug use; and to help parents or other caregivers cope with behavioral problems that can arise.

There are special considerations for children who remain in the home. Drug abuse treatment is necessary for drug-dependent mothers. Among the most alarming statistics in terms of outcome for children born to mothers addicted to cocaine are those associated with child abuse and neglect. Child abandonment is common with infants who require extended care at birth or are later hospitalized. Intoxication from crack is associated with outbursts of violence, which increases the risk for battering. In many urban areas where crack use is prevalent, treatment programs have long waiting lists. Facilities that will accept pregnant women or women with infants are few. Unfortunately, even if treatment is provided, outcome studies suggest that, compared with alcohol and opiate dependence, individuals dependent on cocaine, especially in the form of crack, have much more difficulty maintaining abstinence. Thus, some oversight of children in the home is imperative. However, in urban areas in which child welfare systems are already overburdened, the probability of oversight to identify problems and intervene on the child's behalf is low.

RESOURCES AND FURTHER READING

Basic References

Graham AW, Shultz TK. *Principles of Addiction Medicine*, 3rd ed. Chevy Chase, MD: American Society of Addiction Medicine, 2003.

Johnston LD, O'Makket OM, Bachman JG, Schulenberg JE. *Monitoring the Future. National Survey Results on Drug Use, 1975–2003. Volumes I and II.* Bethesda, MD: National Institute on Drug Abuse, 2004.

Lowinson JH, Ruiz P, Millman RB, Langred JG. *Substance abuse: A comprehensive textbook,* 4th ed. Baltimore, MD: Williams and Wilkins, 2005.

Marnell T, ed. *Drug Identification Bible,* 4th ed. Denver, CO: Drug Identification Bible, 1999.

Office of National Drug Control Policy. *The Economic Costs of Drug Abuse in the United States, 1992–1998.* Washington, DC: Executive Office of the President, 2001. (Note: includes projections through 2002.)

Smith DE, Seymour RB. *Clinicians Guide to Substance Abuse.* New York: McGraw-Hill, 2001.

Tarter RE, Ammerman RT, Ott PJ, eds. *Handbook of Substance Abuse: Neurobehavioral Pharmacology.* New York: Plenum, 1998.

Other Resources and Readings

Buprenorphine and BuprenorphineNaltrexone: A Guide for Clinicians. *Drug and Alcohol Dependence* 70(2, Supplement 1): entire issue, 2003.

Anglin D, Spears KL, Hutson HR. Flunitrazepam and its involvement in date or acquaintance rape. *Academic Emergency Medicine* 4(4):323–326, 1997. (21 refs.)

Anglin MD, Rawson RA, eds. The CSAT Methamphetamine Treatment Project. *Journal of Psychoactive Drugs* 32(2):135–136, 2000.

Brouette T, Anton R. Clinical review of inhalants. *American Journal on Addictions* 10(1):79+, 2001. (66 refs.)

Castro FG, Barrington EH, Walton MA, Rawson RA. Cocaine and methamphetamine: Differential addiction rates. *Psychology of Addictive Behaviors* 14(4):390–396, 2000. (7 refs.)

Center for Substance Abuse Treatment. *Breaking news for the treatment field.* OxyContin, Prescription Drug Abuse 1(1):1–4, 2001.

Davids E, Gastpar M. Buprenorphine in the treatment of opioid dependence (review). *European Neuropsychopharmacology* 14(3):209–216, 2004. (101 refs.)

Freese TE, Miotto K, Reback CJ. The effects and consequences of selected club drugs. *Journal of Substance Abuse Treatment* 23:151–156, 2002.

Fudala PJ, Bridge TP, eds. Buprenorphine and Buprenorphine/Naloxone: A Guide for Clinicians. *Drug and Alcohol Dependence* 70(2, supplement 1), 2003.

Gable RS. Comparison of acute lethal toxicity of commonly abused psychoactive substances (review). *Addiction* 99(6):686–696, 2004. (103 refs.)

Gittler J. The American Drug War, Maternal Substance Abuse and Child Protection: A Commentary. *Journal of Gender, Race & Justice* 7(Spring):237+, 2003. (117 refs.)

Green AR, Mechan AO, Elliott JM, O'Shea E, Colado MI. The pharmacology and clinical pharmacology of 3,4-methylenedioxymethamphetamine (MDMA, "ecstasy") (review). *Pharmacological Reviews* 55(3):463–508, 2003. (414 refs.)

Hahn EJ, Warnick TA, Plemmons S. Smoking cessation in drug treatment programs. *Journal of Addictive Diseases* 18(4):89–101, 1999. (24 refs.)

Hser Y, Hoffman V, Grella CE, Anglin MD. A 33-year follow-up of narcotics addicts. *Archives of General Psychiatry* 58(5):503–508, 2001. (17 refs.)

Hughes JR. An overview of nicotine use disorders for alcohol/drug abuse clinicians. *American Journal on Addictions* 53(2):62–274, 1996. (78 refs.)

Indiana Prevention Resource Center. *Factline on Nonmedical Use of Dextromethorphan aka "DXM"* #14, March 2001.

Iversen L. Cannabis and the brain (review). *Brain* 126(6): 1252–1270, 2003. (195 refs.)

Johnson RE, Strain EC, Amass L. Buprenorphine: How to use it right. *Drug and Alcohol Dependence* 70(2, Supplement 1):559–577, 2003.

Juliano LM, Griffiths RR. A critical review of caffeine withdrawal: Empirical validation of symptoms and signs, incidence, severity, and associated features (review). *Psychopharmacology* 176(1):1–29, 2004. (139 refs.)

Kandall SR. *Improving Treatment for Drug-Exposed Infants, Treatment Improvement Protocol (TIP) Series 5.* Rockville, MD: Center for Substance Abuse Treatment, 1993. (210 refs.)

Lai SH, Lai H, Page JB, McCoy CB. The association between cigarette smoking and drug abuse in the United States. *Journal of Addictive Diseases* 19(4):11–14, 2000. (22 refs.)

McCann MJ, Rawson RA, Obert JL, Hasson AJ. *Treatment of Opiate Addiction with Methadone: A Counselor Manual, Technical Assistance Publication (TAP) Series 7.* Rockville, MD: Center for Substance Abuse Treatment, 1994. (Chapter refs.)

McDonough M, Kennedy N, Glasper A, Bearn J. Clinical features and management of gamma-hydroxybutyrate (GHB) withdrawal: A review. *Drug and Alcohol Dependence* 75(1):3–9, 2004. (25 refs.)

McRae AL, Budney AJ, Brady KT. Treatment of marijuana dependence: A review of the literature (review). *Journal of Substance Abuse Treatment* 24(4):369–376, 2003. (47 refs.)

Mullins ME. Laboratory confirmation of flunitrazepam in alleged cases of date rape. *Academic Emergency Medicine* 6(9):966–968, 1999. (10 refs.)

Nathan KI, Bresnick WH, Batki SL. Cocaine abuse and dependence: Approaches to management. *CNS Drugs* 10(1):43–59, 1998. (94 refs.)

Nicholson KL, Balster RL. GHB: a new and novel drug of abuse. *Drug and Alcohol Dependence* 63(1):1–22, 2001. (218 refs.)

Patkar AA, Vergare MJ, Batra V, Weinstein SP, Leone FT. Tobacco smoking: Current concepts in etiology and treatment (review). *Psychiatry: Interpersonal and Biological Processes* 66(3):183–199, 2003. (120 refs.)

Riley SCE, Hayward E. Patterns, trends, and meanings of drug use by dance-drug users in Edinburgh, Scotland. *Drugs: Education, Prevention and Policy* 11(3):243–262, 2004. (21 refs.)

Simmons MM, Cupp MJ. Use and abuse of flunitrazepam. *Annals of Pharmacotherapy* 32(1):117–119, 1998. (17 refs.)

Uchtenhagen A. Substitution management in opioid dependence. *Journal of Neural Transmission* 88 (supplement):33–60, 2003. (64 refs.)

Valdez A, Cepeda A, Kaplan CD, Yin ZN. The legal importation of prescription drugs into the United States from Mexico: A study of customs declaration forms. *Substance Use and Misuse* 33(12):2485–2497, 1998. (14 refs.)

van den Brink W, van Ree JM. Pharmacological treatments for heroin and cocaine addiction (review). *European Neuropsychopharmacology* 13(6):476–487, 2003. (133 refs.)

van den Brink W, Goppel M, van Ree JM. Management of opioid dependence (review article). *Current Opinion in Psychiatry* 16(3):297–304, 2003. (83 refs.)

Van Etten ML, Anthony JC. Comparative epidemiology of initial drug opportunities and transitions to first use: Marijuana, cocaine, hallucinogens and heroin. *Drug and Alcohol Dependence* 54(2):117–125, 1999. (31 refs.)

CHAPTER 14

Odds 'n' Ends

BEYOND COUNSELING

There are other relevant issues for substance abuse clinicians, beyond patient care. However, space considerations prevent doing little more than mentioning them briefly. Clinicians frequently discover that, although their formal job description is centered around serving clients, there are often other expectations. Such duties fall into the general area of "indirect services," an awkward phrase used to cover all the other things the clinician is often required to do. Educational activities, case consultation, and planning for community programs are just a few examples. These aspects of a therapist's work are vital to the overall success of treatment efforts.

Educational Activities

Counselors are often called on to participate in public and professional education programs. The former includes presentations to high school students or church groups or might entail being a panelist on a radio or television talk show. The latter might take the form of conducting in-service training for other professionals, supervising trainees or students, or assisting with workshops.

Do's

In any educational endeavor, plan ahead—don't just "wing it." An effective presentation takes preparation. Find out from those organizing the program what they have in mind for a topic. You may wish to suggest an alternative. Who will be in the audience, and what will be its size? How long are you expected to speak? Are there others on the program? In choosing a topic, consider what would be of interest; ask yourself what kinds of questions are likely to be on the audience's mind. Do not be overly ambitious and try to cover everything you think someone ought to know about alcohol. If your audience goes away understanding three or four major points, you can consider your presentation successful. Choose a subject about which you are more expert than your audience. A counselor might effectively talk about alcohol's effects on the body to a group of fifth or sixth graders. Any counselor who would attempt to lecture a group of doctors about medical complications is asking for trouble. Leave time for questions, and save some of your choice tidbits for a question-and-answer period.

Feel free to develop several basic spiels. Use films or videotapes. A film can be an excellent vehicle for stimulating conversation, but be sure it is appropriate. Three questions for sparking a discussion afterward are the following: "What kind of response did you [the audience] have?" "What new information did you learn?" and "What surprised you?"

If public speaking doesn't come easily, rather than trying hard to avoid such assignments or just struggling through with one eye on the clock, enroll in a public speaking course. A good place to look for such an offering is at a local community college or an adult education program.

Feel free to borrow from colleagues. One of the things that marks effective speakers is having metaphors that somehow manage to capture the essence of a situation.

Dont's

Avoid crusading, personal accounts, to use AA jargon "drunkalogs," or telling horror stories. These approaches may shock your audience and titillate them, but (and it is an important "but") most audiences will not identify with what you are saying. The presentation will be unconnected to their experience. Such an approach is likely to leave those in the audience with a "That's not me!" response. There seems to be a widespread tendency to share one's personal history of alcohol or other drug use, especially when speaking with teenagers. Perhaps the motivation is to establish credibility. Perhaps it is intended to demonstrate to teenagers that, even though an adult, the speaker is in tune with the teenagers' experience. Whatever the motive, there is reason to question this approach. It is an approach that is out of touch with adolescents' psychology.

Preaching is preaching, whatever the guise. It's also a bit presumptuous. Does the speaker really think that his or her history is so compelling that the recital of past problems should motivate others to change? Another danger is that what the speaker wishes to describe as problems are heard by those in the audience as escapades. There is the danger, too, that a degree of romanticism and bravado creeps into the telling. The speaker lived dangerously, at the edge, and beat the odds. Most important, it doesn't really sit well with kids and accomplish what is intended. A middle school student, in response to a parental query as to what the mandatory drug education program was like, rolled his eyes and groaned. He recounted the "episode of the day," attributed to the educator's "friend." The educator, having grown up in the 1960s, managed

to conjure up a succession of "close friends," each of whom had had some experience with whatever the drug the class happened to be discussing. In summing up what they were learning, the student wryly noted, "I guess what we're really learning is that Mr. J. has some problems picking his friends." Whatever factual information Mr. J had intended to convey was lost. The general impression was that the sessions were contrived. The unfortunate effect, too, was to trivialize the subject.

This raises the question of the appropriateness of situations in which court judges sentence DWI offenders—typically, young drivers involved in fatal accidents—to go on the "speaker circuit," to local schools, or to make videotapes for such presentations. While these sentences are well intentioned, the effectiveness of such presentations needs to be questioned. There are no studies of the results of this endeavor. While a judge may sentence the individual to be available to make such presentations, the judge cannot sentence a school to use these speakers. Anyone in a situation to make a decision to accept such a presentation needs to think carefully before saying yes. Related to this are victim impact panels used in educational programs, which involve not those who caused such an accident but those who were touched by a drinking-driving event—parents, spouse, a child. Victim impact panels have been studied, and the findings are mixed. Some researchers report changes in future drinking-driving behavior among audiences composed of those who have been arrested for DWI. Others have found no change. Others have found that victim impact panels have an effect on some people—for example, those over age 35—but not on others. So it is not clear what situations lend themselves to the use of victim impact panels.

Finally, clinical vignettes are usually inappropriate with lay audiences. With professional audiences, if case material is used, great care must be taken to obscure identifying information. For either audience, avoid using jargon. Instead, look for everyday words to convey what you mean or use examples or metaphors that capture what you are trying to say.

Training Others

Substance abuse professionals have a special contribution to make in the training of other professionals. A common complaint of many substance abuse counselors is how ill equipped some other professional helpers are to work with alcoholics. However, this situation is not likely to change unless and until the experts, such as substance abuse clinicians, begin to participate in education. Consider this a high-priority activity.

It is especially important to stick to your area of expertise. Your single unique skill is your ability to interact therapeutically with those with substance abuse problems. Your specialized knowledge and experience are the most important things you can share. Often this is most effectively communicated by examples of the kinds of questions you ask clients and the way you respond to clients' concerns, rather than by lecturing. However, one trap you should avoid is giving the impression that what you do and know is a mystery, which others could never hope to learn. This can come across to your students in subtle ways, through statements such as "Well, I've been there, so I know what it's like" or the offhanded comment "If you really want to know what alcoholism's all about, what you have to do is (1) spend 2 weeks working on an alcohol unit, (2) go to at least 20 AA meetings, and (3) talk firsthand to recovering alcoholics." Any or all of these might be advisable and valuable educational experiences. However, you ought to be able also to explain in very concrete terms what information such experiences can provide and why they are valuable.

A few words on supervision of trainees or students may be helpful. Do not be fooled by the notion that the arrival of a student or a trainee is going to ease your workload. It shouldn't. Doing a good job of supervision requires a big investment of your time and energy. Whether the student is with you for a single day, several weeks, or a semester, serious thought must be given to structuring the time to ensure a valuable experience for the student. There are some basic questions to consider in planning a reasonable program. Do you want the trainee to acquire specific skills or just become "sensitized" to treatment techniques? What are the student's goals? What will prove most useful to the student later on? What is the student's background in terms of academic training and experience with alcohol problems? The social worker trainee, the clergy member, the recovering person with 10 years of AA experience—each is starting from a different point. Each has different strengths and weaknesses, different things to learn and unlearn. In planning the educational experience, map out how you will incorporate the trainee. In what activities will the trainee participate? Generally you will want to have the student to at least sample a broad range of agency activity but also to have a more in-depth, continuing involvement in selected areas.

Probably the single most important thing is to allow a trainee ample time to discuss what goes on, either with you or with other staff. The idea is not to run a student ragged with a jam-packed schedule and no chance to sit down with anyone to talk about what has been observed. If a student is going to be joining you in a clinical session, be sure you set aside at least 10 to 15 minutes ahead of time as a pre-interview briefing. Also, at the conclusion, spend some time reviewing the session and responding to questions. Do not expect that what the student is to learn is obvious.

Be sure to discuss with clients the presence of trainees. Clients do not need to be provided a student's résumé or be given a brochure describing in complete detail the nature of the training program. However, clients do need to be told who the trainees are and to be reassured that they are working with the staff in a trainee capacity. Clients have every right to be uncomfortable and apprehensive at the thought either that the merely curious are passing through to observe them or that they are being used as guinea pigs. Those who have worked in agencies which include trainees find that most clients do not object to being involved with students if the situation is properly presented and if they recognize they have the right to say no.

Prevention Efforts

"Prevention" is a hot topic at the national, state, and local levels. The first concerted attention to prevention appeared about 2 decades ago, when the NIAAA and NIDA meshed their prevention efforts in what was then known as the Office for Substance Abuse Prevention. Then several years later, this office was renamed the Center for Substance Abuse Prevention (CSAP).

Background and Terminology

Before discussing current efforts, some background on prevention and its terminology is useful. Activities directed at preventing the occurrence of diseases are a long-standing focus of all public health efforts. This is true whether it is the notion of vaccination to prevent polio or measles or efforts to ensure that the town water supply is uncontaminated so as to prevent cholera outbreaks. However, the attention to prevention within the substance abuse field is probably more closely linked to prevention efforts as they developed in the community mental health movement in the 1950s and early 1960s.

The community mental health movement introduced the notion of different levels of prevention: primary, secondary, and tertiary prevention activities. What these three levels of prevention activity all have in common is that each is intended to help reduce the total number of people who suffer from a disease. Consider that there are only three ways that the total number of sick individuals can be lowered. One way is to prevent the illness in the first place; thus, no new cases develop. This is what is meant by *primary prevention.* A second way to lower the number of sick persons is to identify and treat those who contract the disease, as quickly as possible. Restoring health to those with the disease reduces the total number of cases. This is called *secondary prevention.* A third way to keep down the total number of cases is to initiate specific efforts to avoid relapse and to maintain the health of those who have been treated. This is *tertiary prevention.* When prevention was first introduced into the substance abuse field, the emphasis was on preventing alcoholism/alcohol dependence. In applying the public health framework to alcohol dependence, primary prevention efforts are activities directed at reducing the number of people who develop alcohol dependence. Secondary prevention is essentially early detection and intervention. Tertiary prevention efforts include follow-up care and continued monitoring after active, intensive treatment to avoid relapse, reactivating of the disease. Prevention is sometimes thought of as activities that occur outside of the clinical arena. However, in this public health framework, secondary and tertiary prevention involve treatment personnel.

Focus of Prevention Efforts

In addition to the three levels of prevention, other frameworks have also emerged. They are not in conflict but represent other ways of formulating prevention efforts. One model was introduced by CSAP. In this framework the type of prevention activity is defined by the target of the prevention efforts—those at whom the prevention is being directed. Here, too, there are three target categories: the broad, general population; at-risk groups; and then specific individuals identified as being at risk. In this framework the prevention efforts are defined as *universal,* for the general population; *selective,* for at-risk groups; and *indicated,* for high-risk individuals. Examples of general population, universal approaches include broad media campaigns. Selective approaches directed to at-risk groups include pregnant women (to prevent FAS/FAE) or the elderly who use over-the-counter medications. Selective approaches might also be targeted at specific subgroups, such as teenage drivers, teen athletes, parenting teens, or parents of teens. *Indicated approaches,* those directed to at-risk individuals, include those individuals identified as having some problems that are known to place them at risk—for example, school dropouts or children with ADHD or school adjustment problems.

Demand Reduction and Supply Reduction

At the policy level there is even one more set of terms used in respect to prevention: "demand reduction" and "supply reduction." These terms are borrowed from the field of economics. They draw on the notion of the marketplace and the fact that the availability of any commodity is dependent on two factors—one is the amount produced by manufacturers, representing supply, and the other the amount consumers want to purchase, which represents demand. If no one wants to buy a widget, fewer are made. If fewer are manufactured, there are fewer available for people to purchase. To apply this to alcohol and other drugs, *demand reduction initiatives* include any activities that make these substances less attractive to potential users and thus reduce the size of the market. One obvious way is through treatment; abstinence removes a customer. Another demand strategy is to raise taxes on licit drugs, such as alcohol and tobacco, thus increasing their cost and reducing the numbers who purchase them. *Supply reduction efforts,* on the other hand, are those efforts directed at making drugs or alcohol less available. Examples include border patrols to reduce traffic in illicit drugs and reductions in the number of package stores or bars within a neighborhood.

Early Prevention Efforts

The very earliest prevention programs in the alcohol field were directed to prevention of alcohol*ism*. That there were other alcohol problems to be prevented didn't even register. The very earliest prevention programs were conducted by treatment agencies as part of what were often called their outreach efforts. By today's standards, these early programs were rather primitive. There was little research to guide efforts. The programs were clearly "add-ons" to the agencies' basic mission. For the most part the prevention activities were primarily educational efforts explaining what alcoholism was, its signs and symptoms. Then the notion of prevention expanded to include the serious problems that can accompany alcohol or other drug use. Therefore, in terms of alcohol, efforts also included efforts to prevent the negative consequences resulting from drinking. In this context, primary prevention might be directed at achieving low-risk alcohol use—such as "responsible drinking" campaigns. Similarly, secondary prevention can include efforts to prevent problems if/when intoxication occurs, such as designated drivers or call-a-ride.

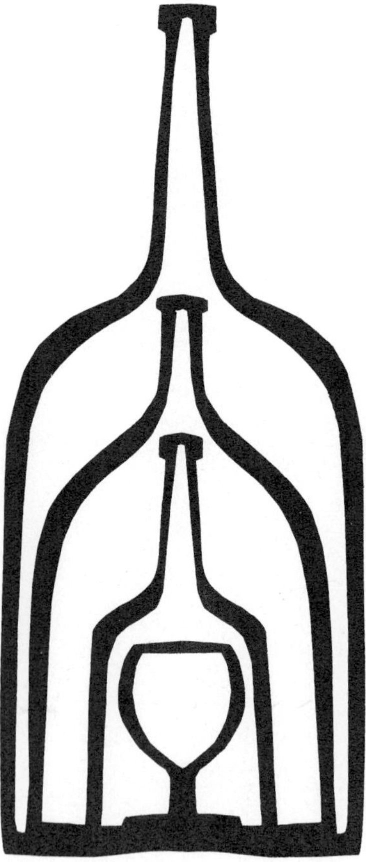

The difference between attempts to prevent dependence and attempts to prevent the problems associated with use may be obvious now, but that was not always the case. Nor is it always fully recognized that efforts that may be effective for preventing acute problems cannot be expected automatically to be effective in dealing with the problems of chronic use. Programs successful at one level of prevention may not work well at another level. Consider SADD (Students Against Drunk Driving). This program may help reduce the toll associated with teenage driving and alcohol use. However, it would not be a promising means by which to prevent alcohol dependence in teenagers. To be successful the program has to target a behavior that causes the condition. As this example illustrates, in any discussion of prevention, it is important to be clear as to what it is we are trying to prevent. In the absence of such specification, people tended to lump different kinds of problems together. As a result, there is the ever-too-likely outcome that the programs implemented will be ill suited to accomplish what the planners had hoped to achieve.

Current Prevention Approaches

Prevention efforts directed at adolescents have always been a priority. The first wave of such efforts were largely educational. The second generation included other elements, such as providing social alternatives or trying to build self-esteem or to teach drink refusal skills. The models now being promoted are seen as multipronged, for example, combining legal approaches, public education, media campaigns, and outreach efforts targeted at specific high-risk groups and individuals. Within these, greater attention is paid to the role of community organizations and their potential role in changing community norms. Community groups, too, may become involved in lobbying to change laws or to increase local services such as getting more police patrols.

Much is being done to mobilize parents to respond collectively to teenagers' substance use. This may involve helping parents define their collective expectations, for example, around issues such as teenagers having parties without parents or other adults present, or parents allowing alcohol to be consumed in their homes. Other activities involving parents may focus on organizing substance-free high school graduation parties or providing mini-courses on parenting skills. What these approaches are doing is making changes in the environment and changing attitudes toward substance use, as well as imparting concrete skills. Handbooks and program guides that outline these approaches are available from CSAP.

Prevention efforts now look considerably different than they did even a decade ago. Special programs and agencies have been established with prevention as their major mission. There is an ever growing body of research to guide activities. In keeping with this, prevention is emerging as a new and separate professional discipline within the substance abuse field. In terms of its evolution and development, the role of prevention specialist may be comparable to the position of substance abuse clinicians a decade or two ago. The expertise required and the knowledge base for this new profession are not yet clearly defined nor agreed upon. However, when one looks at the nature of the work, one can guess what some of the essential elements may prove to be. There is much to be gotten from the substance abuse fields, such as knowledge of the etiology of substance use, abuse, and dependence and the nature of acute problems. At the same time there are critical pieces to be learned from other disciplines, such as the nature of child and adult development, family dynamics, information from health education and promotion as to the underlying principles that influence health habits and behavior, interpersonal skills, educational skills, and principles of community organization. The list could surely be extended.

Prevention Research

As the prevention field has grown, there has been an increasing body of research to help guide these efforts. In general, the research findings have not been very encouraging. There have been a variety of programs particularly directed at adolescents, often organized in the schools, which have involved educational efforts and alternative recreational and social activities, with efforts to build self-esteem and to teach refusal and other coping skills. More often than not, the results have been minimal at best. Behavior changes that may occur immediately after participation in a program tend not to be very long-lasting. Or students learn the material and have more information, yet this doesn't get translated into behavior changes.

There have been programs that have been well funded, popular, widely used, and well loved. Unfortunately, this doesn't make them effective. The prime example of the dearly loved but ineffective program model is D.A.R.E. (Drug Abuse Resistance Education). It involves having police officers go into the schools to conduct sessions with elementary school students. D.A.R.E. simply has no impact on adolescents' substance use. Furthermore, there are even programs that are worse than being ineffective—on completion of the program, the participants are more likely to use alcohol or other drugs than those who did not participate. This has raised the question, not entirely with tongue in cheek, as to whether informed consent is as appropriate in the prevention arena as it is in the treatment realm.

Science-Based Programs

To try to respond to these problems, the Center for Substance Abuse Prevention has been engaged in pilot demonstration efforts, has conducted evaluation studies to identify those known to have positive effects, and has made efforts to disseminate these programs. The programs being advocated for use are termed "science-based" or "research-based" to emphasize that the models are not based on biases, or what people "believe" works. CSAP maintains a directory on its website which outlines several dozen science-based initiatives, the key elements, findings to date, methods, and goals. Earlier, to promote the adoption of these kinds of programs at the local level, the Center for Substance Abuse Prevention made large grants to the states, an effort known as State Incentive Grants. These were intended to get the money to local community groups and to ensure the use of known effective approaches. These grants were for 3-year periods. However, knowing what to do and being able to do it are two different things. Some of the problems encountered are discussed in the following paragraphs.

Challenges in Prevention

While there have been strides in prevention efforts, nonetheless there are number of rough spots. Certainly prevention is a laudable goal. To raise questions may be like criticizing Mom and apple pie.

Abstinence versus Harm Reduction

At this time, most of the energy is being directed at adolescents and preadolescents. Unfortunately, the thrust of these programs has been the prevention of use per se. The goal of the programs is *abstinence.* The underlying theory may be that this is the means by which other problems are ultimately reduced. Indeed, the research clearly suggests that, by delaying the onset of alcohol and other drug use, there is a reduction in later life of a host of problems. But adopting abstinence as a goal rather than a means can cloud thinking. All the rhetoric to the contrary, in too many cases abstinence-oriented programs sound less like public health efforts than quasi-legal policing activities. It seems in some ways that we find ourselves in a box that we have built for ourselves. Yes, there continues to be discussion of "responsible use." For the drinking-age population, and especially around the holidays, there are the predictable "Don't drink and drive" messages, but when one hears the word "prevention" these are not the examples that first come to mind. It's "just say no." Suggestions that efforts be made to teach adolescents to recognize life-threatening alcohol overdoses engender discomfort. Such initiatives are faulted for "giving a mixed message." These objections overlook that it may be the nondrinking kids who, by default, may be the ones in a position to act. Similarly efforts to educate adolescents about the steps they can take to reduce the dangers of drug use at raves are criticized as being enabling.

Too often harm-reduction efforts are seen as out of place. At the same time that more and more resources are being directed at prevention, we need to acknowledge that, in the United States, we are witnessing the highest level of binge drinking seen in adolescents. If the overriding message is abstinence, we need to recognize that we have adopted a message that has little relevance and is unlikely to reach 40% of these students, who may be the most vulnerable, those who are already using alcohol. Similarly, with nicotine, by tenth grade a quarter of students are regular smokers. Where are the smoking cessation programs?

The Question of Focus

Another dilemma is that prevention programs are disproportionately directed at the single element that may carry the least weight—that is, the individual's psychological makeup and functioning. One writer, borrowing from the field of environmental pollution, compares this approach to "downstream" efforts. Possibly this is the only thing that community-based programs can undertake. But there seems to be something wrong-minded about spending large amounts of money on efforts that, even if everything is going well, are likely to have at best a modest effect. There have been a few model community-level initiatives that have focused on institutional changes, and while the results have been promising, this is not the type of program that is being marketed by CSAP.

Jack FiN
e could
drink
NO Wi
Ne—H
iS WiF
E Could
driNK
NO liquo
R—But ST
ill they both
got drunk each nig
ht —though he got d
runk much quicker...
La pauvre presse
Brattleboro, Vt.
from the Collected Do
ggerel of 18th Century
France - by J. ANZOlone

Implementation

The implementation of model programs is not a simple matter. The models that have been identified as research-based typically were developed in research settings. There they were amply funded and were adequately staffed by trained professionals. They had everything going for them. Then there is the real world, where things don't go so smoothly. One problem that has been identified is referred to as "fidelity." When model programs are implemented by others, how faithfully do their efforts adhere to the original model? To what degree do others replicate, or not replicate, the initial demonstration project?

The basic question is "What differences matter?" One may realize that a particular package has a known beneficial impact. However, the components that are most critical in achieving these results are unknown. In some cases all that one can do is make an informed guess. But this requires some careful thinking. An example from one community prevention effort is telling. It entailed efforts being made to increase parental supervision and to change norms around alcohol use. One element of the program was to encourage parents to routinely contact other parents of kids who were hosting parties and, in turn, to invite other parents to feel free to contact them. So a mailing went out to all families, inviting parents to indicate their commitment to do this. From this a list was developed of parents who "signed on," with addresses and phone numbers. Unfortunately, the response rate was low; only a third of parents sent back the survey, but the list was distributed to all parents anyway.

Therefore, rather than showing how concerned the parents were, the short list seemed to indicate exactly the opposite. If those who had not responded had been recontacted or had been called by the parents who had signed up, the result would have been quite different.

The *social influences model* has been seen as having particular promise and is included among the models being promoted by CSAP. However, a recent report of the use of this model in a school-based smoking prevention program found no effect. This study was conducted as perfectly as would be possible. There were more than 8,000 students involved, the teachers involved in the project were trained, and they rated highly on the measures of how closely they adhered to the procedures that had been set. Very few students were lost at follow-up; 94% remained throughout the study. The students were enrolled in the third grade and followed regularly through high school and to 2 years post-graduation. What was the outcome? The program had *no* benefits. The rate of smoking was no lower among those who were in the intervention (when compared with those who were not) at grade 12 or 2 years later. There was no effect on any measures of smoking, such as frequency of smoking or the total cumulative amount smoked between grade 3 and after high school.

Those in the research community, with one exception, see this as an exemplary research study. The exception is the group that has been promoting the social influences model, who has reported 87% lower rates of substance use in its prevention programs. This group has raised the question of whether the smoking prevention program studied was "really" based on the social influences model. If it wasn't, then the question becomes "What is the essential missing ingredient to explain the difference between the no effect and 87% success rates?"

Funding

Another problem for community prevention efforts is funding. Any publicly funded program is subject to ups and downs. A major initiative comes along, accompanied by major funding. This funding lasts a couple of years at best. In theory, the hope is that such programs will be given seed money and will then be able to continue on their own, over the longer haul. It is very difficult for community-based efforts to function effectively in such a climate. The State Incentive Grants from CSAP that were intended to boost prevention efforts by states and promotes research-based programs is a good example. The states distributed these monies in many instances to "community coalitions" over the 3-year grant period. Essentially the first year is directed at getting up and running. The final year is directed at scurrying around to identify sources of future funding to continue the efforts that were barely under way. That leaves 1 year to really work on the program.

In a number of instances the community coalitions formed are not community coalitions at all. A true coalition is a combination of established organizations and groups with disparate goals and purposes that come together on a particular issue that touches each of them, even though it may not be the primary concern of any. A true coalition is a coming together of groups with voluntary membership whose members can be mobilized. Thus, a true coalition is composed of churches, synagogues, or mosques; the American Legion; unions; and other such civic groups. True coalitions are essentially confined to community groups that will be there tomorrow and the next day, whose activities are integral to the life of the community. A true coalition is not simply comprised of different treatment agencies, of those already involved in the substance abuse field, who come together to carve up a new pot of funding. Who do they expect to mobilize? Their employees? Their clients? Their board members? Whatever their plans or goals, generally such pseudo-coalitions are marginal to the lives of their communities. They are dependent on the funding of the moment for their existence. Unlike the religious communities, the unions, and the civic organizations who will be there tomorrow, these coalitions disappear when funding dries up. Or they try to reconstitute themselves to apply for the next round of funding. Accordingly, state incentive grantees turn into tobacco prevention coalitions to tap into the monies available through tobacco settlement monies. So the previous efforts, no longer spearheaded by anyone, flounder and are all too likely to leave little evidence of their fleeting existence.

The Future

At this time prevention efforts, though not in their infancy, may still be fairly characterized as being in their adolescence. What is seemingly apparent is that there is no single wonderful program that will do the whole thing. While these are available as guides, anyone who is involved in prevention efforts needs also to think critically about how to apply any program to a particular situation. A question to be considered is what different components might be combined, without spreading oneself so thin that the likelihood of achieving anything is diminished. Attention needs to be directed at setting priorities. If one can't do everything, what are the most pressing concerns, and what is achievable? Possibly the major impact of current efforts is not in their significantly reducing adolescent alcohol or other drug use. What these initiatives may do is to alter the social climate so that if/when alcohol or other drug problems do occur, there is a greater likelihood for early intervention and treatment.

THE REAL WORLD

Being a Professional Colleague

Historically the substance abuse field developed outside of mainstream medicine and the other helping professions. Alcohol treatment programs,

I'm glad he has taken his first step – but at 47 he's only 46 years late.

for example, initially arose for the very reason that those with alcoholism were excluded or poorly served by the traditional helping professions. The first alcohol treatment programs were often staffed by recovering people. The basic therapeutic program consisted of helping the client establish sobriety and attempting to orient him or her to the fellowship of AA.

With the establishment of the NIAAA, alcohol treatment as we now know it was launched. The alcohol field is no longer staffed by paraprofessions and is no longer functioning in isolation, separate and outside the health and human service mainstream. There are tensions remaining because of that history. The various professions now involved in caring for those with alcohol/drug problems are still learning to collaborate. Being the "new kids on the block," the substance abuse professionals may need to work a bit harder at this. One of the difficulties that may go unrecognized is problems in communication. Each profession has its own distinctive language (terminology and jargon), which often is not understood by the outsider. For example, as a substance abuse clinician, you might report to the client's physician that the client has "finally taken the 'first step.'" You shouldn't be surprised if the physician has no idea what that means. In such situations, it may be tempting to get a little testy: "Well, doctors should know about AA." Of course they should, but they'll not learn if you don't use language they can understand. Remember, you expect them to use language you can understand when discussing your client's medical condition. Return the favor.

Sharing Expertise with Colleagues

Be sensitive also to the fact that many other professionals have a distorted view of alcohol treatment's effectiveness. In large part, this is because they never see the successes. However, those patients who come in again and again in crisis (though this may only be a very small minority of clients) are all too memorable. In fact, Vaillant found that as few as 0.5% of all the clients at one detoxification center accounted for as many program admissions as did 50% of the clients who only entered once. Of the 5,000 clients seen in a 78-month span, the 2,500 who never returned were easily forgotten, while the 25 who were admitted 60 times or more were *always* remembered. Encourage recovering clients to recontact the physician, social worker, or nurse who may have been instrumental in their entering treatment but who have no idea of the successful outcome.

Consider making yourself available to other professionals for consultation. One of the surest ways to establish an ongoing working relationship with someone is to have been helpful in managing a difficult case. Consider offering to join a physician during an appointment with a person he or she thinks has an alcohol problem. Or similarly, sit in with a member of the clergy. Your availability may make the clergy's task of referral far easier. The person may be reluctant to make a referral to an

FOCUS ON DRUGS

Profile of Substance Abuse Workforce

The following data were derived from a survey conducted for the Center for Substance Abuse Treatment in 1997. Those surveyed included a sample of all staff and program directors in state-recognized treatment facilities, as well as directors of state agencies responsible for alcohol and drugs. There was a response rate of about 80% for all three groups, a total of 3,267 respondents.

Years in the Field

1–5	6–10	11–15	16–20	Over 20
14%	24 %	23 %	20%	19%

Years in Current Position

Under 1	1–5	>5–10	>10–15	>15–20	Over 20
10%	41%	27%	12%	5%	5%

Highest Level of Education

	Doctorate	Master's	Bachelor's	Less than Bachelor's
All staff	7%	42%	30%	21%
Counselors	0	32	42	26

Certification or Licensure Rates of Staff

Facility Directors	Clinical Supervisors	Program Counselors
69%	78%	72%

Demographic Characteristics of Staff and Clients

	Staff	Clients
Gender		
Male:	49%	68%
Female	51	32
Race/Ethnicity		
White	72%	57%
Hispanic	11	14
African-American	12	25
Asian	4	1
Am. Indian/Alaska Native	1	3

Observations

A common misconception is that staff of substance abuse treatment programs are recovering persons, many of whom have no professional credentials. While historically true, this is no longer the case. There is a disparity between the racial/ethnic compositions of the workforce and client communities.

Source: Mulvey KP, Hubbard S, Hayashi S. A national study of the substance abuse treatment workforce. *Journal of Substance Abuse Treatment* 24(1):51–57, 2003. (15 refs.)

alcohol treatment program because that would imply that the clergy member had already made a definitive diagnosis. Alcohol clinicians should be sensitive to the fact that in "just making a referral," the counselor, physician, or clergy is being forced to deal with the alcoholic's denial, resistance, and ignorance of the disease. That's the hard part, especially for someone who doesn't do it day in and day out. So anything you can do at that stage will be very helpful.

Being Open to New Approaches

Being a professional also means being open to new ideas. One of the observations made of the alcohol field is that practitioners tend to keep using the tried-and-true, rather than paying attention to new information. One article suggests that there are "taboo topics" that govern how care is provided but that have not been validated by research; furthermore, they are seemingly not even open to question. While we may not like to hear this, there is some truth to this observation. Some of the examples the author cited included questions about the necessity of Alcoholics Anonymous for maintaining abstinence; the existence of spontaneous remission; the lack of empirical support for the addictive personality concept; the value of smoking cessation in early recovery; overuse of the addiction concept; and the lack of empirical support for the disease concept of co-dependency. Some of those concepts we might recognize as no longer in vogue, such as the disease concept of co-dependency or belief in an addictive personality. It is always easier to identify the taboos from a former era. In the future, undoubtedly there will be current approaches similarly seen as taboo topics. Possible nominees include the use of drug therapies for treatment of the addiction as opposed to their use in treating comorbid psychiatric conditions; the insistence on abstinence as the central focus of prevention; and discomfort with harm reduction approaches, be it needle exchange or decriminalization of marijuana use.

Whether the substance abuse field is more guilty of such behavior than other fields is probably not an argument worth waging. And, to the extent these charges are true, there may be an historic explanation. When the alcohol field was founded, care was provided in a manner that contradicted what was then the accepted mainstream way of doing things. In fact, those who remember the early days of the field can recall when alcohol counselors often thought their job, in part, was to protect clients from the established professionals, who, however well intentioned, didn't then have a very good track record in treating alcoholism. But that is now a very old battle, one that no longer needs to be fought. What is true is that it is always easier for any of us to continue doing what we have been doing. Don't our clients effectively remind us of this every day? Part of being a professional is evaluating new information and modifying our approaches based on the evidence.

Selecting a Professional Position

In seeking and selecting professional employment, there are a number of points to consider. By analogy, accepting any employment is almost like entering into a marriage. When it works it's marvelous, but when there's a mismatch, it's quite the opposite. Many positions may have the title of "addictions counselor" or "therapist," but there is considerable variation among them, depending on the agency's setting and clientele. Beyond looking closely at the facility, it is equally important to look closely at yourself. Take a professional inventory. What are your clinical strengths, and what are areas of lesser competence? What are you most comfortable doing, and which things are more stressful? Is "routine" a comfort, or is it likely to invite boredom? Because of the differences between people, one person's perfect job is another person's nightmare.

In considering agencies, you are your own best counsel. But at the same time, consult with colleagues and use the grapevine. What should you give thought to? Among the long list of things worth considering are the following: What is the work atmosphere like? Does the agency have frequent staff turnover, or is it fairly stable? Why do people leave? Is there a sense of camaraderie? How do the various professionals on staff interact with one another? How does the counselor/therapist fit into the hierarchy? What are the opportunities for professional development, both formal and informal? How is clinical supervision handled? Does the agency support and encourage continuing education? Will the agency help cover the costs of attending conferences and workshops? What are the routes for promotion? To what are promotions tied—formal credentials, experience, certification? Is the position part of a well-established program or a new venture just getting off the ground? What kind of security does the position provide? How much security do you want and need? Where do you want to be professionally 5 years from now, and how will the position you are considering facilitate attaining that goal? What are the skills you would like to develop, and can they be learned in the position being considered?

Then there are always the nuts and bolts of personnel practices. Is the salary appropriate for the position, and can you live on it? Are the benefits comparable with those for other professional staff? What are the hours? Is there "on-call" or evening or weekend work? How many hours a week do comparable staff typically work? In both alcohol and human service agencies there is too often chronic understaffing. So conscientious workers pitch in, work extra hours, and somehow never have the opportunity to take that time off later. Before managed care, many clinicians found themselves considering private practice. Now, with the changes that are taking place in health-care delivery, this is a less inviting option. The importance of carefully considering agency characteristics in selecting a potential employer is brought home by a national survey of a representative sample of 175 alcohol and drug agencies. Published in 2003, its findings included the following: Over the 16 months prior to the survey, 15% of facilities had closed or stopped addiction treatment and an additional 29% had been reorganized under a different agency. There was a 53% turnover among directors and a similar rate among counselors within the previous year. Less than half the programs had a full-time physician or nurse, and very few programs had a social worker or psychologist. The dominant form of treatment was abstinence-oriented group counseling. The intake process typically required 2 to 4 hours to collect data required by managed care and city, state, and federal agencies. Very few programs had computers for clinical operations or decision support.

The authors note the disturbing implications for the ability of the nation's treatment system to meet treatment needs. It is similarly disturbing for anyone who envisions seeking professional employment in a treatment agency. Other studies which have looked at the substance abuse treatment workforce, have not identified staff turnover that is as dramatic. However, it does appear that the level of staff turnover exceeds that for other fields; the reasons are not fully clear. Despite job changes, clinicians do appear to remain in the substance abuse field. In fact one of the concerns is that there is a graying of the workforce, as the bulk of clinicians are between the ages of 40 and 55.

Private Practice

On the surface, private practice may seem very attractive. On the other hand, it can be very lonely. Those who are in private practice need to take specific steps to develop and maintain professional contacts. (This is in addition to developing referral sources to assure that your clients get the services they need, beyond those that you can offer.) More than any of us can appreciate is the extent to which our colleagues are responsible for helping us maintain our balance and are invaluable and needed resources for us. While it is difficult to set any minimum length of experience before setting up a private practice, this certainly is not the place for a newcomer to the field.

Being a Professional

What It Is

Addictions counseling is a growing profession. The professional counselor has mastered a body of knowledge, has special skills, and has a code of ethics to guide the work. Being a professional does not mean you have to know it all. Do yourself a favor right now. Give yourself permission to give up any pretense that it is otherwise. Feel free to ask questions, seek advice, request a consultation, say you don't know. Alcohol treatment requires diverse skills and talents. Treatment programs are staffed by people with different kinds and levels of training, for the very reason that no one person or specialty can do the job alone. Being a professional also means constantly looking at what you are doing, evaluating your efforts. There is always more than one approach. You cannot make people sober by grinding drunks through an alcohol treatment machine. Being open to trying new things is easier if you aren't stuck with the notion that you are supposed to be the expert. And, of course, you will make mistakes—everyone does.

What It Isn't

Overwhelming numbers of people need and ask for help. The tendency is to overburden yourself because of the obvious need. Spreading yourself too thin is a problem and a danger. You also need to develop assertiveness to resist agency pressures to take on increasing responsibilities. In either instance, it creates resentment, anger, frustration, and a distorted view of the world: "No one else seems to care! Somebody's got to do it." It's a trap. Unless you're an Atlas, you'll get mashed.

Your personal life must be preserved—try to keep that in mind. The people who live with you deserve some of your attention, too. It is hard to maintain a relationship with anyone if all you can manage is "What a day!" before you lapse into silence and soon fall asleep. Save your own space. Collapsing might give you a nice sense of martyrdom, but it won't help anybody. It's better to be more realistic in assessing just what you can do productively, devoting your energy to a realistic number of clients, and giving your best. Keep a clear eye on your own needs for time off, trips, and visits to people who have nothing to do with your work. Some compromise may be necessary between being your version of the ideal therapist and attending to your own needs.

Give some thought to handling the calls that come after working hours. Some workers ruefully decide to have unlisted home phone numbers. Intoxicated clients and their upset families are notoriously inconsiderate. "Telephone-itis" sets in with a few drinks. You may think you do want to be available at all hours; if so, think it over carefully. Many agencies have emergency services to handle after-hours calls. If there are situations when you decide it is important to be available to a client outside of the working day, have him or her contact the emergency service, which can in turn contact you. You cannot take total responsibility for clients. Rarely does someone make it or not because of one incident. This does not mean that you should adopt a laissez-faire policy; however, just as you cannot take all the credit for a sober, happy alcoholic, neither can you shoulder all the blame when the client fails to remain sober.

Professional Development

Part of the work life of any professional is properly focused not on serving clients, developing programs, or promoting the broad interests of the substance abuse field but to nurturing your own professional growth. This can take many forms—for example, attending workshops, going to conferences, seeking consultation from colleagues, visiting other

programs, and reading. It is important that you provide for your own continuing professional development.

It has been said that the half-life of medical and scientific knowledge is 8 years. This means that half of what will be known 8 years from now has not yet been discovered. On the other hand, half of what is now taken as fact will be out of date. Consequently education must be a continuing process. What can so easily happen is that, in the press of day-to-day work, you find you do not have enough time to keep up. You may have a résumé with 10 years' job experience, but it is the first year's experience repeated 9 more times. As with any specialty, the daily pressures make keeping current a big problem. Get on NIAAA's and NIDA's mailing lists, subscribe to a journal or two, and then make the time to read them. Area or regional meetings of addiction workers of all disciplines are also a way to keep up-to-date.

At the federal level, explicit efforts are being made to promote the dissemination of new knowledge, sometimes referred to either as information dissemination, knowledge transfer, or technology transfer. The counseling field is not a high-technology field, in which one has to keep up with the rapid and new developments or disappear. All fields have a certain amount of inertia. However, this seems to be particularly pervasive in the substance abuse field. The knowledge being gained by the field through first-class research simply isn't getting down to the rank-and-file workers. One example is a study of the extent to which a particular counseling technique, behavioral couples therapy, has been adopted by the field at large. (This technique, which engages the alcoholic and the spouse, has been widely studied and its effectiveness demonstrated in reducing substance use and improving both partners' satisfaction with the relationship.) The results were disheartening. Of the almost 400 programs surveyed, only 27% offered any kind of family- or couples-based treatment. Less than 5% of the agencies used any kind of behavioral therapy approach. None used behavioral couples therapy.

A priority for any clinician is gaining skills in new treatment techniques. The failure to adopt new treatment approaches cannot be laid simply on the shoulders of individual clinicians. The agency and its treatment program are major factors in promoting the use of new approaches. A general surgeon doesn't go to a workshop or two and decide that next week he or she will start doing open heart surgery; neither does the substance abuse clinician decide that he or she will begin doing behavioral couples therapy tomorrow or offer other new treatments. Adopting new therapeutic approaches requires both clinician training and agency support for these efforts. That adopting new approaches isn't necessarily easy is suggested by a survey of staff attitudes about addiction treatment, conducted in 1999 as part of an effort to assess the effectiveness of research-based new initiatives in community settings. Among the findings were that 80% of respondents supported increased use of research-based innovations, 12-step/traditional approaches, and spirituality in addiction treatment. On the other hand, only 39% were in favor of increased use of naltrexone and only 34% increased use of methadone maintenance. Also, over a third of the staff believed confrontation should be used more and almost half (46%) agreed with the notion of discharging noncompliant patients. There were some differences based on the staff's formal education. Those with more formal education tended to be less supportive of confrontation and more supportive of the use of medications.

There is one final factor worth mentioning with respect to remaining current. One of the things that confronts the alcohol counselor is that much of the information that he or she needs to know comes from many fields—medicine, psychology, anthropology, law, and so forth. Because of this, keeping current isn't simply a matter of time. In many instances it means having access to an "interpreter," someone who can explain things in everyday language, in a way that is easy to understand. In turn, part of the counselor's work becomes translating relevant information for clients. Beyond taking part in formal education programs, every substance abuse clinician needs to have someone to whom he or she can turn, with whom he or she is comfortable saying, "Explain this to me."

Certification and Licensure

If you plan to work as a drug and/or alcohol counselor, the issue of certification and licensure is important. In the past, certification by a counselor's association or licensure by a state board may have been primarily important for your own sense of professionalism. Now it is becoming a necessity. More and more frequently, a clinician's being certified or licensed is a hiring requirement. Groups that accredit treatment programs are concerned about staff qualifications, as a way of assessing a program's ability to provide good care. Also, insurance companies are paying attention to the credentials of those who provide care and making this a basis for reimbursement. Clinical agencies may no longer be able to bill for alcohol treatment provided by noncertified or nonlicensed counselors. The same is true for counselors in private practice.

Certification and licensure are two different approaches to accomplishing the same goal. They differ chiefly in terms of the type of group that is certifying that an individual has demonstrated a minimal level of competency, or training, and is therefore qualified to do a particular line of work. "Certification" is the term used when an association or professional group confers the seal of approval. "Licensure" is the term used when an officially designated state governmental body awards the credential. Certification or licensure takes place at a state level, and each state has its own requirements. The same is true for teachers, lawyers, nurses, social workers, barbers, beauticians, and some tradespeople, such as plumbers and electricians. For the established professions, such as law, nursing, and medicine, there is generally reciprocity among states. In part, this is based on the fact that clear professional standards have

Table 14.1 Overview of Certification/Licensure Requirements

Certifying group	The group varies by state, it is most commonly an alcohol counselors' association. Some states have more than one group offering certification.
Types of certification	States typically have different types of certification available. Distinctions may be made between alcohol and other drug counselors. Some states offer an administrative or supervisory certificate as well as a clinician certificate. Levels of certification may distinguish more senior clinicians from those entering the field or those in training.
Requirements	The requirements are counseling experience, education/training, and clinical supervision. The biggest differences among states are in the time requirements for each; whether there is a formula for substituting formal educational programs for work experience; and to what extent the subject area of education and training is stipulated. Several states specify clinical competencies that must be covered; several require specific educational programs in the area of ethics. States may have additional special requirements, such as length of sobriety for those in recovery.
Testing	There is generally a written examination, a personal interview, and a sample of clinical work, whether a portfolio, a case presentation, or a videotape of a clinical encounter.
Recertification	Length of certification ranges from 2 to 4 years. Recertification requires evidence of continuing education.

emerged over the years. Also, there is a national examination that all states use and recognize. In addictions counseling there is much more variation among states, even though the areas assessed are similar. These areas are summarized in Table 14.1. But the differences among states are narrowing. Clearly on the horizon is the requirement that clinicians have master's-level training, rather than only a certificate program or a bachelor's degree. The best way to find out the requirements for a particular state are to contact the state office of alcohol/drug programs, which can provide the name and address of the certifying group.

ETHICS

Basic Principles

Being a helping professional means being allied to a set of ethical standards. National groups and state counselor associations have adopted codes of ethics for their members. The principles that underlie these codes are the same as those for other helping professions. These codes are actually a series of statements of the most basic rules you are striving to follow in working with clients. Ultimately the most basic tool you have to help others is yourself. Therefore, how you think about the responsibilities of working with others is vitally important. Ethical codes are intended to serve as guidelines. They have a history and have developed from experience. The National Association of Alcohol and Drug Abuse Counselors (NAADAC) has a code of ethics that addresses confidentiality, nondiscrimination, interprofessional relationships, legal and moral standards, relationships with clients, the manner in which the substance abuse field is represented in public statements, issues related to payment for services, competence, and obligations to the larger society.

Quite a few years ago, the graduation speaker for a group of counselor trainees at Dartmouth Medical School spoke on what constituted being a professional. The question raised was "How is a professional counselor different from the kindly neighbor who offers advice over the backyard fence?" The answer provided was that the professional counselor is able "to profess." That raised a few eyebrows, the meaning not being immediately obvious. What was being referred to as distinguishing the trained helping person from ordinary well-intentioned people is that the professional is able to state—to "profess"—what it is he or she does. A professional functions deliberately and thoughtfully. The professional doesn't rely merely on intuition or instinctive responses. The other important distinction is that the counselor or therapist has made a commitment to a set of beliefs as to how one interacts with clients. The counselor has an explicit set of ethical standards to guide helping behavior.

While commonly used, the word "ethics" nonetheless warrants a definition. One definition is that ethics encompasses the rules that define the "ought-ness" of our behavior. Ethics is a statement of how we believe we ought to behave. Those who study ethics have identified three basic principles that are germane to determining standards and values with respect to clinical work. If the clinician's behavior does not incorporate these values, there is considerable risk of doing harm. One such ethical principle for those in a helping relationship is a belief in a client's *right to autonomy.* Simply put, this refers to the belief that clients have the ultimate right to make the decisions that affect their lives. Another is the principle of *beneficence.* This represents a commitment to respect clients, compassion, a commitment to "doing good" and not behaving in

a way that places the clinician's interests above those of the client. The third principle is that of *justice.* This, too, means being respectful, but it refers as well to behavior that promotes social justice, a self-imposed obligation both to be fair and to not discriminate in one's clinical work.

Even if a specific code of ethics for counselors did not exist and was not written down, these are basic ethical principles that are presumed by professional coworkers. What is required by those in helping professionals is above and beyond that which may be expected of others or expected of you in other situations. It also needs to be pointed out that how these principles are put into practice is all too often neither clear-cut nor obvious. For example, consider the issue of autonomy. With respect to those who are alcohol dependent and drinking, a clinician struggles with the question of whether a client is capable of acting in his or her own self-interest. If the principle of beneficence is also factored in, it may be felt that some degree of pressure or coercion to prompt treatment is warranted, yet there are limits to the degree of coercion and how it is exercised.

There are two ethical concerns that deserve special comment. One is confidentiality. The other is establishing and maintaining boundaries between what is professional and personal, between work and the rest of your life, and between your professional efforts and your personal participation in AA or other self-help groups.

Confidentiality

For the alcohol professional, as for anyone in the helping professions, confidentiality is a crucial issue. Most of us probably do not consider how much of our conversation includes discussion about other people. When you think about it, it can be quite a shock. It is especially difficult when you are really concerned about someone and are looking for aid and advice. There is only one place for this in a professional relationship with a client. That is with your supervisor or therapist coworkers. It is never okay to discuss a client with a spouse, friends, and even other alcohol workers from different facilities. Even without using names, enough usually slips out to make the client easily identified in the future. Unfortunately, the confidentiality standard is not kept all the time; there are occasional slips by even the most conscientious workers. You will do it accidentally, and you will hear it from time to time. All you can do is try harder in the first instance and deliberately forget what you have heard in the second. What your client shares with you is privileged information. That includes where the client is and how he or she is doing. Even good news is the client's alone to share.

Dear, you'd never guess what happened at work today—and if you could guess, I couldn't tell you whether or not you were right.

If you are heading up an outreach office, rather than functioning within the main agency, it is up to you to inform your secretary and other staff about confidentiality. The same is true for any volunteers working in the office. Of necessity, they have some knowledge about the people being seen, at least who they are. It must be stressed that any information they acquire there is strictly private. You do not need to get huffy and deliver a lecture, but you should make the point very clearly and set some standards in the workplace.

Confidentiality is not simply a noble idea going back to the ancient Greeks. There are laws pertaining to confidentiality and court cases that have helped to define the protections afforded patients. There are specific federal regulations with respect to confidentiality of client information and records in alcohol and drug services. Information cannot be released to any outside party without the client's permission. This means friends, physician, employer, or another treatment facility. A treatment facility is not even allowed to say if anyone has ever been or is currently in treatment. Most agencies have a release of information form used whenever information is provided about a client. This then becomes part of the client or medical record. Similarly, if clinicians want to get information from another facility or party, they need client's permission and a written release to forward to those from whom the information is being requested. The only exception to this is if the life of the client or of someone else is at risk.

One arena in which modern technology has moved at a faster pace than laws and regulations is e-mail. E-mail has become a routine part of most people's daily lives. Not surprisingly, e-mail has become a common part of clinical communications with patients. Clinicians should not slip into the use of e-mail without considering possible limitations. Some things to consider: How private is e-mail from your client's perspective? Is the e-mail address used only by the client or is it a family or household account? If the e-mail address is used by several people, communications are best limited to the kinds of messages that you would feel comfortable leaving on someone's answering machine, when there is the likelihood that others beside the client will hear the message. Aside from privacy, which communications are better handled in person, whether by telephone or in an individual session?

In both hospitals and agencies, electronic records are rapidly replacing paper records. Agencies that use electronic records have a variety of protections in place to help assure privacy and confidentiality. Chief among these is restricted access. One of the potential pitfalls associated with electronic records is the ease with which such materials can be forwarded via e-mail. For example, reports generated by such record-keeping systems can be e-mailed to others within the organization or to staff at other agencies. Interestingly, the very ease of sending such materials creates a danger that materials are sent out a bit indiscriminately. Before forwarding electronic reports, consider whether everyone on the intended recipient list *really* needs all the information included in the particular report. In addition to being overinclusive, there is always the potential for simple error. In large organizations, material may be sent to the wrong person due to selecting the incorrect Jane Smith from an in-house name directory.

Even in the presence of firewalls, and giving careful thought to whom materials are sent electronically, there is at least one other potential problem. Many e-mail systems have the option of forwarding e-mail to another electronic address. People going on vacation or leaving town to attend a meeting may have their workplace e-mail sent to another account. In forwarding electronic reports via e-mail, consider whether it is something that you want going out on a large commercial system, be it Hotmail or AOL. Indeed some medical centers are considering eliminating forwarding of e-mail.

Another issue involving e-mail is the matter of authenticity. This refers to the fact that no e-mail recipient can be certain that the indicated sender is in fact accurate. Anyone can send e-mail with virtually anyone's name attached to it. The inability of e-mail to provide methods of authentication presents a possible risk to patients and health care providers. E-mail authentication has been one of the more difficult issues to address when using e-mail for medical communication. Any user of e-mail is way too familiar with spam. Beyond the unwanted advertisements, some spam involves outright scams: "Send in $20 and get ____." The most recent spam twist encountered by this author pretended to be from her physician. The messages begin, "URGENT: This concerns you as a patient & we have not heard from you." This is followed by a reference to a review of my medical record, and then an offer to order a recommended weight loss product. This suggests that it may be important to emphasize which kinds of communications a client will not ever receive from you and which should be viewed with suspicion.

It's really not much of a gift. It's 2 half empty bottles of gin, 1 bottle of scotch, 2 bottles of sherry, 3 pints of whiskey, two-thirds of a bottle of vodka, one half filled bottle of Kahlua, a martini shaker and 4 wine glasses.

Setting Boundaries

An ever important and ongoing dilemma is establishing appropriate boundaries in relationships with clients. This can turn up in many forms, but ultimately the task is doing what is required to maintain a professional relationship. For example, occasionally clients will present you with gifts. While they are actively working with you, the general guideline is no gifts. This is especially true if something of great monetary value is offered. In such cases, it is important to discuss what is being said by the gift. Use your common sense, though; there are times when clearly the thing to do is accept graciously. (If you have a fantasy of a Hummer being delivered anonymously to your door, and it comes true, unfortunately, most of our experience doesn't cover that.) A bouquet of flowers from someone's garden is different than a huge bouquet from the florist. Even then, placing them in the reception area may be more appropriate than saying you can't wait to take them home.

Similarly, social engagements with a client alone or with the family are not recommended. It could be a "plot" to keep you friendly and avoid problems that have to be worked out. During office time, deal with the invitation and gently refuse.

Helping professionals are expected to avoid romantic entanglements with clients. If a romantic inclination seems to be surfacing, either for you or a client, it should be worked out—and not in bed. This is the time to run, not walk, to an experienced coworker. It may be hard on the ego, but the fact is that people with problems are as confused about their emotions as they are about everything else. They may be feeling so needy that they "love" anyone who seems to be hearing their cry. It really isn't you personally. If they had drawn someone else as their counselor, then that person would be the object of the misplaced emotion right now. So talk it over with a supervisor, guide, or mentor, not just a buddy. Then, follow his or her advice. It may have to be worked through with the client, or referral to another counselor may be necessary if it cannot be resolved. It is never acceptable to have a sexual relationship with a client.

The need to keep counseling and personal relationships separate does not apply only when the client is in actual treatment. It is also applicable afterward. This can be particularly difficult when the paths of a clinician and a former client intersect in other areas of life, possibly if both are members of AA or NA. However, as cruel as it may sound, former clients are forever off-limits.

These ethical standards are not arbitrary nonsense set up by a bunch of Puritans. They are protections designed to protect both you and the client from needless hurt. The hurt can be emotional or range all the way to messy court actions. Those who have walked the road before you have discovered what keeps upsets to a minimum, your sense of self-worth realistic, and your helpfulness at its optimum level.

Another ethical concern is how to keep your professional life and private life separate. Don't counsel your friends; you are likely to end up with fewer of them if you do. When you see a friend exhibiting behavior that you think indicates he or she is heading for trouble, it is hard not to fall into your professional role. Don't. Bite your tongue. A friend knows what business you're in. If that person wants help, he or she will ask. Should that day come, refer him or her to see someone else. And stay out of the picture. Vital objectivity is impossible. No matter how good you are with your clients, almost anyone else will be better equipped to work with your family or friends. If you are concerned about a close friend, then you see a therapist, as a client, to assess whether you want to or can become part of an intervention process. It is just as inappropriate to turn friends or family into clients as it is to turn clients into friends.

Seemingly ethical issues that arise in alcohol and drug counseling are being more widely discussed. This reflects greater attention to medical ethics generally. A formal field of medical ethics has emerged. Ethics Committees have been created in many institutions to help staff consider ethical dilemmas. With the alcohol field a part of health and human service fields, the issues that are raised elsewhere are now also being considered in respect to substance abuse clients. A number of ethical issues have gotten particular attention. One of these arises around illicit drug

Hippocratic Oath—Classical Version

I swear by Apollo Physician and Asclepius and Hygieia and Panaceia and all the gods and goddesses, making them my witnesses, that I will fulfill according to my ability and judgment this oath and this covenant:

To hold him who has taught me this art as equal to my parents and to live my life in partnership with him, and if he is in need of money to give him a share of mine, and to regard his offspring as equal to my brothers in male lineage and to teach them this art—if they desire to learn it—without fee and covenant; to give a share of precepts and oral instruction and all the other learning to my sons and to the sons of him who has instructed me and to pupils who have signed the covenant and have taken an oath according to the medical law, but no one else.

I will apply dietetic measures for the benefit of the sick according to my ability and judgment; I will keep them from harm and injustice.

I will neither give a deadly drug to anybody who asked for it, nor will I make a suggestion to this effect. Similarly I will not give to a woman an abortive remedy. In purity and holiness I will guard my life and my art.

I will not use the knife, not even on sufferers from stone, but will withdraw in favor of such men as are engaged in this work.

Whatever houses I may visit, I will come for the benefit of the sick, remaining free of all intentional injustice, of all mischief, and in particular of sexual relations with both female and male persons, be they free or slaves.

What I may see or hear in the course of the treatment or even outside of the treatment in regard to the life of men, which on no account one must spread abroad, I will keep to myself, holding such things shameful to be spoken about.

(continued on next page)

Hippocratic Oath *(continued)*

If I fulfill this oath and do not violate it, may it be granted to me to enjoy life and art, being honored with fame among all men for all time to come; if I transgress it and swear falsely, may the opposite of all this be my lot.

Translation from the Greek by Ludwig Edelstein. From *The Hippocratic Oath: Text, Translation, and Interpretation,* by Ludwig Edelstein. Baltimore: Johns Hopkins Press, 1943.

use during pregnancy. The question is how one considers and balances the welfare of the unborn child with that of the mother. Another area in which there has been increasing discussion is that of organ transplants. Should alcohol-dependent people be considered candidates for a liver transplant, given that the number of those who need liver transplants far exceeds the number of organs available? If so, should a period of abstinence be required to transplant? If so, what length?

Ethical Issues in Research

Ethics also enters into the area of research. Anyone who works in a setting that conducts research needs to be familiar with the guidelines for ethical research practices. Federal regulations that involve human subjects are very strict. Any research project that involves human subjects is required to take very careful steps to protect the subjects. First, it must be demonstrated that the answers to the questions being raised require human research, that mice, rats, or baboons wouldn't do. With that established, virtually all institutions have a committee to review how the research is to be conducted. These committees are required to review the risks to those involved, to consider how it is proposed that subjects will be recruited, to review the steps to be taken so that potential subjects understand what the research entails and what the risks are, and to ensure that no coercion is involved. This is not as straightforward as it sounds.

Consider the situation in which the researcher is also the potential subject's counselor or doctor. There is an established relationship. Given the trust that is present, the client or patient may agree to virtually anything. It is not that he or she is being pressured; the client is simply apt to comply with any request because the counselor or doctor makes it. The possible research subject may not even really listen to the counselor's explanation of the research but tend to do whatever he or she is asked to do. On the other hand, the subject may not be wild about the idea of participating in the research, but he or she is afraid of the consequences of saying no. Will the counselor be angry or stop seeing the client? These worries may seem unfounded, but they are common.

Another source of confusion is that clients, and patients in general, assume that any research will actually benefit them if they are involved. In an abstract way, all knowledge probably benefits all of us. But that isn't really the case with clinical research conducted in health-care settings. Clinical research is justified only when the answer to the research question is unknown: Is drug A more effective than drug B? Is the use of this counseling approach more effective than another? If the answer is clear—that is, scientifically established, opposed to being based on hunches and impressions—then it is unethical to do research on that question. Occasionally articles appear in the newspaper referring to a research project that has been discontinued early, when it became evident that those receiving an experimental treatment were doing better than those receiving an alternative therapy, or no treatment at all. Thus, the continuation of the research was not necessary and would have been unethical.

Anyone who works in an organization that conducts research is likely to find ethical questions arising. The following is just a smattering of some of the ethical questions being raised in the substance abuse field related to research issues. Should it be permissible for researchers to design a study that involves giving alcohol to alcoholics? What safeguards are needed to do this? What obligations are there to provide or at least offer treatment after the research is completed? What kinds of criteria are necessary to decide who could or could not be included in such a study? Another research-related ethical issue is the role of the liquor and brewing industries, as well as the tobacco industry, in the sponsorship of research. What biases and potential conflicts of interest might this introduce? Another ethical issue in the field centers on the role of drug testing in the workplace and the balance between public safety concerns and an individual's right to privacy.

Cases that raise ethical concerns do not have clear-cut solutions. One can examine the case from different perspectives and potentially arrive at very different conclusions. To further complicate the situation, it is important to recognize that the course of action that different professions deem ethical can differ. This is sometimes the source of unfortunate misunderstandings. It is most likely to come to the forefront around cases that involve resistant clients. Counselors may determine that terminating with a client who is in denial and for whom every reasonable effort has been made to intervene is the best and ethical course of action. To do otherwise may seem to the clinician to facilitate the continuation of drinking or other drug use. One of the hard things that substance abuse clinicians have had to learn to say to clients is "The way things are going, I don't see how I can help you." Counselors may fail to appreciate that this option may not be open to other professionals. The physician who is caring for a patient doesn't have the right to simply say, "I will not see you anymore." The person has a right to medical care, and the physician is ethically required to make a referral before terminating care. The issue is further compounded by the fact that the patient probably did not go to the physician for help with alcohol or other drug problems but for some other condition. Counselors not understanding this have at times erroneously viewed physicians as enabling continued drinking or drug use because the doctor continued to provide medical care even if the patient refused to deal with these issues.

Hopefully, in your first years of counseling, you will have a supervisor to help you through such sticky wickets. Use him or her. The real pros are the ones who used all the help they could get when they needed it. That is how they got to be pros.

COUNSELORS WITH "TWO HATS"

Many workers in the addictions field are themselves recovering people. Long before national attention was focused on alcohol treatment, for example, private rehabilitation centers were operated and often staffed by sober alcoholics. In the course of recovery, today some find themselves working in the field. The days are long gone when simply being a recovering person is considered a qualification as a professional. Differences in philosophy or outlook among staff were evident in the early days of the alcohol and substance abuse fields, depending on whether the person had or did not have a personal history of substance abuse. These divisions have largely evaporated. Studies of staff attitudes and clinical practice styles now show little differences based on recovery status.

However, for someone entering the field, being a recovering person has some potential advantages, but it also has some potential drawbacks. Being a counselor may, at times, be most confusing for the recovering clinician who is also in AA or NA. Doing 12-step work and calling it counseling won't do, from the individual's or the 12-step program's point of view. Twelve-step work is voluntary and has no business being used for bread earning; AA's and NA's traditions are clearly against this. They are not opposed to their members working in the field, if they are qualified to do so. For those who are a member of a 12-step program and a counselor, it is important to keep the dividing line in plain sight. The trade calls it "wearing two hats." There are some good AA/NA pamphlets on the subject, and the AA monthly magazine, *The Grapevine,* publishes articles for two-hatters from time to time.

A particular bind for two-hat counselors occurs when attending meetings of 12-step programs becomes tied to their jobs more than to their own sobriety. You might easily find yourself sustaining clients at meetings and not being there for yourself. A way to avoid this is to find a meeting you can attend where you are less likely to see clients. On the occasions when clients do see you at meetings and bring up problems or questions about their treatment, gently tell them you will discuss it with them in the office. On the other hand if they are questioning some aspect of the meeting, introduce them to another member present.

Taking care of myself. I like it. A good idea. But all the nurturing people I know only nurture clients.

It is too easy for both you and the clients to confuse AA or NA with the other therapy. The client benefits from a clear distinction as much, if not more, than you do. There is always the difficulty of keeping your priorities in order. You cannot counsel if you are drinking yourself. So, whatever you do to keep sober, whether it includes self-help or not, keep doing it. Again, when so many people out there seem to need you, it is very difficult to keep from overextending. A recovering person simply cannot afford this. (If this description fits you, stop reading right now and choose one thing to scratch off your schedule.) It is always easy to justify skimping on your own sober regimen because "I'm working with alcoholics all the time." Retire that excuse. Experience has shown it to be a counselor killer.

Another problem is the temptation to discuss your job at a 12-step or self-help meeting or to discuss clients with other members. The members don't need to be bored by you any more than by a physician member describing the surgical removal of a gallbladder. Discussing your clients, even with another AA or NA member, is a serious breach of confidentiality. This will be particularly hard when a really concerned member asks you point-blank about someone. The other side of the coin is keeping the confidences gained at self-help meetings and not reporting to coworkers about what transpired with clients. Your nonalcoholic coworkers should not put you in a bind by asking. It is probably okay to talk with your AA or NA sponsor about your job if it is giving you fits. However, it is important to stick with the subject of you and to leave out work details and/or details about clients.

Watch out if feelings of superiority creep in toward other "plain" members or colleagues without a personal history of alcohol/drug problems. Recovery from alcohol or other drug dependence does not accord you magical insights. On the other hand, the absence of a personal alcohol or other drug history is not a guaranteed route to knowing what is going on, either. Keep your perspective as much as you're able. After all, you are all in the same boat, with different oars. To quote an unknown source: "It's amazing how much can be accomplished if no one cares who gets the credit."

Before proceeding further, it should be noted that the issue of impairment caused by alcohol and other drug use is not solely a concern for the alcohol and substance abuse fields. While some professions have come further than others, virtually every professional group—physicians, nurses, social workers, psychologists—has recognized the problem and has developed policies and programs to address it. These efforts are conducted under the auspices of an impaired professionals committee, which may be affiliated with the professional association or a state licensing board. The general thrust is to encourage reporting by concerned individuals, be it family members, colleagues, or patients; to initiate a nonprejudicial review; and, where impairment is suspected, to then endeavor to have the individual evaluated and, as indicated, provided with treatment. In many of these instances, considerable leverage is provided by the obligation to report findings to licensing boards and the threat of disciplinary action if treatment is refused.

While every profession has members who are recovering alcoholics or drug-dependent individuals—as well as those who go untreated—the alcohol and substance abuse field is a special case, given its history. There appear to be greater numbers of recovering people in this field, and their recovery status is relevant to the work they perform. For those professionals who are recovering, there are a variety of situations that may spell potential trouble: burnout, inappropriate relationships with clients, slackening self-help attendance, overinvolvement with the job, and unrealistic expectations. For the clinician who is a recovering alcoholic, all of these can lead to a relapse. Becoming a professional in no way confers immunity to relapse. Unfortunately, this fact of life has not been very openly discussed by the alcohol counseling profession. It has

been the profession's big taboo topic. When relapse has occurred, the situation has too often been handled poorly. There is either a conspiracy of silence or a move to drive the counselor out of the field. The coworkers can very readily assume all the roles of "the family," and the counselor's coworkers can get caught up in functioning as enablers.

Ideally, the time to address the issue of possible relapse is at the time of hiring. Both the counselor and the agency have a mutual responsibility to be alert to possible danger signs, and they should agree to address them openly. This does not mean the recovering professional is always under surveillance. It simply is a means of publicly acknowledging that relapses can and do occur and that they are too serious to ignore. If a counselor relapses, it is his or her responsibility both to seek help and to inform the agency. The job status will be dependent on evaluating the counselor's ability to continue serving clients and to participate in treatment for him- or herself. The time to agree on an arbitrator/consultant or referral is before relapse, not in the midst of it.

Some people favor an arbitrary ironclad rule: any drinking and you're out of your job. However, that seems to miss the point. There is the recovering professional, who buys a six-pack, has 1 or 2 beers, sees what is going on, picks up the phone, and calls for help. Another case is the person who "nips" off and on for weeks, who subsequently exhibits loss of control, and shows up at the office intoxicated. Though it is important not to treat the former case lightly, nonetheless the disease process has not been wholly reactivated, as it has in the latter case. Interestingly, some people who have had a single drinking incident, as in the example, have tended to take a brief sick leave and to reengage themselves in a brief period of intensive care. They have interpreted the drinking as a very serious sign that something in their lives was out of balance, warranting serious attention. What is essential in any case is securing adequate treatment for the clinician and not jeopardizing the care of the clients.

If you are a clinician known to your clients as a recovering alcoholic, your relapse can have a profound effect on some of them. If you are off the job and enter treatment, you can count on the news rapidly becoming public knowledge. The agency and the coworkers dealing with your case load have a responsibility to inform your clients. Certainly, any details are a private matter, but that a relapse has occurred cannot be seen as none of their business.

If you happen to become a coworker providing coverage for a relapsed counselor, be prepared to deal with clients' feelings of betrayal, hopelessness, anger, and fear. You will need to provide extra support. Be very clear about who is available to them in their counselor's absence. Also recognize that this can be a difficult, painful experience for you and other coworkers, who may share many of the clients' feelings. Be prepared to call on extra reinforcements in the form of consultation and supervision.

If you are a counselor who has relapsed and you return to work after a leave, there is no way you can avoid dealing with the fact of the relapse.

How this is handled should be dealt with in supervision and with lots of input from more seasoned colleagues. You will be trying to walk along a difficult middle ground. On one hand, your clients do not need apologies, nor will they benefit from hearing all the details or in any way being put in the role of your therapist. Yet neither can it be glossed over, treated as no big deal and of no greater significance than your summer vacation. In short, you have to, in your own counseling, come to grips with the drinking or relapse, so that you do not find yourself working it out on the job with your clients.

A similar situation is posed by the clinician who enters the alcohol field as a nonalcoholic but who comes to recognize his or her own budding alcohol problem. In some cases, the individuals are in very early stages of the disease. This raises interesting questions. Since there has been ample evidence of the wisdom of not having recovering alcoholics enter the field until sober a minimum of 2 years, how does the "2 years of sobriety principle" apply in such situations? Does that automatically mean that those who have been good clinicians must exit from the field for the same length of time? To jump to that conclusion is premature. The profession needs to determine what the dynamics in this situation are, when an extended leave is needed and when it is not. In the meantime, common sense dictates that this situation needs to be carefully evaluated and monitored. Possibly a brief leave of absence is indicated, although not necessarily because the counselor has to enter a residential program. A leave provides the opportunity to work intensely on personal issues, which then reduces the risk that they will be dealt with inappropriately in sessions with clients. At the very least, it is imperative that lots of clinical supervision occurs and that both a sponsor and a therapist for the counselor be an integral part of the recovery.

The foregoing may seem a very grim note on which to conclude this text. It is sobering, but it is reality, too. Maybe one of the hardest things to learn in becoming a clinician is how to take care of yourself. Like everything else, that takes a lot of practice. One aspect of caring for yourself professionally as well as personally is to place yourself in the company of nurturing people.

RESOURCES AND FURTHER READING

Issues of the Profession

Baer JS, Rosengren DB, Dunn CW, Wells EA, Ogle RL, Hartzler B. An evaluation of workshop training in motivational interviewing for addiction and mental health clinicians. *Drug and Alcohol Dependence* 73(1):99–106, 2004. (33 refs.)

Blume SB. *Confidentiality of Patient Records in Alcoholism and Drug Treatment Programs.* New York: American Medical Society on Alcoholism and Other Drug Dependencies and National Council on Alcoholism, 1987.
Note: This pamphlet reviews the 1987 revisions of the federal regulations governing the confidentiality of alcohol and other drug abuse patient records. It addresses the records covered by the regulations; the types of communications covered; written informed consent; the application of consent to situations involving minors,

incompetent persons, and deceased persons; the types of information to be released with consent; and the security of records.

Center for Substance Abuse Treatment, Addiction Technology Transfer Centers Curriculum Committee, Deitch DA. *Addiction Counseling Competencies: The Knowledge, Skills, and Attitudes of Professional Practice (TAP) Series 21.* Rockville, MD: CSAT, 1997. (Chapter refs.)

Chiauzzi EJ, Liljegren S. Taboo topics in addiction treatment: An empirical review of clinical folklore (review). *Journal of Substance Abuse Treatment* 10(3):303–316, 1993.

Forman RF, Bovasso G, Woody G. Staff beliefs about addiction treatment. *Journal of Substance Abuse Treatment* 21(1):1–9, 2001. (34 refs.)

Gallon SL, Gabriel RM, Knudsen JRW. The toughest job you'll ever love: A Pacific Northwest Treatment Workforce Survey. *Journal of Substance Abuse Treatment* 24(3):183–196, (15 refs.)

Gotham HJ. Diffusion of mental health and substance abuse treatments: Development, dissemination, and implementation (review). *Clinical Psychology: Science and Practice* 11(2):160–178, 2004 (117 refs.)

McGovern MP, Fox TS, Xie H, Drake RE. A survey of clinical practices and readiness to adopt evidence-based practices: Dissemination research in an addiction treatment system. *Journal of Substance Abuse Treatment* 26(4):305–312, 2004. (51 refs.)

McLellan AT, Carise D, Kleber HD. Can the national addiction treatment infrastructure support the public's demand for quality care? *Journal of Substance Abuse Treatment* 25(2):117–121, 2003 (26 refs.)

Mulvey KP, Hubbard S, Hayashi S. A national study of the substance abuse treatment workforce. *Journal of Substance Abuse Treatment* 24(1):51–57, 2003. (15 refs.)

NAADAC Education and Research Foundation. *Salary and Compensation Study of Alcoholism and Drug Abuse Professionals, 1995.* Arlington, VA: NAADAC, 1995.

Stoffelmayr BE, Mavis BE, Kasim RM. Substance abuse treatment staff: Recovery status and approaches to treatment. *Journal of Drug Education* 28(2):135–145, 1998. (14 refs.)

Ethics

Doyle K. Substance abuse counselors in recovery: Implications for the ethical issue of dual relationships. *Journal of Counseling and Development* 75(6):428–432, 1997. (16 refs.)

Gerstle RS, Task Force on Medical Informatics. Guidance for the clinician in rendering pediatric care *Pediatrics* 114:317-321, 2004. (18 refs.)

Hall W. The role of legal coercion in the treatment of offenders with alcohol and heroin problems. *Australian and New Zealand Journal of Criminology* 30(2):103–120, 1997. (71 refs.)

Hannum H. The Dublin Principles of Cooperation among the beverage alcohol industry, governments, scientific researchers, and the public health community (editorial). *Alcohol and Alcoholism* 32(6):639–640, 1997.

Scott CG. Ethical issues in addiction counseling. *Rehabilitation Counseling Bulletin* 43(4):209–214, 2000. (31 refs.)

Weinstein BA, Raber MJ. Ethical assessment of structured intervention with chemically dependent clients. *Employee Assistance Quarterly* 13(3):19–31, 1998. (22 refs.)

Prevention

Abt Associates, eds. *Drug Abuse Prevention Research, Dissemination and Application Materials* (6 vol.). Rockville, MD: National Institute on Drug Abuse, 1997. (Volume refs.)

Beck J. 100 years of "just say no" versus "just say know": Reevaluating drug education goals for the coming century (review). *Evaluation Review* 22(1):15–45, 1998. (112 refs.)

Brown JH. Youth, drugs and resilience education (review). *Journal of Drug Education* 31(1):83–122, 2001. (168 refs.)

Hogan JA, Gabrielsen KR, Luna N, Grothaus D. *Substance Abuse Prevention: The Intersection of Science and Practice.* Boston: Allyn & Bacon, 2003.

Lynam DR, Milich R, Zimmerman R, Novak SP, Logan TK, Martin C, et al. Project DARE: No effects at 10-year follow-up. *Journal of Consulting and Clinical Psychology* 67(4):590–593, 1999. (16 refs.)

Midford R. Does drug education work? (review). *Drug and Alcohol Review* 19(4):441–446, 2000. (29 refs.)

Peterson AV Jr., Kealey KA, Mann SL, Marek PM, Sarason IG. Hutchinson Smoking Prevention Project: Long-term randomized trial in school-based tobacco use prevention. Results on smoking. *Journal of the National Cancer Institute* 92(24):1979–1991, 2000. (87 refs.)

Rosenbaum DP, Hanson GS. Assessing the effects of school-based drug education: A six-year multilevel analysis of project DARE. *Journal of Research in Crime and Delinquency* 35(4):381–412, 1998. (60 refs.)

Swisher JD. Sustainability of prevention. *Addictive Behaviors* 25(6):965–973, 2000. (23 refs.)

Wallace SK, Staiger PK. Informing consent: Should "providers" inform "purchasers" about the risks of drug education? *Health Promotion International* 13(2):167–171, 1998. (47 refs.)

APPENDIX A

North American Organizations in the Substance Abuse Field

The following organizations are of interest for two major reasons. These groups provide information services; they also publish quality publications, and most have a variety of materials on their websites. Organizations are listed alphabetically, drawn from the following categories:

- Clearinghouses
- Hotlines
- Library-Related Organizations
- Special Focus of Group by Population
- Self-Help Groups
- Professional Organizations
- Canadian-Based
- U.S.-Based

Addictions Foundation of Manitoba, William Potoroka Memorial Library

Address: 1031 Portage Ave., Winnepeg, MB, Canada R3G OR8
Phone: (204) 944-6233
Fax: (204) 772-0225
Web: www.afm.mb.ca

Description The library has over 4,000 books, 400 videotapes and films, and an in-house database. It collects and disseminates alcohol and drug information on behalf of the Foundation and serves professionals, students, and the general public throughout the province. It responds to short queries from others. Its public service publications are available in multiple languages: English, French, Filipino, Chinese and Vietnamese.

Adult Children of Alcoholics (ACoA) World Service Organization, Inc.

Address: PO Box 3216, Torrance, CA 90510-3216
Phone: (310) 534-1815
E-mail: info@adultchildren.org
Web: www.adultchildren.org

Description A 12-step, 12-tradition program of recovery for those who grew up in an alcoholic or otherwise dysfunctional household. The World Service Organization provides information about and referral to meetings throughout the country and offers assistance to those organizing new groups. Information is available on its website.

Al-Anon Family Group Headquarters, Inc.

Address: 1600 Corporate Landing Parkway, Virginia Beach, VA 23454-5617
Phone: (757) 563-1600
Fax: (757) 563-1655
E-mail: wso@al-anon.org
Web: www.al-anon.alateen.org

Description Al-Anon is a self-help program for family members and friends of those with an alcohol problem. The headquarters serve both Al-Anon and

Alateen. Alateen is directed to teenagers with an alcoholic parent. In 2000 Al-Anon had over 35,000 groups in more than 100 countries, including 3,500 Alateen groups. Al-Anon was founded by Lois Wilson, wife of one of the founders of AA, and was originally known as the AA Auxiliary.

Alcoholic Beverage Medical Research Foundation (ABMRF)

Contact: Robin A. Kroft, Deputy Executive Director
Address: 1122 Kenilworth Dr., Suite 407, Baltimore, MD 21204
Phone: (410) 821-7066
Fax: (410) 821-7065
E-mail: info@abmrf.org
Web: www.abmrf.org

Description Established in 1982 with support from the malt beverage industries of the United States and Canada, supports medical, behavioral, and social research and information dissemination on the use of alcoholic beverages and the prevention of alcohol-related problems. Grant recipients are from U.S. and Canadian academic institutions. The Foundation's Library and Resource Center on Moderate Drinking provides literature searches on request. It publishes the *Journal of the ABMRF.* A free quarterly publication, it includes abstracts of current literature on the psychosocial and medical effects of moderate drinking, news about the Foundation, and selected statistical tables.

Alcoholics Anonymous General Service Office (AA)

Contact: Adrienne Brown (liaison to professional community)
Address: Box 459, Grand Central Station, New York, NY 10163
Phone: (212) 870-3400
Fax: (212) 870-3003
Web: www.alcoholics-anonymous.org

Description The General Service Office responds to inquiries about the Fellowship; prepares and distributes literature, including lists of the thousands of AA groups around the world; and maintains links with each AA group. AA literature and audiovisual materials are directed to alcoholics, AA members, and human service and health-care professionals.

American Academy of Addiction Psychiatry (AAAP)

Contact: Jeanne G. Trumble, MSW
Address: 7301 Mission Road, Suite 252, Prairie Village, KS 66208
Phone: (913) 262-6161
Fax: (913) 262-4311
E-mail: info@aaap.org
Web: www.aaap.org

Description Founded in 1985 to improve education, prevention, treatment, and research in the field of alcoholism and addictions and to strengthen the training of psychiatrists in the addiction field, the Academy holds annual meetings and edits a peer-reviewed journal, *The American Journal on Addictions,* published quarterly.

American Council for Drug Education (ACDE)

Address: 164 West 74th St., New York, NY 10023
Phone: (800) 488-3784
Fax: (212) 595-2553
E-mail: acde@phoenixhouse.org
Web: www.acde.org

Description Founded in 1977, the ACDE provides information on health hazards associated with the use of tobacco, alcohol, marijuana, cocaine, crack, and other psychoactive drugs. It prepares and publishes educational materials for employees and employers, parents, children, educators, students, policy makers, and constituents, all available through its website.

American Society of Addiction Medicine (ASAM)

Contact: James F. Callahan, DPA, Executive Vice President
Address: 4601 North Park Ave., Upper Arcade Suite 101, Chevy Chase, MD 20815

Phone: (301) 655-3920
E-mail: e-mail@asam.org
Web: www.asam.org

Description ASAM is a national medical specialty society of physicians in the field of alcohol and other drug dependencies. It was admitted to the American Medical Association's House of Delegates as a voting member in June 1988, and in June 1990 the AMA added addiction medicine (ADM) to its list of self-designated specialties. Members encompass all medical specialties and subspecialties. Physician certification is offered. It publishes the *Journal of Addictive Diseases,* position statements, and guidelines.

Association for Medical Education and Research in Substance Abuse (AMERSA)

Contact: Doreen Maclane-Baeder
Address: 125 Whipple St., Third Floor, Suite 300, Providence, RI 02908
Phone: (401) 349-0000
Fax: (877) 418-8769
E-mail: doreen@amersa.org
Web: www.amersa.org

Description Started in 1976 by the federally funded Career Teachers in Alcohol and Drug Abuse, AMERSA is a national organization directed to education of health professionals in the field of alcohol and drug abuse. Full membership is available to those holding faculty appointments as well as others, as determined by the membership committee. AMERSA arranges field placements for students and trainees who desire experience in alcohol and drug abuse treatment, research, and education. It publishes the journal *Substance Abuse.*

Brewers Association of Canada

Address: 650-100 Queen St., Ottawa, ON, Canada K1P 159
Phone: (613) 232-9601
Fax: (613) 232-2283
E-mail: info@brewers.ca
Web: www.brewers.ca

Description National trade association for Canadian brewing companies, both conventional and microbreweries. Information primarily serves organizational members. It compiles international statistical information on consumption, taxation, and control policies, and these are posted on its website. It publishes *Alcoholic Beverage Taxation and Control Policies.*

Canadian Centre on Substance Abuse (CCSA)

Address: 75 Albert St., Suite 300, Ottawa, ON, Canada K1P 5E7
Phone: (613) 235-4048
Fax: (613) 235-8101
E-mail: jausten@ccsa.org (for clearinghouse)
Web: www.ccsa.ca

Description CCSA is a national agency, established in 1988 by an Act of Parliament. Funded by Canada's Drug Strategy and through its own revenue-generating efforts, the Centre promotes informed debate on substance abuse issues and encourages public participation in reducing the harm associated with drug abuse; disseminates information on the nature, extent, and consequences of substance abuse; and supports and assists organizations involved in substance abuse treatment, prevention, and educational programming. Its website includes documents and reports on policy.

Canadian HIV/AIDS Clearinghouse

Contact: Ian Culbert, Director
Address: Canadian Public Health Association, 1565 Carling Ave., 4th Floor, Ottawa, ON, Canada K1Z 8R1
Phone: (613) 725-3434, (877) 999-7740
Fax: (613) 725-1205
E-mail: AIDS/SIDA@cpha.ca
Web: www.clearinghouse.cpha.ca

Description The Clearinghouse serves AIDS educators across Canada and throughout the world. It is the central Canadian documentation center on AIDS/HIV in Canada. The Clearinghouse offers distribution of free materials, a lending library, and information and referral services in English and French.

Center for Substance Abuse Prevention (CSAP)

Address: 5600 Fishers Lane, Rockwall II Building, 9th floor, Rockville, MD 20857
Phone: (301) 443-0365 (clearinghouse)
(800) 729-6686
Fax: (301) 443-5447
Web: www.prevention.samhsa.gov

Description CSAP, a part of the Substance Abuse and Mental Health Services Administration (SAMHSA) of the Public Health Service, U.S. Department of Health and Human Services, was created by the Anti-Drug Abuse Act of 1986. It oversees and coordinates national drug prevention efforts, funds demonstration grant programs, coordinates a national training system for prevention, and manages an information clearinghouse. It also runs a regionally based network of programs to promote prevention at the state level, the RADAR (Regional Alcohol and Drug Awareness Resources) Network. Its prevention materials are distributed through NCADI (National Clearinghouse for Alcohol and Drug Information).

Center for Substance Abuse Treatment (CSAT)

Contact: H. Westley Clark, M.D., Director
Address: Rockwall II Bldg., Suite 618, 5600 Fishers Lane, Rockville, MD 20857
Phone: (301) 443-5700
Fax: (301) 434-8751
Web: www.samhsa.gov/csat

Description The Center for Substance Abuse Treatment (CSAT), within the Substance Abuse and Mental Health Services Administration of the U.S. Department of Health and Human Services, was established to direct and coordinate federal efforts to promote treatment of alcohol and other drug problems.

Centers for Disease Control National Prevention Information Network

Address: CDC National Prevention Information Network, PO Box 6003, Rockville, MD 20849-6003
Phone: (800) 458-5231, TTY (800) 243-7012
E-mail: info@cdcnpin.org
Web: www.cdcnpin.org

Description The Network is a major source of information on HIV/AIDS. It offers information on all aspects of prevention, care, and social support. Its collection includes descriptions of AIDS-related programs and materials on topics ranging from general information to education and training programs in over 50 languages. The bilingual, multidisciplinary staff of the Network offer reference and referral services and document delivery. Services are accessible by phone, by Internet services, by FAX, and by mail. The Internet services include E-mail and a listserv.

Centre for Addiction and Mental Health (CAMH)

Address: 33 Russell St., Toronto, ON, Canada M5S 2S1
Phone: (416) 595-6111, (800) 661-1111
U.S. and Canada
E-mail: info@CAMH.net
Web: www.camh.net

Description Originally organized in 1949 as an agency of the government of Ontario, the Addiction Research Foundation was established to provide treatment, conduct research, and disseminate information about alcoholism and drug addiction. In 1998, the Foundation merged with the Clarke Institute of Psychiatry of the Donwood and Queen Street Mental Health Center to form the Centre for Addiction and Mental Health. It is a collaborating center for research and training on drug dependence of the World Health Organization. The Foundation is significant to those beyond the province for its research, educational materials, and information services, available on its website.

Children of Alcoholics Foundation, Inc.

Contact: Director of Public Information
Address: 164 W. 74th St., New York, NY 10023
Phone: (800) 359-2623
Fax: (212) 754-2208

E-mail: coaf@phoenixhouse.org
Web: www.coaf.org

Description A voluntary nonprofit organization established in 1982. Primary purposes are to reach, help, and offer hope to young and adult children of alcoholics; to inform and educate the public and professionals about this group; to disseminate research and new data on the effects of family alcoholism on children; and to encourage federal, state, and local decision-makers to respond to the needs of this high-risk group. It affiliated with Phoenix House in 1997.

Cocaine Anonymous World Services, Inc. (CA)

Address: 3740 Overland Ave., Suite C, Culver City, CA 90034
Phone: (310) 559-5833 (administrative office)
(800) 347-8998 (24-hour referral line)
E-mail: CAWSO@ca.org
Web: www.ca.org

Description Founded in 1982, CA is a fellowship of people who help each other recover from their addiction to cocaine and other mind-altering substances. Its structure is similar to that of AA, with meetings held throughout the United States. The World Service Office maintains a 24-hour referral line. The Co-Anon program is available for affected family members. Its website includes literature, a meeting directory, and other member-related information.

CSAP Workplace Helpline

Phone: (800) 843-4971

Description Operated by the Center for Substance Abuse Prevention, the helpline is staffed Monday through Friday, 9 A.M. to 8 P.M. It offers telephone consultation, resource referrals, and publications to business, industry, and unions to assist in planning, development, and implementation of comprehensive drug-free workplace programs.

Distilled Spirits Council of the United States (DISCUS)

Contact: Matthew Vellucci, Librarian
Address: 1250 Eye Street NW, Washington, DC 20005
Phone: (202) 628-3544
Fax: (202) 682-8888
Web: www.discus.health.org

Description: This trade association for liquor producers and marketers in the United States, monitors national, state, and local alcohol legislation; maintains statistics on production and sales; maintains a library; and welcomes inquiries from the general public.

Drug Information & Strategy Clearinghouse (DISC)

Address: PO Box 8577, Silver Spring, MD 20907
Phone: (800) 578-3472. (Note: There are several voicemail menus before callers reach the Clearinghouse.)
Fax: (301) 519-6655
Web: www.ocsc.org

Description DISC provides housing officials, residents, and community leaders with information and assistance on drug abuse prevention and drug trafficking control techniques. It operates and maintains databases with information about national and community-based antidrug programs. The Clearinghouse acquires and reviews more than 1,500 reports, articles, news items, videos, grant applications, and other materials annually. Information specialists conduct searches of specialized databases for materials about antidrug programs and strategies.

Employee Assistance Professionals Association (EAPA)

Contact: John Maynard, Executive Officer
Address: 2101 Wilson Boulevard, Suite 500, Arlington, VA 22201
Phone: (703) 387-1000
Fax: (703) 522-4585
E-mail: ceo@eap-association.org
Web: www.eapassn.com

Description Founded in 1971 as the Association of Labor-Management Administrators and Consultants on Alcoholism (ALMACA), the organization changed its name in 1989. It currently has over 7,000 members engaged directly in providing employee assistance services. In 1987 it established a Certification Commission for certification of employee assistance professionals under an examination system. The Association publishes an extensive selection of brochures, books, and research publications on prevention, treatment, and education. The Resource Center responds to professional information requests without charge.

Hazelden Foundation, Library and Information Resources

Contact: Barbara Weiner, MLS, Librarian
Address: Box 11, Center City, MN 55012
Phone: (651) 213-4411 (library)
(800) 328-9000 (publishing)
Fax: (651) 213-4411
E-mail: bweiner@hazelden.org
Web: www.hazelden.org

Description Founded in 1949 as a residential treatment program, the Foundation also provides education and training, at its Minnesota Center as well as at other sites. Of special note is a weeklong "Professionals in Residence Program" which offers experiential learning in addition to lectures and discussions with program staff. Hazelden also offers comprehensive prevention training to teachers, counselors, and community leaders working with at-risk youth. Hazelden is a major publisher in the alcohol-drug field. Its library will respond to questions from professionals.

Health Canada

Address: Departmental Library, Jeanne Mance Building, Floor 2, AL 090 C2 Ottawa, ON, Canada K1A 0K9
Phone: (613) 957-2991
Fax: (613) 941-5366
Web: www.hc-sc.gc.ca

Description Health Canada (Federal Department of Health) assists Canadians to maintain and advance their physical and mental well-being. The departmental library was established in 1991. Its collections focus on health policy, health promotion, health financing and service delivery, mental health, as well as health and well-being of specific populations (e.g., aged, children, natives, etc.). All library services are available to the public.

International Lawyers in Alcoholics Anonymous (ILAA)

Contact: Eliseo D.W. Gauna
Address: 14643 Sylvan St., Van Nuys, CA 91411-2327
Phone: (818) 785-6541
Fax: (818) 785-3887
Web: www.ILAA.org

Description ILAA serves as a clearinghouse to assist attorneys seeking help for alcohol and other drug problems and holds an annual convention. The website includes member services.

International Nurses Society on Addictions (IntNSA)

Address: PO Box 10752, Raleigh, NC 27605
Phone: (919) 821-1292
Fax: (919) 833-5743
Web: www.intnsa.org

Description IntNSA is a professional organization for nurses whose field of practice is substance abuse/addictions nursing, including clinicians, educators, managers, and researchers. Full membership is available to registered professional nurses; others may become associate members. The organization is dedicated to providing quality comprehensive care to addicted persons and their families. The website includes information on certification for nurses in the specialty, developed in collaboration with the National Consortium of Chemical Dependency Nurses.

Join Together

Address: 1 Appleton St., 4th Floor, Boston, MA 02116-5223
Phone: (617) 437-1500
Fax: (617) 437-9394
E-mail: info@jointogether.org
Web: www.jointogether.org

Description Started in 1991, Join Together is a national program to help communities fight substance abuse. It is funded by a grant from the Robert Wood Johnson Foundation to the Boston University School of Public Health. Program components include public policy panels, a national leadership fellows program, a national computer network, a communications program, and technical assistance to community programs. Although Join Together does not have a formal information service, professionals respond to phone queries.

Marin Institute

Address: 24 Belvedere St., San Rafael, CA 94901
Phone: (415) 456-5692
Fax: (415) 456-0491
E-Mail: info@marininstitute.org
Web: www.marininstitute.org

Description Established in 1987 and designated to receive long-term core funding from the Beryl Buck Trust, the Institute's goal is to reduce the toll of alcohol and other drug problems on Marin County and on society in general. The Institute develops, implements, evaluates, and disseminates innovative approaches to prevention locally, nationally, and internationally. It has major collections of materials related to alcohol control policy.

NAADAC, Association of Addiction Professionals

Address: 901 Washington St., Suite 600,
Alexandria, VA 22314
Phone: (800) 548-0497
Fax: (800) 377-1136
E-mail: naadac@naadac.org
Web: www.naadac.org

Description NAADAC is a national professional organization for alcoholism and drug abuse professionals with over 14,000 members. It runs a credentialing program with two levels of certification for counselors who are certified in their states. Certification requirements include education, clinical experience, and successful completion of an exam that is offered two times a year. Its website provides information on certification, study guide (for certification exam), and counselor job ads.

Narcotics Anonymous World Services, Inc. (NA)

Contact: Jeff Gershoff, Public Information
Address: PO Box 9999, Van Nuys, CA 91409
Phone: (818) 773-9999, ext. 131
Fax: (818) 700-0700
E-mail: jeffg@na.org
Web: www.na.org

Description Narcotics Anonymous is a 12-step program, modeled after AA, for persons for whom drugs have become a problem and who wish to stop using. The website includes publications, directories, and member information.

National Association for Children of Alcoholics (NACoA)

Address: 1426 Rockville Pike, Suite #100,
Rockville, MD 20852
Phone: (888) 554-2627
Fax: (301) 468-0987
E-mail: info@nacoa.org
Web: www.nacoa.org

Description Founded in 1983 the National Association for Children of Alcoholics (NACoA) provides public and professional information, education, advocacy, and community networking on behalf of children and families affected by alcoholism and other drug dependencies. NACoA programs and members work to increase public awareness and services for children of alcoholics.

National Association of Lesbian and Gay Addiction Professionals (NALGAP)

Address: 901 Washington St., Suite 600,
Alexandria, VA 22314
Phone: (703) 465-0539
Fax: (703) 741-6989
E-mail: clinical@nalgap.org
Web: www.nalgap.org

Description NALGAP is a national membership organization comprised of professionals and other concerned individuals whose mission is to address and counteract the effect of heterosexual bias and homophobia on those affected by substance abuse and addictions through advocacy, training, networking, and resource development.

National Association of State Alcohol and Drug Abuse Directors (NASADAD)

Contact:	Rob Morrison, Director of Public Policy
Address:	808 17th St. NW, Suite 410, Washington, DC 20006
Phone:	(202) 293-0090, ext. 106
Fax:	(202) 293-1250
E-mail:	dcoffice@nasadad.org
Web:	www.nasadad.org

Description NASADAD is a private association that endeavors to facilitate cooperative efforts between the federal government and state agencies and among states on alcohol and drug abuse treatment, prevention, and public policy.

National Center on Addiction and Substance Abuse at Columbia University (CASA)

Contacts:	David Mann, MLS, Librarian
Address:	633 3rd Ave., 19th Floor, New York, NY 10017-6706
Phone:	(212) 841-5200
Fax:	(212) 956-8020
Web:	www.casacolumbia.org

Description Founded in 1992, CASA is an independent, nonprofit corporation affiliated with Columbia University. It works with experts in medicine, law enforcement, business, law, economics, communications, teaching, social work, and the clergy. Its goals are to explain the social and economic cost of substance abuse, identify what prevention and treatment programs work for whom and under what circumstances, and encourage individuals and institutions to take responsibility to prevent and combat substance abuse. The website provides access to center reports and white papers.

National Clearinghouse for Alcohol and Drug Information (NCADI)

Address:	PO Box 2345, Rockville, MD 20847-2345
Phone:	(800) 729-6686, (301) 468-2600
Fax:	(301) 468-6433
E-mail:	info@health.org
Web:	www.health.org

Description NCADI is the information service of the Substance Abuse and Mental Health Services Administration of the U.S. Department of Health and Human Services. It acts as the central point within the federal government for current print and audiovisual materials about alcohol, tobacco, and other drug problems. Information specialists respond to more than 20,000 alcohol and other drug-related inquiries each month. It distributes bibliographies and publications, posters, videotapes, and prevention curricula. NCADI maintains an extensive full-service library. It coordinates the Regional Alcohol and Drug Awareness (RADAR) Network which facilitates access to state and local sources of information about alcohol and other drugs.

National Clearinghouse on Family Violence (Canada)

Address:	1918C2, Floor-18 Jeanne Mance Bld. Tunney's Pasture, Ottawa, ON, Canada K1A 1B4
Phone:	(800) 267-1291, (613) 957-2938 (local), (800) 561-5643 (TTY)
Fax:	(888) 267-1233, (613) 941-8930 (local)
Web:	www.hc-sc.gc.ca./nc-cn

Description The Clearinghouse is a national resource center for information and solutions to violence in the family. It provides information to front-line workers, researchers, and community groups as well as answering queries from individuals. The Clearinghouse maintains a reference collection with online bibliographic searching of approximately 14,000 titles.

National Clearinghouse on Substance Abuse (Canada) (NCSA)

Address:	75 Albert St., Suite 300, Ottawa, ON, Canada K1P 5E7
Phone:	(613) 235-4048
Fax:	(613) 235-8101
E-mail:	webmaster@ccsa.ca
Web:	www.ccsa.ca

Description The National Clearinghouse has a collection of over 10,000 items unique to Canadian substance abuse and addictions issues. It provides information services and maintains specialized databases on Canadian substance abuse resources, treatment services, and organizations. It coordinates the Canadian Substance Abuse Information Network (CSAIN), a nationwide consortium whose members exchange information, share resources, and develop new information products. The NCSA fulfills information requests or directs them to an appropriate source. It develops and produces electronic and printed information products including databases, directories, inventories, and bibliographies. It distributes the publications of the Canadian Centre on Substance Abuse (CCSA).

National Clearinghouse on Tobacco and Health, Canadian Council for Tobacco Control

Address:	75 Albert St., Suite 500, Ottawa, ON, Canada K1P 5E7
Phone:	(613) 567-3050
Fax:	(613) 567-2730
E-mail:	info-services@cctc.ca
Web:	www.cctc.ca

Description Founded in 1989, the Clearinghouse is a program of the Canadian Council for Tobacco Control. Provides information on tobacco use, prevention, and reduction issues, programs, resources, and initiatives to eligible professionals. It is an integral component of the National Strategy to Reduce Tobacco Use in Canada.

National Council on Alcoholism and Drug Dependence, Inc. (NCADD)

Contact:	Jeffrey Hon, Director for Public Information
Address:	20 Exchange Place, Suite 2902, New York, NY 10005
Phone:	(212) 269-7797
Fax:	(212) 269-7510
E-mail:	national@ncadd.org
Web:	www.ncadd.org

Description Founded in 1944, NCADD currently works in partnership with nearly 200 affiliates throughout the nation. It actively advocates government policies to reduce alcohol and other drug addictions and to provide for the treatment needs and rights of affected people. Its annual meetings and publications are excellent continuing education opportunities and information resources.

National Institute on Alcohol Abuse and Alcoholism (NIAAA)

Address:	5655 Fishers Lane, MSC 9304, Bethesda, MD 20892-9304
Phone:	(301) 443-3885
Fax:	(301) 443-7043
Web:	www.niaaa.nih.gov

Description NIAAA is one of 16 research institutes that comprise the National Institutes of Health. NIAAA conducts and supports biomedical and behavioral research, health services research, research training, and health information dissemination regarding the prevention of alcohol abuse and the treatment of alcoholism. The National Clearinghouse for Alcohol and Drug Abuse responds to questions about the NIAAA and distributes its publications.

National Institute on Drug Abuse (NIDA)

Address:	6001 Executive Blvd., Room 5213, Bethesda, MD 20892-9561
Phone:	(301) 443-6480
Fax:	(301) 433-9127
E-mail:	information@lists.nida.nih.gov
Web:	www.nida.nih.gov

Description One of 16 research institutes overseen by the National Institutes of Health. NIDA conducts and supports biomedical and behavioral research, health services research, research training, and health information dissemination regarding the prevention and treatment of drug abuse. The Institute is organized into five divisions: Intramural Research, Extramural Research, Education and Research Training, Research Dissemination, and Epidemiological Studies. The website includes reports and publications.

National Self-Help Clearinghouse

Contact: Audrey Gartner, Executive Director
Address: Graduate School and CUNY, 365 5th Ave., Suite 3300, New York, NY 10016
Phone: (212) 817-1822
Fax: (212) 642-1956
E-mail: info@selfhelpweb.org
Web: www.selfhelpweb.org

Description The Clearinghouse conducts training for professionals and laypeople about self-help methods, carries out research activities, maintains an information and referral databank, publishes materials, and addresses professional audiences about policies affecting self-help groups. Its website provides access to reports and publications.

Nicotine Anonymous World Services (NA)

Address: NAWSO, 419 Main St., PMB 370, Huntington Beach, CA 92648
Phone: (415) 750-0328
E-mail: info@nicotine-anonymous.org
Web: www.nicotine-anonymous.org

Description NA helps members and others to live without smoking using the 12-step self-help program model adapted from Alcoholics Anonymous. Materials for NA are available through its website.

Office of Minority Health Resource Center (OMHRC)

Address: PO Box 37337, Washington, DC 20013-7337
Phone: (800) 444-6472; (301) 565-4020
Fax: (301) 230-7198
Web: www.omhrc.gov

Description The Office of Minority Health (OMH) established the OMH Resource Center as a national resource for minority health information. The Resource Center facilitates access to minority health information, health promotion activities, preventive health services, and public health education. It offers assistance in the analysis of issues and problems that relate to minority health and provides assistance to organizations and individuals working in minority health professions. The Center maintains information, resources, and publications on health-specific topics that target African-American, Asian-American, Alaska Native, Hispanic/Latino, Native American, and Pacific Islander people. It provides information services and maintains five minority health databases.

Prevention Source BC (British Columbia)

Address: Suite 210, 2730 Commercial Dr., Vancouver, BC, Canada V5N 5P4
Phone: (604) 874-8452; (800) 663-1880, British Columbia residents
Fax: (604) 874-9348
E-mail info@preventionsource.bc.ca
Web: www.preventionsource.bc.ca

Description Prevention Source BC is funded by the Province of British Columbia. It provides toll-free information services to residents of the province seeking information about prevention, organizations, programs, materials, and research in the area of substance misuse. In addition, Prevention Source BC has a collection of materials available for on-site use.

Rutgers University Center of Alcohol Studies, Library

Contact: Penny Page, MLS, Library Director
Address: 607 Allison Rd., Smithers Hall, Busch Campus, Piscataway, NJ 08854-8001
Phone: (732) 445-4442 (library)
Fax: (732) 445-5944
E-mail: ppage@rci.rutgers.edu
Web: www.rci.rutgerscas2.edu

Description The Center is internationally recognized for its research, education, clinical services, and information. The Center's library houses the world's largest collection of alcohol information and can provide individualized information services, specialized bibliographies, and document delivery services. The website has many unique resources, from historical material to bibliographies and fact sheets. The Center publishes *The Journal of Studies on Alcohol.*

Substance Abuse Librarians and Information Specialists (SALIS)

Address: Box 9513, Berkeley, CA 94709-0513
Phone: (510) 642-5208 (Andrea Mitchell)
Fax: (510) 642-5208
E-mail: salis@arg.org
Web: www.salis.org

Description An international association of individuals and organizations with special interests in the exchange and dissemination of alcohol, tobacco, and other drug information, created in 1978, SALIS's annual meetings offer members opportunities for professional development, information exchange, and networking. SALIS is an affiliate member of the International Council on Alcohol and Addictions (ICAA). It actively collaborates with the Center for Substance Abuse Prevention (CSAP) RADAR Network and the NIAAA-CSAP Alcohol and Other Drug Thesaurus project.

Electronic Resources

Alcohol Advisory Council of New Zealand

www.alcohol.org.nz

Description An innovative site that provides public information on alcohol and its effects, in a very effective manner. Of particular note are the sections for adolescents with a harm-reduction approach. See the interactive section "FUEL," with sections that include a game, safety tips for teens, even a screen saver that depicts the process of intoxication.

Columbia University Health Service, *Go Ask Alice*

www.alice.columbia.edu

Description Mounted by the Student Health Service at Columbia University, this site deals with sexuality, sexual health, relationships, general health, fitness and nutrition, and emotional well-being. The subsection on substance abuse issues uses a question-and-answer format. It provides factual, authoritative information from a harm-reduction perspective.

Indiana Prevention Resource Center (IPRC)

www.drugs.indiana.edu

Description The IPRC provides technical assistance through the provision of information, materials, and consultations to public and private prevention programs. The site is well organized, and it contains a wealth of information, in many instances unique, such as a dictionary of drug-related slang terms. It maintains several searchable databases and links to other groups, e.g., the National PTA's website, Resources for School Educators.

National Inhalant Prevention Coalition

www.inhalants.org

Description This site is a source of information and resource materials on inhalants, including videos for adults and youth, posters, curriculum, and brochures/comic books. Includes related information for emergency medical personnel, public policy initiatives with retailers, and educational initiatives cosponsored with the U.S. Consumer Product Safety Commission.

Project Cork

www.projectcork.org

Description ProjectCork.org is the continuation of a program founded in 1978, at Dartmouth Medical School to improve medical education on alcohol. The website provides information of interest to health-care and human service professionals, in addition to those in the substance abuse field. The major areas of the website are bibliographies on over 200 topics; quarterly newsletters available for substance abuse agencies to distribute to constituents; clinical tools such as interview guidelines and screening tests; and curriculum materials. Project Cork also maintains a bibliographic database, CORK, with over 65,000 items.

Web of Addictions

www.well.com/user/woa

Description This privately produced site consists primarily of links to web resources. It is one of the best and easiest means to explore substance abuse resources on the Internet.

World Health Organization

www.who.int/substance_abuse

Description Access to programs and materials produced by the World Health Organization. It deals with primary prevention and epidemiology, that focus upon alcohol, nicotine, and other drug use.

APPENDIX B

The Interaction Effects of Alcohol with Other Drugs

Type of Drug	Generic Name	Trade Name	Interaction Effect with Alcohol
Analgesics Nonnarcotic	Salicylates	(Products containing aspirin) Bayer Aspirin Bufferin Alka-Seltzer	Heavy concurrent use of alcohol with analgesics can increase the potential for GI bleeding. Special caution should be exercised by individuals with ulcers. Buffering of salicylates reduces possibility of this interaction.
	Acetaminophen	Tylenol Exedrin	With 2+ drinks per day can cause liver damage.
	Ibuprofen*	Advil Motrin Midol Exedrin IB	Can increase bleeding.
Narcotic	Codeine Morphine Opium	 Pantopon Parepectolin (paregoric)	The combination of narcotic analgesics and alcohol interact to reduce functioning of the CNS and can lead to loss of effective breathing function and respiratory arrest: death may result.
	Oxycodone	Percodan OxyContin	
	Propoxyphene	Darvon Darvon-N	
	Pentazocine Meperidine	Talwin Demerol Tylox	
Antianginal	Nitroglycerin Isosorbide dinitrate	Nitrosat Isordil, Sorbitrate	Alcohol in combination with antianginal drugs may cause the blood pressure to lower—creating a potentially dangerous situation.

*Also classified as non-steroid anti-inflammatory agents.

(continued on next page)

Type of Drug	Generic Name	Trade Name	Interaction Effect with Alcohol
Antibiotics Antiinfective agents	Furazolidone Metronidazole Nitrofurantoin	Furoxone Flagyl Cyantin Macrodantin	Certain antibiotics, especially those taken for urinary tract infections and Trichomonas infections, have been known to produce disulfiram-like reactions (nausea, vomiting, headaches, hypotension) when combined with alcohol.
Anticoagulants	Warfarin sodium Acenocoumarol Coumarin derivatives	Coumadin, Panwarfin Sintrom Dicumarol	With chronic alcohol use, the anticoagulant effect of these drugs is inhibited. With acute alcohol use the anticoagulant effect is enhanced: hemorrhaging could result.
Anticonvulsants	Phenytoin Carbamazepine Primidone	Dilantin Tegretol Mysoline	Chronic heavy drinking can reduce the effectiveness of anticonvulsant drugs to the extent that seizures previously controlled by these drugs can occur if the dosage is not adjusted appropriately.
	Phenobarbital	Luminal	Enhanced CNS depression may occur with concurrent use of alcohol.
Antidiabetic agents Hypoglycemics	Chlorpropamide Acetohexamide Tolbutamide Tolazamide Insulin	Diabinese Dymelor Orinase Tolinase Iletin	The interaction of alcohol and either insulin or oral antidiabetic agents may be severe and unpredictable. The interaction may induce hypoglycemia or hyperglycemia; also disulfiram-like reactions may occur.
Antidepressants Tricyclics	Nortriptyline Amitriptyline Desipramine Doxepin Imipramine	Aventyl Elavil, Endep Pertofrane Sinequan Tofranil	Enhanced CNS depression may occur with concurrent use of alcohol and antidepressant drugs. Alcohol itself can cause or exacerbate clinical states of depression.
Monoamine oxidase inhibitors (MAOI)	Pargyline Isocarboxazid Phenelzine Tranylcypromine	Eutonyl Marplan Nardil Parnate	Alcoholic beverages (such as beer and wines) contain tyramine, which will interact with an MAOI to produce a hypertensive hyperpyrexic crisis. Concomitant use of alcohol with MAOIs may result in enhanced CNS depression.
Antihistamines	Many cold & allergy remedies (Included as examples) Chlorpheniramine Diphenhydramine	 Coricidin Allerest Benadryl	The interaction of alcohol and these drugs enhances CNS depression.

(continued on next page)

Type of Drug	Generic Name	Trade Name	Interaction Effect with Alcohol
Antihypertensive agents	Rauwolfia preparations Reserpine Guanethidine Hydralazine Pargyline Methyldopa	Rauwiloid Serpasil Ismelin Apresoline Eutonyl Aldomet	Alcohol, in moderate dosage, will increase the blood pressure–lowering effects of these drugs, and can produce postural hypotension. Additionally, an increased CNS-depressant effect may be seen with the rauwolfia alkaloids and methyldopa. Alcohol itself causes hypertension and may counteract the therapeutic effect of antihypertensive agents.
Antimalarials	Quinacrine	Atabrine	A disulfiram-like reaction and severe CNS toxicity may result if antimalarial drugs are combined with alcohol.
Anti-psychotic (major)	Thioridazine Chlorpromazine Trifluoperazine Haloperidol	Mellaril Thorazine Stelazine Haldol	The major tranquilizers interact with alcohol to enhance CNS depression, resulting in impairment of voluntary movement such as walking or hand coordination; larger doses can be fatal. Increases incidence and severity of extrapyramidal side effects of these drugs.
Benzodiazepines (minor)	Diazepam Meprobamate Chlordiazepoxide Oxazepam Lorazepam Alprazolam	Valium Equanil Miltown Librium Serax Ativan Xanax	The minor tranquilizers depress CNS functioning. Serious interactions can occur when using these drugs and alcohol.
CNS depressants Barbiturate sedative hypnotics	Phenobarbital Pentobarbital Secobarbital Butabarbital Amobarbital	Luminal Nembutal Seconal Butisol Amytal	Since alcohol is a depressant, the combination of alcohol and other depressants interact to further reduce CNS functioning. It is extremely dangerous to mix barbiturates and alcohol. What would be a nondangerous dosage of either drug by itself can interact in the body to the point of coma or fatal respiratory arrest. Many accidental deaths of this nature have been reported. A similar danger exists in mixing the nonbarbiturate hypnotics with alcohol.
Nonbarbiturate sedative hypnotics	Methaqualone Glutethimide Bromides Flurazepam Chloral hydrate	Quaalude Doriden Neurosine Dalmane Noctec	Disulfiram-like reactions have been reported with alcohol use in the presence of chloral hydrates.

(continued on next page)

Type of Drug	Generic Name	Trade Name	Interaction Effect with Alcohol
CNS Stimulants	Caffeine Amphetamines Methlyphenidate Dextroamphetamine Methamphetamine	(in coffee and cola) Vanquish Benzedrine Ritalin Dexedrine Desoxyn Ritalin	The stimulant effect of these drugs can reverse the depressant effect of alcohol drugs on the CNS, resulting in a false sense of security. They do not help the intoxicated person gain control over coordination or psychomotor activity.
Disulfiram	Disulfiram	Antabuse	Severe CNS toxicity follows ingestion of (anti-alcohol preparation) even small amounts of alcohol. Effects can include headache, nausea, vomiting, convulsions, rapid fall in blood pressure, unconsciousness, and—with sufficiently high doses—death.
Diuretics (also antihypertensive)	Hydrochlorothiazide Chlorothiazide Furosemide Quinethazone	Hydrodiuril, Esidrix Diuril Lasix Hydromax	Interaction of diuretics and alcohol enhances the blood pressure—lowering the effects of the diuretic; could possibly precipitate hypotension.

INDEX

D

E

N

O

P